UNCITRAL Arbitration

UNCITRAL Arbitration

Jan Paulsson and Georgios Petrochilos

Wolters Kluwer

Published by:
Kluwer Law International B.V.
PO Box 316
2400 AH Alphen aan den Rijn
The Netherlands
Email: international-sales@wolterskluwer.com
Website: lrus.wolterskluwer.com

Sold and distributed in North, Central and South America by:
Wolters Kluwer Legal & Regulatory U.S.
7201 McKinney Circle
Frederick, MD 21704
United States of America
Email: customer.service@wolterskluwer.com

Sold and distributed in all other countries by:
Air Business Subscriptions
Rockwood House
Haywards Heath
West Sussex
RH16 3DH
United Kingdom
Email: international-customerservice@wolterskluwer.com

Printed on acid-free paper.

ISBN 978-90-411-2733-4

e-Book: ISBN 978-90-411-4219-1
web-PDF: ISBN 978-90-411-6604-3

Printed in the United Kingdom.

Preface

Acting in the guise of the United Nations, the international community has contributed three achievements that have proved instrumental to the effective resolution of transborder commercial disputes. The first of this triad was *a treaty:* the 1958 New York Convention by which states undertook that their courts would give effect to agreements calling for arbitration and enforce foreign arbitral awards. The last of the three was the text of national legislation in the form of *a model act* recommended to all states: the 1985 UNCITRAL Model Law on International Commercial Arbitration (revised in 2006). In-between came a set of rules for the binding resolution of disputes, recommended as *a voluntary contractual stipulation:* the 1976 UNCITRAL Arbitration Rules, which are the subject of this book.

There was immediate attraction to the UNCITRAL Rules. In the first place, their text was the product of representatives of the international community of States, irrespective of national ideologies and economic power. At the time, arbitral institutions which offered their services to international business managers at best had a regional footprint. As they were not constituted from a universal base, they were not perceived (whatever their qualities) as representative of the international community as a whole. In the second place, the UNCITRAL Rules gave new impetus to ad hoc arbitration. As, ultimately, the UN was not to provide the personnel and facilities to administer arbitrations, the Rules proceed on the basis that the process should to a maximum extent be self-administering. As essential and sensitive functions such as the appointment (and occasionally removal) of arbitrators would be left to "Appointing Authorities" which the parties were free to select, contract drafters could thus choose from an infinite number of potential institutions in which they might have confidence.

These features explain a difficulty pertaining to the capacity for reforming the Rules. Arbitral institutions can react quickly to developments in practice, and do so regularly, for example to deal with originally unanticipated problems (such as cases involving more than two parties when each of them insists on the right to nominate a separate arbitrator) and to curtail undesirable practices (such as the mala fide resignation of unscrupulous arbitrators). Although institutions prefer not to bewilder users of their services by comprehensive reforms, in intervals of less than a decade, significant adjustments in detail may be undertaken more frequently.

The UNCITRAL Rules do not readily accommodate such a pattern of reform for two reasons. First of all, although the institutions that serve as Appointing Authorities may and do in fact enact their own regulations for the way they function when they do so, they are in no position to alter the Rules themselves. Secondly, the process of appraisal and drafting within UNCITRAL itself, conducted with simultaneous translation into all six official languages of the UN by a large number of delegations, is cumbersome. This explains why the Rules did not change for four decades, although this was a period of great change and innovation in practice.

The authors of this book were engaged by the UNCITRAL Secretariat in 2006 to advise it on the need for reform. Their Report is at Annex II in this work, and readers who desire to see the main features of reform may turn to its Introduction section. The Report, discussed in a number of meetings and conferences and in UNCITRAL Working Group II in September 2006, led to the decision to undertake the project of reconsidering the Rules in their entirety while maintaining their key features. The exercise involved delegations of States who were members and observers of the Working Group, as well as invited observers of arbitral institutions and others thought to have useful contributions to make to the discussions. The main work took place in semi-annual sessions alternating between Vienna and New York over four years, culminating in the adoption of the new Rules by the Commission in 2010. Both of the authors participated in the process as representatives of member States.

During these sessions, some delegations proposed that the transparency of arbitral proceedings should be regulated by the Rules. This was however recognized as unsuitable for general prescriptions; although some disputes dealt with under the Rules – notably those under investment treaties – may involve public interests and a concomitant need for transparency, many others concern only private interests which the arbitrants may strongly prefer be handled confidentially. This explains that a regime of transparency was developed through a separate, follow-up exercise leading to the adoption of the Transparency Rules in 2013, as an optional feature of the process applicable in investment-treaty cases. The UNCITRAL Rules incorporate the transparency chapter as part of their text, through a new article 1(4). The entire text, issued as the *UNCITRAL Rules 2013*, was endorsed by UN General Assembly Resolution 68/103 in December 2013. (The present work refers to the generic rules, articles 1-43, as the *2010 Rules*.)

* * *

The present work is organized in the conventional way of article-by-article commentary, for ease of reference. It does not contain a narration of the process revising the Rules, but it frequently refers to the thorough preparatory work (abstracted in Annex III, in respect of the 2010 Rules) better to explain the purpose and effect of the text. This commentary also explains the links – continuities as well as changes – between the 1976 and 2010 versions: in a number of respects, the 2010 text codifies best practice already developed under the 1976 text; and the 1976 text will continue to apply (notably under investment treaties) for many years to come with respect to pre-2010 arbitration agreements. Annex IV is a table of correspondence between the 1976 and the 2010 provisions. Finally, per general usage, we have adopted the stylistic conventions and terminology of the Rules.

* * *

This work was in the making for several years. In that process, we have been assisted by a number of persons. Special mention is due (in chronological order) to Tamara Kraljic, Tunde Oyewole, Milica Kostić, Jenna Meth, Rachel Atkinson, and Patrick Fox. We are glad to acknowledge a debt of gratitude to them.

The authors hope that this work, informed by their own involvement in the process and by observations of the early years of experience under the 2010 Rules, will contribute to a shared and useful understanding of them.

Jan Paulsson and Georgios Petrochilos
Washington and Paris

Table of contents

Tables of authorities

DECISIONS OF INTERNATIONAL COURTS AND TRIBUNALS

Ad hoc and International Tribunals

International Centre for Settlement of Investment Disputes

International Court of Justice and Permanent Court of International Justice

Iran-United States Claims Tribunal

DECISIONS OF MUNICIPAL COURTS

Austria

Bermuda

Canada

England & Wales

France

Germany

Hong Kong

India

New Zealand

Russian Federation

Singapore

Sweden

Switzerland

United States

PART I

Section I
Introductory rules

2010 Rules

Article 1
Scope of application

1976 Rules Article 1: Scope of application	2010 Rules Article 1: Scope of application

1976 Rules

Article 1: Scope of application

1. Where the parties to a contract have agreed in writing* that disputes in relation to that contract shall be referred to arbitration under the UNCITRAL Arbitration Rules, then such disputes shall be settled in accordance with these Rules subject to such modification as the parties may agree in writing.

2. These Rules shall govern the arbitration except that where any of these Rules is in conflict with a provision of the law applicable to the arbitration from which the parties cannot derogate, that provision shall prevail.

**MODEL ARBITRATION CLAUSE*

Any dispute, controversy or claim arising out of or relating to this contract, or the breach, termination or invalidity thereof, shall be settled by arbitration in accordance with the UNCITRAL Arbitration Rules as at present in force.

Note – Parties may wish to consider adding:

(a) The appointing authority shall be ... (name of institution or person);

(b) The number of arbitrators shall be ... (one or three);

(c) The place of arbitration shall be ... (town or country);

2010 Rules

Article 1: Scope of application

1. Where parties have agreed that disputes between them in respect of a defined legal relationship, whether contractual or not, shall be referred to arbitration under the UNCITRAL Arbitration Rules, then such disputes shall be settled in accordance with these Rules subject to such modification as the parties may agree.

2. The parties to an arbitration agreement concluded after 15 August 2010 shall be presumed to have referred to the Rules in effect on the date of commencement of the arbitration, unless the parties have agreed to apply a particular version of the Rules. That presumption does not apply where the arbitration agreement has been concluded by accepting after 15 August 2010 an offer made before that date.

3. These Rules shall govern the arbitration except that where any of these Rules is in conflict with a provision of the law applicable to the arbitration from which the parties cannot derogate, that provision shall prevail.

UNCITRAL Arbitration Rules (with new article 1, paragraph 4, as adopted in 2013):

4. For investor-State arbitration initiated pursuant to a treaty providing for the protection of investments or investors,

(d) The language(s) to be used in the arbitral proceedings shall be …

these Rules include the UNCITRAL Rules on Transparency in Treaty-based Investor-State Arbitration ("Rules on Transparency"), subject to article 1 of the Rules on Transparency.

---

1. Article 1 of the 1976 Rules addressed the scope of application of the Rules. It stipulated the fundamental principle that for the UNCITRAL Rules to apply, the parties must express their intent to arbitrate under the UNCITRAL Rules. This requirement follows from the inherently consensual nature of arbitration. More specifically, article 1(1) of the 1976 Rules required that the agreement to arbitrate under the Rules be 'in writing'. Article 1(1) also clarified that the provisions of the Rules are all 'subject to such modification as the parties may agree in writing'.[1] Notably, the NAFTA Rules and the Tribunal Rules of the Iran-US Claims Tribunal represent modified versions of the UNCITRAL Rules.[2]

2. An important limitation was set out in paragraph (2) of article 1. In case of conflict between the Rules and a mandatory provision of the 'law applicable to the arbitration' (i.e. the controlling arbitration law, or *lex arbitri*), the latter shall prevail. Article 1(2) did not define the controlling law nor give any indication as to how to identify the mandatory provisions from which 'the parties cannot derogate', leaving these matters to the arbitral tribunal, or a controlling court, to decide.[3] It is submitted that the relevant provisions of domestic law must pertain specifically to arbitration, rather than (say) civil procedure, and that compliance with them must be secured through setting aside or equivalent sanction: unless these two requirements are met, the parties' agreement on the Rules must prevail. Article 1(2) of the 1976 Rules has remained unmodified in the revision process and is reproduced verbatim under article 1(3) of the 2010 Rules.

3. By contrast, article 1(1) has undergone substantial changes. The changes pertain to the elimination of the requirements that (i) the parties must agree to the application of the Rules and to any modification thereof 'in writing' and (ii) the relationship between the parties be of a contractual nature. Moreover, a new paragraph (2) has been added, addressing the intertemporal law question

---

1 Though one may doubt the wisdom of such agreements, it is difficult to see an objection of principle to derogating from fundamental and essentially declaratory provisions of the Rules, such as articles 1(3) and 17(1). The extent to which such agreements would be valid and enforceable is another matter – and it is a matter for the *lex arbitri*, not the Rules.

2 *See* modifications to the UNCITRAL Rules in Section B, Chapter 11 of NAFTA; and Article III(2) of the Iran-United States Claims Settlement Declaration (19 January 1981); *see also* Tribunal Rules of Procedure of the Iran-United States Claims Tribunal (3 May 1983); *see also* David D. Caron & Lee M. Caplan, *The UNCITRAL Arbitration Rules, A Commentary*, 5-6 (2nd ed., Oxford University Press 2013).

3 *See* Jan Paulsson & Georgios Petrochilos, *Revision of the UNCITRAL Rules* (September 2006), paras 36-39, < www.uncitral.org >, for situations (i) where the applicable law is a domestic one, the reference is to arbitration law and (ii) the applicable law may be public international law in certain circumstances.

of which version of the Rules shall apply. The model arbitration clause, which used to appear as a footnote to article 1 under the 1976 Rules but is now found in the Annex of the 2010 Rules, has also undergone certain changes.

A. WRITING REQUIREMENT

4. In the context of investment-treaty disputes, difficult questions may arise, and have in fact arisen, with respect to the requirement that the parties must have agreed to submit to UNCITRAL arbitration 'disputes between them'. At the root of the difficulties lies the fact that arbitration clauses in investment treaties are typically analysed as standing offers to arbitrate made by states to investors. Not infrequently investors team up to form a group of claimants, purporting jointly to accept the respondent state's offer in one treaty or (less frequently) several treaties. States on occasion oppose such teaming-up, and there is reported practice by the PCA and the SCC accepting the respondent state's position that investors may present claims jointly (i) under a single treaty, provided that (ii) they are either affiliated among them or allege to have invested in the same project.[4] Nevertheless, there is authority for the proposition that there is in principle no obstacle to investors' jointly accepting a state's offer to arbitrate, at the very least under a single treaty, and commencing proceedings on that basis.[5] The latter analysis must be correct, it is submitted: there is no basis in the Rules to oppose joint acceptance by all purported claimants of a single offer to arbitrate contained in a single treaty. The only conceivable limitation would stem from requirements of good faith and avoidance of abuse of process, notably in manifest cases of an attempt by the claimants to oppress the respondent, or where judicial orderliness requires that proceedings be split because of differing subject-matters. In such exceptional cases, tribunals could intervene under their general powers in article 17(1) of the Rules or the doctrine of inherent powers to dismiss the proceedings as inadmissible or (probably more satisfactorily) split them. By contrast, asymmetric claimant groups – with some claimants acting under one treaty and others under a different one – are impossible to regard as acting under the same arbitration agreement. Thus, if one considers that article 1(1) requires that there be a single arbitration agreement among all arbitrating parties, asymmetric groups could be housed in a single proceeding only on the basis of an agreement to consolidate separate arbitrations.

---

4 *See* Sebastian Perry & Kyriaki Karadelis, *Sun Rises on Czech Energy Claims*, GAR, 19 February 2014, < www.globalarbitrationreview.com >.

5 *See Guaracachi America Inc and Rurelec PLC v. The Plurinational State of Bolivia* (UNCITRAL) Award, 31 January 2014, < www.italaw.com >, paras 3-4. Cf. *Noble Energy Inc and Machalapower Cia Ltda v. The Republic of Ecuador and Consejo Nacional de Electricidad* (ICSID Case No. ARB/05/12) Decision on Jurisdiction, 5 March 2008, < www.italaw.com >, paras 186-194; *Abaclat & Ors v. Argentine Republic* (ICSID Case No. ARB/07/5) Decision on Jurisdiction and Admissibility, 4 August 2011, < www.italaw.com >; *Ambiente Ufficio S.p.A. & Ors v. Argentine Republic* (ICSID Case No. ARB/08/9) Decision on Jurisdiction and Admissibility, 8 February 2013, < www.italaw.com >; *Giovanni Alemanni & Ors v. Argentine Republic* (ICSID Case No. ARB/08/9) Decision on Jurisdiction and Admissibility, 17 November 2014, < www.italaw.com >, para. 141.

5. In the revision process, the Working Group noted that the concept of 'writing' had undergone substantial developments since the advent of electronic means of communication, and that 'issues such as whether the writing requirement had been met and how it could be met had given rise to a substantial amount of litigation'.[6]

6. The Model Law offers guidance in respect of the required form, by clarifying that '[t]he requirement that an arbitration agreement be in writing is met by an electronic communication if the information contained therein is accessible so as to be useable for subsequent reference'.[7] Similarly, UNCITRAL has issued a recommendation on the interpretation of Article II(1) of the New York Convention, which provides that the writing requirement in the said article should be read so as to include modern forms of communication.[8] While the emergence of modern forms of communication is acknowledged in article 2 of the 2010 Rules,[9] a definition of the writing requirement was said to lie 'beyond the usual scope' of the Rules.[10] Indeed, at the outset of the revision process, the Working Group stressed that the writing requirement of article 1 had a limited function:

> [T]he purpose of the requirement that the arbitration agreement be in writing was to set out the scope of application of the UNCITRAL Arbitration Rules and, unlike the function of the form requirement under the UNCITRAL Arbitration Model Law, was separate from the question of the validity of the arbitration agreement (which was governed by the applicable law) or from the question of enforcement under the New York Convention.[11]

7. That is to say, the only purpose of the requirement of an agreement in writing in the Rules was to ensure that there was in fact consensus between the parties as to the application of the Rules. That limited purpose was no longer served by a requirement whose inclusion gave rise to the difficulty of defining what constitutes a 'writing'. In order to adopt an entirely neutral position, the Working Group decided to omit altogether the writing requirement from article 1 of the

---

6 UNCITRAL Report of 46th Session, 20 March 2007, UN Doc A/CN.9/619, para. 29.

7 Article 7, Option I of the UNCITRAL Model Law with a detailed definition of the term 'electronic communication'; *see* UNCITRAL Note by the Secretariat, 13 April 2006, UN Doc A/CN.9/606, para. 4.

8 UNCITRAL Recommendation regarding the interpretation of article II(2) and article VII(1) of the Convention on the Recognition and Enforcement of Foreign Arbitral Awards, 14 July 2006, UN Doc A/61/17, Annex II; *see also* Nigel Blackaby, Constantine Partasides, Alan Redfern & Martin J. Hunter, *Redfern and Hunter on International Arbitration*, para. 1.48 and the references (6th ed., Kluwer 2015). For a summary of case law on this issue, *see* UNCITRAL, *2012 Digest of Case Law on the Model Law on International Commercial Arbitration*, 29 et seq. (United Nations 2012).

9 *See* discussion of article 2 of the 2010 Rules, *infra*.

10 UNCITRAL Report of 46th Session, 20 March 2007, UN Doc A/CN.9/619, para. 28.

11 *Ibid.*

2010 Rules.[12] Of course, this does not dispense compliance with the requirements under the *lex arbitri* or the New York Convention.[13]

B. REQUIREMENT OF A CONTRACTUAL RELATIONSHIP BETWEEN THE PARTIES

8. The wording of article 1(1), which referred to disputes relating to a contract between the parties to 'that contract', implied that the 1976 Rules were intended to be used in contractual disputes only.

9. In practice, however, the UNCITRAL Rules have had much broader use. The Iran-US Claims Tribunal, for instance, specifically modified article 1 of the Rules so as to include disputes relating to expropriations and dispossessions.[14] Further, in *Larsen v. Hawaiian Kingdom*, which sought to place in issue the United States' annexation of the Hawaiian Kingdom, the tribunal noted that 'there appears no reason why the UNCITRAL Rules cannot be adapted to apply to a non-contractual dispute'.[15] An agreement to refer a non-contractual dispute to arbitration under the 1976 Rules is an implied and perfectly valid derogation from article 1(1).[16] Indeed, the UNCITRAL Rules have for a long time been incorporated in BITs and multilateral treaties, such as the Energy Charter Treaty (ECT),[17] where they are used to resolve investor-state disputes involving causes of action under international law. About a third of reported investment arbitration cases have been conducted under the UNCITRAL Rules.[18]

10. The increasing use of the UNCITRAL Rules in investment arbitration has given rise to debate as to whether the Rules should include provisions to cater to the

---

12 *See* UNCITRAL Report of 49th Session, 30 September 2008, UN Doc A/CN.9/665, para. 18. Note that the deletion of the writing requirement with respect to the parties' modification of the 2010 Rules was not extensively discussed, perhaps because it was 'less clearly justified' to begin with. *See* Stewart A. Baker & Mark D. Davis, *The UNCITRAL Arbitration Rules in Practice – The Experience of the Iran-United States Claims Tribunal*, 8 (Kluwer 1992). *See also* Paulsson & Petrochilos, *supra* fn 3, at paras 25-26, for the view that the writing requirement with respect to modifications of the Rules 'would bring about unreasonable results in cases of *de minimis* modifications'.

13 *See* Blackaby, Partasides, Redfern & Hunter, *supra* fn 6, at para. 1.45 and Chapter 2; *see also* Toby Landau, *The Requirement of a Written Form For an Arbitration Agreement When 'Written' Means 'Oral'*, 11 ICCA Congress Series 19 (2003).

14 *See* Caron & Caplan, *supra* fn 2, at 25.

15 *Larsen v. Hawaiian Kingdom* (UNCITRAL) PCA Case No. 1999-01, Award, 5 February 2001, < www.pca-cpa.org > , para. 10.7. *See*, for a more recent example, *AWG Group Ltd v. The Argentine Republic* (UNCITRAL) Decision on Jurisdiction, 3 August 2006, < www.italaw.com > , para. 49.

16 A hypothesis would be an agreement to submit to arbitration a dispute arising from tort, succession, breaches of legal duties, and so on – where such disputes are capable of being submitted to arbitration.

17 *See* Article 26(4)(b) of the Energy Charter Treaty.

18 Norbert Horn, *Current Use of the UNCITRAL Arbitration Rules in the Context of Investment Arbitration*, 24 Arb Int 587, 587 (2008). *See also* Paulsson & Petrochilos, *supra* fn 3, at paras 6, 30-34 and the references.

specific needs of investment arbitration (notably regarding the transparency of proceedings). Ultimately, however, the Working Group decided to continue the revision process of the Rules in their generic form. Further work on the specificity of investor-state arbitrations was to be addressed once the revision process had been completed.[19]

11. The wording of article 1(1) of the 2010 Rules does not include any reference to a 'contractual' relationship, in order to pre-empt 'possible preliminary objections on the arbitrability of non-contractual disputes under the Rules'.[20] Adopting the wording of Article 7 of the Model Law, article 1(1) of the 2010 Rules now states that the Rules will apply to disputes in respect of a 'defined legal relationship, whether contractual or not'. Moreover, the title of the model clause, which now reads 'Model Arbitration Clause *for Contracts*' (emphasis added), makes it clear that the model wording will require adaptation for use in other contexts.

12. The Rules do not specify what a 'defined legal relationship' means. This language follows Article II(1) of the New York Convention and Article 7(1) of the Model Law, as echoed by various national legislations.[21] Its general intent, as used in these instruments, is to negate exceptional cases where the arbitration agreement is couched in indeterminate and imprecise terms. In practice, the language has had little bite and remains rarely tested,[22] largely swallowed by the pro-arbitration attitude of courts and tribunals.[23]

C. THE APPLICABLE VERSION OF THE RULES

13. With the completion of the revision process in 2010, there were, for the first time in the history of the UNCITRAL Rules, two versions of the Rules: the 1976 Rules and the 2010 Rules. Experience shows that investment treaties,[24] in particular, in which an agreement to arbitrate under the UNCITRAL Rules is embedded, rarely specify the 1976 version of the Rules (as opposed to a later version possibly extant at the time of commencement of an arbitration). There are no published empirical data as to how often in commercial contracts parties heed the recommendation of the 1976 drafters to refer to the 'UNCITRAL Arbitration Rules as at present in force'. In any event, the 2010 Rules cannot retroactively legislate for pre-existing agreements. There will certainly be cases where the parties will debate whether

---

19 For a general discussion, *see* UNCITRAL Report of 48th Session, 29 February 2008, UN Doc A/CN.9/646, paras 54-69. The UNCITRAL Working Group II commenced this project in autumn 2010.

20 Paulsson & Petrochilos, *supra* fn 3, at para. 33.

21 *See* Gary B. Born, *International Commercial Arbitration*, 293 (2nd ed., Kluwer 2014) citing Article II(1) of the New York Convention; Article 7, Option I of the UNCITRAL Model Law; Article 1442 of the French Code of Civil Procedure; Articles 807-808 of the Italian Code of Civil Procedure.

22 *Ibid.*, at 294-296. One reported case exists suggesting that an arbitration clause may run afoul of the 'defined legal relationship' language; *see ibid.*, at 295 citing to *Roose Industries Ltd v. Ready Mixed Concrete Ltd* [1974] 2 NZLR 246, 247 (Wellington Court of Appeal).

23 *Ibid.*, at 294.

24 Paulsson & Petrochilos, *supra* fn 3, at para. 27.

they should be taken as having contemplated potential post-1976 revisions of the Rules current at the time of referral of an actual dispute to arbitration, though doubtless most cases will be resolved by explicit agreement of the parties at the time of actual referral to opt for the 1976 or the 2010 version. (That is in fact a common occurrence in the experience of the authors.)

14. Article 1(2) of the 2010 Rules is a deeming provision which concerns arbitration agreements concluded *after* the date of adoption of the 2010 Rules. It has no retroactive effect. It does, however, have a forward-reaching effect, in that it establishes a presumption that the parties have agreed to apply the Rules in effect 'on the date of commencement of the arbitration'. In this way, (i) agreements concluded after the date of the adoption of the 2010 Rules in August 2010 are deemed to refer to the 2010 Rules, and (ii) in addition, parties are deemed to have agreed to arbitrate under any potential future revised version of the Rules in force at the time of commencement of the arbitral proceedings.[25] A number of arbitral institutions have adopted similar provisions when revising their Rules. For example, the ICC added the following provision under Article 6(1) of its 1998 Rules (now Article 6(1) of its 2017 Rules):

> Where the parties have agreed to submit to arbitration under the Rules, they shall be deemed to have submitted ipso facto to the Rules in effect on the date of commencement of the arbitration proceedings, unless they have agreed to submit to the Rules in effect on the date of their arbitration agreement.[26]

15. Article 1(2) is worded in peremptory fashion to set forth an irrefutable presumption: '*shall* be presumed'. A looser formulation would have defeated the purpose of ensuring certainty in the crucial issue of which text applies. Nevertheless, it is clear that there could be room for dispute on whether the parties can be said to have actually envisaged the 2010 Rules (as opposed to the 1976 Rules) at the time of contracting. Conceptually, the rule in article 1(2) can be a non-rebuttable gloss on contractual wording only after establishing a link in the parties' agreement to the 2010 version of the Rules. By contrast, an agreement referring expressly to the 2010 Rules will clearly also encompass the forward-reach rule in favour of potential future revisions of the Rules.

16. The second part of article 1(2) stipulates an exception. No presumption will apply in cases where the offer to arbitrate has been made before the adoption date of the 2010 Rules but the offer has been accepted after that date. Such situations 'could arise in arbitration pursuant to a treaty, as well as in certain commercial contexts'.[27] Where an offer to arbitrate is made as a standing offer

---

[25] As discussed *infra*, however, the UNCITRAL Rules on Transparency in Treaty-based Investor-State Arbitration are only deemed to apply where the treaty in question is concluded on or after 1 April 2014. *See* article 1 of the Transparency Rules.

[26] Article 6(1) of the 2012 ICC Rules introduced a minor linguistic adjustment to the 1998 version, replacing 'commencement of the arbitration proceedings' with 'commencement of the arbitration'. The Preamble to the LCIA Rules contains a similar provision.

[27] UNCITRAL Report of 48th Session, 29 February 2008, UN Doc A/CN.9/646, para. 76.

in an investment treaty or in standard commercial terms issued unilaterally by a party, perfection of the agreement by way of acceptance by another party may occur several years later. It was felt that in such cases one cannot automatically impute an intent to refer to future versions of the Rules.

17. A decision by the Paris Court of Appeal illustrates the kind of tensions which may arise on this point.[28] The claim concerned an allegation by an arbitrating party that the ICC had failed to comply with duties set out in the ICC Rules in the course of an arbitration between the claimant, SNF, and another company, CYTEC. The contract between SNF and CYTEC, which contained the agreement to arbitrate under the ICC Rules, was signed in 1993. At that time, the ICC Rules extant were the 1988 version. A dispute between the two companies arose, leading SNF to commence arbitration in May 2000. By that stage, the ICC had adopted the 1998 version of its Rules.

18. Contrary to the 1988 Rules, the 1998 Rules contain an exclusion of liability clause, under which the ICC is immune from any claims against it.[29] The ICC argued that the 1998 Rules were applicable, on the theory that the ICC emits a permanent offer to contract, which is accepted only once a Request for Arbitration is filed. By contrast, SNF held that the date of acceptance of the ICC's offer was the date of signature of arbitration agreement. The Paris court sided with SNF in holding that the ICC's offer was accepted in 1993, i.e. the year the arbitration agreement was signed. The court indicated that the ordinary analysis would indicate the version of the ICC Rules which the parties 'knew' when they concluded their agreement. Ultimately, however, the court held that the parties had agreed to apply the 1998 version of the ICC Rules by agreeing on Terms of Reference which repeatedly referred to the 1998 version.

D. ADDITION OF THE 2013 UNCITRAL RULES ON TRANSPARENCY

19. In 2013, UNCITRAL adopted the UNCITRAL Rules on Transparency in Treaty-based Investor-State Arbitration (the 'Transparency Rules') for arbitrations initiated pursuant to an investment treaty concluded on or after 1 April 2014, the date on which the Transparency Rules came into effect. After significant debate on the form the Transparency Rules should take, it was decided that they would form part and parcel of the UNCITRAL Rules, while also being available as a stand-alone instrument that could be applied in disputes governed by other arbitration rules.[30] In order to incorporate the Transparency Rules into the existing body of the text, a new article 1(4) was added to the text of the UNCITRAL Rules.[31]

---

[28] *SNF v. Chambre de Commerce Internationale*, CA Paris, 1ère Chambre, 22 January 2009, Case No. 07/19492.

[29] Article 34 of the 1998 ICC Rules.

[30] Article 1(9) of the Transparency Rules states that the Transparency Rules are 'available for use in investor-State arbitrations initiated under rules other than the UNCITRAL Arbitration Rules or in ad hoc proceedings'.

[31] Article 1(4) of the UNCITRAL Rules. *See also* Report of the Commission on its 46th Session, 8-26 July 2013, UN Doc A/68/17, para. 103.

20. The result is that references to the UNCITRAL Rules in treaties concluded on or after the coming into effect[32] of the Transparency Rules are interpreted as including the Transparency Rules, unless the parties to the treaty have agreed otherwise.[33] In contrast, and as noted by the Commission, reference to the UNCITRAL Arbitration Rules as adopted in 1976 or as revised in 2010 in a treaty concluded after the coming into force of the Transparency Rules would have the effect of 'precluding the application of the rules on transparency'.[34] Where an investor-state arbitration is initiated under the UNCITRAL Rules pursuant to a treaty concluded before 1 April 2014, the Transparency Rules only apply where the parties to the arbitration or the Contracting States to the treaty have agreed on their application.[35]

21. Article 1(4) therefore serves a largely mechanical function, including the Transparency Rules in the 2010 Rules where the conditions for inclusion are met. The Working Group discussed the possibility of including 'evolutive' language in article 1(4) (referring to the Rules 'as amended from time to time' or 'as in effect on the date of commencement of the arbitration'), but ultimately decided against it on the basis that this might deter countries from adopting the Transparency Rules in future treaties.[36]

22. The Transparency Rules themselves, as well as their scope of application, are further discussed in Part II of this book.

---

32 Lise Johnson & Nathalie Bernasconi-Osterwalder, *New UNCITRAL Arbitration Rules on Transparency: Application, Content and Next Steps*, 11 (CIEL, IISD, CCSI, August 2013), <http://ccsi.columbia.edu>: 'Notably, UNCITRAL chose April 1, 2014 as the effective date of the Rules on Transparency. This was done in order to give UNCITRAL time to secure necessary resources and develop the capabilities in order to serve as the repository. If an investment treaty is concluded after adoption of the Rules on Transparency ... but before their coming into force in April 2014, the Rules on Transparency will *not* be included by default in UNCITRAL arbitrations'.

33 *See* article 1(4) of the UNCITRAL Rules; article 1 of the Transparency Rules. *See also* Krista N. Schefer, 'Article 1. Scope of Application' in Dimitrij Euler, Markus Gehring & Maxi Scherer (eds), *Transparency in International Investment Arbitration: A Guide to the UNCITRAL Rules on Transparency in Treaty-Based Investor-State Arbitration*, 50 (Cambridge University Press 2015).

34 Report of the Commission on its 46th Session, 8-26 July 2013, UN Doc A/68/17, para. 104.

35 Article 1(2) of the Transparency Rules. *See also* Schefer, *supra* fn 31, at 52; *see also* UNCITRAL Report of 56th Session, 16 February 2012, UN Doc A/CN.9/741, para. 54.

36 Report of the Commission on its 46th Session, 8-26 July 2013, UN Doc A/68/17, paras 107-108.

Article 2
Notice and calculation of periods of time

1976 Rules

Article 2: Notice, calculation of periods of time

1. For the purposes of these Rules, any notice, including a notification, communication or proposal, is deemed to have been received if it is physically delivered to the addressee or if it is delivered at his habitual residence, place of business or mailing address, or, if none of these can be found after making reasonable inquiry, then at the addressee's last-known residence or place of business. Notice shall be deemed to have been received on the day it is so delivered.

2. For the purposes of calculating a period of time under these Rules, such period shall begin to run on the day following the day when a notice, notification, communication or proposal is received. If the last day of such period is an official holiday or a non-business day at the residence or place of business of the addressee, the period is extended until the first business day which follows. Official holidays or non-business days occurring during the running of the period of time are included in calculating the period.

2010 Rules

Article 2: Notice and calculation of periods of time

1. A notice, including a notification, communication or proposal, may be transmitted by any means of communication that provides or allows for a record of its transmission.

2. If an address has been designated by a party specifically for this purpose or authorized by the arbitral tribunal, any notice shall be delivered to that party at that address, and if so delivered shall be deemed to have been received. Delivery by electronic means such as facsimile or e-mail may only be made to an address so designated or authorized.

3. In the absence of such designation or authorization, a notice is:

(a) Received if it is physically delivered to the addressee; or

(b) Deemed to have been received if it is delivered at the place of business, habitual residence or mailing address of the addressee.

4. If, after reasonable efforts, delivery cannot be effected in accordance with paragraphs 2 or 3, a notice is deemed to have been received if it is sent to the addressee's last-known place of business, habitual residence or mailing address by registered

letter or any other means that provides a record of delivery or of attempted delivery.

5. A notice shall be deemed to have been received on the day it is delivered in accordance with paragraphs 2, 3 or 4, or attempted to be delivered in accordance with paragraph 4. A notice transmitted by electronic means is deemed to have been received on the day it is sent, except that a notice of arbitration so transmitted is only deemed to have been received on the day when it reaches the addressee's electronic address.

6. For the purpose of calculating a period of time under these Rules, such period shall begin to run on the day following the day when a notice is received. If the last day of such period is an official holiday or a non-business day at the residence or place of business of the addressee, the period is extended until the first business day which follows. Official holidays or non-business days occurring during the running of the period of time are included in calculating the period.

---

1. Article 2 of the 1976 Rules contains provisions relating to notices and communications, as well as the calculation of periods of time under the Rules. As 'notice' captures virtually any pleading and other document exchanged in an arbitration, these matters are pivotal to the orderly conduct of proceedings, and equivalent provisions can be found in other major sets of arbitration rules.[1]

2. Under the 1976 Rules, a notice is deemed to be received on the day that it is delivered when it is (i) physically delivered to the addressee, (ii) delivered at his place of business, habitual residence or mailing address, or (iii) if none of these can be found after making reasonable enquiry, sent to his last-known place of business, habitual residence or mailing address.[2] The basic notion is that, failing actual receipt of a notice, deemed receipt requires actual delivery of the notice at one of the addresses exhaustively listed in article 2(1). The 2010 Rules retain this basic philosophy but make several significant changes to this article, which has been expanded in article 2(1)-(5) of the 2010 Rules. The thrust of the 2010 changes was to separate three issues that were bundled up in article 2(1)-(2) in the 1976 Rules: means of communicating a notice, address for delivery of

---

1 *See*, e.g., Article 3 of the ICC Rules; Article 10 of the AAA International Arbitration Rules; Article 4 of the LCIA Rules; Articles 4 and 5 of the SCC Rules.

2 Article 2(1) of the 1976 Rules.

a notice, and time at which a notice counts as delivered (which is the starting point for calculating subsequent time-periods).[3] This clear structure is a major improvement achieved in the 2010 version. The wording and the structure were carefully considered over rather lengthy discussion by the Working Group, though it is doubtful whether the 1976 version of article 2 has actually given rise to difficulties.

3. The second paragraph of article 2 under the 1976 Rules provides for the calculation of periods of time. Such periods begin to run on the day following the day of receipt of a notice. Official holidays and non-business days are factored into this calculation.[4] With the exception of one minor editorial change,[5] this paragraph is identically reproduced at the new paragraph 6. It calls for no particular commentary here.

PRINCIPAL CHANGES

4. Paragraph 1 of article 2 now provides that a notice (i.e., any communication in the arbitration) may be transmitted by any means that provides or allows for a record of its transmission. The distinction made is between a means of communication that generates a record within the communication itself (and thus 'provides' a record) and one whose transmission is capable of being recorded separately (and thus 'allows' for a record to be had). This language closely reflects that which is used in several other major sets of arbitration rules.[6] Article 2(2), meanwhile, expressly refers to facsimile and email.[7] The general language of article 2(1) will allow the Rules to remain current as new technology is developed.[8] Although the 1976 Rules do not prohibit such forms of communication, they are silent on the

---

3 *See* UNCITRAL Summary Record of the 908th Meeting, 24 June 2010, UN Doc A/CN.9/SR.908, XLI UNCITRAL Ybk 1256, 1260 para. 61, (Greece): the aim of the revisions to article 2 'was to clarify the details of permitted modes of communication of notices, permitted delivery destinations, actual and deemed receipt, and delivery by electronic means'.

4 Article 2(2) of the 1976 Rules.

5 Article 2(2) of the 1976 Rules provides that a period 'shall begin to run on the day following the day when a *notice, notification, communication or proposal* is received' (emphasis added); article 2(6) of the 2010 Rules simply states that 'a period shall begin to run on the day following the day when a *notice* is received' (emphasis added). This amendment is purely textual, reflecting the fact that a notice is defined in article 2(1) of the 2010 Rules as 'including a notification, communication or proposal'.

6 *See*, e.g., Article 3(2) of the ICC Rules; Article 4.1 of the LCIA Rules; Article 5(2) of the SCC Rules; cf. Article 25(2), Council Regulation (EU) 1215/2012 on jurisdiction and the recognition and enforcement of judgments in civil and commercial matters, OJ L 351 (12 December 2012; in force on 10 January 2015).

7 *See*, e.g., Article 3(2) of the 2012 ICC Rules (Article 3(2) of the 2017 ICC Rules), which replaced 'facsimile transmission, telex, telegram' under Article 3(2) of the 1998 ICC Rules with 'email', reflecting advancements in technology.

8 For the same reason, the Working Group opted not to use the word 'telecommunications' in reference to modern electronic forms of communication, despite the view that such electronic communications might be more satisfactorily referred to in this way. *See*, e.g., Article 3(2) of the ICC Rules; Article 4.1 of the LCIA Rules.

issue; in this sense, paragraphs 1 and 2 are to be seen as an evolution of the 1976 paragraph 1 rather than a departure from it. The principle underpinning this change is uncontroversial: provision for electronic forms of communication, reflecting contemporary arbitral practice.[9]

5. Article 2(2) of the 2010 Rules introduces a new concept: the designation of an address by a party or by the tribunal for the purpose of arbitration-related communications. A number of delegations expressed apprehension about this new concept at first, hence the wording is tight, requiring that an address be 'specifically' designated for delivery of arbitration-related communications. Then any notice *shall* be delivered to that address, to the exclusion of any other one. Accordingly, any notice delivered to a designated address shall be deemed to have been received. Communications delivered to other addresses, while not prohibited, do not benefit from this presumption.

6. Delivery by electronic means such as facsimile or email can only be made to an address which has been 'specifically' designated, or authorized, in order to ensure that important documents are not overlooked – for example, where electronic communications are delivered to a generic business email address. Also, where a party has several electronic addresses, simply providing for any electronic address carries the risk that not all of them are regularly consulted or not even currently used at all.[10]

7. Some concern was expressed during the drafting of the 2010 Rules that the term 'designated' might not be sufficiently clear and unambiguous.[11] In addition, it was noted that although the Working Group had intended there to be a link with the concept of 'an electronic address designated by the addressee' found in article 10(2) of the 2005 United Nations Convention on the Use of Electronic Communications in International Contracts,[12] this may not be immediately apparent to those who are not familiar with the drafting history.[13] In practice, the qualifier '*specifically* designated' is likely to address fully such concerns.

8. Paragraph 3 provides for the default position, where a party has not designated, or a tribunal has not authorized, an address for the purpose of receipt of communications in accordance with paragraph 2. This paragraph basically reiterates the content of paragraph 1 in the 1976 Rules. It uses the concepts of actual and deemed receipt. In the absence of designation or authorization, a

---

9 *See* UNCITRAL Working Paper for 46th Session, 6 December 2006, UN Doc A/CN.9/WG.II/WP.145, para. 25.

10 *See* APRAG Report of 49th Session, 10 October 2008, para. 24. *See also* UNCITRAL Summary Record of the 908th Meeting, 24 June 2010, UN Doc A/CN.9/SR.908, XLI UNCITRAL Ybk 1256, 1260 para. 62, (Greece): the intention of the 2010 Rules was to 'prevent the use of a general mailbox or facsimile number that was not likely to be regularly checked for incoming messages'.

11 *See* APRAG Report of 49th Session, 10 October 2008, para. 23.

12 United Nations Convention on the Use of Electronic Communications in International Contracts (23 November 2005; in force on 1 March 2013).

13 *See* APRAG Report of 49th Session, 10 October 2008, para. 20.

notice is received if it is physically delivered to the addressee,[14] and deemed to have been received if delivered to the place of business, habitual residence or mailing address of the addressee.[15]

9. If for some reason it is not possible to effect delivery of a notice in accordance with paragraphs 2 and 3 (for example, where the address does not exist or no delivery can be made there), under paragraph 4 a notice is deemed to have been received if it is sent to the addressee's last-known place of business, habitual residence or mailing address, by registered letter or any other means that provides a record of delivery or of attempted delivery. This, too, is a new provision, which establishes an address for service of last resort; the need for evidence of delivery or 'attempted delivery' seeks to ensure that some form of delivery notice always exists – even if it is highly unlikely that the addressee will actually be notified or alerted to a notice at such an address. The provision strikes a balance between the natural-justice rights of both parties, respectively to be able to effect notice and to have a reasonable opportunity to receive notice.[16] That said, deemed delivery is the most practical approach to dealing with the situation without stifling the arbitral process. Naturally, after the commencement of proceedings the problem will arise infrequently (if at all) in practice, correspondence usually being transmitted between the parties' lawyers and at designated addresses pursuant to paragraph 2.

10. Finally, paragraph 5 deals with the day on which receipt is deemed to have taken place under article 2 of the 2010 Rules. Here a distinction is drawn between delivery by electronic means and traditional forms of communication. If a notice has been delivered (or if delivery has been attempted under paragraph 4) by traditional means, receipt is deemed to have taken place on the same day. A notice transmitted by electronic means is deemed to have been received on the day that it was sent, except that a notice of arbitration so transmitted is deemed to have been received only on the day when it reaches the addressee's electronic address.[17] The rule of deemed receipt at the time a notice reaches the addressee's electronic address is consistent with other UNCITRAL texts and conducive to the promotion of electronic communications.[18] But concern was expressed that requiring a sender of an electronic notice to confirm the date of delivery to the

---

14 Article 2(3)(a) of the 2010 Rules; cf. article 2(1) of the 1976 Rules.

15 Article 2(3)(b) of the 2010 Rules.

16 It is, however, possible to rebut the presumption of receipt of a notice 'deemed to have been received' pursuant to article 2(3)(b) where a party adduces evidence to establish that the notice has not actually been received: *see Sun Tian Gang v. Hong Kong & China Gas (Jilin) Ltd* [2016] HKEC 2128 (setting aside an award issued in 2007, the Hong Kong High Court held that the claimant had had no actual notice of the arbitration by reason of his imprisonment, and that the notice provisions in Article 3(1) of the Model Law and Article 2 of the Rules cannot be used to derogate from principles of natural justice and fairness).

17 Article 2(5) of the 2010 Rules.

18 *See* Report of the Commission on its 43rd Session, 21 June-9 July 2010, UN Doc A/65/17, para. 24. *See also* UNCITRAL Summary Record of the 909th Meeting, 25 June 2010, UN Doc A/CN.9/SR.909, XLI UNCITRAL Ybk 1262, 1267 para. 63, Mr Castello (United States of America): 'The phrase "reaches the addressee's electronic address" had been taken

addressee's address might be excessively burdensome and not always reliable, whereas the date of sending could be readily ascertained.[19]

11. The Rules make no specific provision for service on states. There is incoherent practice when initiating arbitrations against states, which may be 'prone to cause confusion and does not assist states in receiving notice of proceedings in timely fashion'.[20] Indeed, the Rules do not define who the 'addressee' of a notice should be, this being a matter to be resolved by agreement of the parties, the *lex arbitri*, the tribunal, or common sense in light of the purpose of making effective service of the notice.

12. Turning, finally, to paragraph 6 concerning time-periods, the only comment called for is that while it does not expressly authorize an arbitral tribunal to alter the relevant time-periods under the Rules as necessary for the fair and efficient resolution of the dispute,[21] this is undoubtedly a power within the general provision of article 17(1) of the Rules.

---

from article 10, paragraph 2, of the United Nations Convention on the Use of Electronic Communications in International Contracts'.

19 Report of the Commission on its 43rd Session, 21 June-9 July 2010, UN Doc A/65/17, para. 24.

20 *See* Jan Paulsson & Georgios Petrochilos, *Revision of the UNCITRAL Rules* (September 2006), para. 42, <www.uncitral.org>: 'In practice, claimants initiating arbitrations against states variously serve Notices of Arbitration to the respondent state's Ministry of Foreign Affairs, the Head of Government, other Ministries, an ambassador of the respondent state, or (less frequently) autonomous state agencies'.

21 *Ibid.*, at para 42. Cf. Article 22.1(ii) of the LCIA Rules, pursuant to which a tribunal may 'abridge or extend (even where the period of time has expired) any period of time prescribed under the Arbitration Agreement, any other agreement of the parties or any order made by the Arbitral Tribunal'.

Articles 3 and 4
Notice of arbitration and response to the notice of arbitration

1976 Rules

Article 3: Notice of arbitration

Article 3

1. The party initiating recourse to arbitration (hereinafter called the 'claimant') shall give to the other party (hereinafter called the 'respondent') a notice of arbitration.

2. Arbitral proceedings shall be deemed to commence on the date on which the notice of arbitration is received by the respondent.

3. The notice of arbitration shall include the following:

(a) A demand that the dispute be referred to arbitration;

(b) The names and addresses of the parties;

(c) A reference to the arbitration clause or the separate arbitration agreement that is invoked;

(d) A reference to the contract out of or in relation to which the dispute arises;

(e) The general nature of the claim and an indication of the amount involved, if any;

(f) The relief or remedy sought;

2010 Rules

Article 3: Notice of arbitration

Article 4: Response to the notice of arbitration

Article 3

1. The party or parties initiating recourse to arbitration (hereinafter called the 'claimant') shall communicate to the other party or parties (hereinafter called the 'respondent') a notice of arbitration.

2. Arbitral proceedings shall be deemed to commence on the date on which the notice of arbitration is received by the respondent.

3. The notice of arbitration shall include the following:

(a) A demand that the dispute be referred to arbitration;

(b) The names and contact details of the parties;

(c) Identification of the arbitration agreement that is invoked;

(d) Identification of any contract or other legal instrument out of or in relation to which the dispute arises or, in the absence of such contract or instrument, a brief description of the relevant relationship;

(g) A proposal as to the number of arbitrators (i.e. one or three), if the parties have not previously agreed thereon.

4. The notice of arbitration may also include:

(a) The proposals for the appointments of a sole arbitrator and an appointing authority referred to in article 6, paragraph 1;

(b) The notification of the appointment of an arbitrator referred to in article 7;

(c) The statement of claim referred to in article 18.

(e) A brief description of the claim and an indication of the amount involved, if any;

(f) The relief or remedy sought;

(g) A proposal as to the number of arbitrators, language and place of arbitration, if the parties have not previously agreed thereon.

4. The notice of arbitration may also include:

(a) A proposal for the designation of an appointing authority referred to in article 6, paragraph 1;

(b) A proposal for the appointment of a sole arbitrator referred to in article 8, paragraph 1;

(c) Notification of the appointment of an arbitrator referred to in articles 9 or 10.

5. The constitution of the arbitral tribunal shall not be hindered by any controversy with respect to the sufficiency of the notice of arbitration, which shall be finally resolved by the arbitral tribunal.

Article 4

1. Within 30 days of the receipt of the notice of arbitration, the respondent shall communicate to the claimant a response to the notice of arbitration, which shall include:

(a) The name and contact details of each respondent;

(b) A response to the information set forth in the notice of arbitration, pursuant to article 3, paragraphs 3 (c) to (g).

2. The response to the notice of arbitration may also include:

(a) Any plea that an arbitral tribunal to be constituted under these Rules lacks jurisdiction;

(b) A proposal for the designation of an appointing authority referred to in article 6, paragraph 1;

(c) A proposal for the appointment of a sole arbitrator referred to in article 8, paragraph 1;

(d) Notification of the appointment of an arbitrator referred to in article 9 or 10;

(e) A brief description of counterclaims or claims for the purpose of a set-off, if any, including where relevant, an indication of the amounts involved, and the relief or remedy sought;

(f) A notice of arbitration in accordance with article 3 in case the respondent formulates a claim against a party to the arbitration agreement other than the claimant.

3. The constitution of the arbitral tribunal shall not be hindered by any controversy with respect to the respondent's failure to communicate a response to the notice of arbitration, or an incomplete or late response to the notice of arbitration, which shall be finally resolved by the arbitral tribunal.

---

1. The notice of arbitration, required by article 3(1) of the 2010 Rules, is the pleading by which a dispute is referred to arbitration, at which point proceedings are commenced (article 3(2)).[1] Article 3(3) sets out the elements that must be included in the notice of arbitration, while article 3(4) allows the claimant to include additional elements in order to simplify or accelerate the proceedings. Importantly, article 3(5) ensures that the proceedings move forward regardless of defects in the notice of arbitration, by providing that controversies with respect to the completeness of the notice of arbitration shall not hinder the constitution of the tribunal.[2]

---

1 *See Forminster Enterprises Limited (Cyprus) v. Czech Republic* (UNCITRAL) Final Award, 15 December 2014, <www.italaw.com>, paras 62-64.

2 A number of US investment treaties, as well as the 2012 US Model BIT (Article 24(4)(c)), require for the commencement of proceedings that the investor/claimant submit together with its notice of arbitration 'the statement of claim referred to in Article 20 of the [2010] Rules'. The intention is obviously to avoid bare-bones notices of arbitration which do not provide to the respondent state sufficient particulars to organize its defence. Such a requirement sits uncomfortably within the Rules, which allow but do not compel the claimant to treat its notice of arbitration as a statement of claim, and what is more permit that election to be made only at a later stage of the proceedings; *see* article 20(1) of the Rules. Given that under article 4 of the 2010 Rules the respondent is to submit a response before the statement of claim, if the treaty text is applied to the letter, the response would be followed not by the claimant's statement of claim but by the respondent's statement of defence – which would be eccentric and inefficient, as well as unfair. Thus practice has applied these treaty requirements in a sensible way, whereby the investor/claimant submits a fully fleshed-out notice of arbitration (styled 'notice of arbitration and statement of claim') and in due course an 'amended' statement of claim which fulfils the function of a first-round memorial on the merits as conceived by article 20 of the Rules; *see*, e.g., the

2. The 1976 Rules did not foresee a response to the notice of arbitration. The statement of defence was the respondent's first opportunity to express its views on the claimant's claims and set forth any potential claims of its own. As stated in a previous report, '[n]ot to determine the respondent's position – perhaps for six months – is wasteful. It does not promote reciprocal understanding of the dispute, and therefore impedes efficient preparation for both litigation and amicable settlement'.[3] Knowledge of the respondent's position at an early stage of the proceedings may notably allow for a more targeted selection of the arbitrators and also allow for an orderly process tailor-made from the outset to the complexion of the case, catering for counter-claims or objections to jurisdiction or admissibility.[4] In addition, a response to the notice of arbitration is the appropriate procedural opportunity for the respondent to formulate claims of its own against parties to the jurisdiction agreement other than the claimant (cf. article 4(2)(f)), so that the multi-party configuration of the arbitration can be addressed early on.

3. Considered to be one of the principal changes of the revision process,[5] article 4 of the 2010 Rules now mandates the respondent to submit a response to the notice of arbitration. Article 4(1) of the 2010 Rules addresses the timing and required content of the response, while article 4(2), reproducing verbatim the contents of article 3(4), allows the respondent to include additional information. Article 4(2) also permits the respondent to submit jurisdictional objections (article 4(2)(a)); counter-claims or claims for set-off (article 4(2)(e); and a notice of arbitration in respect of a new party, which is thereby joined by right in the proceedings (article 4(2)(f)). Article 4(3) provides that neither the respondent's failure to respond nor a late or incomplete response will prevent the proceedings from moving forward.

4. Taken together, the notice and response form the opening submissions and define the contours of the case at the outset of the arbitration. Articles 3 and 4 are linked, in that many of the changes made to article 3 of the 1976 Rules have had an impact on the contents of article 4.

---

recent cases of *Gramercy Funds Management LLC, Gramercy Peru Holdings LLC, Gramercy Investment Advisors LLC and Gramercy Advisors LLC v. Peru* (UNCITRAL) <www.italaw.com>; *Cosigo Resources Ltd, Cosigo Resources Sucursal Colombia, Tobie Mining and Energy, Inc v. Colombia* (UNCITRAL) <www.italaw.com>; *Michael Ballantine and Lisa Ballantine v. Dominican Republic* (PCA Case No. 2016-17), <www.italaw.com>; and *Aaron C Berkowitz, Brett E Berkowitz and Trevor B Berkowitz (formerly Spence International Investments and others) v. Republic of Costa Rica* (ICSID Case No. UNCT/13/2) <www.italaw.com>.

3 *See* Jan Paulsson & Georgios Petrochilos, *Revision of the UNCITRAL Rules* (September 2006), para. 14(a), <www.uncitral.org>.

4 *Ibid.*

5 Markus Wirth, 'The Current Revision of the UNCITRAL Rules' in Christoph Müller (ed.), *New Developments in International Commercial Arbitration*, 6 (Schulthess 2007).

A. NOTICE OF ARBITRATION: ARTICLE 3

5. Most arbitration rules provide that the parties must communicate a formal notice of arbitration.[6] The notice of arbitration 'serves to inform the respondent … that arbitral proceedings have been started and that a particular claim will be submitted to arbitration'.[7] This requirement was originally adopted in the 1976 Rules and is reproduced in article 3(1) of the 2010 Rules.

6. The notice of arbitration has two main functions: first, it sets out the *ratione personae* and *ratione materiae* scope of the case, and second, it provides the foundation for submission of the case to arbitration in the form of an arbitration agreement.[8] This explains the list of mandatory items to be addressed in the notice (as set out in article 3(3) of the 1976 Rules). In addition to these mandatory items, a claimant wishing to submit 'more than a bare notice'[9] may also include the optional items listed in article 3(4). The purpose of these optional items was chiefly to anticipate organizational issues, relevant to the set-up and conduct of the arbitral proceedings.

7. Article 3 of the 2010 Rules maintains the dual structure of mandatory and optional items for the notice of arbitration. However, certain modifications to article 3 became necessary as the notice of arbitration would no longer be followed by the claimant's statement of claim, but by the respondent's response.

1. Mandatory items of the notice of arbitration

(i) Demand for arbitration and description of the parties: articles 3(3)(a) and (b)

8. First, and most obviously, article 3(3)(a) of the 1976 Rules required that the notice of arbitration contain 'a demand that the dispute be referred to arbitration'. This requirement is satisfied when it is clear in substance from the notice itself that the dispute is being submitted to arbitration: no specific wording is required. This basic requirement remains unchanged in the 2010 Rules, with only a textual

---

6 *See*, e.g., Article 4 of the ICC Rules; Article 6 of the WIPO Rules; Article 3 of the Swiss Rules; Article 1 of the LCIA Rules.

7 *See* UNCITRAL Report of 8th Session, 4 November 1974, UN Doc A/CN.9/97, 6 UNCITRAL Ybk 163, 167 para. 1. *See also* David D. Caron & Lee M. Caplan, *The UNCITRAL Arbitration Rules, A Commentary*, 361 (2nd ed., Oxford University Press 2013).

8 Note, however, that the Iran-US Claims Tribunal eliminated the requirement that claimants must provide a notice of arbitration (*see* Article 3 of the Tribunal Rules of Procedure (3 May 1983)). The Tribunal considered that a notice was necessary only in ad hoc proceedings in order to notify the respondent of the claimant's intent and the commencement of the proceedings. *See* Gerald Aksen, 'The Iran-United States Claims Tribunal and the UNCITRAL Arbitration Rules, an early comment' in Jan C. Schultz & Albert Jan van den Berg (eds), *The Art of Arbitration*, 1-26 (Kluwer 1982); *see also* Caron & Caplan, *supra* fn 7, at 366.

9 Peter Turner & Reza Mohtashami, *A Guide to the LCIA Arbitration Rules*, para. 3.02 (Oxford University Press 2009) (commenting on article 1 of the LCIA Rules).

change making it applicable to multi-claimant cases: article 3(1) of the 2010 Rules refers to 'the party *or parties* initiating recourse to arbitration' (emphasis added).

9. With respect to the description of the parties, article 3(3)(b) of the 1976 Rules required that the claimant include the 'names and addresses of the parties'. Article 3(3)(b) now requires the 'names and *contact details* of the parties' (emphasis added). This generic formulation is better suited to modern means of communication, as addressed in article 2 of the 2010 Rules.[10] As discussed in the context of article 4(2)(f) below, a significant change in relation to article 3(3)(b) is that, under the revised Rules, the claimant no longer enjoys an exclusive power to dictate the identity of the parties to the arbitration.

(ii) Description of agreements and or relationships: articles 3(3)(c) and (d)

10. Under the 1976 Rules, the notice of arbitration had to contain a 'reference' to the arbitration clause or agreement on the basis of which the claimant initiated the arbitral proceedings. The arbitration agreement evidences the parties' common intention to waive their respective rights to submit disputes to national courts and to turn to arbitration instead. The legitimacy of the entire arbitral proceedings rests on the arbitration agreement; accordingly, most other arbitration rules require that the notice of arbitration include a copy,[11] or at least a description,[12] of this foundational agreement.

11. Against this background, the 2010 Rules are more demanding and require an 'identification' of the arbitration agreement (article 3(3)(c)). Such 'identification' implies that the claimant should provide basic information relating to the agreement, e.g. the conclusion date, identity of the signatories/parties, etc. However, the suggestion that a copy of the arbitration agreement should also be provided with the notice of arbitration was not accepted, for a straightforward reason. The requirement that the parties 'identify' the arbitration agreement is worded broadly enough to call for all relevant particulars, without unduly restricting the claimant in cases where the agreement has been made orally, or via the exchange of several documents, etc.

12. In the same vein, article 3(3)(d) of the 2010 Rules requires the 'identification of' – as opposed to a 'reference to' – the contract out of which or relating to which the dispute arises. However, unlike the 1976 Rules, the 2010 Rules do not assume a contract to be the only potential source of a dispute. Consistent

---

[10] *See* discussion of article 2 of the 2010 Rules, *supra*.

[11] *See*, e.g., Article 1.1(ii) of the LCIA Rules; Article 9(iii) of the WIPO Rules; Article 2(3)(c) of the AAA International Arbitration Rules. *See also* Article 4(3)(e) of the ICC Rules, pursuant to which the request for arbitration must include 'any relevant agreements and, in particular, the arbitration agreement(s)'. *See* on this point, Yves Derains & Eric A. Schwartz, *A Guide to the ICC Rules of Arbitration*, 48 fn 11 (2nd ed., Kluwer 2005) (citing to final Award in ICC Case No. 6784, 8(1) ICC Ct Bull 53, 53-54, where the Tribunal refused to declare as 'inadmissible' a request for arbitration that did not contain a copy of the arbitration agreement).

[12] *See* article 6(iv) of the SCC Rules.

with the new wording used in article 1(1),[13] article 3(3)(d) of the 2010 Rules specifically provides for the identification of any 'other legal instrument out of or in relation to which the dispute arises'. Such a 'legal instrument' could be, for example, an investment treaty referring to arbitration under the UNCITRAL Rules.[14] Article 3(3)(d) also envisages 'the absence' of a contract or instrument. In such a situation, the claimant must submit 'a brief description of the relevant relationship' which the parties have agreed would be subject to arbitration. This wording acknowledges that 'a cause of action can originate not only from a particular contract or a particular legal instrument, but also from a particular act (such as an infringement) or – for example in the context of antitrust laws – from an omission'.[15]

(iii) Description of the claim: articles 3(3)(e) and (f)

13. Under the 1976 Rules, the claimant had to mention the 'general nature of the claim' and indicate the amount involved, if any (article 3(3)(e)). The 'general nature of the claim' is a rather vague formulation which does not require that the dispute be described or summarised, or that the claims against the respondent be spelt out.[16]

14. Although the specific language of article 3(3)(e) was not directly at issue there, the *Grand River* case[17] illustrates the sort of problems that can be encountered when a claim is insufficiently identified. The respondent objected to the tribunal's jurisdiction on grounds that, *inter alia*, the claimant had raised claims that were not specified in the notice of arbitration.[18] The arbitral tribunal disallowed the relevant claims, upholding the objection on the basis that:

---

[13] *See* discussion of article 1(1), *supra*.

[14] *See Link-Trading Joint Stock Company v. Department for Customs Control of the Republic of Moldova* (UNCITRAL) Award on Jurisdiction, 16 February 2001, <www.italaw.com> (in light of the reference to the applicable bilateral investment treaty in the notice of arbitration, it was not necessary to make reference to any contract); *see also* Paulsson & Petrochilos, *supra* fn 3, at para. 6. In the same way that a claim may not be 'in relation to [a] contract' (to satisfy article 1(1) of the 1976 Rules), a contract may not be the relevant instrument under which the claim arises. *See* further on this point, Jan Paulsson, *Arbitration Without Privity*, 10 For Inv LJ 232 (1995).

[15] Marc Blessing, *Comparison of the Swiss Rules with the UNCITRAL Arbitration Rules and Others*, Report submitted to ASA Conference in Zurich, 23 January 2004, 10 (commenting on the deficiencies of article 3(3)(d) of the Swiss Rules).

[16] Cf. Article 1.1(iii) of the LCIA Rules and Article 4(3) of the ICC Rules.

[17] *See Grand River Enterprises Six Nations Ltd and ors v. United States of America* (UNCITRAL) Decision on Objections to Jurisdiction, 20 July 2006, <www.italaw.com>.

[18] Pursuant to Article 1119 of NAFTA, the claimant must submit a 'Notice of Intent to Submit a Claim to Arbitration'. *See also Achmea BV v. The Slovak Republic (Number 2)* (UNCITRAL) Award on Jurisdiction and Admissibility, 20 May 2014, <www.italaw.com>, paras 269-270 (tribunal had 'no difficulty in finding' that elements of the claim fell outside of its jurisdiction on the basis that these elements were not complained of in the claimant's notice of arbitration).

> [F]undamental fairness and good order require that a party receive sufficient notice of the claim that it is expected to answer. The Notice of Arbitration and Particularized Statement of Claim did not do so with respect to the allocable share amendments. The Claimants presumably knew of these amendments when they were preparing these pleadings, but they were not identified as a significant element of the claims in either document. If the Claimants intended the amendments to be a major component of their case ... the Respondent (and the Tribunal) had a right to know this at a much earlier time.[19]

It will be noted that the tribunal disallowed the additional, tardy claims, not simply on the formal basis that they had not been articulated in the notice of arbitration but on the basis that to admit them at the time that they were formulated would run counter to 'fundamental fairness and good order'. Such findings would call for an assessment of all relevant circumstances. In this connection, there is nothing in the text or in the spirit of the 1976 Rules (or the 2010 Rules for that matter) to exclude the possibility of supplementing or amending a notice of arbitration early in the proceedings.

15. Article 3(3)(e) of the 2010 Rules addresses this issue by requiring a 'brief description of the claim', which calls for a greater degree of detail than what was required under the 1976 Rules. The 2010 Rules maintain the requirement that the amount 'involved' be indicated, if possible. The words 'amount involved', as opposed to 'amount claimed', encompass the cases where the claim is not per se monetary – e.g. a declaratory claim or a claim to complete or revise contractual terms – but nevertheless has monetary implications. This is a useful requirement, common in international practice. It means that if the amount in dispute – or, more broadly, at stake – is quantifiable, then an effort should be made to quantify it, be it in a provisional manner. This allows the parties and the tribunal to determine the magnitude of the dispute at the very outset of the arbitration and to plan resources accordingly.[20]

16. Article 3(3)(f) remains unchanged from the 1976 Rules, requiring simply that the relief or remedy sought be indicated in the notice of arbitration. This requirement is also to be read in a pragmatic fashion. What is required is in the nature of an indication of the type and scope of the relief sought. It is not uncommon in practice for such an indication to be framed in programmatic or provisional terms, especially where the dispute continues to evolve.

(iv) Matters relating to the conduct of the arbitration: article 3(3)(g)

17. Article 3(3)(g) of the 1976 Rules required that the claimant propose the number of arbitrators (one or three), unless the parties had previously agreed on this matter. The original wording of this provision is maintained in the 2010 Rules.

---

[19] *Grand River Enterprises Six Nations Ltd and ors v. United States of America, supra* fn 17, at para. 94.

[20] *See The Canadian Cattlemen for Fair Trade v. United States of America* (UNCITRAL) Award on Jurisdiction, 28 January 2008, <www.italaw.com>, para. 5.

Indeed, it is in the parties' interest to articulate their preferences and reach an agreement on the number of arbitrators as soon as possible, in order to avoid the default appointment of three arbitrators (pursuant to article 7 of the 2010 Rules). This is particularly relevant in disputes involving small amounts, which may not warrant three arbitrators.[21]

18. Article 3(3)(g) of the 2010 Rules also requires proposals relating to the language and seat of the arbitration. This brings the UNCITRAL Rules in line with most other sets of arbitration rules. It is important to include these fundamental procedural components in the notice of arbitration as they are relevant to the organization of the arbitration – notably in respect of the identity of the arbitrators.[22]

2. Optional items of the notice of arbitration: streamlining the arbitral process

19. Article 3(4) of the 1976 Rules listed a number of optional items that the claimant 'may' include in its notice of arbitration. The main purpose of this provision was to clarify that the claimant could include additional information in order to accelerate the proceedings. The first three items related to proposals for the appointment of a sole arbitrator (article 3(4)(a)), an appointing authority (article 3(4)(a)), and the notification of a claimant-appointed arbitrator (for three-member arbitral tribunals) (article 3(4)(b)).

20. Article 3(4)(c) of the 1976 Rules, which allowed the claimant to include the statement of claim in the notice of arbitration (or to treat the notice of arbitration as the statement of claim),[23] rather than submitting its statement of claim at a later stage of the proceedings,[24] was omitted in the 2010 Rules. In the preparation of the 1976 text, some delegates favoured consolidating the submission of these two pleadings in the interest of saving time, while others emphasized that requiring the claimant to produce a detailed pleading at such an early stage of the proceedings would be unnecessarily burdensome.[25] Article 3(4)(c) was a compromise between the two views. However, in light of the new dynamics

---

21 *See* Paulsson & Petrochilos, *supra* fn 3, at para. 14(c) (noting that the default appointment of a three-member tribunal 'has the potential to deter small claims from being brought to arbitration on considerations of cost').

22 *See*, e.g., Articles 4(3)(g) and 4(3)(h) of the ICC Rules; Article 1.1(iv) of the LCIA Rules; Article 6(vi) of the SCC Rules.

23 For a recent example of a claimant designating its notice of arbitration as its statement of claim by simple letter to the tribunal, *see Eli Lilly and Company v. The Government of Canada* (UNCITRAL) (ICSID Case No. UNCT/14/2) Claimant's Letter Designating the Notice of Arbitration as the Statement of Claim, 14 May 2014, <www.italaw.com>.

24 *See* UNCITRAL Report of the Secretary General on the Draft UNCITRAL Arbitration Rules, 12 December 1975, UN Doc A/CN.9/112/Add.1, 168. *See also Canfor Corporation v. United States of America and Tembec et al. v. United States of America and Terminal Forest Products Ltd v. United States of America* (UNCITRAL) Decision on Preliminary Question, 6 June 2006, <www.italaw.com>, para. 5.

25 *See* UNCITRAL Report of 9th Session, 15 April 1976, UN Doc A/CN.9/9/C.2/SR.2, paras 32-45. *See also* Caron & Caplan, *supra* fn 7, at 361.

introduced by the respondent's response under article 4 of the 2010 Rules, the Working Group concluded that 'the decision to treat the notice of arbitration as a statement of claim should only be required after the respondent had submitted its response. Otherwise, the claimant would not know whether it should further develop its position'.[26] The claimant may still elect to treat its notice of arbitration as its statement of claim, but only at a later stage of the proceedings, in accordance with article 20(1) of the 2010 Rules.

3. Incomplete notice of arbitration

21. The 1976 Rules do not explicitly address the consequences of an incomplete notice of arbitration. Although this could give rise to an argument that the notice was invalid and incapable of commencing valid arbitration proceedings, the 1976 Rules did not stipulate a sanction for incomplete notices, nor (despite the peremptory wording 'shall include' in article 3(3)) did they explicitly formulate the minimum content of the notice as a formal requirement of validity or admissibility. In the *Link Trading* case, the respondent was therefore unsuccessful in its objection to the jurisdiction of the tribunal on the basis that 'the notice of arbitration was defective since it fail[ed] to make reference to the contract that is the basis of the dispute or to propose the number of arbitrators as required by UNCITRAL Rules'.[27]

22. The issue is addressed to a certain extent in the 2010 Rules. The Working Group was initially undecided as to whether the issue of an incomplete notice of arbitration should be addressed in the revised Rules or left to the tribunal's discretion.[28] Ultimately, it decided to address the issue in part, by providing that 'any controversy with respect to the sufficiency of the notice of arbitration' shall not hinder the constitution of the arbitral tribunal. Whether genuine or purely tactical, any complaints of the respondent relating to the completeness of the notice of arbitration shall now 'be finally resolved by the arbitral tribunal' (article 3(5)). Inspired by article 5.4 of the 1998 LCIA Rules,[29] the new article 3(5) ensures that the arbitral proceedings are conducted in a cost- and time-efficient manner. The Rules steer clear, however, of addressing the consequences, if any, of an incomplete notice of arbitration. Article 3(5) speaks of 'sufficiency', a term which suggests that the matter is not simply one of formal completeness but rather of a necessary content, absent which the document will be incapable of constituting a notice of arbitration. It is submitted that each case should be assessed individually, and the tribunal must inquire whether the alleged defect is so grave as to compromise the essential functions of the notice of arbitration. Any

---

26 *See* UNCITRAL Report of 49th Session, 30 September 2008, UN Doc A/CN.9/665, para. 36; and Paulsson & Petrochilos, *supra* fn 3, at para. 14(a).

27 *Link-Trading Joint Stock Company v. Department for Customs Control of the Republic of Moldova* (UNCITRAL) Award on Jurisdiction, 16 February 2001, <www.italaw.com>, 3. *See also Eureko BV v. Republic of Poland* (UNCITRAL) Partial Award, 19 August 2005, <www.italaw.com>, para. 4.

28 *See* UNCITRAL Report of 45th Session, 5 October 2006, UN Doc A/CN.9/614, para. 54.

29 *See* UNCITRAL Report of 46th Session, 20 March 2007, UN Doc A/CN.9/619, para. 56.

objections with respect to the existence or validity of the arbitration agreement will be dealt with by the tribunal in accordance with article 23.

23. There were proposals within the Working Group to grant the tribunal express powers to request rectification of a notice of arbitration and to determine the consequences of an incomplete notice, such as whether the date of the commencement of the proceedings should be delayed.[30] Ultimately it was considered that such powers were already conferred upon the tribunal pursuant to article 17.[31]

B. RESPONSE TO THE NOTICE OF ARBITRATION: ARTICLE 4

24. As already mentioned, the 1976 version of the Rules did not foresee a response to the notice of arbitration. While, in practice, respondents did on occasion choose to respond to the notice of arbitration *after* the arbitral tribunal had been constituted,[32] the absence of an express requirement for a response to the notice of arbitration was not in step with international practice.

25. By requiring that a response be lodged, article 4 of the 2010 Rules provides 'an appropriate balance between the applicant and the respondent'.[33] The respondent has an opportunity to answer the notice of arbitration and establish its position with respect to the claimant's allegations. The Working Group also considered that allowing the respondent to respond to the notice would have the 'advantage of clarifying at an early stage of the procedure the main issues raised by the dispute'.[34] The response may also include any jurisdictional objections the respondent intends to raise.[35] The response also allows the respondent to raise any counterclaims or set-off claims against any of the parties to the arbitration agreement (article 4(2)(e)), even if the latter were not named in the notice of arbitration.[36] In this case, a notice of arbitration in accordance with article 3 must also be included (article 4(2)(f)).

---

30 *Ibid. See also* Caron & Caplan, *supra* fn 7, at 365.

31 *See* discussion of article 17, *infra*.

32 *See Chevron Corporation (USA) and Texaco Petroleum Company (USA) v. The Republic of Ecuador* (UNCITRAL) Interim Award, 1 December 2008, < www.italaw.com >, para. 16.

33 UNCITRAL Report of 45th Session, 5 October 2006, UN Doc A/CN.9/614, para. 57.

34 *Ibid.*

35 The cut-off time for such objections is the filing of the statement of defence (*see* article 23(2)) but an early indication of any objections will best allow for the proper organization of proceedings, for example by allowing the tribunal to handle the objections 'as a preliminary question' in accordance with article 23(3). *See*, e.g., *National Grid PLC v. The Argentine Republic* (UNCITRAL) Decision on Jurisdiction, 20 June 2006, < www.italaw.com >, para. 8.

36 As to these notions, *see* the commentary to article 21 of the 2010 Rules, paras 13-14, *infra*.

1. Timing

26. Article 4(1) starts out by stating the basic principle that 'the respondent shall communicate to the claimant a response to the notice of arbitration'. The respondent is given 30 days, running from the receipt of the notice of arbitration.

27. The 30-day requirement is in itself unexceptional.[37] However, institutional arbitration rules give the relevant institutions the power to extend deadlines for the response to the notice of arbitration, if need be.[38] The UNCITRAL Rules, designed for ad hoc arbitrations, cannot offer this solution before a tribunal has been constituted, although they permit an arbitral tribunal to amend or extend deadlines,[39] and the tribunal, once constituted, has authority to determine the consequences of an inadequate response.[40]

28. The issue is unlikely to cause problems in the vast majority of cases. The response is intended to define the contours of the respondent's position and therefore may be a relatively brief submission. As such, there is only a small risk that 30 days will be insufficient.[41] Moreover, article 4(3) of the 2010 Rules (discussed below) provides that a late response – or indeed the respondent's failure to communicate a response at all – will not hinder the advancement of the arbitral process.

29. Other time-limits provided under the 1976 Rules were extended in the 2010 Rules to bring them into conformity with the 30-day time-limit in article 4(1). The deadline for the parties to agree on the number of arbitrators pursuant to article 7 of the 2010 Rules, for instance, is now 30 days from the receipt of the notice of arbitration, as opposed to 15 days under article 5 of the 1976 Rules. However, the 15-day time-limit to challenge an arbitrator was not extended, on grounds that the respondent must act promptly on this fundamental matter and that a challenge leads to a further process in which the challenge is examined. Thus, a challenge process will run its course in parallel with the respondent's preparation of its response.

---

37 *See*, e.g., Article 2.1 of the LCIA Rules; Article 11 of the WIPO Rules. Cf. Article 9(1) of the SCC Rules, which gives the Secretariat discretion to 'set a time period within which the Respondent shall submit an Answer to the SCC'.

38 *See*, e.g., Article 5(2) of the ICC Rules ('[t]he Secretariat may grant the respondent an extension of the time for submitting the Answer'). Cf. Turner & Mohtashami, *supra* fn 9, at para. 3.28 (the authors note that the LCIA Rules do not give the LCIA Court the explicit power to extend this deadline).

39 *See* discussion of article 17, *infra*.

40 Caron & Caplan, *supra* fn 7, at 373. Arbitration institutions that administer proceedings under the UNCITRAL Rules – for example, the SCC, PCA and ICSID – do not expressly state whether they offer the possibility of extending the deadline for the response to the notice of arbitration.

41 *See*, however, *Chevron Corporation (USA) and Texaco Petroleum Company (USA) v. The Republic of Ecuador*, *supra* fn 32, at paras 17-18 (the respondent twice sought an extension for the submission of 'a short Reply to the Notice of Arbitration', causing the deferral of scheduled procedural meetings).

2. Mandatory content

30. The content of the response is intended to mirror the mandatory content of the notice of arbitration. The respondent must provide the 'name and contact details' of each respondent (article 4(1)(a)), and must include a response to 'the information set forth in the notice of arbitration, pursuant to article 3, paragraphs 3 (c) to (g)'.

3. Optional items

(i) Jurisdictional objections: article 4(2)(a)

31. Article 4(1) was largely uncontroversial during the revision process and was adopted by the Working Group with minimal discussion. One issue of debate was whether to address in article 4 the respondent's pleas regarding the tribunal's lack of jurisdiction. Some participants noted that requiring the respondent to raise such pleas in its response would contradict article 23(2), which provides that jurisdictional pleas should be raised no later than in the statement of defence.[42] The Working Group finally decided to make such pleas an optional component of the notice of arbitration (article 4(2) of the 2010 Rules).[43]

32. Tactically, the respondent will often have every interest in setting out jurisdictional (or other threshold) objections as early as possible. As put by two commentators:

> It is ... good practice and in the interests of the respondent for it to raise any jurisdictional defences as soon as possible, especially if it wishes the tribunal to determine the issue of its jurisdiction in a preliminary phase of the arbitration and before consideration of the merits of the case.[44]

33. Thus article 4(2)(a) allows the respondent to include in its response 'any plea that an arbitral tribunal to be constituted under these Rules lacks jurisdiction'. This should be read as including objections to admissibility (of the claim or of the notice of arbitration), as these also have the potential to be dealt with in a separate, preliminary phase of the proceedings in accordance with article 23(3) of the Rules.[45] The 2010 Rules encourage the respondent to raise such objections before the establishment of the procedural timetable[46] so that it can be fixed accordingly.[47]

---

42 *See* UNCITRAL Report of 49th Session, 30 September 2008, UN Doc A/CN.9/665, para. 39.

43 *Ibid.*

44 Turner & Mohtashami, *supra* fn 9, at para. 3.34.

45 For discussion of the distinction between jurisdiction and admissibility, *see* Jan Paulsson, 'Jurisdiction and Admissibility' in *Global Reflections on International Law, Commerce and Dispute Resolution – Liber Amicorum in honour of Robert Briner*, 601 (ICC Publication 693) (2005).

46 Cf. APRAG Report of 49th Session, 10 October 2008, para. 30.

47 *See* article 17(2) of the Rules.

(ii) Proposals for the constitution of the tribunal: articles 4(2)(b)-(d)

34. Mirroring articles 3(4)(a)-(c) with respect to the notice of arbitration, articles 4(2)(b)-(d) invite the respondent to make proposals for the appointment of an appointing authority, a sole arbitrator, or to identify its appointee to the tribunal if the tribunal is to comprise three members.[48]

(iii) Raising claims in the response: article 4(2)(e)

35. Article 4(2)(e) enables the respondent to set out in the response, by way of 'brief description', 'counterclaims or claims for the purpose of a set-off'. The language follows article 3(3)(e), which similarly requires a 'brief description' of the claimant's claim, and article 21(3), which refers to counterclaims or set-off claims by the respondent. The essential points to note here are as follows:

   (i) *Optional character:* As is the case with objections to jurisdiction or admissibility, it is desirable, but not mandatory, for the respondent to assert such claims in its response: the last procedural opportunity to do so is the respondent's first substantive pleading, i.e. the statement of defence (see article 21(3)).

   (ii) *Terminology:* The 2010 Rules preserve the terms 'counterclaims' and claims in 'set-off' which were originally in the 1976 Rules.[49] These terms are not defined in the Rules, nor is there uniform terminology in the various legal systems of the world. The Iran-US Claims Tribunal has adopted the reading that counterclaims are stand-alone claims by the respondent against the claimant (i.e. claims which could have been asserted in arbitration proceedings commenced by the respondent against the claimant), whereas set-off claims are claims which are conditional upon the success of the claimant's claims (i.e. claims which could not have been asserted as the subject-matter of separate proceedings initiated by the respondent, but which are allowed under the applicable substantive law to be made in proceedings brought by the other side – time-barred claims being one example under some laws).[50]

   (iii) *Scope of permissible claims:* The purpose of the 1976 Rules, as for the 2010 Rules, was to capture in the same arbitration all the claims that a respondent might assert, so that all possible claims between the parties could be resolved in the arbitration already on foot and may be resolved in a single set of proceedings. Accordingly, it would be wrong to read the terms 'counterclaims' and claims in 'set-off' as unduly limitative of the permissible claims: on the contrary, the terms are used in a non-technical sense and are intended to

---

48 For a criticism of these optional items, *see* Pieter Sanders, *The Revision of the UNCITRAL Arbitration Rules* (August 2009), 6, <www.arbitration-icca.org>.

49 *See* articles 19(3)-(4) of the 1976 Rules.

50 *See* David D. Caron, Lee M. Caplan & Matti Pellonpää, *The UNCITRAL Arbitration Rules, A Commentary*, 424 (Oxford University Press 2006) citing to *Anaconda-Iran Inc v. The Islamic Republic of Iran, et al.*, Case No. 167, Chamber Three, Order of 11 October 1984 (standing for the proposition that counter-claims satisfying the 'transaction or occurrence' test are independent claims not bound by the claimant's initial claims).

cover the field of conceivable types of claims. Claims that might be labelled in one legal tradition as 'cross-claims' or 'substantive objections' – for instance, claims that serve not only as defensive assertions, but also allegations that the claimant committed an offence of some sort – fall in principle within the ambit of article 4(2)(e). Any possible doubt in this regard is dispelled by a combined reading of articles 4(2)(e) and 4(2)(f). It follows from the latter provision that the crucial requirement is that the claim asserted by the respondent be one that can be brought under the same arbitration agreement as the one invoked by the claimant as the basis for the arbitration. Moreover, and in contrast with article 19(3) of the 1976 Rules, article 21(3) no longer requires that counterclaims or claims in set-off 'aris[e] out of the same contract'. However, in practice this will of course almost always be the case, given the requirement that permissible claims by the respondent must come within the ambit of the same arbitration agreement as that which is invoked by the claimant.

(iv) *Claims among various respondents:* For the same reasons, claims within the respondents' group can be freely asserted within the above limitation. A typical example is a claim by which respondent A seeks to pass liability for a claim asserted by the claimant to respondent B, typically in an owner-contractor-subcontractor triangular contract. (This kind of configuration, where respondent A has interests divergent from those of respondent B, has been catered for in respect of the constitution of the tribunal in article 10(3).)

(v) *No consolidation of related claims:* Claims that cannot be brought under the same arbitration agreement, but that can be brought to arbitration under another agreement providing for arbitration under the Rules, would require consolidation in order to be adjudicated together with the claimant's claims. The Working Group discussed and ultimately rejected suggested provisions concerning the non-consensual joinder of parties, as well as consolidation.[51]

(iv) Joinder of additional respondents: article 4(2)(f)

36. Article 4(2)(f) is a novel provision. By permitting the party named as respondent in the notice of arbitration to direct claims against any other party that is not a named claimant in the notice but is a party to the arbitration agreement, article 4(2)(f) provides for a joinder by right – to be distinguished from joinder by leave of the tribunal under article 17(5) at subsequent stages of the proceedings.[52] Here too, the intent is to concentrate as much as possible all possible claims between the parties. Additionally, however, the respondent is now on an equal footing with the claimant in determining the *ratione personae* scope of the proceedings, and

---

[51] For further discussion of consolidation *see* commentary to article 17 of the 2010 Rules, paras 45-47, *infra*. *See* James E. Castello, *Plus Ça Change, Plus C'est la Même Chose: Eight Revisions not Adopted in the 2010 UNCITRAL Rules*, 28(4) ASA Bull 855, 860-62 (2010); *see also* Paulsson & Petrochilos, *supra* fn 3, at paras 125-131.

[52] As such, Article 4(2)(f) is consistent with the practice of the ICC Court: *see* Article 7 of the ICC Rules. Cf. Article 13 of the SCC Rules.

in this way the provision serves both procedural efficiency and party equality. Two examples will illustrate this:

(i) Suppose a triangular contract among A_1, A_2, and B, where A_2 is a wholly-owned corporate vehicle of A_1. The obligations under the contract are defined as flowing from B to both A_1 and A_2 on an equal footing, and from A_1 and A_2 jointly and severally to B. Suppose, further, that A_2 is relatively enforcement-proof and for tactical reasons A_2 commences arbitration against B – i.e. to spare A_1 the risk of a counterclaim by B and force B to commence separate proceedings, which will likely be delayed given the existence of a prior related arbitration. Now, under the 2010 Rules, B may join A_1 in the proceedings as a matter of right.

(ii) In the triangular owner-contractor-subcontractor contract posited in connection with article 4(2)(e) above, the contractor will be able to assert a claim against the subcontractor as a respondent in the arbitration even if the owner/claimant chose to commence proceedings only against the contractor.

37. Neither article 4 nor other provisions in the Rules deals with the specific process to be followed after a joinder by right. This may be because article 4(2)(f) was added at the end of the final reading of the revised Rules,[53] but the reality is that providing for a separate process might have given rise to inconsistencies with other provisions of the Rules and in respect of time-limits. Generally, the procedure under the Rules is configured for the paradigm of two opposed camps, each comprising identical or aligned interests.[54] As such, a degree of adjustment must be made by the tribunal where there are three or more camps in the proceedings.[55] The application of the Rules in that context may be a more delicate matter before the constitution of the tribunal or in the absence of an institution agreed by the parties to administer the proceedings.

38. Moreover, there appears to be nothing standing in the way of a newly-named party deciding to respond to the notice of arbitration. In fact, such a response is desirable, for the same reasons as the response by the original respondent.[56] One may also posit the desirability of a response by the claimant to any counterclaim asserted by the newly-named party against the claimant. Ultimately, these are matters going to the fairness and efficiency of the procedure, which the tribunal may address under its general power pursuant to article 17(1).

---

53 *See* UNCITRAL Report of 52nd Session, 19 February 2010, UN Doc A/CN.9/688, para. 67.

54 *See*, e.g., the provisions on the statement of claim and the statement of defence, articles 20 and 21 of the Rules, respectively.

55 This will be in exercise of the tribunal's general procedural power under article 17(1) of the Rules.

56 It is clear from the Rules that there is a right to respond in substance to any claim or allegation: signally, article 21(3) of the 1976 Rules referred to a 'reply' to a counterclaim to be submitted by the claimant after the statement of claim, apparently as a matter of right, even if the Rules did not expressly envisage any submission by the claimant after the statement of claim.

39. The most important effect of a joinder under article 4(2)(f) is, crucially, one which is felt before the tribunal has been constituted. The newly-joined party will have to take a position on the arbitrator appointments by the original claimant or respondent, depending on which camp it falls in. It will have to determine whether it accepts that nomination as a joint one (see article 10(1)); if not, as may be more likely in practice, the constitution of the tribunal should be left to the appointing authority (see article 10(3)).

4. Missing, incomplete, or late response to the notice of arbitration

40. Article 4(3) of the 2010 Rules addresses the consequences of a 'failure to communicate a response ... or an incomplete or late response' to the notice of arbitration. Essentially mirroring article 3(5), article 4(3) simply states that 'the constitution of the arbitral tribunal shall not be hindered by' a missing, incomplete or late response. Although the filing of a response (be it an incomplete one) may be viewed as a 'procedural obligation',[57] the Working Group was well aware of the reality of defaulting respondents. Article 30(1)(b) treats a failure to submit a response as a species of default, which (as for any default by the respondent) cannot prevent the continuation of the proceedings but does not amount to 'an admission of the claimant's allegations'. Indeed, the possibility of a missing response has been taken into account in article 6(6), which provides that '[w]hen the appointing authority is requested to appoint an arbitrator ... the party making the request shall send to the appointing authority copies of the notice of arbitration and, *if it exists*, any response to the notice of arbitration' (emphasis added).

41. Notwithstanding the provisions of articles 4(3) and 30(1)(b), failure by the respondent to submit a response may well amount to a waiver, notably of objections to the completeness or validity of the notice of arbitration.[58]

---

[57] UNCITRAL Working Paper for 46th Session, 6 December 2006, UN Doc A/CN.9/WG.II/WP.145, para. 39. *See also* UNCITRAL Report of 46th Session, 20 March 2007, UN Doc A/CN.9/619, para. 58.

[58] *See* discussion of article 32, *infra*.

Article 5
Representation and assistance

1976 Rules Article 4: Representation and assistance	2010 Rules Article 5: Representation and assistance
The parties may be represented or assisted by persons of their choice. The names and addresses of such persons must be communicated in writing to the other party; such communication must specify whether the appointment is being made for purposes of representation or assistance.	Each party may be represented or assisted by persons chosen by it. The names and addresses of such persons must be communicated to all parties and to the arbitral tribunal. Such communication must specify whether the appointment is being made for purposes of representation or assistance. Where a person is to act as a representative of a party, the arbitral tribunal, on its own initiative or at the request of any party, may at any time require proof of authority granted to the representative in such a form as the arbitral tribunal may determine.

1. Article 5 of the 2010 Rules reiterates article 4 of the 1976 Rules, with small substantive and textual changes. The new element is a provision expressly requiring proof of representation to be provided if the tribunal requests such proof. While the communication of the identity of representatives/assistants to the receiving party normally suffices to ensure that the other party proceeds safely,[1] in the 2010 revision it was felt that this was not enough to ensure the actual validity of the putative representation.

---

[1] *See* UNCITRAL Report of the Secretary General on the Draft UNCITRAL Arbitration Rules, 12 December 1975, UN Doc A/CN.9/112/Add.1, 168: 'The communication of the name of the counsel or agent is necessary so as to assure the other party that such counsel or agent possesses the requisite authority to act on behalf of the party whom he claims to represent'.

2. The salient element in article 5, as in article 4 of the 1976 Rules, is the rule allowing parties to be represented or assisted in arbitral proceedings by whomever they choose. There is no requirement that the persons chosen be admitted to a particular bar (e.g. that of the place of arbitration), or, for that matter, any bar or other professional association at all. This has the merit of excluding any suggestion that such bar or other affiliation should be inferred from rules of domestic procedural law. This accords well with emerging statements of good practice in international arbitration, which apply to all participants as counsel regardless of whether they are admitted as practising lawyers in a national regulated body.[2] Obviously, mandatory provisions of the *lex arbitri* to opposite effect remain unaffected by article 5, in accordance with the rule in article 1(3).[3]

3. The use of two terms, 'representation' and 'assistance', is not redundant. The latter is intended to account for persons other than counsel of record (or, in an inter-state context, agents) who are also involved in the preparation or presentation of a party's case.[4] However, the term 'assistance' should not be read too broadly, compelling parties to communicate the names and addresses of, for example, 'translators, economists, paralegals, secretaries, perhaps even travel agents'.[5]

4. A change with significant potential lurks in the facially minor change of wording from 'persons of their choice' (article 4 of the 1976 Rules) to 'persons chosen by it' (article 5 of the 2010 Rules). The drafting history indicates that the modification was made 'in order to avoid the implication that the party had an unrestricted discretion, at any time during the proceedings, to impose the presence of any counsel (for example, a busy practitioner who would be unable to meet reasonable time schedules set by the arbitral tribunal)'.[6] True, the exiguously subtle change of wording provides a limited textual foothold for limiting a party's freedom of choice on grounds of maintaining a procedural schedule. Perhaps no wording

---

[2] *See*, e.g., the 2013 IBA Guidelines on Party Representation in International Arbitration (defining a 'Party Representative' or 'Representative' as 'any person, including a Party's employee, who appears in an arbitration on behalf of a Party and makes submissions, arguments or representations to the Arbitral Tribunal on behalf of such Party, other than in the capacity as a Witness or Expert, and whether or not legally qualified or admitted to a Domestic Bar').

[3] For example, under Thai law (Royal Decree No 3 BE 2543) (2000), foreign lawyers may represent parties to an arbitration only where the dispute is not governed by Thai law, or where, irrespective of the governing law, there is no need to apply for enforcement of the arbitral award in Thailand.

[4] *See* Stewart A. Baker & Mark D. Davis, *The UNCITRAL Arbitration Rules in Practice – The Experience of the Iran-United States Claims Tribunal*, 12 and the references (Kluwer 1992). The Iran-U.S. Claims Tribunal clarified the distinction between representation and assistance by specifying that a party's 'representative shall be deemed to be authorized to act' for and to bind that party for all purposes, whereas a party's assistants may neither bind the party nor receive notices or documents on its behalf; *see* Notes to Article 4, Tribunal Rules of Procedure of the Iran-United States Claims Tribunal (3 May 1983).

[5] *See* Baker & Davis, *supra* fn 4, at 12-13.

[6] UNCITRAL Report of 46th Session, 20 March 2007, UN Doc A/CN.9/619, para. 63.

would be capable properly to address this very delicate – and exceedingly rare – issue. The matter turns chiefly on two issues which are inter-linked:

(i) The issue of jurisdiction, i.e. whether the Rules grant the tribunal the power to reject a party's choice: the only arguable bases are the general power under article 17(1) and, possibly, a residual inherent power to safeguard the integrity of the proceedings.[7]

(ii) On what substantive grounds may a tribunal reject a party's choice? It may be the case that certain grounds for recusal of counsel or other participants will be within the exclusive jurisdiction of another body to enforce – for example, the disciplinary arm of a bar, or a court, in the event of a conflict of interests. A case for not accepting the party's choice on grounds related to the arbitral process under the Rules may probably be made only in connection with the general duties of avoiding unnecessary delay and expense and providing a fair and efficient process, under article 17(1). The passage from the drafting history quoted above indicates a tactical or careless change of counsel which stalls the process at a delicate stage or has the potential of frustrating party equality.

Obviously where the issue of resisting a party's choice arises there will be a difficult balance to strike between party equality and natural justice, on the one hand, and the integrity of the process, on the other hand.

5. The names and addresses of each party's representatives are to be communicated to the other party or parties and to the tribunal. Article 5 does not itself explicitly require that this communication be in writing, as was the case under article 4 of the 1976 version, but the general provisions on notices in article 2 apply to this communication as well.[8] It is still a requirement, however, that the communication specify the role of each person as a representative (i.e. agent or counsel of record) or as providing assistance.

6. Finally, article 5 includes an addition which can be expected to have less significance in practice than is perhaps suggested by the fact that the addition was made. The arbitral tribunal may now require proof of the actual authority granted to a person or entity acting as a party's representative (but not as a person offering other forms of assistance). The tribunal may do so either on its own initiative or at the request of any party. Sufficient proof will be in the form that the arbitral tribunal determines: the rule is intended to be flexible.[9] This addition is in itself doubtless sound, and seeks to cater for cases where there are doubts about the putative representative's actual authority to represent a party.[10] It is not clear whether this addition was prompted by an excess of caution or problems actually encountered in practice. But it may be true that such problems may be

---

7 The doctrine of inherent powers is addressed in this work under the rubric of article 17(1).

8 *See* article 2(1) of the Rules and the definition of 'notice' in that provision, which includes any 'communication'.

9 UNCITRAL Report of 46th Session, 20 March 2007, UN Doc A/CN.9/619, paras 64-67.

10 *Ibid.*, at para. 66.

encountered by the proliferation of arbitration in relatively small disputes, and the addition is therefore sound.

Article 6
Designating and appointing authorities

1976 Rules

Articles 6, 7, and 8: Appointment of arbitrators

Article 6

1. If a sole arbitrator is to be appointed, either party may propose to the other:

(a) The names of one or more persons, one of whom would serve as the sole arbitrator; and

(b) If no appointing authority has been agreed upon by the parties, the name or names of one or more institutions or persons, one of whom would serve as appointing authority.

2. If within 30 days after receipt by a party of a proposal made in accordance with paragraph 1 the parties have not reached agreement on the choice of a sole arbitrator, the sole arbitrator shall be appointed by the appointing authority agreed upon by the parties. If no appointing authority has been agreed upon by the parties, or if the appointing authority agreed upon refuses to act or fails to appoint the arbitrator within 60 days of the receipt of a party's request therefore, either party may request the Secretary-General of the Permanent Court of Arbitration at The Hague to designate an appointing authority.

3. The appointing authority shall, at the request of one of the parties, appoint the

2010 Rules

Article 6: Designating and appointing authorities

Article 6

1. Unless the parties have already agreed on the choice of an appointing authority, a party may at any time propose the name or names of one or more institutions or persons, including the Secretary-General of the Permanent Court of Arbitration at The Hague (hereinafter called the 'PCA'), one of whom would serve as appointing authority.

2. If all parties have not agreed on the choice of an appointing authority within 30 days after a proposal made in accordance with paragraph 1 has been received by all other parties, any party may request the Secretary-General of the PCA to designate the appointing authority.

3. Where these Rules provide for a period of time within which a party must refer a matter to an appointing authority and no appointing authority has been agreed on or designated, the period is suspended from the date on which a party initiates the procedure for agreeing on or designating an appointing authority until the date of such agreement or designation.

4. Except as referred to in article 41, paragraph (4), if the appointing authority refuses to act, or if it fails to appoint an arbitrator

sole arbitrator as promptly as possible. In making the appointment the appointing authority shall use the following list-procedure, unless both parties agree that the list-procedure should not be used or unless the appointing authority determines in its discretion that the use of the list-procedure is not appropriate for the case:

(a) At the request of one of the parties the appointing authority shall communicate to both parties an identical list containing at least three names;

(b) Within 15 days after the receipt of this list, each party may return the list to the appointing authority after having deleted the name or names to which he objects and numbered the remaining names on the list in the order of his preference;

(c) After the expiration of the above period of time the appointing authority shall appoint the sole arbitrator from among the names approved on the lists returned to it and in accordance with the order of preference indicated by the parties;

(d) If for any reason the appointment cannot be made according to this procedure, the appointing authority may exercise its discretion in appointing the sole arbitrator.

4. In making the appointment, the appointing authority shall have regard to such considerations as are likely to secure the appointment of an independent and impartial arbitrator and shall take into account as well the advisability of appointing an arbitrator of a nationality other than the nationalities of the parties.

within 30 days after it receives a party's request to do so, fails to act within any other period provided by these Rules, or fails to decide on a challenge to an arbitrator within a reasonable time after receiving a party's request to do so, any party may request the Secretary-General of the PCA to designate a substitute appointing authority.

5. In exercising their functions under these Rules, the appointing authority and the Secretary-General of the PCA may require from any party and the arbitrators the information they deem necessary and they shall give the parties and, where appropriate, the arbitrators, an opportunity to present their views in any manner they consider appropriate. All such communications to and from the appointing authority and the Secretary-General of the PCA shall also be provided by the sender to all other parties.

6. When the appointing authority is requested to appoint an arbitrator pursuant to articles 8, 9, 10 or 14, the party making the request shall send to the appointing authority copies of the notice of arbitration and, if it exists, any response to the notice of arbitration.

7. The appointing authority shall have regard to such considerations as are likely to secure the appointment of an independent and impartial arbitrator and shall take into account the advisability of appointing an arbitrator of a nationality other than the nationalities of the parties.

Article 7

1. If three arbitrators are to be appointed, each party shall appoint one arbitrator. The two arbitrators thus appointed shall choose the third arbitrator who will act as the presiding arbitrator of the tribunal.

2. If within 30 days after the receipt of a party's notification of the appointment of

an arbitrator the other party has not notified the first party of the arbitrator he has appointed:

(a) The first party may request the appointing authority previously designated by the parties to appoint the second arbitrator; or

(b) If no such authority has been previously designated by the parties, or if the appointing authority previously designated refuses to act or fails to appoint the arbitrator within 30 days after receipt of a party's request therefore, the first party may request the Secretary-General of the Permanent Court of Arbitration at The Hague to designate the appointing authority. The first party may then request the appointing authority so designated to appoint the second arbitrator. In either case, the appointing authority may exercise its discretion in appointing the arbitrator.

3. If within 30 days after the appointment of the second arbitrator the two arbitrators have not agreed on the choice of the presiding arbitrator, the presiding arbitrator shall be appointed by an appointing authority in the same way as a sole arbitrator would be appointed under article 6.

Article 8

1. When an appointing authority is requested to appoint an arbitrator pursuant to article 6 or article 7, the party which makes the request shall send to the appointing authority a copy of the notice of arbitration, a copy of the contract out of or in relation to which the dispute has arisen and a copy of the arbitration agreement if it is not contained in the contract. The appointing authority may require from either party such information as it deems necessary to fulfil its function.

2. Where the names of one or more persons are proposed for appointment as arbitrators, their full names, addresses and nationalities shall be indicated, together with a description of their qualifications.

1. It has been rightly pointed out that '[h]ow arbitrators are chosen, challenged, and replaced are among the most important issues in any set of procedural rules'.[1] This is *a fortiori* the case in ad hoc arbitration, where progress of the proceedings mainly rests with the tribunal. To avoid that proceedings may stall – or, worse, remain stillborn – an outside authority may have to intervene in the constitution of the tribunal. National courts may of course perform that function, but it is appropriate that first and foremost the arbitral process cater to that need. While in institutional arbitration this function is performed by the institution itself, the ad hoc UNCITRAL Rules introduced the concept of an 'appointing authority'.[2] Under the Rules, the parties can jointly choose any person or institution to act in this capacity.[3] In case the parties cannot agree, both the 1976 and the 2010 Rules require the Secretary-General of the Permanent Court of Arbitration ('PCA') to act as the 'designating authority' or the appointing authority. The selection of the Secretary-General of the PCA in the 1976 Rules has not been fully documented in the official papers. There was an earlier proposal for a UN body, to be identified by UNCITRAL, to be charged with the functions of the appointing authority.[4] In the end, the PCA was selected on grounds that it is a specialised international organization with a very large number of Member States (larger than the UN, in fact) – and, perhaps crucially, a very small caseload in the 1970s.

2. Despite the importance of both the designating and the appointing authorities in the architecture of the arbitral procedure, elements pertaining to the definition and mechanisms of appointment were scattered in articles 6-8 of the 1976 Rules.[5] The 2010 Rules took a different approach. In particular, article 6 ('designating and appointing authorities') was added, to highlight the 'importance of the role of the appointing authority, particularly in the context of non-administered arbitration ... [and] to better clarify the role of the designating and appointing authorities'.[6] In addition, the changes made to the substantive provisions in article 6 were prompted by a desire to grant additional powers to the appointing authority[7] in

---

1 Stewart A. Baker & Mark D. Davis, *The UNCITRAL Arbitration Rules in Practice – The Experience of the Iran-United States Claims Tribunal*, 15 (Kluwer, 1992).

2 *See* David D. Caron & Lee M. Caplan, *The UNCITRAL Arbitration Rules, A Commentary*, 340 (2nd ed., Oxford University Press 2013): 'The title "appointing authority" as used in the UNCITRAL Rules is somewhat of a misnomer. There are appointing authorities who do only what their name implies: appoint. However, an appointing authority under the UNCITRAL Rules is also called upon to decide challenges to arbitrators'.

3 Neither the 1976 Rules nor the 2010 Rules explicitly dictates criteria that the person or institution must fulfil in order to act as an appointing authority. *See* discussion in section A, *infra*.

4 Report of the Commission on its 9th Session, 12 April-7 May 1976, UN Doc A/31/17, 69 para. 38.

5 *See* articles 6, 7, and 8 of the 1976 Rules.

6 UNCITRAL Working Paper for 49th Session, 6 August 2008, UN Doc A/CN.9/WG.II/WP.151, para. 16.

7 *See*, e.g., article 10 of the 2010 Rules (appointment of arbitrators in multiparty proceedings), article 14 of the 2010 Rules (in exceptional circumstances, appointment of a substitute arbitrator, or, after closure of the hearings, authorization of remaining arbitrators to

light of the growing number of requests being made to the PCA.[8]

3. Article 6 of the 2010 Rules amasses several elements of articles 6, 7 and 8 of the 1976 Rules, while adding new aspects. It now appears as the last article in the 'Introductory rules' section and spells out (i) the mechanics of agreeing on or designating an appointing authority, (ii) the consequences of the appointing authority's refusal or failure to act, (iii) the information that must be provided to the designating and appointing authority, and (iv) the appointing authority's criteria for selecting arbitrators.

A. AGREEMENT ON OR DESIGNATION OF AN APPOINTING AUTHORITY

4. The starting point is that the appointing authority is to be agreed upon by the parties: article 6(1) of the 2010 Rules. The Rules contain no requirement as to any criteria or safeguards that the appointing authority must meet, such as notably independence and impartiality. While an argument may be made that an appointing authority (in particular, a natural person) who fails to fulfil such basic criteria must be replaced, there is no reported instance where the PCA as designating authority acceded to a request by a party to replace an agreed-upon appointing authority. Indeed, there is no such explicit authority under the Rules.[9] This is not a straightforward issue,[10] in two respects in particular. In the first place, the requirements of independence and impartiality concern arbitrators, not the appointing authority, and these essential requirements may always be policed under the Rules and the *lex arbitri*. One may therefore say that there is no gap in the Rules. In the second place, one may conceive that a party could

---

proceed), article 41 of the 2010 Rules (final determination of the fees of arbitrators upon request).

8 *See* UNCITRAL Report of the Secretary-General of the PCA on its activities under the UNCITRAL Arbitration Rules since 1976, 7 December 2006, UN Doc A/CN.9/634. The Annex to the Report indicates that between 1976 and 1990, only 21 cases requested the Secretary-General's designation and appointing services, whereas between 2001 and 2005, the number of requests soared to 101. The Report also indicates at para. 6 that '[t]he significant growth in requests in recent years is partially attributable to arbitrations commenced under bilateral and multilateral investment treaties'. The latest Annual Report from the PCA indicates 44 cases in 2016 alone where the Secretary-General's designation and appointing services were requested; *see* PCA Annual Report 2016, <www.pca-cpa.org>, 8.

9 Cf. *BG Group Plc v. The Republic of Argentina* (UNCITRAL) Final Award, 24 December 2007, <www.italaw.com>, para. 9. Argentina refused to submit an arbitrator challenge to the existing appointing authority (ICC). Following this refusal, the parties attempted to agree on an alternative appointing authority. When this attempt failed, Argentina sought the designation of a new appointing authority by the Secretary-General of the PCA. The Secretary-General of the PCA, however, informed the parties that it had no power to replace the ICC Court as appointing authority.

10 *See* Caron & Caplan, *supra* fn 2, at 342. For a more general discussion on this point in light of the experience of the Iran-US Claims Tribunal, *see ibid.*, at 337-343. On the question of how to determine impartiality and independence, *see* discussion of articles 11 and 12 of the 2010 Rules, *infra*.

resort to the courts at the seat of the arbitration to set aside the agreement on an appointing authority and have the court take upon itself that function.[11] But here too it would not be straightforward to persuade a court of such a novel ground of invalidity. In the practice of the PCA, in any event, independence and impartiality are taken into account in designating an appointing authority.[12]

5. Under the 1976 Rules, either party was invited to propose the 'name or names of one or more institutions or persons, one of whom would serve as appointing authority'. This is retained in article 6(1) of the 2010 Rules, which explicitly adds the Secretary-General of the PCA to the pool of potential appointing authorities.[13] As the Secretary-General of the PCA had acted – even under the 1976 Rules – as appointing authority, this addition reflects well-established practice.[14] However, there was not sufficient support for a proposal 'to provide that, where the parties were unable to agree on an appointing authority, the Secretary-General of the PCA should act directly as the appointing authority, instead of designating an appointing authority'.[15] The proposal was motivated by a desire to streamline the present two-step process by a faster, one-step default solution. Notwithstanding the procedural efficiency gains, the proposal attracted heated opposition and debate – not least on political grounds. Ultimately, and in line with its mandate to respect the original structure and spirit of the Rules, the Working Group decided that the Secretary-General of the PCA should maintain its role as designating authority which was found to operate 'quite satisfactorily'.[16]

B. DESIGNATION OF AN APPOINTING AUTHORITY

6. Under the 1976 Rules the parties were encouraged to agree on the identity of the appointing authority as soon as possible.[17] But they were not compelled to do so, nor could they cause the designation of an appointing authority prudentially, so as to be able to have recourse to it immediately in the event its intervention is required later on. Thus, failure to agree on an appointing authority did not give rise to the possibility of seeking designation of the appointing authority by the Secretary-General of the PCA. Rather, such designation was contingent on

---

11 *See*, e.g., Articles 11(3)-(4), 13(2), 14 and 15 of the UNCITRAL Model Law.

12 *See* UNCITRAL Report of the Secretary-General of the PCA on its activities under the UNCITRAL Arbitration Rules since 1976, 7 December 2006, UN Doc A/CN.9/634, para. 9.

13 When the Secretary-General acts as an appointing authority certain mechanisms of the Rules may become inapplicable. *See* discussion of article 6(4), *infra*.

14 As described in a letter by the Secretary-General of the PCA himself, 'the Secretary-General of the PCA routinely ... acts as Appointing Authority under the UNCITRAL Arbitration Rules'; *see Marks 3 Zet-Ernst Marks GmbH & Co KG v. Presstek Inc*, 455 F.3d 7 (1st Cir. 2006) reproduced in XXXI YCA 1256, 1257 (2006).

15 UNCITRAL Report of 46th Session, 20 March 2007, UN Doc A/CN.9/619, para. 71.

16 APRAG Report of 49th Session, 10 October 2008, para. 37.

17 *See* the model arbitration clause of the 1976 Rules (inviting the parties to indicate the appointing authority) and article 3(4)(a) of the 1976 Rules (inviting, but not compelling, the claimant to add a proposal for the appointing authority in its notice of arbitration).

reaching an impasse in the constitution of the tribunal and in some cases the passage of a 60-day period.[18]

7. The 2010 Rules dispense with a 'cause' requirement for requests to the Secretary-General of the PCA for the designation of an appointing authority.[19] Article 6(1) of the 2010 Rules gives any party the power to propose an appointing authority 'at any time' during the proceedings.[20] The proposal triggers a 30-day time-period during which the parties have the opportunity to agree on an appointing authority. Failing agreement, any party may request the Secretary-General of the PCA to make a designation.[21]

8. The efficacy of this new procedure depends entirely on the proactiveness of the parties. If a party does not propose an appointing authority early on, awaiting an actual impasse, the 2010 Rules do not necessarily lead to a more efficient procedure compared to the 1976 Rules. For example, it is common for an appointing authority to appoint the second arbitrator of a three-member tribunal on behalf of a defaulting respondent.[22] Article 7(2)(b) of the 1976 Rules gives the claimant the right to request the designation of an appointing authority immediately. By contrast, under the 2010 Rules the claimant must first propose an authority and the respondent has 30 days to react. It is likely that the respondent will not agree to this proposal: 'a party who refuses to appoint his own arbitrator is unlikely to agree on a person or institution to appoint an arbitrator for him'.[23] Thus the claimant will have to wait for the expiry of the 30-day period before approaching the Secretary-General of the PCA.

9. Note that after a party proposes an appointing authority – which triggers the 30-day period – other deadlines under the Rules are suspended. Under article 6(3) of the 2010 Rules, if no appointing authority exists, any 'period of time within which a party must refer a matter to an appointing authority ... is suspended' until an appointing authority has been agreed upon or designated. For example, under article 13(4) of the 2010 Rules, a party has 30 days to seek the decision of an appointing authority on the challenge of an arbitrator if the parties have been unable to decide on the challenge or the challenged arbitrator refuses to

---

18 *See* articles 6(2) and 7(2)(b) of the 1976 Rules.

19 Cf. Jan Paulsson & Georgios Petrochilos, *Revision of the UNCITRAL Rules* (September 2006), para. 74, <www.uncitral.org>.

20 The 2010 Rules encourage an agreement on the appointing authority before the start of arbitral proceedings. Indeed, unlike the old model arbitration clause, which stipulated that the parties '*may wish* to consider' (emphasis added) adding the identity of the appointing authority in the arbitration clause, the new model arbitration clause stipulates that the parties '*should* consider' (emphasis added) such an addition. The purpose of this change was 'to emphasize the importance for the parties of considering inclusion of the elements listed'; *see* UNCITRAL Report of 49th Session, 30 September 2008, UN Doc A/CN.9/665, para. 21.

21 *See* articles 6(1) and 6(2) of the 2010 Rules.

22 UNCITRAL Report of the Secretary-General of the PCA on its activities under the UNCITRAL Arbitration Rules since 1976, 7 December 2006, UN Doc A/CN.9/634, para. 5.

23 Baker & Davis, *supra* fn 1, at 23.

withdraw. If a party wishes to seek such a decision from the appointing authority, the 30-day deadline is suspended until an appointing authority is in place.

10. The broader point is that there is no overall time-limit within which the arbitral tribunal must be constituted. Time-limits run sequentially from the last act in the procedural sequence. In the result, if no appointing authority is in place, it is incumbent on the most diligent party to initiate the process for its designation, so that any missing or substitute appointments can be made by the appointing authority. Note, however, that there is *no time-limit* for the designation of an appointing authority by the PCA. All that can be said is that it is incumbent on the PCA to act 'within a reasonable time', by analogy with article 6(4) – this being another provision where it was not considered wise to have an inflexible time-limit. In practice, the PCA stays well within a 30-day window.

C. APPOINTING AUTHORITY'S REFUSAL OR FAILURE TO ACT IN TIME

11. Under the 1976 Rules, an appointing authority has 60 days following a party's request to appoint a sole arbitrator.[24] For a three-member tribunal, the appointing authority has 30 days to appoint the second arbitrator, and if needed, another 60 days to appoint the presiding arbitrator.[25] If an appointing authority refuses or fails to appoint a second arbitrator within 30 days of a party's request to do so, the Secretary-General of the PCA will designate a new appointing authority.[26] It should be noted, however, that no express deadlines are imposed on the PCA under the 1976 Rules. This means, among other things, that it 'can respond flexibly if a party unjustifiably attempts to use the 60-day deadline to oust an appointing authority'.[27]

12. In an effort to harmonise and simplify the various deadlines, article 6(4) of the 2010 Rules stipulates that the operative time-limit for the appointment of an arbitrator by an appointing authority is 30 days, failing which the Secretary-General of the PCA may, at the request of any party, designate another appointing authority. A proposal granting the appointing authority the power to extend this deadline was not passed,[28] which makes it clear that the authority has no powers equivalent to those of an arbitral tribunal under article 17(2). However, nothing prevents the appointing authority from recommending to the parties that they

---

24 Article 6(2) of the 1976 Rules.

25 Article 7(2)(b) and 7(3) of the 1976 Rules. In practice, the party which has not named its arbitrator in a three-member arbitration might still appoint an arbitrator before the appointing authority has had a chance to do so. The appointing authority and the other side in practice prefer to accept an untimely appointment by a party rather than insisting upon causing an 'imposed' appointment, for obvious reasons. *See*, e.g., *Chevron Corporation (USA) and Texaco Petroleum Company (USA) v. The Republic of Ecuador* (UNCITRAL) Interim Award, 1 December 2008, <www.italaw.com>, paras 12-14.

26 Article 7(2)(b) of the 1976 Rules. *See* Pieter Sanders, *Commentary on UNCITRAL Arbitration Rules*, II YCA 172, 188 (1977).

27 Baker & Davis, *supra* fn 1, at 27.

28 *See* UNCITRAL Note by the Secretariat, 5 March 2010, UN Doc A/CN.9/703/Add.1, para. 25.

agree to extend the 30-day period within which the appointing authority must appoint an arbitrator, or that they define a somewhat prolonged 'reasonable time' within which it must decide a challenge to an arbitrator under article 6(4). Given that the 2010 Rules clearly apply this deadline to both agreed-upon and designated appointing authorities,[29] there should be no doubt that it also applies to the Secretary-General of the PCA when acting as appointing authority. Indeed, it is unlikely that any party would request the Secretary-General of the PCA to appoint another appointing authority in its stead, pursuant to article 6(4) of the 2010 Rules, if it had failed to appoint an arbitrator within 30 days.

13 Significantly, as discussed in detail below, article 6(4) of the 2010 Rules adds that in case the appointing authority's failure to act concerns review of the fees and expenses of the tribunal under article 41, any party may refer the matter directly to the Secretary-General of the PCA.[30]

D. INFORMATION PROVIDED TO THE DESIGNATING AND APPOINTING AUTHORITIES

14. Article 8 of the 1976 Rules sets forth what information must be provided to the appointing authority under article 6 and 7 in order for it to perform its functions. Pursuant to article 8(1), the party making the request must provide to the appointing authority copies of the notice of arbitration and the contract underlying the dispute, as well as the arbitration agreement 'if it is not contained in the contract'.[31] The appointing authority has the power to request additional information and should be informed of the 'names, addresses and nationalities ... [and] qualifications' of any arbitrator who may have been proposed.[32] In line with other institutions that offer their services as an appointing authority, such as the ICC and the SCC,[33] the PCA has established guidelines and a procedure

29 The 2010 Rules use the generic form 'the appointing authority'. By contrast, according to the literal text of article 6(2) of the 1976 Rules, the 60-day time-period applies only to appointing authorities 'agreed upon' by the parties. For a discussion of the consequences of this drafting mistake, *see* Baker & Davis, *supra* fn 1, at 26-27.

30 *See* discussion of article 41 of the 2010 Rules, *infra*.

31 In at least one case, the Secretary-General of the PCA described compliance with article 8(1) as a 'condition precedent to the replacement of an appointing authority' and consequently denied a request to replace the appointing authority by a claimant who had not provided a copy of a required document; *see* UNCITRAL Report of the Secretary-General of the PCA on its activities under the UNCITRAL Arbitration Rules since 1976, 7 December 2006, UN Doc A/CN.9/634, para. 12.

32 Article 8(2) of the 1976 Rules.

33 *See* Rules of ICC as Appointing Authority in UNCITRAL or Other *Ad Hoc* Arbitration Proceedings (in force from 1 January 2014), available at < www.iccwbo.org > ; SCC Procedures as Appointing Authority Under the 2010 UNCITRAL Arbitration Rules (in force from 1 January 2015), available at < www.sccinstitute.com > . *See also* UNCITRAL, *Recommendations to assist arbitral institutions and other interested bodies with regard to arbitration under the UNCITRAL Arbitration Rules (as revised in 2010)*, 9-10 and the references (United Nations 2013) (citing further institutions that may act as an appointing authority).

for parties to request that the Secretary-General act in this capacity.[34] This procedure identifies certain documents in addition to those specified in article 6(6) of the 2010 Rules which 'should' be provided when a party requests that the Secretary-General take any action as appointing authority.[35] The need for such materials is obvious and calls for no particular comment.

15. Elements of article 8 of the 1976 Rules have been incorporated in paragraphs 5 and 6 of article 6 of the 2010 Rules. The party requesting the appointing authority to appoint an arbitrator must provide only copies of the notice of arbitration and of the response to the notice of arbitration, if any; the requirement for copies of the contract and the arbitration agreement has been omitted.[36] Such a requirement would not only have been out of step with other modifications of the Rules,[37] but would have also been redundant in view of the appointing authority's power – maintained in the 2010 Rules – to request any information or documents it considers necessary to perform its task. This power has also been given to the Secretary-General of the PCA acting as designating authority.

16. The process before the designating or appointing authority is to a degree inquisitorial and to a degree adversarial. Additional information may be requested of the parties and the arbitrators. The reference to 'the arbitrators' was added to a later draft of article 6, as the Working Group recognized that there are instances, such as a challenge procedure, 'in which the Secretary-General of the PCA and the appointing authorities, in exercising their functions, may require information from the arbitrators (and not only from the parties)'.[38] The parties, and where appropriate the arbitrators, must be given an opportunity to present their views. Article 6(5) provides that views may be presented by the parties 'in any manner [the PCA or the appointing authority] consider appropriate'. The wording makes it plain that there may be written observations (which is of course the norm) or an oral conference or, in appropriate cases of complexity and importance, both.

---

34 *See* Procedure for Requesting the Secretary-General to Act as Appointing Authority, available at < www.pca-cpa.org > .

35 *Ibid.* (providing that requests should be accompanied by copies 'of the arbitration clause, agreement, or other instrument establishing the applicability of the UNCITRAL Arbitration Rules and the designation of the Secretary-General as appointing authority; [a] copy of the notice of arbitration served upon the respondent, as well as the date of such service; [a]n indication of the nationalities of the parties; [t]he names and nationalities of the arbitrators already appointed, if any; [a] power of attorney evidencing the authority of the person making the request; and [p]ayment of the non-refundable appointing authority fee').

36 However, as noted *ibid.*, copies of e.g. the arbitration agreement may still be required under the procedural guidelines of individual appointing authorities.

37 *See* discussion of article 3 of the 2010 Rules (pointing out that requesting copies presumes that the arbitration agreement and contract are in writing) and discussion of article 1(1) of the 2010 Rules (pointing out that the dispute may arise out of a non-contractual relationship, which for present purposes means that a contract might not always be the relevant document of which a copy should be required), *supra*.

38 UNCITRAL Working Paper for 52nd Session, 10 December 2009, UN Doc A/CN.9/WG.II/WP.157, para. 22.

17. Moreover, article 6(5) of the 2010 Rules requires that 'all such communications to and from the appointing authority and the Secretary-General of the PCA shall also be provided by the sender to all other parties'. The specific 'to and from' language covers communications of the appointing authority or the Secretary-General of the PCA with one or all parties: there can be no *ex parte* communication involving a party. By contrast, the provision does not apply (at least on its face) to internal communications between the designating and appointing authority.

E. CRITERIA FOR SELECTING ARBITRATORS

18. Article 6(4) of the 1976 Rules states that '[i]n making the appointment, the appointing authority shall have regard to such considerations as are likely to secure the appointment of an independent and impartial arbitrator and shall take into account as well the advisability of appointing an arbitrator of a nationality other than the nationalities of the parties'. While the significance of the requirements of 'independence and impartiality' is discussed in more detail below,[39] one notes here that article 6(4) of the 1976 Rules has been transposed to article 6(7) of the 2010 Rules. Although the content of the provision remains exactly the same, its impact has slightly changed in two respects. First, unlike in the 1976 Rules, where the principle of an arbitrator's independence and impartiality was embedded in the article dealing with the appointment of a sole arbitrator, the 2010 Rules clarify that the requirement of independence and impartiality applies to all arbitrators named by the appointing authority (including any substitute arbitrator). Second, 'the advisability of appointing an arbitrator of a nationality other than the nationalities of the parties' acquires a new dimension in the 2010 Rules. As already mentioned, the 2010 Rules offer the possibility of joining new parties to the arbitral proceedings.[40] In order to avoid any subsequent challenge, an appointing authority may therefore do well to inquire further about the nationality of any party likely to be joined in the arbitration, before choosing an arbitrator.

19. Inquiries and determinations as to the nationality of a party may well raise questions of dominant beneficial ownership. The reason is that the appointing authority may select an arbitrator of a nationality different from that of the parties, but the same as that of a party's dominant beneficial owner where that party is a corporate entity. Under the ICC Rules, the tribunal may include information regarding each party's 'ownership and control' in its Terms of Reference.[41] The claimant may also submit this information in its Request for Arbitration as part of its description of the parties.[42] Although the 2010 Rules did not adopt an express provision on this point,[43] an appointing authority would be mindful to call for

---

39 *See* discussion of articles 11 and 12 of the 2010 Rules, *infra*.

40 *See* articles 4(2)(f) and 17(5) of the 2010 Rules.

41 Jason Fry, Simon Greenberg & Francesca Mazza, *The Secretariat's Guide to ICC Arbitration*, para. 3-841 (ICC 2012).

42 *Ibid.*, at para. 3-94. *See* Article 4(3)(a) of the ICC Rules.

43 *See* proposed article 6(5) in Paulsson & Petrochilos, *supra* fn 19, at para. 78.

information from the parties as to dominant beneficial ownership in order better to ensure neutrality in appropriate cases.

PART I

Section II

Composition of the arbitral tribunal

2010 Rules

Article 7
Number of arbitrators

1976 Rules Article 5: Number of arbitrators	2010 Rules Article 7: Number of arbitrators
If the parties have not previously agreed on the number of arbitrators (i.e. one or three), and if within 15 days after the receipt by the respondent of the notice of arbitration the parties have not agreed that there shall be only one arbitrator, three arbitrators shall be appointed.	1. If the parties have not previously agreed on the number of arbitrators, and if within 30 days after the receipt by the respondent of the notice of arbitration the parties have not agreed that there shall be only one arbitrator, three arbitrators shall be appointed. 2. Notwithstanding paragraph 1, if no other parties have responded to a party's proposal to appoint a sole arbitrator within the time limit provided for in paragraph 1 and the party or parties concerned have failed to appoint a second arbitrator in accordance with article 9 or 10, the appointing authority may, at the request of a party, appoint a sole arbitrator pursuant to the procedure provided for in article 8, paragraph 2, if it determines that, in view of the circumstances of the case, this is more appropriate.

1. The vast majority of international arbitrations are conducted by either a sole arbitrator or a tribunal comprising three arbitrators, a practice ubiquitously endorsed by institutional and other arbitration rules.[1]

---

1 Cf. e.g. Regulation 3.1 of the Arbitration Regulations of the London Metal Exchange, which provides for the arbitration to be conducted by two arbitrators 'unless the parties to the dispute agree that either one or three arbitrators should form the Tribunal'. Should the two arbitrators fail to agree on any issue, they must request the appointment of a third arbitrator (Regulations 12.2.1 and 3.5).

2. The 1976 Rules dealt with the number of arbitrators in article 5. It stated that, subject to any prior agreement by the parties,[2] and unless the parties agreed on a sole arbitrator within 15 days after the receipt of the notice of arbitration, three arbitrators would be appointed.[3] By contrast, other arbitration rules, such as the ICC, the LCIA and the AAA Rules, prefer a sole arbitrator as the default option.[4]

3. The default number of arbitrators took centre stage during the debate over article 7 of the 2010 Rules,[5] with the Working Group eventually splitting along efficiency vs. legitimacy lines. On the one hand, it was argued that referring a dispute to a sole arbitrator could be less costly and more time-efficient.[6] On the other hand, three-member tribunals were defended as advancing the legitimacy of the arbitral process, pointing to parties' dissatisfaction when not being able to appoint 'their' arbitrator, the greater risk of error or 'rogue decisions', etc.[7] Historically, too, this has been considered a safer option in that it 'yields deliberations that are necessarily more refined and exacting' and offers a larger pool of skills and experiences.[8]

4. With no consensus on the question, the Working Group decided to keep the default rule but to allow[9] a party to request the appointment of a sole arbitrator where the other party fails to respond and appoint a second arbitrator. Once

---

[2] Parties are encouraged to agree on the number of arbitrators in their arbitration agreement. *See* the model arbitration clause of the 1976 Rules and the model arbitration clause for contracts of the 2010 Rules.

[3] It should be noted that under both the 1976 Rules and the 2010 Rules, parties are free to agree on a number of arbitrators other than one or three. This possibility is expressly acknowledged by article 10(2) of the 2010 Rules. *See* discussion of article 10 of the 2010 Rules, *infra*.

[4] *See* Article 12(2) of the ICC Rules; Article 11 of the AAA International Arbitration Rules; Article 5.8 of the LCIA Rules.

[5] *See*, e.g., UNCITRAL Report of 45th Session, 5 October 2006, UN Doc A/CN.9/614, paras 59-61; UNCITRAL Report of 46th Session, 20 March 2007, UN Doc A/CN.9/619, paras 79-83; UNCITRAL Report of 49th Session, 30 September 2008, UN Doc A/CN.9/665, paras 57-67. For a general discussion on the debate relating to the respective benefits and drawbacks of a sole arbitrator or a multiple-member tribunal, *see* Nigel Blackaby, Constantine Partasides, Alan Redfern & Martin J. Hunter, *Redfern and Hunter on International Arbitration*, paras 4.22-4.32 (6th ed., Kluwer 2015); *see also* David D. Caron & Lee M. Caplan, *The UNCITRAL Arbitration Rules, A Commentary*, 157-161 (2nd ed., Oxford University Press 2013).

[6] This discussion should be considered in light of the overarching procedural due process command of article 17(1) of the 2010 Rules: 'The arbitral tribunal, in exercising its discretion, shall conduct the proceedings so as to avoid unnecessary delay and expense and to provide a fair and efficient process for resolving the parties' dispute'.

[7] Blackaby, Partasides, Redfern & Hunter, *supra* fn 5, at paras 4.30-4.31.

[8] Caron & Caplan, *supra* fn 5, at 159. But *see* Jennifer Kirby, *With Arbitrators, Less Can Be More: Why the Conventional Wisdom on the Benefits of Having Three Arbitrators May Be Overrated*, 26(3) J Int Arb 337 (2009).

[9] This is in line with the position taken by the drafters of the UNCITRAL Model Law. *See* Article 10 of the Model Law; *see also* UNCITRAL, *2012 Digest of Case Law on the Model Law on International Commercial Arbitration*, 57 and the references (United Nations 2012).

again, for the sake of consistency the deadline for default appointment of the three-member panel was extended.

A. TIMING FOR THE APPLICATION OF THE DEFAULT RULE

5. Article 5 of the 1976 Rules gave the parties 15 days from the receipt of the notice of arbitration to agree on the number of arbitrators. If this period lapsed, the default three-arbitrators rule became controlling. In practice this 15-day period was often considered to be too short. Claimants who wished to opt for a sole arbitrator found themselves forced into a three-member tribunal when respondents did not respond in time. The insufficiency of the 15-day period was most palpable in cases involving state respondents where co-ordination among various state agencies and outside counsel, and obtaining the necessary authorizations, are often time-consuming.[10]

6. Moreover, a modification of the 15-day time-limit seemed necessary to avoid incongruence with other revised provisions of the Rules. For instance, the 15-day time-limit would have effectively shortened the deadline for proposing the number of arbitrators in the response to the notice of arbitration. Pursuant to article 4, the response needs to be filed within 30 (and not 15) days from receipt of the notice of arbitration.

7. Thus, article 7 of the 2010 Rules extends the time to agree on a sole arbitrator to 30 days, which starts to run from receipt of the notice of arbitration. This way, the deadline is aligned with the time-limit for filing the response to the notice of arbitration. The 30-day period, and the opportunity to express views in the response, allow the respondent 'more fully to articulate the reasons for its proposals on the constitution of the tribunal – for example, how counterclaims affect the nature and magnitude of the dispute, and any particular expertise or qualifications that a sole arbitrator should have'.[11] Note, however, that if the respondent files its response on the expiry of the 30-day time-period (as is often the case), no further exchange between the parties on the number of arbitrators is required before either party may appoint an arbitrator pursuant to article 9(1) of the Rules.[12]

---

10 *See* UNCITRAL Report of 46th Session, 20 March 2007, UN Doc A/CN.9/619, para. 81. *See also Link-Trading Joint Stock Company v. Department for Customs Control of the Republic of Moldova* (UNCITRAL) Award on Jurisdiction, 16 February 2001, <www.italaw.com>, 6-7.

11 Jan Paulsson & Georgios Petrochilos, *Revision of the UNCITRAL Rules* (September 2006), para. 65, <www.uncitral.org>.

12 *See* UNCITRAL Report of 49th Session, 30 September 2008, UN Doc A/CN.9/665, para. 66: 'One proposal was to provide that the 15-day time limit under article 5 [of the 1976 Rules] should commence from the expiration of the time limit for the response to the notice of arbitration. That additional time period was said to be necessary to allow further exchange between the parties on that question'.

B. POSSIBILITY TO REQUEST APPOINTMENT OF SOLE ARBITRATOR

8. As already mentioned, the 1976 Rules provided for the automatic appointment of three arbitrators if the parties failed to agree on a sole-arbitrator tribunal. Practice shows that a non-negligible number of cases under the Rules involve small claims warranting the appointment of a sole arbitrator. Since respondents in small claims frequently fail to participate in the proceedings, this ends up triggering the application of the 'overly burdensome' three-arbitrator default rule.[13]

9. Thus, while the 2010 version of the Rules maintains the default number of three arbitrators, it also provides for a 'corrective mechanism' to address situations where a claimant faces a respondent that fails to appear.[14] Indeed, pursuant to article 7(2), a party may request the appointing authority to appoint a sole arbitrator when (i) a proposal for a sole arbitrator has not been answered and (ii) the respondent party (or parties) have failed to appoint a second arbitrator. The rationale is that in this way, the respondent will have indicated that it has no particular interest in a three-member formation.

10. If these two conditions are fulfilled, it is within the appointing authority's discretion to grant a request for a sole-arbitrator formation 'in view of the circumstances of the case', notably the complexity of the case, the amount in dispute, and any urgency. Most of the information about the circumstances of the case will be available from the claimant's notice of arbitration and related documentation. By application of article 6(5), the appointing authority may also request any additional information it deems necessary and must invite the parties to express their views on the subject.

11. The decision of the appointing authority is whether or not to 'appoint a sole arbitrator'. This is a decision as to the number of arbitrators rather than their identity. It is clear from the text of article 7(2) that the selection and appointment of a sole arbitrator is a separate and subsequent step, to be made 'pursuant to the procedure provided for in article 8, paragraph 2' of the Rules. Practically, these two decisions cannot be made at the same time, unless the list-procedure has been dispensed with in accordance with article 8(2). Even if that procedure has been dispensed with, an appointing authority will in practice be extremely reluctant to appoint a person whose name has been suggested by the moving party (the claimant). It will be prudent in an article 7(2) context to appoint a fresh name.

12. Apart from the exceptional case of article 7(2), unlike arbitral institutions, an appointing authority under the UNCITRAL Rules does not have the power to determine the number of arbitrators in case the parties positively disagree.[15]

---

13 *Ibid.*, at para. 59.

14 *Ibid.*, at para. 63.

15 Cf. Yves Derains & Eric A. Schwartz, *A Guide to the ICC Rules of Arbitration*, 146 (2nd ed., Kluwer 2005): '[I]n cases where the parties cannot agree, [Article 8(2) of the 1998 ICC Rules confers] upon the Court the important function of determining the number [of arbitrators]'. This provision is now found in Article 12(2) of the 2012 and 2017 ICC Rules.

Indeed, the Working Group rejected a proposal to give the appointing authority such powers, on the basis that 'involving an appointing authority at such an early stage of the arbitral proceeding could create unnecessary delays'.[16] There is therefore the potential for a tactical respondent to force the costs up by taking the step of refusing to agree on a sole arbitrator and making an appointment within the time set forth in article 9. As mentioned in a previous report, '[t]hough this would be a risky strategy, it may deter some claimants with good cases but limited resources'.[17]

16 UNCITRAL Report of 49th Session, 30 September 2008, UN Doc A/CN.9/665, para. 60; Cf. Paulsson & Petrochilos, *supra* fn 11, at paras 64 and 67 (the authors proposed that in the absence of the parties' agreement the appointing authority should have the power to decide whether a sole or a three-member tribunal should be appointed).

17 Paulsson & Petrochilos, *supra* fn 11, at para. 64.

Articles 8 and 9
Appointment of arbitrators

1976 Rules

Articles 6 and 7:
Appointment of arbitrators

Article 6

1. If a sole arbitrator is to be appointed, either party may propose to the other:

(a) The names of one or more persons, one of whom would serve as the sole arbitrator; and

(b) If no appointing authority has been agreed upon by the parties, the name or names of one or more institutions or persons, one of whom would serve as appointing authority.

2. If within thirty days after receipt by a party of a proposal made in accordance with paragraph 1 the parties have not reached agreement on the choice of a sole arbitrator, the sole arbitrator shall be appointed by the appointing authority agreed upon by the parties. If no appointing authority has been agreed upon by the parties, or if the appointing authority agreed upon refuses to act or fails to appoint the arbitrator within sixty days of the receipt of a party's request therefore, either party may request the Secretary-General of the Permanent Court of Arbitration at The Hague to designate an appointing authority.

2010 Rules

Articles 8 and 9:
Appointment of arbitrators

Article 8

1. If the parties have agreed that a sole arbitrator is to be appointed and if within 30 days after receipt by all other parties of a proposal for the appointment of a sole arbitrator the parties have not reached agreement thereon, a sole arbitrator shall, at the request of a party, be appointed by the appointing authority.

2. The appointing authority shall appoint the sole arbitrator as promptly as possible. In making the appointment, the appointing authority shall use the following list-procedure, unless the parties agree that the list-procedure should not be used or unless the appointing authority determines in its discretion that the use of the list-procedure is not appropriate for the case:

(a) The appointing authority shall communicate to each of the parties an identical list containing at least three names;

(b) Within 15 days after the receipt of this list, each party may return the list to the appointing authority after having deleted the name or names to which it objects and numbered the remaining names on the list in the order of its preference;

3. The appointing authority shall, at the request of one of the parties, appoint the sole arbitrator as promptly as possible. In making the appointment the appointing authority shall use the following list-procedure, unless both parties agree that the list-procedure should not be used or unless the appointing authority determines in its discretion that the use of the list-procedure is not appropriate for the case:

(a) At the request of one of the parties the appointing authority shall communicate to both parties an identical list containing at least three names;

(b) Within fifteen days after the receipt of this list, each party may return the list to the appointing authority after having deleted the name or names to which he objects and numbered the remaining names on the list in the order of his preference;

(c) After the expiration of the above period of time the appointing authority shall appoint the sole arbitrator from among the names approved on the lists returned to it and in accordance with the order of preference indicated by the parties;

(d) If for any reason the appointment cannot be made according to this procedure, the appointing authority may exercise its discretion in appointing the sole arbitrator.

4. In making the appointment, the appointing authority shall have regard to such considerations as are likely to secure the appointment of an independent and impartial arbitrator and shall take into account as well the advisability of appointing an arbitrator of a nationality other than the nationalities of the parties.

(c) After the expiration of the above period of time the appointing authority shall appoint the sole arbitrator from among the names approved on the lists returned to it and in accordance with the order of preference indicated by the parties;

(d) If for any reason the appointment cannot be made according to this procedure, the appointing authority may exercise its discretion in appointing the sole arbitrator.

Article 7

1. If three arbitrators are to be appointed, each party shall appoint one arbitrator. The two arbitrators thus appointed shall choose the third arbitrator who will act as the presiding arbitrator of the tribunal.

Article 9

1. If three arbitrators are to be appointed, each party shall appoint one arbitrator. The two arbitrators thus appointed shall choose the third arbitrator who will act as the presiding arbitrator of the arbitral tribunal.

2. If within thirty days after the receipt of a party's notification of the appointment of an arbitrator the other party has not notified the first party of the arbitrator he has appointed:

(a) The first party may request the appointing authority previously designated by the parties to appoint the second arbitrator; or

(b) If no such authority has been previously designated by the parties, or if the appointing authority previously designated refuses to act or fails to appoint the arbitrator within thirty days after receipt of a party's request therefore, the first party may request the Secretary-General of the Permanent Court of Arbitration at The Hague to designate the appointing authority. The first party may then request the appointing authority so designated to appoint the second arbitrator. In either case, the appointing authority may exercise its discretion in appointing the arbitrator.

3. If within thirty days after the appointment of the second arbitrator the two arbitrators have not agreed on the choice of the presiding arbitrator, the presiding arbitrator shall be appointed by an appointing authority in the same way as a sole arbitrator would be appointed under article 6.

2. If within 30 days after the receipt of a party's notification of the appointment of an arbitrator the other party has not notified the first party of the arbitrator it has appointed, the first party may request the appointing authority to appoint the second arbitrator.

3. If within 30 days after the appointment of the second arbitrator the two arbitrators have not agreed on the choice of the presiding arbitrator, the presiding arbitrator shall be appointed by the appointing authority in the same way as a sole arbitrator would be appointed under article 8.

1. Articles 8 and 9 of the 2010 Rules deal with the selection of a sole arbitrator and the empanelment of a three-member formation, respectively. The two provisions share as a common feature the list-procedure which is set out in article 8(2). They are thus usefully to be discussed together, in discrete sections below. Article 10, which deals with cases of multi party proceedings and other, residual issues is discussed separately.

A. APPOINTMENT OF A SOLE ARBITRATOR

2. Article 8 of the 2010 Rules dictates the appointment procedure where the parties have agreed, or the appointing authority has decided, that a sole arbitrator is to be appointed but have not selected the person who will serve in that capacity.

1. Appointment of a sole arbitrator where the parties cannot agree

3. Article 8(1) of the 2010 Rules inherits the provisions of article 6(2) of the 1976 Rules. It provides that where the parties fail to agree on the identity of the sole

arbitrator within 30 days 'of a proposal for the appointment of a sole arbitrator', the appointing authority shall appoint the sole arbitrator upon the request of a party. Unlike article 6(2) of the 1976 Rules, article 8(1) of the 2010 Rules makes it plain that the intervention of the appointing authority is contingent upon the request of a party – an uncontroversial but helpful clarification.

4. The earliest time for such a request is 30 days from the relevant 'proposal' – by which article 8(2) means proposed names, as opposed to a proposal within the meaning of article 7(1) that a sole-arbitrator tribunal be constituted. It is therefore conceivable, though not necessary, that there will be a 60 + -day period in all before the appointing authority is charged with selecting and appointing a sole arbitrator: 30 days that the respondent will have in which to consider the claimant's proposal for a sole-arbitrator formation, then one or more names proposed, then 30 days in which to agree on an individual. There is nothing, however, to prevent a claimant from proposing one or more names at the same time as the proposal of a sole arbitrator as a matter of principle; and proposing sensible names that are likely to attract consensus may be an effective approach to secure agreement on both proposals, and early on. Even if no agreement is reached on the individual, if agreement is reached on the principle of a sole-arbitrator formation, the 30-day period starts counting from the date of the receipt of the initial proposals. There is nothing in the text of article 8(1) or in procedural logic to suggest that two proposals require two separate 30-day periods of consideration, one after the other. Indeed, articles 7(2) and 8(1) describe the two proposals in textually near-identical terms, which suggests that they were conceived as practically belonging together although they remain conceptually separate.

2. Selection of a sole arbitrator by the appointing authority

5. Article 8(2) of the 2010 Rules sets out the procedure by which the appointing authority appoints a sole arbitrator. Just as under the 1976 Rules, the appointing authority is to use a list-procedure, unless the parties agree that this should not be used or the appointing authority determines in its discretion that it is not appropriate for the case. The term 'discretion' strongly suggests latitude of judgement in the light of all the circumstances that the appointing authority considers relevant. The most important one is given in the text itself: the appointment is to be made 'as promptly as possible'. It has therefore been suggested that the appointing authority may be justified in forgoing the list-procedure where it is urgent that proceedings be commenced (given the time involved in the list-procedure), or where the appointing authority is concerned that the list-procedure would be thwarted by the systematic rejection of the names on the list by one of the parties.[1] Expense may also be a relevant consideration, in very small cases or where there are clear indications that the parties are practically impecunious and all cost-savings will be justified. In practice, an appointing authority may

---

1 *See* Thomas H. Webster, *Handbook of UNCITRAL Arbitration*, para. 8-13 (2nd ed., Sweet & Maxwell 2015).

start by proposing a name informally, stating at the same time that if that name is not acceptable to the parties, the list-procedure will be applied.

6. Article 8(2) reproduces in substance the list-procedure set out in article 6(3) of the 1976 Rules.[2] The appointing authority must produce a list containing at least three names. The parties must then return the list to the appointing authority within 15 days of receipt, having deleted the names of candidates objected to and numbered the remaining names in order of preference. At the end of the 15-day period following receipt of the parties' lists, the appointing authority is to appoint the sole arbitrator from the remaining names and in accordance with the order of preference indicated by the parties. In the event that the list procedure should fail to result in the appointment of an arbitrator, the appointing authority is permitted to exercise its discretion and directly appoint the sole arbitrator.

7. In practice, in cases of any significance, the list is considerably longer than three names – for example, nine with a possibility for either side to exclude up to three, thus leaving at least three names to be ranked in preference. The reason is simple. A list of three may be reduced to nil if one party 'deletes' two names and the other one. In that connection, the term 'objects' in article 7(2)(b) may mean either a formal objection on grounds of neutrality (see article 12(1)) or fitness to serve, agreed qualifications, etc. (see article 12(3)); or a mere preference that a person not be considered further. The instructions to the parties will indicate the rules of the process. As a matter of good practice, it is desirable to give the parties considerable latitude, since the main objective is to gauge their preferences and allow these to be aired rather fully. Hence the prevailing practice of long lists with liberty to strike out (say) three names without giving reasons.

B. APPOINTMENT OF THREE ARBITRATORS

8. Article 9 sets out the procedure for the appointment of three-member tribunals, reproducing the substance of its corresponding provisions in article 7 of the 1976 Rules.

1. Party-appointment of a three-member panel

9. Article 9(1) of the 2010 Rules reproduces nearly verbatim article 7(1) of the 1976 Rules. The single difference is editorial: the new article reads 'arbitral tribunal' and the old article 7(1) reads simply 'tribunal'. The mechanics remain the same. When there is an express choice of the parties for a three-member formation, or by virtue of the default rule in article 7(1), each party appoints one arbitrator and the two party-appointed arbitrators together appoint the president

[2] One difference between article 6(3) of the 1976 Rules and article 8(2) of the 2010 Rules is that with the latter, the appointing authority is to communicate to each of the parties identical lists containing the names of the potential arbitrators, regardless of whether or not one of the parties has requested that it do so. Given the good sense of communicating the list to the parties (as opposed to, for example, relaying the candidates' names to the parties orally), one assumes that this has always been the rule in practice.

of the tribunal ('presiding arbitrator'). That is a classical way of empanelling a three-member formation. (Equally classical is the methodology of two party appointees and a presiding arbitrator selected jointly by the parties, but it is now confined mostly to ICSID arbitrations.) Although the Rules do not expressly state so in article 9, it is clear from article 1(1) that the parties may choose a different methodology, such as the full empanelment by the appointing authority (as is the default position under the LCIA Rules)[3] or the appointment of the presiding arbitrator only by the appointing authority (as is the default position under the SCC Rules).[4] Appointment of all arbitrators from a roster constituted by *one* of the parties in the proceedings, as will be the case for tribunals under the CETA (Comprehensive Economic and Trade Agreement) between the EU and Canada,[5] may raise broader issues of law and policy, which are outside the ambit of this commentary.

2. Appointment of a second arbitrator by the appointing authority

10. Article 9(2) sets out the appointment procedure for a second arbitrator where a party fails to appoint an arbitrator within 30 days of notification of the other party's appointment. Then, the latter party may request that the appointing authority appoint the second arbitrator in the stead of the defaulting party.

11. The procedure will thus be the same as that envisaged under article 7(2) of the 1976 Rules, so long as the appointing authority is already in place. In the event that it is not, the procedures under the 2010 Rules may be different from the 1976 Rules. Under article 7(2)(b) of the 1976 Rules, when no appointing authority is in place, the first party to appoint an arbitrator has the right to request the Secretary-General of the PCA to designate an appointing authority right away, which once designated can be requested to appoint the second arbitrator. By contrast, under article 6(1)-(2) of the 2010 Rules, the moving party will first have to make a proposal as to the identity of the appointing authority and wait for up to 30 days to receive the other party's reaction. The moving party would only then be able to request that the Secretary-General of the PCA designate the appointing authority, if the parties do not come to an agreement.[6]

---

3 Article 5.6 of the LCIA Rules.

4 Article 17(4) of the SCC Rules.

5 Article 8.27 of the Comprehensive Economic and Trade Agreement (signed 30 October 2016).

6 *See* discussion of article 6 of the 2010 Rules, *supra*. As for the hypothesis where the appointing authority refuses to act, or where it fails to appoint an arbitrator within thirty days after it receives a request to do so, article 6(4) of the 2010 Rules envisages a result nearly identical to that envisaged under article 7(2)(b) of the 1976 Rules: any party (and not only the first party to designate an arbitrator, as under the 1976 Rules) may request the Secretary-General of the PCA to designate a substitute appointing authority.

3. Appointment of a presiding arbitrator by the appointing authority

12. Article 9(3) of the 2010 Rules, which only slightly edits the wording of article 7(3) of the 1976 Rules and updates an internal cross-reference to article 8, provides the mechanism for selection of the president of the arbitral tribunal when the two arbitrators already appointed are unable to identify an individual on whom they agree. If the two arbitrators cannot settle upon the choice of the presiding arbitrator within 30 days following the appointment of the second arbitrator, the appointing authority is to appoint the presiding arbitrator. The appointing authority is to follow the same procedures as those set out under article 8 of the 2010 Rules, discussed above.

Article 10
Appointment of arbitrators

1976 Rules	2010 Rules **Article 10: Appointment of arbitrators**
	1. For the purposes of article 9, paragraph 1, where three arbitrators are to be appointed and there are multiple parties as claimant or as respondent, unless the parties have agreed to another method of appointment of arbitrators, the multiple parties jointly, whether as claimant or as respondent, shall appoint an arbitrator. 2. If the parties have agreed that the arbitral tribunal is to be composed of a number of arbitrators other than one or three, the arbitrators shall be appointed according to the method agreed upon by the parties. 3. In the event of any failure to constitute the arbitral tribunal under these Rules, the appointing authority shall, at the request of any party, constitute the arbitral tribunal and, in doing so, may revoke any appointment already made and appoint or reappoint each of the arbitrators and designate one of them as the presiding arbitrator.

1. Article 10 was added to the 2010 Rules as a new and necessary provision to deal mostly with multiparty proceedings, against the backdrop of the *DUTCO* case in the French *Cour de cassation*.[1] The case arose from the constitution of a

[1] *See Sociétés Siemens & BKMI v. Société DUTCO*, Cass Civ 1, 7 January 1992, Case No. 89-18708, 2 Bull Civ 2 (1992).

three-member tribunal under the 1988 ICC Rules. The claimant had nominated an arbitrator, but the two respondents, who as contractor and sub-contractor had conflicting positions and did not fall neatly within one camp, nominated one arbitrator 'under protest' (or else the ICC Court would have made a single appointment in their stead).[2] The award was challenged, and the French court set it aside on grounds of irregular constitution of the tribunal. It held that the principle of party equality in the appointment of arbitrators and the relevant right were matters of public policy, which could not be 'waived' by agreeing upon arbitration rules that forced a joint appointment (as did the 1988 ICC Rules) except after the dispute had arisen.[3]

2. Multiparty arbitrations, which can lead to tribunal-constitution issues similar to those seen in the *DUTCO* case, are a common feature of today's arbitral practice.[4] The major institutional arbitration rules were quickly modified to address the *DUTCO* issue, which is at core the need to treat equally multiple parties forming effectively three or more camps in a single set of proceedings.[5] If multiple claimants or (more likely, of course) respondents cannot agree on one arbitrator, the arbitral institution has the power to appoint each member of the arbitral tribunal. For example, Article 12 of the ICC Rules now reads in material part:

> 6 Where there are multiple claimants or multiple respondents, and where the dispute is to be referred to three arbitrators, the multiple claimants, jointly, and the multiple respondents, jointly, shall nominate an arbitrator for confirmation pursuant to Article 13 ['Appointment and Confirmation of the Arbitrators'].
>
> 7 Where an additional party has been joined, and where the dispute is to be referred to three arbitrators, the additional party may, jointly with the claimant(s) or with the respondent(s), nominate an arbitrator for confirmation pursuant to Article 13.
>
> 8 In the absence of a joint nomination pursuant to Articles 12(6) or 12(7) and where all parties are unable to agree to a method for the constitution of the arbitral tribunal, the Court may appoint each member of the arbitral tribunal and shall designate one of them to act as president. In such case, the Court shall be at liberty to choose any person it regards as suitable to act as arbitrator, applying Article 13 when it considers this appropriate.[6]

---

2 For a more detailed discussion of the *DUTCO* case, *see* Yves Derains & Eric A. Schwartz, *A Guide to the ICC Rules of Arbitration*, 177-185 (2nd ed., Kluwer 2005).

3 *See Sociétés Siemens & BKMI v. Société DUTCO, supra* fn 1, at 2: '*Attendu que le principe de l'égalité des parties dans la désignation des arbitres est d'ordre public ; qu'on ne peut y renoncer qu'après la naissance du litige*'.

4 One third of the cases registered with the ICC, for instance, involve multiple parties; *see* ICC, *2015 ICC Dispute Resolution Statistics*, 9, 1 ICC Dispute Resolution Bulletin (2016); Jan Paulsson & Georgios Petrochilos, *Revision of the UNCITRAL Rules* (September 2006), para. 14(d) and the references, <www.uncitral.org>.

5 *See*, e.g., Article 12(6)-(8) of the ICC Rules; Article 8 of the LCIA Rules; Article 17(5) of the SCC Rules; Article 18 of the WIPO Rules.

6 Article 12(6)-(8) of the ICC Rules.

3. The 1976 UNCITRAL Rules did not address the situation that gave rise to the *DUTCO* case. This was 'a serious lacuna',[7] now filled by article 10(1) of the 2010 Rules which describes how a tribunal of three arbitrators should be appointed when there are multiple claimants or multiple respondents. Article 10(2) deals with a broader issue, namely situations where parties have agreed to constitute a formation other than one or three arbitrators, and article 10(3) provides a back-stop solution in all cases of a failure to constitute an arbitral tribunal.

4. When a sole arbitrator is to be appointed, all parties are to select them jointly (articles 7(1) and 8(1) of the 2010 Rules). There is therefore equality among all parties, even in multiparty proceedings. Difficulty may arise only in the case of the addition of a new respondent through the response, as discussed above in connection with article 4(2)(f). If the new respondent does not agree to a sole arbitrator already selected by the existing claimant(s) and respondent(s), or even to a sole-arbitrator formation, the matter will have to be resolved by application of article 7. By contrast, where a new party is joined by leave of the tribunal at a later stage, article 17(5) caters for the fact that the new party will not have participated in the constitution of the tribunal, by requiring the tribunal to consider whether any 'prejudice' would be caused to the new party (as discussed in connection with that provision below).

A. PRINCIPLE OF JOINT APPOINTMENT FOR THREE-MEMBER TRIBUNALS

5. Article 10(1) addresses the constitution of a three-member tribunal when the case involves multiple claimants or respondents. It refers to article 9(1), pursuant to which each party appoints one arbitrator on a three-member tribunal. Applying this rule to multiparty situations, article 10(1) stipulates that multiple parties are to appoint an arbitrator jointly.[8] Similarly, Article 12(6) and Article 12(7) of the ICC Rules provide that the joint nomination requirement 'is intended to ensure that all, and not just some, of the multiple parties concerned agree on the nomination'.[9] In the UNCITRAL Rules, too, it is only if such agreement is secured that there will be a joint appointment. In order words, article 10(1) calls for a joint appointment where multiple parties can be characterized as a 'claimant' or a 'respondent' group.

6. Joint appointments constitute the default position, but the parties are free to agree on other methods of appointment.[10] An example of an alternative arrangement

---

[7] Paulsson & Petrochilos, *supra* fn 4, at para. 87.

[8] Each party's right to appoint one arbitrator is thus not contingent on a prior agreement by the parties. Cf. Article 8.1 of the LCIA Rules: 'Where the Arbitration Agreement entitles each party howsoever to nominate an arbitrator…'.

[9] Derains & Schwartz, *supra* fn 2, at 181, referring to Article 10(1) of the 1998 ICC Rules, which is substantively the same as Article 12(6) of the 2017 ICC Rules. Article 12(7) of the 2017 ICC Rules provides for joint appointment in the case of joinder of an additional party, as the 2012 ICC Rules included a new provision on joinder (Article 7).

[10] *See* article 10(1) of the 2010 UNCITRAL Rules.

can be found in *Econet Wireless Ltd. v. First Bank of Nigeria,*[11] a multiparty arbitration where the arbitration clause provided that a three-member tribunal would be empanelled by decision of a senior judge in Nigeria.

B. TRIBUNALS COMPRISING A NUMBER OF ARBITRATORS OTHER THAN ONE OR THREE

7. Tribunals almost invariably are sole-arbitrator or three-member formations. Exceptions are rare and represent only a small fraction of the cases in international practice.[12] This is why the 1976 Rules operated under the assumption that there would be one or three arbitrators.[13] Parties desiring to derogate from this rule were able to do so by virtue of the right to agree to derogations under article 1(1). And there was nothing in the 1976 Rules (or the 2010 Rules for that matter) to forbid umpire formations or even-number formations.[14] However, nothing in the 1976 Rules specifically addressed the constitution of a tribunal comprising two or more than three arbitrators.

8. Article 10(2) of the 2010 Rules offers clarity in this regard. It explicitly mentions that parties are free to agree on a number of arbitrators other than one or three. Article 10(2) also makes it clear that, in such cases, the parties must agree on their own method of appointment. The Rules do not release the parties from any obligations or restrictions concerning the number of arbitrators under the *lex arbitri*.[15] They direct the parties to agree on the method for the constitution of the tribunal. If they fail to reach agreement, the appointing authority may step in pursuant to article 10(3). The provision does not spell out, but it goes without saying, that special provision for forming a majority must be made in case of an even-numbered formation.

---

11 *Econet Wireless Ltd (UK/South Africa) v. First Bank of Nigeria, et al. (Nigeria)* (UNCITRAL) Award, 2 June 2005, excerpt in XXXI YCA 49 (2006).

12 Paulsson & Petrochilos, *supra* fn 4, at para. 63. Cf. the Iran-United States Claims Tribunal, which may sit as a 'Full Tribunal' of nine arbitrators when deciding disputes between the Iranian and United States governments. Article III of the Iran-United States Claims Settlement Declaration (19 January 1981) provides that claims 'may be decided by the full Tribunal or by a panel of three members of the Tribunal as the President shall determine'.

13 Article 5 of the 1976 Rules, in relevant part, provides: 'If the parties have not previously agreed on the number of arbitrators (i.e. *one or three*)' (emphasis added). *See* discussion of article 7 of the 2010 Rules, *supra*.

14 But cf. article 33(1), which requires a 'majority' if 'there is more than one arbitrator'.

15 *See* article 1451 of the French Code of Civil Procedure which applies to domestic arbitration in France (article 1506) and provides that the arbitral tribunal is composed of one or many arbitrators, in uneven numbers. If the arbitration agreement provides for an even number of arbitrators, the tribunal must be 'completed'; Article 37(2)(a) of the ICSID Convention (allowing parties to agree on an uneven number of arbitrators only); Cf. section 15(1) of the Arbitration Act 1996 (England & Wales) (providing that the parties are free to agree on the number of arbitrators to form the tribunal).

C. APPOINTING AUTHORITY'S POWER TO COMPLETE THE CONSTITUTION OF THE TRIBUNAL

1. Scope of the appointing authority's power

9. Article 10(3) states that a party may request the appointing authority to appoint all arbitrators 'in the event of any failure to constitute the arbitral tribunal under these Rules'. As emphasized, article 10(3) is drafted in broad terms to cover 'all possible failures to constitute the arbitral tribunal and not be limited to those circumstances covered by paragraph (1) [failed joint appointments]'.[16] Article 10(3) therefore applies not only where a group of claimants or respondents fails jointly to appoint an arbitrator in accordance with article 10(1), but also where a tribunal is not constituted in accordance with the ad hoc method chosen by the parties under article 10(2).[17] It remains to be tested in practice how complete the parties' agreement must be in respect of the method for the constitution of the tribunal for the appointing authority to feel able to exercise its powers. For instance, a stipulation that there will be two arbitrators may suffice for the appointing authority to appoint them if the parties are unable to agree on their identity. But a stipulation that there will be 'two or more arbitrators as the parties may agree' is a less secure foundation for the appointing authority's intervention. Finally, article 10(3) also serves as a useful 'catch-all' provision, applying as a 'last resort in the event of *any* failure to constitute an arbitral tribunal', including where the parties have been unable to do so pursuant to articles 8 and 9,[18] where the designating authority agreed upon by the parties refuses or is unable to exercise its functions, etc.

2. Timing

10. Article 10(3) does not indicate at what point the constitution of the tribunal must have failed in order to trigger the appointing authority's intervention. This was done on purpose. The Working Group noted that 'there was no need to provide for specific deadlines applicable to the appointment of arbitrators in multiparty arbitration'; this view was based largely on the experience under other arbitration

---

16 *See* UNCITRAL Report of 46th Session, 20 March 2007, UN Doc A/CN.9/619, para. 88. Initial drafts of article 10(3) started with the opening words 'In the absence of appointment pursuant to paragraph 1…'.

17 David D. Caron & Lee M. Caplan, *The UNCITRAL Arbitration Rules, A Commentary*, 170 (2nd ed., Oxford University Press 2013); and James E. Castello, 'UNCITRAL Arbitration Rules, Section II, Article 10' in Loukas A. Mistelis (ed), *Concise International Arbitration*, 199 (2nd ed., Kluwer 2015) ('Art. 10(3) provides a rule for constituting three-member tribunals in multi-party arbitrations where the parties fail to constitute a three-member tribunal according to the appointment method described in art. 10(1) or any alternative method they may agree upon … The same default rule is also to be used for constituting tribunals of irregular size if parties have failed to constitute such a tribunal according to any method that have agreed').

18 Peter Binder, *Analytical Commentary to the UNCITRAL Arbitration Rules*, para. 10-016 (Sweet & Maxwell 2013).

rules showing that the lack of deadlines did not create difficulties.[19] Meanwhile, multiple parties should be given sufficient time to agree on an arbitrator. In any event, the possibility of approaching the appointing authority remains open to any party who is 'concerned about delay and desire[s] some action'.[20] These points are also valid in purely two-party cases as well.

3. Discretion of the appointing authority to select three new arbitrators

11. When asked by a party to appoint afresh each member of the arbitral tribunal pursuant to article 10(3), it is in the appointing authority's discretion to grant the party's request.[21] As expressly indicated in article 10(3), the appointing authority may revoke appointments already made and appoint new arbitrators, or reappoint already appointed arbitrators. Thus, it is possible for all parties to be deprived of their right to appoint an arbitrator, and in this manner to be treated equally.[22] For instance, in situations similar to that in *DUTCO*, where there are multiple parties which do not naturally align into one claimant or respondent group (e.g. a large group of shareholders) or do not share the same interests, (e.g. through joint and several rights and duties), party equality is likely to require that the appointing authority appoint the entire tribunal.[23]

12. However, a tactical choice to fail to make a joint appointment will not harm the other side by leading to the revocation of its appointment. It may be unnecessary for the appointing authority to revoke an arbitral appointment where, for example one respondent is in fact under the common control of the other respondent or 'otherwise [has] identical interests in the outcome of the arbitration', in which case there is no 'legitimate reason why they should not normally be expected to agree upon an arbitrator'.[24] Moreover, while the appointing authority has the power to revoke any appointments already made,[25] it may also 'reappoint' any arbitrator if it considers that it would be inappropriate to deprive a party of its appointed arbitrator, for example, where the individual's particular skills were

---

19 UNCITRAL Report of 49th Session, 30 September 2008, UN Doc A/CN.9/665, para. 70.

20 APRAG Report of 49th Session, 10 October 2008, para. 50.

21 The user of the Rules should not be confused by the mandatory language in article 10(3): '[t]he appointing authority *shall* ... constitute the arbitral tribunal' (emphasis added).

22 Caron & Caplan, *supra* fn 17, at 170.

23 Castello, *supra* fn 17, at 199 (noting that 'seeking to avoid the outcome in Dutco ... The drafters adopted the remedy of having the appointing authority appoint the entire tribunal in the circumstances just described'); *see* UNCITRAL Report of 46th Session, 20 March 2007, UN Doc A/CN.9/619, para. 90.

24 *See* Derains & Schwartz, *supra* fn 2, at 184 (the authors give the example of cases where seemingly multiple parties are, in fact, controlled by the same group). *See also* Castello, *supra* fn 17 ('the drafters determined that, following any such revocation, the appointing authority "should have the discretion to appoint an arbitrator already appointed by a party that was subsequently deprived of its right to appoint"').

25 The appointing authority's ability to revoke appointments already made caused concern amongst certain members of the Working Group. For the discussion of this issue, including a suggested 'two-step' procedure for nominating and appointing arbitrators, *see* UNCITRAL Report of 46th Session, 20 March 2007, UN Doc A/CN.9/619, para. 91.

relevant to the arbitration. Reappointment, however, is unlikely, as the purpose of revocation is 'usually ... to ensure equality of treatment as between the parties', and reappointment could undermine this objective.[26]

13. In contrast to arbitral institutions such as the ICC Court,[27] the appointing authority may exercise its discretionary power to appoint all the arbitrators only if it is requested to do so by a party ('at the request of any party'). This is particularly important for parties who have not been able to participate in the selection of the arbitrators because they were joined in the proceedings after the initial parties had made appointments, especially in the context of a joinder by right through the respondent's response.[28] In that situation, article 10(1) calls for a joint appointment, if the new party may join in a 'claimant' or 'respondent' camp for the purposes of that article. If not, article 10(3) may then be triggered.

---

26 Thomas H. Webster, *Handbook of UNCITRAL Arbitration*, para. 10-31 (2nd ed., Sweet & Maxwell 2015).

27 *See* Article 12(8) of the ICC Rules.

28 *See* discussion of article 4(2)(f) of the 2010 Rules, *supra*.

Articles 11 and 12
Disclosures by and challenge of arbitrators

1976 Rules
Articles 9 and 10: Challenge of arbitrators

Article 9

A prospective arbitrator shall disclose to those who approach him in connexion with his possible appointment any circumstances likely to give rise to justifiable doubts as to his impartiality or independence. An arbitrator, once appointed or chosen, shall disclose such circumstances to the parties unless they have already been informed by him of these circumstances.

2010 Rules
Articles 11 and 12: Disclosures by and challenge of arbitrators

Article 11

When a person is approached in connection with his or her possible appointment as an arbitrator, he or she shall disclose any circumstances likely to give rise to justifiable doubts as to his or her impartiality or independence. An arbitrator, from the time of his or her appointment and throughout the arbitral proceedings, shall without delay disclose any such circumstances to the parties and the other arbitrators unless they have already been informed by him or her of these circumstances.

Model statements of independence pursuant to article 11 of the Rules

No circumstances to disclose: I am impartial and independent of each of the parties and intend to remain so. To the best of my knowledge, there are no circumstances, past or present, likely to give rise to justifiable doubts as to my impartiality or independence. I shall promptly notify the parties and the other arbitrators of any such circumstances that may subsequently come to my attention during this arbitration.

Circumstances to disclose: I am impartial and independent of each of the parties and intend to remain so. Attached is a statement made pursuant to article 11 of the UNCITRAL Arbitration Rules of (a) my past and present professional, business and other relationships with the parties and (b) any other relevant circumstances. [Include statement] I confirm that those circumstances do not affect my independence and impartiality. I shall promptly notify the parties and the other arbitrators of any such further relationships or circumstances that may subsequently come to my attention during this arbitration.

Note. Any party may consider requesting from the arbitrator the following addition to the statement of independence:

I confirm, on the basis of the information presently available to me, that I can devote the time necessary to conduct this arbitration diligently, efficiently and in accordance with the time limits in the Rules.

Article 10	Article 12
1. Any arbitrator may be challenged if circumstances exist that give rise to justifiable doubts as to the arbitrator's impartiality or independence.	1. Any arbitrator may be challenged if circumstances exist that give rise to justifiable doubts as to the arbitrator's impartiality or independence.
2. A party may challenge the arbitrator appointed by him only for reasons of which he becomes aware after the appointment has been made.	2. A party may challenge the arbitrator appointed by it only for reasons of which it becomes aware after the appointment has been made.
[Article 13(2)] In the event that an arbitrator fails to act or in the event of the *de jure* or *de facto* impossibility of his performing his functions, the procedure in respect of the challenge and replacement of an arbitrator as provided in the preceding articles shall apply.	3. In the event that an arbitrator fails to act or in the event of the de jure or de facto impossibility of his or her performing his or her functions, the procedure in respect of the challenge of an arbitrator as provided in article 13 shall apply.

1. The mechanisms to police the essential safeguards of independence and impartiality are set out in articles 11 to 13.[1] Article 11 governs the arbitrators' duty of disclosure while article 12 addresses the grounds for challenge. The standards

[1] On independence and impartiality generally, *see* Sam Luttrell, *Bias Challenges in International Commercial Arbitration* (Kluwer 2009).

applicable to disclosure and to challenges are intrinsically linked; it is therefore appropriate to discuss articles 11 and 12 in tandem.

A. THE 1976 RULES

2. As has been aptly stated, 'the requirements that the arbitrators be impartial and independent ... are essential if the institution of arbitration is to maintain the respect needed to be an effective means of settling international commercial disputes'.[2] In the 1976 Rules, article 9 deals with the duty of arbitrators to disclose any circumstances which might call into question their impartiality or independence, whereas article 10 addresses challenges to arbitrators on the basis of justifiable doubts as to their impartiality or independence.

3. As in other arbitration rules, and arbitration laws for that matter, the notions of independence and impartiality are not defined by spelling out permissible or impermissible situations. Aside from few indirect indications,[3] these remain broad standards calling for an assessment of all relevant circumstances in the light of prevailing perceptions in arbitral practice and (crucially of course) any specific requirements of the *lex arbitri*.

4. The threshold test for challenges, set out in article 10 of the 1976 Rules, is the existence of circumstances 'that give rise to justifiable doubts as to the arbitrator's impartiality or independence'. This is 'an objective standard in that it requires not only a showing of doubt [in fact], but doubt that is *justifiable*' (emphasis added).[4] Doubts are justifiable 'if they give rise to an apprehension of bias that is, to the objective observer, reasonable'.[5] A party may challenge an arbitrator not on grounds that it actually and honestly entertains doubt that it regards as justifiable but on grounds that an objective observer would entertain such doubt.[6]

5. To illustrate, an investor in an arbitration against a state (applying the 1976 Rules) challenged the state's appointed arbitrator in part because she had a 'remarkable record of being appointed mostly by Respondent States in investor-State arbitrations' which, the investor submitted, 'further strengthen[ed]

---

2 David D. Caron & Lee M. Caplan, *The UNCITRAL Arbitration Rules, A Commentary*, 207 (2nd ed., Oxford University Press 2013).

3 *See* article 6(4) of the 1976 Rules, pursuant to which an appointing authority 'shall take into account ... *the advisability* of appointing an arbitrator of a nationality other than the nationalities of the parties' (emphasis added). This prompted commentators to reason that '[under the 1976 Rules] impartiality does not require that the arbitrator's nationality be different from the nationality of the parties'. *See* Stewart A. Baker & Mark D. Davis, *The UNCITRAL Arbitration Rules in Practice – The Experience of the Iran-United States Claims Tribunal*, 47 (Kluwer 1992). Cf. Article 6.1 of the LCIA Rules.

4 *Vito G Gallo v. The Government of Canada* (UNCITRAL) Decision on the Challenge to Mr J. Christopher Thomas QC, 14 October 2009, <www.italaw.com>, para. 19.

5 *Country X v. Company Q* (UNCITRAL) Challenge Decision, 11 January 1995, XXII YCA 227, 234 (1997), para. 24.

6 *See Vito G Gallo v. The Government of Canada, supra* fn 4, at para. 12.

the appearance of bias'.[7] In parallel, the state also challenged the arbitrator nominated by the investor in the same case. It submitted that the arbitrator's consistent representation of investors in a counsel capacity demonstrated that his work was 'sufficiently one-sided' to give rise to the perception that he would be more receptive to investors' claims; and that 'even if Respondent [was] in fact wrong about this, the mere circumstance that Respondent [could] reasonably have this perception' was sufficient for the challenge.[8] Although both arbitrators ultimately resigned before the PCA could issue a decision on the challenges,[9] this case demonstrates that in practice arguments are raised which are founded on subjective perceptions although it is clear that the standard is an objective one.[10]

6. Circumstances giving rise to justifiable doubts may comprise several discrete factors or events which should be considered in the round, qualitatively and quantitatively. In *CC/Devas v. India*,[11] for example, the respondent brought challenges against the presiding arbitrator and the claimant-appointed arbitrator on the basis of an 'issue conflict' – i.e., the arbitrators' previously-expressed views on a subject arising (or expected to arise) in the proceedings. In so doing:

> The Respondent emphasi[zed] that its concern is not related to the substance of the arbitrators' previously stated views, but rather to *the totality of the circumstances*, including their service together on two occasions, as well as the additional decision and chapter by [the party-appointed arbitrator], from which it believes its doubts as to both arbitrators' open-mindedness ... are justifiable. (emphasis added)[12]

Only the challenge against the party appointee was sustained, on the grounds that he had pronounced on the relevant legal concept on four previous occasions

7 *Murphy Exploration & Production Company International v. Republic of Ecuador* (UNCITRAL) Claimant's Challenge to Professor Stern, 28 November 2011, <www.italaw.com>, 7.

8 *Murphy Exploration & Production Company International v. Republic of Ecuador* (UNCITRAL) Respondent's Challenge to Dr Tawil, 21 December 2011, <www.italaw.com>, 13. *See also Valeri Belokon v. Kyrgyz Republic* (UNCITRAL) Decision on Challenges to Arbitrators Professor Kaj Hobér and Professor Jan Paulsson, 6 October 2014, <www.italaw.com>, para. 75 ('As with Professor Hobér, the Respondent submits that it has "so far no reasons to doubt Professor Paulsson's personal intention to act impartially and independently", but that the facts suggest "an appearance of lack of independence and bias that undermines the confidence in the investor-State system"').

9 Ms Stern and Mr Tawil resigned for 'personal' reasons within an hour of each other on 22 February 2012, as reported in Investment Arbitration Reporter, *Bid by US Oil Company to claim that Ecuador's 2006 windfall levy breaches investment treaty continues slow, torturous path to arbitration*, 28 March 2012, <www.iareporter.com>.

10 For an overview of recent investor-state arbitration case-law concerning challenges based on an arbitrator's past or present service as counsel or advocate, *see* ICCA, *Report of the ASIL-ICCA Joint Task Force on Issue Conflicts in Investor-State Arbitration*, 3 ICCA Reports 42, <www.asil.org>, paras 125-133 (2016).

11 *See CC/Devas (Mauritius) Ltd, Devas Employees Mauritius Private Limited and Telecom Devas Mauritius Limited v. India* (UNCITRAL) Decision on the Respondent's Challenge to the Hon. Marc Lalonde and Prof. Francisco Orrego Vicuña, 30 September 2013, <www.italaw.com>.

12 *Ibid.*, at para. 55.

– including by way of an academic 'chapter'. By contrast, the appointing authority held that the presiding arbitrator's 'more limited pronouncements on the relevant text [were] not sufficient to give rise to justifiable doubts regarding his impartiality'.[13] The case serves as authority for the broader proposition that in circumstances where an arbitrator cannot be trusted with reasonable confidence to keep an open mind to a material issue – for example because of repeat service in materially identical cases – one can conclude that there is a justifiable doubt as to his or her impartiality.

7. While a challenge requires a showing of justifiable doubts, the disclosure requirement is governed by a likelihood standard, which is lower. Indeed, article 9 of the 1976 Rules mandated that an arbitrator disclose 'any circumstances *likely* to give rise to justifiable doubts as to his impartiality or independence' (emphasis added). The 'justifiable doubts' wording again indicates that the disclosure standard, like the challenge standard, is an objective one. Even if the arbitrator does not believe himself to be biased in any way, he must disclose any information that, if known, is *likely* to cause a reasonable and neutral observer to have doubts about his or her independence or impartiality. Although 'likely' means something more than 'possibly', in practice it should not be read too restrictively. Thus, a Hong Kong court, interpreting the 'justifiable doubts' standard under Article 12 of the Model Law, held that '[t]he facts to be disclosed are not confined to those warranting or perceiving to be warranting disqualification but those that *might* found or warrant a *bona fide* application for disqualification'.[14] The rationale for this, the court added, is that an arbitrator's 'failure to disclose, of itself, can be one of the circumstances which together with others may give rise to a reasonable apprehension of bias ... A failure to disclose, no matter how unwitting, can undermine public confidence in the integrity of ... the tribunal concerned'.[15]

8. In practice, therefore, the position under the Rules is not significantly different from that under other arbitration rules, which require arbitrators to reveal any information that might 'call into question the arbitrator's independence in the eyes of the parties'.[16]

---

13 *Ibid.*, at para. 66. *See also* ICCA, *supra* fn 10, at paras 118-122.

14 *Jung Science Information Technology Co Ltd v. Zte Corporation* [2008] HKCFI 606, para. 58 (emphasis in the original).

15 *Ibid.*, at para. 57. *See also Valeri Belokon v. Kyrgyz Republic, supra* fn 8, at para. 68 (where the tribunal acknowledged that, '[i]n certain cases, a failure to disclose circumstances that the arbitrator had a duty to disclose can, in itself, give rise to justifiable doubts as to that arbitrator's independence and impartiality').

16 *See*, e.g., Article 11(2) of the ICC Rules. However, while the ICC Rules apply a subjective disclosure standard to the arbitrator's independence, Article 11(2) also includes an additional objective disclosure standard applicable to the arbitrator's impartiality. *See also* General Standard 3(a) of the 2014 IBA Guidelines on Conflicts of Interest in International Arbitration, which foresees a subjective test for disclosure.

B. DISCLOSURES BY ARBITRATORS: ARTICLE 11

1. Clarifications and changes pertaining to the timing and addressees of disclosure

9. Article 9 of the 1976 Rules mandates that 'prospective' arbitrators make disclosure as soon as they are approached for appointment. The purpose of pre-appointment disclosure is 'to prevent the appointment of arbitrators who could later be successfully challenged and to ensure that any challenges occur early in the proceedings, thus producing a minimum of disruption'.[17] An obligation on the part of a prospective arbitrator to investigate whether he or she has potentially problematic relationships or interests is implied in the duty to disclose.[18] In other words, an arbitrator is 'obligated to conduct a conflicts check to see if he must disclose any circumstances that might cause his impartiality to be questioned'.[19] Article 9 also states that arbitrators must continue to comply with the duty to disclose 'once appointed or chosen'. Although not expressly stated, this means that an arbitrator's duty to disclose is a continuing one, consistent with the duty to remain independent and impartial throughout the arbitral proceedings.[20]

10. The revision of the Rules represented an opportunity to make explicit the continuing nature of the duty to disclose, adapting the text of the Rules to 'the modern landscape of international arbitration, in which many arbitrators are members of large international law firms [and where] a duty of continuing disclosure (and thus continuing vigilance) assumes very great significance'.[21] Against this background, article 11 of the 2010 Rules now expressly states that an arbitrator shall make the necessary disclosures 'from the time of his or her appointment and throughout the arbitral proceedings'.

11. An arbitrator therefore bears the duty to disclose in two stages: at the outset, as soon as they are approached; and if appointed, from that time and throughout the proceedings.[22] Article 11 also encourages prompt disclosure by requiring arbitrators to disclose new information 'without delay': there is no meaningful difference between the term 'promptly' used elsewhere in the Rules and 'without

---

17 Baker & Davis, *supra* fn 3, at 46.

18 *See HSMV Corp v. ADI Ltd*, 72 F. Supp. 2d 1122 (CD Cal 1999), 1129.

19 *Ibid.*

20 *See*, e.g., *AWG Group Ltd v. The Argentine Republic* (UNCITRAL) Decision on a Second Proposal for the Disqualification of a Member of the Arbitral Tribunal, 12 May 2008, < www.italaw.com > , para. 25; *Vito G Gallo v. The Government of Canada, supra* fn 4, at para. 24 ('Allowing the Respondent to invoke evidence of constructive knowledge ... would relieve the arbitrator of *the continuing duty to disclose*' (emphasis added)); *See also* Meg N. Kinnear, Andrea K. Bjorklund & John F.G. Hannaford, *Investment Disputes under NAFTA: An Annotated Guide To NAFTA Chapter 11*, 1125-3 (Kluwer 2006) ('The obligation to disclose under UNCITRAL is clearly a continuing one').

21 Peter Turner & Reza Mohtashami, *A Guide to the LCIA Arbitration Rules*, para. 4.39 (Oxford University Press 2009) (commenting on Article 5.3 of the 1998 LCIA Rules).

22 Caron & Caplan, *supra* fn 2, at 195.

delay'. These additions reflect the language used in Article 12(1) of the Model Law[23] and bring the Rules in line with the majority of other arbitration rules.[24]

12. Changes have also been made with respect to the addressees of the disclosed information. Under the 1976 Rules, the two-step structure of pre- and post-appointment disclosure determined the addressees of the disclosed information. Pre-appointment disclosure was made to those who approach an arbitrator for appointment (typically the parties, although this could also apply to an appointing authority). At the post-appointment stage, however, a strict reading of article 9 of the 1976 Rules called for disclosure to the parties only.[25] Under article 11 of the 2010 Rules the addressees at the post-appointment stage explicitly include the other members of the tribunal,[26] because they have every reason to know of circumstances that may lead to a challenge and affect the work and procedural timetable of the tribunal.

2. Model statements of independence

13. Article 9 of the 1976 Rules was silent as to what form disclosures should take. Arbitration rules commonly require that disclosures be made in writing – in the form of a signed statement of independence – and submitted to the arbitral institution.[27]

14. While the 2010 Rules do not require arbitrators to file a written statement,[28] they nevertheless encourage them to do so, and this is obviously good (and standard) practice. Indeed, two model statements of independence are annexed to the Rules to provide guidance. The model statements provide a template for arbitrators in case there are 'no circumstances to disclose' and in case there are 'circumstances to disclose'. By including these statements, the Working Group also

---

23 *See* UNCITRAL Report of 45th Session, 5 October 2006, UN Doc A/CN.9/614, para. 64.

24 *See*, e.g., Article 22(c) of the WIPO Rules; Article 18(4) of the SCC Rules; Article 5.5 of the LCIA Rules.

25 *See* David D. Caron, Lee M. Caplan & Matti Pellonpää, *The UNCITRAL Arbitration Rules, A Commentary*, 200 (Oxford University Press 2006). Cf. Article 9 of the Tribunal Rules of Procedure of the Iran-United States Claims Tribunal (3 May 1983), which mandates arbitrators to disclose any information to the President of the Tribunal, and, only if the latter so determines, to the arbitrating parties. *See*, for discussion, Baker & Davis, *supra* fn 3, at 46–47.

26 Cf. Jan Paulsson & Georgios Petrochilos, *Revision of the UNCITRAL Rules* (September 2006), para. 90, <www.uncitral.org> (the authors propose to extend the disclosure duty to the appointing authority who has appointed the arbitrator in question). *See also* UNCITRAL Report of 49th Session, 30 September 2008, UN Doc A/CN.9/665, para. 74.

27 *See*, e.g., Article 18(3) of the SCC Rules; Article 11(2) of the ICC Rules; Article 13(2) of the AAA International Arbitration Rules.

28 *See* UNCITRAL Report of 45th Session, 5 October 2006, UN Doc A/CN.9/614, para. 65 ('The Working Group did not support a proposal that disclosure should be in the form of a written declaration').

intended to provide guidance 'on the required content of disclosure'.[29] When an arbitral institution or the PCA serves as the appointing authority, it will typically use its own form prepared for UNCITRAL cases.

(i) No circumstances to disclose

15. A declaration that there are 'no circumstances to disclose' does not require a total absence of links between the arbitrator and the parties (and counsel).[30] According to the text of the first model statement, an arbitrator should declare that there are no circumstances to disclose when 'there are no circumstances, past or present, likely to give rise to justifiable doubts as to [his or her] impartiality or independence'. Therefore, in line with the standard set out in article 11, an arbitrator may file a 'no circumstances to disclose' statement where links are, from an objective standpoint, insignificant.

16. The *AWG v. Argentina* case is a good illustration of the type of circumstances that is unlikely to be covered by the disclosure requirement.[31] It is also a good example of the relationship between the challenge and disclosure standards. The case involved a concession for water distribution and treatment services in Buenos Aires, in which *AWG* and two other claimants had invested. Argentina challenged the claimant-appointed arbitrator on the basis that she was a non-executive director of an international bank whose investment portfolio included an interest in one of the claimants. The tribunal[32] rejected the challenge as the arbitrator was not aware of the bank's investment, which in any event could not compromise her impartiality as it was not material.[33] The tribunal identified disclosure obligations as follows:

> Having decided that Professor Kaufmann-Kohler's appointment as a director of UBS did not create a circumstance giving rise to justifiable doubts as to her impartiality or independence in the *AWG Case*, because of the lack of any business relationship ... we also conclude that she had no obligation

[29] UNCITRAL Report of 49th Session, 30 September 2008, UN Doc A/CN.9/665, para. 75. For a criticism of the model statements of independence, *see* Pieter Sanders, *The Revision of the UNCITRAL Arbitration Rules* (August 2009), 17, <www.arbitration-icca.org>.

[30] *See* UNCITRAL Report of 49th Session, 30 September 2008, UN Doc A/CN.9/665, para. 78 (a suggestion was made that to better distinguish the first and second statement of independence, the first statement should 'focus on the absence of any relation between the arbitrator and the parties'; this suggestion was rejected as 'unnecessary' and 'too far-reaching').

[31] *See AWG Group Ltd v. The Argentine Republic, supra* fn 20.

[32] Note that under the UNCITRAL Rules it is the appointing authority, and not the arbitral tribunal, which decides on the challenge of an arbitrator (article 12 of the 1976 Rules; article 13(4) of the 2010 Rules). However, the fact that the *AWG* decision on challenge also involved two ICSID arbitrations allowed the tribunal to decide on challenges (Article 58 of the ICSID Convention).

[33] *AWG Group Ltd v. The Argentine Republic, supra* fn 20, at paras 36-40.

under Article 9 of the UNCITRAL Arbitration Rules to disclose the fact of her directorship in UBS to the parties in the *AWG Case*.[34]

(ii) Circumstances to disclose

17. The second model statement invites arbitrators to disclose 'past and present professional, business and other relationships with the parties' as well as 'any other relevant circumstances'. The purpose of this statement is to provide a template for the disclosure of 'grey-zone' circumstances, which are the most common occurrence in practice. Such circumstances neither are entirely insignificant (so as to justify the use of a 'no circumstances to disclose' statement), nor do they constitute clear grounds for disqualification (so as to prompt an arbitrator to refuse the appointment or to resign). Therefore, a practical test for disclosure is whether negative inferences can be drawn from an arbitrator's failure to disclose. Also, disclosure enables an arbitrator to explain any factors that place in their proper context, and give the proper measure of, the circumstances disclosed, allowing an arbitrator to 'confirm that those circumstances do not affect [his or her] independence and impartiality', while leaving it to the parties to judge for themselves.

18. It should be noted that the Working Group has not issued a guidance note addressing any specific situations that would trigger the disclosure requirement. In practice, arbitrators may easily refer to the ever-increasing number of publicly-available procedural orders and decisions rendered under the UNCITRAL Rules in the context of investment-treaty arbitration. The IBA Guidelines on Conflicts of Interest in International Arbitration (now in their second edition) are obviously instructive and standard terms of discourse in practice. In *ICS Inspection v. Argentina*, the tribunal noted that '[a]lthough the IBA Guidelines have no binding status in the present [UNCITRAL] proceedings, they reflect international best practices and offer examples of situations that may give rise to objectively justifiable doubts as to an arbitrator's impartiality or independence'.[35]

C. GROUNDS FOR CHALLENGE: ARTICLE 12

19. The text of article 10 of the 1976 Rules on the challenge of arbitrators is reproduced, with only minor textual changes, in article 12 of the 2010 Rules. However, a difference between the two sets of Rules lies in the relocation – from article 13(2) of the 1976 Rules to article 12(3) of the 2010 Rules – of the paragraph addressing the challenge of an arbitrator who 'fails to act', or for whom it becomes de jure or de facto impossible to perform his or her functions. Thus, the 2010 Rules group all possible grounds for the challenge of arbitrators into article 12. As no substantial changes have been made to the text of these provisions, the

---

[34] *Ibid.*, at para. 26.

[35] *ICS Inspection and Control Services Ltd v. The Republic of Argentina* (UNCITRAL) Decision on Challenge to Arbitrator, 17 December 2009, <www.italaw.com>, 4; *See also Vito G Gallo v. The Government of Canada, supra* fn 4, at para. 36.

reader is referred to commentaries on the 1976 Rules for further details.[36] It will simply be noted that the terms 'fails to act', which are taken verbatim from the 1976 text, should be read, it is submitted, consistent with the more specific wording of Article 10.2 of the LCIA Rules, namely to capture an arbitrator's failure to 'conduct or participate in the arbitration with reasonable efficiency, diligence and industry'. That reading is consistent with the tribunal's duties under article 17(1) to conduct the proceedings 'so as to avoid unnecessary delay ... and to provide a[n] efficient process for resolving the parties' dispute'. The Rules do not spell out the mechanics of how the parties are to become aware of an arbitrator's impossibility to act. It is possible that the parties learn of such a development through public sources or private information. It is also possible, and in fact entirely permissible at the very least, that the other tribunal members (in a plural formation) alert the parties. It is clear, however, that a unilateral communication from one arbitrator to a party would be impermissible, as it might indicate partiality.[37]

20. However, the 2010 Rules do suggest the addition of a 'declaration of availability'[38] to the statement of independence, whereby the arbitrator confirms that he or she 'can devote the time necessary to conduct this arbitration diligently, efficiently and in accordance with the time limits in the Rules'. (It is emerging practice for arbitrators in fact to disclose major commitments in their schedule to allow parties to judge for themselves an arbitrator's availability in concrete terms.) This is consistent with the practice of major arbitral institutions, and has obvious good sense. If nothing else, a declaration of availability will give parties additional leverage in encouraging arbitrators to act in a timely manner, where necessary. An arbitrator who signs the declaration represents to the parties and the tribunal facts about his or her availability. If the arbitrator then fails to dedicate the time required to conduct an efficient arbitration, he or she may face sanctions for having intentionally misrepresented such facts. Article 16 of the 2010 Rules gives tribunal members general immunity from collateral attacks; however, arbitrators may be liable for intentional wrongdoing.[39]

21. It should also be noted that article 12(2), as article 10(2) of the 1976 Rules, performs two functions. The first is to indicate that a party may challenge its

---

36 *See* Caron, Caplan & Pellonpää, *supra* fn 25, at 209-240 (discussing article 10), 284-297 and 299-318 (discussing article 13(2)). *See also* Baker & Davis, *supra* fn 3, at 37-60 (discussing article 10) and 70 (discussing article 13(2)).

37 Cf. *Symbion Power LLC v. Venco Imtiaz Construction Co* [2017] EWHC 348 (TCC), paras 75 et seq. (arbitrator sent 'confidential' email to the party that had appointed him, stating that 'both party-appointed arbitrators were upset by the conduct of the chairman; ... [and] that he was meeting the chairman and would encourage him to resign'; held at para. 85 that '[a]ny communication by one arbitrator with one party which concerns the arbitration may give rise to concerns that that arbitrator is not acting fairly or impartially for the simple reason that it creates the impression of a close relationship between the arbitrator and the party and raises the spectre of other such communications').

38 A term used by the Working Group: *see* UNCITRAL Report of 52nd Session, 19 February 2010, UN Doc A/CN.9/688, para. 58.

39 *See* the commentary on article 16 of the 2010 Rules, *infra*.

appointee on the tribunal. From a philosophical perspective, this reflects the premise that all parties have a shared interest in the integrity and validity of the arbitral process. Thus a party that did not have the benefit of full disclosure, or learns of a newly-disclosed circumstance, may mount a challenge to its appointee. Secondly, from a practical perspective, the provision prevents parties from tactical or pre-ordained challenges that cause vacancies on the tribunal, delay, or both – a concern also addressed in article 14(2). The policy of the Rules is to place celerity/orderliness of the proceedings above the risk of maintaining an arbitrator who is liable to be recused or pose risk to the validity of the award.

Article 13
Procedure for challenging arbitrators

1976 Rules Articles 11 and 12: Challenge of arbitrators	2010 Rules Article 13: Disclosures by and challenge of arbitrators
Article 11	Article 13
1. A party who intends to challenge an arbitrator shall send notice of his challenge within fifteen days after the appointment of the challenged arbitrator has been notified to the challenging party or within fifteen days after the circumstances mentioned in articles 9 and 10 became known to that party.	1. A party that intends to challenge an arbitrator shall send notice of its challenge within 15 days after it has been notified of the appointment of the challenged arbitrator, or within 15 days after the circumstances mentioned in articles 11 and 12 became known to that party.
2. The challenge shall be notified to the other party, to the arbitrator who is challenged and to the other members of the arbitral tribunal. The notification shall be in writing and shall state the reasons for the challenge.	2. The notice of challenge shall be communicated to all other parties, to the arbitrator who is challenged and to the other arbitrators. The notice of challenge shall state the reasons for the challenge.
3. When an arbitrator has been challenged by one party, the other party may agree to the challenge. The arbitrator may also, after the challenge, withdraw from his office. In neither case does this imply acceptance of the validity of the grounds for the challenge. In both cases the procedure provided in article 6 or 7 shall be used in full for the appointment of the substitute arbitrator, even if during the process of appointing the challenged arbitrator a party had failed to exercise his right to appoint or to participate in the appointment.	3. When an arbitrator has been challenged by a party, all parties may agree to the challenge. The arbitrator may also, after the challenge, withdraw from his or her office. In neither case does this imply acceptance of the validity of the grounds for the challenge.
	4. If, within 15 days from the date of the notice of challenge, all parties do not agree to the challenge or the challenged arbitrator does not withdraw, the party making the challenge may elect to pursue it. In that case, within 30 days from the date of the notice of challenge, it shall seek a decision on the challenge by the appointing authority.

Article 12

1. If the other party does not agree to the challenge and the challenged arbitrator does not withdraw, the decision on the challenge will be made:

(a) When the initial appointment was made by an appointing authority, by that authority;

(b) When the initial appointment was not made by an appointing authority, but an appointing authority has been previously designated, by that authority;

(c) In all other cases, by the appointing authority to be designated in accordance with the procedure for designating an appointing authority as provided for in article 6.

2. If the appointing authority sustains the challenge, a substitute arbitrator shall be appointed or chosen pursuant to the procedure applicable to the appointment or choice of an arbitrator as provided in articles 6 to 9 except that, when this procedure would call for the designation of an appointing authority, the appointment of the arbitrator shall be made by the appointing authority which decided on the challenge.

---

1. Article 13 of the 2010 Rules sets out the procedure for challenging arbitrators. It also provides the procedure for the acceptance or the pursuit of the challenge. It is particularly important that the Rules provide clear guidelines for this process: challenges – especially successful ones – have the potential to delay the arbitral proceedings, as new arbitrators may need to be appointed and hearings may need to be repeated.[1]

A. THE REGIME UNDER THE 1976 RULES

2. Article 11 of the 1976 Rules laid down the process to be followed after a party had challenged an arbitrator. Article 11(1) provided a challenging party with a

---

[1] *See* David D. Caron & Lee M. Caplan, *The UNCITRAL Arbitration Rules, A Commentary*, 242 (2nd ed., Oxford University Press 2013) citing UNCITRAL Report of the Secretary General on the Draft UNCITRAL Arbitration Rules, 12 December 1975, UN Doc A/CN.9/112/ Add.1, 170 ('Challenge of an arbitrator results in an interruption of the course of arbitral proceedings, and a successful challenge will result in a serious interruption arising from the need to appoint a substitute arbitrator and the possible need to repeat hearings held prior to such challenge').

time-limit of 15 days within which to send notice of its challenge after becoming aware of the circumstances giving rise to the challenge. Article 11(2) then specified whom the challenging party had to notify, stating that this notification 'shall be in writing and shall state the reasons for the challenge'. Article 11(3) provided that, upon notification, the other party may agree to the challenge or the arbitrator may withdraw from office. In either eventuality, this did not 'imply acceptance of the validity of the grounds for the challenge'. The rationale for this is eminently pragmatic: a party may have a superior interest in expediting the proceedings than in fighting a position of principle, especially in the early stages of the proceedings. Article 11(3) further stated that the procedures set out in articles 6 and 7 of the Rules – pertaining to the initial appointment of arbitrators – were to be applied to appoint any substitute arbitrator. These procedures were to be used regardless of whether the party had exercised its right to appoint the arbitrator or had otherwise participated in the appointment.

3. Article 12 of the 1976 Rules provided a fairly complex mechanism for the appointing authority to intervene in the challenge process. The appointing authority had to decide on a challenge if (i) the other party did not agree to the challenge and (ii) the challenged arbitrator did not withdraw. Article 12 offered three different hypotheses: (a) where the initial appointment was made by an appointing authority, that authority would resolve the challenge; (b) where the initial appointment was not made by an appointing authority, but one had been previously designated, that authority would resolve the challenge; and (c) in all cases not coming under (a) or (b), an appointing authority was to be designated in accordance with the procedure set out in article 6 of the 1976 Rules, and that appointing authority would then resolve the challenge.

4. These provisions of the 1976 Rules gave rise to certain issues in practice. For example, the absence of a time-limit for the party to designate, or seek a decision by, the appointing authority under article 12(1) opened the door to dilatory tactics.[2] Indeed, during the revision process, it was specifically noted that the absence of such a time-limit had 'on occasion led to delay and uncertainty on the part of the arbitral tribunal on whether the proceedings should be continued' in the face of a pending challenge that had not been referred to an appointing authority.[3]

B. SIGNIFICANT CHANGES UNDER THE 2010 RULES

5. The 2010 Rules have made significant changes to the challenge process. First, the 2010 Rules clarify the connection between the 'challenge' and the 'notice of challenge' provided for in article 11 of the 1976 Rules. Second, article 13(2) clarifies that all other parties have a right to oppose the challenge, as may be

---

2 Jan Paulsson & Georgios Petrochilos, *Revision of the UNCITRAL Rules* (September 2006), paras 100-101, <www.uncitral.org>.

3 James E. Castello, 'UNCITRAL Arbitration Rules, Section II, Article 13' in Loukas A. Mistelis (ed), *Concise International Arbitration*, 204 (2nd ed., Kluwer 2015). *See also* UNCITRAL Working Paper for 45th Session, 20 July 2006, UN Doc. A/CN.9/WG.II/WP.143, para. 49.

relevant in a multiparty case. Third, the role of the appointing authority is clarified in article 13(4); the references to procedures 'in article 6 or 7' for the appointment of the substitute arbitrator, which appeared in 11(3) of the 1976 Rules, as well as the entirety of article 12 of the 1976 Rules, have been removed.[4] Certain ambiguities do, however, remain in the 2010 Rules.

1. Clarification of the 'notice of challenge': articles 13(1) and (2)

6. Articles 13(1) and 13(2) are substantially unchanged from the 1976 provisions (articles 11(1) and 11(2), respectively). Under the 2010 Rules, a party intending to challenge has 15 days after it has been notified of the appointment of the arbitrator whom it intends to challenge, or after the grounds for justifiable doubts became known to the challenging party (article 13(1)).[5] Article 13(2) provides that the notice of challenge must be communicated to the other parties and all arbitrators, and that it must state the reasons for the challenge.

7. It is clear that the time-limit is ordinarily triggered by the receipt of the arbitrator's disclosure under article 11. But the provision is couched, as it must be, in broader terms, referring to the date on which 'the circumstances ... became known to [the challenging] party'. This of course covers instances of incomplete disclosure, where the circumstances founding a challenge become known through independent inquiry or happenstance. This may for instance happen in respect of facts that reveal an arbitrator's lack of impartiality, e.g. through public statements or a separate opinion that became available in the course of the proceedings. A question that arises in this connection is whether the start-date is not that of actual knowledge by the challenging party – as in fact the text of article 13(1) indicates – but the date of presumed knowledge on which a diligent party *should* have known of the circumstances founding a challenge.[6] This is not an easy question, although there is authority against the notion of presumed knowledge.[7] It is important that the wording of the provision – 'became known to that party' – remained unchanged in the 2010 revision. But it is also important

---

[4] Article 14 of the 2010 Rules also plays a role here insofar as it creates a 'global' process for the replacement of arbitrators. This global replacement process thus applies where the parties have agreed to the challenge or where the arbitrator withdraws, as well as where the appointing authority has had to make the decision on the challenge. *See* discussion of article 14 of the 2010 Rules, *infra*.

[5] Other institutions provide for similar time-limits. *See*, e.g., Article 14(2) of the ICC Rules; Article 10.3 of the LCIA Rules; Article 25 of the WIPO Rules.

[6] *See* Stewart A. Baker & Mark D. Davis, *The UNCITRAL Arbitration Rules in Practice – The Experience of the Iran-United States Claims Tribunal*, 62-63 (Kluwer 1992).

[7] *Vito G Gallo v. The Government of Canada* (UNCITRAL) Decision on the Challenge to Mr J. Christopher Thomas QC, 14 October 2009, < www.italaw.com >, para. 24. *See also CC/Devas (Mauritius) Ltd, Devas Employees Mauritius Private Limited and Telecom Devas Mauritius Limited v. India* (UNCITRAL) Decision on the Respondent's Challenge, 30 September 2013, < www.italaw.com >, paras 45-49 (finding that the respondent's challenge – brought following the actual knowledge of its newly-retained counsel – was timely, the appointing authority rejected the claimants' argument that the respondent *could* have known the facts giving rise to the challenge at the time of the arbitrators' appointments).

that the Rules set forth a tight 15-day deadline for challenges, with the obvious objective of resolving issues quickly at the initiative of the interested party, without keeping one's cards up one's sleeve, as it were. The authors submit that although it is clear from article 11 that parties do not have an independent duty of making inquiries, there is scope for the application of the waiver rule in article 32. If a circumstance ought to have been known by a reasonably diligent party in the position of the challenging party, that circumstance cannot be invoked later than 15 days of the date of presumed knowledge; 'unless [the challenging] party can show that, under the circumstances, its failure to [raise a challenge] was justified'.

8. Moreover, it is important to note that the time-limits set out in article 13(1) of the 2010 Rules (and article 11(1) of the 1976 Rules) cannot be extended by the tribunal pursuant to article 17(2), unless a tribunal is already in place. Nor does the appointing authority have any express power under the Rules to grant an extension. In practice, an extension may be needed if further investigations or inquiries are required after the date of initial knowledge, e.g. the date of disclosure. The appropriate solution in such circumstances is to regard as the operative date for article 13(1) purposes the date on which all necessary information was obtained.

9. The Rules do not specify which party bears the burden of demonstrating the specific time at which the challenging party became aware of the circumstances giving rise to the challenge, and this issue has arisen on several occasions before the Iran-US Claims Tribunal.[8] Arguably, the party bringing the challenge should bear the burden of demonstrating that the challenge is timely, as this is consistent with article 27(1) of the Rules.[9] In any event, article 13(1) does not spell out what type of evidence is required to establish knowledge, although the standard has generally been set quite high.[10]

---

8 Caron & Caplan, *supra* fn 1, at 243-245; *see also ibid.* Baker & Davis, *supra* fn 6, at 62-63, and in particular the Briner decision reprinted in (1989) 21 Iran-US CTR 391, as discussed by each of these authors. This case illustrates the ambiguity with respect to the burden of proof and a potential duty to investigate. One of the key issues was whether Iran had been aware of the ground for challenge on which it relied a long time before it decided to bring the challenge. The challenge was based on Judge Briner's professional relationship to Morgan Stanley, which was published in an annual listing of all directorships of Swiss companies. Thus, in principle, Iran could have discovered this long before the challenge was in fact made. The parties also disagreed as to whether or not Iran had the burden of proving that it learned of the circumstances that gave rise to the challenge no later than 15 days before acting on the information (and refute the suspicion that it would have been aware long before because of the public nature of the information). However, as Judge Briner withdrew from Case No. 55, the Appointing Authority had no opportunity to address this issue. *See* Caron & Caplan, *supra* fn 1, at 244 (agreeing with Amoco's attorney that the burden of proof lay on Iran, and analogizing to article 27(1) of the 2010 Rules, which provides that 'each party shall have the burden of proving the facts relied on to support its claim or defence').

9 *See* Caron & Caplan, *supra* fn 1, at 245.

10 For a more detailed analysis of this issue, *see* Caron & Caplan, *supra* fn 1, at 245-248.

10. One notable improvement is that paragraphs 1 and 2 of article 13 clarify that the notice of challenge is the instrument through which a challenge is raised, rather than a notice of intention to challenge. The 1976 Rules gave the impression that there may be a two-step challenge process, comprising a 'notice of challenge' under article 11(1), followed by the 'challenge' itself under article 11(2). The new Rules make clear in articles 13(1) and (2) that there is only a 'notice of challenge' (both paragraphs now use this term) which is the instrument setting forth the grounds for challenge and seeks the recusal of an arbitrator. The requirement to 'state the reasons' under article 13(2) is to be read as requiring both an articulation of the factual and legal grounds for the challenge and to adduce the necessary evidence. This reading is consistent with the general evidential principle in article 27(1) of the Rules.

2. Agreeing to or opposing the challenge: article 13(3)

11. Article 13(3) specifies that, upon notification, the other parties may agree to the challenge or the arbitrator may withdraw from office, and that neither circumstance implies acceptance of the validity of the grounds for the challenge. One notable change is that, unlike article 11(3) of the 1976 Rules, which provided only for the agreement of 'the other party', article 13(3) provides for agreement by 'all parties'. Not only does this account for multiparty arbitrations,[11] it also clarifies that all the parties, regardless of which party appointed the arbitrator, have a right to oppose the challenge.[12] Practically, this allows the parties to oppose an appointment made by the appointing authority – a possibility that is not available under the ICC Rules for example in respect of ICC Court appointments and which may be valuable when both parties consider that the choice of the appointing authority is not suitable for the case.

12. The provision does not spell out the legal consequences of the parties' agreeing to the challenge. A proposal was put forward during the revision process to state that unanimous agreement by the parties had the effect of terminating the mandate of the challenged arbitrator.[13] This proposal was rejected due to concerns that some national arbitration laws contain mandatory provisions regarding the mandate of arbitrators.[14] Article 13(3) therefore implicitly refers to the governing arbitration law with respect to the legal effects of the parties' agreement to the challenge.[15] The effect, in practical terms, is that the recused arbitrator's appointment is revoked; hence article 14 requires that a 'substitute' appointment be made. No provision is made, however, as to the fees and expenses the recused arbitrator may be entitled to for his or her period of service.

---

11 *See* UNCITRAL Report of 49th Session, 30 September 2008, UN Doc A/CN.9/665, para. 85.
12 *Ibid.*, at paras 85-88.
13 *Ibid.*, at para. 89.
14 *Ibid.*, at para. 90.
15 Caron & Caplan, *supra* fn 1, at 255.

3. Clarification of the role of the appointing authority: article 13(4)

13. The role of the appointing authority in the challenge process is set out in articles 11 and 12 of the 1976 Rules. The 2010 Rules amalgamated these provisions in article 13, leaving the question of replacement of an arbitrator to article 14.[16] Article 13(4) provides the mechanism whereby the party making the challenge may choose to pursue it if (i) none of the conditions of article 13(3) is met (resignation of the arbitrator or agreement of the parties), and (ii) the 15-day time-limit from the date of the notice of challenge has not expired. In such a case, the challenging party has 30 days from the date of the notice of challenge to seek a decision from the appointing authority.[17] By imposing this time-limit, article 13(4) prevents the parties from using a contested challenge as a tool to create uncertainty and delay the proceedings.

14. Other relevant provisions, however, now appear in article 6 of the 2010 Rules. For example under article 6(4), if the appointing authority fails to decide a challenge 'within a reasonable time' after receiving a party's request, any party may request that the Secretary-General of the PCA designate a substitute appointing authority. This is an important provision for the avoidance of delay, as there is otherwise no fixed time-limit for the appointing authority to make a decision on the challenge.[18] This mechanism also emphasizes the advantages of designating an appointing authority as early as possible.[19] Early designation of the appointing authority, in conjunction with the time-limit laid down in article 13(4), serves to ensure the rapid resolution of contested challenges.

15. The Rules do not spell out that the decision of the appointing authority is final, that is to say, non-appealable before domestic courts on a stand-alone basis.[20Fn] In any event the matter is subject to mandatory provisions of the *lex arbitri*. Thus, under Article 13(1) and (3) of the Model Law, a decision by the appointing authority is always subject to recourse before the controlling court (such recourse not necessarily having the effect of suspending the arbitral proceedings).

---

16 *See* discussion of article 14 of the 2010 Rules, *infra*.

17 *See* discussion of article 6 of the 2010 Rules, *supra*. Note that where no appointing authority is in place, article 6(3) provides that the 30-day deadline is suspended 'from the date on which a party initiates the procedure for agreeing on or designating an appointing authority until the date of such agreement or designation'.

18 Typically, however, the appointing authority 'will ordinarily resolve the challenge quickly (typically in a matter of days or (more likely) a few weeks'; *see* Gary B. Born, *International Commercial Arbitration*, 2028-2035 (2nd ed., Kluwer 2014). This is perhaps due to the fact that the Rules 'properly [regard] the objective of resuming the arbitration as quickly and cheaply as possible as more important than ascertaining with certainty ... the truth of a challenge' (Caron & Caplan, *supra* fn 1, at 339).

19 Cf. the discussion of article 6 of the 2010 Rules, paras 7-8 *supra*.

20 Cf. Article 19(5) of the SCC Rules, which provides for a final decision of the SCC Board.

4. Progress of arbitration proceedings pending a challenge

16. The Rules do not spell out whether the tribunal is entitled to continue with the proceedings pending a challenge, but nor do they state that the proceedings must be stayed. A number of national laws provide that the tribunal may proceed notwithstanding a challenge.[21] As for the position under the Rules, it is difficult, it is submitted, to make an argument, either way, from article 23(3), which allows a tribunal to proceed pending a court challenge to a jurisdictional ruling it has issued. There is no analogy between the two situations, since the tribunal has no power under the Rules to decide on a challenge to its members, while it does have the power and duty to decide on its jurisdiction. In the authors' submission, the tribunal may, subject to the *lex arbitri*, decide to proceed pending a challenge, taking into account the stage of the arbitration, the perceived seriousness of the challenge, and any possible need to retain its functions for the sake of orderly proceedings, for example to issue interim measures or uncontroversial procedural documents such as the timetable of the proceedings.

---

[21] *See*, e.g., section 24(3) of the Arbitration Act 1996 (England & Wales); Article 10(3) of the Swedish Arbitration Act; cf. Article 13(3) of the Model Law, which allows the tribunal to continue with the proceedings if a party appeals against the rejection of a challenge by the appointing authority or a national court.

Articles 14 and 15

Replacement of an arbitrator and repetition of hearings

1976 Rules	2010 Rules
Article 13: Replacement of an arbitrator	Article 14: Replacement of an arbitrator
Article 14: Repetition of hearings in the event of the replacement of an arbitrator	Article 15: Repetition of hearings in the event of the replacement of an arbitrator

1976 Rules

Article 13

1. In the event of the death or resignation of an arbitrator during the course of the arbitral proceedings, a substitute arbitrator shall be appointed or chosen pursuant to the procedure provided for in articles 6 to 9 that was applicable to the appointment or choice of the arbitrator being replaced.

2. In the event that an arbitrator fails to act or in the event of the de jure or de facto impossibility of his performing his functions, the procedure in respect of the challenge and replacement of an arbitrator as provided in the preceding articles shall apply.

2010 Rules

Article 14

1. Subject to paragraph 2, in any event where an arbitrator has to be replaced during the course of the arbitral proceedings, a substitute arbitrator shall be appointed or chosen pursuant to the procedure provided for in articles 8 to 11 that was applicable to the appointment or choice of the arbitrator being replaced. This procedure shall apply even if during the process of appointing the arbitrator to be replaced, a party had failed to exercise its right to appoint or to participate in the appointment.

2. If, at the request of a party, the appointing authority determines that, in view of the exceptional circumstances of the case, it would be justified for a party to be deprived of its right to appoint a substitute arbitrator, the appointing authority may, after giving an opportunity to the parties and the remaining arbitrators to express their views: (a) appoint the substitute arbitrator; or (b) after the closure of the hearings, authorize the other arbitrators to proceed with the arbitration and make any decision or award.

Article 14

If under articles 11 to 13 the sole or presiding arbitrator is replaced, any hearings held previously shall be repeated; if any other arbitrator is replaced, such prior hearings may be repeated at the discretion of the arbitral tribunal.

Article 15

If an arbitrator is replaced, the proceedings shall resume at the stage where the arbitrator who was replaced ceased to perform his or her functions, unless the arbitral tribunal decides otherwise.

1. Article 13 of the 1976 Rules dealt with the replacement of arbitrators in the event of death, resignation, failure or impossibility to act. The impact of the replacements on the hearings was, in turn, addressed in article 14. Article 13 distinguished death and resignation (13(1)) from the arbitrator's failure or impossibility to act (13(2)). Only the former led to the direct replacement of an arbitrator. By contrast, an arbitrator who failed to act or was incapable of performing his or her functions had to be successfully challenged to be replaced.

2. The procedure for replacing missing or inactive arbitrators has the potential considerably to disrupt the arbitral proceedings – and therein lies the risk that a mala fide litigant could cause such situations. In particular, article 13 of the 1976 Rules did not adequately address situations in which arbitrators were physically prevented from acting, or where they resigned for tactical reasons, or failed to act in order to advance the interests of the party that appointed them. These are difficult and doubtless exceptional cases, but it is precisely because of this that they must be addressed by the Rules.

3. The drafters of the 2010 Rules were largely inspired by the solutions adopted by tribunals in practice, especially those of the Iran-US Claims Tribunal, when applying article 13 of the 1976 Rules.[1] Most significantly, the 2010 Rules allow the remaining arbitrators, in certain exceptional circumstances, to proceed as a 'truncated tribunal' and issue an award without the missing arbitrator.[2]

A. REPLACEMENT OF AN ARBITRATOR: ARTICLE 14

4. The provisions of article 14 apply throughout the life of the tribunal, until it is finally *functus officio* after all deadlines for post-award remedies have been exhausted (articles 37-39). The strict view is that in fact they apply until the very last award or decision of the tribunal has been signed by the arbitrators (article 34(4)) and dispatched to the parties and, if so agreed, made public (article 34(5)). Thus, it is conceivable that the replacement procedure may be applied at these very last stages.

---

[1] *See* Article 13 of the Tribunal Rules of Procedure of the Iran-United States Claims Tribunal (3 May 1983).

[2] *See* Jan Paulsson & Georgios Petrochilos, *Revision of the UNCITRAL Rules* (September 2006), paras 107-111, <www.uncitral.org> (This notion was included in the report and was accepted in substance).

1. The replacement mechanism

5. Pursuant to article 13(1) of the 1976 Rules, in case of death or resignation, a substitute arbitrator had to be appointed following the procedure that was applicable to the appointment (by a party or appointing authority) or choice (by party-appointed arbitrators) of the arbitrator being replaced. Thus, if a sole arbitrator died or resigned, the procedure in article 6 applied, and if a member of a three-member panel died or resigned, the procedure in article 7 applied. Importantly, article 13(1) mandated the use of the procedure that was 'applicable' even if it had not in fact applied, for example because a party had failed to appoint an arbitrator within the relevant time-limit. Thus the second time around, the right to appoint was revived. The information and disclosure requirements set out in articles 8 and 9 respectively, also applied in full.

6. Article 13(2) dealt with situations where an arbitrator failed to act or where it was de jure or de facto impossible for them to act. 'De jure' impossibility may arise where, for example, there is a domestic legal restriction on the arbitrator's performing his duties; 'de facto' impossibility, on the other hand, may arise where an arbitrator causes unacceptable delays to the proceedings, where there is a breakdown of working relations between members of the tribunal, or where an arbitrator refuses to reply to correspondence from the parties, among other causes.[3] In such situations, parties applying the 1976 Rules were given the opportunity to challenge the inactive arbitrator. Thus, rather than providing for direct replacement of the arbitrator, article 13(2) treated the failure or impossibility of an arbitrator's performing of his or her functions as a separate ground for a challenge (as for impartiality or independence).

7. For greater consistency, article 13(2) of the 1976 Rules now appears in article 12 of the 2010 Rules, which addresses the grounds for challenging arbitrators. The provision for the replacement of arbitrators, article 14 of the 2010 Rules, therefore deals exclusively with the replacement mechanism. Moreover, instead of spelling out the hypotheses that may give rise to an arbitrator's absence (death, resignation or successful challenge), article 14 instead uses broader language: it applies 'in any event where an arbitrator has to be replaced'.

---

3 Jason Fry, Simon Greenberg & Francesca Mazza, *The Secretariat's Guide to ICC Arbitration*, paras 3-614-3-621 (ICC 2012). The terms 'de jure' and 'de facto' also appear in Article 14(1) of the Model Law and Article 15(2) of the ICC Rules. *See also* David D. Caron & Lee M. Caplan, *The UNCITRAL Arbitration Rules, A Commentary*, 278-281 (2nd ed., Oxford University Press 2013) (citing the Report of Committee II at the Ninth Session in which the Committee agreed to replace the word 'incapacitated', which was 'unduly ambiguous', with 'an objective statement' which 'extended to all circumstances that made it legally or physically impossible for an arbitrator to perform his functions'. The authors further provide the example of Judge Mångard of the Iran-US Claims Tribunal, who had been physically attacked by his Iranian co-arbitrators. The co-arbitrators were thereafter challenged on the basis that, even if they agreed to continue to act, their conduct had demonstrated 'their incapacity and unfitness to perform—and hence the *de facto* impossibility of performing—their functions as arbitrators').

8. Article 14(1) of the 2010 Rules sets out the general principle of article 13(1) of the 1976 Rules, pursuant to which a substitute arbitrator is to be appointed according to the procedure that was originally applicable to the appointment or choice of their predecessor. Article 14(1) codifies an already-prevailing practice under article 13(2) of the 1976 Rules, namely that a party is entitled to make the appointment of a substitute arbitrator even if that party had failed to make the appointment of the original arbitrator. Thus, article 14(1) 'in effect disregards any default by a party (or by the co-arbitrators) that may have necessitated intervention of the appointing authority in initially constituting the tribunal', and 'appointments of replacement arbitrators will be governed by art. 8 (in the case of sole arbitrators) or by arts. 9 and 10 (in the case of arbitrators on tribunals having more than one member)', except in the limited circumstances provided in paragraph 2.[4]

9. This may prove particularly useful in multiparty arbitrations: a party which was not involved in the selection or appointment of the original arbitrator – because it was joined at a later stage of the proceedings[5] – may fully participate in the appointment of the substitute arbitrator.

2. Abuse and disruption: improvements under the 2010 Rules

(i) The 1976 Rules

10. *Resignations*: Article 13(1) of the 1976 Rules was silent on any potential duties of a resigning arbitrator towards the parties or the other members of the arbitral tribunal. In particular, the 1976 Rules provided no requirement that arbitrators only be able to resign for 'good reasons', as the original drafters felt that there was no effective way to enforce such a limitation.[6] However, as pointed out in a previous report:

> Practically, in cases of resignation of party-appointed arbitrators, application of the appointment process under article 7 means that the relevant party has 30 days in which to make a substitute appointment, failing which the designating authority/Appointing Authority process is to take its course. The potential for delay and disruption is obvious, especially where a hearing, deliberations, or the signature of an award are imminent.[7]

11. Precisely because resignations can cause considerable delay, they have been used as dilatory tactics. One way in which the proceedings can be seriously delayed is through a series of successive resignations, followed by successive appointments within the 30-day period stipulated in article 7(2) of the 1976 Rules, so as to prevent the appointing authority from intervening.[8]

---

4 James E. Castello, 'UNCITRAL Arbitration Rules, Section II, Article 14' in Loukas A. Mistelis (ed), *Concise International Arbitration*, 206 (2nd ed., Kluwer 2015).

5 By operation of article 4(2)(f) or 17(5) of the 2010 Rules.

6 *See* UNCITRAL Summary Record of the 5th Meeting, 16 April 1976, UN Doc A/CN.9/9/C.2/SR.5, para. 32.

7 Paulsson & Petrochilos, *supra* fn 2, at para. 104 fn 104.

8 *See ibid.*, at para. 107 fn 112. This matter is also dealt with in the provision covering the nomination of the appointing authority.

12. The Iran-US Claims Tribunal faced several tactical or (openly) party-imposed resignations, prompting it to establish a practice of 'policing' resignations. Pursuant to this practice, (i) resignations had to be submitted to the Tribunal, not to the party that initially appointed the resigning arbitrator, (ii) resignations were not effective until accepted by the Tribunal, and (iii) the effective date was determined by the Tribunal and not by the resigning arbitrator.[9]

13. Although suggestions were initially made to include a similar policing mechanism by the arbitral tribunal in the 2010 Rules,[10] consensus was reached on other mechanisms to dissuade such tactics. The 2010 Rules do not stipulate that an arbitrator should be able to resign only for 'good reasons', since the Working Group, like the drafters of the 1976 Rules, felt that there was no effective way of policing such a provision.

14. *Failure or impossibility to act*: As already mentioned, under article 13(2) of the 1976 Rules, an arbitrator's failure to act, or the de jure or de facto impossibility for an arbitrator to perform his or her functions, made it possible to challenge the arbitrator in question. The challenging process breaks the flow of the arbitral proceedings and may well cause delay. The subsequent process whereby a new arbitrator is appointed also causes delay, which, once again, can be used for tactical purposes.[11] Unjustified absences at an advanced stage of the proceedings, such as during the hearing or the deliberations, are, for instance, particularly disruptive.

15. The Iran-US Claims Tribunal dealt with attempts to paralyse the Tribunal by allowing the remaining arbitrators to continue in truncated form and issue an award without the missing arbitrator. Because the 1976 Rules did not *explicitly* address truncated tribunals, the Tribunal relied on the 'inherent power' of the remaining arbitrators to continue.[12] In a landmark decision,[13] the Tribunal refused to recognize that article 13(2) was 'the exclusive procedure for dealing with

---

9 Caron & Caplan, *supra* fn 3, at 287.

10 *See* Paulsson & Petrochilos, *supra* fn 2, at paras 107 and 111 (proposing that the remaining arbitrators be required to authorize the resignation of a fellow arbitrator).

11 Note that one way to limit the potential for delays, offered under article 12(2) of the 1976 Rules, is to allow the appointing authority which upheld a challenge to appoint the substitute arbitrator directly when 'the procedure applicable to the appointment or choice of an arbitrator as provided in articles 6 to 9 ... would call for the designation of [a new] appointing authority'. *See* article 12(2) of the 1976 Rules. However, this provision has no equivalent in the 2010 Rules.

12 An implicit basis for the validity of truncated tribunals has been found in article 15(1) of the 1976 Rules, which allows a tribunal to 'conduct the arbitration in such manner as it considers appropriate'. *See* David D. Caron, Lee M. Caplan & Matti Pellonpää, *The UNCITRAL Arbitration Rules, A Commentary*, 288-289 (Oxford University Press 2006). *See also Himpurna California Energy Ltd (Bermuda) v. The Republic of Indonesia* (UNCITRAL) Final Award, 16 October 1999, XXV YCA 186 (2000), paras 59-60.

13 *Uiterwyk Corp v. Iran* (1988) 19 Iran-US CTR 107, Supplemental Opinion of Judges Böckstiegel and Holtzmann.

failure of an arbitrator to act', finding that it 'cannot be invoked to disrupt the orderly process of the Tribunal or to obstruct its functions'.[14]

16. Based on the practice of the Iran-US Claims Tribunal, at least one other tribunal under the UNCITRAL Rules decided to proceed as a truncated tribunal. The *Himpurna* tribunal held that the challenge and replacement procedure foreseen by article 13(2) would be 'manifestly inappropriate' in the light of the timing of the arbitrator's absence and the lack of any valid excuse (the arbitrator was effectively kidnapped by the respondent state that had appointed him).[15] The tribunal concluded that 'an arbitral tribunal has not only the right, but the obligation, to proceed when, without valid excuse, one of its members fails to act, withdraws or ... even purports to resign'.[16]

(ii) Solutions adopted in the 2010 Rules to prevent disruption

17. *Powers of the appointing authority*: Article 14(2) creates an exception to the basic requirement that a missing arbitrator must be replaced in accordance with the procedure that was originally applicable to his or her appointment (regardless of whether that procedure was actually used).[17] Article 14(2) applies only in the 'exceptional circumstances' in which 'it would be justified for a party to be deprived of its right to appoint a substitute arbitrator'. The word 'justified' calls for the exercise of judgement in the totality of the circumstances. And though it is plain that article 14(2) sanctions a party who has attempted to disrupt the arbitral process, the principal purpose of the provision is not to sanction the party but rather to safeguard the integrity of the arbitral process. To do so, the appointing authority may either: (i) appoint the substitute arbitrator directly or (ii) in exceptional circumstances, authorize the remaining arbitrators to proceed as a truncated tribunal.[18] Article 14(2) is drafted in a manner that makes it absolutely clear that, in terms of sequencing, the first possibility is the first exceptional measure while the second is for even more exceptional cases 'after the closure of the hearings' pursuant to article 31, i.e. at the deliberations stage.

18. The provision is clearly of exceptional import. Much of its force lies in its deterrent effect. Depriving the parties of their right to appoint an arbitrator has, for instance, proven particularly successful in arbitrations under the ICSID Rules, where Article 56(3) of the ICSID Convention provides that the Chairman of the Administrative Council shall appoint a substitute arbitrator directly if his or her predecessor had resigned without valid consent.[19] Indeed, Article 56(3) was applied in the very

---

14 *Ibid.*

15 *Himpurna California Energy Ltd (Bermuda) v. The Republic of Indonesia, supra* fn 12, at para. 59.

16 *Ibid.*, at para. 43.

17 Castello, *supra* fn 4, at 206.

18 *See* UNCITRAL Report of 49th Session, 30 September 2008, UN Doc A/CN.9/665, paras 107-117.

19 *See also* Rule 11(2) of the ICSID Rules. Note that the ICSID Convention does not allow truncated tribunals: *see* further Lucy Reed, Jan Paulsson & Nigel Blackaby, *Guide to ICSID*

first ICSID case,[20] which may have contributed to the near-absence of any such instances in subsequent years.[21] Similarly, the appointing authority's power to allow truncated tribunals is intended 'to "hang a sword of Damocles" over the parties to prevent them [from] raising frivolous and unnecessary challenges and [over] arbitrators resigning to delay or prevent the continuation of arbitral proceedings'.[22]

19. While most major arbitration rules now provide for the possibility of truncated tribunals,[23] the validity of awards rendered by truncated tribunals has been questioned in certain jurisdictions. In particular, such awards have been said to violate the parties' right to a proper composition of the tribunal.[24] Moreover, a truncated tribunal may be composed of an even number of arbitrators, giving rise to obvious issues in case of split voting. Illustrating the caveat in favour of the *lex arbitri* set out in article 1(3), the new provision on truncated tribunals may thus be inapplicable in certain jurisdictions.[25]

(iii) Circumstances in which the Tribunal can proceed in a truncated form

20. In the absence of (i) any improper conduct by a party or (ii) other circumstances justifying that the party be 'deprived of its right to appoint a substitute arbitrator',

---

Arbitration, 81 (2nd ed., Kluwer 2010).

20 *Holiday Inns SA and others v. Morocco* (ICSID Case No. ARB/72/1), <www.italaw.com>.

21 *See* Paulsson & Petrochilos, *supra* fn 2, at para. 109 and the references. *See also Hrvatska Elektroprivreda dd v. Republic of Slovenia* (ICSID Case No. ARB/05/24) Order Concerning the Participation of Counsel, 6 May 2008, <www.italaw.com>, para. 27 (the provision in Article 56(3) of the Convention – the 'principle of immutability' – was explicitly considered by the drafters of the Convention and '[a]s Mr. Aaron Broches explained ... "[i]f a party could prevail upon an arbitrator to resign in the course of proceedings without cause he would be able to frustrate or slow down the proceedings"').

22 APRAG Report of 49th Session, 10 October 2008, para. 79.

23 *See*, e.g., Article 21(2) of the SCC Rules; Article 12 of the LCIA Rules; Article 15(3) of the AAA International Arbitration Rules; Article 13(2)(b) of the Swiss Rules.

24 *See* Markus Wirth, 'The Current Revision of the UNCITRAL Rules' in Christoph Müller (ed.), *New Developments in International Commercial Arbitration*, 16 (Schulthess 2007) (the author notes a decision of the Swiss Federal Tribunal in 1991 which found that 'allowing the two remaining arbitrators to proceed and issue an award [after the third arbitrator's formal resignation during the deliberations] would amount to a violation of the parties' rights to a proper composition of the arbitral tribunal – and a violation of a fundamental right both protected by the Swiss Constitution as well as by the European Convention on Human Rights'). However, the 2012 Swiss Rules now provide, in article 13(2)(b), that 'in exceptional circumstances, the Court may, after consulting with the parties and any remaining arbitrators ... after the closure of the proceedings, authorise the remaining arbitrator(s) to proceed with the arbitration and make any decision or award'. *See also* Gary B. Born, *International Commercial Arbitration*, 1957 (2nd ed., Kluwer 2014): 'It is true that a truncated tribunal involves one party not participating in the nomination of an effective member of the tribunal, while the other party has so participated. This is not materially different, however, from a situation where a party fails to exercise its right to nominate a co-arbitrator and the tribunal is constituted with three members, one nominated by one party and the other two selected by the appointing authority'.

25 This is consistent with article 1(3) of the 2010 Rules.

the missing arbitrator will have to be replaced pursuant to article 14(1). By contrast, other arbitration rules do not make the availability of truncated tribunals contingent on a party's conduct, but rather present truncated tribunals as a mechanism to 'finish the proceedings with all due speed'.[26] In the UNCITRAL Rules, a party's right to appoint an arbitrator in principle trumps considerations of the speed and efficiency of the proceedings. However, an inference about improper conduct may well fall to be drawn from a resignation at a late stage of the proceedings, in the light of all other circumstances, such as prior resignations (in particular poorly motivated or unmotivated ones), whether the resignation was unannounced and came at a suspect stage of the deliberations, etc. Nevertheless, it must be borne in mind that the primary test is not improper conduct on the part of a party but rather 'exceptional circumstances'. That there must be such as to justify the loss of the right to appoint speaks to the nature and seriousness of the circumstances and not necessarily to their cause. It is possible to take the view that if a majority has been formed on the key issues, letting the majority proceed without the resigned arbitrator is justified: a new arbitrator would require very considerable time to educate himself or herself, may never be able to do so properly without a fresh hearing, and there is no reason to suppose that he or she will be able to create a new majority.

21. Moreover, contrary to the practice under the 1976 Rules, the Working Group considered that the appointing authority, and not the remaining members of the tribunal, should decide whether or not the tribunal can proceed as a truncated tribunal. The Working Group feared that 'granting the power to the arbitral tribunal to proceed as a truncated tribunal might not provide sufficient safeguards for the parties, in particular in case of collusion between arbitrators'.[27] This was a wise choice. A 2005 Paris Court of Appeal decision seems to support the Working Group's concerns about potential abuse by the remaining arbitrators.[28] The Court refused to recognize an award which had been rendered by a truncated tribunal in an AAA arbitration. Pursuant to the applicable AAA Rules, the remaining arbitrators were able to decide 'in their sole discretion' whether to proceed as a truncated tribunal.[29] In the court's view, this rule could not be construed to amount to consent by the parties to a truncated tribunal, without the parties having been heard on the issue. The court noted that arbitrators must fully inform parties of every procedural step, even where, as was the case here, one of the parties had defaulted. In this case, the third arbitrator's withdrawal

---

26 Peter Turner & Reza Mohtashami, *A Guide to the LCIA Arbitration Rules*, para. 4.147 (Oxford University Press 2009) (commenting on Article 12.1 of the 1998 LCIA Rules).

27 UNCITRAL Report of 46th Session, 20 March 2007, UN Doc A/CN.9/619, para. 109.

28 *Malecki v. Long*, CA Paris, 21 April 2005, 3 Rev Arb 673 (2006). *See also* Denis Bensaude, *Malecki v. Long: Truncated Tribunals and Waivers of Dutco Rights*, 23(1) Journal of International Arbitration 81 (2006).

29 Article 11 of the AAA International Arbitration Rules states in relevant part: 'If an arbitrator on a three-person tribunal fails to participate in the arbitration for reasons other than those identified in Article 15(1), the two other arbitrators shall have the power in their sole discretion to continue the arbitration and to make any decision, ruling, order, or award, notwithstanding the failure of the third arbitrator to participate'.

from the proceedings was not communicated to the parties and the parties had no opportunity to express their views on the constitution of the tribunal. The court therefore found that, by proceeding as a truncated tribunal, the remaining arbitrators had violated their duty to deliberate in a collegial process.

22. Another restriction set out in article 14(2) is that the appointing authority has the power to order the tribunal to proceed in truncated form only 'after the closure of the hearings'.[30] There is general consensus that truncated tribunals should only be resorted to at the last stage of the proceedings, when replacing the missing arbitrator would cause very considerable disruption. This is true even for sets of arbitration rules which do not explicitly state it.[31] One of the Working Group's main motivations for imposing an explicit temporal restriction was that, under the UNCITRAL Rules, 'the identity and experience of any appointing authority is, naturally, unknown. This means that the appointing authority may be very experienced or may, on the other hand, be very inexperienced'.[32] As a result, particular care should be taken in order to 'avoid possible problems with the capriciousness of a truncated tribunal at an early stage in the proceedings'.[33] This temporal restriction thus acknowledges that, in principle, the parties have agreed to have their dispute settled by three arbitrators, not two. However, limiting the use of truncated tribunals to a 'post-hearing' phase excludes cases such as *Himpurna* (in which the arbitrator was prevented from participating in the hearings) from the scope of application of article 14(2).

23. Once a party requests the intervention of the appointing authority, the authority may authorize a truncated tribunal only after giving 'an opportunity to the parties and the remaining arbitrators to express their views'. This requirement is a manifestation of the appointing authority's general duty to take the views of the parties and arbitrators into account.[34] This requirement also increases the legitimacy of the appointing authority's decision, particularly when the appointing authority has not been chosen by the parties or is relatively inexperienced. However, the fact that the appointing authority can only act 'at the request of a party' may give rise to problems when, unbeknownst to the parties, the proceedings are obstructed – whether intentionally or not – during the deliberations phase. If the parties are unaware of the inactivity or absence of an arbitrator during the deliberations, the parties will not be in a position to raise any objections to the appointing authority. This implies that, for the mechanism set out in

---

30 Cf. Article 15(5) of the ICC Rules ('[s]*ubsequent to the closing of the proceedings*, instead of replacing an arbitrator ... the Court may decide, when it considers it appropriate, that the remaining arbitrators shall continue the arbitration' (emphasis added)). *See also* Yves Derains & Eric A. Schwartz, *A Guide to the ICC Rules of Arbitration*, 206-207 (2nd ed., Kluwer 2005) (referring to the 1998 ICC Rules).

31 *See*, e.g., Turner & Mohtashami, *supra* fn 26, at para. 4.149 (with reference to the 1998 LCIA Rules, the authors submit that the power to continue as a truncated tribunal 'should normally only be ... exercised if the procedure has progressed to such a stage that it would be more cost-effective to carry on [without replacing the missing arbitrator]').

32 APRAG Report of 49th Session, 10 October 2008, para. 81.

33 *Ibid.*, at para. 79.

34 *See* article 6(5) of the 2010 Rules.

article 14(2) to work, the remaining arbitrators must communicate to the parties any disruptions or delays encountered during the deliberations without of course betraying the secrecy of deliberations.

B. REPETITION OF HEARINGS IN THE EVENT OF THE REPLACEMENT OF AN ARBITRATOR: ARTICLE 15

24. Article 14 of the 1976 Rules addressed the extent to which previous hearings were to be repeated after the replacement of an arbitrator. It drew a distinction between the replacement of 'the sole or presiding arbitrator' on the one hand, and the replacement of 'any other arbitrator' on the other hand. The text stated that if a sole or presiding arbitrator was replaced, the hearings held previously '*shall* be repeated' (emphasis added). For the replacement of any other arbitrator, 'prior hearings *may* be repeated' (emphasis added). The rationale for this is obvious: hearings were considered to be essential to be attended in person by at least the majority of decision-makers. This may well reflect that in 1976 there was no generalized practice of verbatim transcripts, no expectation of two rounds of written submissions (see article 24(2) of the 1976 Rules), but rather an expectation that documentary evidence could be handed up for the first time at the hearing (id.) and witnesses would testify only at the hearing (article 25(2) of the 1976 Rules). Today's expectations are different.

25. Article 14 was modified in the Tribunal Rules of the Iran-US Claims Tribunal in order to give the Tribunal 'discretion to decide whether to repeat all or any part of the previously held hearings, regardless of the status of the arbitrator who is ... replaced'.[35] Similarly, the ICC and SCC Rules give arbitral tribunals the discretionary power to determine the extent to which hearings held prior to the replacement of an arbitrator shall be repeated, without drawing any distinction between presiding, sole or other arbitrators.[36]

26. Ultimately, the mechanism adopted under the 2004 Swiss Rules is the one that most inspired the Working Group in the revision of article 14, the content of which appears as article 15 of the 2010 Rules.[37] Closely mirroring the text of the corresponding Swiss Rules provision, and reversing the position under the 1976 Rules, article 15 of the 2010 Rules stipulates that 'the proceedings shall resume at the stage where the arbitrator who was replaced ceased to perform his or her functions'.[38] Guided by a desire to reduce the risk of disruption, the new default rule is based on the premise that the continuation of the proceedings is

---

[35] Stewart A. Baker & Mark D. Davis, *The UNCITRAL Arbitration Rules in Practice – The Experience of the Iran-United States Claims Tribunal*, 71 and the references (Kluwer 1992).

[36] *See* Article 15(4) of the ICC Rules; Article 21(3) of the SCC Rules.

[37] *See* UNCITRAL Report of 45th Session, 5 October 2006, UN Doc A/CN.9/614, para. 75.

[38] Article 14 of the 2004 Swiss Rules provided as follows: 'If an arbitrator is replaced, the proceedings shall as a rule resume at the stage where the arbitrator who was replaced ceased to perform his functions, unless the arbitral tribunal decides otherwise'. With minor textual amendments, this provision was retained as Article 14 of the 2012 Swiss Rules.

'important for the sake of preventing obstruction by a resigning arbitrator'.[39] The default rule applies 'unless the arbitral tribunal decides otherwise'; the remaining arbitrators therefore must exercise judgement to determine the point at which the proceedings shall resume.[40] Moreover, and consistently with the majority of other arbitration rules, article 15 applies for the replacement of any arbitrator, whether chairing the tribunal or not.[41]

27. Article 15 of the 2010 Rules is silent as to whether the parties should be consulted on the question of repeating any prior proceedings.[42] Commentary on the Swiss Rules suggests that such consultation may be necessary in light of the parties' right to be heard.[43] The same may be true for the UNCITRAL Rules, where each party's right to be 'given a reasonable opportunity of presenting its case' is safeguarded under article 17(1): a party may feel that a fresh hearing is necessary for the new arbitrator properly to understand and test its case. In the tribunal's deliberations over whether to depart from the default rule, the commentary on the Swiss Rules suggests that the test should be 'whether the replacement arbitrator on the basis of the written records, party submissions and other documents is in a position to form an opinion on the points arising for determination in an appropriate and fair way'.[44] Apart from the availability of documentation, the tribunal should also consider the stage of the proceedings, as repetition will not be necessary where the hearing has not yet occurred.[45] Moreover, partial (final) awards rendered by the previous formation cannot be revisited, unless they have been set aside by a competent court: see article 34(2) of the Rules.[46]

---

39 Marc Blessing, 'Comparison of the Swiss Rules with the UNCITRAL Arbitration Rules and Others' in Gabrielle Kaufmann-Kohler & Blaise Stucki (eds), *The Swiss Rules of International Arbitration, ASA Special Series No. 22*, 38 (ASA 2004) (in relation to Article 14 of the 2004 Swiss Rules).

40 As such, Article 14 reflects common practice in international arbitration. *See*, e.g., Article 14 of the Swiss Rules; Article 21(3) of the SCC Rules. Cf. Article 15(4) of the ICC Rules (providing in pertinent part that '[o]nce reconstituted, *and after having invited the parties to comment*, the arbitral tribunal shall determine if and to what extent prior proceedings shall be repeated ...' (emphasis added)); Article 34 of the WIPO Rules ('[w]henever a substitute arbitrator is appointed, the Tribunal shall, *having regard to any observations of the parties*, determine in its sole discretion whether ... any prior hearings are to be repeated' (emphasis added)).

41 *See also* Article 21(3) of the SCC Rules; Article 15(3) of the AAA International Arbitration Rules.

42 For an overview of arbitration rules on this point, *see* Nigel Blackaby, Constantine Partasides, Alan Redfern & Martin J. Hunter, *Redfern and Hunter on International Arbitration*, paras 4.165-4.166 (6th ed., Kluwer 2015).

43 *See* Tobias Zuberbühler, Christoph Müller & Philipp A. Habegger, *Swiss Rules of International Arbitration: Commentary*, 140 (Kluwer 2005).

44 *Ibid.*, at 142.

45 Blackaby, Partasides, Redfern & Hunter, *supra* fn 42, at para. 4.162.

46 *See* Fry, Greenberg & Mazza, *supra* fn 3, at para. 3-648 (providing that '[i]n general, an award has res judicata effect once rendered and cannot be revisited by either the arbitral tribunal that rendered it or a newly constituted tribunal in the same case').

28. In contrast, repetition of hearings may be necessary where the award is likely to turn on a point that can only be properly assessed at a hearing, such as the credibility of a key witness,[47] or where assessment of the evidence has been controversial among former members of the tribunal.[48] However, given the added expense and inconvenience of repeating proceedings, tribunals rarely will depart from the default rule.[49] This prediction is based in large part on the artificiality of a 'repeat' hearing as the 1976 Rules envisaged. Repeating a witness examination is never a satisfactory experience. By contrast, one can see that giving the opportunity to the newly-constituted tribunal to see key witnesses and experts for itself and examine them, and also to pose questions to counsel may be valuable. That is a follow-up hearing, building on the existing record, rather than a repeat hearing.

---

47 *See* Derains & Schwartz, *supra* fn 30, at 203.

48 *See* Zuberbühler, Müller & Habegger, *supra* fn 43, at 142.

49 *See* Baker & Davis, *supra* fn 35, at 71 (reporting on the experience of the Iran-US Claims Tribunal, where Tribunal Rule 14 altered article 14 of the 1976 Rules to give tribunals the discretion to repeat hearings, regardless of the status of the arbitrator who was replaced. The authors note that, where judges were replaced, new hearings were rare: 'at the time of Judge Virally's death, some eleven cases in which he participated were still pending, but only two of these cases were reheard. In most cases the new Chairman, Judge Arangio-Ruiz, was satisfied that he could adequately proceed on the basis of written record, assisted by Judge Virally's notes and drafts and the recollection of Judge Virally's legal assistants who remained at the Tribunal'). *See also* Blackaby, Partasides, Redfern & Hunter, *supra* fn 42, at paras 4.162-4.164.

Article 16
Exclusion of liability

1976 Rules	2010 Rules Article 16: Exclusion of liability
	Save for intentional wrongdoing, the parties waive, to the fullest extent permitted under the applicable law, any claim against the arbitrators, the appointing authority and any person appointed by the arbitral tribunal based on any act or omission in connection with the arbitration.

1. As was the case for other contemporaneous arbitration rules, the 1976 Rules did not contain provisions concerning the liability of arbitrators. The issue arises rarely, but it is far from being theoretical. Despite their '*nobile officium*' status, arbitrators are providers of services just like other professionals. The importance of the issue is obvious. To avoid collateral attacks by losing parties it is important to clarify the issue of liability of arbitrators in advance, lest they be vulnerable to challenges in courts 'as a means of, in effect, appealing or overturning' an award.[1]

2. Certain national laws set out standards for the liability of arbitrators.[2] With some exceptions, many jurisdictions confer a degree of immunity on arbitrators

[1] APRAG Report of 48th Session, 28 February 2008, para. 29. *See also* UNCITRAL Report of 48th Session, 29 February 2008, UN Doc A/CN.9/646, para. 39. For a recent illustration of losing parties accusing the arbitrators of corruption, *see Gulf Petro Trading Co Inc v. Nigerian National Petroleum Corp*, 512 F.3d 742-745 (5th Cir. 2008) (The appellate court upheld the lower District Court, which granted the defendant's motion to dismiss, reasoning that Gulf Petro's entire complaint constituted a collateral attack on the final award for which the District Court lacked subject matter jurisdiction).

[2] Gary B. Born, *International Commercial Arbitration*, 2028-2035 (2nd ed., Kluwer 2014) (giving examples of national legislations and case law).

akin to those of judges, based on their quasi-judicial function.[3] Jurisdictions which provide for extensive liability are outliers.[4] In addition, some arbitration rules allow for waiver of arbitrators' liability.[5] The UNCITRAL Working Group considered it desirable, as a matter of general policy, to offer arbitrators a degree of immunity under the 2010 Rules. One of the main concerns of the Working Group was to prevent 'the unhealthy situation where the arbitrators would have to negotiate with the parties regarding their immunity after the arbitral tribunal had been constituted'.[6] Article 16 was therefore introduced to address the partial 'exclusion of liability' of arbitrators and other decision-makers in the arbitral proceedings (i.e. 'the appointing authority and any person appointed by the arbitral tribunal' such as a tribunal expert). Article 16 (as all similar provisions in other arbitration rules) makes it plain that the extent of an arbitrator's liability is a matter for the 'applicable law'. That law is normally the *lex arbitri*, whose application is safeguarded by article 1(3) in any event. But article 16 does not take a stance on which law (or possibly laws) is applicable, this being a matter to be determined by that law itself.

A. CONTENT AND SCOPE OF THE RULE OF IMMUNITY

1. Carve-out for intentional wrongdoing

3. By virtue of article 16, the parties to an UNCITRAL arbitration waive any claims against arbitrators and any other participants in the proceedings, 'save for intentional wrongdoing'. This caveat was added late in the revision process to emphasize that immunity from 'intentional wrongdoing' is unacceptable even if the *lex arbitri* were to allow for it. The purpose of this addition was not to establish

---

3 For an updated overview *see* Nigel Blackaby, Constantine Partasides, Alan Redfern & Martin J. Hunter, *Redfern and Hunter on International Arbitration*, paras 5.50-5.66 (6th ed., Kluwer 2015). *See also*, for a jurisdiction-by-jurisdiction analysis, Jan Paulsson (ed.), *International Handbook on Commercial Arbitration* (1984) as electronically available and updated at <www.kluwerarbitration.com>.

4 *See* the amendment made by Federal Decree No. 7 to Article 257 of the United Arab Emirates' Federal Penal Code No. 3 of 1987: 'Anyone who issues a decision, expresses an opinion, submits a report, presents a case or proves an incident in favour of or against a person, in contravention of the requirements of the duty of neutrality and integrity, while acting in his capacity as an arbitrator, expert, translator or fact finder appointed by an administrative or judicial authority or selected by the parties, shall be punished by temporary imprisonment. The aforesaid categories of persons shall be barred assuming once again the responsibilities with which they were tasked in the first instance, and shall be subject to the provisions of Article 255 of this Law'.

5 *See*, e.g., Article 41 of the ICC Rules; Article 31 of the LCIA Rules; Article 52 of the SCC Rules; Article 79 of the WIPO Rules; Article 45 of the Swiss Rules.

6 UNCITRAL Report of 48th Session, 29 February 2008, UN Doc A/CN.9/646, para. 39. In practice, arbitral tribunals under the 1976 Rules could establish their immunity from suits in the form of procedural orders. For an illustration, *see TCW Group Inc and Dominican Energy Holdings LP v. The Dominican Republic* (UNCITRAL) Procedural Order No. 1, 23 June 2008, <www.italaw.com>, para. 12(1).

liability (a matter for the *lex arbitri*) but simply to preserve any liability that might exist, which is also why the terms were formulated in a non-technical way.

4. A number of other arbitration rules contain similar carve-outs.[7] The SCC Rules allow claims against arbitrators and other participants of the proceedings in case of 'wilful misconduct'.[8] By contrast, the 1998 ICC Rules did not limit the immunity of the arbitrators and of the ICC Court in any way, which has attracted much criticism in the past.[9] This concern was addressed in the 2012 ICC Rules which adopted the language of 'limitation of liability' in Article 40 (now Article 41 of the 2017 ICC Rules), rather than the absolute 'exclusion of liability' under Article 34 of the 1998 Rules. Thus the limitation of liability applies 'except to the extent [that it] is prohibited by applicable law', as many jurisdictions prescribe an exclusion of liability for gross or serious negligence.[10]

5. During the drafting process of article 16, a suggestion was made also to carve out liability claims based on gross negligence, as currently foreseen by the Swiss Rules and the SCC Rules.[11] However, observing that 'some States [do] not have a concept of degrees of negligence' the Working Group felt that there was–

> a risk that a "gross negligence" exception might have no operation or might possibly operate as an exception on the basis of negligence generally, which would tend to defeat the purpose of the proposed exclusion of liability provision.[12]

In order better to guarantee the effective and universal applicability of the Rules, it was finally decided to leave the degree of culpability required to national law

---

7 *See* Article 31.1 of the LCIA Rules; Article 79 of the WIPO Rules; Article 45 of the Swiss Rules. For a criticism of the term 'wrongdoing' as giving little practical guidance for establishing liability, *see* Jan Paulsson & Georgios Petrochilos, *Revision of the UNCITRAL Rules* (September 2006), paras 94-95, <www.uncitral.org> (the authors suggested to use the notion of 'manifest bad faith' instead).

8 *See* Article 52 of the SCC Rules. The idea of an arbitrator's wilful and reckless disregard of his or her legal duties is also reflected in the Introductory Note to the 1987 IBA Rules of Ethics for International Arbitrators.

9 For references of the debate surrounding unrestricted immunity for arbitrators, *see* Yves Derains & Eric A. Schwartz, *A Guide to the ICC Rules of Arbitration*, 383 fn 22 (2nd ed., Kluwer 2005).

10 *See* Jason Fry, Simon Greenberg & Francesca Mazza, *The Secretariat's Guide to ICC Arbitration*, para. 3-1535 (ICC 2012).

11 Marc Blessing, *Comparison of the Swiss Rules with the UNCITRAL Arbitration Rules and Others*, Report submitted to ASA Conference in Zurich, 23 January 2004, 42 (commenting on article 44(1) of the 2004 Swiss Rules): 'Can you expect parties/users of the rules to be happy with a provision that tells them: No matter how negligent your Arbitrator will be, he will benefit from immunity?'. Article 45(1) of the 2012 Swiss Rules adopts the language 'intentional wrongdoing or gross negligence', instead of 'deliberate wrongdoing or extremely serious negligence' as used in Article 44(1) of the 2004 Rules. *See also* Article 52 of the SCC Rules; Cf. Article 21(a) of the ICSID Convention (providing that arbitrators 'shall enjoy immunity from legal process ... in the exercise of their functions, except when the Centre waives this immunity').

12 APRAG Report of 48th Session, 28 February 2008, para. 28.

without spelling out a concept of negligence.[13] This consideration may also explain why Article 40 of the 2012 ICC Rules (now Article 41 of the 2017 ICC Rules) similarly does not specifically mention negligence, but simply refers to the confines of applicable law.

2. Exclusion of liability to the fullest extent possible under applicable law

6. Article 16 specifies that parties waive any potential claims to 'the fullest extent permitted under the applicable law'. For the establishment of liability, the applicable law can be the *lex arbitri* or, alternatively, the national law of the arbitrator concerned, or the law of the place where the act giving rise to the liability has been committed.[14]

7. The practice under other arbitration rules, and in particular the 1998 ICC Rules, shows that certain courts do not hesitate to strike contractual liability exonerations instead of reducing them 'to a legally acceptable standard' under the applicable law.[15] The wording 'to the extent permitted under applicable law' was therefore added in the UNCITRAL Rules in order to–

> preserve a degree of exoneration in cases where the applicable law would allow contractual exoneration from liability only up to a threshold *lower* than that of "conscious and deliberate wrongdoing" and, at the same time, treat as *unwritten* any clause that would exonerate liability *above* that threshold (emphasis added).[16]

---

13 *See* UNCITRAL Report of 48th Session, 29 February 2008, UN Doc A/CN.9/646, para. 43.

14 *See* Paulsson & Petrochilos, *supra* fn 7, at para. 91 and the references.

15 *See* Derains & Schwartz, *supra* fn 9, at 383 fn 23 where they state that 'it has been suggested that in certain countries, Article 34 [of the 1998 ICC Rules] may be void and not susceptible ... to being reduced to a legally acceptable standard of exclusion'. *See also* Julian D. M. Lew, Loukas A. Mistelis & Stefan M. Kröll, *Comparative International Commercial Arbitration*, para. 12-47 (Kluwer 2003), who point out that under German law, for example, complete exclusions of liability are void and cannot be reduced to an acceptable standard of exclusion, noting a decision by the Austrian Supreme Court in *H GmbH v. Hon*, RPS 7 (2/1999), Rev Arb 392 (1999). *See also* Philippe Fouchard, *Final Report on the Status of the Arbitrator*, 7/1 ICC Court Bull. 42 (1996) stating: 'Does the substantive law allow the arbitrator to exclude his liability contractually? Usually, the general law considers that only clauses excluding liability simply for error, and devoid of any fraudulent intention or deceit, are unlawful. Any other contractual exclusion of liability would contravene public policy (France, Sweden, Norway, Germany, Switzerland, Japan, etc...). Accordingly, it only allows the arbitrator a possibility of limiting his liability that is both narrow and uncertain'. *See also* Pierre Lalive, *Irresponsibility in International Commercial Arbitration*, 7(2) Asia Pacific Law Review 171 (1999) referring to Article 34 of the 1998 ICC Rules: 'The ICC Commission of Arbitration has finally opted for enacting such total immunity—while entertaining no illusion, it would seem, about the legality of such a solution in many jurisdictions. Let me state at the outset that I believe this solution in the new ICC Rules to be legally misconceived ... it appears to ignore deliberately the fact ... that the majority of national legal systems ... do not admit the absolute immunity of arbitrators'.

16 UNCITRAL Report of 48th Session, 29 February 2008, UN Doc A/CN.9/646, para. 44.

Article 41 of the 2017 ICC Rules contains similar language, for the same reason of avoiding complete invalidation of the exclusion clause 'by granting as much protection against liability as is available under the applicable law, but never more'.[17]

B. PERSONS WHO ENJOY IMMUNITY UNDER THE RULES

8. As pointed out in *Redfern & Hunter*, '[a]ggrieved parties who have lost an arbitration may look indiscriminately for defendants, and arbitral institutions have not escaped this trend'.[18] In light of this reality, most institutional arbitration rules do not exonerate from liability *arbitrators* only but also *arbitral institutions*.

9. The extent to which various jurisdictions permit the waiver of liability of arbitral institutions varies greatly. Most common-law jurisdictions allow for the immunity of arbitral institutions, because otherwise 'liability would merely shift from the arbitrator to the arbitral organisation'.[19] By contrast, civil-law jurisdictions often draw a clear distinction between arbitrators and their quasi-judicial power, on the one hand, and arbitral institutions and other persons exercising for the most part administrative powers, on the other hand. The latter category will likely attract liability (if any) on general contractual grounds.[20]

10. The civil-law distinction was stressed by the Paris Court of Appeal in a decision concerning the ICC.[21] The claimant contended that the ICC had not complied with its duties set out in the 1998 ICC Rules, in that it had notably failed (i) to control the form of the draft award (pursuant to Article 27 of the ICC Rules) and (ii) to ensure the celerity of the arbitral process. The ICC countered by pointing

---

17 Fry, Greenberg & Mazza, *supra* fn 10, at para. 3-1536.

18 Blackaby, Partasides, Redfern & Hunter, *supra* fn 3, at para. 5.62. *See*, e.g., *Société Cubic Defense Systems Inc v. Chambre de Commerce Internationale*, Cass Civ 1, 20 February 2001, Rev Arb 511 (2001); *SNF v. Chambre de Commerce Internationale*, CA Paris, 1ère Chambre, section C, 22 January 2009, Case No. 07/19492. *See*, for a recent example, *Landmark Ventures Inc v. Stephanie Cohen and the International Chamber of Commerce*, Case No. 13 Civ. 9044 (JGK), 26 November 2014 (SD New York) (losing party to ICC arbitration filed action against the arbitrator and the ICC, which the District Court dismissed, stating that the alleged conduct fell directly within Article 40 of the 2012 Rules and finding that the arbitrator and ICC were therefore immune from suit). Note that the cases cited on this point usually arise from the ICC Rules, perhaps because the ICC's exclusion of liability 'is the only provision which excludes all liability of the arbitrators and all participants in the ICC Court's activities for any act or omission, without exception': *See* Detlev Kühner & Gustav Flecke-Giammarco, 'Part IV: Selected Areas and Issues of Arbitration in Germany, ICC Arbitration in Germany' in Patricia Nacimiento, Stefan Michael Kröll, et al. (eds), *Arbitration in Germany: The Model Law in Practice*, 781 (2nd ed., Kluwer 2015).

19 Blackaby, Partasides, Redfern & Hunter, *supra* fn 3, at para. 5.64 and the references. Most notably, section 74 of the Arbitration Act 1996 (England & Wales) provides for immunity of all acts of arbitral institutions and their employees and agents in relation to their arbitral functions. *See also* Peter Turner & Reza Mohtashami, *A Guide to the LCIA Arbitration Rules*, paras 9.31-9.33 (Oxford University Press 2009).

20 Blackaby, Partasides, Redfern & Hunter, *supra* fn 3, at para. 5.63 and the references.

21 *SNF v. Chambre de Commerce Internationale*, *supra* fn 18.

to the waiver of liability set forth in Article 34 of the ICC Rules. Although the Paris Court of Appeal found that the ICC had properly performed its duties in that case, it held that Article 34 should be deemed not written because it would exclude liability even when the ICC failed to perform its core obligations in administering arbitration cases, a duty which the ICC agreed to undertake in the arbitration agreement. The court said:

> In order to perform its obligations in exchange for compensation, the ICC must organize and administer the arbitration and for this purpose, provide a structure which allows for an efficient arbitration. The arbitration must be administered promptly, developed according to the chosen rules, and likely to be enforceable.[22]
>
> Article 34 of the 1998 ICC Rules provides: "Neither the arbitrators, nor the Court and its members, nor the ICC and its employees, nor the ICC National Committees shall be liable to any person for any act or omission in connection with the arbitration".[23]
>
> [T]he limitation-of-liability clause which permits the ICC not to comply with its essential duty *as a provider of non-judicial services*, must be considered as not written in relation to the dealings between the ICC and [the claimant] since it runs contrary to the arbitration agreement. (emphasis added)[24]

This decision prompted, in part, the qualifications to the waiver of liability in the 2012 ICC Rules.[25]

11. Against this background, article 16 of the 2010 Rules contains a waiver of any claims against the appointing authority and any person appointed by the arbitral tribunal, such as experts. In drafting article 16, the Working Group wished to–

> cover the *broadest possible range of participants* in the arbitration and preserve exoneration *in cases where the applicable law allows contractual exoneration from liability*, to the fullest extent permitted by such law. (emphasis added)[26]

---

22 *Ibid.*, at para. 18 ('*Considérant que pour exécuter ses obligations moyennant rémunération, la CCI doit organiser et administrer l'arbitrage et à cette fin fournir une structure propre à permettre un arbitrage efficace c'est-à-dire intervenant avec la célérité escomptée, élaborée conformément aux règles choisies et susceptible de recevoir exécution*').

23 *Ibid.*, at para. 19 ('*Considérant que selon l'article 34 du règlement d'arbitrage 1998, « ni les arbitres, ni la Cour ou ses membres ni la Chambre de commerce Internationale ou son personnel, ni les comités nationaux de la Chambre de commerce internationale, ne sont responsables envers quiconque de tout fait, acte ou omission en relation avec un arbitrage »*').

24 *Ibid.*, at para. 20 ('*Considérant que la clause élisive de responsabilité qui autorise la CCI à ne pas exécuter son obligation essentielle en tant que prestataire de services non-juridictionnels doit être réputée non écrite dans les rapports entre la CCI et la société SNF dès lors que la clause contredit la portée du contrat d'arbitrage*').

25 *See* Fry, Greenberg & Mazza, *supra* fn 10, at para. 3-1531 fn 92.

26 UNCITRAL Working Paper for 52nd Session, 10 December 2009, UN Doc A/CN.9/WG.II/WP.157, para. 42. Note that while initial drafts of article 16 also included the Secretary-General of the PCA in the list of persons who enjoy immunity under the Rules,

In addition to the appointing and designating authorities, this provision also covers the repository under article 8 of the Transparency Rules. Revisions incorporated in the 2012 ICC Rules similarly extended the protection of limitation of liability to a wider class of persons and bodies than existed under the 1998 ICC Rules.[27]

the reference to the Secretary-General was taken out in the very last phase of the revision process. *See* UNCITRAL Summary Record of the 902nd Meeting, 21 June 2010, UN Doc A/CN.9/SR.902, XLI UNCITRAL Ybk 1213, 1218 para. 63, The Chairperson. The PCA had indicated in its comments regarding draft article 16 (UNCITRAL Compilation of comments by Governments and international organizations, 4 May 2010, UN Doc A/CN.9/704) that it enjoyed legal immunity under various international instruments, that such immunity provided sufficient protection against liability, and that a specific waiver under the revised Arbitration Rules was therefore unnecessary. The PCA also noted that some scholars and practitioners interpreted the words 'save for intentional wrongdoing' at the beginning of article 16 as an acknowledgment of liability in cases of intentional acts, and expressed that it wished to avoid the misunderstanding that it had waived its immunity by accepting to undertake the functions delegated to it under the UNCITRAL Rules. The PCA therefore requested that the reference to the Secretary-General be removed.

27 In addition to the 'arbitrators', 'the Court and its members', and 'the ICC and its employees' (Article 34 of the 1998 ICC Rules), Article 40 of the 2012 ICC Rules (now Article 41 of the 2017 ICC Rules) also limits the liability of 'any person appointed by the arbitral tribunal', 'the emergency arbitrator' and 'the ICC National Committees and Groups and their employees and representatives'.

PART I

Section III
Arbitral proceedings

2010 Rules

Article 17
General provisions

1976 Rules Article 15: General provisions	2010 Rules Article 17: General provisions
1. Subject to these Rules, the arbitral tribunal may conduct the arbitration in such manner as it considers appropriate, provided that the parties are treated with equality and that at any stage of the proceedings each party is given a full opportunity of presenting his case.	1. Subject to these Rules, the arbitral tribunal may conduct the arbitration in such manner as it considers appropriate, provided that the parties are treated with equality and that at an appropriate stage of the proceedings each party is given a reasonable opportunity of presenting its case. The arbitral tribunal, in exercising its discretion, shall conduct the proceedings so as to avoid unnecessary delay and expense and to provide a fair and efficient process for resolving the parties' dispute.
2. If either party so requests at any stage of the proceedings, the arbitral tribunal shall hold hearings for the presentation of evidence by witnesses, including expert witnesses, or for oral argument. In the absence of such a request, the arbitral tribunal shall decide whether to hold such hearings or whether the proceedings shall be conducted on the basis of documents and other materials.	2. As soon as practicable after its constitution and after inviting the parties to express their views, the arbitral tribunal shall establish the provisional timetable of the arbitration. The arbitral tribunal may, at any time, after inviting the parties to express their views, extend or abridge any period of time prescribed under these Rules or agreed by the parties.
3. All documents or information supplied to the arbitral tribunal by one party shall at the same time be communicated by that party to the other party.	3. If at an appropriate stage of the proceedings any party so requests, the arbitral tribunal shall hold hearings for the presentation of evidence by witnesses, including expert witnesses, or for oral argument. In the absence of such a request, the arbitral tribunal shall decide whether to hold such hearings or whether the proceedings shall

be conducted on the basis of documents and other materials.

4. All communications to the arbitral tribunal by one party shall be communicated by that party to all other parties. Such communications shall be made at the same time, except as otherwise permitted by the arbitral tribunal if it may do so under applicable law.

5. The arbitral tribunal may, at the request of any party, allow one or more third persons to be joined in the arbitration as a party provided such person is a party to the arbitration agreement, unless the arbitral tribunal finds, after giving all parties, including the person or persons to be joined, the opportunity to be heard, that joinder should not be permitted because of prejudice to any of those parties. The arbitral tribunal may make a single award or several awards in respect of all parties so involved in the arbitration.

A. THE BROAD POWERS OF THE TRIBUNAL TO CONDUCT THE ARBITRATION

1. Article 15 of the 1976 Rules establishes general but fundamental principles that form the framework for the elaboration of more specific rules, tailor-made for the specific arbitral proceedings. Hence this provision is said to be 'one of the most important sections of the [1976] UNCITRAL Rules [as it] provide[s] the key to a variety of problems not regulated elsewhere in the Rules'.[1]

2. Perhaps most importantly, article 15(1) provided that 'the arbitral tribunal may conduct the arbitration in such a manner as it considers appropriate'. Relying on the arbitrators' expertise and the flexibility of the arbitral process – the two 'hallmarks of arbitration'[2] – article 15(1) gave tribunals wide procedural-regulation powers, always within the bounds of ensuring the due process rights of the parties[3] and mandatory limitations of the *lex arbitri* under article 1(2). Crucially – and this is an essential feature retained in article 17(1) of the 2010 Rules – article 15(1) does not direct the tribunal to any national law (e.g. procedural law) as a

---

1 David D. Caron, Lee M. Caplan & Matti Pellonpää, *The UNCITRAL Arbitration Rules, A Commentary*, 26 (Oxford University Press 2006).

2 Jan Paulsson & Georgios Petrochilos, *Revision of the UNCITRAL Rules* (September 2006), para. 116 and the references, <www.uncitral.org>.

3 Most other sets of arbitration rules contain a similar provision: *see*, e.g., Article 23(1) of the SCC Rules; Article 37(a) of the WIPO Rules; and Article 20(1) of the AAA International Arbitration Rules.

source to draw upon.[4] Arbitrators have thus relied on this broad authority for a variety of procedural decisions; for example, to hold pre-hearing conferences or admit amicus curiae submissions.[5]

3. It may be helpful at the outset to examine the broad authority of the tribunal under article 15(1) of the 1976 Rules in the light of the doctrine of inherent powers.[6] The doctrine was primarily developed in public international law (although there are domestic precursors in the law of certain jurisdictions), and holds that tribunals possess certain powers that are not expressly conferred upon them, but which are nevertheless necessary for the proper discharge of their adjudicatory function or for the preservation of the integrity of the proceedings. A number of important elements remain open to discussion, including the precise justification for such powers and, by the same token, their precise remit and whether they can be overridden by contrary party agreement. The Iran-US Claims Tribunal has invoked inherent powers since its landmark decision on the authority to issue binding interim measures, *E-Systems*,[7] evidently perceiving a need to add to the express terms of article 26(1) of the 1976 Rules.[8] The Tribunal has also relied on the doctrine in the context of its power to revise awards tainted by forged documents or perjury.[9]

---

4 Nevertheless, a proposal to spell this out further by adding wording similar to that of the current Article 42 of the ICC Rules ('In all matters not expressly provided for in the Rules, the ... arbitral tribunal shall act in the spirit of the Rules') was defeated; *see* UNCITRAL Working Paper for 52nd Session, 10 December 2009, UN Doc A/CN.9/WG.II/WP.157/Add.2, paras 34-35; UNCITRAL Report of 52nd Session, 19 February 2010, UN Doc A/CN.9/688, paras 39-44.

5 *See* David D. Caron & Lee M. Caplan, *The UNCITRAL Arbitration Rules, A Commentary*, 30 fn 68 (2nd ed., Oxford University Press 2013). *See*, for a recent example, *Eli Lilly and Company v. The Government of Canada* (UNCITRAL) (ICSID Case No. UNCT/14/2) Procedural Order No. 4, 23 February 2016, < www.italaw.com >.

6 *See* generally Chester Brown, 'Inherent Powers in International Adjudication' in Cesare P. R. Romano, Karen Alter & Yuval Shany (eds), *The Oxford Handbook of International Adjudication*, Chapter 38 (Oxford University Press 2013). The doctrine has also been studied by the International Commercial Arbitration Committee of the ILA. In 2016, the ILA adopted a series of recommendations for parties, arbitral tribunals and courts, acknowledging the existence of inherent powers and providing guidance as to their appropriate use. *See* ILA International Commercial Arbitration Committee Resolution No. 4/2016, 7-11 August 2016, < www.ila-hq.org >.

7 *E-Systems Inc v. The Islamic Republic of Iran, Bank Melli Iran* (1982) 2 Iran-US CTR 51, 57 ('This tribunal has an inherent right to issue such orders as may be necessary to conserve the respective rights of the Parties and to ensure this Tribunal's jurisdiction and authority are made fully effective').

8 For discussion, *see* David D. Caron, *Interim Measures of Protection: Theory and Practice in Light of the Iran-United States Claims Tribunal*, 46 ZaöRV 465, 473 et seq. (1986).

9 *See Henry Morris v. Government of the Islamic Republic of Iran* (1983) 3 Iran-US CTR 364, 365; and *Dames & Moore v. Islamic Republic of Iran* (1985) 5 Iran-US CTR 107, 117-118. *See also Iran v. United States of America (Cases A3, A8, A9, A14, and B61)*, Decision No. DEC 134-A3/A8/A9/A14/B61-FT (2011), < www.iusct.net >, para. 64 and fn 105 (while the Tribunal was 'not prepared to hold that it has an inherent power to revise a final and binding award', it left open the question whether it might have such a power if the decision

4. When powers are expressly conferred by the Rules, whether in broad or specific terms, it is difficult to see the need to resort to inherent powers. This applies not only to the broad remit of a tribunal under article 15(1) of the 1976 Rules to 'conduct the arbitration in such manner as it considers appropriate' – there is nothing implied about this explicitly broad authority – but also to other powers for which the doctrine of inherent powers has historically been cited as a source (*compétence de la compétence*; interim measures; power to exclude evidence; etc.). However, it is important to recognize that the doctrine may have a residual role to play, at the very least as an overarching justification if not a legal source for powers – for example, where the tribunal proposes to take a procedural measure that is unusual (even if covered by the broad authority under article 15(1))[10] or to afford a remedy not provided for in the Rules (such as the summary dismissal of a claim that has no colourable basis).[11]

B. CODIFICATION OF THE POWERS OF THE TRIBUNAL

5. The basic tenets of article 15 are incorporated in article 17 of the revised Rules. However, as pointed out by Professor Sanders, 'this article has grown up during the revision process'.[12] Indeed, article 17 of the 2010 Rules explicitly spells out certain powers and (signally) also duties of the tribunal which were implied under the 1976 Rules, or for which the only source of guidance were the 1996 UNCITRAL Notes.[13] The revisions include additions underlining the tribunal's duty to ensure a fair and efficient arbitral process, and a new provision on the joinder of third parties.

6. There was intense debate within the Working Group as to whether article 17(1) provides the tribunal the power to grant temporary interim relief on an *ex parte*

---

was proven to have been induced by fraud or perjury). *See also* the discussion in *Riahi v. Iran* (2004-2009) 38 Iran-US CTR 19, 32 et seq.

10 Cf. the Order to exclude one counsel for the parties in the unusual circumstances of *Hrvatska Elektroprivreda dd v. Republic of Slovenia* (ICSID Case No. ARB/05/24) Order Concerning the Participation of Counsel, 6 May 2008, < www.italaw.com > .

11 Cf. *Waste Management Inc v. United Mexican States ('Number 2')* (ICSID Case No. ARB(AF)/00/3) Decision on Venue of the Arbitration, 26 September 2001, < www.italaw.com > , para. 3 (in Procedural Order No. 1, tribunal had ordered respondent to submit its preliminary objections to the claim based on the previous proceedings and on the decision of the previous tribunal, which had dismissed the case for lack of jurisdiction); and *id.*, Decision on Mexico's Preliminary Objection concerning the Previous Proceedings, 26 June 2002, para. 46 ('there is no indication in the Award of the first Tribunal that it considered any issue pertaining to the merits, let alone that it decided any such issue … there was no decision by the first Tribunal between the parties which would constitute a *res judicata* as to the merits of the claim now before us').

12 Pieter Sanders, *The Revision of the UNCITRAL Arbitration Rules* (August 2009), 23, < www.arbitration-icca.org > .

13 UNCITRAL, *Notes on Organizing Arbitral Proceedings*, (United Nations 1996). An updated version of the UNCITRAL Notes was released in 2016.

basis ('preliminary orders'),[14] and whether this should be explicitly addressed in the Rules. The view was strongly advanced that article 17(1), in the broad terms in which it is formulated, encompasses the power to issue preliminary orders, subject of course to the *lex arbitri*.[15] But it was countered that extending the tribunal's general power to the granting of preliminary orders could run counter to the tribunal's duty to treat parties equally, also safeguarded in article 17(1).[16] Unable to reach consensus, the Working Group drafted a 'non-rule' to reflect its neutral stance as to whether article 17(1) provides a foundation for a power to grant preliminary orders, which was eventually not retained,[17] as discussed further in connection with article 26. So it is likely that any support for a power to grant preliminary orders will have to be derived, not from the interstices of article 17(1), but from some higher principle that may be said to underpin it, or perhaps the doctrine of inherent powers (discussed at paragraph 3 above).

7. Certain additional powers (notably confidentiality and consolidation), while not as contentious as the power to grant preliminary orders, were not explicitly codified. There is no doubt that such powers do fall within the broad remit of procedural organization of the proceedings; as is in fact made clear by the inclusion of the tribunal's more far-reaching power to join a party in the proceedings, codified in article 17(5). However, it is also clear that the exercise of a number of such powers, notably in respect of consolidation of parallel related proceedings and confidentiality protections, will also require consent by the parties under many national arbitration laws. The 2010 Rules do not provide such advance consent, leaving the matter to be dealt with on a case-by-case basis. A number of other powers, well established in practice, were not codified even though they do not seem to raise concerns with regard to party consent. These include the tribunal's power to issue a general direction on specific procedural rules for the proceedings (typically the first procedural order), to convene case-management conferences,[18]

---

14 *See* generally Yves Derains, *The View against Arbitral Ex Parte Interim Relief – Confirmation that the best may be the enemy of the good*, 58(3) Dispute Resolution Journal 61 (2003); and James E. Castello, *Arbitral* Ex Parte *Interim Relief – The view in favour*, 58(3) Dispute Resolution Journal 60 (2003).

15 *See* UNCITRAL Report of 47th Session, 25 September 2007, UN Doc A/CN.9/641, para. 59: 'The Working Group was generally of the view that, unless prohibited by the law governing the arbitral procedure, bearing in mind the broad discretion with which the arbitral tribunal was entitled to conduct the proceedings under article 15(1) [of the 1976 Rules], the Rules, in and of themselves, did not prevent the arbitral tribunal from issuing preliminary orders'.

16 *See* UNCITRAL Report of 50th Session, 9 March 2009, UN Doc A/CN.9/669, para. 101.

17 Draft article 26(5) read: 'Nothing in these Rules shall have the effect of creating a right, or of limiting any right which may exist outside these Rules, of a party to apply to the arbitral tribunal for, and any power of the arbitral tribunal to issue, in either case without prior notice to a party, a preliminary order that the party not frustrate the purpose of a requested interim measure'. *See* UNCITRAL Report of 50th Session, 9 March 2009, UN Doc A/CN.9/669, para. 112.

18 *See* paras 24-25, *infra*.

to conduct enquiries,[19] to order a party to make property available for inspection,[20] and to appoint an administrative secretary to the tribunal.[21] Finally, the tribunal's power to appoint an expert has been specifically regulated in article 29.

C. THE DUTY OF THE TRIBUNAL TO ENSURE EQUAL TREATMENT AND A REASONABLE OPPORTUNITY TO BE HEARD

8. The principal limitation to the tribunal's broad powers under article 15(1) of the 1976 Rules was that the parties must be 'treated with equality'; and equal treatment is of course not a mechanistic concept, but rather imports the requirement of treating the parties fairly in the light of all the circumstances.[22] As an additional limitation, tribunals had to ensure that parties received a 'full opportunity' to present their case. This language corresponds to Article 18 of the UNCITRAL Model Law,[23] a provision which the Secretary of UNCITRAL has hailed as the '*Magna Carta* of arbitration'.[24] Article 22(4) of the 2012 ICC Rules,[25] which is couched in similar language, was likewise said to affirm 'an overriding and fundamental principle of arbitration'.[26] The basic notions of due process, equal treatment and a full opportunity to present one's case were further developed

---

[19] This power is codified in, e.g., Article 22.1(iii) of the LCIA Rules (providing the arbitrators with the power 'to conduct such enquiries as may appear to the Arbitral Tribunal to be necessary or expedient, including whether and to what extent the Arbitral Tribunal should itself take the initiative in identifying relevant issues and ascertaining relevant facts and the law(s) or rules of law applicable to the Arbitration Agreement, the arbitration and the merit of the parties' dispute').

[20] *See*, e.g., Article 22.1(iv) of the LCIA Rules (giving the tribunal the power 'to order any party to make any documents, goods, samples, property, site or thing under its control available for inspection by the Arbitral Tribunal, any other party, any expert to such party and any expert to the Tribunal').

[21] *See* Paulsson & Petrochilos, *supra* fn 2, at para. 138 (explaining that the tribunal's power to designate a secretary is well-established in practice). *See also* Constantine Partasides, *The Fourth Arbitrator? The Role of Secretaries to Tribunals in International Arbitration*, 18(2) Arb Int 147 (2002).

[22] *See* Paulsson & Petrochilos, *supra* fn 2, at para. 116 fn 127.

[23] Indeed, the terms of article 18 'were modelled on Article 15(1) of the UNCITRAL Arbitration Rules'; *see* Howard M. Holtzmann & Joseph E. Neuhaus, *A Guide to the UNCITRAL Model Law on International Commercial Arbitration, Legislative History and Commentary*, 551 (Kluwer 1989).

[24] Gerold Herrmann, *The UNCITRAL Model Law – Its Background, Salient Features, and Purposes*, 1(1) Arb Int 6, 19 (1985).

[25] Article 22(4) of the 2012 ICC Rules (Article 22(4) of the 2017 ICC Rules) reads: 'In all cases, the arbitral tribunal shall act fairly and impartially and ensure that each party has a reasonable opportunity to present its case'. *See also* Article 15(1) of the Swiss Rules ('Subject to these Rules, the arbitral tribunal may conduct the arbitration in such manner as it considers appropriate, provided that it ensures equal treatment of the parties and their right to be heard'); and Article 23(2) of the SCC Rules ('In all cases, the Arbitral Tribunal shall conduct the arbitration in an impartial, efficient and expeditious manner, giving each party an equal and reasonable opportunity to present its case').

[26] Jason Fry, Simon Greenberg & Francesca Mazza, *The Secretariat's Guide to ICC Arbitration*, para. 3-814 (ICC 2012).

in the remaining paragraphs of article 15 of the 1976 Rules: article 15(2) gave each party the right to request a hearing 'at any stage of the proceedings'; and article 15(3) required that any information or document supplied by one party to the tribunal also had to be communicated to the other party.[27]

9. Equal treatment and the opportunity to be heard of course continue to be safeguarded explicitly under article 17(1) of the 2010 Rules, with the change that the opportunity to be afforded to the parties must be 'reasonable' rather than 'full'. The intention is to avoid giving foothold for delaying tactics on the pretext that one further opportunity to submit a pleading or evidence is required to satisfy the facially-unqualified requirement of a 'full' opportunity. So the term 'reasonable' effectively means 'as full an opportunity as is reasonable in the circumstances' and in light of the duties of equality and efficiency.[28] Similarly, the duties incumbent upon the tribunal under articles 15(2) and 15(3) of the 1976 Rules are reproduced in the new articles 17(3) and 17(4) respectively, with some changes to provide the tribunal greater flexibility to conduct the proceedings efficiently.

10. The tribunal's duty to ensure due process will often involve a delicate balancing exercise in which the principles of equal treatment and a reasonable opportunity to be heard may be seen as leading to opposing outcomes. A frequently encountered example, to which the answer ought to be straightforward, is where one party requires more time to be given to it at a hearing, in order to examine a larger number of witnesses proffered by the other side. Similarly, a tribunal's exercise of its power to request the parties to deposit an equal amount as an advance for costs under article 43(1) may effectively deprive an impecunious party from affording participation in the proceedings.[29] The broader point is that tribunals may have to eschew formal equality in favour of a substantively equal opportunity for each party to present its case;[30] or limit one party's opportunity to present its case to achieve the equivalent duty of equality. Article 17(1) requires both of these objectives to be achieved in the round: this is not a tick-box, mechanistic exercise.

11. The importance of these general due process duties laid out in article 17(1) cannot be understated, as they must guide the tribunal's exercise of powers throughout the arbitral proceedings and under various provisions of the Rules, such as articles 40-43 on costs. Furthermore, a flagrant and grave breach[31] of

---

27 For the modifications of article 15(3) of the 1976 Rules, *see* discussion of article 26 of the 2010 Rules, *infra*.

28 *See* further *infra*, paras 18 et seq.

29 *See*, e.g., *Reginald H Howe v. Bank of International Settlements*, PCA Case No. 2000-04) Order on Request for Exceptional Remedies, 31 August 2001, <www.pca-cpa.org>, para. H2: 'An allocation of deposits and costs that had the effect of not providing a party with a "full opportunity of presenting its case" would not meet the test of [the relevant Arbitration Rules]'.

30 *See*, e.g., Tobias Zuberbühler, Christoph Müller & Philipp A. Habegger, *Swiss Rules of International Arbitration: Commentary*, 146 (Kluwer 2005) (in relation to Article 15(1) of the 2004 Swiss Rules (Article 15(1) of the 2012 Swiss Rules).

31 Cf. UNCITRAL, *2012 Digest of Case Law on the Model Law on International Commercial Arbitration*, 98, para. 7 (United Nations 2012) (the purpose of Article 18(1) of the Model

the mandatory duties in article 17(1) not only threatens the enforceability of the award,[32] but in exceptional cases it may also give rise to arbitrator liability within the confines of article 16.

D. THE DUTY OF THE TRIBUNAL TO ENSURE EFFICIENT PROCEEDINGS

12. Article 15 of the 1976 Rules did not explicitly spell out a duty to ensure efficient conduct of the arbitral proceedings.[33] However, efficiency in planning and conducting the arbitral proceedings was considered intrinsically linked to or incorporated in the overarching fairness requirement. To take an example mentioned in the 1996 UNCITRAL Notes, the planning of the aggregate amount of time each party will have for oral argument and examining witnesses 'will make it easier for the parties to plan the presentation of the various items of evidence and arguments, reduce the likelihood of running out of time towards the end of the hearings and avoid that one party would unfairly use up a disproportionate amount of time'.[34] More broadly, the 1996 Notes stress the 'need for a just and cost-efficient resolution of the dispute'.[35]

13. A broad duty of efficiency is also reflected in arbitral case-law.[36] In *Glamis Gold v. United States*, the respondent requested that the tribunal bifurcate the proceedings into jurisdictional and merits phases pursuant to its general powers under article 15(1) of the 1976 Rules. The tribunal rejected the request, on grounds (*inter alia*) that the jurisdictional issue identified was so intertwined with the merits that it was 'very unlikely that there will be any savings in time or cost'.[37]

Law is said to be 'to protect a party from egregious and injudicious conduct by an arbitral tribunal').

32 *See* Article V(1)(b) of the New York Convention; and for cases of challenges to awards based on alleged breaches of Article 18(1) of the UNCITRAL Model Law, *see Attorney-General v. Tozer (No 3)*, HC Auckland M1528-IM02, 2 September 2003; and *Front Row Investment Holdings (Singapore) Pte Ltd v. Daimler South East Asia Pte Ltd* [2010] SGHC 80.

33 *See*, e.g., Article 14.4(ii) of the LCIA Rules; Article 23(2) of the SCC Rules; Article 37(c) of the WIPO Rules; and article 20(2) of the AAA International Arbitration Rules. *See also* Article 14(1) of the UNCITRAL Model Law (which cautions against the failure of an arbitrator to act 'without undue delay'); and section 1(a) of the Arbitration Act 1996 (England & Wales) ('the object of arbitration is to obtain the fair resolution of disputes by an impartial tribunal without unnecessary delay or expense').

34 UNCITRAL, *supra* fn 13, at paras 78-79. These paragraphs are substantially reproduced at paras 118-119 of the 2016 Notes.

35 UNCITRAL, *supra* fn 13, at para. 4. The corresponding paragraph of the 2016 Notes, para. 8, does not replicate this wording, referring instead to the observance of 'a fair, equitable and efficient process'.

36 *See*, e.g., *S D Myers Inc v. Government of Canada* (UNCITRAL) Procedural Order No. 18, 26 February 2001, <www.italaw.com>, para. 11 ('it is the duty of this Tribunal to *both* of the Disputing Parties to determine the disputes between them as expeditiously and efficiently as practicable').

37 *Glamis Gold Ltd v. The United States of America* (UNCITRAL) Procedural Order No. 2, 31 May 2005, <www.italaw.com>, para. 25; Cf. *Caratube International Oil Company LLP v. The Republic of Kazakhstan* (ICSID Case No. ARB/08/12) Award, 5 June 2012, <www.

14. Article 17(1) now clearly spells out the duty of the arbitral tribunal to 'avoid unnecessary delay and expense and to provide a fair and efficient process for resolving the parties' dispute'. This was consistent with an overall objective of the Working Group,[38] and was achieved primarily through strengthening the role of the arbitral tribunal rather than through detailed over-regulation of discrete aspects of the arbitral proceedings.[39]

15. It is clear on the face of article 17(1) that the overall duty of fairness and efficiency is subordinate to party equality and the right to be heard. It is also clear that this duty imports broad judgement – 'discretion', says article 17(1) – to be exercised in the circumstances of each case. The duty is of course on-going and applies to every aspect of the arbitration, but article 17 explicitly addresses fairness and efficiency in three respects, addressed in turn below.

1. The duty to promote efficiency and avoid delay

16. One outcome of the inclusion of an express provision requiring the arbitral tribunal to deal with matters expeditiously is to 'provide leverage for arbitral tribunals to take certain steps both vis-à-vis the other arbitrators and the parties'.[40] But the tribunal's duty of course goes further than justifying an effort to persuade participants to move with all due expedition. It seems to have three principal manifestations:

(i) First, all things being equal, and notably if fairness does not command otherwise, a tribunal should elect the promptest and most cost-efficient processes. Thus the permissibility of amendments to the parties' pleaded cases (article 22) and of second-round written pleadings (article 24) should be seen in this light.

(ii) Secondly, article 17(1) places upon tribunals a practical duty to consider measures and processes that increase efficiency and decrease cost. These may be simply logistical (e.g. to have parts of the pleadings only in electronic form, rather than paper copies) or more far-reaching procedurally (e.g. to

---

italaw.com >, para. 487 ('With the wisdom of hindsight, the majority of the costs and expenses of each party and of the dispute, both in duration and expense, would have been avoided had Respondent opted for bifurcation'); *see also Philip Morris Asia Limited v. The Commonwealth of Australia* (UNCITRAL), PCA Case No. 2012-12, Procedural Order No. 8 Regarding Bifurcation of the Procedure, 14 April 2014, para. 106 (in ordering that the proceedings be bifurcated, the Tribunal acknowledged that 'should preliminary objections prevail with the result that no procedure on the merits becomes necessary, this would result in a major saving of work and costs'); *see also* discussion of article 23 of the 2010 Rules, *infra*.

38 *See* Report of the Commission on its 40th Session, 23 July 2007, UN Doc A/62/17 (Part I), para. 174 (the Commission invited the Working Group to make changes which would 'promote greater efficiency in arbitral proceedings'). This guiding principle of efficiency was regularly repeated in the work of the Working Group.

39 *See* Michael E. Schneider, *The Revision of the UNCITRAL Arbitration Rules – Some observations on the process and the results*, 4/2011 Les Cahiers de l'Arbitrage 903, 924 (2011).

40 UNCITRAL Report of 45th Session, 5 October 2006, UN Doc A/CN.9/614, para. 76.

have the parties' experts produce joint reports, to appoint a person assisting the tribunal with on-going document production,[41] to instruct the parties to address specific issues in written or oral pleadings,[42] or to order a stay of the arbitration proceedings).[43] Doubtless the tribunal will wish to have the parties assist it in devising and considering such measures or processes; and in fact, as most such measures will affect the timetable of the proceedings, at the very least the tribunal will have to elicit the parties' views in that regard (see article 17(2)). But article 17(1) requires the tribunal to be proactive in ensuring efficient conduct, guiding the parties rather than simply being reactive to requests by them.

It merits note that exactly how much proactiveness is required and in what respects are matters ultimately controlled by the *lex arbitri*; see article 1(3). It is possible, for instance, for the controlling law to take the approach that tribunals are required to identify a viable legal basis for a claim, even if not pleaded by the claimant, and put it to both parties for submissions.[44] That approach might be underpinned by a policy to ensure the broadest res

41 Cf. *Guyana v. Suriname* (PCA Case No. 2004-04) Procedural Order No 3, 12 October 2005, and Award, 17 September 2007, <www.pca-cpa.org>. The tribunal appointed an independent expert to aid it in resolving the dispute between the parties concerning access to certain documents in the archives of The Netherlands Ministry of Foreign Affairs. The expert would, 'at the request of the Party producing the file or document, review any proposal by that Party to remove or redact parts of that file or document', as each Party may 'have a legitimate interest in the non-disclosure of information that does not relate to the present dispute, or which, for other valid reasons, should be regarded as privileged and confidential'. The expert could also be engaged by the tribunal to aid in its determination of whether files or documents requested of one party by the other were relevant and had been identified with reasonable specificity. The expert would also resolve any disputes concerning a party's failure or refusal to produce such files or documents. The tribunal subsequently adopted the expert's recommendations.

42 *See* the example of the *Aminoil* case (*The Government of the State of Kuwait v. The American Independent Oil Company* (*Aminoil*) Award, 24 May 1982, 21 ILM 976 (1982)), described in Nigel Blackaby, Constantine Partasides, Alan Redfern & Martin J. Hunter, *Redfern and Hunter on International Arbitration*, paras 6.61-6.62 (6th ed., Kluwer 2015).

43 *See*, applying the 1976 Rules, *S D Myers Inc v. Government of Canada* (UNCITRAL), *supra* fn 36, at para. 7 (under article 15.1, the power to grant or deny Canada's application for a stay 'was a matter for the Tribunal's discretion'); and *William Ralph Clayton, William Richard Clayton, Douglas Clayton, Daniel Clayton and Bilcon of Delaware Inc v. Government of Canada* (UNCITRAL), PCA Case No. 2009-04, Procedural Order No. 19, 10 August 2015, <www.italaw.com>, para. 16 ('it is within the scope of [the Tribunal's] discretion to grant a stay'); *see*, applying the 2010 Rules, *Aaron C Berkowitz, Brett E Berkowitz and Trevor B Berkowitz (formerly Spence International Investments and others) v. Republic of Costa Rica* (ICSID Case No. UNCT/13/2) Procedural Order on Stay Application, 28 February 2017, <www.italaw.com>, para. 45 (in addition to the Tribunal's inherent competence, the discretionary power to grant a stay of the arbitration proceedings 'is properly derived from ... Article 17(1) [of the 2010 Rules]').

44 Cf. ILA Resolution No. 6/2008, Recommendations on Ascertaining the Contents of the Applicable Law in International Commercial Arbitration (August 2008), paras 6, 13: tribunals should not 'introduce propositions of law that may bear on the outcome of the dispute ... that the parties have not raised' except in respect of public policy and mandatory norms.

judicata effect for awards. If that is the mandatory approach, the tribunal will have to follow it.

(iii) Thirdly, article 17(1) does not mandate efficiency as an exclusive or absolute objective: rather, efficiency goes hand-in-hand with fairness and, as noted, it is to serve the primary objectives of equality and a fair hearing. There are doubtless trade-offs and compromises to be made, as it is plain from article 17(1) that all these objectives are to be pursued by the tribunal concurrently.

2. Articles 17(1) and 17(3): right to present one's case, and hearings

17. Another way in which article 17 promotes greater efficiency in the proceedings is by reducing the scope for delay and dilatory tactics, through small but significant changes to the wording of provisions relating to a party's right to present its case and the right to a hearing.[45] On the wording of articles 15(1) and 15(2) of the 1976 Rules, there was a 'full' right to present one's case at 'any stage of the proceedings', and a hearing could be requested by right at 'any stage of the proceedings'. This broad wording created a basis for potential abuse, for instance by requesting a hearing on the eve of the closing of the proceedings.[46] In order to minimise the risk of disruptive requests, the wording 'at any stage of the proceedings' has been replaced by the phrase 'at any appropriate stage of the proceedings' in articles 17(1) and 17(3).

(i) Right to present one's case

18. Rather than a 'full' opportunity, the 2010 Rules require arbitrators to afford parties a 'reasonable' opportunity to present their case. It was felt that the qualifier 'reasonable' 'corresponded to a commonly used and well-accepted standard'.[47] While the Working Group had no evidence that the phrase 'full opportunity' had created undesirable results, it was concerned that the phraseology could give rise to contention,[48] and replacing it with the word 'reasonable' would help avoid excessive pleadings.[49] After all, 'a full opportunity to present one's case might be understood as requiring the arbitral tribunal to allow each and every procedural request of a party. Balancing all parties' interests and the need for efficiency rather requires that each party be granted a *reasonable* opportunity to present its case'.[50]

---

45 *See* Schneider, *supra* fn 39, at 924.

46 *See* Caron & Caplan, *supra* fn 5, at 51-52.

47 Report of the Commission on its 43rd Session, 21 June-9 July 2010, UN Doc A/65/17, para. 81. *See*, e.g., Article 22(4) of the ICC Rules; Article 14.4(i) of the LCIA Rules; and section 33(1)(a) of the Arbitration Act 1996 (England & Wales).

48 *See* UNCITRAL Report of 45th Session, 5 October 2006, UN Doc A/CN.9/614, para. 77.

49 *See*, e.g., UNCITRAL Summary Record of the 904th Meeting, 22 June 2010, UN Doc A/CN.9/SR.904, XLI UNCITRAL Ybk 1228, 1233 para. 60, Mr Castello (United States of America).

50 Fry, Greenberg & Mazza, *supra* fn 26, at para. 3-817 (commenting on the 'reasonable' requirement under Article 22(4) of the ICC Rules).

19. It must be noted that, under Article 18 of the Model Law, the 'full' opportunity requirement is considered 'fundamental … for procedural justice'.[51] While courts have thus held that parties may not derogate from this requirement,[52] they have also interpreted it in a manner that has brought its meaning close to the meaning of the 'reasonable' opportunity standard provided for in the 2010 Rules. Thus the Singapore Court of Appeal has held that 'arid, technical or procedural objections that do not prejudice any party should not be tolerated in the context of fairness'; and that overturning an award is called for '[o]nly when the alleged breach of natural justice has surpassed the boundaries of legitimate expectation and propriety, resulting in actual prejudice to a party'.[53]

(ii) Right to hearing

20. The potential for abuse under the wording of article 15(2) of the 1976 Rules led the Iran-US Claims Tribunal to interpret 'any stage of the proceedings' as applying 'in light of the particular circumstances of each case', and to assess hearings requests in light of the 'stage of the proceedings'.[54] Thus, the change in wording in article 17(3) of the 2010 Rules is in line with the practice established under the 1976 Rules, and additionally, reflects the language used in the Model Law.[55]

21. The scope of application of article 17(3) appears clear-cut at first blush. On closer examination it is less so. The references in article 17(3) to fact- and expert-witness evidence suggest that the right to a hearing does not cover purely procedural matters. These references make it plain that hearings on the merits (where witness evidence is tested and oral submissions made on that evidence) are certainly covered. The same is true of matters of jurisdiction and admissibility, which require substantial 'oral argument' within the meaning of article 17(3). Interim measures applications would certainly fall within article 17(3) to the extent they involve witness evidence or substantial oral argument.

22. As for procedural matters, clearly it is necessary to give a party an opportunity to express a view on such matters (see article 17(1)), and article 17(2) provides so expressly in respect of the procedural timetable and changes to deadlines. In some cases, a procedural issue may be of such importance as to warrant a hearing for 'oral argument';[56] thus, bifurcation of proceedings into different phases may have very considerable implications on cost, timing, and the litigation tactics of

---

[51] UNCITRAL, *supra* fn 31, at 97, para. 4.

[52] *See Soh Beng Tee & Co Pte Ltd v. Fairmount Development Pte Ltd* [2007] 3 SLR 86; and *Noble China Inc v. Lei Kat Cheong* [1998] CanLII 14708 (ON SC) 91.

[53] *Soh Beng Tee & Co Pte Ltd v. Fairmount Development Pte Ltd, supra* fn 52, at para. 98.

[54] *World Farmers Trading Inc v. GTC* (1989) 22 Iran-US CTR 204, para. 16.

[55] *See* Article 24(1) of the UNCITRAL Model Law.

[56] Cf. Article 15, Note 2 of the Tribunal Rules of Procedure of the Iran-US Claims Tribunal (3 May 1983) ('the arbitral tribunal shall determine without hearing any written requests or objections of the concerned arbitrating parties with respect to procedural matters unless it grants or invites oral argument in special circumstances').

the parties. In other cases, hearings by telephone or video conference (cf. article 28(4)) are often the appropriate solution.

23. The tribunal may also order a hearing of its own initiative.[57] In practice, it is rare for there not to be a hearing on the merits, especially on the evidential aspects of the case.[58] The tribunal may also perceive a need for a hearing if it finds after the written pleadings that it requires the parties to clarify or further develop certain matters orally.

3. Article 17(2): setting up a provisional timetable and arbitrators' power to extend and abridge time-periods

24. Although the 1976 Rules did not contain any explicit provision to this effect, in practice UNCITRAL tribunals establish provisional timetables as a matter of course, at or following 'preparatory meetings' pursuant to the UNCITRAL Notes.[59] Similarly, pre-hearing conferences, which are expressly provided for in the procedure of the Iran-US Claims Tribunal, are used for the purpose of fixing schedules for written submissions and hearings.[60] While a proposal to codify the tribunal's power of holding preparatory conferences was rejected by the Working Group as over regulation,[61] article 17(2) sets forth the requirement that arbitrators establish a provisional timetable for the proceedings as soon as practicable after the formation of the tribunal. The 2010 Rules include article 17(2) as a codification of 'good practice', based on the belief 'that [this] would enhance [the] efficiency of the proceedings'.[62] The 2010 Rules are entirely concordant with other sets of arbitration rules.[63] Scheduling is expressed as a mandatory requirement, as it ensures that an orderly process can be defined early in the arbitration.[64] The basic parameters and phases of arbitral proceedings are well understood internationally,[65] but that certainly cannot mean a one-size fits all

---

57 The tribunal's power to order hearings of its own motion is also expressly provided for in Article 25(2) of the ICC Rules. The LCIA Rules do not contain such an explicit right in Article 19.1; but *see* Peter Turner & Reza Mohtashami, *A Guide to the LCIA Arbitration Rules*, para. 5.88 (Oxford University Press 2009) (suggesting that such a power may be implied).

58 *See* Blackaby, Partasides, Redfern & Hunter, *supra* fn 42, at para. 6.156.

59 *See* UNCITRAL, *supra* fn 13, at paras 39 (scheduling of written submissions), 48 (time-limits for submission of documentary evidence) and 77 (setting dates for hearings). *See*, in the 2016 Notes, corresponding paras 65-66, 73 and 116.

60 *See*, e.g., *The Austin Company v. Machine Sazi Arak*, Case No. 295, Chamber Two, Order of 30 July 1982, Annex.

61 *See* UNCITRAL Report of 46th Session, 20 March 2007, UN Doc A/CN.9/619, para. 114; and UNCITRAL Report of 52nd Session, 19 February 2010, UN Doc A/CN.9/688, para. 90. Cf. Paulsson & Petrochilos, *supra* fn 2, at paras 120-124 (highlighting the useful purpose of preparatory meetings).

62 UNCITRAL Report of 52nd Session, 19 February 2010, UN Doc A/CN.9/688, para. 85.

63 Cf. Article 24(2) of the ICC Rules; Article 15(3) of the Swiss Rules; and Article 28 of the SCC Rules.

64 *See* Fry, Greenberg & Mazza, *supra* fn 26, at paras 3-915 and 3-924.

65 *See* Blackaby, Partasides, Redfern & Hunter, *supra* fn 42, at paras 6.22 et seq.

approach: 'each arbitral tribunal is different, each dispute is different, and each case deserves to be treated differently'.[66]

25. In practice, a case-management conference will in many cases (though perhaps not in all) undoubtedly be the most appropriate mechanism for the tribunal to obtain the parties' views in respect of the provisional timetable, as it is required to do under article 17(2). Such a conference may also be an appropriate consultation mechanism in respect of the tribunal's fees and expenses: article 41(3) imposes a duty on the tribunal, promptly after its constitution, to inform the parties as to how it proposes to determine its fees and expenses, and there is nothing to suggest that the tribunal should not consult with the parties before making its proposal (and in practice tribunals do in fact consult routinely).

26. Article 17(2) is notable in setting forth a power for the tribunal (after hearing the parties) to alter 'any period of time' even if specifically agreed upon by the parties. The value of such a power, which is doubtless to be used in compelling cases and is always subject to the *lex arbitri* pursuant to article 1(3), lies especially in allowing a tribunal to extend unviably short time-periods for the conclusion of the entire case that parties occasionally agree upon in contracts, whether out of optimism or inexperience. In institutional arbitrations, the administering institution can authorize extensions and generally alter time-limits set forth in the relevant arbitrations rules or agreed by the parties.[67] But on the face of the relevant provisions there is some uncertainty as to whether the institution can also alter time-limits specifically agreed upon by the parties in their contract. Article 17(2) of the Rules is crystal-clear in that regard. The second part of article 17(2) gives the arbitral tribunal the power to shorten or lengthen 'any period of time prescribed under these Rules or agreed by the parties'. While divergent views were expressed in the Working Group as to whether the tribunal has an inherent power to alter procedural time-limits, it was sensibly agreed that there should be a provision expressly providing for such power.[68] In any case, making this power express enabled the Working Group to underline 'the significance of not amending periods of time without the parties being involved in that decision-making process':[69] article 17(2) specifies that the tribunal may make such a decision only after it has invited 'the parties to express their views'. The right of the parties to express their views applies not just when the tribunal alters time-periods set by the parties themselves, but also time-periods prescribed under the Rules.[70]

27. 'Any period under these Rules', although it seems to cover all periods, logically might cover only deadlines and time-periods before which one cannot act that apply after the constitution of the tribunal and are relevant to the tribunal's work,

[66] *Ibid.*, at para. 6.19.

[67] *See*, e.g., Articles 31(2) and 39(2) respectively of the ICC Rules.

[68] *See* UNCITRAL Report of 46th Session, 20 March 2007, UN Doc A/CN.9/619, para. 135.

[69] UNCITRAL Report of 49th Session, 30 September 2008, UN Doc A/CN.9/665, para. 122.

[70] Contrast UNCITRAL Report of 46th Session, 20 March 2007, UN Doc A/CN.9/619, para. 136 with UNCITRAL Report of 49th Session, 30 September 2008, UN Doc A/CN.9/665, paras 122-123.

including those concerning the post-award remedies in articles 37-39. Thus, the power to amend time-periods is vested only in the tribunal. As for periods of time relevant to the proceedings before the tribunal has been constituted, the Rules do not vest in the appointing authority any power to extend or abridge them. Indeed, a proposal to give an equivalent power to the appointing authority in respect of the constitution of the arbitral tribunal (or to decide on a challenge) was raised in the Working Group but dismissed on the grounds that it 'could create a risk of delaying the constitution of the tribunal'.[71] A similar proposal made in connection with the appointing authority's (or the PCA's) costs-review power under article 41(4) was also dismissed.[72] However, as mentioned in our commentary on article 6(4), this does not prevent the appointing authority from recommending that the parties agree to extending time-limits within which the appointing authority or the Secretary-General of the PCA must act.

28. There is a good question as to whether the tribunal's power to amend time-limits extends to time-limits in respect of post-award remedies, namely interpretations, corrections and additional awards, especially considering that article 39 on additional awards explicitly allows for an extension, unlike the other articles on post-award remedies (see articles 37-39 and the discussion in respect of these provisions). The a contrario argument from article 39 apart, where such remedies are exercised with regard to the final award in the proceedings, it may be possible to argue that a tribunal that is *functus officio* cannot modify the applicable time-limits before the relevant remedy has been sought. But on the face of article 17(2) ('*any* period of time prescribed under these Rules' (emphasis added)), a tribunal may extend the time-periods set out in articles 37-39, at the very least in advance, before it has issued its final award.

29. Finally, it is clear that time-limits which are set by the law applicable to the arbitration, and are not modified by the provisions of the Rules themselves or by the parties through specific agreement, are not within the tribunal's power to extend or abridge. Naturally, time-limits set forth by mandatory law (e.g. the three-month period for a setting-aside application in Article 34(3) of the Model Law) are preserved under article 1(3) of the Rules.

E. COMMUNICATIONS WITH THE TRIBUNAL

30. Article 15(3) of the 1976 Rules codifies the prohibition of *ex parte* approaches to the tribunal, which was and remains 'the current practice in international arbitration':[73] thus, any communication sent to the arbitral tribunal must be sent at the same time to the other party or parties. This is of course to safeguard an award from being challenged on the ground that the process or resulting

---

71 *See* UNCITRAL Report of 46th Session, 20 March 2007, UN Doc A/CN.9/619, para. 135.

72 As discussed in our commentary on article 41, the language of article 17(2) suggests that the tribunal can extend or abridge the time-limits applicable to the appointing authority or Secretary General of the PCA for the review of tribunal fees. However, this seems incongruous with the independent function of review provided for under these provisions.

73 UNCITRAL Report of 49th Session, 30 September 2008, UN Doc A/CN.9/665, para. 127.

award was based on information unknown to one party and so in violation of due process.[74] Recognizing that this 'method contributed to the facilitation of arbitral proceedings',[75] the provision is retained in article 17(4) of the 2010 Rules, with the important caveat that simultaneous communication may be derogated from when 'otherwise permitted by the arbitral tribunal if it may do so under applicable law'.

31. This caveat of course addresses the practical considerations in obtaining preliminary orders, if such orders are available under the law applicable to the arbitration: by definition, the whole purpose would be defeated by informing the other party of the request for *ex parte* relief.[76] The caveat also covers the situation where one party submits to the tribunal materials for the very purpose of assessing whether such materials are to be provided to the other party at all, for example whether they are subject to legal privilege or some other impediment to document production. Another situation where the caveat comes into play is where an arbitral institution requires that all communications to the tribunal and the other party be routed through the institution,[77] a practice catered for in Article 24(3) of the Model Law (which for that reason does not contain the simultaneous-communication requirement).[78] Clearly, that the exception is made subject to applicable law provides 'a safeguard and a limit to the possibility for delayed communications'.[79]

32. The rule in article 17(4) applies to 'communications to the arbitral tribunal'. The term 'communication' is broad and non-technical: it encompasses all and any materials given to the tribunal, whatever their purpose or form. However, the rule does not apply to communications that are made in the context of the arbitration to other organs or authorities (e.g. disclosures to regulatory bodies, applications to courts), where any requirement to give notice to the other party will be governed by the rules pertaining to the relevant process or remedy.

---

74 *See* Caron & Caplan, *supra* fn 5, at 53-54; and Jacomijn J. van Hof, *Commentary on the UNCITRAL Arbitration Rules, The Application by the Iran-U.S. Claims Tribunal*, 103 (Kluwer 1991).

75 UNCITRAL Report of 49th Session, 30 September 2008, UN Doc A/CN.9/665, para. 127.

76 Cf. UNCITRAL Report of 52nd Session, 19 February 2010, UN Doc A/CN.9/688, para. 87.

77 *See* Report of the Commission on its 43rd Session, 21 June-9 July 2010, UN Doc A/65/17, para. 88.

78 *See* Howard M. Holtzmann & Joseph E. Neuhaus, *A Guide to the UNCITRAL Model Law on International Commercial Arbitration, Legislative History and Commentary*, 674 (Kluwer, 1989); and UNCITRAL Summary Record of the 907th meeting, 24 June 2010, UN Doc A/CN.9/SR.907, XLI UNCITRAL Ybk 1249 para. 9 (the caveat was 'intended to bring the Rules into line with provisions of the Model Law, which allowed for exceptions to the simultaneous communication requirement in certain cases').

79 Report of the Commission on its 43rd Session, 21 June-9 July 2010, UN Doc A/65/17, para. 89.

F. JOINDER

1. Third-party intervention: *amici curiae* and joinder distinguished

33. Third-party intervention in the arbitral proceedings is not addressed (and was not even discussed) in the 1976 Rules.[80] As pointed out in the *travaux* of the 2010 Rules,[81] third-party interventions involve two distinct situations: (i) when a person wishes to be heard in the arbitral proceedings as a non-party, for example in support of one party or as an amicus curiae;[82] and (ii) when a person seeks to be joined or is requested to be joined in the proceedings as a party for whom the award may produce res judicata effects. Although it is clear that an amicus curiae is not a litigant in the arbitration, while a party being joined in the proceedings is, as we will see, article 17(5) does not stipulate that a joined party be the holder of rights or duties in the dispute on the merits as a matter of substantive law. That is to say, the joined party may be intervening to make its position known and recorded with formal binding effect in an award, or to support one of the original parties, or both. Both guarantors and sub-contractors (to give just two examples) may have an interest in interventions of this type. The tribunal's decision as to the joinder will have to specify the status of the party being joined and the attendant procedural rights and duties pursuant to the procedural schedule of the arbitration (which will have to be revised accordingly).

34. Article 17(5) deals with the joinder of a party, while article 17(1) remains formulated in a fashion that allows for the admission of amicus curiae interventions under the tribunal's broad power to 'conduct the arbitration in such manner as it considers appropriate'. Distinct from both of these possibilities, which require permission by the tribunal, is the joinder of a party by right, regulated in article 4(2)(f). Under that provision, the respondent may include in its response the particulars of a notice of arbitration against a party other than the claimant, provided that party is also bound by the arbitration agreement between the claimant and the respondent. In this way, the respondent may add a new party to the proceedings, against which party the respondent formulates claims. If

---

80 Until recently, most arbitration rules were entirely silent on the subject; *see* Gary B. Born, *International Commercial Arbitration*, 2595 (2nd ed., Kluwer 2014). Note that while the 1998 ICC Rules were silent on the subject, the 2012 version included a new provision (Article 7, now Article 7 of the 2017 Rules) on the joinder of additional parties.

81 *See* UNCITRAL Report of 45th Session, 5 October 2006, UN Doc A/CN.9/614, para. 81. For a general overview of the issues involved in third-party intervention, *see* Bernard Hanotiau, *Complex Arbitrations: Multiparty, Multicontract, Multi-Issue and Class Actions*, Chapter IV (Kluwer 2005).

82 *See Methanex Corporation v. United States of America* (UNCITRAL) Decision on *Amici Curiae*, 15 January 2001, < www.italaw.com >, para. 30 ('In the Tribunal's view, its receipt of written submissions from a person other than the Disputing Parties is not equivalent to adding that person as a party to the arbitration'). *See also United Parcel Service of America Inc v. Government of Canada* (UNCITRAL) Decision on *Amici Curiae*, 17 October 2001, < www.italaw.com >, para. 61 (by allowing third-party submissions, 'the Tribunal has exercised its power to permit that person to make the submission. It is a matter of its power rather than of third party right').

joinder is sought after the submission of the respondent's response, it will have to be on the basis of article 17(5), even if it could have been formulated earlier as an article 4(2)(f) addition of a new respondent.

35. A number of proposals were made during the revision process to add a provision expressly allowing amicus curiae submissions, thus codifying a power that has been held to exist under article 15(1) of the 1976 Rules.[83] In fact, amicus curiae submissions in investment arbitration had their debut in the *Methanex* case, where a NAFTA tribunal constituted under the 1976 Rules held that its jurisdiction to admit briefs from NGOs which were non-disputing parties was 'inferred ... from its more general procedural powers' under article 15(1).[84] The tribunal found that the 'wording of ... article 15(1) suffices ... to support its conclusion',[85] but considered also that its approach was supported by the analogous practice of the Iran-US Claims Tribunal.[86] This conclusion was endorsed in *UPS v. Canada*, where the tribunal found that receiving submissions offered by third parties with the purpose of assisting the tribunal was within the scope of its powers under article 15(1), which 'powers are to be used to facilitate the Tribunal's process of inquiry into, understanding of, and resolving' the dispute.[87] Both tribunals made clear that the exercise of the tribunal's power to permit amicus curiae submissions must comply with due process limitations under article 15(1) and is 'not to be used in a way which is unduly burdensome for the parties or which unnecessarily complicates the Tribunal process'.[88] Further, amici curiae are not exempted from the requirement of respecting the privacy of hearings under the Rules,[89] and are in principle not granted access to confidential materials.[90]

---

[83] *See* UNCITRAL Report of 45th Session, 5 October 2006, UN Doc A/CN.9/614, paras 81-82.

[84] *Methanex Corporation v. United States of America, supra* fn 82, at para. 25.

[85] *Ibid.*, at para. 31.

[86] *See* Article 15, Note 5 of the Tribunal Rules of Procedure of the Iran-US Claims Tribunal: 'The arbitral tribunal may, having satisfied itself that the statement of one of the two Governments – or, under special circumstances, any other person – who is not an arbitrating party in a particular case is likely to assist the tribunal in carrying out its task, permit such Government or person to assist the tribunal by presenting oral or written statements'. For examples of its application, *see Iran v. United States of America (Case A15)* (1984) 2 Iran-US CTR 40.

[87] *United Parcel Service of America Inc v. Government of Canada, supra* fn 82, at para. 60. For further discussion on the issue of non-disputing parties within NAFTA *see Glamis Gold Ltd v. The United States of America* (UNCITRAL) Procedural Order No. 6, 15 October 2005, < www.italaw.com >, paras 11-12. Note also the Statement of the Free Trade Commission on non-disputing party participation, 7 October 2003, < www.state.gov > (expressly confirming the discretionary power of NAFTA tribunals to accept written submissions from non-disputing parties).

[88] *United Parcel Service of America Inc v. Government of Canada, supra* fn 82, at para. 69.

[89] *See Methanex Corporation v. United States of America, supra* fn 82, at para. 42 (tribunal has no power to undermine the effect of article 25(4) of the 1976 Rules under which hearings are to be held *in camera* unless disputing parties consent otherwise). Article 25(4) is reproduced as article 28(3) of the 2010 Rules.

[90] *See ibid.*, at para. 46; and *United Parcel Service of America Inc v. Government of Canada, supra* fn 82, at para. 68 (as the UNCITRAL Rules do not expressly deal with confidentiality,

36. Certain of the proposals expressly to codify the tribunal's power to accept amicus curiae submissions were made in the context of a broader proposal for transparency rules for investment-treaty arbitrations under the Rules.[91] These proposals were rejected, leaving this matter to be dealt with as part of the follow-up project on provisions for transparency in investment arbitrations,[92] which resulted in the Transparency Rules, addressed in Part II of this book.

37. As to joinder of a party, doubts were expressed during the revision process on whether provision should at all be made for this in the Rules.[93] In fact, joinder has been held to be within article 20 of the 1976 Rules (amendments to pleaded case, citing an additional party). In *Biloune v. Ghana*, the tribunal used article 20 to allow the joinder of the Government of Ghana to an arbitration that had originally been commenced against the Ghana Investments Centre (GIC). The tribunal held:

> Under the UNCITRAL Rules, Art. 20, a claimant may amend his claim at any time, unless such factors as undue delay or prejudice suggest that such amendment is inappropriate or the amended claim would fall outside the arbitration clause. In the present case, the amendment was made in the claimants' first submission on the merits following the Statement of Claim, and in any case confirmed the obvious conclusion. From the outset of these proceedings, it was clear to all concerned that the claim was addressed in large part to alleged acts and omissions of the Government of Ghana. Indeed, several responses to the Tribunal's communications and Orders were submitted not by GIC itself (although some were) but by the Solicitor General of the Government of Ghana. Moreover, the first communication of the respondents' Washington's counsel to the Tribunal introduced counsel as representing both GIC and the Government. Given these clear indications of the Government's awareness of and participation in the proceedings prior to the claimant's amendment, no prejudice appears.
>
> ...
>
> Of course, in order to be subject to the Tribunal's jurisdiction, the Government must have consented to the arbitration, either now or previously ... [T]he Agreement [between claimant] with GIC, an agency of the Government of Ghana, clearly binds the Government; indeed, the Agreement speaks explicitly of disputes between the investor "and the Government", and the expropriation clause expressly prohibits expropriation "by the Government".

access of an amicus curiae to confidential materials depends on any agreement between the parties or any order in respect of confidentiality).

[91] *See* UNCITRAL Report of 46th Session, 20 March 2007, UN Doc A/CN.9/619, para. 61; and UNCITRAL Report of 48th Session, 29 February 2008, UN Doc A/CN.9/646, para. 64. Cf. Jan Paulsson & Georgios Petrochilos, *supra* fn 2, at para. 133 (proposing that the tribunal's power to accept amicus curiae briefs be made explicit 'especially in light of the frequent use of the UNCITRAL Rules in arbitrations under international investment treaties').

[92] *See* UNCITRAL Report of 48th Session, 29 February 2008, UN Doc A/CN.9/646, para. 69; and Report of the Commission on its 43rd Session, 21 June-9 July 2010, UN Doc A/65/17, paras 190-191.

[93] *See* UNCITRAL Report of 45th Session, 5 October 2006, UN Doc A/CN.9/614, para. 82.

> Thus the relevant clauses both engage the Government of Ghana, and contemplate claims against it.[94]

Article 20 of the 1976 Rules was also used by the Iran-US Claims Tribunal to add additional respondents.[95] In *Kimberly-Clark Corp v. Bank Markazi Iran*,[96] the Tribunal allowed the joinder of parties who had already been identified in the original statements of claim, in which some assertions concerning their nationality and responsibility had already been made. By contrast, in *Re Ministry of Economic Affairs and Finance of Iran*,[97] the attempt to join the US Government was not considered a permissible amendment under article 20, as the original claim against several US banks had not indicated that any claims against that Government were being raised.

38. Whether or not one agrees with the jurisdictional analysis in *Biloune*, the practice under article 20 of the 1976 Rules seems to allow for a sort of correction or regularisation – i.e. the formal addition as a named respondent of a party against which claims were in substance already asserted in the notice of arbitration or statement of claim. The better view would seem to be that such cases will now fall under article 17(5), not only because this provision is *lex specialis* compared to article 20, but also because the successor to article 20 of the 1976 Rules, article 22 of the 2010 Rules, is formulated with a focus on the amendment of the claims that are being asserted rather than the party against which they are asserted.[98]

2. Conditions for joinder under article 17(5)

(i) At the request of any party

39. Article 17(5) expressly allows for joinder to be initiated 'at the request of any party', giving this right of initiative to any of the existing arbitrants[99] but also, in the submission of the authors, a third person seeking to join in the

94 *Antoine Biloune and Marine Drive Complex Ltd v. Ghana Investments Centre and the Government of Ghana* (UNCITRAL) 27 October 1989, XIX YCA 11 (1994), paras 14-15.

95 *See* van Hof, *supra* fn 74, at 139-140.

96 *Kimberly-Clark Corp v. Bank Markazi Iran* (1983) 2 Iran-US CTR 338.

97 *Re Ministry of Economic Affairs and Finance of Iran* (1984) 6 Iran-US CTR 28.

98 *See*, on this point, *Enkev Beheer BV v. Republic of Poland* (PCA Case No. 2013-01), First Partial Award, 29 April 2014, <www.pca-cpa.org>, para. 304 ('the Tribunal does not consider that Enkev Polska could be joined as an additional party under Article 22 of the [2010] UNCITRAL Arbitration Rules. That provision addresses only amendments to a claim or defence by an existing party: it does not address the addition … of a third party to the arbitration').

99 The Working Group considered the comments received from the ICC, that while it had generally taken a conservative view that only the claimant is entitled to join parties under the 1998 ICC Rules, a more moderate approach had been reflected in recent cases; *see* Anne-Marie Whitesell & Eduardo Silva-Romero, 'Multiparty and Multicontract Arbitration: Recent ICC Experience' in *Complex Arbitrations: Perspectives on their Procedural Implications*, 7 ICC ICA Bull. Spec. Supp. (2003), considered in UNCITRAL Working Paper for 49th Session, 6 August 2008, UN Doc A/CN.9/WG.II/WP.151, para. 37.

proceedings. That is to say, the words 'any party' in article 17(5) do not refer simply to any party in the existing proceedings but also to any party that may join in the proceedings. The contrary view retorts that the term 'party' in the Rules normally connotes an arbitrant and that similar wording in the 1998 LCIA Rules was read accordingly.[100] It is also true, however, that the *travaux* do not support a narrow reading and that the purpose and object of the provision are paramount. While 'any party' in article 17(5) is perhaps not as explicit a reference to 'one or more third persons [requesting] to participate in arbitral proceedings already pending' as in article 4(2) of the Swiss Rules, there is no compelling reason to read article 17(5) restrictively. First, 'any party' is not as clear a reference to existing arbitrants as is Article 7(1) of the 2012 ICC Rules[101] or as is Article 22.1(viii) of the LCIA Rules.[102] Second, situations where a third person may seek to join in the proceedings were clearly contemplated by the Working Group, who noted that 'insofar as parties agreed to arbitration under Rules containing the proposed joinder provision, they would have consented to the voluntary joinder of a third party'.[103]

40. The Working Group also commented that the provision on joinder 'might need to remain as flexible as possible to accommodate the varying circumstances in which a third party might seek joinder'.[104] The narrow reading has no satisfactory answer to situations where a third party has a legitimate interest in intervening – where, for example, there is a multiparty project agreement with a limitation-of-liability clause, and C seeks to present its position on the clause in proceedings where this is a live issue between A and B, and C has a separate dispute with A on that same legal issue under the same contract. It is no satisfactory answer for C to be told that the A-B award will not be res judicata when it is clear that if A obtains a favourable award it will invoke it against C as persuasive authority. Another way to describe the right approach

---

[100] Caron & Caplan, *supra* fn 5, at 57; Peter Binder, *Analytical Commentary to the UNCITRAL Arbitration Rules*, paras 17-044–17-046 (Sweet & Maxwell 2013).

[101] Now Article 7(1) of the 2017 ICC Rules. *See* Fry, Greenberg & Mazza, *supra* fn 26, at para. 3-294. *See also* Yves Derains & Eric A. Schwartz, *A Guide to the ICC Rules of Arbitration*, 72 (2nd ed., Kluwer 2005) (commenting on the practice under the 1998 ICC Rules which did not allow an interested third party to seek to intervene if it was not named by the arbitrating parties).

[102] *See* Turner & Mohtashami, *supra* fn 57, at para. 6.44 (the authors define the power in Article 22.1(h) of the 1998 LCIA Rules as a power of the 'applicant party ... without the consent of the other original party or parties to the arbitration, [to] apply to join a third party "as a party" to the arbitration').

[103] UNCITRAL Report of 46th Session, 20 March 2007, UN Doc A/CN.9/619, para. 122 (in connection with UNCITRAL Working Paper for 46th Session, 6 December 2006, UN Doc A/CN.9/WG.II/WP.145/Add.1, article 15(4)(b): 'The arbitral tribunal may, on the application of any party, allow one or more third persons to be joined in the arbitration as a party and, provided such a third person and the applicant party have consented, make an award in respect of all parties involved in the arbitration').

[104] UNCITRAL Report of 46th Session, 20 March 2007, UN Doc A/CN.9/619, para. 124. *See also* UNCITRAL Report of 45th Session, 5 October 2006, UN Doc A/CN.9/614, para. 81 (referring to the situation 'where a party sought to be joined to the proceedings').

is to regard joinder requests by third parties as admissible in principle but to be scrutinized closely for legitimate interest, procedural efficiency, and from the perspective of prejudice to the existing parties (as discussed below).

(ii) Third person to be joined must be a party to the arbitration agreement

41. Article 17(5) of the 2010 Rules allows joinder only if the party sought to be joined or seeking to join is a party to the arbitration agreement between the original parties. Article 17(5) uses broad language[105] and leaves it to the applicable law to determine when a person may be considered 'a party to the arbitration agreement' (whether by being a signatory to the arbitration agreement or on any other possible basis).[106] Thus, by agreeing to an arbitration agreement which incorporates the 2010 Rules, the third person accepts the possibility of being joined, or joining, in proceedings between any other parties to the agreement. Similarly, the original arbitrants have also consented to such potential joinder.[107]

42. By contrast, initial drafts of article 17(5) also required the third party to consent in express terms to the joinder.[108] This was intended to reduce potential problems at the enforcement stage, in particular arguments that the award is invalid on the ground that the joined party had not been involved in the constitution of the arbitral tribunal. However, it was rightly countered that any person entering into an arbitration agreement under the 2010 Rules is deemed to have accepted that it might be joined after the arbitrators have been chosen.[109] The express consent requirement was finally rejected because it was thought to give the joining party an unjustified 'veto right'.[110] As noted at paragraph 44, however,

---

105 Contrast the practice that developed under the 1998 ICC Rules, requiring that the party to be joined had signed the arbitration agreement; *see* Derains & Schwartz, *supra* fn 101, at 70-71. Under Article 7 of the 2012 ICC Rules (which remains unchanged as Article 7 of the 2017 Rules), the test is more broadly whether the party to be joined is or has become bound, on any basis, by the arbitration agreement; *see* Fry, Greenberg & Mazza, *supra* fn 26, at para. 3-292.

106 *See* generally Nathalie Voser, 'Multi-party Disputes and Joinder of Third Parties' in Albert Jan van den Berg (ed.), *50 Years of the New York Convention: ICCA International Arbitration Conference*, 343 (Kluwer 2009); and Hanotiau, *supra* fn 81, at Chapter II.

107 UNCITRAL Report of 49th Session, 30 September 2008, UN Doc A/CN.9/665, para. 130 ('The agreement of parties to apply the UNCITRAL Arbitration Rules would imply their consent to the application of the joinder provision and to the possibility of the arbitral tribunal being constituted without their consent. Requiring additional agreement by the party to be joined would provide that party with a veto right, which might not be justified').

108 *See* UNCITRAL Working Paper for 49th Session, 6 August 2008, UN Doc A/CN.9/WG.II/WP.151, article 15(4) ('The arbitral tribunal may, on the application of any party, allow one or more third persons to be joined in the arbitration as a party provided such person is a party to the arbitration agreement *and has consented to be joined*' (emphasis added)).

109 *See* UNCITRAL Report of 49th Session, 30 September 2008, UN Doc A/CN.9/665, para. 130; and APRAG Report of 49th Session, 10 October 2008, para. 95.

110 UNCITRAL Report of 49th Session, 30 September 2008, UN Doc A/CN.9/665, para. 130. By contrast, Article 22.1(viii) of the LCIA Rules requires the applicant and the joining party expressly to consent to the joinder in writing. This writing requirement seems necessary

non-participation in the constitution of the tribunal is to be taken into account in determining a joinder request.

(iii) Process; no prejudice to any of the parties involved

43. Article 17(5) gives each party, including the party to be joined, an opportunity to state its views on the prospective joinder. The request may then be granted, 'unless the arbitral tribunal finds ... that joinder should not be permitted because of prejudice to any of [the] parties'. The formulation indicates the direction of the tribunal's inquiry in two respects: first, the test is a high one – 'prejudice' is clearly stronger than 'convenience'; secondly, the test is formulated as an exception – if the tribunal does have jurisdiction over the person to be joined, that person being a party to the arbitration agreement, the presumption under article 17(5) is that the tribunal should exercise its jurisdiction 'unless' this would prejudice any party.

44. The reference to 'prejudice' imports a number of possible issues, which chiefly fall within the overarching duties of the tribunal under article 17(1). An obvious type of prejudice, mostly from the perspective of the original parties in the arbitration, is the overall delay of the proceedings that is likely to result from the joinder of a new party.[111] Another type of prejudice, mostly from the perspective of the party to be joined, may be that the proceedings are too far advanced to allow that party to participate meaningfully, i.e. give it a 'reasonable opportunity of presenting its case' in terms of article 17(1). A further prejudice may be said to arise by depriving the person to be joined of the right to participate in the constitution of the arbitral tribunal. Such prejudice is conceivable at least in a *DUTCO*-like hypothesis, i.e. in a situation where the party to be joined has distinct and opposing interests from those of all existing arbitrants.[112] The Committee of the Whole also noted that failure to take part in the constitution of the tribunal could have a possible impact on the validity or the enforcement of the award, and should therefore be considered when assessing possible prejudice to a party, which includes prejudice to the enforceability of the award.[113] In practice, a tribunal would doubtless wish to have the third party take a position on whether it falls into the camp of one of the existing parties and on whether it accepts the appointments already made by the parties and/or the appointing authority. If the tribunal has been totally empanelled by the appointing authority under article 10(3), then the new joiner will be in a position of perfect equality with the existing parties in the constitution of the tribunal. Conversely, a party seeking to join in proceedings between other parties must be regarded as thereby waiving such objections.

---

since by virtue of article 22.1(viii) the joining party does not need to be a party to the arbitration agreement.

111 *See* APRAG Report of 49th Session, 10 October 2008, para. 96.

112 *See* discussion of article 10 of the 2010 Rules, *supra*.

113 *See* Report of the Commission on its 43rd Session, 21 June-9 July 2010, UN Doc A/65/17, para. 94; and UNCITRAL Summary Record of the 905th Meeting, 23 June 2010, UN Doc A/CN/.9/SR/905, XLI UNCITRAL Ybk 1235, 1235 paras 2-4.

45. Overall, the no-prejudice test requires the tribunal to weigh a number of factors in deciding whether to exercise its power under article 17(5). The provision is premised on an assumption that having all parties relevant to the dispute in a single process and bound by the same res judicata is conducive to overall fairness and efficiency, especially given the absence of a consolidation provision in the Rules. One must also consider that the tribunal will have the power to issue procedural directions consequential upon a joinder, ensuring that party equality and the right to be heard are given effect to in the new procedural context. A particularly helpful tool in that regard is the explicit power in article 17(5) to issue 'a single award or several awards', coupled with the general power to issue awards on separate issues under article 34(1). Thus, a tribunal may be able to address in a first award issues of priority interest to the initial arbitrants, leaving to a subsequent award issues which concern also the joined party. (It is clear, however, both from the wording of article 17(5) and from its very rationale that all awards must be issued as between *all* parties. If a party is to be joined after a partial award has been issued, e.g. on the validity of the contract or the applicable law to it, this may be only on the basis that this party expressly accepts the award. It is difficult to see on what other basis joinder would be allowed in such circumstances without causing prejudice to that party.)

46. One must also recognize that all initial parties have an unfettered right to name respondents to their claims (see article 4(2)(f)), from which it follows logically that a request by either of them to join a further party later must be specifically motivated.

G. CONSOLIDATION

47. As noted by the Working Group, the consolidation of separate but related arbitral proceedings increases efficiency 'in situations where several distinct disputes [arise] between the same parties under separate contracts (e.g. related contracts or a chain of contracts) containing separate arbitration clauses'.[114] By the same token, consolidation is useful 'to avoid a situation where a party [initiates] a separate arbitration in respect of a distinct claim under the same contract in order to gain a tactical advantage'.[115] More generally, consolidation reduces the possibility of inconsistent awards in relation to the same dispute.[116] While there

---

114 UNCITRAL Report of 46th Session, 20 March 2007, UN Doc A/CN.9/619, para. 117. But *see* Article 1126 of NAFTA, which permits consolidation even when the parties are not the same. For an application of Article 1126, *see Canfor Corporation v. United States of America and Tembec et al. v. United States of America and Terminal Forest Products Ltd v. United States of America* (UNCITRAL) Order of the Consolidation Tribunal, 7 September 2005, <www.italaw.com>.

115 UNCITRAL Report of 46th Session, 20 March 2007, UN Doc A/CN.9/619, para. 117.

116 The *causes célèbres* for consolidation are the contrasting outcomes in *CME Czech Republic BV v. The Czech Republic* (UNCITRAL) Partial Award, 13 September 2001, <www.italaw.com> and *Ronald Lauder v. The Czech Republic* (UNCITRAL) Final Award, 3 September 2001, <www.italaw.com>. The same dispute was arbitrated under two different bilateral investment treaties, but CME, a company controlled by Mr Lauder, was awarded USD 270

are obvious advantages to consolidating claims, the 2010 Rules, like the 1976 Rules, do not contain a provision on consolidation.[117]

48. There are several reasons for this.[118] For one, doubts were expressed as to the workability of a consolidation process in ad hoc proceedings. In prominent sets of rules expressly providing for consolidation (e.g., the ICC Rules, the LCIA Rules and the SCC Rules), it is the arbitral institution – and not the tribunal – that decides and supervises the consolidation.[119] A specific provision on consolidation also seemed less necessary in the light of other modifications to the Rules.[120] Thus the mechanism of joinder may prevent parallel proceedings in disputes involving the same arbitration agreement but a different party. For cases involving different contracts between the same parties, the innovations in articles 21 and 22 of the 2010 Rules may play a similarly remedial role. Under article 19 of the 1976 Rules, a counterclaim or set-off claim arising out of a different, but closely related, contract was inadmissible: only claims arising 'out of the same contract' were allowed. By contrast, article 21 of the 2010 Rules allows any counterclaim or set-off claim, 'provided that the arbitral tribunal has jurisdiction over it', and

---

million in damages, while Mr Lauder received no compensation despite a finding that there had been a breach of the relevant treaty. These conflicting awards have been decried as 'the ultimate fiasco in investment arbitration': August Reinisch, 'The Proliferation of International Dispute Settlement Mechanisms: The Threat of Fragmentation vs the Promise of a More Effective System? Some Reflections From the Perspective of Investment Arbitration' in Isabelle Buffard, James Crawford, Alain Pellet & Stephan Wittich (eds), *International Law Between Universalism and Fragmentation – Festschrift in Honour of Gerhard Hafner*, 116 (Brill 2008). It is of some interest perhaps that the respondent State in that case rejected a proposal for consolidation which, had it been accepted, would have seen it obtain an award of nil damages. The rejection seems to have been based on a theory, for which there seems to be no authority, that 'it [is] never conceivable to consolidate ... under bilateral investment treaties'; *see* Jeremy Carver, *How to Avoid Conflicting Awards: The Lauder and CME Cases*, 5(1) J World Inv & Trade 28 (2004). Contrast *Archer Daniels Midland Company and Tate & Lyle Ingredients Americas Inc v. The United Mexican States* (ICSID Case No. ARB (AF)/04/5) Order of the Consolidation Tribunal, 20 May 2005, < www.italaw.com > and *Corn Products International Inc v. United Mexican States* (ICSID Case No. ARB (AF)/04/1) Award, 18 August 2009, (unreported) (consolidation denied, on factors such as the competition between the claimants, the claimants' preference against consolidation, the issue of one of the claims being delayed, that distinct issues of state responsibility and quantum as between the two cases confirmed the need for separate proceedings, and that there was little risk of inconsistent awards because the claims appeared to be sufficiently different from each other).

117 Prior drafts of article 17 of the 2010 Rules contained a provision on consolidation; *see* UNCITRAL Working Paper for 46th Session, 6 December 2006, UN Doc A/CN.9/WG.II/WP.145/Add.1, article 15(4)(a).

118 *See* UNCITRAL Report of 46th Session, 20 March 2007, UN Doc A/CN.9/619, paras 117-120.

119 *See* Article 10 of the ICC Rules; Article 22.1(ix) and (x) of the LCIA Rules; and Article 15 of the SCC Rules. Cf. Article 1126(5) of NAFTA, which gives the Secretary-General of NAFTA the responsibility to establish the consolidation tribunal; Article 8 of the AAA International Arbitration Rules, which gives a 'consolidation arbitrator' appointed by the ICDR the responsibility to decide whether to consolidate.

120 *See* UNCITRAL Report of 45th Session, 5 October 2006, UN Doc A/CN.9/614, para. 80.

article 22 allows a counterclaim or set-off claim to be amended or supplemented unless it falls outside the tribunal's jurisdiction. This formulation is much broader and is not limited to the arbitration agreement on which the main claim was based.[121] As no parallel proceedings will have to be commenced in such cases, the need for a consolidation provision is weaker.

49. The upshot seems to be this: as consolidation under the Rules would require specific party consent in the form of an authorization to the tribunal to effect consolidation, it seems clear that in the absence of such an authorization in the law of the arbitration or in a specific agreement of the parties, article 17(1) would not be an adequate source of such an authorization.

H. CONFIDENTIALITY

50. There can be little doubt that it is within a tribunal's authority under article 17(1) to make orders preserving the confidentiality of aspects of the proceedings which are not already covered by more specific provisions (article 28(3) on 'in camera' hearings, and article 34(5) on conditions for disclosure of awards).[122] Such orders might therefore cover the existence of the arbitration, the pleadings of the parties, and evidential and other materials before the tribunal.[123] The question is in what circumstances a tribunal is to exercise its authority to make such orders.

51. It is clear that the Working Group did not intend to establish a general default rule either for or against confidentiality,[124] despite precedents in other sets of

---

[121] *See* UNCITRAL Report of 50th Session, 9 March 2009, UN Doc A/CN.9/669, paras 30-32. *See also* UNCITRAL Report of 46th Session, 20 March 2007, UN Doc A/CN.9/619, para. 160 (when revising article 19 of the 1976 Rules, the Working Group was fully aware of its connection with and impact on a potential provision on consolidation).

[122] *See Pope & Talbot Inc v. The Government of Canada* (UNCITRAL) Decision and Order No 5, 11 March 2002, < www.italaw.com > (in respect of article 15(1) of the 1976 Rules). *See also* James Crawford, 'Report on Confidentiality of Proceedings in International Arbitration' in *re Democracy Watch et al. v. Attorney General of Canada*, Ontario Superior Court of Justice, Court File No. 01CV211576 (2003), para. 91. Cf. Article 22(3) of the ICC Rules (expressly granting tribunals the power, upon the request of any party, to 'make orders concerning the confidentiality of the arbitration proceedings or of any other matters in connection with the arbitration and ... take measures for protecting trade secrets and confidential information').

[123] The rule that deliberations of the tribunal are secret is 'a fundamental principle which constitutes one of the mainsprings of arbitration': Matthieu de Boisséson, *Le Droit Français de l'Arbitrage National et International*, para. 343 (GLN-éditions 1990). This rule is also provided for in national laws; *see* Born, *supra* fn 80, at 2809-2810. *See also* Article 31, Note 2 of the Tribunal Rules of Procedure of the Iran-US Claims Tribunal ('deliberations shall be and remain secret').

[124] For discussion within the Working Group on whether to include a general provision regarding confidentiality, *see* UNCITRAL Report of 45th Session, 5 October 2006, UN Doc A/CN.9/614, paras 84-86; and UNCITRAL Report of 46th Session, 20 March 2007, UN Doc A/CN.9/619, paras 127-133. Note that the Working Group did not adopt the suggestion of including a footnote to the model arbitration clause drawing parties' attention to the possibility of adding a provision on confidentiality.

arbitration rules[125] and recent national court decisions declining to confirm a legal duty of confidentiality.[126] This was only in part due to the pro-transparency momentum in respect of investment-treaty arbitrations. There was simply no consensus that confidentiality is a necessary, or even presumed, attribute of the arbitral process. Equally importantly, in the light of lack of uniform treatment of confidentiality in the various domestic laws,[127] it would have been difficult to form consensus on default rules regarding the scope of (and exceptions to) a duty of confidentiality, its temporal scope, and the persons to whom it would extend other than the tribunal and the parties in the arbitration (such as witnesses and experts).[128] It was therefore concluded to retain the flexibility of the UNCITRAL Rules in accommodating evolving law and practice on confidentiality, and to leave the issue to be addressed by parties and tribunals on a case-by-case basis, taking into account the particulars of the case and its subject-matter.[129] Against this background, it may be difficult to suggest that the discrete provisions on confidentiality in the 2010 Rules are expressive of a general rule that ought to guide the tribunal's discretion under article 17(1).[130]

---

125 *See* Article 3 of the SCC Rules; and Article 30 of the LCIA Rules. For more detailed provisions on confidentiality, *see* Articles 75-78 of the WIPO Rules, tailored for intellectual-property disputes. Cf. Article 22(3) of the ICC Rules, which does not provide for a general rule, but instead adopts a tailor-made approach of leaving the issue for the parties or the tribunal to address.

126 *See* UNCITRAL Report of 46th Session, 20 March 2007, UN Doc A/CN.9/619, para. 128.

127 While some jurisdictions assume that an arbitration agreement gives rise to an implied duty of confidentiality subject to exceptions, other jurisdictions start from the contrary premise that there is no general duty but only specific duties of confidentiality regarding aspects of the proceedings; *see*, e.g., Caron & Caplan, *supra* fn 5, at 37; and Blackaby, Partasides, Redfern & Hunter, *supra* fn 42, at paras 2.161-2.176.

128 *See* generally Filip de Ly, Mark Friedman & Luca Radicati di Brozolo, *International Law Association International Commercial Arbitration Committee's Report and Recommendations on 'Confidentiality in International Commercial Arbitration'*, 28(3) Arb Int 355 (2012).

129 *See*, e.g., *The Louis Berger Group Inc/Black & Veatch Special Projects Corp Joint Venture et al. v. Symbion Power, LLC* (ICC Case No. 16383/VRO) (the tribunal ruled that the new French arbitration law of 2011 has no presumption of confidentiality. The new French law specifically provides for confidentiality in domestic arbitration, but remains silent as to confidentiality in international arbitration. In reaching this decision, the tribunal took into account the public interest in the dispute and lack of compelling reasons to keep the award confidential). Cf. UNCITRAL Report of 45th Session, 5 October 2006, UN Doc A/CN.9/614, para. 86 (confidentiality to be addressed on a case-by-case basis); and UNCITRAL Report of 46th Session, 20 March 2007, UN Doc A/CN.9/619, para. 131 (certain cases, e.g. intellectual-property disputes, may warrant confidentiality more than others).

130 It was certainly difficult to suggest so on the basis of articles 25(4) and 32(5) of the 1976 Rules (which are retained as articles 28(3) and 34(5) of the 2010 Rules, with the added clarification that the disclosure of awards may be required by 'legal duty, to protect or pursue a legal right or in relation to legal proceedings before a court or other competent authority'); *see* Caron & Caplan, *supra* fn 5, at 36-37. But cf. the position under English law, where courts have held that an implied duty of confidentiality is a natural extension of the privacy of the hearing, because disclosure of documents and evidence given at a hearing 'would be almost equivalent to opening the door of the arbitration room to that third party': *Hassneh Insurance Co of Israel v. Mew* [1993] 2 Lloyd's Rep 243, 247.

52. In the result, in each case it will be necessary for the tribunal to invite views from the parties and to consider, in this order: whether there is specific party agreement on confidentiality;[131] failing such agreement, whether under the law of the arbitration there is a generalized duty of confidentiality or, conversely, no such duty but only an obligation to protect the confidentiality of certain aspects of the process or particular materials (e.g. trade secrets); and, within the parameters of the law of the arbitration, whether in the circumstances of the case there are good reasons to preserve the confidentiality of specific materials or information. In that regard, the exceptions to confidentiality of awards stated in article 34(5) do seem to codify broader and generally accepted rules, and would be a useful source of guidance to tribunals.

[131] *See* UNCITRAL, *supra* fn 13, at paras 31-32 (suggesting that the tribunal discuss the issue of confidentiality with the parties and outline certain matters that an agreement on confidentiality might cover). In the 2016 Notes, para. 51 explicitly provides that 'should confidentiality be a concern ... the parties may agree on the desired confidentiality regime to the extent not precluded by the applicable arbitration law'.

Article 18
Place of arbitration

1976 Rules Article 16: Place of arbitration	2010 Rules Article 18: Place of arbitration
1. Unless the parties have agreed upon the place where the arbitration is to be held, such place shall be determined by the arbitral tribunal, having regard to the circumstances of the arbitration. 2. The arbitral tribunal may determine the locale of the arbitration within the country agreed upon by the parties. It may hear witnesses and hold meetings for consultation among its members at any place it deems appropriate, having regard to the circumstances of the arbitration. 3. The arbitral tribunal may meet at any place it deems appropriate for the inspection of goods, other property or documents. The parties shall be given sufficient notice to enable them to be present at such inspection. 4. The award shall be made at the place of arbitration.	1. If the parties have not previously agreed on the place of arbitration, the place of arbitration shall be determined by the arbitral tribunal having regard to the circumstances of the case. The award shall be deemed to have been made at the place of arbitration. 2. The arbitral tribunal may meet at any location it considers appropriate for deliberations. Unless otherwise agreed by the parties, the arbitral tribunal may also meet at any location it considers appropriate for any other purpose, including hearings.

1. The term 'place', in articles 16(1) and 16(4) of the 1976 Rules, refers to the legal seat of the arbitration, which, in the vast majority of cases, imports the 'law applicable to the arbitration' within the meaning of article 1(3), i.e. the *lex arbitri*.[1] Under article 16(1), the parties have a primary right to choose the place

[1] UNCITRAL Report of 45th Session, 5 October 2006, UN Doc A/CN.9/614, para. 88. *See also* Pieter Sanders, *Commentary on UNCITRAL Arbitration Rules*, II YCA 172, 194 (1977) (pointing out that the parties are free to choose an applicable arbitration law other than

of arbitration.[2] The arbitral tribunal has a subsidiary right (indeed, duty) to do so, 'unless' the parties have agreed on this matter. When the arbitral tribunal is called upon to determine the place of arbitration, it is to 'hav[e] regard to the circumstances of the arbitration'. Articles 16(2) and 16(3) of the 1976 Rules go on to address the practical (and legally significant) issue of hearings and other acts of the process at a 'locale' other than the place/seat of the arbitration.[3] Finally, article 16(4) wisely reiterated the juridical link between the award and the arbitral seat by providing that the award 'shall be *made* at the place of arbitration'. The wording raised the question whether the provision compelled the physical making of the award at the place of arbitration (i.e. the affixing of signatures), a notional such process (i.e. the inclusion of a mention that the award was 'done at' the place of arbitration), or a deeming rule.[4]

2. The 2010 revision did not bring wholesale change to the time-tested and sound 1976 text. Article 18 of the 2010 Rules is succinct in its restatement of article 16 of the 1976 Rules, with a number of subtle yet important textual revisions that clarify areas of potential ambiguity. Article 18(1) consolidates the content of articles 16(1) and 16(4), whereas article 18(2) consolidates the substance of articles 16(2) and 16(3). An important improvement is in article 18(1), to the effect that '[t]he award *shall be deemed to have been made* at the place of arbitration' (emphasis added).

A. PLACE OF ARBITRATION

1. 'Place' as the arbitral seat

3. Although the term 'juridical seat' arguably may have better denoted the legal connection that the arbitral seat entails,[5] the term 'place' is much more commonly

---

that of the place of arbitration, but that this freedom of choice is 'seldom used by the parties'). *See also* the discussion in section A, *infra*.

2 The Notes to the model arbitration clauses that accompany both the 1976 Rules and the 2010 Rules encourage the parties to consider designating the place of arbitration. Sanders, however, cautions that 'opinions vary as to the usefulness and advisability of designating the place of arbitration before the circumstances of a particular dispute referred to arbitration are known'; *see* Sanders, *supra* fn 1, at 179. Sanders additionally advises that parties choosing to designate the seat in advance take into account the advantage of having the place of arbitration coincide with the seat of the arbitral institution that may serve as appointing authority; *see ibid.*, at 193. Forty years later, these views are minoritarian and out of step with contemporary realities.

3 Sanders, *supra* fn 1, at 195, notes that the phrase 'having regard to the circumstances of the arbitration' was inserted at article 16(1) of the 1976 Rules 'to avoid the choice of attractive meeting places such as the Riviera or the Bahamas which have no relationship whatsoever with the arbitration or the domicile of the arbitrators'.

4 *See* UNCITRAL Report of 45th Session, 5 October 2006, UN Doc A/CN.9/614, para. 90; *see also* David D. Caron & Lee M. Caplan, *The UNCITRAL Arbitration Rules, A Commentary*, 92 (2nd ed., Oxford University Press 2013).

5 *See*, e.g., section 3 of the Arbitration Act 1996 (England & Wales) (the seat of the arbitration 'means the juridical seat of the arbitration').

used and it is maintained in the 2010 Rules[6] for consistency with the UNCITRAL Model Law.[7] As is the case under the 1976 Rules, the 'place of arbitration' under the 2010 Rules concerns the anchorage of an arbitration in a national legal system, as opposed to a geographical attachment.

4. It was clear already under the 1976 text that the place of arbitration is a jurisdiction, not a place on the map: article 16(2) refers to a 'country'. The place of arbitration has important legal consequences: in all but highly exceptional cases, the place of arbitration determines the law applicable to the arbitration (i.e. the *lex arbitri*),[8] and article 1(3) of the 2010 Rules clearly provides that mandatory provisions of the 'law applicable to the arbitration' prevail over the Rules in the event that a conflict arises. The place of arbitration also imports the jurisdiction, notably the supervisory jurisdiction, of the courts of that country as well as the application of the country's national arbitration law. Article 18(1) does not spell out the legal consequences that arise from the choice of a place of arbitration: these differ among legal systems, and the Rules are 'not the appropriate instrument to codify that matter'.[9]

5. The term 'place', rather than 'seat', has the advantage of indicating that a geographical designation by the parties (e.g. a city or province) should be interpreted as a choice of a country as the legal seat.[10] This accords with a line of authority in several legal systems whereby limited effect is given to a reference to the 'arbitration law' or 'procedural law' of a third country to the extent possible.[11] In one of the classic cases of this type, *Union of India v. McDonnell Douglas Corp*,[12] a contract provided that 'the seat of the arbitration proceedings shall be London' and that 'the arbitration shall be conducted in accordance with the procedures provided in the Indian Arbitration Act 1940'. The English court considered that

---

6 *See* UNCITRAL Report of 46th Session, 20 March 2007, UN Doc A/CN.9/619, para. 141 ('it was cautioned that the use of new terminology might lead to unintended consequences to existing contractual drafting practices that used different expressions, including the "place of arbitration", with the intention of referring to the legal seat of arbitration').

7 *See* Article 20(1) of the Model Law. Note that Article 20(2) of the Model Law also uses the word 'place' to refer to the geographical location of meetings and hearings. The use of the word 'location' in article 18(2) of the 2010 Rules thus reflects the Working Group's efforts 'to distinguish between the legal and physical places of arbitration'; *see* UNCITRAL Report of 46th Session, 20 March 2007, UN Doc A/CN.9/619, para. 138.

8 *See* UNCITRAL Report of 45th Session, 5 October 2006, UN Doc A/CN.9/614, para. 88.

9 UNCITRAL Report of 46th Session, 20 March 2007, UN Doc A/CN.9/619, para. 143.

10 *See*, e.g., *Shashoua and others v. Sharma* [2009] 2 All ER (Comm) 477 (where the English Commercial Court held that, in the absence of 'significant contrary indicia', an arbitration agreement under the 1998 ICC Rules which designated London as the 'venue' of the arbitration led to the 'inexorable conclusion ... that London is the juridical seat and English law the curial law').

11 For a discussion on the ability of parties to choose a foreign procedural law (other than the law of the seat) and the significance of such a choice, *see* generally Gary B. Born, *International Commercial Arbitration*, 1601-1603 (2nd ed., Kluwer 2014); and Nigel Blackaby, Constantine Partasides, Alan Redfern & Martin J. Hunter, *Redfern and Hunter on International Arbitration*, paras 3.65-3.68 (6th ed., Kluwer 2015).

12 *Union of India v. McDonnell Douglas Corp* [1993] 2 Lloyd's Rep 48.

'seating' the arbitration in one country while subjecting it to the procedural laws of another, although theoretically possible, would be 'highly unsatisfactory'.[13] It thus concluded that the proper construction of the agreement was this:

> The parties have chosen English law as the law to govern their arbitration proceedings, while contractually importing from the Indian Act those provisions of that Act which are concerned with the internal conduct of their arbitration and which are not inconsistent with the choice of English arbitral law.[14]

2. Determination of the arbitral seat

6. As was the case under the 1976 Rules, article 18(1) of the 2010 Rules gives the parties a primary right to choose the place of arbitration, with the arbitral tribunal retaining a subsidiary obligation to 'determine' the place of arbitration where the parties have not agreed. This ensures that national courts do not have to intervene to establish the seat. Article 18(1) improves on article 16(1) of the 1976 Rules by clarifying that, once the tribunal has made its determination as to the place of arbitration, it is no longer open to the parties to reach a different agreement on this point. Under article 16(1) of the 1976 Rules, a tribunal was to determine the place of arbitration '[u]nless the parties have agreed'; under article 18(1) of the 2010 Rules, the tribunal is seised of the matter 'if the parties have not *previously* agreed' (emphasis added), i.e. prior to the tribunal's determination.[15] There is a good, and apparently untested, question as to whether the parties may then agree on a different seat, or cause the tribunal to take a new article 18(1) decision adopting the seat agreed between them. Article 18(1) conceives of the tribunal's decision as a one-off event. It is arguable that through article 18(1) the parties have irrevocably delegated to the tribunal their right to elect the seat. And formal legal logic apart, there can be no split *lex arbitri* and concomitant supervisory court jurisdiction between various phases of a single arbitration.

7. Article 18(1) uses the word 'determine' not only because the tribunal must issue a decision in formal terms (see article 33(1)),[16] but also because the arbitrators must reach their choice through a process of judicial determination. Article 18(1) accordingly provides that the tribunal is to 'hav[e] regard to the circumstances of the arbitration'.[17] Practice under the 1976 Rules and the

---

13 *Ibid.*, at 51.

14 *Ibid.*

15 For a discussion of this view under the 1976 Rules, *see* Sanders, *supra* fn 1, at 193.

16 *See*, e.g., *Pope & Talbot Inc v. The Government of Canada* (UNCITRAL) Decision by Tribunal, 6 September 2000, <www.italaw.com> (signed '[o]n behalf of and after deliberation with the members of the Tribunal'); *United Parcel Service of America Inc v. Government of Canada* (UNCITRAL) Decision on Amici Curiae, 17 October 2001, <www.italaw.com> (signed 'for the Tribunal').

17 For general considerations when selecting the seat of the arbitration, *see* Born, *supra* fn 11, at 2054-2062. In the context of investment treaty arbitration, *see Vito G Gallo v. Government of Canada* (UNCITRAL) Decision on Place of Arbitration, 4 June 2008, <www.investorstatelawguide.com>, para. 15 ('In the Tribunal's opinion, the perfect place of

UNCITRAL Notes[18] indicates that the circumstances to be considered include notably:

(i) the neutrality of the seat;[19]
(ii) the national arbitration law that would apply;
(iii) any other legal consequences of the choice of place, such as any impact on the enforceability of the award as a matter of the New York Convention; and
(iv) practical considerations, including the availability of proper hearing rooms, competent interpreters, and (importantly) ability to rely on the local bar as may be needed.[20]

B. AWARD DEEMED TO HAVE BEEN MADE AT PLACE OF ARBITRATION

8. Article 16(4) of the 1976 Rules did not clarify whether the words 'shall be made at the place of arbitration' meant that the arbitrators were required physically to travel to the place of arbitration to sign (and thus 'make') the award. As Caron and Caplan acknowledge, the wording 'shall be made at the place' 'could have been construed to require the signing at the place of arbitration',[21] whereas the drafters' intention was rather to establish the legal framework within which the award was made.[22]

arbitration in an international investment arbitration is a jurisdiction which is neither that of the investor nor that of the host State, which has a high quality, independent judiciary, with experience in providing support to, and reviewing and setting aside decisions from international arbitral tribunals, and which has the capability of handling disputes in the language of the arbitration').

18 *See* UNCITRAL, *Notes on Organizing Arbitral Proceedings*, para. 29 (United Nations 2016) (listing, among the 'more prominent legal factors' influencing the selection of the place of arbitration: '(a) The suitability of the arbitration law at the place of arbitration; (b) The law, jurisprudence and practices at the place of arbitration regarding: (i) court intervention in the course of arbitral proceedings; (ii) the scope of judicial review or of grounds for setting aside an award; and (iii) any qualification requirements with respect to arbitrators and counsel representation; and (c) Whether the State where the arbitration takes place and hence where the arbitral award will be made is a Party to the … "New York Convention" … and/or to any other multilateral or bilateral treaty on enforcement of arbitral awards').

19 *See* Caron & Caplan, *supra* fn 4, at 88-89 (the authors suggest that 'the increased harmonization of national arbitration laws' has made the neutrality of the seat of the arbitration less of a concern).

20 *See ibid.*, at 81 et seq. *See also* Sanders, *supra* fn 1, at 193 (stating that the 'circumstances of the arbitration' referred to in article 16(1) of the 1976 Rules 'not only refers to practical considerations in connection with the arbitral proceedings, such as the least possible displacement of parties, witnesses and arbitrators, but also … to the legal consequences of the choice, and more especially to the recognition and enforcement of the award').

21 Caron & Caplan, *supra* fn 4, at 92.

22 *See* Sanders, *supra* fn 1, at 194 (stating that article 16(4) of the 1976 Rules makes clear 'the legal consequences of the place of arbitration … The law of the country where the arbitration takes place and where the award is made applies to the arbitral procedure and to the award unless the parties have chosen another applicable arbitration law').

9. Article 18(1) resolves this ambiguity with its new wording. The drafters derived the terminology from section 53 of the English Arbitration Act 1996,[23] which was adopted in response to the decision of the House of Lords in *Hiscox v. Outhwaite*.[24] In that case, it was held that the award had been 'made' in Paris (where it was physically signed by the presiding arbitrator, affixing his signature last), despite the fact that the arbitration had been conducted in London under English substantive and curial law.[25] Section 53 of the Act addresses this issue by providing that the award 'shall be treated' as made at the seat of arbitration. The tribunal cannot override the parties' choice of seat or its own prior choice of seat: such a choice, once made, is irrevocable. Indeed, despite the slight discrepancy between the wording of section 53 ('shall be treated as made') and article 18(1) of the 2010 Rules ('shall be deemed to have been made'), the language adopted in the 2010 Rules is consistent with that in other arbitration rules.[26]

10. The notion of 'award' in article 18 comprises of course all documents designated and issued as such by the tribunal, including partial and interim awards.

C. VENUE OF ARBITRATION

11. Article 18(2) of the 2010 Rules concerns the physical location for various acts/processes in the arbitration, providing that the arbitral tribunal 'may meet at any location it considers appropriate for deliberations'. Unless otherwise agreed by the parties, this extends to any location that the arbitral tribunal considers appropriate 'for any other purpose, including hearings'. In contrast with article 16(2) of the 1976 Rules, there is no longer a requirement that hearings be held 'within the country agreed upon by the parties'.[27]

---

[23] Section 53 of the Arbitration Act 1996 (England & Wales) reads: 'Unless otherwise agreed by the parties, where the seat of the arbitration is England and Wales or Northern Ireland, any award in the proceedings shall be treated as made there, regardless of where it was signed, dispatched or delivered to any of the parties'.

[24] *Hiscox v. Outhwaite* [1992] 1 AC 562.

[25] This precise situation had been imagined by F. A. Mann some years previously. *See* Francis A. Mann, *Where is an award 'made'?*, 1(1) Arb Int 107, 108 (1985) ('If a place other than the seat is held to be decisive, unacceptable consequences could ensue. An arbitration which in every possible sense is an English one could suddenly become foreign, merely because the arbitrator has gone to Paris and signed and, perhaps, dispatched the award there. ... The award, it is submitted, is no more than a part, the final and vital part of a procedure which must have a territorial, central point or seat. It would be very odd if, possibly without the knowledge of the parties or even unwittingly, the arbitrators had the power to sever that part from the preceding procedure and thus give a totally different character to the whole').

[26] *See*, e.g., Article 32(3) of the ICC Rules; Article 25(3) of the SCC Rules; Article 16.3 of the LCIA Rules; and Article 16(4) of the Swiss Rules.

[27] Article 16(2) of the 1976 Rules stated that '[t]he arbitral tribunal may determine the locale of the arbitration *within the country agreed upon by the parties*' (emphasis added). As one commentator on the 1976 Rules noted, '[t]he motivation for this appears to be that the place where the award is made is an element in determining the applicability of the New York Convention, and thus may have an important role in relation to recognition and

12. There is authority for the proposition that the choice of place raises no presumption in favour of the location of the hearings.[28] The tribunal in *Salini v. Ethiopia*[29] considered that its decision to hold the hearing in Paris rather than in Addis Ababa (the seat of the arbitration) was reasonable, given that the majority of the participants in the hearing were based in Europe, and that the terms of reference specifically empowered it to conduct hearings 'at any other appropriate place', which would have no effect on Addis Ababa as the seat. The tribunal was of the opinion that the Ethiopian Supreme Court would reach the same decision, and continued the proceedings despite a temporary injunction issued by an Ethiopian court, pending an appeal by the respondent challenging the arbitrators' decision to hold the hearing in Paris.[30] In *Karaha Bodas*,[31] both US and Hong Kong courts also considered that statements in the contract that the 'site of the arbitration shall be Geneva' were intended to establish the seat in Switzerland, as opposed to the venue of the hearing, and that the hearings could therefore be held in Paris.

13. The better view is that tribunals should not be too astute in deciding that various acts, such as hearings, should be outside the agreed seat. That the parties agreed on a seat or (as noted above) the tribunal elected one, connotes an assessment or expectation that the seat has 'appropriate' venues.[32] It is certainly the case that application of article 18(2) is justified where there are compelling reasons for holding hearings in a place other than the seat. This is well-illustrated by the facts of the *Himpurna* arbitration,[33] in which the courts of Jakarta (the seat of the arbitration) had issued an injunction enjoining the arbitral proceedings, with breach of the injunction punishable by a fine of US$1 million per day. The

enforcement of the award'; *see* Alan Redfern, *Law and Practice of International Commercial Arbitration*, para. 6-24 (Sweet & Maxwell 2004).

28 *See* Georgios Petrochilos, *Procedural Law in International Arbitration*, para. 3.30 (Oxford University Press 2004) (modern international arbitration law is premised on the 'fundamental proposition' that 'because a choice of seat operates as a choice of a legal system to regulate an arbitration, it is entirely without prejudice to the actual locale where various procedural acts take place and an award is made').

29 *Salini Costruttori SPA v. The Federal Democratic Republic of Ethiopia, Addis Ababa Water and Sewerage Authority* (ICC Case No 10623/AER/ACS) Award regarding the Suspension of Proceedings and Jurisdiction, 7 December 2001, < www.italaw.com >.

30 *See ibid.*, at para. 69 (respondent challenged on the ground that, by choosing to hold the hearing in Paris rather than in Addis Ababa, 'the Tribunal had "improperly" and "abusively" had regard to its own convenience and to the convenience of the Claimant and its witnesses, and had disregarded the convenience of the Respondent and its witnesses').

31 *Karaha Bodas Company LLC v. Perusahaan Pertambangan Minyak Dan Gas Bumi Negara*, 18(4) Mealey's Int Arb Rep B-1 (2003) 17 (SD Texas); *Karaha Bodas Company LLC v. Perusahaan Pertambangan Minyak Dan Gas Bumi Negara*, 18(6) Mealey's Int Arb Rep C-1 (2003) (5th Cir.); and *Karaha Bodas Company LLC v. Perusahaan Pertambangan Minyak Dan Gas Bumi Negara (Pertamina)*, Hong Kong SAR CFI, 27 March 2003.

32 *See* Caron & Caplan, *supra* fn 4, at 96 ('very loose ties between the legal place of arbitration and the actual proceedings may, depending on the nature of the domestic laws involved, have negative repercussions').

33 *Himpurna California Energy Ltd (Bermuda) v. The Republic of Indonesia* (UNCITRAL) Interim Award, 26 September 1999, XXV YCA 111, 142 (2000), para. 73 et seq.

tribunal elected to hold the hearing at The Hague, while Jakarta remained the seat of the arbitration.[34] The test is however one of 'appropriateness', which is a lower threshold, and primarily directed to practicality and efficiency: the duty under the second sentence of article 17(1) applies in full.

Determination of location

14. Under article 18(2), the tribunal's determination of the location of the arbitration must be 'appropriate'. This standard requires that the arbitral tribunal take all relevant circumstances into account (as was expressly provided under article 16(2) of the 1976 Rules), including in particular cost- and time-savings. The tribunal must also comply with its duty to ensure efficient proceedings under article 17(1) of the 2010 Rules. Thus a venue that may be appropriate for deliberations (because convenient for the tribunal) may be inappropriate for hearings (because inconvenient for other participants). In any event, again in the light of article 17(1), tribunals should do well to explore in full electronic means of communication that 'do not require ... physical presence' (article 28(4)) for procedural conferences, short hearings, and the like. The UNCITRAL Notes recognize that 'it may be more expeditious or convenient for the parties and the arbitral tribunal to hold hearings ... remotely via technological means of communication'.[35]

15. Where hearings are to be held in the country in which the arbitration is seated, the UNCITRAL Notes provide that the tribunal should consider inter alia 'the convenience of the location' for both the parties and the arbitrators; the 'availability and cost of support services' (for example, meeting rooms and the venue of the hearing); the 'location of the subject matter in dispute and proximity of any evidence';[36] and 'qualification restrictions with respect to counsel representation'.[37] These last are rare but a very important consideration. If the agreed seat is, say, Nigeria, where only locally-qualified 'legal practitioners' may appear as counsel (with foreign lawyers assisting them) at hearings, one can see why a non-Nigerian party would have a sound basis to suggest that hearings take place elsewhere, so its non-Nigerian counsel may also plead.

16. Where the tribunal determines that hearings are to be held outside the country of the seat, the tribunal should additionally consider whether this 'may create difficulties at the stage of judicial review, setting aside or enforcement of the arbitral award'.[38]

---

[34] Jan Paulsson & Georgios Petrochilos, *Revision of the UNCITRAL Rules* (September 2006), para. 153 and fn 169, <www.uncitral.org>, also making reference to *PT Garuda Indonesia v. Birgen Air* [2002] 1 SLR 393 (CA) (where the Singapore Court of Appeal held that the award was made in Jakarta, the agreed seat of the arbitration, despite the hearings having been held in Singapore, as a convenient location to avoid unrest in Jakarta).

[35] UNCITRAL, *supra* fn 18, at para. 31.

[36] *See* Caron & Caplan, *supra* fn 4, at 90-91 (suggesting that 'evidence' may comprise witness testimony or, in construction cases, site visits).

[37] *See* UNCITRAL, *supra* fn 18, at para. 30.

[38] *Ibid.*, at para. 31.

Article 19
Language

1976 Rules Article 17: Language	2010 Rules Article 19: Language
1. Subject to an agreement by the parties, the arbitral tribunal shall, promptly after its appointment, determine the language or languages to be used in the proceedings. This determination shall apply to the statement of claim, the statement of defence, and any further written statements and, if oral hearings take place, to the language or languages to be used in such hearings.	1. Subject to an agreement by the parties, the arbitral tribunal shall, promptly after its appointment, determine the language or languages to be used in the proceedings. This determination shall apply to the statement of claim, the statement of defence, and any further written statements and, if oral hearings take place, to the language or languages to be used in such hearings.
2. The arbitral tribunal may order that any documents annexed to the statement of claim or statement of defence, and any supplementary documents or exhibits submitted in the course of the proceedings, delivered in their original language, shall be accompanied by a translation into the language or languages agreed upon by the parties or determined by the arbitral tribunal.	2. The arbitral tribunal may order that any documents annexed to the statement of claim or statement of defence, and any supplementary documents or exhibits submitted in the course of the proceedings, delivered in their original language, shall be accompanied by a translation into the language or languages agreed upon by the parties or determined by the arbitral tribunal.

1. The provision on language in the 2010 Rules is identical to the corresponding provision of the 1976 Rules, as the latter did not give rise to any practical difficulties. Moreover, the ability to have more than one procedural languages has proved important in practice;[1] the text of the 1976 Rules was rather innovative in

[1] For example, in the case of the Iran-US Claims Tribunal, both English and Persian were used because of the political consequences of choosing one language over the other, and the impracticalities of choosing a neutral language; *see* David D. Caron & Lee M. Caplan, *The UNCITRAL Arbitration Rules, A Commentary*, 378 (2nd ed., Oxford University Press 2013); *see also* Stewart A. Baker & Mark D. Davis, *The UNCITRAL Arbitration Rules in Practice – The*

this respect. Although in general the use of a single language may be preferable in terms of simplicity, the Working Group recognised the necessity of having multiple languages in arbitrations involving parties from different countries (and/or with a bilingual evidential record),[2] and rejected a proposal to delete the reference to 'languages' in the plural.[3] However, in the Note to the model arbitration clause contained in the Annex to the 2010 Rules, the drafters replaced the reference to 'language(s)' with 'language', as they did not want to appear to encourage parties to choose multiple languages, which can unnecessarily complicate the arbitral proceedings.[4]

A. ARTICLE 19(1)

2. The language(s) of the arbitration should be established from the outset, as this affects the choice of arbitrators and counsel; the effectiveness of testimony by and the cross-examination of witnesses; and the cost and efficiency of the proceedings more generally.[5] Article 19(1) provides that the parties may choose the language(s) to be used in the proceedings: if they fail to do so, the tribunal will decide this 'promptly after its appointment'. Although the Rules do not expressly require the tribunal to consult with the parties in making this determination, it is clearly 'consistent with the spirit of arbitration and the principle of party autonomy' that it does so.[6]

Experience of the Iran-United States Claims Tribunal, 80 and the references (Kluwer 1992) (noting that 'virtually all pleadings were submitted in two versions, English and Persian, and all hearings and other oral proceedings were translated into both languages'); and Jacomijn J. van Hof, *Commentary on the UNCITRAL Arbitration Rules, The Application by the Iran-U.S. Claims Tribunal*, 113 (Kluwer 1991).

2 *See* UNCITRAL Working Paper for 49th Session, 6 August 2008, UN Doc A/CN.9/WG.II/WP.151, para. 39. For examples of arbitrations employing the use of two procedural languages, *see Gami Investments Inc v. The Government of the United Mexican States* (UNCITRAL) Procedural Order No. 1, 31 January 2003, < www.ouplaw.com >, paras 10.1-10.4 (applying the 1976 Rules, the tribunal ordered that the languages of the arbitration be English and Spanish, with translations of written submissions to be provided by the parties 'as they see fit'); and *Lone Pine Resources Inc v. The Government of Canada* (ICSID Case No. UNCT/15/2) Procedural Order on Two Disputed Issues, 6 February 2015, < www.italaw.com >, para. 18 (applying the 2010 Rules, the tribunal considered the central role of Québec as the location of the alleged investment, and ordered that English and French be the languages of the arbitration).

3 *See* UNCITRAL Report of 46th Session, 20 March 2007, UN Doc A/CN.9/619, para. 145 (the Working Group agreed to delete the reference to 'languages' on the basis that parties are free to agree as to whether more than one language is required in the proceedings); and UNCITRAL Report of 49th Session, 30 September 2008, UN Doc A/CN.9/665, paras 140-141 (the Working Group reinstated the reference to 'languages', concerned that deletion 'could have the negative consequence of depriving the arbitral tribunal of the possibility to have more than one language').

4 James E. Castello, 'UNCITRAL Arbitration Rules, Section III, Article 19' in Loukas A. Mistelis (ed), *Concise International Arbitration*, 219 (2nd ed., Kluwer 2015).

5 *See* Gary B. Born, *International Commercial Arbitration*, 2230 (2nd ed., Kluwer 2014).

6 Caron & Caplan, *supra* fn 1, at 377.

3. Although there is some authority for the suggestion that, by failing to come to a prior agreement, the parties have waived their right to choose the language and left this issue to be decided by the tribunal,[7] the tribunal should nevertheless base its decision on any expressed preference of the parties.[8] In fact, a proposed change, suggested in the first draft of the 2010 Rules, was to amend article 17(1) of the 1976 Rules expressly to require the tribunal to consult the parties before determining the language(s) of the arbitration.[9] However, the Working Group found that such an express requirement was unnecessary, considering that 'the Rules did not affect the advisability of consulting the parties before the arbitral tribunal took such or any other procedural decision'.[10] In fact, a similar suggestion had been made during the drafting process of the 1976 Rules, but was deemed unnecessary because 'any competent arbitrator would invariably consult with the Parties before determining the language to be used'.[11]

4. With respect to the factors that should be taken into account when determining the language(s) of the proceedings, tribunals should consider factors similar to those that the parties themselves would have considered. An important consideration is the language previously used in the commercial agreement(s) or dealings between the parties, followed by the language(s) of the parties, arbitrators, counsel, and other participants, such as witnesses.[12] During the discussions on the Preliminary Draft of the 1976 Rules, one proposal was that, where the parties had not chosen a language, it should be implied that the language of the contract or the language of the correspondence between the parties should apply to the arbitral proceedings (as was standard practice at the

7 *See* Jacomijn J. van Hof, *supra* fn 1, at 113.

8 *See* Caron & Caplan, *supra* fn 1, at 377, fn 8.

9 *See* UNCITRAL Working Paper for 45th Session, 20 July 2006, UN Doc A/CN.9/WG.II/WP.143/Add.1, para. 3. *See also* provisions to this effect in Article 17.4 of the LCIA Rules; Article 26(1) of the SCC Rules; Article 39(a) of the WIPO Rules.

10 UNCITRAL Report of 45th Session, 5 October 2006, UN Doc A/CN.9/614, para. 91.

11 UNCITRAL Summary Record of the 6th Meeting, 19 April 1976, UN Doc A/CN.9/9/C.2/SR.6, para. 91, Mr Guest (United Kingdom).

12 *See* Caron & Caplan, *supra* fn 1, at 378. Article 20 of the ICC Rules may provide a helpful comparison; in the absence of the parties' agreement, it gives the tribunal discretion to determine the applicable language, 'due regard being given to all relevant circumstances, including the language of the contract'. The ICC Secretariat suggests that tribunals may identify the language which the parties would have expected to govern when they made the arbitration agreement, considering the language of the arbitration agreement as a strong indication, alongside the language of the communications between the parties. Another approach, which the Secretariat suggests may be used in combination with the first, is to consider the language of the arbitrators, counsel, likely witnesses and documentary evidence; *see* Jason Fry, Simon Greenberg & Francesca Mazza, *The Secretariat's Guide to ICC Arbitration*, paras 3-735-3-739 (ICC 2012). *See also* UNCITRAL, *Notes on Organizing Arbitral Proceedings*, para. 20 (United Nations 2016) (stating that 'common criteria' for determining the language of the arbitration 'are the primary language of the contract(s) or other legal instruments under which the dispute arose, and the language commonly used by the parties in their communication').

time). This suggestion was not accepted due to concerns that the rule was too rigid and may have given rise to difficulties in practice.[13]

B. ARTICLE 19(2)

5. Having determined the applicable language(s), the next issue for the tribunal is whether and to what extent to order translations of annexes, exhibits, and other supplementary documents. On the face of article 19(2), the following implications are immediately apparent:

   (i) On grounds of equality and efficiency (general principles under article 17(1) of the 2010 Rules), translations, usually limited to relevant extracts, must in the first instance be made by the party putting forward the relevant materials.

   (ii) The tribunal's power to order translations applies not only to documents annexed to the statement of claim or statement of defence (as article 19(2) provides), but also to 'any further written statements' required from or presented by the parties under article 24 (to which article 19(1) refers). It also applies to witness and expert evidence presented during the 'oral hearings' (to which article 19(1) refers).

   (iii) 'Exhibits' includes all materials annexed to the written pleadings, witness statements, and expert reports. 'Supplementary documents' is a catch-all term intended to encompass any documents that may be exchanged between the parties and submitted to the arbitral tribunal.

6. The tribunal's decision as to whether or not to order a translation will depend on the nature of the document in question. The Iran-US Claims Tribunal issued 'Guidelines for the Translation of Documentary Evidence'.[14] These guidelines list the following as documents requiring translation: written evidence prepared or submitted for the purpose of the arbitration; documents which are new to the other party (such as internal reports and correspondence between a party and a third party); and correspondence between the parties which creates or alters contractual rights or obligations or which is relied on as evidence. The guidelines also list documents which do not require translation, such as correspondence between the parties and contemporaneous materials not requiring translation at the time of their creation (e.g. invoices, blueprints and technical reports).[15] In considering this list, however, one should bear in mind the unique features of the Iran-US Claims Tribunal, which is composed of arbitrators versed in English and at least one member in each formation who is versed in Persian, and which

---

[13] Report of 8th Session, 1-17 April 1975, UN Doc A/10017, Annex I, VI UNCITRAL Ybk 9, 36, paras 111-113. Cf. Article 18 of the AAA International Arbitration Rules (providing that '[i]f the parties have not agreed otherwise, the language(s) of the arbitration shall be the language(s) of the documents containing the arbitration agreement'. Importantly, however, Article 18 also includes the caveat that this is 'subject to the power of the arbitral tribunal to determine otherwise').

[14] Reproduced in, e.g., *Fluor Corporation v. Iran*, Case No. 810, Chamber One, Order of 16 February 1987. *See also* Caron & Caplan, *supra* fn 1, at 388-389.

[15] *See* Caron & Caplan, *supra* fn 1, at 388-389.

also includes a standing Secretariat that may assist with translations. As such features are not present in most ad hoc tribunal formations, the list of materials reasonably requiring translation will often be longer.

7. In addition, the tribunal has discretion to determine the consequences of a party's failure to produce a document in the required language. A party may be allowed to correct this failure without repercussions, to the extent that correction 'is possible without undue prejudice to the other party or the overall proceedings'.[16] Alternatively, the other party may prepare a translation and seek to recover the cost under article 40(2)(e). The maximum sanction one can conceive is for the non-translated document to be ignored by the tribunal. A persistent and systematic failure to present translations may also be a consideration in the allocation of costs pursuant to article 42(2).

8. Article 19(2) does not address the issue of contested translations on which the tribunal needs to make a decision, or defective documents that need to be corrected. These are issues of detailed regulation, normally dealt with in procedural directions (typically agreed by the parties) early on, issued under article 17(1). It is not infrequently the case that the precise meaning of a statutory, treaty, or contractual term will be central to the dispute and closely debated.

16 Castello, *supra* fn 4, at 220.

Article 20
Statement of claim

1976 Rules

Article 18: Statement of claim

1. Unless the statement of claim was contained in the notice of arbitration, within a period of time to be determined by the arbitral tribunal, the claimant shall communicate his statement of claim in writing to the respondent and to each of the arbitrators. A copy of the contract, and of the arbitration agreement if not contained in the contract, shall be annexed thereto.

2. The statement of claim shall include the following particulars:

(a) The names and addresses of the parties;

(b) A statement of the facts supporting the claim;

(c) The points at issue;

(d) The relief or remedy sought.

The claimant may annex to his statement of claim all documents he deems relevant or may add a reference to the documents or other evidence he will submit.

2010 Rules

Article 20: Statement of claim

1. The claimant shall communicate its statement of claim in writing to the respondent and to each of the arbitrators within a period of time to be determined by the arbitral tribunal. The claimant may elect to treat its notice of arbitration referred to in article 3 as a statement of claim, provided that the notice of arbitration also complies with the requirements of paragraphs 2 to 4 of this article.

2. The statement of claim shall include the following particulars:

(a) The names and contact details of the parties;

(b) A statement of the facts supporting the claim;

(c) The points at issue;

(d) The relief or remedy sought;

(e) The legal grounds or arguments supporting the claim.

3. A copy of any contract or other legal instrument out of or in relation to which the dispute arises and of the arbitration agreement shall be annexed to the statement of claim.

4. The statement of claim should, as far as possible, be accompanied by all documents and other evidence relied upon by the claimant, or contain references to them.

1. The vast majority of cases begin with an exchange of comprehensive written submissions, typically sequential but not rarely simultaneous.[1] These are essential to determining the issues between the parties and defining their scope. As such, written submissions are generally given 'primary emphasis' throughout the arbitral proceedings.[2] In this context, the statement of claim is the first opportunity for the claimant to set out in detail full particulars of its case.

2. The developments below address the distinction between the notice of arbitration and the statement of claim, and the content requirements of the statement of claim (as well as the evidence required in support of it), with a focus on the changes brought about by the 2010 Rules. In general, the amendments made during the revision process have clarified the scope of article 20 of the 2010 Rules.[3] Other modifications reflect the fact that the respondent may now submit a response to the notice of arbitration under the 2010 Rules.

A. COMMUNICATION OF THE STATEMENT OF CLAIM: ARTICLE 20(1)

3. Under the 1976 Rules, the statement of claim was the next pleading submitted after the notice of arbitration,[4] unless it was 'contained' in the notice of arbitration (see article 18(1) of the 1976 Rules). Under the 2010 Rules, the order of written pleadings has changed. The statement of claim now follows the respondent's response to the notice of arbitration under article 4 of the 2010 Rules, unless the claimant 'elect[s] to treat' the notice of arbitration as its statement of claim. Thus, as under the 1976 Rules, the claimant may still choose to treat the notice of arbitration as its statement of claim,[5] but under article 20(1) of the 2010 Rules it may now do so only after having received the respondent's response to the notice of arbitration.[6]

---

1 *See* Nigel Blackaby, Constantine Partasides, Alan Redfern & Martin J. Hunter, *Redfern and Hunter on International Arbitration*, para. 6.65 (6th ed., Kluwer 2015).

2 David D. Caron & Lee M. Caplan, *The UNCITRAL Arbitration Rules, A Commentary*, 409-410 (2nd ed., Oxford University Press 2013).

3 *See* UNCITRAL Working Paper for 52nd Session, 10 December 2009, UN Doc A/CN.9/WG.II/WP.157/Add.1, paras 11-13.

4 *See*, e.g., *Forminster Enterprises Limited (Cyprus) v. Czech Republic* (UNCITRAL) Final Award, 15 December 2014, <www.italaw.com>, para. 65 ('In the UNCITRAL Rules (1976) there is no opportunity for a respondent to answer a claimant's Notice of Arbitration until after the arbitral tribunal has been constituted and the claimant has filed its statement of claim. This was changed in the latest version of the UNCITRAL Rules (2010) in which a respondent is entitled to file a Response to the notice of arbitration (Art. 4)').

5 *See* discussion of article 3 of the 2010 Rules, *supra*. *See also*, for a recent example of a claimant designating the notice of arbitration as its statement of claim under the 1976 Rules, *Eli Lilly and Company v. The Government of Canada* (UNCITRAL) (ICSID Case No. UNCT/14/2) Claimant's Letter Designating the Notice of Arbitration as the Statement of Claim, 14 May 2014, <www.italaw.com>.

6 *See* UNCITRAL Report of 49th Session, 30 September 2008, UN Doc A/CN.9/665, para. 36; and UNCITRAL Report of 50th Session, 9 March 2009, UN Doc A/CN.9/669, para. 19.

4. The rationale is that an informed decision to treat the notice of arbitration as the statement of claim may be made only after the claimant has become aware of the contents of the response to the notice of arbitration. Only at this point can the claimant make an informed decision that there is 'truly nothing further that it wishes to include' in the statement of claim.[7] The Working Group further identified the separation of the notice of arbitration and the statement of claim as beneficial insofar as it provided for 'the right level of procedural flexibility'.[8]

5. Although it is clear that the claimant may choose to treat the notice of arbitration as the statement of claim at any time after the response, article 20 does not set out a time-limit for this decision. Logic dictates that it could be made up to the date on which the statement of claim is due. Indeed, there is no apparent prejudice to the respondent from the claimant's announcing this decision at the last minute. Nevertheless, if the claimant elects to treat the notice of arbitration as its statement of claim at an earlier point in time, this should, in principle, bring forward the milestones in the procedural schedule.[9] It may therefore be more efficient for the claimant to announce any such election prior to the fixing of the procedural schedule under article 17(2). Note that the claimant's choice to treat the notice of dispute as the statement of claim does not oblige the respondent to do the same; see article 21(1).

6. In highly exceptional cases, it may be more efficient for the respondent to submit its first-round memorial first. Such an exceptional case is where a party resorts to arbitration seeking a negative declaration (e.g. of no liability or that the other side has no entitlement to certain alleged rights). The named respondent certainly has an affirmative case on the issues and, had it commenced proceedings first, it would have articulated it in a statement of claim. It may be more natural for the named respondent, then, to go first in framing the dispute, rather than for the named claimant to present a wholly negative case of no liability, etc.

7. If the claimant fails to submit a statement of claim within the time-limit directed by the tribunal, article 30(1), which provides for the termination of the arbitral proceedings, will apply, unless sufficient cause for such failure is shown.[10] However, it is accepted in scholarship and in practice that a claimant 'who has submitted a defective statement of claim may cure the shortcomings by submitting supplementary information',[11] through submissions authorized under article 24.

---

7 James E. Castello, 'UNCITRAL Arbitration Rules, Section III, Article 20' in Loukas A. Mistelis (ed), *Concise International Arbitration*, 220 (2nd ed., Kluwer 2015).

8 UNCITRAL Report of 45th Session, 5 October 2006, UN Doc A/CN.9/614, para. 49.

9 *See also* Michael McIlwrath & John Savage, *International Arbitration and Mediation: A Practical Guide*, para. 5-015 (Kluwer 2010) (the authors note that, in addition to leading to time savings, combining the notice of arbitration and statement of claim 'may also put the respondent under pressure, as it may have to file its defence sooner than would have been the case had the claimant submitted a separate Statement of Claim').

10 Castello, *supra* fn 7, at 221; Caron & Caplan, *supra* fn 2, at 414-415. *See also* discussion of article 30 of the 2010 Rules, *infra*.

11 Caron & Caplan, *supra* fn 2, at 414. Note that this is also consistent with article 17(1) of the 2010 Rules.

B. CONTENTS OF THE STATEMENT OF CLAIM

8. As was the case under article 18(2) of the 1976 Rules, article 20(2) of the 2010 Rules lays down the necessary contents in the statement of claim. The provision is framed in mandatory terms ('shall include') but may also be characterized as a statement of good practice in guiding the parties as to a simple but logical structure that is easy for a tribunal to follow. Article 20(2)(e) is a new addition, providing that the statement of claim shall include 'the legal grounds or arguments supporting the claim'. Under the practice of the 1976 Rules, the requirement in article 18(2)(c) that the statement of claim include 'the points at issue' presupposed 'explication of the legal arguments', but was not taken to 'necessitate a final elaboration of the legal theories supporting the claim'.[12] The position is similar under the 2010 Rules: it is not strictly required that the claimant set out its definitive, 'fully elaborated' arguments.[13] Nevertheless, the Working Group through the revision process sought to 'encourage the parties to substantiate their claims from a legal point of view',[14] and felt that there was a need expressly to require this through article 20(2)(e). The addition was considered particularly necessary in the light of the divergence in international legal practice regarding the necessary content for the statement of claim.[15] From the perspective of efficiency, as well, it is highly desirable that the statement of claim set out a fully factual and legal case, leaving for subsequent written pleadings (article 24) or the hearing (article 28) responsive arguments. In this way, the parties join cases early on and surprises are avoided, which is helpful to the process. Directions to that effect may usefully be made, and are increasingly often made in practice, in the first procedural order.

9. A necessary component of the statement of claim is a defence to a counterclaim or a claim in set-off that has been set forth in the respondent's response (article 4(2)(e)). The Rules conceive that this is a procedural duty, attracting default if the claimant has failed to observe it; see article 30(1)(b). By contrast, the Rules allow a jurisdictional objection to a counterclaim or set-off claim to be made at the latest in a pleading called the 'reply'; see article 23(2). That is one of the pleadings generically envisaged as possible 'further written statements' in article 24. It is strongly arguable however that the reply time-limit applies only

---

12 David D. Caron, Lee M. Caplan & Matti Pellonpää, *The UNCITRAL Arbitration Rules, A Commentary*, 396 (Oxford University Press 2006).

13 *See* Caron & Caplan, *supra* fn 2, at 412-413; and, referring to the 1976 Rules, Nigel Blackaby, Constantine Partasides, Alan Redfern & Martin J. Hunter, *Redfern and Hunter on International Arbitration*, para. 6.61 (5th ed., Kluwer 2009).

14 UNCITRAL Report of 46th Session, 20 March 2007, UN Doc A/CN.9/619, para. 149.

15 *See* UNCITRAL Report of 46th Session, 20 March 2007, UN Doc A/CN.9/619, para. 150. *See also* Jeffrey Waincymer, *Procedure and Evidence in International Arbitration*, 219 (Kluwer 2012) ('civilian systems typically apply the *iura novit curia* principle whereby the judge must know the law, hence parties need not necessarily include legal argument in their documentation'); Article 18(2) of the Swiss Rules (corresponding closely to article 20(2) of the 2010 Rules, without the requirement that the claimant include the legal grounds or arguments supporting its claim).

where the respondent chooses to formulate counterclaims or set-off claims in its statement of defence pursuant to article 21(3), rather than in its response pursuant to article 4(2)(e). Parity of treatment between the parties would suggest that in the latter hypothesis, jurisdictional objections must be formulated with the statement of claim, just as the respondent must do in its statement of defence under article 23(2).

10. The 2010 drafters also made a minor amendment to the requirement that the statement of claim provide the 'addresses' of the parties (see article 18(2)(a) of the 1976 Rules). Article 20(2)(a) of the 2010 Rules now requires the provision of parties' 'contact details', a broader formulation that reflects modern means of communication.[16] This change is also consistent with the language used in articles 3(3)(b) and 4(1)(a) of the 2010 Rules.[17]

11. Regarding multiparty arbitrations, the Working Group considered that it was unnecessary to make amendments to the statement of claim provisions.[18] The 2010 Rules already allow for a notice of arbitration to be submitted by multiple parties under article 3(1), and likewise for a joint response by multiple respondents under article 4(1). In cases of multiple parties falling into two camps, the basic format of first-round statements under articles 20-21 will apply without difficulty. Such statements will also be necessary in triangular multiparty disputes (with parties joined pursuant to article 4(2)(f) or 17(5)). It is possible in such disputes that, as described in Article 8(1) of the ICC Rules, claims are 'made by any party against any other party'. Doubtless first-round statements as conceived by articles 20-21 will be needed, for reasons described above. The only question will be how to sequence them and what further pleadings pursuant to article 24 will be needed. There can be no generally valid answer to this question: all will depend on the nature of the claims and their logical sequencing in the light of what is conducive to a fair and efficient resolution of the entire dispute. It may even be sensible to hold some of the claims in suspense, pending the resolution of logically prior issues between some only of the multiple parties; and to sequence the first-round statements accordingly, provided that any and all awards be issued 'in respect of all parties so involved in the arbitration', as required by article 17(5).

C. EVIDENTIAL SUPPORT

12. Under the 1976 Rules, it was possible for the claimant to present the evidence upon which it relied a fair amount of time after the submission of the written pleadings, and possibly even at the hearing itself: article 18(2) granted the claimant the option of providing or simply referring to documentary evidence.[19]

---

16 *See* discussion of articles 3 and 4 of the 2010 Rules, *supra*.

17 *See* UNCITRAL Report of 46th Session, 20 March 2007, UN Doc A/CN.9/619, para. 148.

18 *Ibid.*, at para. 155.

19 *See* James E. Castello, *Unveiling the 2010 UNCITRAL Arbitration Rules*, 65(2) Dispute Resolution Journal 21, 152 (2010) (noting that articles 18(2) and 19(4) of the 1976 Rules permitted a claimant or respondent to submit evidence for the first time at a hearing by adding a reference, in the statement of claim or defence, to evidence '*he will submit*').

In contrast, article 20(3) and 20(4) of the 2010 Rules set out the claimant's evidential duties in a manner which, despite retaining some flexibility, requires it to substantiate its position evidentially 'as far as possible' in its first comprehensive pleading. The intent is to crystallize the disputed issues at the first possible opportunity, and concomitantly to avoid surprise tactics leading to inorderly pleadings and delay later. Article 20(3)-20(4) spells out the effect intended – but poorly articulated – by article 24(1) of the 1976 Rules. The latter provided that '[e]ach party shall have the burden of proving the facts relied on to support his claim of defence', which on its face suggested that this was a provision about the burden of proof. But the *travaux* show the intent to have been to direct parties to adduce the evidence of factual allegations together with the relevant pleadings.[20]

13. Article 20(3) of the 2010 Rules prescribes that the claimant 'shall' provide with its statement of claim 'a copy of any contract or other legal instrument out of or in relation to which the dispute arises', as well as a copy of the arbitration agreement. These are obviously very minimal exigencies; cf. article 3(3)(c)-(d). This obligation was also present in article 18(1) of the 1976 Rules, it being necessary to 'apprise the arbitrators of the scope of their jurisdiction and of the frame of reference for the dispute'.[21] However, linguistic amendments have been made in order to accommodate the application of the Rules in an investment-treaty context.[22] In particular, the addition of the phrase 'other legal instrument out of or in relation to which the dispute arises', alongside 'any contract', contemplates that the claim may be based on, for example, an alleged breach of a bilateral investment treaty obligation. Further, the addition brings article 20(3) in line with the language of article 3(3)(d) of the 2010 Rules.[23]

14. In contrast to the mandatory wording of article 20(3), however, article 20(4) provides merely that the statement of claim 'should, as far as possible', be accompanied by all documents and evidence that the claimant has relied upon, or at least contain references to them. The words 'as far as possible' indicate that this is a procedural duty and every effort to comply with it should be made. For example, evidence anticipated through tribunal-ordered production (article 27(3)) or from the respondent (article 21(3)) is not possible to adduce with the statement of claim. While the wording therefore is not as strong as that of article 20(3), this provision may nevertheless be considered a step forward from the overly-permissive language of article 18(2) of the 1976 Rules, which stated that the claimant 'may' (or may not) annex such documents to its statement of claim,

---

20 *See* Stewart A. Baker & Mark D. Davis, *The UNCITRAL Arbitration Rules in Practice – The Experience of the Iran-United States Claims Tribunal*, 109 and the references (Kluwer 1992).

21 UNCITRAL Report of the Secretary General on the Draft UNCITRAL Arbitration Rules, 12 December 1975, UN Doc A/CN.9/112/Add.1, 173.

22 *See* discussion of article 1 of the 2010 Rules, *supra*; *see also* Jan Paulsson & Georgios Petrochilos, *Revision of the UNCITRAL Rules* (September 2006), para. 6, <www.uncitral.org>.

23 *See* UNCITRAL Report of 46th Session, 20 March 2007, UN Doc A/CN.9/619, para. 147. *See also* discussion of article 3 of the 2010 Rules, *supra*.

or add a reference to them. This amendment brought the UNCITRAL Rules in line with the provisions of other arbitration rules.[24]

15. Nevertheless, the language of article 20(4) is the result of a compromise. Earlier drafts used the term 'shall' instead of 'should', but the drafters were concerned that 'shall' would 'impos[e] rigid consequences' if the requirements of the provision were not followed.[25] Hence, the compromise wording 'should, as far as possible', which indicates that the requirement to provide all documents and evidence upon which the claimant relies is a procedural duty, rather than a rule pertaining to the burden of proof. In other words, it does not automatically follow from the fact that a claimant has not provided the evidence upon which it purports to rely in the statement of claim that it has failed to satisfy its burden of proof, or that an unsupported allegation must automatically be dismissed by virtue of article 20(4) there and then. Furthermore, this procedural duty is intended to apply to all 'other evidence' that may be submitted at the stage of the statement of claim, including, for example, 'testimony or written witness statements'.[26]

16. In analysing article 20(3) and 20(4), the following provisions should also be borne in mind:

(i) the arbitral tribunal may, typically at the request of the respondent, require that the claimant provide relevant materials under article 27(3);
(ii) a failure to comply with article 20(3)-(4) may have an impact on the procedural schedule, as the general requirement that the parties be treated equally (pursuant to article 17(1)) may require that the respondent be granted additional time or permission to file further pleadings; and

---

24 *See*, e.g., Article 15.6 of the 1998 LCIA Rules (providing that '[a]ll Statements referred to in this Article *shall* be accompanied by ... all essential documents on which the party concerned relies' (emphasis added). Note that Article 15.2 of the 2014 LCIA Rules provides, in similarly mandatory terms, that the claimant 'shall deliver ... its written Statement of Case ... together with the relief claimed against all other parties, and all essential documents'); *see also* Article 41(c) of the 2002 WIPO Rules (providing that '[t]he Statement of Claim *shall, to as large an extent as possible*, be accompanied by the documentary evidence upon which the Claimant relies ...' (emphasis added). The provision is substantially reproduced as Article 41(c) of the 2014 WIPO Rules, which provides that '[t]he Statement of Claim shall, to as large an extent as possible, be accompanied by the evidence upon which the Claimant relies ...'); *see also* Article 18(3) of the 2004 Swiss Rules (providing that '[a]s a rule, the Claimant *shall* annex to its Statement of Claim all documents it deems relevant' (emphasis added). The provision is reproduced with minor modifications as Article 18(3) of the 2012 Swiss Rules, which provides that '[a]s a rule, the Claimant shall annex to its Statement of Claim all documents and other evidence on which it relies'). Cf. Article 4(3) of the 2017 ICC Rules ('The claimant may submit such other documents or information with the Request as it considers appropriate or as may contribute to the efficient resolution of the dispute').

25 *See* UNCITRAL Report of 46th Session, 20 March 2007, UN Doc A/CN.9/619, para. 153; and UNCITRAL Working Paper for 46th Session, 6 December 2006, UN Doc A/CN.9/WG.II/WP.145/Add.1, para. 13. Cf. the provisions of other arbitration rules at fn 24, *supra*.

26 *See* UNCITRAL Report of 50th Session, 9 March 2009, UN Doc A/CN.9/669, para. 24.

(iii) the claimant's failure to adduce evidence associated with the statement of claim in a timely manner may well be a relevant circumstance considered by the tribunal when allocating costs pursuant to article 42(1).

17. As explicitly provided for in article 20(1), the evidential requirements of article 20(4) must be met by the notice of arbitration for the claimant to be able to treat it as a statement of claim.

Article 21
Statement of defence

1976 Rules
Article 19: Statement of defence

1. Within a period of time to be determined by the arbitral tribunal, the respondent shall communicate his statement of defence in writing to the claimant and to each of the arbitrators.

2. The statement of defence shall reply to the particulars (b), (c) and (d) of the statement of claim (article 18, para. 2). The respondent may annex to his statement the documents on which he relies for his defence or may add a reference to the documents or other evidence he will submit.

3. In his statement of defence, or at a later stage in the arbitral proceedings if the arbitral tribunal decides that the delay was justified under the circumstances, the respondent may make a counter-claim arising out of the same contract or rely on a claim arising out of the same contract for the purpose of a set-off.

4. The provisions of article 18, paragraph 2, shall apply to a counter-claim and a claim relied on for the purpose of a set-off.

2010 Rules
Article 21: Statement of defence

1. The respondent shall communicate its statement of defence in writing to the claimant and to each of the arbitrators within a period of time to be determined by the arbitral tribunal. The respondent may elect to treat its response to the notice of arbitration referred to in article 4 as a statement of defence, provided that the response to the notice of arbitration also complies with the requirements of paragraph 2 of this article.

2. The statement of defence shall reply to the particulars (b) to (e) of the statement of claim (art. 20, para. 2). The statement of defence should, as far as possible, be accompanied by all documents and other evidence relied upon by the respondent, or contain references to them.

3. In its statement of defence, or at a later stage in the arbitral proceedings if the arbitral tribunal decides that the delay was justified under the circumstances, the respondent may make a counterclaim or rely on a claim for the purpose of a set-off provided that the arbitral tribunal has jurisdiction over it.

4. The provisions of article 20, paragraphs 2 to 4, shall apply to a counterclaim, a claim under article 4, paragraph 2 (f), and a claim relied on for the purpose of a set-off.

1. The statement of defence is the respondent's pleading equivalent to the claimant's statement of claim. Article 21(1), (2) and (4) therefore mirrors the content of article 20(1)-(4); the reader is referred to the discussion above in respect of article 20. The only point worth highlighting is that the time-period allocated for this purpose (set at the outset of the proceedings, pursuant to article 17(2)) 'should not normally exceed 45 days' (article 25) and 'would normally match the period of time given to the claimant' for submission of the statement of claim.[1]

A. COUNTERCLAIMS AND SET-OFF CLAIMS

1. Tribunal's jurisdiction over counterclaims and set-off claims

2. The Rules (both in the 1976 and in the 2010 version) explicitly address the typical hypothesis where counterclaims or claims in set-off are formulated by the respondent only. There is no reason to suppose, however, that such claims (and in particular set-off claims) may not be raised by the claimant reactively to those of the respondent. Indeed, that this is a possibility covered by the Rules is borne out by article 22, which deals with amendments or supplements to a party's case. These expressly include counterclaims and set-off claims. The prospect of such additional claims by the respondent is covered in article 21(3). Article 22 therefore recognizes by necessary implication the prospect of such claims by the claimant. That will create no fundamental difficulty under the Rules, provided an appropriate pleading schedule is put in place. This will certainly involve further 'written statements' pursuant to article 24.

3. Article 19(3) of the 1976 Rules limits any counterclaims and set-off claims raised by the respondent to those 'arising out of the same contract' as the original dispute. Article 21(3) of the 2010 Rules widens the scope of this provision, allowing the respondent to raise any counterclaims or set-off claim over which 'the arbitral tribunal has jurisdiction', a requirement to be assessed pursuant to article 1(1) of the Rules.[2]

4. As noted in connection with article 4(2)(e), above, counterclaims and set-off claims are distinct concepts. A counterclaim is a stand-alone claim that may be

---

1 James E. Castello, 'UNCITRAL Arbitration Rules, Section III, Article 21' in Loukas A. Mistelis (ed), *Concise International Arbitration*, 222 (2nd ed., Kluwer 2015).

2 *See*, e.g., *Oxus Gold plc v. Republic of Uzbekistan, the State Committee of Uzbekistan for Geology & Mineral Resources, and Navoi Mining & Metallurgical Kombinat* (UNCITRAL) Award, 17 December 2015, <www.italaw.com>, para. 972 ('In light of the clear wording of Article 21(3) UNCITRAL Rules, the Arbitral Tribunal considers that it cannot rely on a set-off defence in the present arbitration, given that the Arbitral Tribunal does not have jurisdiction over the claims upon which Respondent relies for the purpose of its set-off defence'). *See also* Howard M. Holtzmann & Joseph E. Neuhaus, *A Guide to the UNCITRAL Model Law on International Commercial Arbitration, Legislative History and Commentary*, 649 (Kluwer 1989) (noting that amendments to a counterclaim under Article 23(2) of the UNCITRAL Model Law 'cannot expand the dispute beyond the scope of the arbitration agreement, which is the source of the arbitral tribunal's jurisdiction').

asserted by the respondent against the claimant irrespective of the merits of the original claim. A set-off claim is 'purely a defensive claim' that the applicable substantive law allows a respondent to bring for the eventuality that the original claim may succeed, e.g. a claim that is time-barred.[3] Typically the value of the set-off claim may not exceed the amount of the original claim itself.[4] The Working Group acknowledged this distinction and rejected a proposal that the jurisdiction of the tribunal be defined to extend to simply 'any counterclaim', as there were concerns that this may not include set-off claims, 'which can be understood as a form of payment' and which therefore differ from counterclaims.[5]

5. The Working Group also discussed a proposal by Switzerland, which sought to establish jurisdiction in the Rules over counterclaims that 'fell within the scope of the arbitration agreement and had a sufficient link to the main claim'.[6] This latter requirement was said to be justified because a counterclaim 'was viewed as a different claim going beyond a mere defence'.[7] In contrast, according to the proposal, jurisdiction over a set-off claim could be assumed if the requirements for a set-off under the substantive law applicable to the main claim were fulfilled (as the set-off claim forms a part of the defence).[8] However, the Working Group considered that 'claims for set-off and counterclaims were matters of procedural domestic law and it might not be appropriate to provide substantive universal rules on those questions'.[9] The Working Group also considered that, in any event, the tribunal 'would have to first decide on its competence, treating both claims for set-off and counterclaims alike'.[10] It was finally concluded that 'a better approach would be to avoid substantive rules on the determination of the arbitral tribunal's competence, which could be understood in a variety of manners under different legal systems'.[11]

6. Therefore, article 21(3) lets a tribunal presented with counterclaims or set-off claims determine the scope of its jurisdiction, 'based on the arbitration agreement, the provisions of an applicable treaty or the applicable law, as the case may be'.[12]

---

3 David D. Caron & Lee M. Caplan, *The UNCITRAL Arbitration Rules, A Commentary*, 424 (2nd ed., Oxford University Press 2013).

4 *See* Stewart A. Baker & Mark D. Davis, *The UNCITRAL Arbitration Rules in Practice – The Experience of the Iran-United States Claims Tribunal*, 89 and the references (Kluwer 1992).

5 UNCITRAL Report of 45th Session, 5 October 2006, UN Doc A/CN.9/614, para. 95 ('the function of set-off, which could be understood as a form of payment, differed from that of a counter-claim and different legal principles applied to it').

6 UNCITRAL Report of 50th Session, 9 March 2009, UN Doc A/CN.9/669, para. 30.

7 *Ibid.*, at para. 28.

8 *See* UNCITRAL Working Paper for 49th Session, 9 September 2008, UN Doc A/CN.9/WG.II/WP.152, article 19, para. 3 (proposed amended version); and UNCITRAL Report of 50th Session, 9 March 2009, UN Doc A/CN.9/669, para. 28. *See also* Caron & Caplan, *supra* fn 3, at 427-428.

9 Castello, *supra* fn 1, at 223, citing UNCITRAL Report of 50th Session, 9 March 2009, UN Doc A/CN.9/669, para. 29.

10 UNCITRAL Report of 50th Session, 9 March 2009, UN Doc A/CN.9/669, para. 29.

11 *Ibid.*, at para. 31.

12 Castello, *supra* fn 1, at 223. *See also* Caron & Caplan, *supra* fn 3, at 426.

By allowing the respondent to bring all claims that are within the confines of the tribunal's jurisdiction against the claimant, the arbitration is more likely to encapsulate the parties' disputes, promoting procedural economy.

7. Article 21(3) represents a compromise between the need to 'adopt a particularly broad understanding of the range of counterclaims and set-off claims that could be dealt with in the same proceedings' in the context of investment disputes,[13] on the one hand, and the need for a minimal connection between the original claim and the counterclaim or set-off claim in commercial arbitrations, on the other hand.[14] In particular, the reference to the underlying 'contract' in article 19(3) of the 1976 Rules gave rise to doubt regarding investment tribunals' jurisdiction over counterclaims or set-off claims. In *Saluka v. Czech Republic*,[15] the tribunal turned to ICSID and Iran-US Claims Tribunal decisions for guidance, deciding that, as a matter of principle, it had jurisdiction over counterclaims where consent to arbitration was expressed in broad terms, not limited to treaty-based claims, in an investment treaty.[16] Recognizing that the 1976 Rules imposed no such limitation, the Iran-US Claims Tribunal modified article 19(3) to encompass any counterclaim arising 'out of the same contract, *transaction or occurrence that constitutes the subject matter of the national's claim*' (emphasis added).[17]

8. The broadened jurisdiction of UNCITRAL tribunals under the 2010 Rules thus provides greater certainty with respect to counterclaims in an investor-state context, especially when contrasted with the ICSID regime.[18]

---

13 UNCITRAL Report of 45th Session, 5 October 2006, UN Doc A/CN.9/614, para. 96.

14 *See* UNCITRAL Report of 46th Session, 20 March 2007, UN Doc A/CN.9/619, para. 158 (the Working Group rejected a suggestion that the 'provision should not require that there be a connection between the claim and the counter-claim or set-off', as this 'might accommodate the needs of specific situations such as investment disputes involving States but might not sufficiently meet the needs of more general commercial disputes').

15 *See Saluka Investments BV v. The Czech Republic* (UNCITRAL) Decision on Jurisdiction over the Czech Republic's Counterclaim, 7 May 2004, < www.italaw.com >. < wwwfenceby the Respondent again deal with the der nse stage. to the notice of arbitration as its defence by the Respondent again

16 *Ibid.*, at para. 39 ('The Tribunal agrees that, in principle, the jurisdiction conferred upon it by Article 8, particularly when read with Article 19.3, 19.4 and 21.3 of the UNCITRAL Rules, is in principle wide enough to encompass counterclaims'). The *Saluka* tribunal further found that 'a legitimate counterclaim must have a close connection with the primary claim to which it is a response' (*ibid.*, at para. 61). Note, however, that on the facts of this case, the tribunal decided that it was nevertheless without jurisdiction to hear the respondent's counterclaim.

17 Article 19(3) of the Tribunal Rules of Procedure of the Iran-United States Claims Tribunal (3 May 1983); Article II, para. 1 of the Iran-US Claims Settlement Declaration (19 January 1981).

18 Contrast, for example, *Spyridon Roussalis v. Romania* (ICSID Case No. ARB/06/1) Award, 7 December 2011, < www.italaw.com > with *Antoine Goetz & Others and SA Affinage des Metaux v. Republic of Burundi* (ICSID Case No. ARB/01/2) Award, 1 June 2012, < www. italaw.com >, where the tribunals reached different conclusions on the issue of jurisdiction over counterclaims advanced by the state parties (the *Roussalis* tribunal finding that it

2. Raising counterclaims and set-off claims in the response and the statement of defence

9. Article 4(2)(e) of the 2010 Rules provides that the respondent may include 'a brief description of counterclaims or claims for the purpose of a set-off' in the response to the notice of arbitration. If the respondent elects not to do so in the response, it has a second (and last) chance to raise such claims in the statement of defence. This is to allow the respondent a reasonable opportunity to present its case: the respondent may be able to formulate counterclaims only after having reviewed the statement of claim.[19] Moreover, evidence which the respondent needs in order to develop its counterclaims may be unavailable at the time of submission of the response to the notice of arbitration ('[w]ithin 30 days of the receipt of the notice of arbitration', per article 4(1)).[20]

10. There is no uniformity among the various sets of arbitration rules.[21] Under the LCIA Rules 'it is not unusual for respondents simply to foreshadow the prospect of future counterclaims without further elucidation'[22] in the Response, as the Statement of Defence offers a further opportunity to introduce a counterclaim or set-off claim. By contrast, under the ICC Rules, a Respondent must submit any counterclaims through a Reply,[23] or else formulate them as new claims before the establishment of the Terms of Reference[24] (or later, if authorized by the tribunal).[25]

3. Delay justified under the circumstances

11. The respondent may have a third opportunity to raise counterclaims or set-off claims, after its statement of defence, if the tribunal determines that 'the delay

---

lacked jurisdiction, the *Goetz* tribunal finding that it was competent to hear Burundi's counterclaim).

19 *See* article 3(3)(e) of the 2010 Rules.

20 *See* Baker & Davis, *supra* fn 4, at 90.

21 *See*, e.g., Article 2.1(ii) of the LCIA Rules (providing that the respondent shall deliver 'if not full confirmation, a statement briefly summarising the nature and circumstances of the dispute ... and also indicating whether any cross-claim will be advanced') and Article 15.3 (providing that cross-claims may be submitted with the Statement of Defence); *see also* Article 11 of the WIPO Rules (providing that the respondent's answer to the request for arbitration 'may include indications of any counter-claim or set-off') and Article 42(c) (providing for any such counterclaim or set-off claim to be 'made or asserted in the Statement of Defence'). Cf. Article 9(1) of the SCC Rules (providing that the respondent's answer to the request for arbitration '*shall include*: (iii) a preliminary statement of any counterclaims or set-offs' (emphasis added)) and Article 29(2) (providing that the statement of defence 'shall include, unless previously submitted: (iv) any counterclaim or set-off and the grounds on which it is based').

22 *See*, referring to the 1998 LCIA Rules, Peter Turner & Reza Mohtashami, *A Guide to the LCIA Arbitration Rules*, para. 3.31 (Oxford University Press 2009).

23 *See* Article 5(5) of the ICC Rules.

24 *See* Jason Fry, Simon Greenberg & Francesca Mazza, *The Secretariat's Guide to ICC Arbitration*, para. 3-892 (ICC 2012).

25 *See* Article 23(4) of the ICC Rules.

was justified under the circumstances': article 21(3). That provision overlaps in part with article 22, which deals with the broader topic of amendments (to all types of claims) and supplementations (to existing claims of all types, but also by adding new claims of any type). The practical result is that article 22 adds additional requirements of no-prejudice and appropriateness in view of 'any other circumstances'. As we now turn to see, these additional requirements are imported through the practice of tribunals into article 21(3) in any event.

12. This aspect of article 21(3) of the 2010 Rules is unchanged from article 19(3) of the 1976 Rules. The practice of the Iran-US Claims Tribunal illustrates that determinations as to whether a delay is 'justified' depend on (i) the respondent's reasons for the delay; (ii) the possible prejudice caused to the claimant by such delay; and (iii) the effect of the delay on the arbitral proceedings.[26] These considerations are consistent with the tribunal's general duty to consider, under article 17(1) of the 2010 Rules, (i) the respondent's right to a reasonable opportunity to present its case; (ii) the equal treatment of the parties; and (iii) the provision of 'a fair and efficient process for resolving the parties' dispute'. In particular, the tribunal must weigh any procedural disruption caused by the admission of a late counterclaim – the Rules envisage that a dedicated 'reply' by the claimant will be authorized (see article 23(2)) – against the duplication of proceedings if the respondent has to initiate separate proceedings.[27]

13. It is clear, for the purposes of article 21(3), that the burden of justifying any delay lies with the respondent.[28] Valid justifications for delay could include, for example, the discovery of evidence after the statement of defence has been submitted. Tribunals have considered this to be a valid justification for delay even where the evidence in question was available but not 'detectable' due to the large volume of surrounding materials.[29] Another example identified is where the statement of claim is not 'sufficiently specific' for the respondent to formulate a counterclaim at the time of the statement of defence.[30]

---

26 *See* Caron & Caplan, *supra* fn 3, at 425.

27 *See* Nigel Blackaby, Constantine Partasides, Alan Redfern & Martin J. Hunter, *Redfern and Hunter on International Arbitration*, para. 6.81 (5th ed., Kluwer 2015) ('The arbitral tribunal must decide whether the introduction of new claims would be an abuse of process that will lead to unnecessary delay and expense, or whether (assuming the counterclaim falls within its jurisdiction) the legitimate interest of resolving all issues in dispute between the parties in the proceedings should prevail').

28 *See*, e.g., *Harris International Telecommunications Inc v. Iran* (1987) 17 Iran-US CTR 31, para. 91 (where the tribunal stated that 'the Respondent has the burden of justifying the delay'); and *General Dynamics Corp v. Iran* (1984) 5 Iran US CTR 386, 400 (where the tribunal dismissed a late-filed counterclaim because the respondent failed to demonstrate circumstances justifying the delay).

29 *See*, e.g., *American Bell International Inc v. Iran* (1986) 12 Iran-US CTR 170, para. 183 (the tribunal accepted the late-filed counterclaim, considering that 'respondents may not, at the time of the presentation of the Statement of Defence, have detected the evidence ... supporting this counter-claim among voluminous documentary evidence').

30 *See* Baker & Davis, *supra* fn 4, at 90.

14. The primary prejudice for a claimant faced with a late counterclaim is that it may have less time to respond to it in later stages of the proceedings. The prejudice may be higher where the claimant has lost or destroyed relevant evidence on the assumption that the counterclaim had been waived.[31]

15. There is no strict cut-off date for an article 21(3) application. However, it is submitted that, for obvious reasons, the Iran-US Claim Tribunal's practice of being 'particularly reluctant to accept late counterclaims filed shortly before the Hearing, during the Hearing, or after the Hearing'[32] is a sound one.[33]

4. Reply to counterclaim or set-off claim; further pleadings

16. Like the 1976 Rules, the 2010 Rules do not specifically regulate the claimant's defensive pleading, leaving the matter to be addressed under article 24 in the context of the procedural schedule. (In contrast, mandatory provisions provide for the claimant's reply to a counterclaim in proceedings conducted under, for example, the ICC Rules or the LCIA Rules.[34]) There has never been any doubt that the claimant is to have an opportunity to respond through written submissions. In his commentary to the 1976 Rules, Sanders noted that '[i]t is obvious that the claimant must get an opportunity to reply to the counter-claim', but that the Rules 'only say so indirectly' – i.e. by way of a reference contained in article 21(3).[35] This remains the case under the 2010 Rules: article 23(2) refers to 'the reply to the counterclaim or to the claim for the purpose of a set-off'.[36]

---

31 *Ibid.* Cf. *Phillips Petroleum Co Iran v. Iran* (1989) 21 Iran-US CTR 79 (where the tribunal accepted a late-filed counterclaim filed more than two and a half years prior to the hearing, as the parties had had adequate opportunity to respond to it); *Starrett Housing Corporation v. Iran* (1987) 4 Iran-US CTR 143 (where the tribunal found that the respondent had had sufficient opportunity to answer to counterclaims filed six weeks before the hearings; although Holtzmann, in his dissenting opinion, disagreed that this constituted sufficient time); and *American Bell International Inc v. Iran* (1986) 12 Iran-US CTR 170 (where the tribunal found that the claimant had had adequate opportunity to respond to counterclaims filed a month before the hearing, in a rebuttal memorial due a week before the hearing. Judge Brower, in his concurring opinion, noted that the counterclaim was 'documented at that time with admissions of Claimant in its correspondence as well as contemporaneous memoranda of meetings. In a subsequent Rebuttal Memorial and evidence Claimant would appear at least tacitly to have conceded this liability').

32 *Harris International Telecommunications Inc v. Iran* (1987) 17 Iran-US CTR 31, para. 93.

33 Cf. Article 23(4) of the ICC Rules, where the tribunal must consider 'the stage of the arbitration' in authorising new claims subsequent to the terms of reference.

34 *See* Article 5(6) of the ICC Rules; Article 15.4-15.5 of the LCIA Rules.

35 Article 21(3) of the 1976 Rules, which concerns the jurisdiction of the tribunal, references 'the reply to the counterclaim', a term for which no express provision is made and which does not appear elsewhere in the 1976 Rules. *See* Pieter Sanders, *Commentary on UNCITRAL Arbitration Rules*, II YCA 172, 204 (1977); *see also* Jan Paulsson & Georgios Petrochilos, *Revision of the UNCITRAL Rules* (September 2006), para. 177, <www.uncitral.org>.

36 This reply may consist of a stand-alone written pleading or be part of second-round responsive pleadings by the parties (i.e. followed by a rejoinder and likely a sur-reply).

Article 22
Amendments to the claim or defence

1976 Rules **Article 20: Amendments to the claim or defence**	2010 Rules **Article 22: Amendments to the claim or defence**
During the course of the arbitral proceedings either party may amend or supplement his claim or defence unless the arbitral tribunal considers it inappropriate to allow such amendment having regard to the delay in making it or prejudice to the other party or any other circumstances. However, a claim may not be amended in such a manner that the amended claim falls outside the scope of the arbitration clause or separate arbitration agreement.	During the course of the arbitral proceedings, a party may amend or supplement its claim or defence, including a counterclaim or a claim for the purpose of a set-off, unless the arbitral tribunal considers it inappropriate to allow such amendment or supplement having regard to the delay in making it or prejudice to other parties or any other circumstances. However, a claim or defence, including a counterclaim or a claim for the purpose of a set-off, may not be amended or supplemented in such a manner that the amended or supplemented claim or defence falls outside the jurisdiction of the arbitral tribunal.

1. Article 22 of the 2010 Rules provides the parties a right to amend or supplement their claims, defences, counterclaims or claims for the purpose of a set-off. However, this is not an unqualified right: the amendment or supplementation must not result in the claim or defence 'fall[ing] outside the jurisdiction of the arbitral tribunal', and the tribunal must not consider that the amendment or supplementation is inappropriate, in the light of 'the delay in making it or prejudice to other parties or any other circumstances'.

2. The object and purpose of article 22 are facially identical to those of article 20 of the 1976 Rules. It is procedurally efficient for the parties to have the ability to modify their pleadings, as 'the alternative may be the commencement of new

arbitral proceedings'.[1] The tribunal must be able to exercise control over this ability, however, in order to ensure that parties do not '[obstruct] the course of the arbitral proceedings, either by making frequent changes in [their] position ... or by making frivolous or vexatious amendments'.[2]

3. There is, however, a meaningful difference between the 1976 and 2010 versions of the Rules, which informs the ambit of article 22. Article 20 of the 1976 Rules is the only way to introduce new parties to the proceedings, either on the same side as the party moving for an amendment (e.g. an additional claimant) or opposite (e.g. an additional respondent). The latter possibility is now regulated specifically in articles 4(2)(f) and 17(5) of the 2010 Rules. These specific provisions should be regarded as exclusively governing the issue of joinder, although in substance both article 17(5) and article 22 rely centrally on a test of 'prejudice' to the other side (which is why the practice in respect of the latter will also be relevant to the former). There is also a view, however, that article 22 remains available as a process through which to introduce new parties, done through an amended pleading which will name them as parties, *and* complying in substance with article 17(5).[3] With respect, we regard such procedural duplication anomalous and unnecessary. Article 20 of the 1976 Rules was by design directed to amendments to the object of the proceedings, not the composition of the parties.[4] The possibility of adding new parties was developed organically, mostly through the practice of the Iran-US Claims Tribunal. The 2010 Rules gave a special procedural route for this practice, thereby acknowledging its validity but placing it in its own procedural box, article 17(5). It is true, however, that the addition of new claimants will have to continue being housed under article 22.

4. A clarification that the parties' right to amend or supplement also extends to counterclaims and set-off claims[5] represents the principal change made through the 2010 Rules. This codifies the practice of the Iran-US Claims Tribunal.[6] There are less important changes, consequential upon the broadened scope of the Rules

---

1 David D. Caron & Lee M. Caplan, *The UNCITRAL Arbitration Rules, A Commentary*, 467 (2nd ed., Oxford University Press 2013).

2 *See* Report of 8th Session, 1-17 April 1975, UN Doc A/10017, VI UNCITRAL Ybk 9, 37, para. 126.

3 Caron & Caplan, *supra* fn 1, at 469.

4 *See* Pieter Sanders, *Commentary on UNCITRAL Arbitration Rules*, II YCA 172, 205 (1977) (where no reference is made to new parties).

5 *See* Caron & Caplan, *supra* fn 1, at 475 and the references ('Although these types of defensive pleadings were not specifically identified in original Article 20, there is no doubt that their amendment or supplementation must also be treated according to principles enunciated in the article').

6 The Iran-US Claims Tribunal applied article 20 of the 1976 Rules to both claims and counterclaims. *See*, e.g., *Sylvania Technical Systems Inc v. The Islamic Republic of Iran*, Case No. 64, Chamber One, Order of 10 May 1983 (where the tribunal accepted the submission of a supplementary statement of counterclaim where no objection was filed); *Anaconda-Iran Inc v. Government of the Islamic Republic of Iran* (1986) 13 Iran-US CTR 199 at 228 (permitting the respondent's amendment to the counterclaim, to which the tribunal found that the claimant would have sufficient opportunity to respond before the hearing).

to include investor-state arbitrations in accordance with article 1(1).[7] These revisions, as well as the limitations imposed by article 22 of the 2010 Rules, are discussed in further detail below.

5. It should also be noted at the outset that article 22 (as article 20 of the 1976 Rules) addresses the substantive aspect of the parties' procedural entitlement to amend their pleaded cases. The procedural modalities for doing so – whether it be in second-round written pleadings, or other 'further written statements' pursuant to article 24, or in oral submissions – are a separate matter, to be decided and regulated in accordance with article 17(1)-(2) of the Rules.

A. 'AMENDMENTS' AND 'SUPPLEMENTATIONS'

6. Article 22 makes a distinction between additional items pleaded ('[to] supplement [a] claim or defence') and 'amendments', the latter being either changed or abandoned items. The chapeau captures all these possibilities with the term 'amendments'. 'Amendments' to claims or defences are to be distinguished from additional arguments (including legal ones, such as an alternative legal ground or characterization)[8] or allegations one may expect to see developed over the course of the arbitral proceedings. A pleading item that may be characterized as a claim or cause of action and attract res judicata effect will, if amended, certainly fall within article 22. Ultimately, however, a central objective of article 22 is to ensure procedural fairness and avoid ambush tactics. It is therefore more important to construe the provision accordingly, and thus pragmatically, rather than by focusing on fine distinctions between new arguments and new claims. For there to be an amendment, 'one would usually expect the party filing the document to change the structure of its case', for example by adding a new party or an additional request for relief.[9] In *EnCana v. Ecuador*, the arbitral tribunal considered that the claimant's post-hearing brief did not constitute an amendment insofar as:

---

7 Other textual modifications were also made, reflecting, e.g., the application of the 2010 Rules in the context of multiparty arbitrations, as well for consistency between the first and second sentences of article 22. *See* Caron & Caplan, *supra* fn 1, at 475.

8 *See* Jason Fry, Simon Greenberg & Francesca Mazza, *The Secretariat's Guide to ICC Arbitration*, para. 3-898 (ICC 2012) (noting that ICC arbitral tribunals typically 'do not consider a change in argument as a new claim'. The authors cite the example of a case administered under the 1998 ICC Rules in which a claimant was permitted to amend its cause of action to argue the tort of deceit rather than contractual misrepresentation; the tribunal found that this 'did not result in the making of a new claim' as the 'argument was based on the same set of facts [and] ... the claimant did not seek additional forms of relief').

9 Thomas H. Webster, *Handbook of UNCITRAL Arbitration*, para. 22-7 (2nd ed., Sweet & Maxwell 2015) citing to *Methanex Corporation v. United States of America* (UNCITRAL) Final Award of the Tribunal on Jurisdiction and Merits, 3 August 2005, <www.italaw.com> (amendment sought to add a new request for relief); and *Merrill & Ring Forestry L P v. Government of Canada* (ICSID Case No. UNCT/07/1) Decision on a Motion to Add a New Party, 31 January 2008, <www.italaw.com> (amendment sought to add a new party and claims against that party). *See also* Article 23 of the ICC Rules; and Fry, Greenberg & Mazza, *supra* fn 8, at paras 3-896-3-902.

> [T]he events ... were relied upon by EnCana not for the purpose of introducing a new claim or cause of action, but in order to inform the Tribunal of matters which might be of relevance in relation to the claims which had already been identified when the arbitration proceedings were commenced.[10]

Clarifications of the amount claimed in respect of specific items, as well as adjustments of the calculation methodology applied, will not normally constitute amendments or supplementations of a pleading under article 22 of the Rules.[11]

7. The tribunal may decide on the amendment or supplementation 'as a preliminary issue or as an issue joined to the merits'.[12] In the former case, typically the tribunal will issue a 'decision' pursuant to article 33(1), setting forth reasons and taken by a majority. That avoids any implications that the additional or modified claim has thereby been determined on its merits. As illustrated by the case-law of the Iran-US Claims Tribunal, and in accordance with article 17(1) of the 2010 Rules, tribunals should provide other parties with an opportunity to comment on the proposed amendment or supplementation.[13]

B. JURISDICTION OF THE TRIBUNAL

8. The arbitral tribunal's jurisdiction, as defined by the arbitration clause, agreement, or other instrument (such as an investment treaty) sets a '*prima facie* absolute limitation' on the parties' ability to amend a claim or defence.[14] The 2010 Rules have recast the limitations contained in article 20 of the 1976 Rules, which specified that permissible amendments or supplementations must not take the claim in question 'outside the scope of the *arbitration clause* or separate *arbitration agreement*' (emphasis added). The wider formulation in article 22 of the 2010 Rules, which refers instead to 'the jurisdiction of the tribunal', reflects the fact that determination of the tribunal's jurisdiction over the amendment

---

[10] *EnCana Corporation v. Republic of Ecuador* (LCIA Case No. UN3481) Award, 3 February 2006, <www.italaw.com>, para. 165.

[11] Webster, *supra* fn 9, at 22-7.

[12] Caron & Caplan, *supra* fn 1, at 474.

[13] *Tai Inc v. Islamic Republic of Iran*, Case No. 421, Order of 12 August 1986 (tribunal ordered the respondent to file comments as to whether the amendment should be admitted); *see also EnCana Corporation v. Republic of Ecuador* (LCIA Case No. UN3481) Award, 3 February 2006, <www.italaw.com>, para. 18 (tribunal provided the respondent with an opportunity to reply to the claimant's allegations); *see also Grand River Enterprises Six Nations Ltd and ors v. United States* (UNCITRAL) Decision on Objections to Jurisdiction, 20 July 2006, <www.italaw.com>, paras 95-96 ('The Respondent had no opportunity to respond to [the claimant's] motion made in the final presentation at the hearing. Accordingly, the Tribunal gave the Respondent two weeks in which to comment on the motion in light of the requirements of Article 20 of the [1976] UNCITRAL Arbitration Rules').

[14] Caron & Caplan, *supra* fn 1, at 469, citing to *Merrill & Ring Forestry L P v. Government of Canada* (ICSID Case No. UNCT/07/1) Decision on a Motion to Add a New Party, 31 January 2008, <www.italaw.com>, para. 18 (where the tribunal held that article 20 of the 1976 Rules contained 'an overall and absolute prohibition against introducing amendments which go beyond the scope of the arbitration clause').

may depend on an investment treaty or the applicable law.[15] The Working Group sought to 'accommodate the expansion of the ambit of the Rules beyond merely contract claims and to enable related claims ... to be dealt with as part of the arbitration of the principal claim', thereby avoiding the time, expense and 'risk of inconsistent findings of fact and law arising in separate proceedings'.[16] For consistency with the revised wording of article 21(3),[17] which provides that the respondent may make a counterclaim or set-off claim 'provided that the arbitral tribunal has jurisdiction over it', the Working Group decided to 'avoid substantive rules on the determination of the arbitral tribunal's competence'.[18]

9. Not all arbitration rules deal with jurisdictional limitations in the same way. Article 23(4) of the ICC Rules[19] does not expressly provide that the tribunal's jurisdiction operates as an absolute limit to the parties' right to amend or supplement their pleadings. Instead, the tribunal has discretion to authorize new claims falling outside the Terms of Reference, although a party opposing this may contest the tribunal's jurisdiction over the claim, which is treated as a separate issue to be considered by the tribunal.[20]

10. A claim or defence may '[fall] outside the jurisdiction of the tribunal' where, for example, an amendment attempts to add to the proceedings a third person that is not a party to the agreement forming the basis of the arbitration. As noted at the outset, this is not to say that new parties cannot be brought into the proceedings by way of an amendment; they can, provided that the amendment 'keeps within the limits of the arbitration agreement (i.e. the new party is bound by the agreement)' and satisfies the other conditions set out in article 22 (and arguably also article 17(5) regarding joinder) of the 2010 Rules.[21] There may of course be borderline cases, for example where a wholly-owned subsidiary of a claimant is targeted by the amendment as the proper party to the arbitration.[22] In

15 James E. Castello, 'UNCITRAL Arbitration Rules, Section III, Article 22' in Loukas A. Mistelis (ed), *Concise International Arbitration*, 226 (2nd ed., Kluwer 2015).

16 Clyde E. Croft, Christopher Kee & Jeffrey Waincymer, *A Guide to the UNCITRAL Arbitration Rules*, 246 (Cambridge University Press 2013). The Working Group felt that the tribunal's competence to consider counterclaims and set-off claims 'should, under certain conditions, extend beyond the contract from which the principal claim arose and apply to a wider range of circumstances'. The Working Group concluded that the revised wording was broad enough and did not require substantive definitions of the notions of counterclaims and set-off claims: *see* UNCITRAL Report of 50th Session, 9 March 2009, UN Doc A/CN.9/669, paras 27 and 31.

17 *See* UNCITRAL Report of 50th Session, 9 March 2009, UN Doc A/CN.9/669, para. 34.

18 *Ibid.*, at para. 31. *See also* Croft, Kee & Waincymer, *supra* fn 16, at 240 and 246.

19 Article 23(4) of the ICC Rules provides: 'After the Terms of Reference have been signed or approved by the Court, no party shall make new claims which fall outside the limits of the Terms of Reference unless it has been authorized to do so by the arbitral tribunal, which shall consider the nature of such new claims, the stage of the arbitration and other relevant circumstances'.

20 *See* Fry, Greenberg & Mazza, *supra* fn 8, at para. 3-909.

21 Caron & Caplan, *supra* fn 1, at 469.

22 Castello, *supra* fn 15, at 225, citing to *Refusal to File Claim of AMF Overseas Corp* (1982) 1 Iran-US CTR 392 (Refusal Case No. 20) (tribunal allowed the introduction of a new party

the practice of the Iran-US Claims Tribunal, '[i]f the new party had been "referred to sufficiently clearly in the original statement of claim", the Tribunal treated the claimant's later specification of the new party as a mere "clarification" of the proper claimant or respondent'.[23]

11. In order to avoid court challenges on jurisdictional grounds,[24] a tribunal may be cautious in admitting new or amended claims, lest it compromise its award in respect of claims over which its jurisdiction is secure.

C. APPROPRIATENESS OF THE AMENDMENT

12. Both the 1976 and the 2010 Rules provide that an amendment or supplementation falling within the tribunal's jurisdiction may be made 'unless the arbitral tribunal considers it inappropriate'. By contrast, the Preliminary Draft of the 1976 Rules provided that such amendments could only be made 'with the permission of the arbitrators'.[25] The deliberate shift in wording clarifies two things. First, that, 'in principle, the parties [are] entitled to amend'[26] without prior authorization by the tribunal. The tribunal's intervention may be caused by application of the party opposing what it regards as an 'inappropriate' amendment. Secondly, that acceptance of amendments by the arbitral tribunal is not purely discretionary. Indeed, the parties' right to make amendments under the 1976 Rules existed insofar as the amendment (or supplementation) remained within 'the limits defined by article 20', thereby embodying a 'liberal approach'[27] which remains unchanged in the 2010 Rules.

---

to the proceedings as it was a wholly-owned subsidiary of the party named in the original claim). Cf. *Refusal to Accept the Claim of Raymond International (UK) Ltd* (1982) 1 Iran-US CTR 394, 395 (Refusal Case No. 21) (tribunal did not allow the claimant to amend the named respondent after the filing deadline had passed).

23 Stewart A. Baker & Mark D. Davis, *The UNCITRAL Arbitration Rules in Practice – The Experience of the Iran-United States Claims Tribunal*, 93 (Kluwer 1992) citing to *St Regis Paper Co v. Iran* (1987) 14 Iran-US CTR 86, 92 (Award No. 291-10706-1); and *Re: Refusal to File Claim of AMF Overseas Corp* (1982) 1 Iran-US CTR 392 (Refusal Case No. 20).

24 *See* Caron & Caplan, *supra* fn 1, at 470 (the authors note that 'a court challenge on the ground of lack of jurisdiction is a concrete risk which may affect the validity and enforceability of an international arbitral award'). *See also* Pieter Sanders, *Commentary on UNCITRAL Arbitration Rules*, II YCA 172, 205 (1977) ('[T]he arbitrators should not hesitate to reject an amendment of the claim which falls outside the scope of the arbitration agreement. If not, the other party might attack their award on this ground in Court').

25 UNCITRAL Report of 8th Session, 4 November 1974, UN Doc A/CN.9/97, VI UNCITRAL Ybk 163, 173, article 16(3).

26 *See* UNCITRAL Summary Record of the 7th Meeting, 19 April 1976, UN Doc A/CN.9/9/C.2/SR.7, para. 29, Mr. Holtzmann (United States of America).

27 Caron & Caplan, *supra* fn 1, at 468. *See also International Schools Services, Inc v. Iran* (1986) 10 Iran-US CTR 6, 12 (where the tribunal acknowledged that article 20 afforded the parties broad scope to amend or supplement their pleadings, to the extent that there was no delay, prejudice or 'concrete circumstances'); Baker & Davis, *supra* fn 23, at 92; Jacomijn J. van Hof, *Commentary on the UNCITRAL Arbitration Rules, The Application by the Iran-U.S.*

13. Article 22 sets out the grounds on which the tribunal may consider an amendment inappropriate: delay; prejudice; or 'any other circumstances'. Each of these grounds may suffice, and an accumulation thereof normally will lead to refusal of the amendment.[28] As stated by the Iran-US Claims Tribunal:

> [T]he Tribunal must consider whether the other Party would be prejudiced by the proposed amendment, whether the other party has had an opportunity to respond to the newly-added or amended claim, and whether the proposed amendment would needlessly disrupt or delay the arbitral process.[29]

One may expect that an abandonment of an item pleaded will ordinarily be unproblematic for the other side, except if in the complexion of the case it requires the other side extensively to modify or recast its own pleaded case.

14. The practice of the Iran-US Claims Tribunal demonstrates that an amendment should be rejected where there has been a 'significant lapse of time involved',[30] especially where the delay prejudices the other party by depriving it of an opportunity to defend itself (for example, where an amendment is made after the case has been heard on the merits).[31] Indeed, delay will be 'inappropriate' where it causes some form of prejudice to a material degree. The acceptability of the delay may depend on the reasons for which the amendment was not submitted at an earlier point in time. A tribunal may consider the delay is not inappropriate where, for example, it is due to circumstances beyond the control of the party in question, or where the evidence upon which the amendment is based only became available at a later stage in the proceedings.[32] The nature of

---

Claims Tribunal, 136-141 (Kluwer 1991) (noting that the tribunal highlighted the 'liberal approach' of the 1976 Rules with respect to a party's right to make amendments).

28 Caron & Caplan, *supra* fn 1, at 471.

29 *Harris International Telecommunications Inc v. Islamic Republic of Iran* (1987) 17 Iran-US CTR 31, 55-57, para. 85.

30 *Mohsen Asgari Nazari v. Government of the Islamic Republic of Iran* (1994) 30 Iran-US CTR 123, 126, para. 11.

31 *See* Caron & Caplan, *supra* fn 1, at 471-472. *See also ECE Projektmanagement v. The Czech Republic* (UNCITRAL) Award, 19 September 2013, <www.italaw.com>, paras 4.731-4.733 (where, despite the respondent not having raising a formal objection, the tribunal rejected various claims introduced by the claimants during and after the hearing on the basis that the respondent was not afforded a proper opportunity to prepare a response to them, and to accept the amendment or supplementation would therefore be inappropriate pursuant to article 20 of the 1976 Rules). Cf. *Sanum Investments Limited v. Lao People's Democratic Republic* (UNCITRAL) Award on Jurisdiction, 13 December 2013, <www.italaw.com>, paras 359-368 (where the tribunal permitted amendments submitted within the time-limit of the relevant procedural order and 'nearly two months before the Statement of Claim and the Respondent's Memorial on Jurisdiction').

32 Caron & Caplan, *supra* fn 1, at 471. *See European American Investment Bank AG (EURAM) v. Slovak Republic* (UNCITRAL) Second Award on Jurisdiction, 4 June 2014, <www.italaw.com>, paras 115-117 (applying the 1976 Rules, the tribunal noted that '[t]o preclude a respondent from making a jurisdictional objection after it submitted its statement of defence when that objection concerned facts which arose only after the date on which that statement was filed would involve a grave injustice').

the proposed amendment will also be taken into account, as prejudice to the other party is more likely to arise where the claimant 'seeks an amendment adding a different kind of relief, which raises new factual and legal issues'.[33]

15. In assessing prejudice, the reaction of the party who would suffer from it has proved important in practice. Indeed, in certain cases before the Iran-US Claims Tribunal, the absence of objections to a proposed amendment was a contributing factor to the tribunal's decision to accept the amendment.[34] Amendments that do not radically change the original allegations are 'acceptable' (less likely to cause prejudice),[35] whereas a new claim which is, for example, based on factual circumstances wholly different from those in the original claim is more likely to be regarded as causing prejudice.[36]

16. Consistent with the liberal approach under article 20 of the 2010 Rules, the Iran-US Claims Tribunal has generally 'interpreted "any other circumstances" to require [that] "concrete circumstances"' be demonstrated in order for an amendment to be rejected.[37] Commentators acknowledge the unlikelihood of an arbitral tribunal rejecting an amendment in the absence of prejudice or delay, but rightly note that article 20 may be interpreted as giving the arbitral tribunal discretion to do so, 'if accepting the amendment (with the consequent opportunity for the other party to respond) would be per se prejudicial to orderly proceedings'.[38] In

---

33 *Arthur Young & Company v. Iran* (1987) 17 Iran-US CTR 245, 253-254, para. 37. Cf. *Litton Systems, Inc. v. Iran* (1986) 12 Iran-US CTR 126, 131 (where the tribunal accepted a claim for warehousing charges added to an original claim based on the alleged cost of repairs to equipment held in the warehouse, as the factual basis of the claim was unchanged).

34 *See McCullough & Co Inc v. Ministry of Post, Telegraph and Telephone* (1986) 11 Iran-US CTR 3, 17-18, para. 46; and *Sylvania Technical Systems Inc v. Islamic Republic of Iran*, Case No. 64, Order of 10 May 1983.

35 Caron & Caplan, *supra* fn 1, at 472 ('The presentation of "unjust enrichment" as an alternative legal theory for what originally has been put forward as a contract or expropriation claim in our view is acceptable, provided the other party has an opportunity to respond to it. Nor should the introduction of new facts be considered an amendment of the claim when they merely support existing claims. An amendment seeking an increase in the amount of relief sought should not automatically be barred either, provided that relief is sought on the basis of the original allegations').

36 *See Methanex Corporation v. United States of America* (UNCITRAL) Final Award of the Tribunal on Jurisdiction and Merits, 3 August 2005, < www.italaw.com >, paras 19-21.

37 Baker & Davis, *supra* fn 23, at 92, citing to *International Schools Services, Inc v. Iran* (1986) 10 Iran-US CTR 6, 12 ('[Article 20] affords wide latitude to a party who seeks to amend a claim, and the Tribunal's practice is in accord with this liberal approach. As Article 20 directs, the Tribunal will permit an amendment unless delay, prejudice or other concrete circumstances make it inappropriate to do so'). *See also Harris International Telecommunications Inc v. Islamic Republic of Iran* (1987) 17 Iran-US CTR 31, 55-57, paras 85-87.

38 Caron & Caplan, *supra* fn 1, at 473. *See also Merrill & Ring Forestry L P v. Government of Canada* (ICSID Case No. UNCT/07/1) Decision on a Motion to Add a New Party, 31 January 2008, < www.italaw.com >, paras 27-30 (where the tribunal, considering that the provisions of NAFTA Articles 1119 and 1120 were more than 'merely procedural niceties', found that 'there would indeed be a serious procedural prejudice' if proceedings were delayed until the claimant complied with them).

simple terms, there are circumstances where it is preferable to have separate proceedings than an expansion of existing ones.

17. In contrast to the 2010 Rules and a number of other institutional rules,[39] Article 22.1(i) of the LCIA Rules simply provides that the tribunal may decide 'to allow a party to supplement, modify or amend any claim, defence, cross-claim, defence to cross-claim and reply, including a Request, Response and any other written statement, submitted by such party', without reference to factors that should feature in the tribunal's considerations.

39 *See*, e.g., Article 30 of the SCC Rules; Article 20 of the Swiss Rules; Article 9 of the AAA International Arbitration Rules; and Article 44 of the WIPO Rules.

Article 23
Pleas as to the jurisdiction of the arbitral tribunal

1976 Rules

Article 21: Pleas as to the jurisdiction of the arbitral tribunal

1. The arbitral tribunal shall have the power to rule on objections that it has no jurisdiction, including any objections with respect to the existence or validity of the arbitration clause or of the separate arbitration agreement.

2. The arbitral tribunal shall have the power to determine the existence or the validity of the contract of which an arbitration clause forms a part. For the purposes of article 21, an arbitration clause which forms part of a contract and which provides for arbitration under these Rules shall be treated as an agreement independent of the other terms of the contract. A decision by the arbitral tribunal that the contract is null and void shall not entail ipso jure the invalidity of the arbitration clause.

3. A plea that the arbitral tribunal does not have jurisdiction shall be raised not later than in the statement of defence or, with respect to a counter-claim, in the reply to the counter-claim.

4. In general, the arbitral tribunal should rule on a plea concerning its jurisdiction as a preliminary question. However, the arbitral tribunal may proceed with the arbitration and rule on such a plea in their final award.

2010 Rules

Article 23: Pleas as to the jurisdiction of the arbitral tribunal

1. The arbitral tribunal shall have the power to rule on its own jurisdiction, including any objections with respect to the existence or validity of the arbitration agreement. For that purpose, an arbitration clause that forms part of a contract shall be treated as an agreement independent of the other terms of the contract. A decision by the arbitral tribunal that the contract is null shall not entail automatically the invalidity of the arbitration clause.

2. A plea that the arbitral tribunal does not have jurisdiction shall be raised no later than in the statement of defence or, with respect to a counterclaim or a claim for the purpose of a set-off, in the reply to the counterclaim or to the claim for the purpose of a set-off. A party is not precluded from raising such a plea by the fact that it has appointed, or participated in the appointment of, an arbitrator. A plea that the arbitral tribunal is exceeding the scope of its authority shall be raised as soon as the matter alleged to be beyond the scope of its authority is raised during the arbitral proceedings. The arbitral tribunal may, in either case, admit a later plea if it considers the delay justified.

3. The arbitral tribunal may rule on a plea referred to in paragraph 2 either as a preliminary question or in an award on the merits. The arbitral tribunal may continue the arbitral proceedings and make an award, notwithstanding any pending challenge to its jurisdiction before a court.

1. Article 23 of the 2010 Rules retains all the elements of article 21 of the 1976 Rules, but, inspired mainly by Article 16 of the UNCITRAL Model Law, also expands on a number of points. The old and new elements have been streamlined and structured into three paragraphs, addressing: (i) *compétence de la compétence* and separability; (ii) the timing of an objection to the jurisdiction of the tribunal; and (iii) procedural aspects of objections to jurisdiction, such as bifurcation and court control. The Rules do not address the questions of temporal co-ordination or priority vis-à-vis state courts (including the 'negative effect' of *compétence de la compétence*); nor do they set out rules on the validity or effectiveness of arbitration agreements. These matters, whose importance cannot be overstated, are addressed by the 1958 New York Convention and the law governing the arbitration.

A. *COMPÉTENCE DE LA COMPÉTENCE* AND SEPARABILITY[1]

2. The 1976 Rules set forth in article 21 two rules of elemental importance to arbitration: the rule that the tribunal has the power – indeed, the duty – to pronounce on objections to its jurisdiction (*compétence de la compétence*); and the rule that pathologies affecting the validity or effectiveness of the main agreement, which memorialises the substantive obligations of the parties, do not automatically affect an arbitration clause which is included in or which accompanies the main agreement (separability). While neither of these rules was revolutionary at the time, the 1976 Rules were notable for including both of them in a set of arbitration rules[2] and articulating them with forceful clarity. These two rules are maintained in article 23 of the 2010 Rules, with minor amendments mostly for precision. Before examining the revised provisions, it may be useful to outline the basic functions they serve, which are distinct but complementary.

3. *Compétence de la compétence* is logically the more important of the two rules, hence it was set forth in article 21(1) of the 1976 Rules. It not only permits but in fact mandates the tribunal to determine objections to its jurisdiction, and in doing so it deprives a recalcitrant party of an opportunity to stall the arbitral process at

[1] *See* generally William W. Park, *The Arbitrator's Jurisdiction to Determine Jurisdiction*, 13 ICCA Congress Series 55 (Kluwer 2007); and Pierre Mayer, *L'autonomie de l'arbitre international dans l'appréciation de sa propre compétence*, 217 RdC 320 (1989-V).

[2] The 1955 ICC Rules (Article 13(3)) and the 1966 ECE Rules (Article 18) provided for *compétence de la compétence*. The provision on separability (the final sentence of article 21(2)) was lifted almost verbatim from article 18(2) of the Uniform Law annexed to the 1966 European Arbitration Convention.

its very beginning by challenging the foundation of the tribunal's jurisdictional power and removing the matter to state courts.[3] The power of a tribunal to rule on its own jurisdiction has been rightly characterized as a necessary power of any judicial formation in order properly to discharge its functions,[4] and indeed historically it was the first power that international tribunals claimed as part of their 'inherent powers' when their constitutive instrument did not set it out expressly.[5] But it is straightforward to see why it is a power that should be set out expressly in the case of tribunals whose jurisdiction is the creature of party agreement: it is logically possible to say that if the very agreement on which their jurisdiction is allegedly founded is put in question, that question must be decided by a third party whose power to decide the matter is not in question – here, a court. Thus the respondent could say, 'I have never agreed to arbitration, and if an arbitral tribunal were to sit in judgment of this issue, it would be hoisting itself up by its own bootstraps'. Article 21(1) of the 1976 Rules preserves the tribunal's jurisdictional power in the face of such arguments.

4. Moreover, the power to pronounce upon one's own jurisdiction encompasses the duty not only to affirm it when jurisdiction is extant but also to reject it when it is not.[6] That is to say, *compétence de la compétence* is the basis on which a tribunal has jurisdiction to say that there is no foundation for it to exercise jurisdiction on the merits of the case. Absent that rule, a tribunal would have to stand down without being able to pronounce on its jurisdiction if it were to conclude that it had no jurisdiction because of a defect in the arbitration agreement: the tribunal's finding that it has no jurisdiction would automatically cancel any power to make that pronouncement. (As explained at paragraph 6, the rule of separability does not suffice to give that power in all cases.)

5. Ultimately, the proper source for a power to make negative rulings on jurisdiction cannot be the parties' arbitration agreement (including the UNCITRAL Rules, which are incorporated by reference in the parties' agreement), because in that

---

3 Pieter Sanders, *Model Rules for International Commercial Arbitration: UNCITRAL Arbitration Rules*, Report for 7th ICCA Congress (1974), <www.arbitration-icca.org>. In the words of Professor Sanders: 'Arbitrators are instructed to give their opinion on the validity of the arbitration agreement. They cannot suspend the proceedings and refer parties to Court in case an objection to their competence has been raised. This would be a too easy way for a recalcitrant party to frustrate arbitral proceedings'; *ibid.*, at para. 6.

4 *See* Nigel Blackaby, Constantine Partasides, Alan Redfern & Martin J. Hunter, *Redfern and Hunter on International Arbitration*, para. 5.104 (6th ed., Kluwer 2015). The concept is now well established and widely accepted in domestic laws; *see* generally *ibid.*, at paras 5.105-5.109.

5 Cf. *Nottebohm, Liechtenstein v. Guatemala*, Judgment, ICJ Rep 111, 119 (1953).

6 As the German Supreme Court put it in a celebrated decision in 1970: 'There is every reason to presume that reasonable parties will wish to have the relationships created by their contract and the claims arising therefrom, irrespective of whether their contract is effective or not, decided by the same tribunal and not by two different tribunals'. Peter Schlosser, *The Decision of 27 February 1970 of the Federal Supreme Court of the Federal Republic of Germany (Bundesgerichtshof)*, 6 Arb Int 79, 84 (1990). The passage was quoted with approval by Lord Hoffmann in *Premium Nafta Products Ltd (20th Defendant) & Ors v. Fili Shipping Company Ltd & Ors* [2007] UKHL 40 ('*Fiona Trust*'), para. 14.

hypothesis there will have been no such valid agreement in the first place. The consequences of any defects in the parties' agreement cannot be conclusively regulated by that agreement if the agreement is found to be defective. The ultimate source of this power must therefore be the law, and the UNCITRAL Model Law reprises the text of the Rules in article 16(1).[7]

6. The rule of separability, set out in article 21(2) of the 1976 Rules, performs complementary functions to those of *compétence de la compétence*. Separability means nothing more than that defects of the arbitration clause must be demonstrated specifically, separately from any equivalent defects in the parties' main agreement; and that, conversely, a defect in the main agreement will not automatically entrain the existence of the same defect in the arbitration clause. Separability does not mean that no defect affecting the validity or effect of the main agreement can ever affect the arbitration clause.[8] Rather, it means that any such effect must be specifically demonstrated and will not be presumed.[9] Indeed, it is possible that a defect will affect *only* the arbitration clause but leave the main agreement unaffected. This kind of 'obverse severability'[10] may occur for example when a vice of form or capacity (writing requirement, need for authorized signatories, etc.) concerns only the arbitration clause but not the main agreement. Other examples include the designation of a bogus arbitral institution or self-serving procedures imposed by one party to the detriment of the other.[11]

7. In the *Fiona Trust* case, Lord Hoffmann articulated separability under section 7 of the English Arbitration Act 1996[12] as follows:

> The principle of separability enacted in section 7 means that the invalidity or rescission of the main contract does not necessarily entail the invalidity or rescission of the arbitration agreement. The arbitration agreement must be treated as a 'distinct agreement' and can be void or voidable only on grounds which relate directly to the arbitration agreement. Of course there may be

---

7 *See* further, e.g., Section 30 of the Arbitration Act 1996 (England & Wales) ('the arbitral tribunal may rule on its own substantive jurisdiction, that is, as to— (a) whether there is a valid arbitration agreement'); Article 1465 of the French Code of Civil Procedure ('The arbitral tribunal has exclusive jurisdiction to rule on objections to its jurisdiction').

8 *See*, e.g., Mark S. McNeill & Ben Juratowitch, *Agora: Thoughts on Fiona Trust – The doctrine of separability and consent to arbitrate*, 24 Arb Int 475, 477-478 (2008).

9 It is therefore correct to say that '[an arbitration clause's] validity does not depend on the validity of the contract as a whole' (Blackaby, Partasides, Redfern & Hunter, *supra* fn 4, at para. 5.101), in the sense that proving that the contract is invalid will in principle not suffice to prove that the arbitration clause is also invalid.

10 *See* Adrian Briggs, *Agreements on Jurisdiction and Choice of Law*, paras 3.44-3.48 (Oxford University Press 2008); and Jan Paulsson, *The Idea of Arbitration*, Chapter 3.1(c) (Oxford University Press 2013).

11 *See* Paulsson, *ibid.*

12 Section 7: 'Unless otherwise agreed by the parties, an arbitration agreement which forms or was intended to form part of another agreement (whether or not in writing) shall not be regarded as invalid, non-existent or ineffective because that other agreement is invalid, or did not come into existence or has become ineffective, and it shall for that purpose be treated as a distinct agreement'.

cases in which the ground upon which the main agreement is invalid is identical with the ground upon which the arbitration agreement is invalid. For example, if the main agreement and the arbitration agreement are contained in the same document and one of the parties claims that he never agreed to anything in the document and that his signature was forged, that will be an attack on the validity of the arbitration agreement. But the ground of attack is not that the main agreement was invalid. It is that the signature to the arbitration agreement, as a 'distinct agreement', was forged. Similarly, if a party alleges that someone who purported to sign as agent on his behalf had no authority whatever to conclude any agreement on his behalf, that is an attack on both the main agreement and the arbitration agreement.

On the other hand, if (as in this case) the allegation is that the agent exceeded his authority by entering into a main agreement in terms which were not authorized or for improper reasons, that is not necessarily an attack on the arbitration agreement. It would have to be shown that whatever the terms of the main agreement or the reasons for which the agent concluded it, he would have had no authority to enter into an arbitration agreement. Even if the allegation is that there was no concluded agreement (for example, that terms of the main agreement remained to be agreed) that is not necessarily an attack on the arbitration agreement. If the arbitration clause has been agreed, the parties will be presumed to have intended the question of whether there was a concluded main agreement to be decided by arbitration.[13]

8. The rule of separability affords the foundation for a tribunal to make a holding that the parties' main contract was invalid without by the same stroke of the pen cancelling its own jurisdiction, when that jurisdiction is to be found in an arbitration clause in the main contract.[14] That is of course true so long as either the validity of the arbitration clause has not been impeached or, if it has been, the clause has been found to be valid. But if the arbitration clause is invalid – and a ruling on that point is logically prior to a ruling on the validity of the main agreement[15] – separability will provide no foundation for the tribunal's jurisdiction. That is why *compétence de la compétence* is the more important of the two basic rules in article 21 of the 1976 Rules.

9. As is the case for *compétence de la compétence*, the ultimate source for a rule of separability must be extrinsic to the parties' agreement: the ultimate source must be the law. Hence Article 16(1) of the Model Law reprises the two key propositions of the three that are set out in article 21(2) of the 1976 Rules.

---

13 *Fiona Trust*, *supra* fn 6, at paras 17-18.

14 *See*, e.g., Blackaby, Partasides, Redfern & Hunter, *supra* fn 4, at paras 5.100-5.102. Interestingly the Secretary-General did not spell this out during the drafting of the 1976 Rules; *see* UNCITRAL Report of the Secretary General on the Draft UNCITRAL Arbitration Rules, 12 December 1975, UN Doc A/CN.9/112/Add.1, 174 para. 5.

15 Hence under article 21(4) of the 1976 Rules the tribunal '[i]n general ... should rule' on it 'as a preliminary question'. Although article 23(3) of the 2010 Rules has removed this recommendation in respect of bifurcation of the proceedings, issues of jurisdiction (such as the validity of the arbitration agreement or clause) logically precede issues of the merits (such as the validity of the parties' main agreement).

1. *Compétence de la compétence* under article 23(1)

10. Article 23 of the 2010 Rules speaks broadly of the tribunal's 'jurisdiction'. It is plain from paragraphs (1) and (2) that the term 'jurisdiction' encompasses both (i) comprehensive objections to the tribunal's jurisdiction to examine any of the claims between the parties and (ii) partial objections to the effect that some claims before the tribunal are not covered by the arbitration agreement and are thus 'beyond the scope of its authority'. The latter category of objections would include questions as to whether the tribunal can entertain a particular remedy (for example, where the parties have stipulated that specific performance is not available, or that the tribunal may adjust certain aspects of the contract but not others in certain circumstances)[16] or adjudicate upon a class of claims (for example, claims in tort or unjust enrichment, rather than claims on a contract).

11. Further, the *travaux* make clear that the tribunal's power to 'rule on its own jurisdiction' encompasses the power to rule on whether in the circumstances it should exercise a jurisdiction that it has – in other words, the power to pronounce on the admissibility of the claim before it.[17] The Working Group 'confirmed its understanding that the general power of the arbitral tribunal ... to decide upon its jurisdiction should be interpreted as including the power ... to decide upon the admissibility of the parties' claims'.[18] To illustrate, issues of timeliness of claims; res judicata defences;[19] compliance with pre-arbitration 'cooling-off' periods or similar requirements;[20] and absence of necessary parties will fall within

---

16 Cf. *Quintette Coal Ltd v. Nippon Steel Corp* [1990] 47 BCLR (2d) 201 (SC), aff'd 50 BCLR (2d) 207 (CA) (British Columbia); and *Gas Natural Aprovisionamientos SDG SA v. Atlantic LNG Co of Trinidad and Tobago*, 2008 WL 4344525 (SD New York).

17 For the distinction between jurisdiction and admissibility *see* Jan Paulsson, 'Jurisdiction and Admissibility' in *Global Reflections on International Law, Commerce and Dispute Resolution – Liber Amicorum in honour of Robert Briner*, 601 (ICC Publication 693) (2005); Gerald Fitzmaurice, *The Law and Procedure of the International Court of Justice*, 438-439 (Grotius Publications 1986) ('There is a clear jurisprudential distinction between an objection to the jurisdiction of the tribunal, and an objection to the substantive admissibility of the claim. The latter is a plea that the tribunal should rule the claim to be inadmissible on some ground other than its ultimate merits; the former is a plea that the tribunal itself is incompetent to give any ruling at all whether as to the merits or as to the admissibility of the claim'); and Zachary Douglas, *The International Law of Investment Claims*, paras 306-311 (Cambridge University Press 2009).

18 UNCITRAL Report of 50th Session, 9 March 2009, UN Doc A/CN.9/669, para. 39.

19 *See* UNCITRAL Report of the Secretary-General, Analytical commentary on draft text of a model law on international commercial arbitration, 25 March 1985, UN Doc A/CN.9/264, XVI UNCITRAL Ybk 104, 122 para. 8 (1985); *see also Apotex Holdings Inc and Apotex Inc v. United States of America* (ICSID Case No. ARB(AF)/12/1) Award, 25 August 2014, <www.italaw.com>, Part VII (NAFTA Chapter Eleven tribunal analysed international jurisprudence before taking a flexible approach in upholding respondent's jurisdictional objections on the grounds of res judicata).

20 Cf. the notion of procedural arbitrability in US law: *Howsam v. Dean Witter Reynolds Inc*, (01-800) 537 U.S. 79 (2002) 261 F.3d 956. *See also BG Group PLC v. Republic of Argentina*, (12-138) 572 U.S. __ (2014) (noting that the Argentina-UK BIT did not expressly state whether issues of arbitrability should be decided by courts or the arbitrators, the US Supreme

the rubric of admissibility. Thus the tribunal in *Larsen v. Hawaiian Kingdom* held that 'the nature of the arbitral function requires the Tribunal carefully to scrutinise the submissions of the parties in order to ensure that they do in fact disclose the existence of a dispute and to decline to exercise jurisdiction if it is not satisfied on that score'.[21] It was not sufficient that both parties claimed that there was a dispute; indeed, the tribunal found that, properly understood, the dispute submitted to it was in fact not one between the parties to the arbitration agreement, as required under article 1(1) of the 1976 Rules, but a dispute between each of them and a third party, the United States.

12. Nevertheless, article 23(1) of the 2010 Rules does not provide a definition of matters that go to 'jurisdiction', and it has never been suggested that such a definition would be desirable.[22] The Model Law also speaks in terms of 'jurisdiction' in Article 16. It is therefore possible to include in the concept of jurisdiction any impediment to the tribunal's examination of the merits of the dispute.[23] Such impediments would *not* include defects in the constitution of the tribunal: whether such defects arise from lack of independence/impartiality (see the challenge procedure under article 12 of the 2010 Rules) or on other grounds (e.g. lack of agreed qualifications for arbitrators), under the Rules the tribunal has no competence to consider such complaints. An objection must be entered by the complaining party on pain of waiver (see Article 32), but the tribunal is not the forum for it. Nevertheless, an objection to the effect that the parties' agreement does not provide for arbitration under the UNCITRAL Rules but under other rules (cf. article 1(1)) does go to the tribunal's jurisdiction within the meaning of article 23(1).

13. Article 23(1) adopts from article 21(1) of the 1976 Rules the express stipulation that the tribunal's jurisdiction extends to 'any objections with respect to the existence or validity of the arbitration agreement'. This has the effect of making this competence part of the tribunal's jurisdiction even if the parties have not stipulated so in their arbitration agreement,[24] and even if it is not the controlling forum's policy to construe arbitration agreements in this way.[25] Indeed, depriving

Court applied the presumptions in *Howsam v. Dean Witter Reynolds Inc* and found that the arbitrators had not exceeded their authority by deciding a condition precedent to an obligation to arbitrate).

21 *Larsen v. Hawaiian Kingdom* (UNCITRAL) PCA Case No. 1999-01, Award, 5 February 2001, < www.pca-cpa.org >, para. 11.7.

22 *See* generally on the issue of jurisdictional questions, William W. Park, *supra* fn 1, at 65-84.

23 Pieter Sanders, *Commentary on UNCITRAL Arbitration Rules*, II YCA 172, 198 (1977) (referring to objections 'that the arbitrators are not entitled at all to serve in that capacity').

24 Cf. the model arbitration clause for contracts, Annex to the 2010 Rules, which provides that a dispute, controversy or claim relating to the 'invalidity' of the contract shall be settled in accordance with the UNCITRAL Rules.

25 Cf. *Fiona Trust*, *supra* fn 6, at para. 13 ('the construction of an arbitration clause should start from the assumption that the parties, as rational businessmen, are likely to have intended any dispute arising out of the relationship into which they have entered or purported to enter to be decided by the same tribunal. The clause should be construed in accordance

arbitral tribunals of jurisdiction to deal with issues affecting their very standing to adjudicate the dispute would render arbitral tribunals toothless.

14. Nevertheless, the competence granted to an arbitral tribunal by article 23(1) will have to yield to a specific contrary party agreement. Although article 23(1) is formulated in mandatory terms ('The arbitral tribunal *shall have* the power' (emphasis added)), there can be no question that a specific agreement whereby the parties exclude the tribunal's competence to rule on the validity or effect of the arbitration agreement and instead agree that article 23(1) of the Rules will not apply is a valid 'modification' of the Rules within the meaning of article 1(1). The wisdom of such a stipulation is of course dubious, but the point is that it would be a valid one under the Rules and 'comparatively simple'[26] to make.

15. Given that the tribunal's competence to adjudicate issues of jurisdiction extends to the very 'existence or validity of the arbitration agreement' (article 23(1) of the Rules), lesser issues going to the effectiveness of the arbitration agreement are also encompassed. Such issues include potential waiver or termination or expiry of the arbitration agreement, the identity of the parties to the agreement, and (as noted) whether it refers to the UNCITRAL Rules.

2. Tribunal's mandatory power to rule on its jurisdiction

16. At the risk of stating the obvious, the competence of the tribunal set out in article 23 means that neither one of the parties to the putative arbitration agreement, nor any one of the arbitrators, nor the appointing authority or the PCA as the designating authority can refuse to perform a function under the Rules on grounds that there is no valid arbitration agreement in place. Such a determination under the Rules can only be made by the tribunal, once constituted.[27]

17. A crucial element of article 23(1) of the 2010 Rules, as in article 21(1) of the 1976 Rules, is that it is drafted in mandatory terms: 'The arbitral tribunal shall have the power to rule on its own jurisdiction'. As noted at paragraph 3, this tribunal power is in fact clearly a duty when objections to the existence, scope, or exercise of its jurisdiction are raised by a party. By contrast, it is in principle not for the tribunal to identify of its own initiative objections to its jurisdiction which the parties could have raised but did not raise in a timely fashion.[28] A failure by a party to raise a jurisdictional defence available amounts to a choice to accept the tribunal's jurisdiction in the course of the proceedings, which is of course a time-tested and valid form of forming an arbitration agreement. A legally equivalent analysis is that a failure to advance an objection amounts to a waiver (as discussed at paragraph 28 below). Nevertheless, it is clear from the

with this presumption unless the language makes it clear that certain questions were intended to be excluded from the arbitrator's jurisdiction').

26 *Fiona Trust & Holding Corp & Ors v. Yuri Privalov & Ors* [2007] EWCA Civ 20, para. 17 (per Longmore LJ).

27 *See also* discussion of article 6 of the 2010 Rules, *supra*.

28 As to time-limits, *see* discussion of article 23(2) of the 2010 Rules, *infra*.

revisions made to article 23(1) of the 2010 Rules, compared to article 21(1) of the 1976 Rules, that the tribunal's power is no longer dependent on 'objections that it has no jurisdiction' (article 21(1) of the 1976 Rules).[29] The tribunal's ability 'to rule on its own jurisdiction', including *sua sponte*, is consistent with other major arbitration rules,[30] and removes the limitation imposed by article 21(1) of the 1976 Rules.[31]

18. The tribunal may thus of its own motion identify jurisdictional issues arising from inarbitrability (due to the subject-matter of the dispute or arising from a party's inability validly to submit to arbitration)[32] or contrariety of the arbitral process to public policy (for example, when the contract is a façade for a money-laundering scheme and the illegality may extend to the arbitration clause therein).[33] The same is true of impediments to the tribunal's proper exercise of its adjudicatory function on grounds of manifest absence of a genuine or

---

29 *See* UNCITRAL Report of 45th Session, 5 October 2006, UN Doc A/CN.9/614, para. 97 (such a revision was required because arbitrators need to decide on their jurisdiction *sua sponte* 'where one party did not participate in the proceedings or where complex issues of arbitrability were at stake [e.g. competition issues, of which] the parties were not necessarily aware').

30 *See*, e.g., Articles 6(3) and 6(5) of the ICC Rules; Article 23.1 of the LCIA Rules; and Article 19(1) of the AAA International Arbitration Rules. Cf. Article 21(1) of the Swiss Rules and Article 36(a) of the WIPO Rules which adopt the same language used in article 21(1) of the 1976 Rules.

31 On a strict reading, article 21(1) of the 1976 Rules did not allow arbitrators to rule on their own jurisdiction if no jurisdictional objection had been raised by the parties. *See*, e.g., *Telenor Mobile Communications AS v. Storm LLC* (SD New York) Petition for Enforcement of Final Award, 2 November 2007, XXXIII YCA 1041 (2008), para. 24: 'The UNCITRAL rules only allow arbitrators to rule on objections to that authority [jurisdiction]. Thus, while incorporation of the ICC and AAA rules may be "clear and unmistakable evidence" that the parties intended for the arbitrators to have sole jurisdiction over the arbitrability of the dispute, the UNCITRAL language, standing alone, is insufficient to strip [respondent] of its ability to "present evidence of [the agreement's] ... invalidity" to this Court').

32 *See* UNCITRAL Report of the Secretary-General, Analytical commentary on draft text of a model law on international commercial arbitration, 25 March 1985, UN Doc A/CN.9/264, XVI UNCITRAL Ybk 104, 121 para. 3 (1985).

33 Cf. *CME Czech Republic BV v. The Czech Republic* (UNCITRAL) Partial Award, 13 September 2001, <www.italaw.com>, paras 99-100; and Article V(2)(a)-(b) of the New York Convention. The view articulated here is consistent with the Recommendations of the International Law Association on ascertaining the contents of the applicable law in international commercial arbitration (Resolution No 6/2008). Recommendation 6 of this text reads as follows: 'In general, and subject to Recommendation 13, arbitrators should not introduce legal issues – propositions of law that may bear on the outcome of the dispute – that the parties have not raised'. Recommendation 13 reads: 'In disputes implicating rules of public policy or other rules from which the parties may not derogate, arbitrators may be justified in taking measures appropriate to determine the applicability and contents of such rules, including by making independent research, raising with the parties new issues (whether legal or factual), and giving appropriate instructions or ordering appropriate measures insofar as they consider this necessary to abide by those rules or to protect against challenges to the award'.

justiciable dispute between the parties.[34] As such issues may be raised by the controlling or enforcement courts of their own initiative,[35] and therefore by the parties themselves for the first time in such proceedings, it is appropriate for the arbitral tribunal also to be able to raise them of its own initiative, consistent with the general precept that it is incumbent on the tribunal to ensure that its award will be valid and enforceable. It is difficult, however, to speak of a legal *duty* on the tribunal, such that failure to identify impediments to jurisdiction which the parties did not raise can attract liability (cf. article 16).

19. If the tribunal does identify a jurisdictional or admissibility issue of its own initiative, it goes without saying that it will have to ask the parties to address it, giving them a fair and sufficient opportunity to do so.[36] As to when the tribunal should raise such issues, it seems clear from article 23(2) that it should not do so before the respondent's statement of defence or the claimant's defence to counterclaims ('reply') but, according to the general rule of efficiency in article 17(1), it should do so as soon as possible thereafter.

20. One further point that arises from the 'shall have the power' mandatory wording of article 23(1) is the extent to which the tribunal's decisional power is exclusive of any such power for the domestic courts – i.e., the 'negative effect' of *compétence de la compétence*.[37] Although the Rules confine themselves to the powers of arbitral tribunals, it is clear that they were conceived from the outset on the premise that the ultimate say on issues of jurisdiction belonged to the controlling courts. As Professor Sanders put it: 'The final word on the competence of arbitrators is for the court: Where the competence of arbitrators is involved, the jurisdiction of the courts cannot be excluded'.[38] This would seem to suggest that a national court may pronounce – and pronounce conclusively – upon an arbitral tribunal's jurisdiction but only after the tribunal has done so: after all, if the court were to take temporal priority in addition to decisional precedence, nothing would be left of the decisional power that the Rules say a tribunal 'shall' have.

21. However, such a reading would be wrong in two respects. First, the Rules were conceived with Article II(3) of the New York Convention in mind. That provision allows a court 'when seized of an action in a matter in respect of which the parties have made an agreement within the meaning of this article' to proceed to decide on the merits if it finds that the putative arbitration agreement 'is null and void, inoperative, or incapable of being performed'.[39] True, article II(3) is

---

[34] *See* the discussion of *Larsen v. Hawaiian Kingdom, supra* at para. 11.

[35] *See*, e.g., articles 34(2)(a)(i), 34(2)(b), 36(1)(a)(i) and 36(1)(b) of the UNCITRAL Model Law.

[36] *See* articles 17(1)-(4) of the 2010 Rules.

[37] For an overview *see* Emmanuel Gaillard & Yas Banifatemi, 'Negative Effect of Competence-Competence: The Rule of Priority in Favor of the Arbitrators' in Emmanuel Gaillard & Domenico Di Pietro (eds), *Enforcement of Arbitration Agreements and International Arbitral Awards – The New York Convention in Practice*, 257 (Cameron May 2008).

[38] Pieter Sanders, *Procedures and Practices under the UNCITRAL Rules*, 27 Am J Comp L 453, 462 (1979).

[39] *See* to the same effect Article 8(1) of the Model Law.

formulated in language which clearly indicates that arbitration agreements are presumed valid and effective, and have to be shown to be otherwise. In addition, there is authority for the proposition that the court should hear the action on the merits only in cases of manifest invalidity or ineffectiveness.[40] But, restricted as it may be in scope and modality, incidental court review under Article II(3) of the New York Convention clearly allows a court to determine the foundation of an arbitral tribunal's putative jurisdiction before the tribunal has done so.[41]

22. The second reason is to be found in article 1(3) of the Rules, which preserves the primacy of mandatory provisions of the *lex arbitri*. Court control of arbitral jurisdiction is under most laws a matter that cannot be altered by contrary party agreement. Of course many laws permit the tribunal[42] to complete its jurisdictional review and only then allow for challenges to be made to the tribunal's determination.[43] But this is not the position everywhere,[44] and in arbitrations governed by laws that give temporal priority to the courts, clearly the tribunal's power under article 23(1) of the Rules may have to give way.

3. Separability

23. Article 21(2) of the 1976 Rules addresses the concept of separability. It states that the arbitration agreement is 'independent' from the main contract and that 'a decision by the arbitral tribunal that the [main] contract is null and void shall not entail *ipso jure* the invalidity of the arbitration clause'. This rule applies to all defects of the main agreement, whether *ab initio* or supervening.[45] The rule of separability in the Rules is one of procedural, not substantive, law. Its primary objective is to permit the arbitral tribunal to pronounce on its jurisdiction. As already noted (paragraph 9), the substantive separability rule will have to be found in the law governing the arbitration.

---

40 *See* Albert Jan van den Berg, *The New York Arbitration Convention of 1958, Towards a Uniform Judicial Interpretation*, 155 (Kluwer 1981).

41 Hence Gaillard and Banifatemi put the matter as follows: 'Accepting [the] positive effect of the principle of competence-competence and the arbitrators' inherent power to determine their jurisdiction on the basis of the arbitration agreement entails the consequence that domestic courts should not, in parallel and with the same degree of scrutiny, rule on the same issue, at least at the outset of the arbitral process. In other words, the courts should limit, at that stage, their review to a prima facie determination that the agreement is not "null and void, inoperative or incapable of being performed"': *see supra* fn 37, at 259.

42 Even if the tribunal is seized while an action on the merits is pending before a national court: thus Article 8(2) of the Model Law.

43 *See*, e.g., Article 16(3) of the Model Law; sections 32(1)-(2) of the English Arbitration Act 1996.

44 *See*, e.g., China (article 20 of the Arbitration Law of the PRC allowing jurisdictional objections to be raised either before the tribunal or a people's court), Pakistan, Egypt and Israel (which allow national courts to rule on arbitral jurisdiction before the tribunal itself decides).

45 Cf. UNCITRAL Report of the Secretary-General, Analytical commentary on draft text of a model law on international commercial arbitration, 25 March 1985, UN Doc A/CN.9/264, XVI UNCITRAL Ybk 104, 121 para. 2 (1985).

24. During the revision process, the Working Group revisited the expression 'null and void', which is also found in the Model Law and in the New York Convention.[46] Although no major issues had arisen from the term 'null and void' in practice, some common-law countries expressed concerns about whether the term excluded agreements that are voidable (and thus give rise to a right to avoid them).[47] To accommodate these concerns, the Working Group decided to omit the term 'void' in article 23. The Working Group found that 'the term "null" was wide enough to cover all contractual defects'.[48] The intent therefore is for 'null' to cover all possible grounds on which a putative agreement may fail to produce legal effect, whether *ab initio* or later (including that the agreement has expired). Thus 'null' was chosen with the distinct purpose of being an all-encompassing autonomous term that should *not* be read in the light of any particular domestic law.[49]

25. While the principle of separability is established with regard to commercial contracts, it is not necessarily recognized in respect of international treaties. For that reason the Working Group was careful not to add the words 'or other legal instrument' after the word 'contract' in the second and third sentences of article 23(1).[50]

26. In addition, as a point of formulation, '*ipso jure*' under article 21(2) of the 1976 Rules was modernized to 'automatically'.[51]

B. TIME-LIMITS FOR RAISING JURISDICTIONAL ISSUES

27. Article 23(2) of the 2010 Rules adopts the time-limits set out in article 21(3) of the 1976 Rules, establishing that objections to jurisdiction have to be raised no

46 Articles 8(1) and 16(1) of the Model Law; and Article II(3) of the New York Convention.

47 *See* APRAG Report of 50th Session, 27 February 2009, para. 30 (use of the term 'null and void' may 'lead to issues and questions as to whether a contract is void or voidable and hence may raise issues as to the right to avoid'). In support of this view, delegates referred to *Harbour Assurance Co (UK) v. Kansa General International Insurance Co* [1993] QB 701, 723, where the Court of Appeal recognized that while the principle of separability applies, 'there will obviously be cases in which a claim that no contract came into existence necessarily entails a denial that there was any agreement to arbitrate. Cases of non est factum or denial that there was a concluded agreement, or mistake as to the identity of the other contracting party suggest themselves as examples'. Cf. *Buckeye Check Cashing Inc v. Cardegna*, 546 US 440 (US SCt 2006), where the US Supreme Court held that separability applies both where the main agreement is allegedly void and voidable.

48 UNCITRAL Report of 50th Session, 9 March 2009, UN Doc A/CN.9/669, para. 42.

49 *See* APRAG Report of 50th Session, 27 February 2009, para. 31 (use of the word 'non-existent' was rejected as it 'would be contrary to the usual approach applied to the UNCITRAL Rules ... which is usually to try and avoid terms that have particular meanings in one jurisdiction').

50 *See* UNCITRAL Report of 50th Session, 9 March 2009, UN Doc A/CN.9/669, paras 36-37.

51 *See* UNCITRAL Report of 46th Session, 20 March 2007, UN Doc A/CN.9/619, para. 162; and UNCITRAL Report of 50th Session, 9 March 2009, UN Doc A/CN.9/669, para. 44. While earlier drafts adopted the wording 'of itself', 'automatically' was thought to be a more accurate translation of '*ipso jure*'.

later than the statement of defence or, with respect to a counterclaim by the respondent, in the claimant's reply to the counterclaim. When the pleading sequence is different, for example in a triangular multiparty dispute, objections are to be formulated with the first comprehensive written pleading defending against a substantive claim/counterclaim. In case jurisdictional objections have been set down from the outset for separate pleadings in a preliminary phase, the cut-off date will naturally be that which is set in the procedural schedule. Indeed, it is in everyone's best interests to raise such objections as early as possible, in the response to the notice for arbitration (expressly contemplated in article 4(2)(a) of the 2010 Rules), so that the attendant procedural issues such as bifurcation can be addressed in the procedural timetable to be established under article 17(2).[52] By contrast, the ICSID Arbitration Rules allow jurisdictional objections to be raised as late as the first substantive pleading,[53] while the ICC Rules do not provide any time limitation.[54] However, the Rules do not spell out the temporal rule that should be applied to a jurisdictional objection to the respondent's claim against an additional respondent (pursuant to article 4(2)(f)). We submit that such a jurisdictional objection may be raised in the response to the respondent's notice of arbitration (if any is submitted), and no later than in the statement of defence by the additional respondent.

28. There is thus a general duty in article 23(2) to formulate jurisdictional objections early, which extends not only to comprehensive objections that the arbitral tribunal totally lacks jurisdiction but also to objections that some claims fall astride a jurisdiction that is otherwise admitted. Hence, article 23(2) includes a new sentence explicitly encouraging parties to raise any 'plea that the arbitral tribunal is exceeding the scope of its authority' as soon as possible, in line with Article 16(2) of the Model Law. Although article 23(2) does not state so explicitly, the parties' failure to raise jurisdictional objections in a timely fashion may lead to the finding that the right to object has been irrevocably waived.[55] Indeed, it follows from the waiver provision in the Rules (article 32) that it is incumbent on a party contesting the tribunal's jurisdiction to avail itself of the opportunity to raise such objections in a timely fashion, on pain of waiver. In fact, the *travaux*

---

52 Cf. Article 21(3) of the Swiss Rules which reads: 'As a rule, any objection to the jurisdiction of the arbitral tribunal shall be raised in the Answer to the Notice of Arbitration, and in no event later than in the Statement of Defence ... or, with respect to a counterclaim, in the reply to the counterclaim'.

53 Rule 41(1) of the ICSID Arbitration Rules provides in material part: 'a party shall file the objection [that the dispute or ancillary claim is not within the jurisdiction of the Centre, or for other reasons, is not within the competence of the Tribunal] with the Secretary-General no later than the expiration of the time limit fixed for the filing of the counter-memorial, or, if the objection relates to an ancillary claim, for the filing of the rejoinder'.

54 *See* Articles 6(3)-(5) of the ICC Rules; cf. Article 23.3 of the LCIA Rules which sets a similar time-limit to that in the UNCITRAL Rules.

55 *See* Sanders, *supra* fn 23, at 198; and Nigel Blackaby, Constantine Partasides, Alan Redfern & Martin J. Hunter, *Redfern and Hunter on International Arbitration*, para. 5.119 and fn 170 (5th ed., Kluwer 2009).

to the Model Law[56] and subsequent case law[57] have affirmed such a preclusive effect, unless the challenge to the tribunal's jurisdiction is based on public policy grounds, including arbitrability.[58] The main intention of imposing time-limits is to make the arbitral proceedings more efficient. After all:

> It is axiomatic that a respondent should not be able to raise an objection to jurisdiction at a late stage of the arbitration, at a point when time and costs will have been expended, possibly uselessly. To allow this would be to open the possibility of serious abuse of the arbitral process.[59]

29. Indeed, the drafting history of the 1976 Rules shows that untimely jurisdictional objections could be admitted only in very rare circumstances, under the general powers granted to arbitrators to conduct the arbitration by article 15(1) (now article 17(1)).[60] The practice under article 21(3) of the 1976 Rules confirms the intention of the original drafters. Arbitral tribunals have generally relied on the time-limits set out in article 21(3) to bar tardy objections, with very limited exceptions.[61] For example, the tribunal in *CME v. Czech Republic* held that 'according to the UNCITRAL Rules, a defence of jurisdiction is deemed to be waived, if not raised in time'.[62] Nevertheless, wishing to harmonise the 2010 Rules with Article 16(2) of the Model Law,[63] the Working Group decided explicitly to set forth the arbitral tribunal's ability to 'admit a later plea if it considers the delay justified'.

---

[56] *See* UNCITRAL Report of the Secretary-General, Analytical commentary on draft text of a model law on international commercial arbitration, 25 March 1985, UN Doc A/CN.9/264, XVI UNCITRAL Ybk 104, 122 paras 8-9 (1985).

[57] *See* Oberlandesgericht Celle, Germany, 8 Sch 11/02, 4 September 2003, <www.dis-arb.de/en/ >; Oberlandesgericht Stuttgart, Germany, 1 Sch 16/01 (1), 20 December 2001, <www.dis-arb.de/en/ >; CLOUT Case No. 148 [Moscow City Court, Russian Federation, 10 February 1995]. *See also* CLOUT Case No. 562 [Hanseatisches Oberlandesgericht Hamburg, Germany, 6 Sch 04/01, 8 November 2001] (where a party was allowed to raise jurisdictional objections in setting aside proceedings although it had not previously done so before the tribunal, in light of the unusual circumstance that the party had never been properly informed of the commencement of the arbitration).

[58] Under the Model Law, challenges on public policy grounds in the setting aside and recognition and enforcement proceedings are provided for under Articles 34(2)(b) and 36(1)(b). *See also* Article V of the New York Convention.

[59] Peter Turner & Reza Mohtashami, *A Guide to the LCIA Arbitration Rules*, para. 6.98 (Oxford University Press 2009) (commenting on Article 23.2 of the 1998 LCIA Rules).

[60] *See* David D. Caron, Lee M. Caplan & Matti Pellonpää, *The UNCITRAL Arbitration Rules, A Commentary*, 449 and the references (Oxford University Press 2006).

[61] *See ibid.*, at 456-463. *See also Canfor Corporation v. United States of America and Tembec et al. v. United States of America and Terminal Forest Products Ltd v. United States of America* (UNCITRAL) Order of the Consolidation Tribunal, 7 September 2005, <www.italaw.com>, para. 103 (application of article 21(4) of the 1976 Rules in the context of a consolidation tribunal pursuant to Article 1126 of NAFTA. The tribunal found that if a party has not timely raised a plea as to jurisdiction in the Article 1120 arbitration, it is in principle barred from raising the plea in the consolidation proceedings).

[62] *CME Czech Republic BV v. The Czech Republic* (UNCITRAL) Partial Award, 13 September 2001, <www.italaw.com>, para. 380.

[63] Article 16(2) of the Model Law provides in material part: 'The arbitral tribunal may, in either case, admit a later plea if it considers the delay justified'.

Codification of a power that had been admitted to exist in practice should not alter the applicable test for the exercise of the power: an untimely jurisdictional objection should be admissible only in exceptional circumstances, primarily if it is based on newly discovered facts.[64]

30. In addition, article 23(2) incorporates another new sentence from Article 16(2) of the Model Law, clarifying that the objecting party has every interest in cooperating in the constitution of the arbitral tribunal, as such cooperation does not imply acceptance of the tribunal's jurisdiction.[65] In practice, some respondents would proactively address this issue by stating that their participation in the constitution of the tribunal does not amount to acceptance of the tribunal's jurisdiction.[66] Such reservations are easy enough to formulate if concerns about implied acceptance are honestly held. In fact, the express clarification in article 23(2) essentially serves the purpose of depriving recalcitrant parties of an excuse for not co-operating in the constitution of the tribunal.

C. PROCEDURAL ASPECTS OF OBJECTIONS TO JURISDICTION

1. Possibility of bifurcating the proceedings

31. Article 21(4) of the 1976 Rules expresses a preference 'in general' for the bifurcation of the proceedings into a jurisdictional (or 'preliminary') and merits phase, but ultimately leaves the decision to the arbitrators' discretion pursuant to article 15(1).[67] The preference was stated as a broad principle and without specific guidance as to how it should be exercised in practice.

---

[64] During the drafting of the 1976 Rules, the Conference provided only this one example of when a delay may be justified; *see* UNCITRAL Report of the Secretary General on the Draft UNCITRAL Arbitration Rules, 12 December 1975, UN Doc A/CN.9/112/Add.1, 174 para. 6. *See also* Rule 41(1) of the ICSID Arbitration Rules, which provides that parties must comply with the time-limits for submitting jurisdictional objections 'unless the facts on which the objection is based are unknown to the party at that time'. *See also European American Investment Bank AG (EURAM) v. Slovak Republic* (UNCITRAL) Second Award on Jurisdiction, 4 June 2014, <www.italaw.com>, para. 115: 'The Tribunal considers that what is now explicit in Article 23(2) of the 2010 Rules was implicit in the 1976 Rules. To preclude a respondent from making a jurisdictional objection after it submitted its statement of defence when that objection concerned facts which arose only after … that statement was filed would involve a grave injustice'.

[65] Sanders, *supra* fn 23, at 197 (taking the view that participation without specific objection/reservation in the constitution of the tribunal should amount to a waiver of objections to jurisdiction).

[66] *See Romak SA (Switzerland) v. The Republic of Uzbekistan* (UNCITRAL) Award, 26 November 2009, <www.italaw.com>, para. 77.

[67] The 1976 Rules do not give the parties a *right* to bifurcation. *See* David D. Caron & Lee M. Caplan, *The UNCITRAL Arbitration Rules, A Commentary*, 457-458 (2nd ed., Oxford University Press 2013); and *Glamis Gold Ltd v. The United States of America* (UNCITRAL) Procedural Order No. 2, 31 May 2005, <www.italaw.com>, para. 11 ('The Tribunal reads the presumption in favor of preliminarily considering an objection to jurisdiction as an

32. The preference for an early resolution of jurisdictional issues is rooted in the desire to make the proceedings more efficient, as it may save considerable time and money by either narrowing the scope of the dispute or disposing of the case entirely without entering the merits. The *Glamis v. US* tribunal identified several considerations an arbitral tribunal should take into account when assessing the potential for increasing the efficiency of proceedings in that context. These include asking: (i) whether the jurisdictional objection is non-frivolous; (ii) whether subsequent proceedings would be considerably narrowed by the granting of the request for bifurcation; and (iii) whether the jurisdictional and the merits issues are intertwined to the extent that a bifurcation would be impractical and savings in time or costs unlikely.[68]

33. An early determination of jurisdictional issues does not always lead to greater efficiency. The experience of the Iran-US Claims Tribunal is instructive in this regard. The 'initial enthusiasm of the Tribunal for bifurcation soon waned',[69] partly because this practice bore a significant disadvantage:

> If jurisdiction was ultimately sustained, bifurcation inevitably meant an additional round of written statements, a second deliberation, another award, and, unless the jurisdictional issue had been decided on the papers, a second hearing. Thus, far from saving time and money ... bifurcation potentially added hundreds of thousands of dollars to the expense and years of delay to the resolution of a claim.[70]

Thus, it will normally be more efficient for the tribunal to consider the objection to jurisdiction together with the merits when the entire case is relatively simple[71] or when jurisdictional considerations are too closely intertwined with the

---

instruction to the Tribunal [to ensure efficiency of the proceedings] and *clearly not as an absolute right of the requesting party*' (emphasis added)).

68 *Glamis Gold Ltd v. The United States of America* (UNCITRAL) Procedural Order No. 2, 31 May 2005, < www.italaw.com >, para. 12(c). These considerations constitute one prong of a three-prong test established by the *Glamis* tribunal for the bifurcation of proceedings. The other prongs are: (i) the claim must be taken as alleged by the claimant; and (ii) the plea must be one going to jurisdiction. In applying the 2010 Rules, however, at least one tribunal has referred to the substantive effect of the reformulation of article 21(4) of the 1976 Rules; *see Josias Van Zyl, Josias Van Zyl Family Trust, and Burmilla Trust v. Kingdom of Lesotho* (UNCITRAL) PCA Case No. 2016-21, Procedural Order No. 1, 3 November 2016, < www.italaw.com > (noting that the reformulated article 23(3) of the 2010 Rules signified a shift away from the presumption in favour of bifurcation evidenced in the 1976 Rules, the Tribunal stated that a different approach would be required. In particular the Tribunal took the view that its discretion should be guided by the procedural imperatives of efficiency and fairness, acknowledging that the criteria in the *Glamis* test, albeit 'perhaps less stringently stated, are helpful in identifying the factors that may bear on efficiency and fairness' (*ibid.*, at para. 46)).

69 Stewart A. Baker & Mark D. Davis, *The UNCITRAL Arbitration Rules in Practice – The Experience of the Iran-United States Claims Tribunal*, 107 (Kluwer 1992).

70 *Ibid.*

71 *See Fung Sang Trading Limited v. Kai Sun Sea Products and Food Company Limited* [1991] HKCFI 190.

substantive issue.[72] Conversely, however, if in addition to questions of jurisdiction there are preliminary merits questions as well (e.g. applicable law to the merits, applicable statute of limitations, etc.), it may be efficient to regroup all these questions into a single preliminary phase.

34. Against this background, the 2010 Rules do not express any preference on bifurcation.[73] Consistent with Article 16(3) of the Model Law, article 23(3) simply leaves it to the tribunal to rule on jurisdictional objections either as a preliminary question or in an award on the merits, guided by article 17(1). Evidently the practice that has developed under article 21(4) of the 1976 Rules retains its validity.

35. Article 23(3) of the 2010 Rules thus states that the tribunal may rule on jurisdiction in an 'award of the merits' (which under article 34 includes any award, including a partial one)[74] or in a ruling on 'a preliminary question'. It is clear that such a 'ruling' would be a decision, which must be made by a majority of the arbitrators under article 33(1), and not a procedural ruling, which may be issued by the presiding arbitrator alone under article 33(2). However, article 23(3) does not expressly require the arbitral tribunal to issue its ruling in the form of an award to which the requirements in article 34 apply, although it will of course be ordinarily the appropriate solution to do so. Moreover, there is authority for the proposition that, under Article 16 of the Model Law, a tribunal's ruling on jurisdiction as a preliminary question will be reviewable by the courts whether or not the tribunal issues its ruling in the form of an award.[75]

36. An article 23(3) ruling concerns pleas on jurisdiction 'referred to in paragraph 2 [of article 23]'. Thus, this is not a process for strike-out applications in respect of manifestly unmeritorious claims on the merits.[76] This is not to say, however, that

---

72 *See* UNCITRAL Report of the Secretary-General, Analytical commentary on draft text of a model law on international commercial arbitration, 25 March 1985, UN Doc A/CN.9/264, XVI UNCITRAL Ybk 104, 122 para. 11 (1985). *See also International Thunderbird Gaming Corporation v. The United Mexican States* (UNCITRAL) Order No. 4, 24 December 2003, < www.italaw.com > ; Cf. *Philip Morris Asia Limited v. The Commonwealth of Australia* (UNCITRAL), PCA Case No. 2012-12, Procedural Order No. 8 Regarding Bifurcation of the Procedure, 14 April 2014, para. 106 (in ordering that the proceedings be bifurcated, the Tribunal acknowledged that 'should preliminary objections prevail with the result that no procedure on the merits becomes necessary, this would result in a major saving of work and costs').

73 *See Josias Van Zyl, Josias Van Zyl Family Trust, and Burmilla Trust v. Kingdom of Lesotho, supra* fn 68, at para. 43 ('Article 23(3) of the current UNCITRAL Rules ... does not appear to contemplate any presumption, leaving the Tribunal with an even discretion to decide whether to bifurcate proceedings or not').

74 *See* article 34(1) of the 2010 Rules: 'The arbitral tribunal may make separate awards on different issues at different times'.

75 UNCITRAL, *2012 Digest of Case Law on the Model Law on International Commercial Arbitration*, 79, para. 16 (United Nations 2012).

76 Cf. Rule 41(5) of the ICSID Arbitration Rules which allows a party 'no later than 30 days after the constitution of the Tribunal, and in any event before the first session of the Tribunal, [to] file an objection that a claim is manifestly without legal merit'.

such a process cannot be set up in exercise of the general power of the arbitral tribunal to conduct the proceedings under article 17(1). Such a decision would be a special form of an award on the merits.

2. Court control need not lead to suspension of proceedings

37. As already mentioned, arbitral tribunals' decisions on jurisdiction may be challenged in national courts. Depending on the *lex arbitri*, a party wishing to raise jurisdictional issues before national courts may do so either at the beginning of the arbitration, during the arbitral proceedings, or after an award on the merits has been issued.[77]

38. The 1976 Rules were silent as to the impact on the arbitral proceedings of a court challenge against a 'preliminary' jurisdictional ruling. Article 23(3) now addresses the issue, in a manner consistent with Article 16(3) of the Model Law. (Note that Article 16(3) of the Model Law allows recourse to the courts only if the tribunal 'rules ... that it has jurisdiction'; rulings declining jurisdiction cannot be reviewed.) The Model Law allows national courts to be involved before the tribunal has issued a final award on the merits, but after the tribunal has issued an award on jurisdiction.[78] The question was how to address the concurrence of proceedings that would result.

39. The Working Group was reluctant to adopt a provision that would limit a fundamental right to have recourse to courts (save that, by operation of article 1(3) of the Rules, any such limitation would yield to the mandatory requirements of the applicable law).[79] Thus, it was decided, subject to mandatory contrary provisions in the *lex arbitri*, to allow the arbitral tribunal to proceed with the merits and render its award, 'notwithstanding any pending challenge to its jurisdiction before a court'.[80] The arbitral tribunal may thus prevent delay by continuing with the arbitration while the national court decides on jurisdiction – a process which may be time-consuming if it is subject to one or two appeals. By the same token, moving forward without waiting for the court to render its decision will translate into higher and unnecessary costs if the court eventually does not uphold the jurisdiction of the arbitral tribunal.[81] The guiding criterion will likely be similar

---

77 *See* Park, *supra* fn 1; and Blackaby, Partasides, Redfern & Hunter, *supra* fn 4, at para. 5.112.

78 Article 16(3) of the Model Law reads in relevant part: 'If the arbitral tribunal rules as a preliminary question that it has jurisdiction, any party may request, within thirty days after having received notice of that ruling, the court specified in article 6 to decide the matter ...'. *See also* Jan Paulsson & Georgios Petrochilos, *Revision of the UNCITRAL Rules* (September 2006), para. 187, <www.uncitral.org>.

79 *See* UNCITRAL Report of 45th Session, 5 October 2006, UN Doc A/CN.9/614, para. 100.

80 Article 23(3) of the 2010 Rules.

81 This concern was the basis on which the Court of Appeal for Bermuda held that arbitral tribunals should normally await a decision by the court, but in circumstances where (as the court stressed) a court hearing on the jurisdictional issue was to be had shortly after the tribunal's decision on jurisdiction. *See Christian Mutual Insurance Company & Central United Life Insurance Company & Connecticut Reassurance Corporation v. Ace Bermuda Insurance Limited* [2002] Bda LR 56.

to that under Article VI of the New York Convention, i.e. whether the challenge has serious prospects of success.[82]

[82] Article VI of the New York Convention reads as follows: 'If an application for the setting aside or suspension of the award has been made to a competent authority referred to in article V(1)(e), the authority before which the award is sought to be relied upon may, if it considers it proper, adjourn the decision on the enforcement of the award and may also, on the application of the party claiming enforcement of the award, order the other party to give suitable security'.

Articles 24 and 25
Further written statements and periods of time

1976 Rules Article 22: Further written statements Article 23: Periods of time	2010 Rules Article 24: Further written statements Article 25: Periods of time
Article 22 The arbitral tribunal shall decide which further written statements, in addition to the statement of claim and the statement of defence, shall be required from the parties or may be presented by them and shall fix the periods of time for communicating such statements.	**Article 24** The arbitral tribunal shall decide which further written statements, in addition to the statement of claim and the statement of defence, shall be required from the parties or may be presented by them and shall fix the periods of time for communicating such statements.
Article 23 The periods of time fixed by the arbitral tribunal for the communication of written statements (including the statement of claim and statement of defence) should not exceed 45 days. However, the arbitral tribunal may extend the time limits if it concludes that an extension is justified.	**Article 25** The periods of time fixed by the arbitral tribunal for the communication of written statements (including the statement of claim and statement of defence) should not exceed 45 days. However, the arbitral tribunal may extend the time limits if it concludes that an extension is justified.

1. Articles 24 and 25 replicate, without modification, the corresponding provisions, articles 22 and 23, in the 1976 Rules. No modifications were suggested in the revision process. While the 1976 provisions reflect a mode of skeletal written pleading that is not favoured by the 2010 Rules (as discussed below), very considerable procedural flexibility is built into them and thus they have hardly given rise to problems in practice. As the Working Group made clear that 'the focus of the revision should be on updating the Rules to meet changes that had

taken place over the last thirty years in arbitral practice',[1] it can be safely expected that practice under the 2010 Rules will follow the broad principles developed in the practice under the 1976 Rules.

A. ADDITIONAL PLEADINGS

2. Article 24 grants the tribunal the power to order 'written statements', in addition to the statement of claim and the statement of defence, at its own initiative or at the request of a party.[2] A few provisions in the Rules imply a duty on the part of the tribunal to call for certain specific pleadings, as discussed below. However, article 24 is an authorising provision which may serve as the foundation for the tribunal to discharge its duty under other provisions but which does not in itself contain a duty to accept additional pleadings.[3] Note also that article 24 does not regulate the order and number of pleadings by each party. Typically the claimant/ applicant will go first, with the respondent having the last word, on grounds of procedural efficiency and equality, consistent with article 17(1). But as noted below (paragraph 11), there are exceptional cases in which these fundamental duties compel that one party be given an additional pleading opportunity.

3. The provision is directed to pleadings – whether they be called 'briefs', 'memoranda', 'applications', 'motions', or anything else – at various stages and for various purposes. Such pleadings are separate from evidential materials – 'documents, exhibits, or other evidence', to use the terms of article 27(3) – which may be lodged either separately or (as is typically the case) together with pleadings relying upon and advancing submissions in respect of them.

4. Article 24 distinguishes between pleadings which are 'required' from the parties and those which 'may' be submitted by them. To illustrate, pleadings which the parties may choose whether to submit or not are envisaged by articles 29 (appointment and terms of reference of tribunal-appointed experts), 31(1) (possible inquiries regarding 'further proof', 'witnesses', or 'submissions'), and 36(2) (consultation regarding termination of proceedings). Pleadings which are required will be those which the tribunal has designated as such, in particular in the procedural timetable established under article 17(2).[4] Thus it is not to be thought that article 24 requires the tribunal first to receive the statements of claim and defence and only then to decide whether additional pleadings are necessary. Indeed, procedural efficiency – an article 17(1) duty – compels in most cases that the number, nature, scope, and timing of written pleadings be fixed in advance.

5. It is not required by article 24 that any and all pleadings by the parties be pre-authorized by the tribunal. Notably, applications for joinder (article 17(5)),

---

1 UNCITRAL Report of 45th Session, 5 October 2006, UN Doc A/CN.9/614, para. 16.

2 *See* Pieter Sanders, *Commentary on UNCITRAL Arbitration Rules*, II YCA 172, 204 (1977).

3 *See* Jacomijn J. van Hof, *Commentary on the UNCITRAL Arbitration Rules, The Application by the Iran-U.S. Claims Tribunal*, 152 (Kluwer 1991).

4 Nevertheless, only the failure to submit a statement of claim is a species of default that may lead to termination of the proceedings; *see* article 30(1)(a).

interim measures (article 26), and post-award remedies (articles 37-39) are of necessity spontaneous pleadings to be regarded as pre-authorized by the Rules themselves. Applications for unscheduled eventualities – e.g. an extension of time pursuant to article 17(2) or 25, or an opposition to an impermissible amendment of the other side's case under article 22 – by definition also require no prior authorization. The same may be said of a response by a third party named in the respondent's response pursuant to article 4(2)(f), which in the spirit of the Rules appears as an appropriate pleading and which may be filed either shortly before the tribunal's constitution (without its authorization) or shortly thereafter (with its authorization).[5] Subject to such exceptions, the ordinary position is that pleadings filed after the tribunal's constitution must have been authorized by the tribunal, either as part of the procedural schedule or by specific authorization on application by one or all parties. In both instances, the tribunal will be guided by its article 17(1) general duties.[6] Thus, for example, the Iran-US Claims Tribunal was reluctant to accept unauthorized filings not provided for in the schedule of the proceedings, except when this would not cause prejudice to the other side.[7]

6. The wording of article 24 may suggest that it applies only to pleadings filed after the statements of claim and defence, but the term 'further written statements' is to be read as meaning statements 'other than' or 'in addition to' the statements of claim and defence. There is no other provision in the Rules which may serve as foundation for the multitude of pleadings which are typically lodged in arbitrations, and these include pleadings filed before the statements of claim or defence. Thus article 24 covers notably:

(i) responses to claims brought by the respondent against a party to the arbitration agreement other than the claimant (under article 4(2)(f) of the Rules);
(ii) jurisdiction or admissibility pleadings;
(iii) second-round memorials (reply and rejoinder),[8] commonplace in all cases of any substantial complexity or value;
(iv) third- or fourth-round pleadings, including skeleton arguments for hearings (as in the practice of the Iran-US Claims Tribunal);[9]

---

5 *See* the analysis under article 4, para. 38, *supra*.

6 *See United Parcel Service of America Inc v. Government of Canada* (UNCITRAL) Award on Jurisdiction, 22 November 2002, < www.italaw.com >, para. 131.

7 *See* Stewart A. Baker & Mark D. Davis, *The UNCITRAL Arbitration Rules in Practice – The Experience of the Iran-United States Claims Tribunal*, 97 (Kluwer 1992). *See also Alan Craig v. Ministry of Energy of Iran* (1983) 3 Iran-US CTR 280, 281 (unauthorized submissions disregarded because of fairness, orderliness, and possible prejudice).

8 Cf., e.g., Article 15.4 of the LCIA Rules (expressly requiring a statement of reply to be sent by the claimant in response to the respondent's statement of defence).

9 The Tribunal typically allows four rounds of pleadings: after the statement of claim and the statement of defence (which may include one or more counterclaims), the claimant then submits a reply (including a defence to the counterclaims), followed by a rejoinder by the respondent. The third round ('hearing memorials') summarises the parties' positions and includes all documentary evidence, and is followed by the fourth round ('rebuttal memorials') which is supposed to allow only comments in relation to the third-round

(v) additional particulars to supplement a failure to comply with the requirements of a statement of claim set out in article 20(2) of the 2010 Rules, as preferable to dismissing the claim based on procedural non-compliance under article 30(1)(a);[10]
(vi) the defence to counterclaims or set-off claims (which pursuant to article 21(3) are in principle to be articulated no later than the statement of defence): the Rules anticipate in articles 23(2) and 30(1)(b) that this pleading is necessary and will be called a 'reply', in all likelihood because it will also commonly serve as the second-round pleading on the claimant's affirmative claims;
(vii) second-round pleadings by both parties in respect of counterclaims or set-off claims;[11]
(viii) amendments to claims, defences, counterclaims or set-off claims (pursuant to article 22 of the 2010 Rules), whether through fresh stand-alone pleadings or through 'amended' or 'restated' pleadings;
(ix) written submissions by amici curiae admitted pursuant to article 17(1) of the Rules (although article 24(1) speaks of pleadings 'required from the parties or [which] may be presented by them'), as well as submissions by the parties in response to applications by prospective amici and to the substantive submissions that amici subsequently file;[12]
(x) generally, memorials on procedural or evidential matters, e.g. document production; and
(xi) post-hearing briefs, replacing or complementing closing oral argument.

Like other arbitration rules,[13] the Rules thus give the tribunal flexibility in respect of the types of pleadings appropriate in the particular circumstances. The Rules are more prescriptive than the Model Law, which does not contain an equivalent provision.

---

pleadings. The third and fourth rounds are set down as simultaneous; *see* van Hof, *supra* fn 3, at 153. *See also* David D. Caron & Lee M. Caplan, *The UNCITRAL Arbitration Rules, A Commentary*, 493 (2nd ed., Oxford University Press 2013) (explaining that this practice was allowed because the Iran-US Claims Tribunal's case-load did not allow for long hearing sessions).

10 *See* Caron & Caplan, *supra* fn 9, at 415 ('defects in what purports to be the original statement of claim rarely justify termination of the proceedings under Article 30 [of the 2010 Rules]'). *See also* the content requirements for the statements of claim and defence, discussed in connection with article 20 (para. 8 et seq.) and article 21 (para. 1), *supra*.

11 Cf., e.g., Article 15.5 of the LCIA Rules (giving the respondent the right to submit a reply to the claimant's defence to counterclaim).

12 Although article 24 does not expressly allow for amicus curiae briefs to be submitted by non-parties, the Rules also do not prohibit it; *see* Baker & Davis, *supra* fn 7, at 98; and discussion of article 17(1) of the 2010 Rules, *supra*.

13 *See*, e.g., Article 43(b) of the WIPO Rules ('The tribunal may, in its discretion, allow or require further written statements'); and Article 29(3) of the SCC Rules ('The arbitral tribunal may order the parties to submit additional written submissions').

B. PERIODS OF TIME

7. Article 25 has been said to 'reflect a compromise between two partly conflicting considerations: the need for speedy proceedings on the one hand and the practical impossibility of prescribing rigid time-limits ... on the other'.[14] While the provision stipulates that time-periods for written pleadings 'should not exceed 45 days', it is clear from the precatory 'should'[15] (rather than a mandatory 'shall') that it is 'merely intended to serve as a general guideline'.[16] The tribunal may therefore 'conclude' – i.e. exercise judgement – that 'an extension is justified'; or that, pursuant to article 17(2), a time-limit is to be shortened. These rules apply to all pleadings ('written statements'), including the statements of claim and defence but also additional pleadings pursuant to article 24.

8. A 45-day time-period[17] indicates that, especially for the main pleadings, the submission envisaged will not be detailed. This is borne out by comparing this time-period with the 30 days given to the respondent to prepare its initial response to the notice of arbitration, a pleading which has limited required content (see article 4(1)). It is also borne out by the ability of both parties to treat their notice of arbitration or response as a statement of claim or statement of defence, respectively (articles 20(1) and 21(1)). As has been pointed out in connection with the 30-day time-period under the LCIA Rules,[18] substantive pleadings prepared in such short periods are 'unlikely ... [to] do much more than to identify the material facts and to clarify the principal legal arguments on which the parties' respective cases are based'.[19] This kind of bare-bones pleading comports well with the original design of the 1976 Rules, which permitted documentary evidence to be simply 'refer[red] to' in the statements of claim and defence (articles 18(2) and 19(2) of the 1976 Rules) and presented for the first time at the hearing (article 24(2) of the 1976 Rules) together with witness evidence (article 25(2) of the 1976 Rules). Where a different process is followed, as will invariably be

---

14 Caron & Caplan, *supra* fn 9, at 505.

15 Cf. article 21(4) of the 1976 Rules ('In general, the arbitral tribunal should rule on a plea concerning its jurisdiction as a preliminary question. However, the arbitral tribunal may proceed with the arbitration and rule on such a plea in their final award').

16 UNCITRAL Report of the Secretary General on the Draft UNCITRAL Arbitration Rules, 12 December 1975, UN Doc A/CN.9/112/Add.1, 175.

17 The original proposal was for 30 days, but 45 days were considered preferable. *See* Report of 8th Session, 1-17 April 1975, UN Doc A/10017, VI UNCITRAL Ybk 9, 39, para. 151.

18 The default procedure under the 2014 LCIA Rules imposes a 28-day time-limit between: receipt of notification of the formation of the tribunal and the statement of case (Article 15.2); the statement of case and the statement of defence (Article 15.3); the statement of defence and the statement of reply (Article 15.4); and the defence to counterclaim (if contained in the statement of reply) and the statement of reply to defence to counterclaim (Article 15.5).

19 Peter Turner & Reza Mohtashami, *A Guide to the LCIA Arbitration Rules*, para. 5.51 (Oxford University Press 2009) (explaining the impact of the 30-day time-limits under Article 15 of the 1998 LCIA Rules, with statements 'more likely to resemble English-style pleadings' – i.e. concise submissions typically submitted before a lengthy hearing – rather than full memorials, which are meant to reduce the length of hearings; *see ibid.*, at para. 5.40).

the case in disputes of any complexity or where hearing time is very limited, it will be 'justified' for the tribunal to adopt time-periods longer than 45 days, especially for the statements of claim and defence.

9. Nevertheless, the 45-day default position indicates the general spirit of the Rules that parties should proceed with all due expedition reasonable in the circumstances of the case. That now forms part of the general injunction to the tribunal, set out in article 17(1) of the Rules. That injunction informs also the tribunal's power to 'extend or abridge any period of time prescribed under these Rules' in article 17(2).

10. Article 25 does not state the date from which a time-period should be calculated. It follows from article 17(2) that the very first such date is that on which the procedural timetable is fixed; and all subsequent time-periods start from the date of the immediately prior procedural stage (e.g. a decision on jurisdiction) or act (e.g. a pleading by a party). In that connection, article 25 does not take a view on whether pleadings should be sequential or simultaneous. Practice bears out the wisdom of sequential presentations, at least for the main pleadings, in order for the parties to join cases comprehensively.[20] But there are pleadings – especially post-hearing briefs, submissions on costs, and (rare) cases of factually and legally independent affirmative claims asserted by both sides – which may well be timed simultaneously.

11. It is not expressly required by Article 25 that the parties be given equal time. The cardinal principle of party equality, set out in article 17(1), will in most cases compel equal allocation. But there are circumstances where it will be obvious that one party had considerably more time at its disposal for the preparation of its pleading (for example, the claimant had an unusually long time for the statement of claim because the constitution of the tribunal was delayed;[21] or, conversely, the respondent ambushed the claimant by presenting a host of new factual and legal arguments in its rejoinder). There, again by virtue of article 17(1), the other party will require more time if it is to be treated fairly and to have a reasonable opportunity of presenting its case. As has been held, for example, it would not be fair for one party to be 'permitted to present an extensive memorial and additional exhibits in the 45 day time limit, without providing the other party with an opportunity to file a memorial in response'.[22]

12. Additional time can be built into the procedural timetable from the outset, or be granted later by way of an extension. Article 25 speaks of 'an extension', but one may well envisage successive extensions in exceptional circumstances. Requests

---

[20] *See* Baker & Davis, *supra* fn 7, at 96; and van Hof, *supra* fn 3, at 153.

[21] Cf. Caron & Caplan, *supra* fn 9, at 506. During the drafting of the 1976 Rules, it was suggested that a 15-day time-limit should apply specifically to the statement of claim (*see* UNCITRAL Report of the Secretary General on the Draft UNCITRAL Arbitration Rules, 12 December 1975, UN Doc A/CN.9/112/Add.1, 175) but this was eliminated for uniformity with the communication of other written statements (*see* Report of the Commission on its 9th Session, 12 April-7 May 1976, UN Doc A/31/17, 75 para. 120).

[22] *See Foremost Tehran Inc v. Islamic Republic of Iran* (1983-II) 3 Iran-US CTR 361, 362.

for extension will require the tribunal to be satisfied that, in the light of 'the complexity of the case' and 'any special circumstances, including demonstrated hardship to a claimant or respondent'[23] an extension is justified. The burden of proof on the factual predicate and the burden of persuasion on the legal test lie with the requesting party.[24] Reasons commonly invoked include the complexity of the other party's written submissions; problems with counsel; difficulties with communications; unexpected problems in gathering evidence; etc.[25]

13. It is open to the parties to modify the default 45-day time-period by party agreement under article 1(1) of the Rules. This was done by the United States and Iran, who agreed on 90 days for the statement of claim and 135 days for the statement of defence in Iran-US Claims Tribunal proceedings.[26] There was a special context for this asymmetric extension, but the general point is that parties may agree upon any time-limits, including time-limits that would resemble expedited proceedings available under various institutional rules.[27] Such agreements remain under the tribunal's article 17(2) power to 'extend or abridge any period of time ... agreed by the parties', except if it is plain that the parties intended to withhold that power from the tribunal by virtue of article 1(1) of the Rules.

---

23 Article 19, Note 1 of the Tribunal Rules of Procedure of the Iran-US Claims Tribunal (3 May 1983). In practice, however, the Tribunal routinely granted three-month extensions without explanation; *see* Baker & Davis, *supra* fn 7, at 99-101.

24 James E. Castello, 'UNCITRAL Arbitration Rules, Section III, Article 25' in Loukas A. Mistelis (ed), *Concise International Arbitration*, 231 (2nd ed., Kluwer 2015).

25 *See* Caron & Caplan, *supra* fn 9, at 506; and Jason Fry, Simon Greenberg & Francesca Mazza, *The Secretariat's Guide to ICC Arbitration*, para. 3-141 (ICC 2012) (discussing common reasons why the respondent may request a time extension for submission of the answer under Article 5(2)).

26 *See* Articles 19(1) and 23 of the Tribunal Rules of Procedure of the Iran-US Claims Tribunal.

27 Cf. Article 39(1) of the ICC Rules ('The parties may agree to shorten the various time limits set out in the Rules'); *see also*, e.g., Article 30 ('Expedited Procedure') and Appendix VI of the 2017 ICC Rules; the SCC Rules for Expedited Arbitrations; and the AAA International Expedited Procedures.

Article 26
Interim measures

1976 Rules

Article 26: Interim measures of protection

1. At the request of either party, the arbitral tribunal may take any interim measures it deems necessary in respect of the subject-matter of the dispute, including measures for the conservation of the goods forming the subject-matter in dispute, such as ordering their deposit with a third person or the sale of perishable goods.

2. Such interim measures may be established in the form of an interim award. The arbitral tribunal shall be entitled to require security for the costs of such measures.

3. A request for interim measures addressed by any party to a judicial authority shall not be deemed incompatible with the agreement to arbitrate, or as a waiver of that agreement.

2010 Rules

Article 26: Interim measures

1. The arbitral tribunal may, at the request of a party, grant interim measures.

2. An interim measure is any temporary measure by which, at any time prior to the issuance of the award by which the dispute is finally decided, the arbitral tribunal orders a party, for example and without limitation, to:

(a) Maintain or restore the status quo pending determination of the dispute;

(b) Take action that would prevent, or refrain from taking action that is likely to cause, (i) current or imminent harm or (ii) prejudice to the arbitral process itself;

(c) Provide a means of preserving assets out of which a subsequent award may be satisfied; or

(d) Preserve evidence that may be relevant and material to the resolution of the dispute.

3. The party requesting an interim measure under paragraphs 2 (a) to (c) shall satisfy the arbitral tribunal that:

(a) Harm not adequately reparable by an award of damages is likely to result if the measure is not ordered, and such harm substantially outweighs the harm that is likely to result to the party against whom the measure is directed if the measure is granted; and

(b) There is a reasonable possibility that the requesting party will succeed on the merits of the claim. The determination on this possibility shall not affect the discretion of the arbitral tribunal in making any subsequent determination.

4. With regard to a request for an interim measure under paragraph 2 (d), the requirements in paragraphs 3 (a) and (b) shall apply only to the extent the arbitral tribunal considers appropriate.

5. The arbitral tribunal may modify, suspend or terminate an interim measure it has granted, upon application of any party or, in exceptional circumstances and upon prior notice to the parties, on the arbitral tribunal's own initiative.

6. The arbitral tribunal may require the party requesting an interim measure to provide appropriate security in connection with the measure.

7. The arbitral tribunal may require any party promptly to disclose any material change in the circumstances on the basis of which the interim measure was requested or granted.

8. The party requesting an interim measure may be liable for any costs and damages caused by the measure to any party if the arbitral tribunal later determines that, in the circumstances then prevailing, the measure should not have been granted. The arbitral tribunal may award such costs and damages at any point during the proceedings.

9. A request for interim measures addressed by any party to a judicial authority shall not be deemed incompatible with the agreement to arbitrate, or as a waiver of that agreement.

---

1. Article 26 retains the 1976 title, 'interim measures'. The notion is defined in article 26(2) as a 'temporary measure [issued] at any time prior to the issuance of the

award by which the dispute is finally decided'. Thus the tribunal's authority to issue such measures extends up to the issuance of the last award in the case (i.e. the 'final award' within the meaning of articles 43(5) and 42(2)) or a termination order under article 36(2) or, at the earliest, up to the time a disputed issue is decided by way of a partial final award (cf. article 34(1)). The tribunal's power is of course subject to the *lex arbitri* and may also be limited, or in theory altogether excluded, by agreement of the parties.

2. Under the Rules, there is no particular emphasis on the 'conservatory' nature that provisional measures may take, by contrast to the ICC Rules, for example.[1] There is of course no doubt that interim measures under the 1976 Rules may encompass cease-and-desist measures to preserve the status quo generally or measures to preserve perishable evidence or property in particular.[2] That is now made explicit in article 26(2) of the 2010 Rules.

3. Article 26 of the Rules contains as comprehensive a codification of interim-measures regulation as one may find in arbitration rules.[3] In so doing, it takes the '*lignes directrices*',[4] i.e. the essential elements, in great part verbatim, of the corresponding provisions of the Model Law (Articles 17-17G), which were adopted after lengthy work in 2002-2006.[5] Modifications were made as necessary for clarity in the context of arbitration rules; for example in article 26(8) (compared to Article 17G of the Model Law).[6] The intention of a comprehensive regulation was to give 'necessary guidance and legal certainty' with respect to the definition of and conditions for granting interim measures,[7] especially for tribunals and parties operating in legal systems 'which were unfamiliar with the use of interim measures in the context of international arbitration'.[8] Thus a proposal to adopt short and simplified wording, 'leaving to applicable domestic

---

1 *See* Article 28 of the ICC Rules.

2 *See* Jan Paulsson & Georgios Petrochilos, *Revision of the UNCITRAL Rules* (September 2006), para. 202, < www.uncitral.org >.

3 *See* on article 26 generally Georgios Petrochilos, *Interim Measures Under the Revised UNCITRAL Arbitration Rules*, 28(4) ASA Bulletin 878 (2010); David D. Caron & Lee M. Caplan, *The UNCITRAL Arbitration Rules, A Commentary*, 513 et seq. (2nd ed., Oxford University Press 2013); Peter Binder, *Analytical Commentary to the UNCITRAL Arbitration Rules*, para. 26-001 et seq. (Sweet & Maxwell 2013); James E. Castello, 'UNCITRAL Arbitration Rules, Section III, Article 26' in Loukas A. Mistelis (ed), *Concise International Arbitration*, 231 et seq. (2nd ed., Kluwer 2015); Thomas H. Webster, *Handbook of UNCITRAL Arbitration*, para. 26-1 et seq. (2nd ed., Sweet & Maxwell 2015).

4 The starting point was that the Rules should 'anticipate the *lignes directrices*' of Article 17 of the UNCITRAL Model Law, rather than mirroring it directly; *see* Paulsson & Petrochilos, *supra* fn 2, at para. 205.

5 *See* the provisions dealing with the modification, suspension and termination of interim measures (Article 17D of the Model Law, article 26(5) of the 2010 Rules); the provision of security (Article 17E of the Model Law, article 26(6) of the 2010 Rules); and disclosure by the applicant (Article 17F of the Model Law, article 26(7) of the 2010 Rules).

6 *See* paras 38-41, *infra*.

7 UNCITRAL Report of 50th Session, 9 March 2009, UN Doc A/CN.9/669, para. 88.

8 *Ibid.*

law matters of definition of interim measures and conditions for granting such measures', was not adopted.[9]

4. Because of its comprehensive treatment, article 26 (and the corresponding provisions of the Model Law) is often in practice relied upon as a codification which expresses general principles universally accepted, even in arbitrations under other rules, including in the ICSID system.

5. Nevertheless, article 26 does not pick up elements of the Model Law which are to be set forth in 'an instrument of legislative nature, directed to legislators'[10] – namely the recognition and enforcement of interim measures (Articles 17H and 17I of the Model Law) and court-ordered measures (Article 17J of the Model Law).[11] Also, article 26 gives no authorization to grant *ex parte* 'preliminary orders' (Articles 17B-17C of the Model Law) but it does anticipate that a tribunal may find authority to issue such measures under the *lex arbitri*[12] and/or under powers implied by article 17(1). This matter was extensively debated in the Working Group and is addressed in connection with article 17(1) at the end of the present discussion of article 26.

A. CONDITIONS FOR GRANTING INTERIM MEASURES: ARTICLE 26(3)

6. Article 26 of the 1976 Rules was mostly directed to the authority of the tribunal to issue interim measures – at the time, an authority not universally accepted – and perhaps for that reason it gave little guidance on the requirements for the granting of interim measures.[13] The 2010 Rules codify many of the requirements which have proved important in practice,[14] such as the requirement that the applicant have a prima facie case on the merits (article 26(3)(b)) and the requirements of necessity and proportionality (article 26(3)(a)). Other conditions, in particular those of urgency and prima facie jurisdiction, are largely inherent in the Rules or generally accepted in practice.

---

9 The proposal is contained in UNCITRAL Working Paper for 49th Session, 9 September 2008, UN Doc A/CN.9/WG.II/WP.152; for the decision *see* UNCITRAL Report of 50th Session, 9 March 2009, UN Doc A/CN.9/669, paras 85-90.

10 UNCITRAL Report of 50th Session, 9 March 2009, UN Doc A/CN.9/669, para. 101.

11 The only reference to court-ordered interim measures in the 2010 Rules is in article 26(9), which reproduces article 26(3) of the 1976 Rules without modification. Under the Rules, the relationship of the tribunal's power to take interim measures vis-à-vis that of judicial authorities is left to be addressed by the applicable national arbitration law; *see* Jacomijn J. van Hof, *Commentary on the UNCITRAL Arbitration Rules, The Application by the Iran-U.S. Claims Tribunal*, 176 (Kluwer 1991).

12 As for example is the case in England notwithstanding no express authorization in the Arbitration Act 1996; *see* Nigel Blackaby, Constantine Partasides, Alan Redfern & Martin J. Hunter, *Redfern and Hunter on International Arbitration*, para. 5.42 (6th ed., Kluwer 2015).

13 That is a feature of most arbitration laws and rules though; *see ibid.*, at para. 5.31.

14 *Ibid.* ('Traditionally, arbitrators have looked to concepts common to most legal systems in the granting of such measures—such as the need to establish a prima facie case on the merits and the risk of serious and irreparable harm if the measure is not granted').

7. It is submitted that all the necessary requirements operate 'in the round',[15] in that a tribunal must be satisfied that they are met in the aggregate to a degree which justifies an interim measure being given.

1. Urgency

8. A need to show a degree of urgency is inherent in a request for provisional intervention by the tribunal. The requesting party must show that the tribunal's intervention cannot await 'the award by which the dispute is finally decided' (article 26(2)). The nature and degree of urgency required will depend of course on the specific measure that is being sought, as is further discussed below in respect of the need to show a risk of harm. But as a general proposition the requirement of urgency will bar, for example, an application whose object is to prevent from occurring that which is the gravamen of the claim on the merits – for example, a registration of title that merely completes a dispossession which is the pleaded basis for an expropriation claim.

2. *Prima facie* jurisdiction

9. Requests for interim measures are often (or even typically) made at the beginning of the arbitral proceedings, i.e. at a time when the tribunal has not yet rendered a decision on jurisdiction.[16] This gives rise to a dilemma:

> On the one hand, a party may have legitimate objections to an arbitral tribunal's ordering interim measures against it if it is unclear whether the tribunal ultimately has jurisdiction to grant the relief sought. On the other hand, the very purpose of interim measures serving as a means of conservation and protection of parties' rights could be forfeited if such measures were postponed pending a full jurisdictional determination.[17]

10. The only solution for tribunals is to seek to satisfy themselves on a prima facie test. Prima facie is shorthand for a preliminary analysis, based on the pleadings and evidence available (as opposed to a full record), and subject to a final determination in due course. A prima facie finding on jurisdiction does not prejudge the final decision on jurisdiction, and this is now spelt out in the second sentence of article 26.[18] The Iran-US Claims Tribunal adopted such a test,

---

15 Cf. Sam Luttrell, *ICSID provisional measures 'in the round'*, 31(3) Arb Int 393 (2015).

16 Cf. Article 28(1) of the ICC Rules, which specifies that unless the parties have otherwise agreed, an arbitral tribunal may order interim measures 'as soon as the file has been transmitted to it'.

17 Caron & Caplan, *supra* fn 3, at 522-523.

18 *See*, e.g., *Perenco Ecuador Ltd v. The Republic of Ecuador and Empresa Estatal Petróleos del Ecuador (Petroecuador)* (ICSID Case No. ARB/08/6) Decision on Provisional Measures, 8 May 2009, <www.italaw.com>, para. 39 ('While the Tribunal need not satisfy itself that it has jurisdiction to determine the merits of this case for the purposes of ruling on the application for provisional measures, it will not order such measures unless there is at least a prima facie basis upon which such jurisdiction might be established'); *Quiborax SA, Non Metallic Minerals SA and Allan Fosk Kaplún v. Plurinational State of Bolivia*

pursuant to which a prima facie showing of jurisdiction was sufficient for the grant of interim measures.[19] It is rightly said that such a requirement now follows from article 26(3)(b), which requires a 'reasonable possibility' of success 'on the merits', because this encompasses 'that the tribunal have both a reasonable possibility of possessing jurisdiction over the claim and a reasonable possibility that the substance of the claim is meritorious'.[20]

3. Prima facie case on the merits

11. Under the 1976 Rules tribunals have required applicants to make a showing of a prima facie case on the merits (or a *fumus boni iuris*). This is a necessary predicate for any claim to interim protection: '[t]here can be no prejudice if there is little or no prospect that the alleged right threatened will be recognised as a right'.[21]

12. The threshold that the applicant's substantive case needs to cross has been a matter of substantial debate in the revision of the Model Law. National traditions differ, with some procedural systems contending themselves to a 'good arguable case' (i.e. not a frivolous case) and others providing for a more demanding standard. The Rules follow the compromise solution adopted in the Model Law. The applicant's obligation to establish a prima facie case on the merits is now codified in article 26(3)(b), which stipulates that the applicant shall 'satisfy the tribunal that ... [t]here is a *reasonable possibility* that the requesting party will succeed on the merits of the claim' (emphasis added). Ruling on the equivalent provision under the Model Law, a New Zealand court has held that the test for a 'reasonable possibility' is akin to that of a 'serious question to be tried' (which filters out obviously unmeritorious claims but not much more).[22] Naturally, the test will be harder to satisfy the greater the adverse effect of the requested interim measure on the respondent.

13. By contrast, the requirement of a prima facie case on the merits may not be necessary, or may in fact be inapposite, when the interim measure sought is to 'preserve evidence that may be relevant and material to the resolution of the dispute' under article 26(2)(d). This explains why article 26(4) of the 2010 Rules grants tribunals the discretion to require a prima facie case on the merits as may be

---

(ICSID Case No. ARB/06/2) Decision on Provisional Measures, 26 February 2010, < www.italaw.com > , para. 108 ('It is undisputed by the Parties that the Arbitral Tribunal has the power to order provisional measures prior to ruling on its jurisdiction. The Tribunal will not exercise such power, however, unless there is a *prima facie* basis for jurisdiction'); *see also Sergei Paushok, CJSC Golden East Company and CJSC Vostokneftegaz Company v. The Government of Mongolia ('Paushok v. Mongolia')* (UNCITRAL) Order on Interim Measures, 2 September 2008, < www.italaw.com > , paras 47-54.

19 *See Bendone-Derossi International v. Islamic Republic of Iran*, Interim Award (1984) 6 Iran-US CTR 130; Caron & Caplan, *supra* fn 3, at 523 and the references; Gary B. Born, *International Commercial Arbitration*, 2481-2482 (2nd ed., Kluwer 2014).

20 Caron & Caplan, *supra* fn 3, at 522.

21 David D. Caron, Lee M. Caplan & Matti Pellonpää, *The UNCITRAL Arbitration Rules, A Commentary*, 537 (Oxford University Press 2006).

22 *Safe Kids in Daily Supervision Limited v. McNeill* [2010] NZHC 605.

'appropriate' in relation to measures to preserve evidence. The general proposition is that measures which seek to preserve the integrity of the proceedings (such as the protection of a witness, for example) are not taken for the sake of a party and therefore do not in principle require a showing of a case on the merits.[23]

14. Where the prima facie case on the merits requirement applies, it may be seen as being justified by a number of other provisions of article 26:
   (i) The tribunal's power to 'modify, suspend or terminate' an interim measure on its own initiative in exceptional circumstances (article 26(5));
   (ii) The tribunal's ability to 'require the party requesting an interim measure to provide appropriate security in connection with the measure' (article 26(6)) (the ordering of this security is at the tribunal's discretion);[24] and
   (iii) The requesting party's possible liability for 'costs and damages' caused by the interim measure if the tribunal later determines that the measure should not have been granted, for example if the claim on the merits is ultimately held to have been unfounded (article 26(8)).

4. Risk of harm

15. The only condition for the grant of interim measures imposed under article 26(1) of the 1976 Rules was that an arbitral tribunal may issue measures it deems 'necessary'. That was interpreted to import a number of requirements, namely the urgency of the tribunal's intervention, connected with a serious risk of substantial harm occurring unless the tribunal intervenes, and a weighing of the relative hardship that will be caused to one side or the other by the tribunal's decision. The relevant requirements are now spelt out in article 26(3)(a) of the 2010 Rules.

16. The requirement to show a risk of harm occurring to the applicant is often combined with the requirement of urgency as a requirement of 'current or imminent harm' (as in article 26(2)(b)). Nevertheless, the two are notionally separate. There are two points to be considered under the rubric of harm: first, whether the harm should be 'irreparable'[25] and secondly, how serious the prospect of its occurrence should be. Both points are addressed in article 26(3)(a).

---

23 *See*, e.g., *Perenco Ecuador Ltd v. Republic of Ecuador and Empresa Estatal Petróleos del Ecuador* (ICSID Case No. ARB/08/6) Decision on Provisional Measures, 8 May 2009, < www.italaw.com >, para. 43; and *Biwater Gauff (Tanzania) Ltd. v. United Republic of Tanzania* (ICSID Case No. ARB/05/22) Procedural Order No. 3, 29 September 2006, < www.italaw.com >, para. 135. *See also* Luttrell, *supra* fn 15, at 402 (addressing the notion of 'axiomatic' urgency, and noting that 'where the procedural integrity of the arbitration is seriously threatened, there will be an argument that the harm is necessarily irreparable (and the need for provisional measures self-evident)').

24 *See* UNCITRAL Report of 39th Session, 8 December 2003, UN Doc A/CN.9/545, XXXV UNCITRAL Ybk 463, 474 para. 33.

25 *See*, e.g., *Behring International Inc v. Islamic Republic of Iran Air Force* (1985) 8 Iran-US CTR 238; and *Iran v. United States* (1989) 22 Iran-US CTR 105. More recently, the expression was used in *EnCana Corporation v. Republic of Ecuador* (LCIA Case No. UN3481) Interim Award, 31 January 2004, < www.italaw.com >, para. 17.

17. As to the first, the Rules make clear that the harm must be one that is 'not *adequately* reparable by an award of damages'. This is a salutary definition, because in economic cases it will nearly always be possible to the respondent to say that economic compensation in a final award can make the applicant whole and thus there is no irreparable harm in the literal meaning of the term (as in the common-law tradition).[26] Such literal conceptions of 'irreparability' are not current,[27] but they do remain possible.[28] Helpfully, article 26(3)(a) eliminates any possible doubt. The 'not adequately reparable' standard includes both harm that is not economic in nature (e.g. pre-emptive parallel proceedings in the courts, or the destruction of records) and harm which, though economic, is difficult to repair through an eventual award of damages (e.g. further aggravation of the dispute through economic measures that ruin the applicant's entire business, and make calculation of damages disproportionately difficult or even unreliable).

18. Article 26(3) does not speak of 'current or imminent harm', but article 26(2)(a) does, in the context of describing one particular type of injunctive interim measures. Nevertheless, it is believed that, as a showing of urgency is inherent in any request for interim measures, a showing of 'current or imminent harm' will to some extent be necessary in all cases. This statement requires a qualification in respect of procedural rights (as distinct from the parties' substantive rights in dispute). Harm to a procedural right may have the consequence that a party will be precluded from having a realistic opportunity to obtain an award in its favour, or that the arbitral process as a whole will be frustrated. For that reason, it can be said that averting such serious harm is 'axiomatically' urgent.[29]

---

[26] Stewart A. Baker & Mark D. Davis, *The UNCITRAL Arbitration Rules in Practice – The Experience of the Iran-United States Claims Tribunal*, 139-140 (Kluwer 1992) (noting that the 'US definition of "irreparable harm" is a harm that cannot readily be compensated by an award of damages. If this standard were strictly applied, most commercial disputes arbitrated under the UNCITRAL Rules would not qualify for interim protection under Article 26, since the award of money damages can, at least in theory, rectify nearly all commercial losses').

[27] *See*, e.g., *Paushok v. Mongolia*, *supra* fn 18, at para. 68 ('The possibility of monetary compensation does not necessarily eliminate the possible need for interim measures'); Klaus P. Berger, *International Economic Arbitration*, 336 (Kluwer 1993).

[28] *See*, e.g., *Tokios Tokelés v. Ukraine* (ICSID Case No. ARB/02/18), Procedural Order No. 3, 18 January 2005, < www.italaw.com >, para. 8. *See also Plama Consortium Ltd v. Republic of Bulgaria* (ICSID Case No. ARB/03/24) Order, 6 September 2005, < www.italaw.com >, para. 38 (provisional measures are appropriate 'to avoid the occurrence of irreparable harm or damage'); *Dawood Rawat v. The Republic of Mauritius* (UNCITRAL) Order Regarding Request for Interim Measures, 11 January 2017, < www.italaw.com >, para. 45 ('As for irreparable harm, it is well-established that harm claimed is not irreparable if it can be compensated by monetary damages').

[29] *See*, e.g., *Abaclat & Ors v. Argentine Republic* (ICSID Case No. ARB/07/5) Procedural Order No, 11, 27 June 2012, < www.italaw.com >, para. 20; *Quiborax SA, Non Metallic Minerals SA and Allan Fosk Kaplún v. Plurinational State of Bolivia* (ICSID Case No. ARB/06/2) Decision on Provisional Measures, 26 February 2010, < www.italaw.com >, para. 153; *Marfin Investment Group Holdings S.A., Alexandros Bakatselos and others v. Republic of Cyprus* (ICSID Case No. ARB/13/27), Procedural Order No. 6, 13 September 2016, paras 157-160, 230-246, and 253-257.

19. As to the second point, the Rules require a showing of 'likelihood', and that normally turns on a showing of greater-than-even chances that the harm will occur.[30] But the test is not purely statistical or mechanical. There will be cases where, in the light of the gravity of the potential harm, it is appropriate to demand 'a substantial risk, rather than a 50% or greater likelihood'.[31] Conversely, there will be cases that the harm per se seems so improbable in nature that it should not be considered as likely merely on a balance of probabilities.

5. Proportionality or 'balance of (in)convenience/hardship'

20. A requirement of reasonableness or proportionality is also explicitly provided for in article 26(3)(a) of the Rules. This calls for the applicant to satisfy the tribunal that the harm it invokes 'substantially outweighs the harm that is likely to result to the party against whom the measure is directed if the measure is granted'. The term 'substantially' is rightly pointed out as a significant one in this balancing exercise.[32] It is one that can be expected to feature heavily in cases under the Rules where a sovereign state's regulatory and other powers are sought to be restrained to prevent allegedly greater harm on the part of an investor.

6. Connection with the subject-matter of the claim

21. Article 26 does not expressly require a connection between the measure sought and the subject-matter of the claim or a particular right of the requesting party. The *travaux* indicate that the article 26(1)(a) phrase 'in respect of the subject-matter of the dispute' was considered too restrictive, and that the intended purpose of article 26 is to broaden the focus of interim measures.[33]

22. The matter is a delicate one, because although interim protection was traditionally sought in respect of the substantive rights of the parties that are in contention – hence the oft-encountered formulation that interim measures may 'preserve

---

30 *See* Born, *supra* fn 19, at 2468, citing ICJ and ICSID cases, including *Passage Through the Great Belt (Finland v. Denmark)*, Provisional Measures, Order of 29 July 1991, ICJ Rep 12 (1991), para. 23 (provisional measures are justified when 'action prejudicial to the rights of either party is likely to be taken before [a] final decision is given'); *Burlington Resources Inc v. Republic of Ecuador* (ICSID Case No. ARB/08/5) Procedural Order No. 1, 29 June 2009, < www.italaw.com >, para. 72 (provisional measures are justified when 'actions prejudicial to the rights of the petitioner are likely to be taken before the Arbitral Tribunal decides on the merits of the dispute'); *Perenco Ecuador Ltd v. The Republic of Ecuador and Empresa Estatal Petróleos del Ecuador (Petroecuador)* (ICSID Case No. ARB/08/6) Decision on Provisional Measures, 8 May 2009, < www.italaw.com >.

31 *Ibid.*, at 2468; and *see* Caron & Caplan, *supra* fn 3, at 542 ('Given the exceptional urgency involved and the very provisional nature of the measure, however, the arbitral tribunal should be very sympathetic to the applicant in borderline cases in applying both the *prima facie* and grave/substantial damage (or "irreparable" harm) tests').

32 Caron & Caplan, *supra* fn 3, at 522.

33 UNCITRAL Report of 45th Session, 5 October 2006, UN Doc A/CN.9/614, paras 104-105.

the respective rights of either party'[34] – protection of procedural rights and the integrity of the proceedings is increasingly sought in practice, especially in investment-treaty cases.[35] Thus it is appropriate to leave to the assessment of the tribunal, in light of all the circumstances, the requisite degree of connection between the interim relief sought and the 'subject-matter of the dispute'[36] – although there is of course authority for the proposition that such a nexus is necessary,[37] on occasion being said that a 'direct connection' is required between the requested interim measure and the main claim.[38]

---

[34] *See* Article 41 of the ICJ Statute; Article 47 of the ICSID Convention and Rule 39 of the ICSID Rules, which states that the party needs to 'specify the rights to be preserved' in its request for provisional measures. Commentary on the ICJ practice in relation to interim measures explains: 'By requiring the parties themselves to formulate the rights they might wish to have protected, the Court could expect to attain two goals. First, the parties were given the opportunity to reflect upon the stringency of their possible requests in relation to their main claims. Secondly, the specification of the rights in question might facilitate a prompt and univocal identification of the issues at stake, so that at least differences of opinion as to the basic question: what the applicant seeks to obtain from the Court? – as Judge Anzilotti put it – perhaps could be avoided'. *See* Jerzy Sztucki, *Interim Measures in The Hague Court*, 91 (Kluwer 1983).

[35] *See Plama Consortium Ltd v. Republic of Bulgaria* (ICSID Case No. ARB/03/24) Order, 6 September 2005, <www.italaw.com>, paras 40-41; *see Quiborax SA, Non Metallic Minerals SA and Allan Fosk Kaplún v. Plurinational State of Bolivia* (ICSID Case No. ARB/06/2) Decision on Provisional Measures, 26 February 2010, <www.italaw.com>, para. 117 (tribunal agreed with the claimants in finding that 'the rights to be preserved by provisional measures are not limited to those which form the subject matter of the dispute, but may extend to procedural rights, including the general right to the preservation of the status quo and to the non-aggravation of the dispute'); *see also Biwater Gauff (Tanzania) Ltd v. United Republic of Tanzania* (ICSID Case No. ARB/05/22) Procedural Order No. 1, 31 March 2006, <www.italaw.com>, para. 71 ('The type of rights capable of protection by means of provisional measures are not only substantive rights but also procedural rights').

[36] *See* UNCITRAL Report of 43rd Session, 12 October 2005, UN Doc A/CN.9/589, paras 28-29 (in connection with article 26(2)(d), 'It was noted that the phrase ["relevant and material"] had taken on a meaning such that the term "relevant" required that the evidence be connected to the dispute and the term "material" referred to the significance of the evidence'); *see also* Caron & Caplan, *supra* fn 3, at 520.

[37] *See*, e.g., *Polish Agrarian Reform and German Minority (Germany v. Poland)* PCIJ Series A/B No 58, Order, 29 July 1933, <www.worldcourts.com>, para. 17 (where the Court expounded the principle that 'the essential condition which must necessarily be fulfilled in order to justify a request for the indication of interim measures, should circumstances require them, is that such measures should have the effect of *protecting the rights forming the subject of the dispute submitted to the Court*' (emphasis added). The German request was rejected on the basis that 'the interim measures asked for would result in a general suspension of the agrarian reform in so far as concerns Polish nationals of German race, and cannot therefore be regarded as *solely designed to protect the subject of the dispute and the actual object of the principal claim*' (emphasis added) at paras 21-22). *See also Emilio Agustin Maffezini v. The Kingdom of Spain* (ICSID Case No. ARB/97/7) Decision on Request for Provisional Measures, 28 October 1999, <www.italaw.com>, para. 23.

[38] *See Fisheries Jurisdiction Case (Germany v. Iceland)* Order, 17 August 1972, <www.icj-cij.org>, para. 14 (where the Court pointed out that 'the contention of the Applicant ... is part of the subject-matter of the dispute submitted to the Court, and *the request for*

B. TYPES OF INTERIM MEASURES

23. Article 26(1) of the 1976 Rules grants arbitrators the power to take 'any interim measures … in respect of the subject-matter of the dispute'. The only example provided referred to the conservation of goods – an example that was apt and critical in the 1970s world where trade disputes were the staple of arbitration. That limited example, however, could raise apprehension about the type of interim measures that may be granted under article 26(1).[39] On one view, the sole reference to such conservatory measures made tribunals 'unsure of [their] authority to act', 'where the relief requested was something other than the "conservation of goods"'.[40]

24. A similar issue arose from the term 'in respect of the subject-matter of the dispute'. These terms are unproblematic in the context of conservatory measures (for example, an order to sell perishable goods) but less so when the measure sought is an injunction to protect a party or the arbitral process itself. This potential ambiguity was acute for the Iran-US Claims Tribunal, which granted interim measures in the form of anti-suit injunctions to restrain proceedings in other fora.[41] The Tribunal preferred to rely on 'inherent powers'[42] rather than on article 26. A related issue in this connection was whether orders for security for costs, which can be seen as purely procedural, were 'interim measures' for the purposes of article 26. A strict reading of article 26(1) could exclude them,[43] although some tribunals held that they had the power to grant such orders.[44]

---

provisional measures designed to protect such rights is therefore directly connected with the Application' (emphasis added)).

39 *See* Baker & Davis, *supra* fn 26, at 138 ('doubts about the scope of Article 26 are understandable given the ambiguous formulation of this article').

40 *Ibid.*, at 133-134. Other commentators gave less weight to the 'conservation of goods' example; *see* Caron, Caplan & Pellonpää, *supra* fn 21, at 539; and Pieter Sanders, *Commentary on UNCITRAL Arbitration Rules*, II YCA 172, 195-196 (1977).

41 *See* Caron & Caplan, *supra* fn 3, at 518; Baker & Davis, *supra* fn 26, at 135. For a general discussion on the practice of the Iran-US Claims Tribunal on interim measures, *see* Baker & Davis, *ibid.*, at 133-143.

42 The seminal case regarding the issuance of stay of proceedings orders is *E-Systems Inc v. The Islamic Republic of Iran, Bank Melli Iran* (1982) 2 Iran-US CTR 51, where the Tribunal observed that it had '[a]n *inherent power* to issue such Orders as may be necessary to conserve the respective rights of the Parties and to ensure that this Tribunal's jurisdiction and authority are made fully effective' (emphasis added) (para. 57).

43 Noah Rubins, *In God We Trust, All Others Pay Cash: Security for Costs in International Commercial Arbitration*, 11(3) Am Rev Int Arb 307, 343-344 (2000).

44 *See* Jakob Ragnwaldh & Nils Eliasson, 'Security for Costs in Investment Arbitration' in Kaj Hobér, Annette Magnusson, Marie Öhrström & Christopher Goddard (eds), *Between East and West: Essays in Honour of Ulf Franke*, 395 (Juris 2010) (describing two unreported cases where UNCITRAL tribunals found that article 26 of the 1976 Rules gave them the power to order security for costs). Cf. *Libananco Holdings Co Limited v. Republic of Turkey* (ICSID Case No. ARB/06/08) Decision on Preliminary Issues, 23 June 2008, < www.italaw.com >, paras 56-60 (orders for security for costs may be granted in exceptional circumstances); *RSM Production Corporation v. Saint Lucia* (ICSID Case No. ARB/12/10) Decision on Saint Lucia's Request for Security for Costs, 13 August 2014, < www.italaw.com >, para. 55

25. True, the reference to 'any interim measures' was mostly (and rightly) read to import broad powers to issue any type of provisional measures, including injunctive relief,[45] but the 2010 revision was the opportunity to clarify these matters. After the broad wording of the present article 26(2), which covers 'any temporary measure', there then follows an enumeration of examples which are given emphatically 'without limitation'.[46] The enumeration is a modern classic, being lifted directly from Article 17(2) of the Model Law.[47] It includes measures:

- to preserve the status quo (such as cease-and-desist injunctions, or even a general injunction not to aggravate the dispute in any way);
- to prevent imminent harm (e.g. by preventing or by compelling the disposition of assets) or prejudice to the arbitral proceedings (such as stays of duplicative proceedings on the merits[48] or of enforcement proceedings);[49]
- to provide 'a means of preserving assets out of which a subsequent award may be satisfied' (such as freezing orders but also orders to 'make an interim payment on account of the costs of the arbitration'[50]);[51] and
- to preserve relevant and material evidence (e.g. to prevent the destruction of documents or to obtain the testimony of a witness).

(orders for security for costs are within an ICSID tribunal's power 'provided exceptional circumstances exist').

45 *See* Born, *supra* fn 19, at 2440. *See*, e.g., *Paushok v. Mongolia*, *supra* fn 18, at para. 36 (tribunal issued an order directing Mongolia to suspend enforcement of legislation and a stay of proceedings Mongolia had initiated in national courts); and *Chevron Corporation (USA) and Texaco Petroleum Corporation (USA) v. The Republic of Ecuador* (UNCITRAL) Second Interim Award on Interim Measures, 16 February 2012, <www.italaw.com>, para. 3 (tribunal granted interim relief impacting on non-parties to the arbitration, directing Ecuador '(whether by its judicial, legislative or executive branches) to take all measures necessary to suspend or cause to be suspended the enforcement and recognition within and without Ecuador' of judgments against Chevron in Ecuadorian legal proceedings ('the Lago Agrio Case')).

46 The non-exhaustive character of the list is underlined by the addition of the term 'without limitation'; *see* UNCITRAL Report of 50th Session, 9 March 2009, UN Doc A/CN.9/669, paras 92-94.

47 Castello, *supra* fn 3, at 234.

48 Caron & Caplan, *supra* fn 3, at 518; *Ford Aerospace and Communications Corp v. Government of Iran* (1983) 2 Iran-US CTR 281.

49 *Chevron Corporation (USA) and Texaco Petroleum Corporation (USA) v. The Republic of Ecuador* (UNCITRAL) Second Interim Award on Interim Measures, 16 February 2012, <www.italaw.com>.

50 *See* section 39(2)(b) of the Arbitration Act 1996 (England & Wales).

51 Blackaby, Partasides, Redfern & Hunter, *supra* fn 12, at para. 5.37; *see also Guaracachi America Inc and Rurelec PLC v. The Plurinational State of Bolivia* (UNCITRAL) Procedural Order No. 14, 11 March 2013, <www.italaw.com>; *South American Silver Limited v. Bolivia* (UNCITRAL) Procedural Order No. 10, 11 January 2016, <www.italaw.com>, paras 51-52 ('The UNCITRAL Rules do not expressly provide for the Tribunal's powers to order security for costs ... However, several decisions ... confirm that arbitral tribunals are [so] empowered. The Parties cite these decisions and ... agree that this Tribunal has powers to order the measure').

26. In short, although article 26(2) does not state this expressly, a tribunal may by way of provisional measure order any kind of relief that it might grant in a final award. The only limitation – which goes without saying and is not set out in terms in the provision – is that an interim measure may not amount to an early disposition that renders moot a decision on the merits. That is not to say that (for example) provisional payments under a contested contractual obligation are to be excluded axiomatically. Indeed, the express power a tribunal has to terminate, suspend, or modify a measure issued, pursuant to article 26(5), diminishes the need for a no-preemption principle.

27. Article 26(2) is an authorising provision. It does not compel the tribunal to take any of the measures there listed. What measures a tribunal should take will turn on an assessment of all the relevant circumstances, as discussed under section A above. It will also turn on any specific substantive rights under the law applicable to the merits and the parties' substantive contract. For example, the parties may have agreed that their contract price may be revised by a tribunal only by a final award. Conversely, the applicable law may specifically entitle the buyer to sell a perishable good. In that connection, it is noted that certain laws entitle parties to take measures (e.g. terminate a prior contract) without court intervention. Such substantive-law entitlements are not affected by article 26. That is to say, an additional tribunal intervention to authorize such measures may be unnecessary. But the other side may have recourse to the tribunal to seek interim relief to counter measures already taken.

C. ORDER OR AWARD

28. While it is clear from article 33(1) that a decision on interim measures is to be taken by a majority of the tribunal, and from article 26(2) that such decision is binding on the parties and to be carried out, the Rules do not spell out that such a decision may take the form of an award. This is in contrast to article 26(2) of the 1976 Rules, which expressly provides that 'interim measures may be established in the form of an interim award'.[52] Similarly, Article 17(2) of the Model Law provides that an interim measure may be 'in the form of an award or in another form'.

29. It should not be thought that the 2010 Rules are more restrictive than the 1976 Rules in that regard. Indeed it is right to say that it is 'generally accepted' that under the 2010 Rules a tribunal may frame a decision on interim measures as an award.[53] In practice, tribunals have framed decisions on interim measures both as awards[54] and as orders (or procedural orders),[55] and will continue to do

52 As to the rationale for which *see* the discussion in connection with article 34, *infra*.

53 Caron & Caplan, *supra* fn 3, at 525.

54 *See*, e.g., *Chevron Corporation (USA) and Texaco Petroleum Corporation (USA) v. The Republic of Ecuador* (UNCITRAL) First Interim Award on Interim Measures, 25 January 2012; Second Interim Award on Interim Measures, 16 February 2012.

55 *See*, e.g., *South American Silver Limited v. Bolivia* (UNCITRAL) Procedural Order No. 10, 11 January 2016, <www.italaw.com>.

so. As more fully discussed in the context of article 34, it may be appropriate for the tribunal to opt for an award, especially when there is a prospect that its decision will be enforceable as an award under the national law of a state that is connected with the case (as is the case in Israel and Malaysia for example).[56]

30. The rationale for the difference in formulation between the 2010 and the 1976 Rules is simply that–

> while in the past some practitioners might have used the form of an award for interim measures with a view to enhancing their enforceability, this no longer had much purpose given that the UNCITRAL Arbitration Model Law now contained provisions permitting enforcement of interim measures regardless of the form in which they were issued. As well, it was noted that issuing an interim measure in the form of an award under the Rules could create confusion, particularly in light of article 26 (5) of the Rules, which permitted the arbitral tribunal to modify or suspend an interim measure [without resorting to articles 37-39].[57]

31. It is recognized that interim measures awards are not 'final' in the full sense of article 34(2); that matter is discussed in connection with that provision, below.

D. THIRD PARTIES; NATIONAL COURTS

32. The powers of the arbitral tribunal to order interim measures are 'virtually always' limited to the parties to the arbitration and the arbitration agreement.[58] Thus a tribunal does not have the power to order, for example, the attachment or preservation of property owned by a third party.[59] In accordance with Article 17 of the Model Law, the Rules recognize this principle. Although both versions of article 26 on their face grant the tribunal broad powers by using wording such as 'any interim measures it deems necessary' (1976 Rules) and 'any temporary

---

56 Blackaby, Partasides, Redfern & Hunter, *supra* fn 12, at paras 7.19-7.20.

57 UNCITRAL Report of 47th Session, 25 September 2007, UN Doc A/CN.9/641, para. 51.

58 Born, *supra* fn 19, at 2444. *See also* Caron & Caplan, *supra* fn 3, at 517 ('an arbitral tribunal's jurisdiction encompasses only the parties before it, interim measures may not be directed to non-parties'); *Atlantic Richfield Company v. The Islamic Republic of Iran* (1985-I) 8 Iran-US CTR 179, 181-182 ('The Tribunal holds that, as to the claim for interim relief against the Government of the United States of America, it cannot grant the relief sought because the Government of the United States of America is not a party to Case No. 396'); *Chevron Corporation (USA) and Texaco Petroleum Corporation (USA) v. The Republic of Ecuador* (UNCITRAL) Third Interim Award on Jurisdiction and Admissibility, 27 February 2012, <www.italaw.com>, para. 4.65 ('[T]his Tribunal does not have jurisdiction over the Lago Agrio plaintiffs ... in the context of applications for interim measures ... and cannot order them to do or to abstain from doing anything').

59 *See*, e.g., Final Award in ICC Case No. 7828, cited in Julian D. M. Lew, *Commentary on Interim and Conservatory Measures in ICC Arbitration Cases* 11(1) ICC Ct Bull 23, 25 (2000). *See also* Born, *supra* fn 19, at 2444.

measure ... at any time' (2010 Rules), article 26(2) of the 2010 Rules specifies that an interim measure must be directed at 'a party'.[60]

33. However, the Working Group noted that, even if not directed at a third party an interim measure may practically affect third persons, for example holders of funds or other assets of the respondent, as the third party may be obliged to take some action in respect of that property by virtue of the order directed at the party to the arbitration.[61] This was also recognized in connection with Article 17 of the Model Law.[62] The authors agree with the proposition that a tribunal does have the power to order a party in the arbitration to take steps which involve third parties,[63] either as an obligation to achieve a certain result (when the third party plainly must follow the directions of the respondent, as is the case for a bank holding the respondent's funds), or as an obligation of best efforts to take all steps available to it and report to the tribunal as to these steps.[64] That is different from a direct third-party order, 'for example, addressed to a bank holding deposits of a party [which] would not be enforceable against the bank'.[65] Such an order will require a party to enlist the assistance of national courts or other competent domestic authorities, pursuant to article 26(9).[66]

34. Indeed, article 26(9) addresses the possible role of domestic courts and ensures that a party requesting the intervention of domestic courts will not be taken to have violated or waived the arbitration agreement by resorting to them. From

---

60 Similar wording can be found in other rules; *see*, e.g., Austrian ZPO, para. 593(1) ('against the other party'); Swedish Arbitration Act, para. 25(4) ('the opposing party must undertake').

61 UNCITRAL Report of 32nd Session, 10 April 2000, UN Doc A/CN.9/468, XXXI UNCITRAL Ybk 477, 484 para. 64.

62 It was recognized during the 2006 revision process that the Model Law as it stood in 1985 'did not take into account the special features of interim measures of protection ... [such as the possibility] ... that the measure would affect the interests of third parties'. *See* UNCITRAL Report of 32nd Session, 10 April 2000, UN Doc A/CN.9/468, XXXI UNCITRAL Ybk 477, 485 para. 70.

63 *See* Born, *supra* fn 19, at 2446.

64 *See*, e.g., *Millicom International Operations B.V. and Sentel GSM SA v. The Republic of Senegal* (ICSID Case No. ARB/08/20) Decision on the Application for Provisional Measures, 9 December 2009, para. 52, <www.italaw.com> (where the tribunal directed the parties jointly to address the Dakar Regional Court to have pending proceedings in Senegal suspended).

65 Blackaby, Partasides, Redfern & Hunter, *supra* fn 12, at para. 7.18.

66 Commentary on provision 26(3) of the 1976 Rules (which was retained from the original text, but renumbered as article 26(9)) states: 'This paragraph makes it clear that a party to the arbitral proceedings may, if he so wishes, request an appropriate judicial authority to take interim protective measures, without thereby violating the agreement to arbitration contained in the arbitration clause or separate arbitration agreement under which the arbitral proceedings arose'. *See* UNCITRAL Report of the Secretary General on the Draft UNCITRAL Arbitration Rules, 12 December 1975, UN Doc A/CN.9/112/Add.1, 176. *See also* Jason Fry, Simon Greenberg & Francesca Mazza, *The Secretariat's Guide to ICC Arbitration*, para. 3-1039 (ICC 2012): 'An arbitral tribunal has no power over third parties (i.e. entities or individuals who are not parties to the arbitration). Interim relief against a third party can be granted, if at all, only by a state court'.

this follows that the domestic court's intervention does not negate the tribunal's jurisdiction to issue complementary interim measures, or measures that revise the court's measures or, finally, measures that enjoin the parties to take action to terminate court-ordered interim measures (and the authors are aware of at least one case where this has happened).[67]

35. Equivalent provisions are invariably found in arbitration rules,[68] and their function is three-fold: first, to permit a party to have access to interim measures before the constitution of the tribunal; secondly, to permit a party to compel compliance with interim measures granted by the tribunal;[69] thirdly, where the *lex arbitri* restricts the tribunal's power to grant interim measures (whether at all or in respect of certain types of interim measures). The Rules are notable only in one respect, namely that they do not establish any priority between recourse to the arbitral tribunal and to domestic courts. By contrast, the ICC Rules provide that recourse to a domestic court may be had '[b]efore the file is transmitted to the arbitral tribunal, and in appropriate circumstances even thereafter'.[70]

E. TERMINATION, SUSPENSION, MODIFICATION

36. Article 26(5), imported directly from Article 17D of the Model Law, provides that interim measures remain subject to modification, suspension or termination, either upon the application of a party or, in exceptional circumstances and with advance notice to the parties, at the tribunal's own motion. The Rules eliminate the distinction under the 1976 Rules between orders and awards, only the former being subject to revision.[71] Thus, unlike other awards, which are subject only to the articles 37-39 remedies, interim measures awards are liable to revision, suspension or termination if new elements arise or circumstances change.[72]

37. Consistent with article 26(5), article 26(7) allows a tribunal to 'require a party to notify the tribunal if there is any change in the circumstances either cited by that party when requesting an interim measure or relied upon by the tribunal in granting the measure'.[73] This ensures that an interim measure that is no longer justified does not remain in effect.

---

67 Cf. Article 28(2) of the ICC Rules: recourse to a domestic court 'shall not affect the relevant powers reserved to the arbitral tribunal'.

68 *See*, e.g., Article 6(7) of the AAA International Arbitration Rules; Article 28(2) of the ICC Rules; Article 26(5) of the Swiss Rules; Article 37(5) of the SCC Rules.

69 Especially given that '[a]n order or award of interim measures is ... unlikely to satisfy the requirement of finality under the New York Convention, which may render it unenforceable internationally'. *See* Blackaby, Partasides, Redfern & Hunter, *supra* fn 12, at para. 7.19.

70 Article 28(2) of the ICC Rules.

71 Petrochilos, *supra* fn 3; *see also* Caron & Caplan, *supra* fn 3, at 525.

72 Petrochilos, *supra* fn 3, at 886; *see also Chevron Corporation (USA) and Texaco Petroleum Corporation (USA) v. The Republic of Ecuador* (UNCITRAL) Order on Interim Measures, 14 May 2010, <www.italaw.com>, para. 1.

73 Castello, *supra* fn 3, at 234.

F. LIABILITY FOR COSTS AND DAMAGES

38. Article 26(8) of the 2010 Rules addresses the potential liability of the applicant for costs and damages resulting from the interim measure. The provision allows a tribunal to impose on the party that obtains an interim measure liability for the cost and damage caused by the measure, if it later determines that 'in the circumstances then prevailing, the measure should not have been granted'. In short, this is a mechanism 'for compensating a party that, through no "fault" of its own, has been forced to bear expenses or even incur damages because of an interim measure that the tribunal ultimately concludes it should not have granted'.[74] The provision substantially mirrors Article 17G of the Model Law, except that it clarifies that a claim for costs/damages must be assessed in the light of the situation that was 'then prevailing', i.e. at the time the request for interim measures was made.

39. One may envisage liability for costs/damages in two situations. First, if the applicant withheld material information which, had it been provided to the tribunal, would have prevented the issuance of interim measures, whether fully or partly. Secondly, where 'in light of the outcome of the case [the interim measure granted] turns out to have been an undue measure'[75] – i.e. one that was disproportionate or outright unwarranted. The applicant is best-placed to evaluate such risks from the outset and should bear the economic cost associated with them. Nevertheless, it does not follow that if the claimant fails to prevail on the merits, there will be automatically a claim for costs/damages.[76] The tribunal has a judgement to exercise. That is why the provision, in line with the corresponding Model Law provision, makes no reference to the merits of the case.[77] This also explains the reference to 'the circumstances then prevailing'.[78] It must be shown that, while not necessarily amounting to a wrongful act, the seeking of interim measures in the circumstances placed the burden on the applicant to make good any costs/damage entrained. In sum, the provision places the applicant on notice of a duty to seek interim measures with all necessary disclosures and appreciating the prejudice that they may cause on the respondent.

40. A further function of the phrase 'in the circumstances then prevailing' is to ensure that the original grant of interim measures is not impugned by a subsequent determination that the measure should not have been granted. The

---

[74] *Ibid.*, at 235; *see also* UNCITRAL Report of 50th Session, 9 March 2009, UN Doc A/CN.9/669, paras 116-118; UNCITRAL Report of 52nd Session, 19 February 2010, UN Doc A/CN.9/688, paras 92-95.

[75] APRAG Report of 50th Session, 27 February 2009, para. 67.

[76] UNCITRAL Report of 39th Session, 8 December 2003, UN Doc A/CN.9/545, XXXV UNCITRAL Ybk 463, 481 para. 65.

[77] *See* UNCITRAL Working Paper for 51st Session, 23 July 2009, UN Doc A/CN.9/WG.II/WP.154/Add.1, para. 32. For a discussion of Article 17G of the UNCITRAL Model Law, *see* UNCITRAL Report of 39th Session, 8 December 2003, UN Doc A/CN.9/545, XXXV UNCITRAL Ybk 463, 481 para. 65.

[78] UNCITRAL Report of 50th Session, 9 March 2009, UN Doc A/CN.9/669, paras 116-118; UNCITRAL Report of 52nd Session, 19 February 2010, UN Doc A/CN.9/688, paras 92-95.

later determination may only result in monetary reparation. That is why, also, the provision does not speak of an interim measure that should not have been 'granted' by the tribunal, but rather of a measure the seeking of which appears in retrospect not to have been 'justified' in the first place.

41. Finally, while the Model Law states that the applicant 'shall' be liable, the Rules provide that the applicant 'may' be liable. This formulation was largely driven by a desire to account for differing liability regimes provided in various national arbitration laws. In that regard, the Working Group had at its disposal a note by the Secretariat describing how various national laws deal with the potential liability of applicants for interim measures.[79] The Rules set forth no rules regarding such substantive liability.

G. 'PRELIMINARY ORDERS'[80]

42. There was intense and repeated debate within the Working Group on whether the Rules should follow the Model Law by including provisions on preliminary orders.[81] These are orders made on an *ex parte* basis (i.e. without notice to the respondent) before the issuance of the main interim measures. Article 17B(1) of the Model Law provides for such orders in the following terms:

> Unless otherwise agreed by the parties, a party may, without notice to any other party, make a request for an interim measure together with an application for a preliminary order directing a party not to frustrate the purpose of the interim measure requested.

Article 17B(2) specifies that preliminary orders may be issued when 'prior disclosure of the request for the interim measure to the party against whom it is directed risks frustrating the purpose of the measure'.

43. A typical example is an order to freeze liquid assets, such as bank accounts, or ships and aircraft, where there is a risk of dissipation if the respondent receives notice of the application. A preliminary order will secure these assets pending the tribunal's decision on the main application. However, as with any *ex parte* remedy, preliminary orders are in tension with the cardinal principles of equal treatment and a reasonable opportunity to be heard under article 17(1) – although it will be noted that article 17(1) says that the latter applies 'at an appropriate stage of the proceedings'. Most arbitration rules do not expressly provide for *ex parte* interim relief,[82] and under most national laws it is not clear whether

---

79 This note, which is found in the UNCITRAL Working Paper for 40th Session, 27 January 2004, UN Doc A/CN.9/WG.II/WP.127, was initially prepared to assist the Working Group in its revision of Article 17 of the Model Law.

80 *See* generally Caron & Caplan, *supra* fn 3, at 530 et seq.

81 *See* UNCITRAL Report of 50th Session, 9 March 2009, UN Doc A/CN.9/669, paras 100-112. *See also* APRAG Report of 50th Session, 27 February 2009, paras 63-66.

82 Some arbitration rules prohibit *ex parte* orders; *see*, e.g., Rule 39(4) of the ICSID Rules ('The tribunal shall only recommend provisional measures, or modify or revoke its recommendations, after giving each party an opportunity of presenting its observations').

arbitrators have such powers.[83] This lack of clarity does pose a concern. Although *ex parte* orders of this nature are typically within the power of national courts to give, often the court that is in a position to intervene (e.g. where the assets are located) will be in a jurisdiction other than the seat of the arbitration and may therefore require persuasion as to its jurisdiction. And in investment-treaty cases, the respondent's home courts will be its own domestic courts.

44. Under the 1976 Rules there is practice and scholarly opinion indicating that preliminary orders may be granted, though in narrow circumstances.[84] This practice developed separately from the discussion on the revision of the Rules.

45. The Working Group was not persuaded that preliminary orders should be expressly provided for in the Rules, mostly because they are not universally recognized as a power arbitral tribunals should have. Concerned, therefore, about the impact that the inclusion of such a contentious power might have on the 'universal applicability' of the Rules,[85] particularly with respect to states involved in investor-state disputes,[86] the Working Group came to the conclusion that the Rules should remain neutral. On the other hand, there was pressure not to foreclose a power which tribunals may regard themselves to possess. At one stage, the solution adopted was what has been called a 'non-rule':[87]

> Nothing in these Rules shall have the effect of creating a right, or of limiting any right which may exist outside these Rules, of a party to apply to the arbitral tribunal for, and any power of the arbitral tribunal to issue, in either case without prior notice to a party, a preliminary order that the party not frustrate the purpose of a requested interim measure.[88]

This provision was eliminated at the final stage of the revision process. It was considered cumbersome and difficult to understand, especially by those who were not aware of the negotiating compromises that had led to its formulation.[89]

---

83 There are exceptions: for England *see supra* fn 12; for Switzerland *see* Daniel Wehrli, 'The Swiss Rules and the Revision of the UNCITRAL Arbitration Rules' in Rainer Füeg (ed.), *The Swiss Rules of International Arbitration – Five Years of Experience*, 93 (Swiss Chambers' Court of Arbitration and Mediation 2009).

84 *See* Caron & Caplan, *supra* fn 3, at 530-532 and the references (noting that '[p]reliminary orders were granted in the context of the Iran-US Claims Tribunal and have been granted since 2006 under the 1976 Rules in the context of two investment arbitrations'); Born, *supra* fn 19, at 2508-2510. Cf. *Paushok v. Mongolia, supra* fn 18, at paras 15-16 (tribunal issued temporary restraining order after the parties and the tribunal had exchanged various communications).

85 UNCITRAL Report of 50th Session, 9 March 2009, UN Doc A/CN.9/669, para. 101.

86 *See* UNCITRAL Report of 47th Session, 25 September 2007, UN Doc A/CN.9/641, para. 55.

87 UNCITRAL Summary Record of the 905th Meeting, 23 June 2010, UN Doc A/CN/.9/SR.905, XLI UNCITRAL Ybk 1235, 1240 para. 75, Mr Moollan (Mauritius).

88 UNCITRAL Working Paper for 52nd Session, 10 December 2009, UN Doc A/CN.9/WG.II/WP.157/Add.1, para. 25.

89 *See* Report of the Commission on its 43rd Session, 21 June-9 July 2010, UN Doc A/65/17, paras 121-125. *See also* UNCITRAL Summary Record of the 905th Meeting, 23 June 2010, UN Doc A/CN/.9/SR.905, XLI UNCITRAL Ybk 1235, 1238-1239 para. 58, (Greece); and para. 61, Mr Moollan (Mauritius) (explaining that 'many Governments and organizations

It was also considered unnecessary in light of article 1(3), which safeguards the primacy of the law of the arbitration.[90]

46. The current position under the Rules is that they do not bar arbitrators, subject to the *lex arbitri*, from concluding that an *ex parte* measure is warranted in the exceptional circumstances of the particular case. This they may do in exercise of the tribunal's general procedural power in article 17(1), inherent powers, or specific authorization by the applicable arbitration law. In fact, the wording of article 17(4) preserves the possibility for a party to apply to the tribunal for a preliminary order,[91] providing as follows:

> All communications to the arbitral tribunal by one party shall be communicated by that party to all other parties. Such communications shall be made at the same time, *except as otherwise permitted by the arbitral tribunal if it may do so under applicable law.* (emphasis added)

– future users of the Rules – had commented that draft article 26, paragraph 9, was incomprehensible').

90 *See* Report of the Commission on its 43rd Session, 21 June-9 July 2010, UN Doc A/65/17, paras 121-125. *See also* UNCITRAL Summary Record of the 905th Meeting, 23 June 2010, UN Doc A/CN/.9/SR.905, XLI UNCITRAL Ybk 1235, 1238 para. 58, (Greece).

91 *See* Report of the Commission on its 43rd Session, 21 June-9 July 2010, UN Doc A/65/17, para. 87.

Article 27
Evidence

1976 Rules Article 24: Evidence and hearings	2010 Rules Article 27: Evidence
1. Each party shall have the burden of proving the facts relied on to support his claim or defence.	1. Each party shall have the burden of proving the facts relied on to support its claim or defence.
2. The arbitral tribunal may, if it considers it appropriate, require a party to deliver to the tribunal and to the other party, within such a period of time as the arbitral tribunal shall decide, a summary of the documents and other evidence which that party intends to present in support of the facts in issue set out in his statement of claim or statement of defence.	2. Witnesses, including expert witnesses, who are presented by the parties to testify to the arbitral tribunal on any issue of fact or expertise may be any individual, notwithstanding that the individual is a party to the arbitration or in any way related to a party. Unless otherwise directed by the arbitral tribunal, statements by witnesses, including expert witnesses, may be presented in writing and signed by them.
3. At any time during the arbitral proceedings the arbitral tribunal may require the parties to produce documents, exhibits or other evidence within such a period of time as the tribunal shall determine.	3. At any time during the arbitral proceedings the arbitral tribunal may require the parties to produce documents, exhibits or other evidence within such a period of time as the arbitral tribunal shall determine.
	4. The arbitral tribunal shall determine the admissibility, relevance, materiality and weight of the evidence offered.

1. The evidential record is of cardinal importance in arbitration proceedings. As stated by the learned authors of *Redfern & Hunter*, 'the majority of international arbitrations (perhaps 60 to 70 per cent) usually turn on the facts rather than on

the application of the relevant principles of law'.[1] Article 27 gathers together a number of procedural and evidential rules. These do not constitute an exhaustive treatment of the subject of evidence – documentary and testimonial – but they do set forth basic principles that are essential to the process. Proof of that is that although several aspects of article 27 were the subject of lively debates, the Working Group was not able to add much to the core evidential provisions that were already to be found in the 1976 version of the Rules.

2. Through article 27 the 2010 Rules effected a reorganization of evidence-related rules which were to be found in articles 24-25 of the 1976 Rules under the chapeau 'evidence and hearings'.[2] This is a neater division of the subject of evidence, but it also reflects a basic difference between the 2010 and 1976 versions. The 1976 text proceeds on the premise that evidence may well be presented for the first time at the hearing or shortly before it. This applies to both testimonial evidence (see article 25(2) of the 1976 Rules) and documentary evidence (see article 24(2) of the 1976 Rules). That is no longer standard practice, nor is it good practice in the authors' submission. Evidential hearings serve to present and test the evidence already on record, not to adduce evidence for the first time. Although the 2010 Rules do not contain a provision to that effect (other than the rule that in principle testimonial evidence should be adduced through written statements),[3] they have eliminated all the indications which were to contrary effect in the 1976 Rules. Notable in this connection is the elimination of article 24(2) of the 1976 Rules on pre-hearing summaries of the evidence 'that a party intends to present' at the hearing, so that there would be no 'trial by ambush'. Although the tribunal may still call for such summaries (by directions issued under article 17(1) of the 2010 Rules),[4] it was judged that preserving article 24(2) would be out of step with contemporary practice.[5] The absence of provisions allowing for evidence to be presented at the hearing for the first time is to be read in the light of articles 20(4) and 21(2), which set forth a duty for the parties to adduce 'all documents and other evidence relied upon' by them in their substantive written pleadings. In addition, the Rules should not contain any indication that a hearing is necessary for evidential reasons, for in a number of simple cases considerations of efficiency under article 17(1) will compel a documents-only disposition; see article 17(3). Thus the provisions in the Rules regarding evidence and hearings – articles 27 and 28 – have been properly sequenced and aligned.[6]

---

1 Nigel Blackaby, Constantine Partasides, Alan Redfern & Martin J. Hunter, *Redfern and Hunter on International Arbitration*, para. 6.75 (6th ed., Kluwer 2015).

2 *See* UNCITRAL Report of 50th Session, 9 March 2009, UN Doc A/CN.9/669, paras 69-71; UNCITRAL Working Paper for 51st Session, 23 July 2009, UN Doc A/CN.9/WG.II/WP.154/Add.1, para. 38.

3 *See* article 27(2).

4 UNCITRAL Report of 50th Session, 9 March 2009, UN Doc A/CN.9/669, para. 51; *See also* Sophie Nappert, *Commentary on the UNCITRAL Arbitration Rules 2010: A Practitioner's Guide*, 105 (Juris Publishing 2012).

5 UNCITRAL Report of 47th Session, 25 September 2007, UN Doc A/CN.9/641, paras 22-23. *See also* APRAG Report of 50th Session, 27 February 2009, para. 38.

6 *See* UNCITRAL Report of 50th Session, 9 March 2009, UN Doc A/CN.9/669, paras 70-71.

3. As already noted, article 27 is not an evidential code. It does not, for example, address specifically evidential privileges and other exceptions to disclosure, the tribunal's power to seek evidence from third parties, the manner in which evidential material is to be organized and presented (e.g. as 'exhibits' or otherwise), how legal materials are to be presented and by whom, etc. These are matters for the tribunal to address, in consultation with the parties, at the outset of the proceedings, typically in its first procedural order. These matters may of course be revisited in the light of evolving needs of the proceedings and eventual disagreements between the parties.

4. Two texts in particular serve as codifications of good practice in respect of detailed procedural arrangements regarding evidence. Tribunals do have regard to these texts in practice. The first is the IBA Rules on the Taking of Evidence in International Arbitration (the 'IBA Rules'), particularly with respect to documentary evidence.[7] The IBA Rules were revised in 2010 and may apply in both investment-treaty and commercial arbitrations. They are adopted in practice almost as a matter of course, usually described in a procedural order as a 'source of inspiration' or 'guide' for the tribunal, to preserve discretion to derogate from or supplement them; but they tend to be treated as an authoritative text in actual fact. The second text is the UNCITRAL Notes, which were also recently revised and (inter alia) provide tribunals with useful guidance on how to exercise their powers under article 17(1) in respect of evidence.[8]

5. As the main new provision in article 27 is to be found in paragraph (2), we start first with an overview of paragraphs (1), (3), and (4) which are identical to the corresponding provisions in the 1976 Rules before we turn to the new elements in article 27.

A. THE CONSTITUTION AND ASSESSMENT OF THE EVIDENTIAL RECORD

6. Article 27(1) provides that '[e]ach party shall have the burden of proving the facts relied on to support his claim or defence'. What needs to be proved therefore depends on the factual components that the applicable law sets out as essential ingredients of the legal claim or defence that is pleaded. In particular, there are cases where the applicable law sets forth a factual presumption (for example that a defect identified in a good within a period from its delivery to the buyer is presumed to have existed at the time of delivery) and therefore shifts the evidential burden to the other side.[9] It was recognized in the Working Group that the 'application of regulations on the burden of proof in the applicable

---

[7] *See Walter Bau AG (In Liquidation) v. The Kingdom of Thailand* (UNCITRAL) Award, 1 July 2009, <www.italaw.com>, para. 1.27. *See also* Blackaby, Partasides, Redfern & Hunter, *supra* fn 1, at para. 6.95 (describing the IBA Rules as 'the international standard for an effective, pragmatic, and relatively economical document production regime').

[8] *See* UNCITRAL, *Notes on Organizing Arbitral Proceedings*, paras 73-107 (United Nations 2016).

[9] James E. Castello, 'UNCITRAL Arbitration Rules, Section III, Article 27' in Loukas A. Mistelis (ed), *Concise International Arbitration*, 237 (2nd ed., Kluwer 2015).

law' is unaffected by article 27(1), and therefore there was no need expressly to safeguard the applicable law in the text of this article.[10] By contrast, if the facts necessary to make out are uncontested, what needs to be evidenced under article 27(1) is the lack of contestation. In practical terms, the scope of contested facts should in the main be clear after the exchange of the notice of arbitration and the response: facts which are contested, or not accepted, or in respect of which one party puts the other to proof, are covered by the article 27(1) evidential burden.

7. Article 27(1) practically means that responsibility for the constitution of the factual record rests primarily with the parties. The tribunal's power to call on the parties to adduce additional evidence (article 27(3)) is supplementary, and in principle to be exercised after the parties have had an opportunity to adduce the evidence they rely upon in their main pleadings, as they must under articles 20(4) and 21(2). The importance of this sequencing of party duties and tribunal powers cannot be overstated: it is not the function of the tribunal to substitute for the parties in marshalling the facts that are asserted by the parties. Stated differently, tribunal-ordered production of evidence is neither the primary method nor an invariably-applicable method of evidence-gathering under the Rules.

8. That is not to say that article 27(1) excludes an inquisitorial mode altogether. The provision applies to 'facts', as opposed to law, and therefore leaves it to the tribunal and the parties to address the issue of evidential support for legal arguments such as case-law and scholarly materials. In practice, such materials are adduced much in the same way as factual evidence, with the primary responsibility resting with the parties.[11] Nevertheless, it is possible for the parties to leave the identification of applicable legal rules and corresponding authority entirely or primarily to the tribunal, by adopting a *iura novit curia* approach. Whatever the approach to be adopted, adversarial, inquisitorial or a combination of the two, it is essential that the position be clear in advance to all participants in the arbitration.

9. The main function of article 27(1) is a procedural one. As may be seen from the *travaux* to the 1976 text, the concern was to prevent parties from making factual assertions without providing evidential support for them.[12] This was an acute concern, as articles 18(2) and 19(2) of the 1976 version allowed the parties merely to 'reference ... documents or other evidence' in their main pleadings and submit such materials at the hearing or shortly before. Nevertheless, this procedural duty ('burden') by necessary implication carries an evidential consequence: if a party fails to provide evidential support for its allegations without a satisfactory explanation, the allegations will be unproved and therefore dismissed.

---

[10] *See* UNCITRAL Report of 52nd Session, 19 February 2010, UN Doc A/CN.9/688, paras 96-98.

[11] *See* Recommendations annexed to ILA International Commercial Arbitration Committee Resolution No. 6/2008, 17-21 August 2008, <www.ila-hq.org>.

[12] Stewart A. Baker & Mark D. Davis, *The UNCITRAL Arbitration Rules in Practice – The Experience of the Iran-United States Claims Tribunal*, 109 and the references (Kluwer 1992).

10. A number of further points follow. First, article 27(1) does not address the standard of proof, that is to say, whether the evidence adduced should rise to a preponderance of probabilities or to a level beyond reasonable doubt, or a *conviction intime*, or any other standard. Indeed, it would seem to follow from the tribunal's broad power to assess the evidence that the applicable standard of proof is for the tribunal to determine, as discussed below. Secondly, there are circumstances where evidence may be unavailable to one party (for example, it has been destroyed) but in the possession or control of the other party. That is the kind of justified explanation for a party's failure to adduce evidence, seeking instead the tribunal's intervention to call for disclosure by virtue of article 27(3). Thirdly, and in a related vein, it is also possible for a tribunal to draw adverse inferences from a party's failure to adduce evidence that one expects in the regular course to exist and to be in a party's possession or control.[13] Such inferences may be called for not only in circumstances where a party has been required by the tribunal to produce the relevant materials (under article 27(3)) but also where one party has adduced evidence that is probative to an extent, thereby shifting the burden to the other party to adduce contrary evidence.[14]

11. The power of the tribunal under article 27(3) covers all types of evidential materials: 'documents, exhibits, or other evidence'.[15] This is not an accurate formulation, as the term 'exhibits' refers merely to the mode of presentation of evidence, exhibited (i.e. annexed) to pleadings which rely upon and cite this evidence. Nevertheless, as the provision reiterates verbatim article 24(3) of the 1976 version, the text was left intact.

12. It will be noted that article 27(3) allows a tribunal to call upon 'the parties' to produce evidence. Requests to third parties, including public authorities, are not covered by the wording. There is a sound reason for this: third parties are not bound by the arbitration agreement and cannot be 'require[d]' by the tribunal to produce evidence. This applies also to witnesses and party-appointed experts, except for witnesses who are officers or employees of a party or otherwise within the control of a party. Accordingly, requests for third-party evidence will either have to be routed through the parties, in the sense that the tribunal may require

---

[13] There is venerable authority for this proposition; *see*, e.g., WTO Panel Report on *Argentina – Textiles and Apparel* (DS56), 25 November 1997, para. 6.40; *William A Parker (USA) v. United Mexican States* (1926) IV RIAA 35, paras 6, 41 (tribunals do not recognize 'the "right" of the respondent merely to wait in silence in cases where it is reasonable that it should speak'); *Ahmadou Sadio Diallo (Republic of Guinea v. Democratic Republic of the Congo)* [2010] ICJ Reports 639, para. 55 (where the Applicant alleged that it had not been afforded certain procedural guarantees by a public authority, 'it cannot as a general rule be demanded of the Applicant that it prove the negative fact which it is asserting').

[14] *See* David D. Caron & Lee M. Caplan, *The UNCITRAL Arbitration Rules, A Commentary*, 558 (2nd ed., Oxford University Press 2013) (citing to *Reza Said Malek v. Islamic Republic of Iran* (1992) 28 Iran-US CTR 246: 'It is the Claimant who carries the initial burden of proving the facts upon which he relies. There is a point, however, at which the claimant may be considered to have made a sufficient showing to shift the burden of proof to the respondent').

[15] *See* generally *ibid.*, at 566-567 and the references.

them to make every reasonable effort to obtain such evidence from a third party; or else be framed as invitations to a third party, and be founded on the tribunal's general procedural power under article 17(1) of the Rules. This issue has arisen in investment-treaty arbitrations, concerning negotiating records of an investment treaty available to the investor's home state, and is discussed in the context of article 5 of the Transparency Rules below.

13. Article 27(4) is a provision common to many arbitration rules.[16] It provides that the tribunal has the broadest authority to decide on evidential matters, that is, to 'determine the admissibility, relevance, materiality and weight of the evidence offered'. Importantly, the provision contains no reference to a national law. This applies notably to the standard of proof, covered by the terms 'relevance, materiality and weight' of the evidence. For example, a national rule of civil procedure that regards certain evidence as dispositive (e.g. a report by a state-supervised auditor) does not automatically apply. The rule also applies to the admissibility of evidence. For example, the tribunal is not bound by technical rules about hearsay or parol evidence in deciding whether or not to admit evidence. That is not to say that the tribunal should not have regard to the *lex arbitri* or applicable substantive law; and indeed in many cases it should do so[17] or would even be compelled to do so[18] (for example, when evidence has been procured by fraud or is in itself a fraud). It is simply to say that 'rigid rules of evidence are unsuitable for international arbitration proceedings'.[19] Such rigid rules have a place within comprehensive codes of civil procedure which allocate specific duties and responsibilities to the tribunal and the parties as part of an overall procedural system. Arbitral tribunals do not operate under such comprehensive codes, and one can see the wisdom of not importing automatically isolated elements of those codes into arbitral proceedings.

14. Article 27(4) also provides foundation for a tribunal's power to draw adverse evidential inferences, as discussed above. The provision allows the tribunal to assess the 'materiality and weight of the evidence offered'. This means that the tribunal may, and in fact must, assess the totality of the evidential file. In so doing, the tribunal must assess evidence that could or ought to have been offered but was not in fact offered, by either or both parties.

15. It must be noted that article 27(4) does not import licence for disorderly or unfair proceedings. The article 27(4) power is fully controlled by the cardinal duties in article 17(1). The latter provision makes it plain that each party is to have a 'reasonable', not unlimited, opportunity to make out its case. Thus article 27(4) cannot be abused to allow 'unrestricted admission of evidence',

---

16 *See*, e.g., Article 31(1) of the SCC Rules; Article 24(2) of the Swiss Rules; Article 20(6) of the AAA International Arbitration Rules; Article 50(a) of the WIPO Rules.

17 *See* Castello, *supra* fn 9, at 238. The tribunal may choose to exercise its own policy, or to apply, e.g., the formal rules of evidence of a national system familiar to both parties.

18 *See* article 1(3) of the Rules.

19 Caron & Caplan, *supra* fn 14, at 571-572.

for example, where deadlines for submitting documentary evidence have been set and disrespected. In such cases, the evidence should normally be rejected.[20]

B. WITNESSES OF FACT AND EXPERT WITNESSES

16. Witnesses are regulated in article 27(2), a new provision. It covers both witnesses of fact and witnesses of 'expertise', i.e. party-appointed expert witnesses. (Tribunal-appointed experts are covered in article 29.)[21]

17. In most cases there is no difficulty in distinguishing between fact- and expert-evidence: the latter is opinion evidence, typically based on facts which are the responsibility of the parties to gather and provide to the expert. Nevertheless, there are cases where a person purports to offer factual evidence, often their own experience, as representing industry usage or best practice. These cases may present delicate questions as to whether the expert should be treated as a witness of fact, at least in part, with attendant duties on the expert's part to satisfy the tribunal that the factual predicate for their opinion is complete. Such questions are not touched upon by the Rules other than through article 27(4).

18. Article 27(2) has two limbs, and the second one was uncontroversial in the revision process. It is contained in the second sentence of article 27(2), which allows for written witness statements and expert reports 'unless otherwise directed by the arbitral tribunal'. While it is true that the provision grants the tribunal discretion in the management of witness evidence,[22] as noted above, there is a notable shift from the corresponding provision in article 25(5) of the 1976 Rules. The latter provision allowed for written statements as an additional possibility ('[e]vidence of witnesses may also be presented' in writing), the primary mode of presentation being through oral testimony at the hearing; see article 25(2) of the 1976 Rules. By contrast, article 27(2) provides for written statements/reports as the primary form of testimony, which is then to be tested at an evidential hearing (see article 28(2)). Article 27(2) requires the tribunal to issue 'directions' if it is to disallow written statements. This means that exclusively oral testimonial evidence is an exception, which has to be specifically justified through a decision taken by the tribunal under article 17(1). Doubtless the decision will have to explain how a process of exclusive orality would comport with the rule of substantiated pleadings to be found in articles 20(4) and 21(2).

19. The first limb of article 27(2) proved, unexpectedly, somewhat controversial. Although the 1976 Rules did not specify any necessary qualities for a person to serve as a witness, it was well-established in arbitral practice generally that there are no such qualities and that unreliable witness evidence (e.g. of a witness who had a strong financial or other incentive to be less than truthful) would be filtered

---

[20] *Ibid.*, at 572.

[21] *See* UNCITRAL Report of 50th Session, 9 March 2009, UN Doc A/CN.9/669, para. 72.

[22] Caron & Caplan, *supra* fn 14, at 574.

out through the application of article 25(6) (now article 27(4)) of the Rules.[23] That was the solution under a number of arbitration rules.[24] Nevertheless, the absence of a specific provision in the 1976 Rules had given rise to difficulties. In a number of civilian legal systems, there are clear (and important) civil-procedure rules that testimony by officers and employees of a corporate entity amounts to a party's assertions rather than witness testimony. Thus:

> While in the common law system it is not unusual for a party to be called as a witness, the civil law tradition generally is reluctant to accept testimony from a party or a person who, because of his affiliation to a party, is likely to have a financial interest in the matter.[25]

20. The Iran-US Claims Tribunal was a forum in which these legal traditions clashed. The result was a pragmatic compromise: while parties and their representatives were not treated as regular witnesses, in that some rules were not applicable to them, they were, in general, allowed to give 'information' as 'party representatives' (article 4 of the 1976 Rules).[26] The rationale was that, rather than refusing to admit 'evidence of questionable value, the Tribunal [should rely] on its authority under [article 25(6) of the 1976] UNCITRAL Rules to weigh such evidence in light of its origins and circumstances'.[27] Indeed, it should not be thought that as a general rule such persons will always give unreliable evidence. Financial and other ties are not the only duties which people perceive to be bearing on them. And on occasion the evidence of a party, whether a natural-person litigant or an officer/employee of a corporate entity, will be the only source of knowledge available to the tribunal for certain facts.

21. The 2010 revision was thought a good opportunity to codify settled practice and clarify the position.[28] That was ultimately done, through article 27(2), but not without considerable discussion. As against the proposed rule it was said that the enforcement of an award could be jeopardised because parties are prohibited from appearing as witnesses in certain jurisdictions. To this it was rightly riposted that in that case article 1(3) would give primacy to mandatory *lex arbitri* rules.[29]

---

23 Jan Paulsson & Georgios Petrochilos, *Revision of the UNCITRAL Rules* (September 2006), para. 193 and the references, <www.uncitral.org>. *See also* Blackaby, Partasides, Redfern & Hunter, *supra* fn 1, at para. 6.129; Charles N. Brower & Jason D. Brueschke, *The Iran-United States Claims Tribunal*, 186 (Martinus Nijhoff 1998).

24 *See* Article 4.2 of the 1999 IBA Rules (now Article 4.2 of the 2010 IBA Rules), Article 25(2) of the 2004 Swiss Rules (now Article 25(2) of the 2012 Swiss Rules) and Article 20.7 of the 1998 LCIA Rules (now Article 20.6 of the 2014 LCIA Rules).

25 Caron & Caplan, *supra* fn 14, at 562.

26 *Ibid.*, at 563 (the authors explain *inter alia* that the notice requirement of article 25(2) of the Tribunal Rules of Procedure was generally not applied to 'party witnesses').

27 Baker & Davis, *supra* fn 12, at 114-115.

28 Paulsson & Petrochilos, *supra* fn 23, at paras 193-194; UNCITRAL Working Paper for 46th Session, 6 December 2006, UN Doc A/CN.9/WG.II/WP.145/Add.1, paras 23-24.

29 *See* UNCITRAL Report of 50th Session, 9 March 2009, UN Doc A/CN.9/669, para. 77 and UNCITRAL Report of 47th Session, 25 September 2007, UN Doc A/CN.9/641, paras 30 and 35. *See also* Peter Binder, *Analytical Commentary to the UNCITRAL Arbitration Rules*, paras 27-013-27-014 (Sweet & Maxwell 2013).

Consensus was reached on this basis, in the light of the practice under other arbitration rules. The Working Group was satisfied that article 27(2) offers helpful clarity, especially for arbitrations seated in jurisdictions which do not regulate who may testify as a witness.[30]

22. Article 27(2) is drafted in broad terms, allowing 'any individual, notwithstanding that the individual is a party to the arbitration or in any way related to a party' to be presented as a witness, whether called by a party under article 27(1) or as called upon by the tribunal under article 27(3). The reference to an individual who is 'a party to the arbitration' covers both individual claimants/respondents and also officers, employees, or shareholders who are regarded in some legal systems as indistinguishable from a corporate party. But references in previous drafts to the capacity of 'an officer, employee or shareholder of any party'[31] were eliminated, as they could be thought to exclude other potential witnesses such as the parties' associates, partners or external advisors.[32]

23. On its face, article 27(2) allows for 'any individual' to be not only a fact-witness but also a party-appointed expert.[33] Thus presenting as an expert an individual affiliated with a party is possible, and on occasion, within bounds, seen in practice. It is accepted that an expert's primary duty is normally to assist the tribunal, not the party who retained them, by offering their best professional opinion. It is for this reason that Article 5.2(c) of the IBA Rules requires that an expert report produced by a party-appointed expert should include 'a statement of his or her independence from the Parties, their legal advisors and the Arbitral Tribunal'. The IBA's commentary states that this requirement 'is intended to emphasise the duty of each party-appointed expert to evaluate the case in an independent and neutral fashion rather than to exclude experts with some connection to the participants or the subject-matter of the case'.[34] Thus a party may proffer as an expert a highly specialized employee, or former employee, and the tribunal will be able to assess such ties as the expert may have with the party as part of the reliability of their evidence as a whole.

---

30 *See* UNCITRAL Report of 47th Session, 25 September 2007, UN Doc A/CN.9/641, para. 35.

31 *See* UNCITRAL Working Paper for 46th Session, 6 December 2006, UN Doc A/CN.9/WG.II/WP.145/Add.1, paras 23-24.

32 *See* UNCITRAL Report of 47th Session, 25 September 2007, UN Doc A/CN.9/641, para. 32.

33 Cf. Article 4.2 of the 2010 IBA Rules on the Taking of Evidence in International Arbitration (addressing only 'Witnesses of Fact').

34 *See* IBA, *Commentary on the revised text of the 2010 IBA Rules on the Taking of Evidence in International Arbitration*, <www.ibanet.org>, 19.

Article 28
Hearings

1976 Rules Article 25: Evidence and hearings	2010 Rules Article 28: Hearings
1. In the event of an oral hearing, the arbitral tribunal shall give the parties adequate advance notice of the date, time and place thereof.	1. In the event of an oral hearing, the arbitral tribunal shall give the parties adequate advance notice of the date, time and place thereof.
2. If witnesses are to be heard, at least 15 days before the hearing each party shall communicate to the arbitral tribunal and to the other party the names and addresses of the witnesses he intends to present, the subject upon and the languages in which such witnesses will give their testimony.	2. Witnesses, including expert witnesses, may be heard under the conditions and examined in the manner set by the arbitral tribunal.
3. The arbitral tribunal shall make arrangements for the translation of oral statements made at a hearing and for a record of the hearing if either is deemed necessary by the tribunal under the circumstances of the case, or if the parties have agreed thereto and have communicated such agreement to the tribunal at least fifteen days before the hearing.	3. Hearings shall be held in camera unless the parties agree otherwise. The arbitral tribunal may require the retirement of any witness or witnesses, including expert witnesses, during the testimony of such other witnesses, except that a witness, including an expert witness, who is a party to the arbitration shall not, in principle, be asked to retire.
4. Hearings shall be held in camera unless the parties agree otherwise. The arbitral tribunal may require the retirement of any witness or witnesses during the testimony of other witnesses. The arbitral tribunal is free to determine the manner in which witnesses are examined.	4. The arbitral tribunal may direct that witnesses, including expert witnesses, be examined through means of telecommunication that do not require their physical presence at the hearing (such as videoconference).
5. Evidence of witnesses may also be presented in the form of written statements signed by them.	

6. The arbitral tribunal shall determine the admissibility, relevance, materiality and weight of the evidence offered.

1. Article 25 of the 1976 Rules dealt with basic aspects of organising and conducting a hearing and with the management of witness evidence (which was in principle expected to be given orally).[1] It addressed matters such as the notice of a hearing, the notice of witnesses (to be provided to the other party and tribunal) as well as preparatory measures taken by the tribunal in relation to translations and the recording of hearings. Guidance for arbitrators in this area is important: while there is a growing trend towards fuller written submissions and increasingly document-based arbitrations, the majority of cases are still conducted with at least one hearing.[2] However, during the revision process, concerns were expressed that article 25 over-regulated the conduct of the hearings and that arbitration rules were not the appropriate instrument for detailed guidance in this respect.[3]

2. Accordingly, article 25 (now article 28 of the 2010 Rules) has changed in two ways. First, and as discussed in connection with article 27, the provisions relating to evidence have been grouped together under one article in the 2010 Rules (article 27).[4] Second, the remaining provisions of article 25 have been simplified and streamlined for the purpose of 'establishing a general framework',[5] as opposed to detailed rules for the conduct of hearings.

3. Article 28(1), which provides that the tribunal must give the parties 'adequate advance notice of the date, time and place' of the hearing, is unchanged from the corresponding article 25(1) of the 1976 Rules. The reader is referred to commentary on this provision of the 1976 Rules for further discussion.[6]

A. TRIBUNAL'S CONTROL OVER THE HEARING

4. Pursuant to article 25(2) of the 1976 Rules, a party intending to present a witness had to communicate to the other party and to the arbitral tribunal, at least 15 days before the hearing, the contact details of the witness and the subject-matter and language of the testimony. The purpose of this provision was

---

1 Cf. article 17 of the 2010 Rules, which deals with a party's right to a hearing.

2 *See*, e.g., Peter Turner & Reza Mohtashami, *A Guide to the LCIA Arbitration Rules*, para. 5.86 (Oxford University Press 2009); and Nigel Blackaby, Constantine Partasides, Alan Redfern & Martin J. Hunter, *Redfern and Hunter on International Arbitration*, paras 6.155-6.156 (6th ed., Kluwer 2015).

3 *See* UNCITRAL Report of 50th Session, 9 March 2009, UN Doc A/CN.9/669, para. 69.

4 These provisions are articles 25(5) and 25(6) of the 1976 Rules. Note that the wording of article 25(5) has been slightly modified in article 27(2) of the 2010 Rules. The wording of article 25(6) remains unchanged as article 27(4) of the 2010 Rules.

5 UNCITRAL Report of 50th Session, 9 March 2009, UN Doc A/CN.9/669, para. 70.

6 *See*, e.g., David D. Caron & Lee M. Caplan, *The UNCITRAL Arbitration Rules, A Commentary*, 602 et seq. (2nd ed., Oxford University Press 2013); Peter Binder, *Analytical Commentary to the UNCITRAL Arbitration Rules*, Chapter 28 (Sweet & Maxwell 2013).

to ensure the fairness of the proceedings, by giving the opposing party advance notice.[7] Pursuant to article 25(3), it was within the tribunal's responsibility and discretion to arrange for the translation of oral statements made during the hearings and for the recording of the hearings. However, either arrangement became mandatory where the parties had so agreed at least 15 days before a hearing and 'communicated such agreement to the tribunal'.

5. Apart from the issue of who could be regarded as a witness under the Rules (now addressed in article 27(2) of the 2010 Rules), the application of articles 25(2) and 25(3) did not give rise to any particular problems in practice. Nevertheless, a case was made for their revision since they were considered partly redundant[8] and, more importantly, overly-detailed.[9] Concerns were expressed that these provisions 'could overburden the Rules, reduce their flexibility and were not commonly found in modern arbitration rules'.[10] In light of these considerations, the Working Group decided to retain the portions of the original provisions that expressed fundamental principles and delete those that addressed procedural details. Opposition to this approach was based on fears that tribunals may be left without guidance, but supporters of the proposal argued that 'the Rules were not an instrument designed primarily for [an] educational purpose'.[11] Moreover, the Working Group recalled that there was no need to develop the new article on hearings in detail, as the UNCITRAL Notes already provide guidance for tribunals with respect to the conduct of hearings.[12] Article 28(2) of the 2010 Rules was therefore drafted with a view to establishing the broad authority of arbitrators to determine the conditions under which witnesses are to be heard.[13]

6. The authority granted under article 28(2) of the 2010 Rules is in line with the general principle that the arbitral tribunal has the power to control the proceedings, under article 17(1). This power is of course 'subject to the twin duties of treating both parties fairly and equally and of providing each with a full [now

7 Some commentators posit that this advance requirement, which is not expressly reproduced in article 28(2) of the 2010 Rules, did not apply to rebuttal witnesses, as 'the very definition of a rebuttal witness requires that the subject matter of the testimony is not a surprise' (Caron & Caplan, *supra* fn 6, at 612). Cf. Article 25, Note 2 of the Tribunal Rules of Procedure of the Iran-US Claims Tribunal (3 May 1983) (making this exclusion explicit); Article 20.1 of the LCIA Rules (notice requirement specifically including rebuttal witnesses).

8 In particular, references to the language and any translations of the hearings were considered to be already covered by the provision on language in the Rules (i.e. article 17 of the 1976 Rules; article 19 of the 2010 Rules).

9 UNCITRAL Report of 50th Session, 9 March 2009, UN Doc A/CN.9/669, para. 63.

10 *Ibid.*, at para. 69.

11 *Ibid.*, at para. 56. *See also* Binder, *supra* fn 6, para. 28-003.

12 *See* UNCITRAL Report of 50th Session, 9 March 2009, UN Doc A/CN.9/669, paras 55-56; UNCITRAL, *Notes on Organizing Arbitral Proceedings*, paras 74-85 (United Nations 1996) (paras 114-136 of the 2016 Notes).

13 Cf. article 25(4) of the 1976 Rules, which provides in pertinent part that '[t]he arbitral tribunal is free to determine the manner in which witnesses are examined'. For a discussion of this provision *see* David D. Caron, Lee M. Caplan & Matti Pellonpää, *The UNCITRAL Arbitration Rules, A Commentary*, 617-619 (Oxford University Press 2006).

reasonable] opportunity to be heard'.[14] It is in accordance with these 'twin duties', and having regard to the specific circumstances of each case, that the tribunal is to decide matters such as the cut-off date for presenting witnesses and the necessity of translations and/or recordings of the hearings.

7. Article 28(2) also encompasses the tribunal's freedom to determine the manner in which witnesses should be 'examined', a subject previously addressed by article 25(4) of the 1976 Rules. This provision recognizes divergences in the procedures for examining witnesses across different legal cultures.[15] Thus article 28(2) signals to the tribunal that it is responsible for establishing the necessary rules for the case, by way of directions (often in the form of an order). 'Conditions' for examination include issues such as the necessity or not of a written statement, the ability of a witness to address evidence that was adduced after their last written statement, failure to appear at a hearing, the language of oral testimony, translation or interpretation facilities, ability to hear other witnesses' evidence, physical or remote attendance, etc. The 'manner' of examinations refers to who will examine (the tribunal or counsel, or both), in what sequence, whether there will be an examination in chief/direct examination followed by cross-examination (and normally re-examination), whether there will be witness conferencing (typically for experts) or witness confrontation,[16] whether a witness may be recalled after other witnesses have been heard, etc. The Rules accommodate all these possibilities and favour none as a matter of principle.

B. CONDUCT OF THE HEARINGS 'IN CAMERA' AND RETIRING OF WITNESSES

8. Article 25(4) of the 1976 Rules stated that the '[h]earings shall be held in camera unless the parties agree otherwise'. This wording gave effect to the non-public nature of the hearings. This provision was left untouched during the revision process, despite a long debate as to whether to allow third parties to attend the hearings as amici curiae or audience, particularly in the context of investment-treaty arbitration.[17] These issues were ultimately addressed in article 6 of the Transparency Rules.

9. One modification was made to the rule set forth in the second part of article 25(4) of the 1976 Rules, which permitted the tribunal to 'require the retirement of any witness ... during the testimony of other witnesses'.[18] The tribunal's power in this respect was necessarily limited by the provision in the 2010 Rules that a party to

---

[14] Stewart A. Baker & Mark D. Davis, *The UNCITRAL Arbitration Rules in Practice – The Experience of the Iran-United States Claims Tribunal*, 120-121 (Kluwer 1992).

[15] *See* Caron & Caplan, *supra* fn 6, at 606.

[16] Wolfgang Peter, *Witness Conferencing*, 18(1) Arb Int 47 (2002).

[17] *See* proposals of the Center for International Environmental Law (CIEL) and the International Institute for Sustainable Development (IISD), in UNCITRAL Report of 48th Session, 29 February 2008, UN Doc A/CN.9/646, Annex III. *See also* Jan Paulsson & Georgios Petrochilos, *Revision of the UNCITRAL Rules* (September 2006), paras 199-200, < www.uncitral.org >.

[18] *See*, for guidance on this point, UNCITRAL, *Notes on Organizing Arbitral Proceedings*, paras 131-132 (United Nations 2016).

the arbitration (or an officer, employee, etc. of the party) may testify on behalf of that party. The Working Group considered that requiring a party who is also a witness to retire during the testimony of another witness 'would affect [that] party's ability to present its case' because of the need for counsel to be able to take instructions from party representatives in the course of a hearing.[19] In the practice of the Iran-US Claims Tribunal, '[w]itnesses in the strict sense were not allowed to be present except during their testimony, whereas party representatives who may give evidence de facto as witnesses were allowed to stay'.[20] That is the general practice as well, with all party representatives who also testify as witnesses normally being examined before all other witnesses. Accordingly, article 28(3) of the 2010 Rules provides the tribunal with the general power to order the retirement of any witness, subject to the provision that a witness who is also a party to the arbitration 'shall not, in principle, be asked to retire'.

C. PHYSICAL PRESENCE OF WITNESSES NOT REQUIRED

10. Witnesses attending hearings in person often incur significant travel costs, and it can prove difficult to accommodate everyone's schedule.[21] Such considerations persuaded the Working Group to add article 28(4), which specifies that the examination of witnesses may be conducted through 'means of telecommunication that do not require their physical presence at the hearing (such as videoconference)'.[22] Any such arrangements are subject to the approval of the tribunal.[23] Furthermore, article 28(4) is drafted in broad terms in order to avoid becoming obsolete through the advent of new technology that will increasingly facilitate remote attendance. The Committee of the Whole rejected a proposal that examination by means of telecommunication should be confined to limited circumstances, as such a restriction would be inappropriate 'in the light of technological developments in the field of communication'.[24]

---

19 UNCITRAL Report of 47th Session, 25 September 2007, UN Doc A/CN.9/641, para. 41.

20 Caron & Caplan, *supra* fn 6, at 612 fn 72.

21 *See* Blackaby, Partasides, Redfern & Hunter, *supra* fn 2, at paras 6.160-6.161.

22 In general, other major arbitration rules do not make explicit mention of the possibility of videoconferencing. Nevertheless, videoconferencing is far from a rare practice in international arbitration; it is commonly used for, e.g., preliminary meetings. *See ibid.*, at para. 6.41. *See also* Article 25(4) of the Swiss Rules; Article 3(5) of the ICC Rules.

23 UNCITRAL Report of 50th Session, 9 March 2009, UN Doc A/CN.9/669, para. 66: 'It was observed that the right of the parties to present witnesses by means that did not require their presence should be subject to the agreement of the tribunal. To that end, it was proposed to insert the words "unless the arbitral tribunal determines that it is not appropriate to do so" at the end of paragraph (5). Doubts were expressed regarding the need to add the proposed wording, as paragraph (4) already expressed the general principle that the arbitral tribunal was free to determine the manner in which witnesses and experts were to be examined'. *See also* earlier comments made regarding the use of technology during hearings: UNCITRAL Report of 47th Session, 25 September 2007, UN Doc A/CN.9/641, para. 43.

24 Report of the Commission on its 43rd Session, 21 June-9 July 2010, UN Doc A/65/17, paras 130-131. *See also* UNCITRAL Working Paper for 51st Session, 23 July 2009, UN Doc A/

11. Article 28(4) does not regulate the broader topic of virtual hearings conducted through telephonic or video conferencing. Such hearings, normally on procedural or discrete/urgent matters (such as interim measures), are a regular occurrence in practice. The legal foundation for such measures of efficiency is article 17(1) of the Rules.

CN.9/WG.II/WP.154/Add.1, para. 46; UNCITRAL Report of 50th Session, 9 March 2009, UN Doc A/CN.9/669, paras 65-67 and 84.

Article 29
Experts appointed by the arbitral tribunal

1976 Rules Article 27: Experts	2010 Rules Article 29: Experts appointed by the arbitral tribunal
1. The arbitral tribunal may appoint one or more experts to report to it, in writing, on specific issues to be determined by the tribunal. A copy of the expert's terms of reference, established by the arbitral tribunal, shall be communicated to the parties. 2. The parties shall give the expert any relevant information or produce for his inspection any relevant documents or goods that he may require of them. Any dispute between a party and such expert as to the relevance of the required information or production shall be referred to the arbitral tribunal for decision. 3. Upon receipt of the expert's report, the arbitral tribunal shall communicate a copy of the report to the parties who shall be given the opportunity to express, in writing, their opinion on the report. A party shall be entitled to examine any document on which the expert has relied in his report. 4. At the request of either party the expert, after delivery of the report, may be heard at a hearing where the parties shall have the opportunity to be present and to interrogate the expert. At this hearing either party may present expert witnesses in order to testify on the points at issue. The	1. After consultation with the parties, the arbitral tribunal may appoint one or more independent experts to report to it, in writing, on specific issues to be determined by the arbitral tribunal. A copy of the expert's terms of reference, established by the arbitral tribunal, shall be communicated to the parties. 2. The expert shall, in principle before accepting appointment, submit to the arbitral tribunal and to the parties a description of his or her qualifications and a statement of his or her impartiality and independence. Within the time ordered by the arbitral tribunal, the parties shall inform the arbitral tribunal whether they have any objections as to the expert's qualifications, impartiality or independence. The arbitral tribunal shall decide promptly whether to accept any such objections. After an expert's appointment, a party may object to the expert's qualifications, impartiality or independence only if the objection is for reasons of which the party becomes aware after the appointment has been made. The arbitral tribunal shall decide promptly what, if any, action to take. 3. The parties shall give the expert any relevant information or produce for his or her

provisions of article 25 shall be applicable to such proceedings.

inspection any relevant documents or goods that he or she may require of them. Any dispute between a party and such expert as to the relevance of the required information or production shall be referred to the arbitral tribunal for decision.

4. Upon receipt of the expert's report, the arbitral tribunal shall communicate a copy of the report to the parties, which shall be given the opportunity to express, in writing, their opinion on the report. A party shall be entitled to examine any document on which the expert has relied in his or her report.

5. At the request of any party, the expert, after delivery of the report, may be heard at a hearing where the parties shall have the opportunity to be present and to interrogate the expert. At this hearing, any party may present expert witnesses in order to testify on the points at issue. The provisions of article 28 shall be applicable to such proceedings.

---

1. International arbitrations often involve sophisticated technologies, complex chains of events, and formula-laden quantifications demanding a highly-technical analysis. Arbitrators may well require expertise that goes far beyond their own in order to assess the parties' evidence, including the expert evidence led by the parties.[1] The role of experts, however, is viewed differently in various legal cultures. The more adversarial common-law systems typically rely on party-appointed experts, in accordance with the notion that the parties are solely responsible for making and presenting their case successfully, with little intervention from

[1] The Iran-US Claims Tribunal has appointed experts to provide advice on a variety of issues. *See* Nigel Blackaby, Constantine Partasides, Alan Redfern & Martin J. Hunter, *Redfern and Hunter on International Arbitration*, para. 6.135 (6th ed., Kluwer 2015). *See also* David D. Caron & Lee M. Caplan, *The UNCITRAL Arbitration Rules, A Commentary*, 637 fn 3 (2nd ed., Oxford University Press 2013) citing to, inter alia, *Harza v. Iran* (1983) 2 Iran-US CTR 68 (geology and hydraulics); *Chas T Main International Inc v. Khuzestan Water and Power Authority* (1983) 3 Iran-US CTR 156, 164-166 (hydroelectric engineering); *Behring International Inc v. Islamic Republic of Iran* (1983) 4 Iran-US CTR 89, 92 (inventory); *Starrett Housing Corporation v. Government of the Islamic Republic of Iran* (1983) 4 Iran-US CTR 122 (accounting and valuation); *International Technical Products Corp v. Government of the Islamic Republic of Iran* (1985) 9 Iran-US CTR 10, 32-35 (linguistics); *Paul Donin de Rosiere v. Islamic Republic of Iran*. Case No. 498, Chamber One, Order of 6 September 1985, 3 (property evaluation); *Arco Exploration Inc et al. v. National Iranian Oil Company*, Case Nos 20 and 21, Order of 13 June 1990, 4 (petroleum engineering); *Shahin Shaine Ebrahimi v. Government of the Islamic Republic of Iran* (1994) 30 Iran-US CTR 170, 204-205 (accounting and valuation).

the adjudicators. In contrast, civil-law systems are generally more inquisitorial, with adjudicators having the sole power to appoint experts who can testify to the court,[2] consistent with the role of the judge as 'truth seeker'. The drafters of the 1976 Rules attempted to accommodate the expectations of both systems by adopting a 'dual approach'. As Sanders explains:

> In practice, the parties may bring expert witnesses not only to hearings at which an expert appointed by the arbitrators will testify, but they may also bring expert witnesses to a hearing when no such expert witnesses have been appointed previously by the arbitrators. Since both parties may bring expert witnesses and the latter are not uncommonly of a different opinion, it is even quite possible that the arbitral tribunal may appoint an expert of its own only after the parties' expert witnesses have been heard.[3]

The 2010 Rules continue with this approach, providing for both party-appointed experts under articles 27(2) and 28,[4] and tribunal-appointed experts under article 29.

2. Tribunal-appointed experts can provide to the tribunal 'any technical information that might guide it in the search for the truth'.[5] Experts can also assist the arbitral tribunal in assessing the parties' respective cases and claims and in fashioning the relief the tribunal considers appropriate (e.g. constructing a price formula or arriving at a quantum of damages after complex calculations).[6] The tribunal is not, however, obliged to appoint an expert. Indeed, case-law developed under the UNCITRAL Model Law,[7] which also gives the tribunal the option of appointing experts, demonstrates that expert appointments are not mandatory, and therefore that the tribunal's decision not to appoint an expert will not violate the parties' right to be heard, save in exceptional circumstances.[8] Signally, the expert is merely

---

2 *See* Kap-You Kim & John P. Bang, 'Commentary on Using Legal Experts in International Arbitration' in Albert Jan van den Berg (ed), *International Arbitration 2006: Back to Basics?*, 13 ICCA Congress Series 779-785 (2006).

3 Pieter Sanders, *Commentary on UNCITRAL Arbitration Rules*, II YCA 172, 203 (1977). *See also* Charles N. Brower & Jason D. Brueschke, *The Iran-United States Claims Tribunal*, 200 (Martinus Nijhoff 1998). Other sets of institutional arbitration rules similarly provide for both party- and tribunal-appointed experts: *see*, e.g., Articles 25(3) and 25(4) of the ICC Rules; Articles 20.3 and 21.1 of the LCIA Rules; Articles 33 and 34 of the SCC Rules.

4 Under the 1976 Rules, party-appointed witnesses were dealt with under article 15(2), which applies to witnesses generally.

5 *See Starrett Housing Corporation v. Government of the Islamic Republic of Iran* (1987) 16 Iran-US CTR 112, para. 264, citing to *UK v. Albania* (the '*Corfu Channel Case*'), ICJ 4, 20 (1949).

6 Caron & Caplan, *supra* fn 1, at 637.

7 Article 26(1)(a) of the UNCITRAL Model Law provides that '[u]nless otherwise agreed by the parties, the arbitral tribunal may appoint one or more experts to report to it on specific issues to be determined by the arbitral tribunal'.

8 *See* UNCITRAL, *2012 Digest of Case Law on the Model Law on International Commercial Arbitration*, 116-117, (United Nations 2012) citing to CLOUT Case No. 375 [Bayerisches Oberstes Landesgericht, Germany, 4 Z Sch 23/99, 15 December 1999] (where the German Court rejected the respondent's argument that the arbitral tribunal had a duty to call for a neutral expert opinion as it did not possess the required knowledge of Italian patent law,

an advisor, and as such 'cannot usurp the judicial function of the tribunal'.[9] Or, as the Iran-US Claims Tribunal phrased the issue: '[n]o matter how well qualified the expert may be, ... it is fundamental that an arbitral tribunal cannot delegate to him the duty of deciding the case'.[10]

3. We start with an overview of the major amendments brought about by the 2010 Rules with respect to tribunal-appointed experts before turning to two of the most important changes: the requirements of independence and impartiality for tribunal-appointed experts, and the expanded role of the parties in the selection process. Finally, the costs of tribunal-appointed experts are addressed.

A MAJOR AMENDMENTS IN THE 2010 RULES

4. Article 27(1) of the 1976 Rules addressed the appointment of an expert by the arbitral tribunal,[11] as well as the terms of reference that establish the parameters of the expert's mission.[12] Article 27(2) provided that the expert could require the

and that, by not calling an expert, the tribunal had violated the respondent's right to be heard. 'The Court mentioned that, in the absence of any indication to the contrary, it had to be assumed that the arbitral tribunal had complied with its duty to hear all submissions by the parties and that a violation of the right to be heard could only be assumed under special circumstances). *See also National Thermal Power Corporation Ltd v. Wig Brothers Builders and Engineers Ltd* [2009] INDLHC 1466, OMP 16/2003, available at <www.indiankanoon.org> (where the Indian courts underscored the non-mandatory nature of this provision clarifying that it is not an obligation for the arbitral tribunal to call for expert evidence, particularly in cases where the arbitrators themselves are experts in the field). *See also* Georg von Segesser & Petra Rihar, *The Right to a Tribunal Appointed Expert*, <www.kluwerarbitrationblog.com> (discussing a 2011 Swiss Federal Supreme Court case in which one of the parties argued that the arbitral tribunal, by relying solely on the expert report of the other party and by not appointing an expert of its own, violated that party's right to equal treatment and its right to be heard, as well as public policy (Articles 190(2)(d) and (e), Swiss Federal Statute on Private International Law). The Supreme Court dismissed the appeal, finding inter alia that the party had waived its right to object).

9 *See* Caron & Caplan, *supra* fn 1, at 638, citing Gillian M. White, *The Use of Experts by International Tribunals*, 164 (Syracuse University Press 1965). White further states that '[i]t is not for [the expert] to 'identify' which facts are "relevant and significant", nor to examine and weigh them "for the purpose of determining liability and assessing damages". These responsibilities remain those of the tribunal'.

10 *Starrett Housing Corporation v. Government of the Islamic Republic of Iran* (1987) 16 Iran-US CTR 112, para. 197.

11 Note that this provision is entirely distinct from the appointment of experts by the parties. *See* discussion of article 27 of the 2010 Rules, *supra*.

12 *See* UNCITRAL, *supra* fn 8, at 117 ('When appointing a tribunal expert, it is advisable that the role and scope of the expert's duty in arbitral proceedings be clearly defined'). The Digest refers to *Luzon Hydro Corp v. Transfield Philippines Inc* [2004] SGHC 204 (where a party attempted to set aside an arbitral award on the ground that the expert's involvement in the case went beyond what had been agreed upon, namely, that the expert had performed tasks which ought to have been carried out by the arbitral tribunal. The court refused this argument and held that 'unless there was strong and unambiguous evidence of irregularity in the manner in which the arbitration was conducted, the integrity of the tribunal should

production of any relevant information or documents from the parties, and that the tribunal would decide 'disputes' between a party and a tribunal-appointed expert regarding the relevance or production of such information. Article 27(3) provided the parties with an opportunity to express views on the expert's report. Finally, article 27(4) regulated the presence of the expert at a hearing (at the request of either party), and also provided that either party could present its own expert witness at the hearing to testify on the points at issue. The provision further specified that article 25 of the 1976 Rules – which provides the guidelines for hearings – applied to all such proceedings.

5. The absence of an expressly stipulated mechanism to establish the impartiality and independence of tribunal-appointed experts was a cause for concern. The Iran-US Claims Tribunal dealt with this issue by requiring the expert to take an oath before commencing their work, and, in some instances, retaking the oath again before testifying at a hearing.[13] In addition, the Tribunal has also required the experts to submit disclosure statements prior to their appointment, similar to those required of the arbitrators, pursuant to article 9 of the Tribunal Rules.[14] Article 29(2) of the 2010 Rules addresses this lacuna in the 1976 Rules by introducing standards for the assessment of experts' qualifications, impartiality, and independence.

6. Another issue under the 1976 Rules regarding tribunal-appointed experts was that they accorded the parties a fairly minor role in the tribunal's decision-making process with respect to both the need for an expert in the first place and the identity or profile of the expert to be appointed. Commentators acknowledged that party involvement in the process of selecting an expert, and the parties' confidence in that expert's skills and competency, could prevent disputes and thereby enhance the expediency and fairness of the arbitral proceedings.[15] Furthermore, as explained in *The Secretariat's Guide to ICC Arbitration*, 'the costs and potential delays resulting from the appointment of an expert mean that the question of whether to make the appointment can be important to the parties'.[16] Article 27 of the 1976 Rules contemplated little party-participation aside from

---

not be questioned'. The court emphasized that it would not permit parties to 'mount what appeared to be a 'back-door' appeal by attacking the manner in which the tribunal had made use of [the expert] when there was no evidence but only speculation that [the expert] had overstepped his bounds'). *See also* Caron & Caplan, *supra* fn 1, at 640-641.

13 *See* Article 27, Note 2 of the Tribunal Rules of Procedure of the Iran-United States Claims Tribunal (3 May 1983). *See*, e.g., *Starrett Housing Corporation v. The Government of the Islamic Republic of Iran* (1983) 4 Iran-US CTR 122, C(1)(a).

14 *See Shahin Shaine Ebrahimi v. The Government of the Islamic Republic of Iran*, Chamber Three, Order of 20 July 1992, C(1)(a), where the Tribunal determined that experts are subject to the general challenge procedures set forth in articles 10 and 11 of the Tribunal Rules of Procedure – with the important distinction that the Tribunal, not the Appointing Authority, has the power to decide the validity of any challenge.

15 Michael Straus, *The Practice of the Iran-U.S. Claims Tribunal in Receiving Evidence from Parties and from Experts*, 3 JIA 57, 65-67 (1986).

16 Jason Fry, Simon Greenberg & Francesca Mazza, *The Secretariat's Guide to ICC Arbitration*, para. 3-973 (ICC 2012).

the parties' opportunity to express opinions on the report (article 27(3)), and to request that the expert attend a hearing to discuss the report (article 27(4)).[17]

7. The approach taken by the Iran-US Claims Tribunal demonstrates that it was alive to the need for greater party-involvement. The Tribunal's approach to the expert-selection process began by requesting the parties to select an expert on whom they both agreed.[18] In some instances, the Tribunal would first ask the parties to submit a list of three acceptable expert candidates in a sealed envelope, which the Tribunal would keep in confidence. If a match existed between the two lists, that expert would be appointed. If not, the Tribunal would appoint an expert of its own choosing.[19]

8. Under the 2010 Rules, article 29(1) governs the appointment of the expert and the establishment of the terms of reference. The Rules do not say when a tribunal may or should resort to article 29. In practice, the initiative may come either from the tribunal or a party and consistent with the fact that the primary evidential burden is carried by the parties (see article 27(1)-(2)), it is logical that in all but very exceptional cases the appointment of a tribunal-expert should follow the parties' pleadings and any expert-evidence, often after the evidential hearing (as in fact is suggested by the placement of article 29 after article 28 on hearings). Any such appointment may only be made '[a]fter consultation with the parties'. The parties are to be consulted on the need for an expert, the 'specific' expert disciplines (see article 29(1)), and the identity of the expert. The tribunal may adopt any suitable procedure for broaching these issues and eliciting the parties' views. It may for example identify experts for the parties' consideration or (as the Iran-US Claims Tribunal) leave it to the parties at first instance to make joint or separate proposals. The latter approach will in many cases be preferable. Further, article 29(1) also calls for consultation with the parties on the expert's terms of reference. This follows from the first sentence of article 29(1), which speaks of 'specific issues' on which the expert is to report to the tribunal: these issues are the main object of the expert's terms of reference.

9. It is submitted that, given the comprehensive wording of article 29(1), the tribunal cannot resort to outside knowledge or insight without going through an article

---

17 *See* Stewart A. Baker & Mark D. Davis, *The UNCITRAL Arbitration Rules in Practice – The Experience of the Iran-United States Claims Tribunal*, 127-128 (Kluwer 1992). The Iran-US Claims Tribunal attempted to increase party participation by inserting the following provision at Article 27(2) of the Tribunal Rules of Procedure: 'The expert shall invite a representative of each arbitrating party to attend any site inspection, and, when the arbitral tribunal so determines, a representative of each arbitrating party shall be invited to attend other inspections made by the expert'.

18 *See, e.g., Shahin Shaine Ebrahimi v. The Government of the Islamic Republic of Iran* (1994) 30 Iran-US CTR 170, C(1)(a).

19 *See* Richard C. Allison & Howard M. Holtzmann, 'The Tribunal's Use of Experts' in David D. Caron & John R. Crook (eds), *The Iran-United States Claims Tribunal and the Process of International Claims Resolution*, 271 (Transnational Publishers 2000); *see also* Caron & Caplan, *supra* fn 1, at 640; Jacomijn J. van Hof, *Commentary on the UNCITRAL Arbitration Rules, The Application by the Iran-U.S. Claims Tribunal*, 194-195 (Kluwer 1991).

29 process. The ICJ does on occasion do this, for example in order to prepare indicative boundary maps, employing outside specialists as temporary members of the Registry. UNCITRAL tribunals not only lack such an institutional set-up but are also banned from having the benefit of outside assistance, be it minor or merely in matters of technical implementation of their decisions, without submitting it to the parties' scrutiny in adversarial process.

10. An additional issue under the 1976 Rules was the absence of any means by which to control the costs of tribunal experts, which proved problematic in practice. Commentators note that the 'great expense in time and money' of tribunal-appointed experts caused the Iran-US Claims Tribunal to virtually abandon the practice after two years, instead relying on party-appointed experts.[20] Article 40(2)(c) of the 2010 Rules speaks of 'the reasonable costs of expert advice ... required by the tribunal', which is a clear hint to the tribunal that it has a responsibility to control costs. But in practice such difficulties will be pre-empted in great part by the establishment of clear rules in the expert's terms of reference.

11. Only minor modifications were made to the 1976 corresponding text in articles 29(3), 29(4) and 29(5) of the 2010 Rules, which address, respectively, the relevant information that must be provided to an expert, the expert's report, and the hearing of experts. Article 29(5) also replaces the wording of article 27(4) – 'either party' – with 'any party', in order to account for multiparty arbitrations. It also updates the cross-reference, formerly to article 25 of the 1976 Rules, to provide that the provisions of article 28 of the 2010 Rules – establishing the guidelines for hearings – apply to expert hearings.

12. Overall, the 2010 Rules improve on the procedures governing tribunal-appointed experts under the 1976 Rules. The title of the section is in itself an improvement, as it specifies that it is exclusively concerned with experts appointed by the tribunal, thus making it clear that a party has the right to 'present expert evidence on its own initiative irrespective of whether the arbitral tribunal appointed an expert'.[21] More significantly, article 29 of the 2010 Rules provides a mechanism that bolsters the impartiality and independence of the experts appointed by the arbitral tribunal. Also, the increased role of the parties and the cost-control process are valuable additions to the Rules. Further examination of these particular features follows below.

B. IMPARTIALITY AND INDEPENDENCE

13. Under article 29(2), the expert must provide the parties and the tribunal with a description of his or her qualifications, as well as a statement of impartiality and independence. 'In principle', this should occur before the expert accepts his or her appointment. The choice of the words 'in principle' in article 29(2) grants the tribunal the flexibility needed to accommodate situations in which it urgently requires an expert, for example for the assessment of perishable evidence, while

20 *See* Baker & Davis, *supra* fn 17, at 128 and the references.

21 *See* UNCITRAL Report of 47th Session, 25 September 2007, UN Doc A/CN.9/641, para. 61.

also indicating that proceeding without a statement of independence should occur only in exceptional circumstances.[22] Similarly-strict requirements as to the impartiality and independence of tribunal-appointed experts can be found in other sets of arbitration rules.[23]

14. Some commentators have expressed the view that the standard of neutrality expected from tribunal-appointed experts should be stricter than that which is expected of party-appointed experts, as the latter are to some extent expected to assist the parties' position.[24] In any event, the basis upon which a party may object to the tribunal's appointed expert is broader than that for challenging an arbitrator. Objections may not only be made as to a tribunal-appointed expert's alleged lack of independence and impartiality (as applies to arbitrators, pursuant to articles 11 and 12 of the 2010 Rules),[25] but also for insufficient qualifications in terms of expertise and experience.[26]

C. INCREASED ROLE OF THE PARTIES

1. Consultation with the parties

15. The requirement that the tribunal consult the parties before appointing an expert brings the 2010 Rules in line with other arbitration rules and good practice.[27]

---

22 *See* UNCITRAL Report of 52nd Session, 19 February 2010, UN Doc A/CN.9/688, para. 54. The Working Group preferred the wording 'in principle before accepting appointment' to the alternative suggestion of 'or, as soon as practical' before the word 'submit', as this better highlighted the exceptional character of the procedure.

23 *See*, e.g., Article 21.2 of the LCIA Rules; Article 57(a) of the WIPO Rules; Article 25(1) of the AAA International Arbitration Rules.

24 *See* Kim & Bang, *supra* fn 2, at 783. *See also* James W. Barratt, 'Lost in Translation? The Independence of Experts under the 2010 IBA Rules' in *The European & Middle Eastern Arbitration Review 2012*, < www.globalarbitrationreview.com >, Chapter 2.

25 *See* UNCITRAL Working Paper for 52nd Session, 10 December 2009, UN Doc A/CN.9/WG.II/WP.157/Add.1, para. 37 (where the Working Group noted a proposal to amend article 29 to include the provision that '[e]xperts appointed by the arbitral tribunal may be challenged for the same reasons and in the same way as the arbitrators'. The Working Group opted to adopt alternative wording in line with Article 6 of the 1999 IBA Rules on the Taking of Evidence in International Commercial Arbitration).

26 *See* Caron & Caplan, *supra* fn 1, at 643 (noting that challenges based on a perceived lack of qualifications 'do not generally arise in the context of the appointment of arbitrators').

27 *See*, e.g., Article 25(4) of the ICC Rules; Article 57(a) of the WIPO Rules; Article 27(1) of the Swiss Rules; and Article 6.1 of the IBA Rules. The underlying principle of these articles is to ensure 'the substantial involvement of the parties in the process, even though the expert is being appointed by the arbitral tribunal itself': *see Commentary on the revised text of the 2010 IBA Rules on the Taking of Evidence in International Arbitration*, < www.ibanet.org >, 21. *See also* Sophie Nappert, *Commentary on the UNCITRAL Arbitration Rules 2010: A Practitioner's Guide*, 115 (Juris Publishing 2012); *see* also Chartered Institute of Arbitrators, *Practice Guideline 10: Guidelines on the use of Tribunal-Appointed Experts, Legal Advisers and Assessors*, para. 3.3.2 (2011), < www.ciarb.org > (recommending that terms of reference for a tribunal-appointed expert be drawn up in consultation with the parties); Mark Kantor, *Valuation for Arbitration*, 17 Int Arb Law Library 313 (2008) (noting

Nevertheless, in its first review of the Rules, the Working Group demonstrated little interest in including such wording, due to opposing views as to whether or not such an obligation was already implied under the Rules.[28] There was concern that the addition of such an explicit obligation would create confusion regarding whether the parties should also be consulted on other matters, such as the content of the expert's report.[29] Hence, the Working Group at first decided that the original wording of the article (as under article 27(1) of the 1976 Rules) 'should remain unaltered'.[30] The Secretariat rightly insisted on the requirement of prior consultation, however, and this reappeared in the Secretariat's penultimate draft iteration of the Rules.[31] As a result, the *travaux* do not provide insight as to why this wording suddenly appeared in the text of the 2010 Rules, and certain consequences of its inclusion were not debated for instance, the consequences (if any) in case the tribunal does not consult with the parties prior to appointing an expert.[32] The involvement of a tribunal-appointed expert is a matter of substantial importance given the potential for the expert's contribution to affect the outcome of the case. It may not be excluded that a tribunal's unauthorized appointment, unless waived (within the meaning of article 32) may lead to setting aside on grounds that 'the arbitral procedure was not in accordance with the agreement of the parties'.[33]

16. The plain wording of article 29(1) leaves little doubt that tribunals applying the 2010 Rules must consult with the parties.[34] This clarifies an issue that was left open in the 1996 UNCITRAL Notes, which suggested that the tribunal could choose whether to consult the parties or just proceed directly to select an expert.[35]

---

that 'one very important aspect of the process of selecting a tribunal-appointed expert is the involvement of the opposing parties in the selection process'). Cf. Article 24 of the ICDR Inter-American Commercial Arbitration Commission Rules; and Article 44 CIETAC Rules (which do not provide for the parties' input in the expert appointment or consultation process).

28 UNCITRAL Report of 45th Session, 5 October 2006, UN Doc A/CN.9/614, para. 106.

29 *Ibid.*

30 UNCITRAL Report of 45th Session, 5 October 2006, UN Doc A/CN.9/614, para. 107. *See also* Peter Binder, *Analytical Commentary to the UNCITRAL Arbitration Rules*, para. 29-013 (Sweet & Maxwell 2013).

31 *See* UNCITRAL Working Paper for 46th Session, 6 December 2006, UN Doc A/CN.9/WG.II/WP.145/Add.1, para. 27; UNCITRAL Working Paper for 48th Session, 30 November 2007, UN Doc A/CN.9/WG.II/WP.149, paras 32-34; UNCITRAL Working Paper for 49th Session, 6 August 2008, UN Doc A/CN.9/WG.II/WP.151/Add.1, para. 17.

32 *See* Binder, *supra* fn 30, at para. 29-013.

33 Article 34(2)(a)(iv) of the UNCITRAL Model Law.

34 *See* Yves Derains & Eric A. Schwartz, *A Guide to the ICC Rules of Arbitration*, 279 (2nd ed., Kluwer 2005) (where the authors make a similar argument in their discussion of the consultation requirement under Article 20(4) of the 1998 ICC Rules (now Article 25(4) of the 2017 ICC Rules, with minor textual modification).

35 The 1996 UNCITRAL Notes proposed various methods of consultation, e.g., the presentation of a list of candidates, or soliciting proposals from the parties: *see* UNCITRAL, *Notes on Organizing Arbitral Proceedings*, para. 70 (United Nations 1996). Cf. the 2016 UNCITRAL Notes, which provide that '[t]he arbitral tribunal usually gives the parties an opportunity to

Moreover, the practice of ICC tribunals in applying a similar provision[36] offers guidance as to how this wording is expected to be interpreted in future cases. In particular, the 'consultation with the parties' requirement has been interpreted to encompass not only consultation regarding the appointment of an expert, but also the precise nature of the expert's mission (i.e. the terms of reference), as well as the identity of the expert and the fees payable.[37] This, as noted above, is also the natural textual reading of article 29(1).

2. Party objections

17. In its second and third sentences, article 29(2) of the 2010 Rules introduces a right for the parties to object to experts appointed by the arbitral tribunal, a possibility for which no express provision is found in either the 1976 Rules or the Model Law. Once the description of qualifications and the statement of impartiality and independence have been transmitted to the parties and the tribunal, the parties can object to either of these communications, with the objections to be 'promptly' decided by the tribunal. Although no specific time-frame is provided, several commentators reasonably suggest that the 15-day period that applies to arbitrator challenges is a 'useful model for modifying the Rules to address the timing for raising similar objections to a proposed expert'.[38] Objections may also be made after the expert's appointment, on a more limited basis, in accordance with the last sentence of article 29(2).[39] Once the expert is appointed by the tribunal, parties may only object for reasons of which they become aware after the appointment has been made, such as a conflict of interest or a 'serious question concerning an expert's credentials that has come to light only after his or her appointment'.[40] This is consistent with Article 6.2 of the IBA Rules.[41]

18. In fact, the *travaux* indicate that the Working Group modelled article 29(2) of the 2010 Rules closely on Article 6 of the 1999 IBA Rules on the Taking of Evidence in International Commercial Arbitration (as the IBA Rules were then known).[42] Nevertheless, article 29 differs from its IBA counterpart in a number of ways. First, article 29(2) sets forth both impartiality and independence as grounds for objecting against tribunal-appointed experts, whereas the IBA Rules only

comment on the expert's proposed mandate, qualification, impartiality and independence': *see* UNCITRAL, *Notes on Organizing Arbitral Proceedings*, para. 102 (United Nations 2016).

36 *See* Article 25(4) of the ICC Rules.

37 *See* Derains & Schwartz, *supra* fn 34, at 279 and the references.

38 *See* Caron & Caplan, *supra* fn 1, at 642 and the references; *see also* Thomas H. Webster, *Handbook of UNCITRAL Arbitration*, para. 29-17 (2nd ed., Sweet & Maxwell 2015).

39 Caron & Caplan, *supra* fn 1, at 642.

40 *Ibid.*

41 Article 6.2 of the IBA Rules on the Taking of Evidence in International Arbitration provides, in pertinent part, that '[a]fter the appointment of a Tribunal-Appointed Expert, a Party may object to the expert's qualifications or independence only if the objection is for reasons of which the Party becomes aware after the appointment has been made'.

42 *See* UNCITRAL Report of 52nd Session, 19 February 2010, UN Doc A/CN.9/688, paras 50-53.

refer to independence. Second, when stating the grounds for objecting to the tribunal-appointed expert, article 29(2) does not indicate from whom the expert should be independent, unlike article 6.2 of the IBA Rules, which specifies that an expert must be independent from 'the Parties, their legal advisers and the Arbitral Tribunal'.[43] The omission was intentional: by leaving the scope of the independence requirement undefined, the Working Group sought to ensure a 'broaden[ed] application of the provision' as compared with the IBA Rules.[44] The third difference, as discussed above,[45] is the Working Group's addition of the words 'in principle' as a qualifier to the requirement that an expert shall provide a description of qualifications and statement to the tribunal and parties 'before accepting appointment'. The IBA Rules do not afford such flexibility.[46]

D. COSTS OF TRIBUNAL EXPERTS

19. Tribunal-appointed experts naturally entail increased costs, especially where (as will normally be the case) party-appointed experts are already involved.[47] Article 40(2)(c) of the 2010 Rules states that the costs of arbitration fixed by the arbitral tribunal should include 'the *reasonable* costs of expert advice and of other assistance required by the arbitral tribunal' (emphasis added).[48] This represents an improvement on article 38(c) of the 1976 Rules, which does not contain a reasonableness requirement.[49] As already noted above, the main safeguard for runaway costs is the process of establishing terms of reference in consultation with the parties (who have every interest to keep costs within reasonable bounds).

---

43 *See* Article 6.2 of the 2010 IBA Rules. Note that Article 6.2 of the 1999 IBA Rules required only that arbitrators be independent from 'the Parties and the Arbitral Tribunal'.

44 UNCITRAL Report of 52nd Session, 19 February 2010, UN Doc A/CN.9/688, para. 53. *See also* Nappert, *supra* fn 27, at 117.

45 *See* para. 13, *supra*.

46 *See* Nappert, *supra* fn 27, at 117.

47 Jeffrey Waincymer, *Procedure and Evidence in International Arbitration*, 937 (Kluwer 2012). *See also* Mark Kantor, *supra* fn 27, at 304 (2008) (noting that '[t]he costs of a tribunal-appointed expert may be considerable').

48 *See also* discussion of article 42 of the 2010 Rules, *infra*.

49 Article 38(c) of the 1976 Rules states that '[t[he arbitral tribunal shall fix the costs of arbitration in its award. The term "costs" includes only ... (c) The costs of expert advice and of other assistance required by the arbitral tribunal'.

Article 30
Default

1976 Rules Article 28: Default	2010 Rules Article 30: Default
1. If, within the period of time fixed by the arbitral tribunal, the claimant has failed to communicate his claim without showing sufficient cause for such failure, the arbitral tribunal shall issue an order for the termination of the arbitral proceedings. If, within the period of time fixed by the arbitral tribunal, the respondent has failed to communicate his statement of defence without showing sufficient cause for such failure, the arbitral tribunal shall order that the proceedings continue. 2. If one of the parties, duly notified under these Rules, fails to appear at a hearing, without showing sufficient cause for such failure, the arbitral tribunal may proceed with the arbitration. 3. If one of the parties, duly invited to produce documentary evidence, fails to do so within the established period of time, without showing sufficient cause for such failure, the arbitral tribunal may make the award on the evidence before it.	1. If, within the period of time fixed by these Rules or the arbitral tribunal, without showing sufficient cause: (a) The claimant has failed to communicate its statement of claim, the arbitral tribunal shall issue an order for the termination of the arbitral proceedings, unless there are remaining matters that may need to be decided and the arbitral tribunal considers it appropriate to do so; (b) The respondent has failed to communicate its response to the notice of arbitration or its statement of defence, the arbitral tribunal shall order that the proceedings continue, without treating such failure in itself as an admission of the claimant's allegations; the provisions of this subparagraph also apply to a claimant's failure to submit a defence to a counterclaim or to a claim for the purpose of a set-off. 2. If a party, duly notified under these Rules, fails to appear at a hearing, without showing sufficient cause for such failure, the arbitral tribunal may proceed with the arbitration. 3. If a party, duly invited by the arbitral tribunal to produce documents, exhibits

or other evidence, fails to do so within the established period of time, without showing sufficient cause for such failure, the arbitral tribunal may make the award on the evidence before it.

1. Failure by one of the parties to participate in the arbitration is always problematic, and arbitration rules necessarily focus on the necessary procedures and tribunal powers to ensure the legal validity of the process notwithstanding any non-participation, including outright default.[1] A balance must be struck between efficiency and fairness: arbitration rules must recognize the tribunal's duty to ensure equal treatment and a fair opportunity to be heard, but they should also ensure that a party cannot culpably fail to participate in the proceedings and subsequently be able to claim that it was unable to present its case.[2] Article 30 of the 2010 Rules sets out the extent of the tribunal's powers in this regard.

A. OVERVIEW

2. The provisions in article 30 address three hypotheses of non-participation: failure to submit a pleading (article 30(1)), failure to appear at a hearing (article 30(2)) and failure to produce evidence (article 30(3)). If such a failure (i) occurs after the expiry of the time-limit fixed by the Rules[3] or by the arbitral tribunal, and (ii) the defaulting party cannot demonstrate 'sufficient cause', its failure amounts to a default, empowering the tribunal to continue or to terminate the proceedings, depending on whether the defaulting party is the claimant or the respondent.

3. When deciding whether to exercise this power, the tribunal should consider any mandatory requirements of the *lex arbitri* and may also consider the law of the place of probable enforcement of the award. The New York Convention requires that the defaulting party must have been given notice of a hearing, and the absence of sufficient notice could constitute a ground to oppose enforcement.[4] Model Law countries, as well as France, the United States and England, normally

1 *See* article 17 of the 2010 Rules ('The arbitral tribunal ... shall conduct the proceedings so as to avoid unnecessary delay and expense and to provide a fair and efficient process for resolving the parties' dispute').

2 *See* David D. Caron & Lee M. Caplan, *The UNCITRAL Arbitration Rules, A Commentary*, 47 (2nd ed., Oxford University Press 2013) (noting that 'the Rules seek to strike a careful balance between efficiency of the proceedings and fairness to the parties'); Peter Binder, *Analytical Commentary to the UNCITRAL Arbitration Rules*, para. 30-004 (Sweet & Maxwell 2013).

3 The 1976 Rules referred only to 'the period of time fixed by the arbitral tribunal' and did not refer to any time-limit set by the Rules.

4 *See* Nigel Blackaby, Constantine Partasides, Alan Redfern & Martin J. Hunter, *Redfern and Hunter on International Arbitration*, para. 6.192 (6th ed., Kluwer 2015). *See also* Articles 34(2)(a)(ii) and 36(1)(a)(ii) of the UNCITRAL Model Law; Article V(1)(b) of the New York Convention.

permit a tribunal to continue the proceedings in the event of default as long as the defaulting party has been properly notified.[5]

4. The notion of 'sufficient cause' and the requirement that the parties be duly notified of their procedural duties ensure that the tribunal does not abuse its authority when exercising its powers pursuant to article 30.[6] In the light of these requirements, it is clear that a merely temporary or one-off failure to comply with a submission deadline may not necessarily fall to be characterized as a default which attracts serious consequences.

5. Article 30 of the 2010 Rules is substantially the same as article 28 of the 1976 Rules, save for certain additions and clarifications emphasized below. Sections B, C and D below address the consequences of default, whereas section E addresses the notion of sufficient cause.

6. Only the statements of claim and defence, i.e. the comprehensive pleadings envisaged in articles 20 and 21, are specifically addressed by the Rules in connection with default. And only the former is regarded as a necessary pleading absent which the proceedings will in principle be terminated. The Rules thus regard a comprehensive, evidence-backed memorialization of the claimant's case as indispensable; cf. article 20(2)-(4). By parity of reasoning, the same must apply to counterclaims or claims in set-off that fall to be developed in the respondent's statement of defence. By contrast, the absence of defensive pleadings, as well as any further pleadings due under the procedural schedule (see articles 17(2) and 24), does not affect the tribunal's duty to continue with the arbitration and conclude it by issuing an award.

B. FAILURE TO SUBMIT A PLEADING: ARTICLE 30(1)

1. Claimant's default: article 30(1)(a)

7. Article 30(1)(a) concerns a claimant's failure to submit its statement of claim.[7] Such a failure may be the result of the claimant's failure to indicate that its notice of arbitration should be treated as a statement of claim, pursuant to article 20(1). Under the 2010 Rules, the tribunal is empowered to terminate the arbitral proceedings in these circumstances, unless a two-fold requirement is met. First, the tribunal must consider whether there are 'remaining matters' for

---

5 Thomas H. Webster, *Handbook of UNCITRAL Arbitration*, para. 30-6 (2nd ed., Sweet & Maxwell 2015), citing to *Dovert et Tabourdeau v. Confex*, CA Paris, 7 February 1991, 4 Rev Arb 625, 625-684 (1992) (where the Paris Court of Appeal held that an award rendered by default is not contrary to public international order if the respondent was properly informed of the proceedings and it was not 'materially impossible for the party to be represented'). Note that section 41 of the Arbitration Act 1996 (England & Wales) also requires that 'due notice' be given.

6 The importance of notice is reflected in the three paragraphs of article 30, which refer to deadlines for submissions, notice of hearings and filing deadlines for evidentiary documents; *see* Caron & Caplan, *supra* fn 2, at 674.

7 *See* article 3 of the 2010 Rules.

it to decide – in this context, notably costs. Second, the tribunal may consider it 'appropriate' to decide these matters notwithstanding the claimant's default.[8] This marks an important departure from the 1976 Rules, pursuant to which the tribunal had no discretion and was obliged to terminate the proceedings where the claimant failed to submit its statement of claim.[9] The tribunal may therefore choose to continue the proceedings where, notably, the respondent has formulated a counterclaim or set-off claim, or raised an objection to the jurisdiction of the tribunal.[10] The common elements in these examples is that the respondent has raised an affirmative claim or defence, which may be determined in its own terms, and in the determination of which the respondent will normally have the legitimate interest of obtaining a decision with res judicata effect. There is therefore a combination of factors to consider, both of a procedural nature and of a broader nature such as the respondent's legitimate interest.

8. The Working Group recognized that, in some cases, it may be in the parties' interests for the proceedings to continue.[11] In any event, however, a termination order does not prevent the claimant from commencing fresh proceedings, because, by this stage, 'the tribunal has not assessed the merits of the case'.[12] A termination order is intended to have no res judicata effect, hence it is styled as an exclusively procedural closure. As the Working Group acknowledged, this potentially exposes the respondent to 'harassing claims' by the claimant, and leaves any counterclaims or jurisdictional issues unanswered.[13] Under the 1976 Rules, the tribunal nevertheless had to terminate the proceedings in such cases.

9. The Working Group considered a proposed version of article 30 that confined the tribunal's power to proceed in the absence of a statement of claim to cases in which the respondent had submitted a counterclaim.[14] However, the consensus was that such a formulation was 'too limited'.[15] One concern was that it could lead

---

8 Article 30(1)(a) of the 2010 Rules. *See also* Clyde E. Croft, Christopher Kee & Jeffrey Waincymer, *A Guide to the UNCITRAL Arbitration Rules*, 342 (Cambridge University Press 2013).

9 Article 28(1) of the 1976 Rules provided that 'the arbitral tribunal *shall* issue an order for the termination of the arbitral proceedings' (emphasis added).

10 Caron & Caplan, *supra* fn 2, at 676.

11 UNCITRAL Report of 51st Session, 10 November 2009, UN Doc A/CN.9/684, paras 22-26.

12 Caron & Caplan, *supra* fn 2, at 675.

13 UNCITRAL Report of 51st Session, 10 November 2009, UN Doc A/CN.9/684, paras 22-24. A termination order pursuant to article 36 of the 2010 Rules is not an award, and, as such, there is no 'role' for res judicata effect. *See* Webster, *supra* fn 5, at para. 30-17. *See also* James E. Castello, 'UNCITRAL Arbitration Rules, Section III, Article 30' in Loukas A. Mistelis (ed), *Concise International Arbitration*, 243 (2nd ed., Kluwer 2015) ('A termination order pursuant to art. 30(1)(a) will not prevent re-filing of the claim at a later date').

14 Under the proposed provision, the tribunal would have been obliged to terminate the proceedings 'unless the responded has submitted a counterclaim': *see* Jan Paulsson & Georgios Petrochilos, *Revision of the UNCITRAL Rules* (September 2006), para. 221, <www.uncitral.org>; UNCITRAL Working Paper for 46th Session, 6 December 2006, UN Doc A/CN.9/WG.II/WP.145/Add.1, article 28.

15 UNCITRAL Report of 51st Session, 10 November 2009, UN Doc A/CN.9/684, para. 22. *See also* Binder, *supra* fn 2, at para. 30-012.

to the proceedings continuing every time a counterclaim was submitted; which was thought by some to be too mechanical to capture the 'appropriateness' test. That observation was not valid: under article 30(1)(b), a counterclaim which has not been answered compels the continuation of the proceedings. Another fear was that the interests of the respondent or other parties may require the tribunal to make a decision 'carrying value as *res judicata*', and that the proposed formulation unduly restricted the tribunal's options in this regard.[16] In light of these concerns, the Working Group preferred wording that granted the tribunal discretion in the exercise of its power to terminate or continue the proceedings.[17]

10. Note that in multiparty proceedings with three or more camps, the reasonableness of continuing may be self-evident. If Respondent A has claims against Respondent B, it may be that these claims are all that needs to be decided – and these can indeed be decided without any concern arising from the claimant's default. That hypothesis resembles an ordinary two-party arbitration and requires no further comment.

11. If the tribunal determines that there are no 'remaining matters', it will issue an order for the termination of the proceedings, pursuant to article 36 of the 2010 Rules. The tribunal may, however, also attach an award for costs to the termination order pursuant to article 42(2), and the defaulting claimant could well be allocated the full costs of the arbitration.[18] Alternatively, the issue of costs could be considered a 'remaining matter' pursuant to article 36(2) of the 2010 Rules, requiring a separate costs award. Either course of action is appropriate so long as all parties be given a reasonable opportunity to be heard on costs.

2. Respondent's default: article 30(1)(b)

12. Article 30(1)(b) concerns a respondent's failure to communicate its response to the notice of arbitration or its statement of defence. There are several reasons for which a respondent may neglect to file a response: for example, it may be confident that the tribunal lacks jurisdiction over the dispute such that the effort of participating in the proceedings is not worth the cost; it may lack the necessary financial resources; or it may believe that any award rendered would be unenforceable against it.[19] As clarified in the 2010 Rules, the provisions of article 30(1)(b) also apply to a claimant's failure to submit a defence to a counterclaim or set-off claim (through the claimant's statement of claim or in a subsequent 'reply to the counterclaim' (cf. article 23(2))).

---

16 UNCITRAL Report of 51st Session, 10 November 2009, UN Doc A/CN.9/684, para. 22.

17 *Ibid.*, at para. 26.

18 Binder, *supra* fn 2, at para. 30-015.

19 The respondent may also fail to communicate its response because it believes itself not to be bound by the arbitration clause, or it may fail to file its statement of defence on the basis that it is bound by an anti-arbitration injunction. *See* Webster, *supra* fn 5, at para. 30-25.

13. An arbitral tribunal faced with a respondent default under article 30(1)(b) of the 2010 Rules is required to order that the proceedings continue. This was also the case under article 28(1) of the 1976 Rules, emphatically giving effect to the principle that respondent default has no impact on the proceedings. However, a key addition to the 2010 Rules, and one which replicates the wording found in Article 25(b) of the Model Law, is that failure to produce a response or statement of defence is not treated 'in itself as an admission of the claimant's allegations'.[20] As such, arbitral tribunals acting under the Rules are unable to render the equivalent of a national court's 'default judgment'.[21] The claimant or counterclaimant must make out both the jurisdictional and substantive merits of its case, without benefiting from a lighter burden of proof.[22] The tribunal should, 'without substituting itself for the defaulting party, satisfy itself that the claimant's claims are well-founded in law and fact', and produce a reasoned award.[23] Moreover, while a respondent's failure to submit its statement of defence may not prevent the respondent from responding to the claimant's allegations at a later stage of the proceedings, it normally bars it from raising counterclaims and jurisdiction/admissibility objections; see articles 23(2), 21(2) and 22.[24]

14. Although the tribunal will inevitably be forced to take a 'necessarily more active'[25] role in testing the claims of the remaining party, the tribunal 'has no duty to act as advocate for a party who has elected not to appear'.[26] How much inquisitorial testing of the case by the tribunal is within these bounds is obviously a matter of philosophical preference. Nevertheless, it is absolutely incumbent on the tribunal to give a reasonable opportunity to the remaining party to address any grounds that have not been addressed by that party but may, in the tribunal's estimation, lead to a dismissal of its case. There is a limit as to the defences or

20 Article 25(b) of the UNCITRAL Model Law provides that: 'Unless otherwise agreed by the parties, if, without showing sufficient cause, ... (b) the respondent fails to communicate his statement of defence in accordance with article 23(1), the arbitral tribunal shall continue the proceedings without treating such failure in itself as an admission of the claimant's allegations'. *See also* Paulsson & Petrochilos, *supra* fn 14, at para. 219 (noting the need to clarify 'that where the respondent has failed to communicate his Statement of Defence, such failure cannot and should not be treated by the tribunal as an admission of the claimant's allegation').

21 *See* Webster, *supra* fn 5, at para. 30-29; Caron & Caplan, *supra* fn 2, at 673.

22 Gary B. Born, *International Commercial Arbitration*, 2297 (2nd ed., Kluwer 2014) ('[A]n arbitral tribunal is not a court, empowered to issue a default judgment predicated simply on one party's non-participation. Rather, the tribunal is responsible for evaluating the evidence and arguments presented to it and making a reasoned decision; one party's non-participation does not abrogate that obligation').

23 *Ibid.*, at 2298.

24 Caron & Caplan, *supra* fn 2, at 676, 684-685 citing to *Amoco Intl Finance Corp v. National Iranian Oil Co*, Case No. 56, Chamber Three, Order of 22 February 1984 (where the Iran-US Claims Tribunal, when granting an Iranian respondent an extension to submit its statement of defence and counterclaim, stated that the Iranian respondent would be barred from filing any further counterclaim if the Tribunal's deadline was not respected).

25 Webster, *supra* fn 5, at para. 30-34.

26 Blackaby, Partasides, Redfern & Hunter, *supra* fn 4, at para. 6.197.

objections the continuing party may proactively raise. And more importantly, default cannot be allowed to procure a procedural advantage to the defaulting party. Also, the fact remains that the respondent has forfeited the opportunity to formulate its position in the context of what is intended to be an adversarial process. The tribunal can draw inferences from the respondent's silence in the manner it sees fit:[27] as reflected in the *travaux préparatoires* relating to Article 25(b) of the Model Law, the tribunal is free 'to draw those conclusions from the silence of the respondent that appear most probable'.[28]

15. A concern was raised during the adoption of the Rules by the Commission as to a potential inconsistency between article 30(1)(b) and article 32. Whereas article 30(1)(b) provides that a default does not amount to an admission of the claimant's allegations, article 32 provides that a party who does not 'object promptly' to non-compliance with the Rules or with the arbitration agreement is deemed to waive the right to make such an objection at a later time (unless it can prove that such failure was justified).[29] In response to this concern, 'it was explained that those two provisions dealt with different matters: draft article 30, paragraph 1 (b), addressed matters pertaining to the substance of the case, whereas draft article 32 related to matters of a procedural nature'.[30]

C. FAILURE TO APPEAR: ARTICLE 30(2)

16. Article 30(2) of the 2010 Rules deals with the failure of a party to appear at a hearing. This includes evidential hearings as well as hearings for argument.[31] In this case, provided the absent party has been 'duly notified' under the Rules, the tribunal is empowered to proceed with the arbitration.[32] This is consistent with the practice of the Iran-US Claims Tribunal, which proceeded with hearings notwithstanding the absence of respondents.[33]

---

27 *See*, e.g., Binder, *supra* fn 2, at para. 30-021.

28 Howard M. Holtzmann & Joseph E. Neuhaus, *A Guide to the UNCITRAL Model Law on International Commercial Arbitration, Legislative History and Commentary*, 700 (Kluwer 1989). *See also* Paulsson & Petrochilos, *supra* fn 14, at para. 220 and the reference.

29 *See* article 32 of the 2010 Rules.

30 Report of the Commission on its 43rd Session, 21 June-9 July 2010, UN Doc A/65/17, para. 133.

31 Webster, *supra* fn 5, at para. 30-33.

32 Article 30(2) of the 2010 Rules should be read in conjunction with article 28(1), which provides that the parties must be given 'adequate advance notice of the date, time and place' of a hearing. Article 2 also provides certain requirements for notices under the Rules.

33 *See*, e.g., *Figgie International Inc (Geo. J. Meyer Manufacturing Division) v. Zam Zam Bottling Company*, Case No. 299, Chamber One, Order of 22 March 1984 (where the Iranian respondent failed to appear at the hearing, providing various explanations for its absence before subsequently requesting a new hearing. The tribunal denied the request and proceeded with the arbitration pursuant to Article 28(2) of the Tribunal Rules of Procedure of the Iran-United States Claims Tribunal (3 May 1983). The respondent was, however, permitted to submit a memorial into the record after the default. *See* Caron & Caplan, *supra* fn 2 at 677.

17. In the unlikely case that both parties fail to appear at the hearing, the tribunal may order a second hearing or terminate the proceedings on grounds that continuation is unnecessary or impossible.[34]

D. FAILURE TO PRODUCE DOCUMENTS, EXHIBITS OR OTHER EVIDENCE: ARTICLE 30(3)

18. Article 30(3) of the 2010 Rules provides that where the tribunal requests a document, exhibit or other evidence and the requested party fails to produce it within the period of time provided by the tribunal, the tribunal may 'make the award on the evidence before it'. The term 'documentary evidence' in article 28(3) of the 1976 Rules was replaced with 'documents, exhibits or other evidence' in order to ensure consistency with article 27(3) of the 2010 Rules (pertaining to the tribunal's powers to order the production of evidence).[35] Article 30(3) seeks to ensure that non-production of evidence does not hold up the proceedings or prevent the tribunal from rendering its award.

19. Beyond the principle that the tribunal may decide on the basis of the evidence before it, article 30(3) does not provide for any other consequence of a party's failure to produce documents or evidence.[36] One could interpret article 30(3) as empowering the tribunal to refuse new evidence on the matters covered by the tribunal's direction to produce being submitted by the defaulting party after the production deadline. Such an argument would effectively read 'must' for 'may' in the wording of article 30(3) that 'the arbitral tribunal may make the award on the evidence before it'. It would thus treat article 30(3) as equivalent to article 31(1), which addresses the closure of the evidential file as part of the closing proceedings. Also, the suggestion appears inconsistent with the practice of the Iran-US Claims Tribunal, which, on several occasions, allowed the respondent to submit evidence after it had initially failed to do so, in accordance with Article 28(3) of the Tribunal Rules of Procedure. In light of this practice, one author concludes that a 'more reasonable approach' for a tribunal when determining the admissibility of new evidence is to 'weigh the utility of sanctions against the value of late-filed evidence to the resolution of the dispute'.[37] It is submitted that timing and potential prejudice to the other sidewill be highly relevant in such assessments.

20. Article 30(3) also does not expressly state whether the tribunal may draw adverse inferences from the defaulting party's failure to produce evidence. This lacuna was specifically discussed by the Working Group, which ultimately rejected a

---

34 Castello, *supra* fn 13, at 244, citing Report of 8th Session, 1-17 April 1975, UN Doc A/10017, VI UNCITRAL Ybk 9, 40, paras 171-172.

35 Caron & Caplan, *supra* fn 2, at 679.

36 Depending on the *lex arbitri*, it may be possible to obtain an order forcing the production of documents: *see*, e.g., section 42 of the Arbitration Act 1996 (England & Wales) (providing that 'the court may make an order requiring a party to comply with a peremptory order made by the tribunal'). *See also* Webster, *supra* fn 5, at para. 30-38.

37 Caron & Caplan, *supra* fn 2, at 678.

proposal that a provision providing for the tribunal's power to draw adverse inferences be added to article 30(3). The reasons given for this rejection were that such an addition could overcomplicate the Rules; that article 27 sufficiently addressed the question of the assessment of the 'weight of evidence'; and that the 1976 formulation had not caused difficulties in practice.[38] Some authors have observed that the *force probante* of the evidence as addressed in article 27(4) is an issue distinct from that of adverse inferences.[39] But there can be little doubt that tribunals may draw adverse inferences from a party's failure to produce evidence that in the ordinary course exists and is in its possession or control,[40] a fortiori when directed to do so and fails 'without satisfactory explanation'.[41] Article 27(4) gives the broadest power to assess 'the evidence offered', which must logically encompass conclusions about what evidence one would expect to see in the record but are absent.

E. SUFFICIENT CAUSE

21. The consequences of default provided in the three limbs of article 30 are triggered only if the defaulting party cannot demonstrate 'sufficient cause' for its failure. The existence of 'sufficient cause' is a decision for the tribunal to make judicially, on any evidence available, principally of course from the defaulting party.[42] The *travaux préparatoires* for the 1976 Rules provide no guidance as to the definition of 'sufficient cause'.[43] However, the meaning of this term was addressed – under article 28 of the 1976 Rules – in the context of the *Himpurna* arbitration.[44]

22. In *Himpurna*, a tribunal had found in a first arbitration that Indonesia's state-run electricity corporation had breached an energy sales contract it had concluded

---

38 *See* UNCITRAL Report of 51st Session, 10 November 2009, UN Doc A/CN.9/684, para. 32. *See also* Croft, Kee & Waincymer, *supra* fn 8, at 345.

39 *See* Croft, Kee & Waincymer, *supra* fn 8, at 346 (noting that '[t]he reports of the Working Group indicate that it did not take a view on this matter either way').

40 Born, *supra* fn 22, at 2311, 2313 ('Tribunals are permitted to rely on presumptions or inferences regarding evidence. Examples include negative inferences drawn from a party's failure to produce obviously material documents or witnesses in its control, a party's failure to comply with disclosure orders ... [M]ost arbitrators will conclude that "[w]hen a party ... has access to relevant evidence, the Tribunal is authorized to draw adverse inferences from the failure of that party to produce such evidence"').

41 *See* Article 9.5 of the 2010 IBA Rules on the Taking of Evidence in International Arbitration. The parties may expressly adopt these rules to govern evidentiary matters in the arbitration. Even where this is not the case, tribunals frequently turn to the IBA Rules for guidance as to best practices in international arbitration: *see* Caron & Caplan, *supra* fn 2, at 556-557.

42 Castello, *supra* fn 13, at 243.

43 As noted in Binder, *supra* fn 2, at paras 30-007-30-008 ('Only the Secretariat's Special Consultant on the 1976 Rules commented that, when determining whether there is sufficient cause for a failure, the arbitral tribunal should give the defaulting party an opportunity for justification by asking for what reason the latter's communication was not received'). *See also* Pieter Sanders, *Commentary on UNCITRAL Arbitration Rules*, II YCA 172, 206 (1977).

44 *See Himpurna California Energy Ltd (Bermuda) v. The Republic of Indonesia* (UNCITRAL) Final Award, 16 October 1999, XXV YCA 186 (2000).

with Himpurna, a US company. The tribunal rendered a damages award in Himpurna's favour. The electricity corporation refused to pay, so Himpurna undertook a second arbitration against the Republic of Indonesia. Indonesia failed to submit its case-in-chief after a state-run oil company under its control (Pertamina) sought and obtained an anti-arbitration injunction. Indonesia justified its failure to submit the pleading on the basis that the injunction by the Indonesian courts had suspended the arbitral proceedings.

23. A decisive element for the tribunal was that Indonesia could have prevented the circumstances on which it relied in seeking to justify its default under the force majeure doctrine, holding that Pertamina was not independent from the Indonesian state.[45] The existence of the injunction therefore did not constitute 'sufficient cause', and the tribunal proceeded with the arbitration in default proceedings.

24. Other tribunals have also had to grapple with parties refusing to participate in the proceedings in the context of anti-arbitration injunctions.[46] Ultimately, the tribunal must decide whether it should continue with the proceedings in the circumstances of the case, ensuring in particular that the defaulting party is not merely attempting to escape the arbitration agreement. The notion of 'sufficient cause' must be given a meaning appropriate to the purpose of article 30. The cause must not only be founded in fact and legitimate per se but also proportionate to the failure. The tribunal is also to form a view as to whether the cause is such as to justify the sanctions in article 30. If the conclusion is that the cause is merely temporary (e.g. approval for a filing by a court-appointed administrator) and can be cured, the cause may be sufficient. If the defaulting party does not even purport to give a cause, that may be a very strong indication of the absence of a sufficient cause.

---

45 *Ibid.*, at paras 107-114. *See also* Blackaby, Partasides, Redfern & Hunter, *supra* fn 4, at para. 7.54 ('[T]he arbitral tribunal found that the Indonesian injunction did not constitute "sufficient cause", because (a) it was sought and obtained by a state agency that was under the *de jure* control of the Government of Indonesia, and (b) the Government of Indonesia had *de facto* made no attempt to rein in those actions that were inconsistent with its obligations under the parties' arbitration agreement').

46 *See*, e.g., Webster, *supra* fn 5, at para. 30-14, citing to *Telenor Mobile Communications v. Storm LLC* (UNCITRAL) Final Award, 2 July 2007.

Article 31
Closure of hearings

1976 Rules Article 29: Closure of hearings	2010 Rules Article 31: Closure of hearings
1. The arbitral tribunal may inquire of the parties if they have any further proof to offer or witnesses to be heard or submissions to make and, if there are none, it may declare the hearings closed.	1. The arbitral tribunal may inquire of the parties if they have any further proof to offer or witnesses to be heard or submissions to make and, if there are none, it may declare the hearings closed.
2. The arbitral tribunal may, if it considers it necessary owing to exceptional circumstances, decide, on its own motion or upon application of a party, to reopen the hearings at any time before the award is made.	2. The arbitral tribunal may, if it considers it necessary owing to exceptional circumstances, decide, on its own initiative or upon application of a party, to reopen the hearings at any time before the award is made.

1. Article 31 of the 2010 Rules empowers the tribunal to declare the 'hearings' closed, or, in exceptional circumstances and before the award is made, reopen them. It is clear from the substantive content of this provision (which is verbatim the 1976 text) that the intention is to capture the closure of the proceedings more generally.[1] It is simply the case that the 1976 Rules conceived the hearing (or hearings, especially in case there was a special expert hearing after the appointment of a tribunal expert) as the final procedural act that closed the file before the tribunal deliberations commenced. This provision therefore ensures that the proceedings are not delayed by 'repeated requests for hearings and the taking of further evidence',[2] and allows the tribunal to set limits on the rights

[1] Accord: Thomas H. Webster, *Handbook of UNCITRAL Arbitration*, paras 31-1, 31-7 (2nd ed., Sweet & Maxwell 2015).

[2] Report of the Commission on its 9th Session, 12 April-7 May 1976, UN Doc A/31/17, 77 para. 149. *See also* Pieter Sanders, *Commentary on UNCITRAL Arbitration Rules*, II YCA

which the Rules confer upon the parties.[3] Despite recommendations that the provision be modified or even deleted as self-evident,[4] article 31 of the 2010 Rules is exactly the same as its predecessor, article 29 of the 1976 Rules, except for a minor change in terminology in article 31(2), which is of no real significance.[5]

A. 'HEARINGS'

2. One proposal for modification of article 31 was to replace the word 'hearings' with 'proceedings' in order to address this ambiguity.[6] An argument in favour of this amendment was that the broader term 'proceedings' would be more consistent with the French version of the provision, which provided for 'closure of the arguments',[7] as well as with the terminology of other sets of arbitration rules.[8] However, the Working Group rejected the proposal due to a concern that it would lead to inconsistencies with other provisions. Notably, article 43(2) of the 2010 Rules refers to the tribunal's power to request supplementary deposits from the parties 'during the course of the arbitral proceedings', which must be read as continuing to apply after the 'closure' of the hearing phase.[9] Thus the Working Group agreed that the provision as drafted was generally acceptable.[10] The Working Group reiterated that the term 'hearings' in article 31 was not limited to oral hearings, but also encompassed the presentation of written evidence.[11]

172, 206 (1977) (the 'rather broad wording' of article 29(1) of the 1976 Rules 'should not be interpreted as giving a party the opportunity to drag out the proceedings indefinitely').

3 *See*, e.g., article 17(3) (right to request oral hearings); article 22 (right to amend or supplement claims or defences).

4 The drafters of the Model Law opted for deletion.

5 The 2010 drafters changed the wording 'on its own motion' in article 29(2) of the 1976 Rules to 'on its own initiative' in article 31(2) of the 2010 Rules.

6 *See* Jan Paulsson & Georgios Petrochilos, *Revision of the UNCITRAL Rules* (September 2006), para. 228, <www.uncitral.org> (recommending the use of the term 'proceedings' instead of 'hearings', in line with Rule 38 of the ICSID Arbitration Rules).

7 UNCITRAL Report of 51st Session, 10 November 2009, UN Doc A/CN.9/684, para. 37.

8 *See*, e.g., Article 27 of the ICC Rules (referring to the closure of 'the proceedings'); Article 29 of the Swiss Rules ('When it is satisfied that the parties have had a reasonable opportunity to present their respective cases on matters to be decided in an award, the arbitral tribunal may declare *the proceedings* closed with regard to such matters' (emphasis added)). *See also* Article 40 of the SCC Rules (similarly providing for closure of 'the proceedings', as distinguished from 'the hearings', expressly referred to in Article 32).

9 UNCITRAL Report of 51st Session, 10 November 2009, UN Doc A/CN.9/684, para. 38. *See also* James E. Castello, 'UNCITRAL Arbitration Rules, Section III, Article 31' in Loukas A. Mistelis (ed), *Concise International Arbitration*, 244-245 (2nd ed., Kluwer 2015); *see also* David D. Caron, Lee M. Caplan, *The UNCITRAL Arbitration Rules, A Commentary*, 625 (2nd ed., Oxford University Press 2013) ('[T]he change in terms might raise doubts as to whether deposits could be requested after the hearing phase had passed').

10 UNCITRAL Report of 51st Session, 10 November 2009, UN Doc A/CN.9/684, para. 40.

11 *Ibid.*, at para. 39.

B. CLOSURE OF THE HEARINGS

3. The arbitral tribunal must establish a procedural timetable in accordance with article 17(2), and is to declare the hearings closed after an oral hearing or after the submission of post-hearing briefs.[12] Article 31(1) cannot be viewed in isolation from the procedural timetable. The tribunal *may* inquire of the parties whether they 'have' further evidence or submissions, either in oral or in written form. If the parties have made their submissions as provided for in the procedural timetable, the tribunal would normally conclude that it is not necessary to undertake this inquiry.[13] It may wish to do so to have a record that it gave the parties a full opportunity to be heard (cf. article 17(1) which requires a reasonable opportunity) and head off any challenges to its award.[14]

4. If the tribunal does make an inquiry before closing the proceedings and the parties wish to submit further evidence, the tribunal will have to determine whether there is a 'legitimate need to further develop a material aspect' of that party's case.[15] The tribunal has broad discretion in this regard; any request to submit further evidence is governed by article 27(4), pursuant to which the tribunal determines the admissibility and potential materiality of evidence offered.[16] The mere assertion by a party that it has further evidence will not prevent closure of the hearings.[17] It is clear from the discretionary 'may' that the whole process is an exceptional one.

5. Although the tribunal may proceed to deliberation without formal closure of the hearings, it is at the very least good practice to declare the hearings or 'evidentiary record' closed.[18] Such a declaration is in fact mandatory under some

---

12 Webster, *supra* fn 1, at para. 31-3.

13 *Ibid.*, at para. 31-5 (noting that, '[a]s a general matter, it would be unusual in international arbitration for a Tribunal to ask the parties if they wish to be heard or to make further submissions after the submissions have been made in accordance with the procedural timetable').

14 Indeed, the practice of the Iran-US Claims Tribunal demonstrates that tribunals typically adhered to the scheduled closing time for hearings, with any requests to the parties regarding additional statements largely ceremonial: see Stewart A. Baker & Mark D. Davis, *The UNCITRAL Arbitration Rules in Practice – The Experience of the Iran-United States Claims Tribunal*, 131 (Kluwer 1992).

15 Castello, *supra* fn 9, at 245. *See also* Report of the Commission on its 9th Session, 12 April-7 May 1976, UN Doc A/31/17, 77 para. 149.

16 Webster, *supra* fn 1, at para. 31-8.

17 The 2010 drafters considered deleting the wording 'if there are none' from article 31(1) in order to eliminate any doubt as to whether a party may prevent closure of the hearings by expressing an intention to submit further evidence. However, the Working Group decided that this revision was unnecessary, because article 27(4) already resolved any ambiguity: *see* UNCITRAL Report of 51st Session, 10 November 2009, UN Doc A/CN.9/684, para. 34.

18 Nigel Blackaby, Constantine Partasides, Alan Redfern & Martin J. Hunter, *Redfern and Hunter on International Arbitration*, para. 6.200 (6th ed., Kluwer 2015). For the proposition that the tribunal *should* formally close the proceedings, *see* Caron & Caplan, *supra* fn 9, at 626.

institutional arbitration rules.[19] Formal closure of the proceedings may also be particularly useful where the parties are prone to make frivolous requests, or where the proceedings have been split into various phases. In such cases, the tribunal may – and, according to some authors, should – close the hearings with respect to each particular phase of the arbitral proceedings.[20]

6. Finally, it is also possible for the tribunal to declare the proceedings closed subject to certain exceptions; for example, proceedings are often closed subject to further submissions on costs.[21]

C. DISCRETION TO REOPEN

7. The second paragraph of article 31 was adopted with a view to ensuring enforcement of the award. The drafters of the 1976 Rules raised the concern that enforcement under the New York Convention may be jeopardised if the fair resolution of a dispute required an additional hearing due to exceptional circumstances, but the arbitration rules did not provide for this possibility.[22]

8. Article 31(2) of the 2010 Rules therefore empowers the tribunal, on its own motion or upon application of a party, to reopen the hearings in 'exceptional circumstances'.[23] The application will have to spell out the exceptional circumstances alleged, i.e. why there is at this late stage a need for a fresh/additional hearing and why the applicant party was unable to identify and address that need pursuant to the procedural timetable. The narrow scope of this provision is further limited by its potential temporal scope: by definition, the tribunal's power

---

19 *See*, e.g., Article 27(a) of the ICC Rules; Article 40 of the SCC Rules; Article 32.1 of the SIAC Rules. *See also* Paulsson & Petrochilos, *supra* fn 6, at para. 228 (the authors recommended amending article 31 of the 2010 Rules to make the closure of the hearings mandatory, in line with Rule 28 of the ICSID Arbitration Rules. In particular, it was suggested that the following wording be inserted at the end of article 31(1): 'when the parties have completed the presentation of the case, or of a phase of the case, the Tribunal shall declare the proceedings closed with respect to the whole case or its relevant phrase').

20 *See* Webster, *supra* fn 1, at para. 31-4; Paulsson & Petrochilos, *supra* fn 6, at para. 228 (recommending closure 'when the parties have completed the presentation of the case, *or of a phase of the case*' (emphasis added)).

21 *See* Webster, *supra* fn 1, at para. 31-6.

22 In such a case, a national court may consider that a party unable to reopen the hearings in the light of fresh evidence was not given an opportunity to present its case for the purposes of Article V of the New York Convention: *see* Report of the Commission on its 9th Session, 12 April-7 May 1976, UN Doc A/31/17, para. 149.

23 Note that a party may not attempt to reopen the hearings on the basis of article 17(3) of the 2010 Rules, which provides a right to request a hearing at 'an appropriate stage of the proceedings', as this would undermine the 'exceptional circumstances' limitation provided in article 31. *See also* Caron & Caplan, *supra* fn 9, at 628 (noting that the same position was also taken under the 1976 Rules); and *Dadras International v. Iran* (1995) 31 Iran-US CTR 127, 145 paras 56-57 (where the Tribunal found that article 15(2) of the Tribunal Rules of Procedure of the Iran-United States Claims Tribunal (the equivalent of article 17(3) of the 1976 Rules) 'is primarily applicable to the situation where there has not yet been a hearing' and 'does not oblige the Tribunal to accede to any request by a party for a hearing').

to 'reopen' the hearings only exists after the closure of the hearings, with article 31(2) further providing that any such reopening must occur 'before the award is made'. Thus article 31(2) plainly excludes the possibility of invoking the process of reopening hearings as a means to have the tribunal reconsider an award.[24]

'Exceptional circumstances'

9. The Rules are silent as to the circumstances that qualify as 'exceptional' for the purposes of article 31(2). The case-law of the Iran-US Claims Tribunal emphasizes that such circumstances must be 'extraordinary' – particularly if deliberations have begun[25] – and the Tribunal has rarely granted requests to reopen hearings, 'never formally or explicitly invok[ing] Article 29' (of the 1976 Rules).[26] The requirement of 'exceptional circumstances' is justifiable given that reopening the hearings will almost certainly delay the proceedings and lead to additional costs for the parties. Given the adversarial nature of the arbitral proceedings, a tribunal may be reluctant to reopen the case on its own initiative unless it regards the issue as one of central importance.[27]

10. The tribunal may consider there to be 'exceptional circumstances' where:

(i) it is considering applying a principle of law that has not been argued by the parties;[28]
(ii) it becomes clear during deliberations that an important point of law has not been sufficiently developed by the parties;[29] or
(iii) new evidence, potentially of central importance, is discovered.[30]

---

24 If article 31(2) could be used in that way, it would usurp the rule of finality of awards (article 34(2)) and the exclusivity of post-award remedies (articles 37-39). The position is that if a hearing is required on any post-award remedy, that is a separate hearing and not a reopened hearing of the prior phase. Cf. *Perenco Ecuador Ltd v. The Republic of Ecuador and Empresa Estatal Petróleos del Ecuador (Petroecuador)* (ICSID Case No. ARB/08/6) Decision on Remaining Issues of Jurisdiction and on Liability, 12 September 2014, <www.italaw.com>; *ConocoPhillips Petrozuata B.V., ConocoPhillips Hamaca B.V. and ConocoPhillips Gulf of Paria B.V. v. Bolivarian Republic of Venezuela* (ICSID Case No. ARB/07/30) ('ConocoPhillips') Decision on Jurisdiction and Merits, 3 September 2013, <www.italaw.com>.

25 Castello, *supra* fn 9, at 245.

26 Baker & Davis, *supra* fn 18, at 131.

27 Webster, *supra* fn 1, at para. 31-11.

28 *Ibid.*, at para. 31-12 (citing to *X KFT v. Y AG*, 4A_108/2009 (9 June 2009), <www.swissarbitrationdecisions.com> (where the claimant appealed an arbitral award to the Swiss Federal Supreme Court on the basis that the tribunal's reasoning had come as a surprise and was 'based on legal arguments which the parties could not reasonably expect'. The Court rejected the appeal, stating that 'it is only when the arbitral tribunal *intends to rely on some legal grounds which none of the parties argued* and that they could not have reasonably expected that a violation of the right to be heard may take place' (emphasis added)).

29 Caron & Caplan, *supra* fn 9, at 626; *See also* Sanders, *supra* fn 2, at 206-207.

30 Caron & Caplan, *supra* fn 9, at 626.

11. One notable example is the *Dadras International* arbitration.[31] The central issue in that case was whether a contract had been validly concluded between the claimants' and respondents' representatives. The respondents had claimed early on in the proceeding that the signature on the contract was a forgery, but had been unable to obtain an affidavit from the signatory of the contract. Almost a year and a half after the hearing and in the course of the tribunal's deliberations, the respondents produced an affidavit by their representative, Mr Golzar, attesting that the signature on the contract was not his. The respondent's request to reopen the hearings to address this point was accepted, and the new evidence and post-hearing pleadings on the forgery issue were admitted. The tribunal considered that the circumstances were exceptional because Mr Golzar's evidence was at the heart of the dispute, and the veracity of the affidavit, if proved, might result in the dismissal of the claim.[32]

12. Thus it is unlikely that evidence that was or could have been discovered before the closure of the hearings would constitute 'exceptional circumstances' justifying the reopening of the hearings.[33] Moreover, if the tribunal finds, after reopening the hearings, that the new evidence is without merit, it should doubtless take this into account when deciding on costs under article 42(1).[34]

---

31 *Dadras International v. Iran* (1995) 31 Iran-US CTR 127; *Dadras International v. Iran* (1994) 30 Iran-US CTR 112. *See also* Webster, *supra* fn 1, at para. 31-16 (citing an unreported AAA arbitration decision in which 'know how and patent rights' of the claimant were at issue. The European Patent Office rendered a decision holding the patent invalid during the tribunal's deliberations, which led to the tribunal's reopening of the hearings to allow submissions on this point).

32 Caron & Caplan, *supra* fn 9, at 626. *See* also *Dadras International v. Iran* (1994) 30 Iran-US CTR 112, 118, para. 27 ('the disposition of the dispute was highly dependant on the credibility of these two "key players", which emphasised the importance of reopening the hearing').

33 Webster, *supra* fn 8, at para. 31-15.

34 *See* Blackaby, Partasides, Redfern & Hunter, *supra* fn 18, at para. 6.203.

Article 32
Waiver of right to object

1976 Rules Article 30: Waiver of rules	2010 Rules Article 32: Waiver of right to object
A party who knows that any provision of, or requirement under, these Rules has not been complied with and yet proceeds with the arbitration without promptly stating his objection to such non-compliance, shall be deemed to have waived his right to object.	A failure by any party to object promptly to any non-compliance with these Rules or with any requirement of the arbitration agreement shall be deemed to be a waiver of the right of such party to make such an objection, unless such party can show that, under the circumstances, its failure to object was justified.

1. Legal instruments which recognize the autonomy of the parties to enter into arbitration agreements also recognize 'the parties' capacity to waive or abandon' their right to object to non-compliance with certain procedural protections.[1] The predicate is that it is incumbent upon the parties to take the steps necessary to ensure procedural compliance, on pain of waiver. That may be called a duty of procedural loyalty and co-operation, aimed at preserving the procedural rectitude of arbitral proceedings and at limiting challenges before national courts.

2. That is the function of article 30 of the 1976 Rules, a provision that has been recast in article 32 of the 2010 Rules, in part to ensure alignment with Article 4 of the Model Law.[2] As the formulation of article 32 makes plain, the object of a waiver under that provision is not the Rules themselves but rather a party's right to insist upon compliance with the Rules by raising the appropriate objection

[1] *See* Gary B. Born, *International Commercial Arbitration*, 2186 (2nd ed., Kluwer 2014) (referring to the New York Convention and to national arbitration legislation).

[2] *See* UNCITRAL Report of 47th Session, 25 September 2007, UN Doc A/CN.9/641, paras 66-67. *See also* Peter Binder, *Analytical Commentary to the UNCITRAL Arbitration Rules*, paras 32-005-32-009 (Sweet & Maxwell 2013).

'promptly'.[3] The waiver rule is formulated as a deeming rule, in that a failure to formulate an objection 'shall be deemed to be a waiver'. This means that such a failure legally amounts to a waiver. As we will see, however, not all instances of non-compliance are capable of being waived; which ones are and which ones not is ultimately a matter for the *lex arbitri* or the New York Convention,[4] and article 32 does not take a position on this.

3. The rule practically operates in respect of instances of non-compliance that can be rectified by the arbitral tribunal (e.g. by ordering a fresh round of pleadings, or admitting new evidential materials, or revising the procedural schedule) or sanctioned by a national court through challenges to awards, challenges to arbitrators, opposition to recognition or enforcement of awards, or a claim against the arbitrators (within the confines of article 16). It is academic to discuss, for example, whether article 32 covers a pre-announced decision by the arbitrators, not opposed by the parties, to ignore the body of 'rules of law' chosen by the parties under article 35(1) – save if the controlling forum regards this as a ground for setting aside. Similarly, a decision by the arbitrators to act as *amiable compositeurs* without the 'express authorization' by the parties required by article 35(2) will be relevant in article 32 terms only if the resulting award can be challenged as an excess of jurisdiction in the controlling forum.

A. SCOPE OF APPLICATION AND OPERATION OF THE WAIVER RULE

4. Article 32 purports to cover 'any non-compliance with these Rules or with any requirement of the arbitration agreement'. These terms are capacious (as are those of corresponding provisions in other arbitration rules),[5] and they mirror the formulation of the grounds for setting aside/non-recognition found in Article 34(2)(b)(iv) of the Model Law and Article V(1)(d) of the New York Convention respectively.

5. The 2010 formulation is substantially equivalent to that of 1976 ('any provision of, or requirement under, these Rules') in that both texts cover:

(i) requirements directly under the Rules (e.g. the necessary content of statements of claim and defence under articles 20 and 21, or the rules regarding the constitution of the tribunal in articles 7-14);
(ii) requirements imposed by direction of the tribunal pursuant to powers granted to them by the Rules (e.g. a document-production order under article 27(3), or time-limits in a procedural timetable fixed under article 17(2));[6]

---

[3] *See* UNCITRAL Report of 47th Session, 25 September 2007, UN Doc A/CN.9/641, para. 66.

[4] Thomas H. Webster, *Handbook of UNCITRAL Arbitration*, para. 32-9 (2nd ed., Sweet & Maxwell 2015); David D. Caron & Lee M. Caplan, *The UNCITRAL Arbitration Rules, A Commentary*, 692 (2nd ed., Oxford University Press 2013); Binder, *supra* fn 2, at paras 32-010-32-011.

[5] *See*, e.g., Article 40 of the ICC Rules; Article 36 of the SCC Rules; Article 30 of the Swiss Rules; Article 60 of the WIPO Rules.

[6] The authors had recommended that such directions be expressly covered; *see* Jan Paulsson & Georgios Petrochilos, *Revision of the UNCITRAL Rules* (September 2006), para. 230,

(iii) 'any requirement of the arbitration agreement',[7] including an agreement made by the parties to 'modify', i.e. to derogate from or to supplement, the Rules (see article 1(3)),[8] whether this be contained in the arbitration agreement itself or in a subsequent special agreement.[9]

6. An example of the range of issues that the waiver rule is intended to cover is provided by the *Bombardier v. Siemens* case in the French courts. There, the tribunal had relied in its award on documents that were lodged only in German without translation. Bombardier had failed properly to object to this in the course of the arbitration, and on this basis unsuccessful in trying to have the award annulled in the courts.[10]

7. Note that the waiver rule is stated to operate objectively, that is, it is not stated to require invocation by a party: '[a] failure ... to object promptly ... shall be deemed to be a waiver'. Nevertheless, it is believed that there can only be very exceptional cases where a tribunal or court would take it upon themselves to apply the waiver rule without having been prompted by a party to do so. Another way to put this would be to say that a party's choice not to raise article 32 is to be taken as an indication that it considers its opponent's failure to object to have been justified – a concession that a tribunal or court should in principle accept. A further way to put it is that the right of invoking article 32 is capable of being waived.

B. WAIVABLE RIGHTS AND WAIVABLE INSTANCES OF NON-COMPLIANCE

8. The Rules textually cover 'any' instance of 'non-compliance', whatever its gravity or nature. The *travaux* indicate that both in 1976 and in 2010 the drafters envisaged run-of-the-mill or 'minor' procedural mishaps.[11] It must be right to say that whether article 32 may or may not apply will 'depend upon the importance of the procedural right at stake'.[12] Nevertheless, one should not be too astute in characterizing a party's right as fundamental in order to exclude the application of the waiver rule. Equal treatment and a reasonable opportunity to be heard are doubtless fundamental rights under article 17(1) of the Rules. If a party was content to see its opponent file a submission several weeks after the deadline

<www.uncitral.org>. This recommendation was not adopted, but the final text seems to us to create no real difficulty; but *see* Binder, *supra* fn 2, at para. 32-013.

7 Cf. Article 4 of the UNCITRAL Model Law.

8 *See* UNCITRAL Report of 47th Session, 25 September 2007, UN Doc A/CN.9/641, para. 67.

9 Although it is said that there is some doubt in that regard (Binder, *supra* fn 2, at paras 32-013-32-014), the authors believe that there is no real room for debate on this score. *See also* in respect of Article 4 of the Model Law UNCITRAL Report of 7th Session, Note by the Secretariat, 6-17 February 1984, UN Doc A/CN.9/WG.II/WP.50, XV UNCITRAL Ybk 218, 231-232 para. 12 (1984).

10 *See* fn 21, *infra*.

11 Report of the Commission on its 9th Session, 12 April-7 May 1976, UN Doc A/31/17, 77 para. 146. *See also* UNCITRAL Report of 51st Session, 10 November 2009, UN Doc A/CN.9/684, para. 46 (referring to 'situations of mischief and procedural manoeuvres').

12 Caron & Caplan, *supra* fn 4, at 692.

without claiming any corresponding extension for itself, there can be no doubt that the party has waived any right to complain thereafter. The general point is that a number of procedural rights have to take shape in the specific circumstances of the proceedings, and the parties are best-placed to take these decisions.

9. At any rate, a waiver will be effective only insofar as the controlling or recognition forum considers that the relevant right is capable of being waived. It is clear that violations which result in awards that would not pass muster under the tests of public policy or arbitrability cannot be waived: under Article 34(2)(b) of the Model Law and Article V(2) of the New York Convention parties do not have free disposition of these matters and therefore cannot waive the relevant rights. Parties may not by way of waiver settle on an arrangement that they could not effect by way of express agreement. Thus, as Born notes, '[a]greements involving outright corruption and grossly abusive procedural arrangements should in principle not be valid, even where a party fails to object to them at the time'.[13]

10. Jurisdiction and admissibility merit special mention. Although it is true that the waiver rule applies 'principally to procedural aspects of the arbitration rather than substantive rights',[14] there is little doubt in case-law[15] and scholarship[16] that a party may waive its right to object to the tribunal's jurisdiction or the admissibility[17] of a claim. The foundation for this is that matters of jurisdiction and admissibility are for the parties to raise, and indeed to do so in their first substantive defensive pleading at the latest; see article 23(2) of the Rules. Indeed, there cannot even be a question of 'non-compliance' with the Rules if a party fails to raise such an objection, for the tribunal will not have failed in its duty to make a jurisdictional determination. Also, matters of jurisdiction and admissibility may be regarded either as issues of 'compliance with the Rules', i.e. the jurisdictional requirement in article 1(1), or as 'requirement[s] of the arbitration agreement' within the meaning of article 32. In the submission of the authors, under article 23(2) any such requirements are for the parties to raise before the tribunal rather than operating on their own. That is consistent with

[13] Born, *supra* fn 1, at 2187.

[14] Jason Fry, Simon Greenberg & Francesca Mazza, *The Secretariat's Guide to ICC Arbitration*, para. 3-1522 (ICC 2012) (discussing the application of Article 39 of the 2012 ICC Rules (now Article 40 of the 2017 ICC Rules, without modification)).

[15] *See*, e.g., *CME Czech Republic BV v. The Czech Republic* (UNCITRAL) Partial Award, 13 September 2001, <www.italaw.com>, 99-100 ('The Respondent, in respect to this investment of the Claimant in the Czech Republic, expressly did not raise the defence of lack of jurisdiction ... Any possible defence in respect to lack of jurisdiction ... therefore, must be deemed as waived. That also would be consistent with Rule 21.3 of the [1976] UNCITRAL Rules, according to which objections in respect to jurisdiction must have been made in the Statement of Defence ... According to the [1976] UNCITRAL Rules, a defence of jurisdiction is deemed to be waived, if not raised in time. This concept derives from the assumption that defences on jurisdiction can be waived by the Parties').

[16] *See* Nigel Blackaby, Constantine Partasides, Alan Redfern & Martin J. Hunter, *Redfern and Hunter on International Arbitration*, para. 10.30 (6th ed., Kluwer 2015).

[17] E.g., insisting on the observance of a waiting period, or a prior attempt at a negotiated settlement, or the exhaustion of remedies in local courts, etc.

the position under a number of national laws.[18] There are only limited exceptions where it is incumbent on the tribunal to examine questions of jurisdiction or admissibility of its own motion, as discussed in the context of article 23 in this work. In respect of such exceptions, article 32 does not operate at all, as they concern essentially matters of public policy which cannot be waived.

C. PROMPT OBJECTION

11. A right may be waived only if a party was in a position to 'object' to the relevant non-compliance. If so, a party must have objected 'promptly'. The rule therefore operates at a time when a party is in a position to react (normally up to the closure of the hearings pursuant to article 31),[19] hence the 1976 text provided expressly that the waiving party must have 'proceed[ed] with the arbitration', for example by appearing at a hearing or filing submissions.[20] This requirement has been deleted from the 2010 Rules, as it goes without saying.

12. The notion of *objection* that is used in article 32 is substantive in nature: no particular form or separate pleading seems to be required (except as required under article 23(2)). Nevertheless, the opposition must be clearly signalled and amount to something more than a mere complaint or criticism. The tribunal must be clearly made aware that a party regards the situation as non-compliant and seeks measures to redress the non-compliance. Thus the Paris Court of Appeal rejected an annulment suit based on untranslated documents that were relied upon by the tribunal, on grounds that a party's mere 'criticisms' or 'allegations' in order to 'keep its options open' were insufficient to constitute an objection.[21] The objection must therefore also be directed to a specific issue or issues. An objection to the general conduct of the proceedings, or a statement to the effect that provisions of the Rules or the arbitration agreement have been violated, is unlikely to meet the test under article 32.[22] One might go so far as to say that a generalized complaint will be a good indication that no proper objection could have been formulated.

---

18 *See* Arbitration Act 1996 (England & Wales), sections 31 (Objection to substantive jurisdiction of tribunal) and 73 (Loss of right to object); Blackaby, Partasides, Redfern & Hunter, *supra* fn 16, at para. 10.30 ('English law requires an objection to jurisdiction to be raised at the earliest possible opportunity and provides that if this is not done, the right to object is lost. Accordingly, the award would be a valid award under the law of England (as the law of the seat of arbitration) and, in principle, enforceable under the New York Convention'). *See also* Article 1466 of the French Code of Civil Procedure ('A party which, knowingly and without a legitimate reason, fails to object to an irregularity before the arbitral tribunal in a timely manner shall be deemed to have waived its right to avail itself of such irregularity'). *See also* Webster, *supra* fn 4, at paras 32-32–32-46.

19 Webster, *supra* fn 4, at para. 32-15.

20 Caron & Caplan, *supra* fn 4, at 695.

21 Webster, *supra* fn 4, at para. 32-33, citing to *La société Bombardier Transportation Switzerland v. La société Siemens AG*, CA Paris, 23 June 2005, RG 2004/04732, Juris-Data: 2005-287132.

22 Webster, *supra* fn 4, at paras 32-12–32-13.

13. By contrast, in another French case an objection was held to have been properly formulated. The tribunal had admitted counterclaims by the respondent through a procedural order, to which the claimant had formulated an objection at the hearing. The objection was that the counterclaims were tardy and the claimant would have no opportunity to respond to them at all in written pleadings. The tribunal dismissed the objection and, ruling on the counterclaims, awarded sums to the respondent. The French court held that the claimant had properly registered an objection and had not waived its right to challenge the award.[23]

14. The requirement of promptness in article 32, as in other instances where the term is used (articles 19(1), 26(7), and 29(2)), generally means something more than 'without undue delay' (as in Article 4 of the Model Law)[24] or 'without delay' (as in articles 11 and 34(2)) but something less than 'as promptly as possible' (as in article 8(2)). 'With all expedition reasonably to be expected in the circumstances' is a good long-form paraphrase. This calls for an assessment case-by-case, in all the circumstances.[25] For example, parties may require several days to consult with counsel to object to a procedural order or other decision, whereas an objection that a witness is being asked to disclose privileged information should in principle be raised immediately or in any event before the end of the hearing.[26]

15. The requirement of promptness also means that it is incumbent upon the parties to object spontaneously, rather than waiting for a scheduled procedural opportunity. However, it is good practice for tribunals to take the opportunity at the 'closure of the hearings' under article 31 to ask the parties if they have objections to the proceedings until that time. (The possibility provided for in article 32(2) is much for the same purpose.) The value of confirmations that no objections lie is shown by the practice of the Iran-US Claims Tribunal, which dealt with this issue on at least two occasions, denying objections that were 'untimely' since the party had 'failed promptly to react' when given the opportunity to do so.[27]

D. KNOWLEDGE OR JUSTIFICATION

16. Waiver under article 30 of the 1976 Rules operates when '[a] party knows' of the relevant non-compliance.[28] On its face, the provision requires actual knowledge on

---

23 *Ibid.*, at paras 32-41–32-43. *See Merial SAS v. Klocke Verpackungs – Service GmbH*, Cass Civ 1, No. 08-21288, 3 February 2010.

24 Note that the UNCITRAL Model Law adopts the term 'without undue delay' in order to 'soften the more restrictive approach of the 1976 Rules'; Caron & Caplan, *supra* fn 4, at 695.

25 Caron & Caplan, *supra* fn 4, at 694.

26 Webster, *supra* fn 4, at para. 32-19.

27 *See Varo Intl Corp v. Government of the Islamic Republic of Iran* (1990) 25 Iran-US CTR 3, 6 ('[t]he request of 15 August 1985 is untimely and is therefore denied'); and *Cook Industries Inc v. Foreign Transactions Co et al.*, Case No. 393, Chamber Two, Order of 6 September 1985 ('[b]y failing promptly to react, in any way, ... the Claimant waived its right to object').

28 But does not require that the non-objecting party must also have known that it could have objected to it.

the part of the waiving party, and seems to place the burden of proving that on the other party.[29] Although there was no known instance where actual knowledge was imposed as a requirement in practice, at the outset of the revision process it was suggested that it be clarified in the 2010 Rules that knowledge includes constructive knowledge (i.e. 'ought to have known' or equivalent terms).[30]

17. Although that is believed to be the right position under the 1976 Rules, in the 2010 Rules a better solution was adopted. A requirement of knowledge has been altogether eliminated: all that needs to be shown is a failure to object promptly.[31] Consistent with other provisions (e.g. articles 21(3) and 23(2)), the onus is then on the party that failed to object to show that 'its failure was justified'.[32] It was said that a constructive-knowledge requirement would call for an assessment of possibly subjective circumstances and might also create a cleavage with Article 4 of the Model Law (who uses the 'knows' formulation of the 1976 Rules).[33] On the latter point, as has already been noted, the position is that if the controlling or recognition forum has a higher standard for waiver than the Rules, that standard is likely to prevail.[34] But in any event, the solution ultimately adopted in article 32 is practically and conceptually tidier than a constructive-knowledge requirement. It is also a better solution than another alternative which was considered, namely to require that the non-objecting party must prove that it did not know of the non-compliance.[35]

18. Turning now to the justification that will have to be tendered for a failure to object, the standard is again case-specific but it is plainly an objective one. Thus lack of knowledge will be justified if the non-objecting party can show that it did exercise the requisite degree of diligence expected of a party in its position (or, equivalently, that it would not have known even if it had exercised such diligence).

---

29 *See* UNCITRAL Report of 51st Session, 10 November 2009, UN Doc A/CN.9/684, para. 44; Caron & Caplan, *supra* fn 4, at 693-694.

30 *See* Paulsson & Petrochilos, *supra* fn 6, at para. 229.

31 Cf. Article 40 of the ICC Rules, which reads: 'A party which proceeds with the arbitration without raising its objection to a failure to comply with any provision of the Rules, or of any other rules applicable to the proceedings, any direction given by the arbitral tribunal, or any requirement under the arbitration agreement relating to the constitution of the arbitral tribunal or the conduct of the proceedings, shall be deemed to have waived its right to object'.

32 UNCITRAL Report of 51st Session, 10 November 2009, UN Doc A/CN.9/684, paras 49-51.

33 *See* UNCITRAL Report of 51st Session, 10 November 2009, UN Doc A/CN.9/684, para. 45; *see also* APRAG Report of 51st Session, 30 October 2009, para. 23.

34 *See* Fry, Greenberg & Mazza, *supra* fn 14, at para. 3-1526 (the applicable standard 'will be determined by a court of law called upon to consider the effect of this provision').

35 UNCITRAL Report of 51st Session, 10 November 2009, UN Doc A/CN.9/684, para. 49; Caron & Caplan, *supra* fn 4, at 694.

PART I

Section IV

The award

2010 Rules

Article 33
Decisions

1976 Rules Article 31: Decisions	2010 Rules Article 33: Decisions
1. When there are three arbitrators, any award or other decision of the arbitral tribunal shall be made by a majority of the arbitrators.	1. When there is more than one arbitrator, any award or other decision of the arbitral tribunal shall be made by a majority of the arbitrators.
2. In the case of questions of procedure, when there is no majority or when the arbitral tribunal so authorizes, the presiding arbitrator may decide on his own, subject to revision, if any, by the arbitral tribunal.	2. In the case of questions of procedure, when there is no majority or when the arbitral tribunal so authorizes, the presiding arbitrator may decide alone, subject to revision, if any, by the arbitral tribunal.

1. Article 33 of the Rules deals with decision-making, rather than with the form and content that various decisions should have (a matter dealt with in article 34). It lays down in paragraph (1) the rule that in a plural formation 'any award or other decision' must be made by a majority, subject to specific exceptions which are set out in paragraph (2). The provision remains virtually identical with its counterpart in the 1976 Rules,[1] although the Working Group considered the possibility of granting the presiding arbitrator the power to decide on their own when no majority can be formed. The provision does not deal with the deliberative process of the tribunal or minority opinions. A few observations are called for here in respect of the tribunal's deliberation, while the issue of individual arbitrator opinions is addressed in the context of article 34.

---

1 Article 33(1) of the 2010 Rules replaces the reference to 'three arbitrators' in the 1976 wording with 'more than one arbitrator' to ensure consistency with the changes made to article 10(2) of the 2010 Rules (allowing tribunals to be constituted of more than three arbitrators). In article 33(2), the 2010 drafters also replaced 'on his own' with 'alone', with no apparent impact.

A. DELIBERATIONS AND SECRECY

2. The Rules do envisage that the tribunal will 'meet … for deliberations' (article 18(1)). This step of the process will inevitably, though not exclusively, take place between the closure of the hearings (article 31) and the tribunal's making of an award or other decision (article 33). Unlike a number of other arbitration rules,[2] the Rules treat this matter as an *internum corporis* that is self-evident and need not be expressly regulated (other than in respect of the reasonableness of the tribunal's costs and fees).[3] There are therefore no requirements of process, form, frequency, timing, or record-keeping set out in the Rules.

3. Indeed, it goes without saying that in order for a tribunal to reach a decision as a collegial formation, whether in the end unanimously or otherwise, there must be a deliberative process. It is submitted that the duty to deliberate is a basic obligation which arbitrators owe to the parties, and that failure to discharge it may engage their liability. It is also right to say that violation of that duty amounts to a breach of procedural public policy.[4] However, it will be difficult to argue that an instrument purporting to be an 'award' but which was not preceded by deliberation does not even amount to one. The requirements for an award set out in article 34(4), although constitutive in nature, take a formal expression in the form of signatures etc.: this is intended precisely to avoid ambiguity on whether an instrument is or is not an award.

4. It is clear from article 18(1) but also, more importantly, from first principles that deliberation is a collegial process that involves all tribunal members. *Ex parte* discussions excluding one of the tribunal members are impermissible, save (in exceptional circumstances where this is absolutely necessary) with the advance authorization of the member who is unable to participate and with them being kept informed of the discussion in which they were unable to participate.

5. Deliberations are treated as a purely internal ('in camera')[5] matter for the tribunal, in order to guarantee the full and frank exchange of views, to avoid pressure on arbitrators to justify their positions or concessions, and to ensure that there will be no leakage of information which might influence settlement negotiations between the parties. That exchange must take place out of sight of the parties, other participants (such as tribunal assistants), and the world at large; save of course for court-reporters or translators if necessary. The requirement of secrecy was not even discussed in the preparation of the 1976 Rules (or the 2010 Rules),

---

[2] *See*, e.g., Rule 15 of the ICSID Rules; Article 30.2 of the LCIA Rules; Article 44(2) of the 2012 Swiss Rules; and Article 31, Note 2 of the Tribunal Rules of Procedure of the Iran-United States Claims Tribunal (3 May 1983).

[3] *See* articles 40(2)(a)-(b) and 41(4) of the 2010 Rules.

[4] *See*, e.g., John Savage & Emmanuel Gaillard (eds), *Fouchard, Gaillard, Goldman on International Commercial Arbitration*, para. 1369 (Kluwer 1999) (where proper deliberations are considered 'a requirement of international procedural public policy').

[5] This is the term used in article 28(3) of the Rules.

being so widespread and accepted in practice that it was unnecessary to do so.[6] (The Rules of the Iran-US Claims Tribunal do, however, expressly provide for secrecy.)[7] One might even say that secrecy is an inherent duty of arbitrators, in common to all persons exercising judicial functions.[8] Thus a dissenting opinion which reveals, be it obliquely, the content of deliberations commits 'a most serious error'.[9] Secrecy applies for all time:[10] it is a necessary part of the perennity of res judicata.

6. By contrast to the contents of deliberations, however, the existence or inexistence of deliberations may not be covered by confidentiality. It may be necessary to divulge to the parties that an arbitrator has been unable to participate in scheduled deliberations and thus unable to fulfil their functions, for article 12(3) purposes. It may also be necessary to do so when there have been breaches of the rule of collegial deliberation.[11] That such disclosures are not violations of the confidentiality of deliberation seems to have been accepted by a decision of Judge Moons (the President of the Dutch Supreme Court) in his capacity as the appointing authority for the Iran-US Claims Tribunal. The question was whether a 'secret memorandum' that the presiding arbitrator had allegedly passed to only one of his two colleagues on a Chamber of the Tribunal could be considered in the context of a challenge to the presiding arbitrator. The appointing authority held that the secrecy rule did not prevent him from considering whether the award had been based on the memorandum, and thus whether the rule of collegial

---

6 Stewart A. Baker & Mark D. Davis, *The UNCITRAL Arbitration Rules in Practice – The Experience of the Iran-United States Claims Tribunal*, 157 (Kluwer 1992).

7 Note 2 to Article 31 of the Tribunal Rules of Procedure of the Iran-United States Claims Tribunal (3 May 1983) provides that '[t]he arbitral tribunal shall deliberate in private. Its deliberations shall be and remain secret. Only the members of the arbitral tribunal shall take part in the deliberations. The Secretary-General may be present. No other person may be admitted except by special decision of the arbitral tribunal'.

8 David D. Caron & Lee M. Caplan, *The UNCITRAL Arbitration Rules, A Commentary*, 712 (2nd ed., Oxford University Press 2013); Decision of the appointing authority ('*Briner decision*'), 19 September 1989, 21 Iran-US CTR 384, 387.

9 Decision of Sir Robert Jennings, Appointing Authority to the Iran-US Claims Tribunal, 7 May 2001, reprinted in 16(5) Mealey's Int Arb Rep 2 (2001).

10 *See* Rule 9 of the 1987 IBA Rules of Ethics for International Arbitrators, which provides, in pertinent part, that '[t]he deliberations of the arbitral tribunal, and the contents of the award itself, remain confidential in perpetuity unless the parties release the arbitrators from this obligation'.

11 *See Victor Pey Casado and President Allende Foundation v. Republic of Chile* (ICSID Case No. ARB/98/2) ICSID Secretary-General Letter, 2 December 2005, <www.italaw.com>, which led to the recusal of one arbitrator; and *CME Czech Republic BV v. The Czech Republic* (UNCITRAL) Dissenting Opinion of Arbitrator JUDr Jaroslav Hándl against the Partial Award, 13 September 2001, <www.italaw.com>, which in part served as foundation for an (unsuccessful) challenge to the award in the Swedish courts; *see Czech Republic v. CME Czech Republic BV*, Challenge of Arbitral Award, Judgment of SVEA Court of Appeal (15 May 2003), 42 ILM 919.

deliberation had been violated; but that he was prevented from taking account of the internal discussions within the tribunal as to that memorandum.[12]

7. Similarly, in the recent *Tapie* case the French courts did have regard to communications between a party, its appointee on the tribunal, and the tribunal president, in order to establish whether the deliberative process was free of external influence (and concluded that the tribunal had been misled through impermissible influence).[13] It is true that addressing such instances of fraud, forgery, or corruption within the tribunal – highly exceptional as they are of course – may call for an understanding of the substance of the deliberations. This, it is submitted, will be a justified exception for such grave cases.

B. MAJORITY RULE

8. Article 33(1) primarily addresses decision-making by three arbitrators, although the rule can apply without modification if the tribunal is comprised of a greater number of arbitrators.[14] Thus, when there are three arbitrators, at least two must agree for a majority to be formed. This rule applies to all 'decisions', whether or not they be framed as awards under the requirements of article 34(3)-(4). The term 'decisions' in the Rules encapsulates everything that the tribunal decides or determines, as is discussed in the context of article 34 in this work. Thus the term includes procedural orders, directions, decisions, rulings, etc. The only distinction that article 33 makes is in respect of 'procedural' matters which fall within the ambit of paragraph 2.[15]

9. The majority rule is of course the traditional rule in arbitration. It is intended to force continued deliberation in order to reach compromise.[16] Its drawback stems precisely from this intended characteristic: it may 'sacrifice principle' and cogency or coherence of reasoning to the altar of accommodation,[17] in circumstances where there is deadlock and the presiding arbitrator must side with the arbitrator whom they consider the least-unreasonable in order to form

---

12 *Briner decision*, 21 Iran-US CTR 384, 387. For an account of the events, *see* Baker & Davis, *supra* fn 6, at 160-161.

13 Arrêt n° 842 du 18 mai 2017 (15-2.683, 16-10.339, 16-10.344), Cass Comm, 18 May 2017, < www.courdecassation.fr > .

14 For example, the Iran-US Claims Tribunal adhered to the majority rule principle when sitting as a Full Tribunal of nine members; *see* Article 31, Note 1 of the Tribunal Rules of Procedure of the Iran-United States Claims Tribunal (3 May 1983); Article III(2) of the Iran-United States Claims Settlement Declaration (19 January 1981). Decisions by sole arbitrators are not addressed by the provision as these are straightforward.

15 *See* Caron & Caplan, *supra* fn 8, at 700.

16 *See* Pieter Sanders, *Commentary on UNCITRAL Arbitration Rules*, II YCA 172, 207 (1977) ('The arbitrators are therefore forced to continue their deliberations until a majority, and probably a compromise solution, has been reached').

17 In fact, the practice whereby arbitrators concur in an award while adopting different reasoning has been accepted by the International Court of Justice as validly forming a 'majority': *see Case Concerning the Arbitral Award of July 31, 1989 (Guinea-Bissau v. Senegal)*, ICJ Rep 40 (1991). *See also* Caron & Caplan, *supra* fn 8, at 702.

a majority.[18] This is a particular concern in cases that are highly politicized (e.g. boundary cases)[19] or have broader policy implications (as may be the case in investor-state arbitrations). Negotiating 'acceptable outcomes', as opposed to the legally optimal solution compelled by one's professional conscience, is inimical to decision-making.[20] The jigsaw majorities formed in the Iran-US Claims Tribunal on a 'something is better than nothing' basis are well-known.[21] That is not to say that a plurality of opinions within a decision is necessarily a bad thing: several supreme courts frequently reach decisions through individual opinions a majority of which concur in the result (though not in the reasoning). It is simply to say that it does not accord with the traditional conception of awards issued by small formations of three arbitrators.

10. It was therefore suggested at the outset of the revision process to include in the Rules a provision to the effect that the presiding arbitrator's opinion will prevail when no majority can be formed.[22] Such a rule would technically be based on authorizations by the *lex arbitri*, as is the case under Article 29 of the Model Law, to derogate from the requirement of a majority. A rule of this kind is a traditional feature of the ICC Rules[23] (and more recently the LCIA

---

18 Jan Paulsson & Georgios Petrochilos, *Revision of the UNCITRAL Rules* (September 2006), para. 233, <www.uncitral.org>. *See also* UNCITRAL Report of 47th Session, 25 September 2007, UN Doc A/CN.9/641, para. 69.

19 Cf. *The Republic Srpska v. The Federation of Bosnia and Herzegovina* (UNCITRAL) Award on Control over the Brcko Corridor, 14 February 1997, 36 ILM 396 (1997) (where, in a highly-politicised arbitration, in which it was 'clear from the outset that any party-appointed arbitrator would encounter significant difficulties in conducting himself with the usual degree of detachment and independence' (para. 5), the parties amended article 31(1) of the 1976 Rules to allow the presiding arbitrator to make unilateral decisions when a majority could not be formed). Similarly, concerned that a majority formed by the presiding arbitrator and the US-appointed arbitrator would result in the inflation of amounts awarded against it, Iran proposed modifying article 31(1) of the 1976 Rules, allowing the presiding arbitrator in Iran-US Claims Tribunal cases to determine the amount of compensation sought in the event of a dispute. However, this was rejected by the Full Tribunal: *see* Caron & Caplan, *supra* fn 8, at 704.

20 Caron & Caplan, *supra* fn 8, at 702.

21 *See Economy Forms Corp v. Government of the Islamic Republic of Iran* (1983) Concurring Opinion of Judge Holtzmann, 3 Iran-US CTR 42, 55 (where Judge Holtzmann concurred despite considering that double the amount of damages should have been awarded).

22 Nigel Blackaby, Constantine Partasides, Alan Redfern & Martin J. Hunter, *Redfern and Hunter on International Arbitration*, para. 9.122 (6th ed., Kluwer 2015) ('there may be cases in which it is genuinely impossible to achieve a majority. In construction industry arbitrations, for example, there are often many different issues in relation to separate claims and it is possible for each individual arbitrator to have a different view on these different issues. Furthermore, the arbitrators may have widely differing views on questions of quantum in such cases, with no real possibility of a compromise solution being achieved in order to obtain a majority award').

23 Article 32(1) of the ICC Rules provides that: 'When the arbitral tribunal is composed of more than one arbitrator, an award is made by a majority decision. If there is no majority, the award shall be made by the president of the arbitral tribunal alone'.

Rules)[24] and works well in practice by dissuading party appointees from taking extreme positions. As for presiding arbitrators, they are understandably reluctant to issue awards under their sole authority (especially in the face of two likely individual opinions appended to the award) other than in extremis. Thus in the authors' experience president-only awards are an exceedingly rare occurrence, of which they have seen only two examples.[25] The only known reported example is the *RAKTA* arbitration, under the 1955 ICC Rules.[26] The suggestion for president-only decisions was therefore intended to strengthen, rather than to dilute, the requirement that decisions must be made by at least a majority.[27]

11. In the Working Group it was said that president-only decisions could lead to the other arbitrators' being 'reduced to the position of mere assessors'.[28] There was, more generally, apprehension that there would be too much power in the hands of the presiding arbitrator and that, in investor-state arbitrations in particular, a ruling by the president alone would not have the necessary standing. Specifically, the Working Group considered: (i) preserving the 'majority requirement', but with an opt-out provision, similar to that found in Article 29 of the Model Law;[29] (ii) adopting the 'presiding arbitrator solution';[30] and (iii) adopting the 'presiding arbitrator solution' if the parties choose to opt-in.[31] No consensus could be reached

---

24 Article 26.6 of the LCIA Rules provides that: 'If any arbitrator refuses or fails to sign the award, the signatures of the majority or (failing a majority) of the presiding arbitrator shall be sufficient, provided that the reason for the omitted signature is stated in the award by the majority or by the presiding arbitrator'.

25 *See* Peter Turner & Reza Mohtashami, *A Guide to the LCIA Arbitration Rules*, para. 7.14 (Oxford University Press 2009) ('we understand that no chairman of an LCIA arbitration has ever been required to decide alone any issue dealt with in an award'); and Jason Fry, Simon Greenberg & Francesca Mazza, *The Secretariat's Guide to ICC Arbitration*, para. 3-1142 (ICC 2012) (noting that the provision in the ICC Rules authorising the presiding arbitrator to render an award alone 'does not in any way undermine the importance of the co-arbitrators' views, as confirmed by the rarity of awards made by presidents alone').

26 ICC Case No. 1703/1971, summarised in W. Laurence Craig, William W. Park & Jan Paulsson, *International Chamber of Commerce Arbitration*, 370 (3rd ed., Oceana Publications 2000).

27 UNCITRAL Report of 47th Session, 25 September 2007, UN Doc A/CN.9/641, para. 68.

28 UNCITRAL Summary Record of the 11th Meeting, 21 April 1976, UN Doc A/CN.9/9/C.2/SR.11, para. 7, Mr Boston (Sierra Leone).

29 *See* UNCITRAL Working Paper for 49th Session, 6 August 2008, UN Doc A/CN.9/WG.II/WP.151/Add.1, draft Article 31, Option 1 ('When there is more than one arbitrator, any award or other decision of the arbitral tribunal shall be made, unless otherwise agreed by the parties, by a majority of the arbitrators'); *see also* UNCITRAL Report of 47th Session, 25 September 2007, UN Doc A/CN.9/641, para. 73.

30 *See* UNCITRAL Working Paper for 49th Session, 6 August 2008, UN Doc A/CN.9/WG.II/WP.151/Add.1, draft Article 31, Option 2, Variant 1 ('When there is more than one arbitrator and the arbitrators are not able to reach a majority on the substance of the dispute, any award or other decision shall be made by the presiding arbitrator alone'). This is similar to the wording of, e.g., Article 32(1) of the ICC Rules; Article 31(1) of the Swiss Rules; and Article 63 of the WIPO Rules.

31 *See* UNCITRAL Working Paper for 49th Session, 6 August 2008, UN Doc A/CN.9/WG.II/WP.151/Add.1, draft Article 31, Option 2, Variant 2 ('When there is more than one arbitrator and the arbitrators are not able to reach a majority on the substance of the dispute, any

in the end to depart from the majority rule. In particular, some members of the Working Group were concerned that modifying the strict 'majority requirement' could weaken the arbitrators' resolve to form a majority and thus 'change the internal dynamics of an arbitral tribunal's deliberation'.[32] Another cause for reticence was the issue of defining the point at which it would be deemed certain that a majority could not be formed.[33] Finally, some members of the Working Group considered that the need for a majority decision may be heightened in investment-treaty cases.[34] Such concerns are of course entirely legitimate, but they ignore the experience from practice described above.

12. Article 33(1) of the 2010 Rules therefore retains the majority rule in article 31(1) of the 1976 Rules.[35] Parties may of course consider modifying article 33(1) in order to remove the majority requirement in the event of a deadlock.[36]

C. 'QUESTIONS OF PROCEDURE'

13. Article 33(2) empowers the presiding arbitrator to decide 'questions of procedure' alone where (i) a majority fails to be formed, or (ii) the presiding arbitrator has been authorized to do so by the tribunal. These unilateral powers remain 'subject to revision, if any, by the arbitral tribunal'. The power conferred on the president is not merely to sign on their own a full-tribunal decision with the mention that they are acting on behalf of the tribunal, as is often the case for procedural directions and the like for reasons of practicality and speed. Rather, the power is to take the decision alone.

14. The notion of 'questions of procedure' is not defined in the Rules; nor is its opposite (e.g. 'questions of substance') spelt out. It is generally accepted that it is basically for the tribunal to determine which matters fall within 'procedure' and which not.[37] In practice tribunals tend to grant advance authorization to the president through a procedural order early in the proceedings, sometimes specifying further conditions, such as that the issue must be minor in importance or very urgent, or both. Also, if the president intends to act alone in the absence of a majority, the other arbitrators will have been able to express a view on whether the contentious issue may be characterized as one of procedure.

award or other decision shall be made, if previously agreed by the parties, by the presiding arbitrator alone'); *see also* UNCITRAL Report of 47th Session, 25 September 2007, UN Doc A/CN.9/641, paras 74-75.

32 UNCITRAL Report of 47th Session, 25 September 2007, UN Doc A/CN.9/641, para. 70.

33 *Ibid.*, at para. 72.

34 *See* Caron & Caplan, *supra* fn 8, at 703.

35 *Ibid.*, at 704; *see also* UNCITRAL Report of 51st Session, 10 November 2009, UN Doc A/CN.9/684, paras 52-62.

36 *See* UNCITRAL Report of 51st Session, 10 November 2009, UN Doc A/CN.9/684, para. 61 ('the Working Group emphasized that the parties had the ability in such situations to agree to another method of decision-making').

37 The drafters of the Model Law were of the view that the tribunal may define the difference between questions of procedure and substance: *see* Caron & Caplan, *supra* fn 8, at 709 fn 62.

Generally, however, it is right to say that matters going to the 'creation, definition and regulation and rights of the parties to the dispute' are substantive, while the 'technical steps of the arbitral process' are of a procedural nature.[38] Thus, interim measures, creating as they do duties and obligations, should not be covered by article 33(2).

15. There are cases where the line is less than bright[39] and which call for caution. A number of matters of process have serious implications for the arbitration as a whole and, by extension, for the parties' rights. It is thus the better view that the tribunal's decision as to the place of the arbitration pursuant to article 18(1) is substantive in that it determines the *lex arbitri* and thus entitlements and remedies for the parties.[40] Also, in respect of requests for correction, interpretation or supplementation of an award under articles 37-39, the practice has not been uniform.[41] We agree with the view that article 33(2) powers should be exercised with caution, as is consistent with the fact that they are set out as an exception to the majority rule and in practice have been used rarely.[42] Arbitrators would do well to ask themselves if a decision is likely to have 'a measureable impact on the rights of one or both of the parties, which could result in unfair advantage or prejudice'.[43] If so, they may well decline to treat it as one of procedure.[44]

16. The power of revision extends to the entire decision that was taken by the presiding arbitrator. Thus the original decision may be revoked and substituted by a fresh one, amended, or supplemented. A revision may not, however, amount to a simple retraction: a revised decision must be issued by the tribunal. As for the time within which revisions may occur, it is submitted that it must be as promptly as possible in the circumstances, consistent with the general duty of efficiency in article 17(1) of the Rules.

---

38 *Ibid.*, at 709.

39 Jacomijn J. van Hof, *Commentary on the UNCITRAL Arbitration Rules, The Application by the Iran-U.S. Claims Tribunal*, 214 (Kluwer 1991); Clyde E. Croft, Christopher Kee & Jeffrey Waincymer, *A Guide to the UNCITRAL Arbitration Rules*, 375 (Cambridge University Press 2013).

40 Sanders, *supra* fn 16 at 193 (expressing the view that the decision on the place of arbitration is not a question of procedure).

41 *See* Baker & Davis, *supra* fn 6, at 156 (explaining that the Iran-US Claims Tribunal sometimes treated such requests as procedural matters, and at other times as substantive issues resolved by an award or decision signed by all three arbitrators).

42 The practice of the Iran-US Claims Tribunal provides few examples of presidential decision-making under Article 31(2) of the Tribunal Rules of Procedure; *see* Caron & Caplan, *supra* fn 8, at 707-708.

43 Caron & Caplan, *supra* fn 8, at 709.

44 *Ibid.*, at 709-710. *See also* James E. Castello, 'UNCITRAL Arbitration Rules, Section IV, Article 33' in Loukas A. Mistelis (ed), *Concise International Arbitration*, 247 (2nd ed., Kluwer 2015).

Article 34
Form and effect of the award

1976 Rules Article 32: Form and effect of the award	2010 Rules Article 34: Form and effect of the award
1. In addition to making a final award, the arbitral tribunal shall be entitled to make interim, interlocutory, or partial awards.	1. The arbitral tribunal may make separate awards on different issues at different times.
2. The award shall be made in writing and shall be final and binding on the parties. The parties undertake to carry out the award without delay.	2. All awards shall be made in writing and shall be final and binding on the parties. The parties shall carry out all awards without delay.
3. The arbitral tribunal shall state the reasons upon which the award is based, unless the parties have agreed that no reasons are to be given.	3. The arbitral tribunal shall state the reasons upon which the award is based, unless the parties have agreed that no reasons are to be given.
4. An award shall be signed by the arbitrators and it shall contain the date on which and the place where the award was made. Where there are three arbitrators and one of them fails to sign, the award shall state the reason for the absence of the signature.	4. An award shall be signed by the arbitrators and it shall contain the date on which the award was made and indicate the place of arbitration. Where there is more than one arbitrator and any of them fails to sign, the award shall state the reason for the absence of the signature.
5. The award may be made public only with the consent of both parties.	5. An award may be made public with the consent of all parties or where and to the extent disclosure is required of a party by legal duty, to protect or pursue a legal right or in relation to legal proceedings before a court or other competent authority.
6. Copies of the award signed by the arbitrators shall be communicated to the parties by the arbitral tribunal.	6. Copies of the award signed by the arbitrators shall be communicated to the parties by the arbitral tribunal.
7. If the arbitration law of the country where the award is made requires that the award be filed or registered by the arbitral tribunal, the tribunal shall comply with this requirement within the period of time required by law.	

Possible waiver statement

Note. If the parties wish to exclude recourse against the arbitral award that may be available under the applicable law, they may consider adding a provision to that effect as suggested below, considering, however, that the effectiveness and conditions of such an exclusion depend on the applicable law.

Waiver

The parties hereby waive their right to any form of recourse against an award to any court or other competent authority, insofar as such waiver can validly be made under the applicable law.

---

1. Article 34 deals with the requirements of form and content for arbitral awards. It also addresses exceptions to the confidentiality of arbitral awards. This is one of the several new features compared to the 1976 text. It should not be thought, however, that article 34 is intended as a full exposition of all issues regarding the finality of arbitral awards; nor can it be, as cognate issues are also addressed by the *lex arbitri*, not infrequently with mandatory force. Such issues include the res judicata effect of awards[1] and the time at which an award becomes final and binding.[2]

A. THE NOTION AND TYPES OF 'AWARDS': ARTICLE 34(1)

2. The Rules use the terms 'decision' or 'rul[ing]' in respect of matters of substance (see, e.g., article 23(1)), jurisdiction (see article 23), or procedure (see, e.g., article 29(3)). It is clear from article 33(1), which speaks of 'award or other decision', that not all decisions/rulings by the tribunal need be in the form of an award. There is in fact latitude for the tribunal – and this has always been a feature of the Rules – to adopt the form of an award or another form. Notably, as already discussed in connection with article 26(1), the 1976 drafters were concerned to grant tribunals express authorization to issue interim measures in the form of an award (often titled 'interim award'),[3] to encourage compliance with them. This latitude is preserved in article 34(1) of the 2010 Rules.

---

1 Cf. *Apotex Holdings Inc and Apotex Inc v. United States of America* (ICSID Case No. ARB(AF)/12/1) Award, 25 August 2014, <www.italaw.com>, paras 7.33 et seq. (where the tribunal relied on article 32 of the 1976 Rules, and more general rules of public international law, to conclude that its prior decisions issued in *Apotex I* and *Apotex II* had a preclusive effect as to claims arising out of Apotex's advance approvals).

2 *See* UNCITRAL Report of the Secretary General on the Draft UNCITRAL Arbitration Rules, 12 December 1975, UN Doc A/CN.9/112/Add.1, 177, Section IV, para. 1; Peter Binder, *Analytical Commentary to the UNCITRAL Arbitration Rules*, para. 34-003 (Sweet & Maxwell 2013).

3 *See* Pieter Sanders, *Commentary on UNCITRAL Arbitration Rules*, II YCA 172, 210 (1977).

3. The provision is an improvement on article 32 of the 1976 Rules by way of simplification. The substantive import of article 32 has been retained. The 1976 provision referred to 'interim, interlocutory, or partial awards',[4] not in order to assign a specific function to each of these types of awards but simply to connote that '[a]rbitrators are entitled to make any kind of award they deem appropriate for the proper conduct of the arbitration'.[5] This procedural latitude is better served by the present wording, which avoids bare labels that are prone to differing interpretations by referring to 'separate awards on different issues at different times'.

4. Furthermore, the 1976 version's introductory phrase 'in addition to making a final award' has been deleted. Although in its context the term 'final award' merely means the chronologically last award (as in articles 40(1) and 43(5)),[6] it was felt that the phrase might be read to suggest that all prior awards were not final in the substantive sense of article 34(2).[7] It was on such considerations that article 34(1) was revised along the lines of Article 26.7 of the 1998 LCIA Rules, whose intention is to head off the same kind of difficulties.[8] The corollary is that the Rules, as most other arbitration rules[9] and arbitration laws,[10] avoid specifying the various types and functions of 'awards'. Nevertheless, there are a number of parameters to be taken into account.

5. Under the Rules it is clear that a decision expressed in the form of an award must set forth its reasons and also have the requisite form, as set out in articles 34(2)-(3) (discussed separately below). An award must contain a decision, even if it is on a narrow discrete issue. A communication that contains no decision but merely information cannot be an award. It is also clear that only decisions issued by the entire tribunal can be awards. This may include president-only

---

4 Cf. the definition in Article 2 of the ICC Rules: '"award" includes, *inter alia*, an interim, partial or final award'.

5 Sanders, *supra* fn 3, at 210.

6 *See* David D. Caron & Lee M. Caplan, *The UNCITRAL Arbitration Rules, A Commentary*, 739 (2nd ed., Oxford University Press 2013).

7 Some delegates were concerned that the wording in the 1976 provisions may be misleading as they differ across legal systems and that 'final award' could be subject to various interpretations. *See* UNCITRAL Report of 45th Session, 5 October 2006, UN Doc A/CN.9/614, para. 113; UNCITRAL Report of 47th Session, 25 September 2007, UN Doc A/CN.9/641, paras 79-80; and UNCITRAL Report of 51st Session, 10 November 2009, UN Doc A/CN.9/684, para. 63.

8 Article 26.7 of the 1998 LCIA Rules provided as follows: 'The Arbitral Tribunal may make separate awards on different issues at different times. Such awards shall have the same status and effect as any other award made by the Arbitral Tribunal'. Note that this provision is reproduced as Article 26.1 of the 2014 LCIA Rules, with additional wording at the end of the first sentence: 'including interim payments on account of any claim or cross-claim (including Legal and Arbitration Costs)'. *See* Caron & Caplan, *supra* fn 6, at 733.

9 *See*, e.g., Article 26.1 of the LCIA Rules; Article 29 of the AAA International Arbitration Rules; Rule 47 of the ICSID Rules; Article 64 of the WIPO Rules; Article 42 of the SCC Rules.

10 *See*, e.g., Article 189 of the Swiss Private International Law Act; Article 1481 of the French Code of Civil Procedure; section 52 of the English Arbitration Act 1996 (England & Wales).

procedural decisions made pursuant to article 33(2), as these are by definition issued on behalf of the tribunal.

6. At first glance, it also appears that any and all awards without exception have a necessary legal consequence, namely that they are 'final', as well as binding, pursuant to article 34(2). That would be the wrong conclusion. As already noted, interim measures may be given in the form of an award – e.g. an 'interim' or 'provisional' award – when the tribunal considers it appropriate to do so,[11] and that is not infrequently the case in practice. Such awards cannot be final in the sense of containing rulings intended to stand for all time: their maximum temporal reach is the date of the final award on the relevant issue, and they are subject to modification, suspension, or revocation at all times (see article 26(2) and (5)). Thus interim measures awards, though indisputably binding and to be carried out (article 26(2) contains the injunctive verb 'orders'), may be final only in that qualified sense; and certain such awards expressly state this.[12] That the characterisation 'final' does not properly fit interim measures awards was well understood by the Working Group, but in the end the rule that '[a]ll awards shall be final and binding' was maintained in article 34(2), largely in order to avoid any confusion or dilution of the finality that attaches to awards as a general rule.[13]

7. Further, the Rules require that certain decisions must be made and issued as awards. That is the case for: the last decision by which the proceedings are concluded, which must be framed as a 'final award' even if it deals only with issues of jurisdiction/admissibility or costs; awards setting out sums due from one party to the other by way of costs (article 40(2)); awards on agreed terms (article 36(1)); and additional awards (article 39(1)) – in the last two cases if the tribunal agrees or decides to issue such decisions. By parity of reasoning with article 40(2), it may also be said that incidental decisions awarding to one party sums it advanced by way of deposits in the stead of the other side,[14] should also be framed as awards, so they can be enforced. Conversely, the Rules require that an article 30(1) decision terminating proceedings must be in the form of an order, rather than an award, to make it plain that the termination of proceedings by such an order has no bearing on the merits of a claim.

8. Within the above parameters, a tribunal has latitude. Under the Rules, a tribunal may, for example, choose to decide by way of an award a purely procedural

---

11 This is the formulation adopted in Article 28(1) of the ICC Rules: 'Any such measure shall take the form of an order, giving reasons, or of an award, as the arbitral tribunal considers appropriate.'

12 For example, in *Chevron Corporation (USA) and Texaco Petroleum Corporation (USA) v. The Republic of Ecuador* (UNCITRAL) First Interim Award on Interim Measures, 25 January 2012, < www.italaw.com >, the tribunal rendered what it called an 'interim award' pursuant to article 32 of the 1976 Rules, while stating that such award 'is and shall remain subject to modification (including its extension or termination) by the Tribunal' (at section VI(3)).

13 *See* UNCITRAL Report of 51st Session, 10 November 2009, UN Doc A/CN.9/684, para. 68; Caron & Caplan, *supra* fn 6, at 741.

14 *See* the discussion in connection with article 43(1) and the references to decided cases there, *infra*.

matter, such as the venue of the hearing, suspension of the proceedings, or a party's default.[15] This would be explained by the importance of the matter in the context of the proceedings and the tribunal's intention to adopt a correspondingly solemn, final form of decision-making and decisional instrument. The same may be said of a decision on the place of arbitration (article 18(2)) and on joinder (article 17(5)), as neither of these issues is purely procedural and both have important repercussions.[16] Decisions on discrete issues but with repercussions on the disposition of the claim on the merits, such as which party bears the burden of proof or what the applicable law is, may well also be expressed in the form of an award. What particular appellation a tribunal chooses to use for such awards – e.g., 'interim' or 'interlocutory' award (both connoting a decision *pendente lite*) – will turn in part on the tribunal's and the parties' legal backgrounds: there is no uniform terminology.[17] The salient necessary characteristic of such awards follows from the rule of finality in article 34(2): they must be final and binding,[18] in the sense that they bind both the parties and the tribunal, and will not be capable of being revisited except if and to the extent that they state so expressly.

9. A question that arises in that context is whether the tribunal should have regard to the *lex arbitri* and the New York Convention in exercising its discretion as to the form and title of the decisional instrument it will employ. The *lex arbitri* will be concerned mostly with what decisions may be subject to setting aside; the New York Convention with what decisions may be recognized or enforced. Most jurisdictions will take the view that an award for such purposes is a decision that finally disposes, partially or fully, of the substantive dispute that has been referred to arbitration,[19] whether on grounds of jurisdiction/admissibility or on the merits.[20] This excludes decisions which regulate exclusively matters of process and settle related disputes, as they have limited temporal scope and do not dispose

15 *See Himpurna California Energy Ltd (Bermuda) v. The Republic of Indonesia* (UNCITRAL) Interim Award, 26 September 1999, XXV YCA 111, 142 (2000) (where, by way of interim award, the tribunal decided the issue of whether the respondent had defaulted on its obligation to submit a statement of defence).

16 Typically, however, such decisions are styled 'Decisions'; *see*, e.g., *Vito G Gallo v. Government of Canada* (UNCITRAL) Decision on Place of Arbitration, 4 June 2008, < www.investorstatelawguide.com >; *Merrill & Ring Forestry L P v. Government of Canada* (ICSID Case No. UNCT/07/1) Decision on Place of Arbitration, 13 September 2007, < www.italaw.com >.

17 For an overview *see* Gary B. Born, *International Commercial Arbitration*, 3014-3020 (2nd ed., Kluwer 2014). On the fluctuating practice of the Iran-US Claims Tribunal *see* Stewart A. Baker & Mark D. Davis, *The UNCITRAL Arbitration Rules in Practice – The Experience of the Iran-United States Claims Tribunal*, 163-165 (Kluwer 1992).

18 James E. Castello, 'UNCITRAL Arbitration Rules, Section IV, Article 34' in Loukas A. Mistelis (ed), *Concise International Arbitration*, 248 (2nd ed., Kluwer 2015). *See also Methanex Corporation v. United States of America* (UNCITRAL) Final Award of the Tribunal on Jurisdiction and Merits, 3 August 2005, < www.italaw.com >, Part II, Chapter E, para. 31.

19 *See* article 1(1) of the Rules.

20 *See*, e.g., UNCITRAL, *2012 Digest of Case Law on the Model Law on International Commercial Arbitration*, 126-127 (United Nations 2012); and Marike R.P. Paulsson, *The 1958 New York Convention in Action*, 114-120 (Kluwer 2016).

of the substantive dispute. But decisions that set forth procedural directions and are framed as such (typically as orders) may be regarded as awards to the extent that by necessary implication they contain a decision on jurisdiction[21] or the merits.[22] (The recognition and enforceability of awards on interim measures remains an open question, as discussed in the context of article 26(2).)

10. This, then, suggests that tribunals should be circumspect in selecting their decisional instrument when they have discretion to do so. Although a number of jurisdictions will or will not characterize a decision as an award based on its substance rather than its title,[23] an instrument framed as an award is apt to create the expectation that it can be the object of setting aside or enforcement proceedings. It will certainly create an entitlement under the Rules for a party to make requests for interpretation, correction, or an additional award (articles 37-39). Thus, in exercising its judgement on the form of its decision it is 'appropriate' for the tribunal – to use the terms of article 17(1) of the Rules – to provide an indication to the parties as to the remedies available to them in respect of that decision. It may even be suggested that the tribunal should motivate its choice in the text of the decision itself.[24] It is at the very least good practice for a tribunal to issue an award when resolving with finality portions of the dispute, which award may well be titled 'partial final award' for clarity. Partial awards may dispose of discrete issues such as jurisdiction or applicable law, certain claims in their entirety, or parts of (all or some of) the claims (e.g., liability in principle but not quantum of compensation). By contrast, decisions on document production (article 27(3)) or the admission of evidence or the closure of the proceedings (article 31), however pivotal they may be to the outcome of the case, should not in principle be framed as awards.

B. 'SEPARATE AWARDS ON DIFFERENT ISSUES AT DIFFERENT TIMES'

11. Article 34(1) sets forth the tribunal's power to 'make separate awards on different issues at different times'. This necessarily implies a concomitant procedural power to split the proceedings into discrete phases – such as jurisdiction/admissibility, liability, quantum, costs, etc. It also implies that where the tribunal exercises that procedural power, it should be reasonably confident that at the conclusion of each phase it will be able to issue an award (i) resolving with finality (ii) all the issues pleaded in that phase. Permeable phases lead to inefficiency or worse. A good illustration of the difficulties that may arise is provided by a case where the tribunal felt compelled in its final award to remove one of the decisions it

21 *See* Tribunal Fédéral, Arrêt du 4 novembre 2014, 4A_446/2014, <www.bger.ch>.

22 *See Publicis Communication v. True North Communications, Inc.*, 3 F.3d 725 (2d Cir., 2000): order to produce documents 'was not just some procedural matter – it was the very issue True North wanted arbitrated'.

23 See, e.g., *Braspetro Oil Services Co v. The Management and Implementation Authority of the Great Man-Made River Project*, CA Paris, 1 July 1999, 14 Mealey's Int Arb Rep 8, at [G-1]–[G-7] (1999); Caron & Caplan, *supra* fn 6, at 735.

24 *See* Rolf Trittmann, *When Should Arbitrators Issue Interim or Partial Awards and or Procedural Orders?*, 20(3) Journal of International Arbitration 255, 264 (2003).

had given in a partial award, on grounds that in the light of new evidence the issue had become 'moot'. This led to a dispute in the courts on whether the tribunal had exceeded its powers by reopening a matter in respect of which it was *functus officio*.[25]

12. More generally, whether and to what extent issues should be hived off into separate phases always turns on two main considerations, both to be found in article 17(2): efficiency and fairness.[26] That assessment falls to be made uniquely in the circumstances of each case; tribunals should resist one-size-fits-all solutions. The analysis set out under article 23(3) applies here as well. Of course, pursuant to article 1(3) any limitations imposed by the *lex arbitri* are to be taken into account above all else.[27]

C. REQUIREMENTS OF FORM AND CONTENT

13. The requirements set forth in article 34(2)-(4) apply to all decisions framed as 'awards'. There is of course nothing to prevent a tribunal from complying with these requirements in other decisions, such as 'decisions' or 'procedural orders', and for reasons discussed above it may well be appropriate to do so. In respect of reasons, in particular, it is believed that unless there is urgency (in which case reasons may be supplied later), there is a general expectation that tribunals should provide reasons for any decision on a contested issue.

1. Writing, date and signature: articles 34(2) and 34(4)

14. Article 34 provides for straightforward, formal requirements which are constitutive of an award. The award must be made in writing (article 34(2)); include the date of the award (article 34(4)); indicate the place of arbitration (rather than the place(s) at which the arbitrators happened to sign) and thus the *lex arbitri* (article 34(4)); and be signed by the arbitrators (article 34(4)).

15. In a plural arbitral formation, if one of the arbitrators fails to sign, the award must also 'state the reason for the absence of the signature'. The drafters had in mind an arbitrator's inability (rather than refusal) to sign,[28] given that the

---

25 *See* Castello, *supra* fn 18, at 249.

26 *See*, e.g., Baker & Davis, *supra* fn 17, at 163; Caron & Caplan, *supra* fn 6, at 733; Sanders, *supra* fn 3, at 209. *See also* UNCITRAL Summary Record of the 10th Meeting, 21 April 1976, UN Doc A/CN.9/9/C.2/SR.10, para. 59, Mr Sanders (Special Consultant to the UNCITRAL secretariat).

27 Caron & Caplan, *supra* fn 6, at 736.

28 *See* article 34(4) of the 2010 Rules; *see also* Caron & Caplan, *supra* fn 6, at 748. *See also* UNCITRAL Summary Record of the 11th Meeting, 21 April 1976, UN Doc A/CN.9/9/C.2/SR.11, para. 40, Mr. Roehrich (France) ('There was no reason for an arbitrator who disagreed with the majority decision not to sign the award; his signature would not signify agreement with the majority decision but would simply render the award valid. If, however, an arbitrator was physically unable to sign the award, his failure to sign should not invalidate the award').

absence of a signature may raise questions as to the participation of the arbitrator in the award or, in certain jurisdictions, as to the whether the document is to be treated as an award at all.[29] Whatever the reason for which an arbitrator failed to sign the award, however, signature by the necessary majority will suffice: article 34(4) does not state that the award must be signed by 'all' arbitrators. (And of course a president-only decision, if exceptionally framed as an award on 'matters of procedure', pursuant to article 33(2), need be signed only by the president.)

16. The rule about signatures of tribunal members does not go merely to the formal requirements of an award. As with all similar requirements in article 34(2) and (4), there is a duty on all arbitrators to affix their signatures on the award, even if they disagree with it in substance. As discussed below, the ability of individual arbitrators to issue separate (dissenting or concurring) opinions is intended precisely to pre-empt disagreement being put forward as an excuse for one's failure to sign an award. The same may be said of the ability to include minority reasons in the body of the award itself, pursuant to article 34(3), as also discussed below.

2. Reasons: article 34(3)

17. Unless the parties have explicitly or impliedly agreed otherwise, the tribunal must provide reasons in the award.[30] Reasons may include the minority's reasons for its disagreement. The Rules do not address what form reasons should take, but it is general and sound practice for the reasoning to precede the dispositive section of the award (*dispositif*).[31] Nor do the Rules require any particular intellectual sufficiency or textual length to meet the requirement: unless there is no text at all that can be characterized as a reason on a reasonable definition, it will be difficult to argue that a purported award does not meet the article 34(3) requirement. Thus, a statement to the effect that the tribunal 'carefully considered' the parties' arguments and evidence is not a reason, even if the arguments and evidence are copiously described in the award. It is possible, however, that the *lex arbitri* may have additional requirements, for example that the reasons given cannot be arbitrary or cancelling each other out, in order for an award properly to be said to contain reasons.

18. The wording of article 32(3) of the 1976 Rules was adopted with a view to reaching a solution acceptable to both civil law countries, whose laws generally required reasons to be given, and common law countries, where the prevailing practice was not to require reasons.[32] One view of the provision is that by agreeing on a place of arbitration whose law does not require reasons to be given, the parties

29 Caron & Caplan, *supra* fn 6, at 749.

30 Report of the Commission on its 9th Session, 12 April-7 May 1976, UN Doc A/31/17, 77 para. 157. *See also* Castello, *supra* fn 18, at 250.

31 However, the reasons may also be in a separate statement annexed to the award; *see* Sanders, *supra* fn 3, at 208.

32 Caron & Caplan, *supra* fn 6, at 750-751; *see also* Sanders, *supra* fn 3, at 208.

may be taken to have impliedly agreed to dispense with reasons.[33] That view does not seem to be altogether sound: it is clear from article 1(3) that specific provisions in the Rules, such as the requirement of reasons, prevail over the corresponding provisions of the *lex arbitri* (unless 'the parties cannot derogate' from them).

D. SEPARATE OPINIONS

19. The 'award' envisaged in article 34(4) is a decisional instrument issued by the tribunal as a sole-arbitrator or collegial formation. It contains the reasons adopted by the tribunal – unanimously, by a majority, or in exceptional cases under article 33(2) by the president alone. It must (again subject to the limited exception of article 33(2)) contain the signatures of the arbitrators; and, conversely, arbitrators have a duty to sign it, even if they are in the minority. Thus an award is the *only* instrument which carries the tribunal's decisional authority on the issues decided therein.

20. That is not to suggest that awards may not within their text record minority reasons and opinions, so long as it is clear from the *dispositif* what the effect of the award is. That is legitimate, and in the authors' view in principle a more satisfactory way of handling plurality or divergence of views within the collegial formation that a tribunal is. Nevertheless, separate opinions by individual arbitrators (or, in panels of more than three arbitrators, possibly joint opinions) are permitted. The possibility for such opinions to be issued and 'included' in, i.e. appended to, the award is not expressly foreseen in the Rules, but from their inception it was accepted as a permitted practice. Thus the initial proposal that the text of article 32 (now article 34) should provide that '[t]he award ... shall not include any dissenting opinion'[34] was not accepted,[35] the Committee of the Whole later stating that the silence of the text means that such opinions are 'in effect permit[ed] but not require[ed]'.[36] The 1976 *travaux* indicate that a strongly-expressed motivation for permitting dissenting opinions was that, with their separate views recorded, dissentients would have no incentive to refuse to sign awards, and indeed no justification for withholding their signature.[37] Separate opinions are thus permitted, subject to any mandatory requirements of the *lex arbitri*.[38] Again, these are individual texts: they do not carry res

33 *See* Report of the Commission on its 9th Session, 12 April-7 May 1976, UN Doc A/31/17, 77 para. 157; Caron & Caplan, *supra* fn 6, at 751.

34 UNCITRAL Report of the Secretary-General on the Preliminary Draft Set of Arbitration Rules, 4 November 1974, UN Doc A/CN.9/97, VI UNCITRAL Ybk 163, 177.

35 UNCITRAL Report of the Secretary General on the Draft UNCITRAL Arbitration Rules, 12 December 1975, UN Doc A/CN.9/112/Add.1, 177-178.

36 Report of the Commission on its 9th Session, 12 April-7 May 1976, UN Doc A/31/17, para. 166. For a fuller account, *see* Baker & Davis, *supra* fn 17, at 165-166.

37 *See ibid.*, at 166 and the references.

38 *See generally* Born, *supra* fn 17, at 3053 et seq. The *lex arbitri* may either permit or disallow separate opinions and also deal with the form that they are to take and whether they should be 'included' in the award (i.e. appended to it); *see* Castello, *supra* fn 18, at 250.

judicata effect, nor are they necessarily an authoritative interpretation of what the award decided.[39]

21. Separate opinions are a fact of life in UNCITRAL arbitration, especially in investment-treaty cases. There is no uniform culture of *en bloc* awards with the minority silently rallying behind the majority.[40] In practice such opinions mostly take the form of dissenting opinions, although they may also be concurring opinions (subscribing to the outcome on different grounds), or a combination of the two. There is a wealth of views and lively discourse on the permissible uses and value that dissenting opinions may have, notably in forcing the majority to prepare a more cogent award and in pointing out (for a reviewing court) serious due-process errors.[41] We do not propose to enter this policy debate here at any length.[42] Suffice it to say that while at the level of principle one can see value to the possibility of separate opinions, there is room for misuse and abuse. When a 'mandatory' separate opinion is being proffered for reasons of perception or politics, there is no added value. Indeed such opinions may also be used, and have in fact been used, as a device to breach confidentiality of deliberations, to stall the issuance of the award, or place obstacles to the validity of an award or compliance with it. In that regard, the empirical evidence is that dissenting opinions in investment-treaty cases have so seldom been used to record a position different from that advanced by one's appointing party that they may be said to confirm a rule of foreordained dissents with a small exception of cogent disagreements.[43] On the other hand, other than occasional problems at the stage of post-award remedies, the experience in both the Iran-US Claims Tribunal[44] (where separate opinions are expressly authorized)[45] and investment-treaty cases suggests that dissenting opinions are to be assessed on their own merits – often to be discounted, but in some cases likely to stand as the jurisprudentially better view.

---

39 *See Waste Management Inc v. United Mexican States ('Number 2')* (ICSID Case No. ARB(AF)/00/3) Decision of the Tribunal on Mexico's Preliminary Objection concerning the Previous Proceedings, 26 June 2002, <www.italaw.com>, para. 23.

40 As is the case, e.g., in the European Union courts.

41 *See also*, regarding bounds imposed by the secrecy of deliberations, article 33, *supra*.

42 *See* notably Laurent Lévy, *Dissenting Opinions in International Arbitration in Switzerland*, 5 Arb Int 35 (1989); Alan Redfern, *The 2003 Freshfields – Lecture Dissenting Opinions in International Commercial Arbitration: The Good, the Bad, and the Ugly*, 20(3) Arb Int 223 (2004); Albert Jan van den Berg, 'Dissenting Opinions by Party-Appointed Arbitrators in Investment Arbitration' in *Looking to the Future: Essays on International Law in Honor of W. Michael Reisman*, 820 (Brill 2010); Charles N. Brower & Charles B. Rosenberg, *The Death of the Two-Headed Nightingale: Why the Paulsson – van den Berg Presumption that Party-Appointed Arbitrators are Untrustworthy is Wrongheaded*, 29(1) Arb Int 7 (2013); Albert Jan van den Berg, *Charles Brower's problem with 100 per cent – dissenting opinions by party-appointed arbitrators in investment arbitration*, 31 Arb Int 381 (2015).

43 *See* notably the papers by van den Berg and Brower & Rosenberg, *ibid*.

44 As to which *see* Baker & Davis, *supra* fn 17, at 166 et seq.

45 See Article 32(3) of the Tribunal Rules of Procedure of the Iran-United States Claims Tribunal (3 May 1983), providing, in pertinent part, that '[a]ny arbitrator may request that his dissenting vote or his dissenting vote and the reasons therefor be recorded'.

E. AWARDS ARE FINAL AND BINDING: ARTICLE 34(2)

22. Article 34(2) states that 'all awards shall be final and binding on the parties', who shall 'carry out all awards without delay'. During the revision of the Rules, there was general agreement that the 'final and binding' character of the award 'should be envisaged at three levels': (i) 'in respect of the arbitral tribunal, which could not modify the award after it was rendered'; (ii) 'in respect of the parties, who were bound by the findings of the award'; and (iii) 'in respect of the courts, which were under a duty not to entertain any recourse against the award, save in the exceptional circumstances that justified the setting aside of the award'.[46] In sum, an award is res judicata. The quality of finality comprises the first two aspects, and the binding nature of an award the third. These two qualities are discussed separately below.

1. Finality

23. An award, whether titled 'partial' or 'final' as discussed above,[47] is final in quality 'when the ability of the parties to bring direct and collateral challenges against the award ceases'.[48] The challenges foreseen in the Rules are set out in articles 37-39. Thus an 'award' within the meaning of article 34(2) is one in respect of which such remedies are no longer available. As these are exceptional remedies, an award is presumptively final from the time it has been perfected by the signature(s) of the tribunal. By contrast, the communication of an award is conceived as a separate act in article 34(6), rather than a constitutive requirement among those listed in article 34(2) and (4).

24. The remedies provided for in articles 37-39 are in principle an exhaustive list. Reconsideration of the substantive rectitude of an award is impermissible under any guise, including under cover of one of the permitted remedies.[49] As one ICC tribunal put it, there is 'virtual unanimity that an application [for interpretation] cannot be used to seek revision, reformulation or additional explanations of a given decision'.[50] Thus there can be no reconsideration of a partial award on account of the successful recusal of an arbitrator.[51]

---

46 UNCITRAL Report of 47th Session, 25 September 2007, UN Doc A/CN.9/641, para. 81.

47 *See CME Czech Republic BV v. The Czech Republic* (UNCITRAL) Final Award, 14 March 2003, <www.italaw.com>, para. 425 (where the tribunal noted that, pursuant to article 32(2) of the 1976 Rules, it was not authorized to reconsider its partial award, which was expressly stated to be 'final and binding in respect to the issues decided' therein). *See also Ultrasystems Inc v. Islamic Republic of Iran* (1983-I) 1 Iran-US CTR 100, 101; *RJ Reynolds Tobacco Co v. Iranian Tobacco Co* (1984) 7 Iran-US CTR 181, 183.

48 Caron & Caplan, *supra* fn 6, at 738.

49 *See* Caron & Caplan, *supra* fn 6, at 803; Baker & Davis, *supra* fn 17, at 200-204.

50 Born, *supra* fn 17, at 3148 (citing to Procedural Order of 6 January 2003, ICC Case 11451 (Extract), in ICC, *Decisions on ICC Arbitration Procedure: A Selection of Procedural Orders Issued by Arbitral Tribunals Acting Under the ICC Rules of Arbitration (2003-2004)*, 18-20 (ICC Ct. Bull. Spec. Supp. 2010).

51 *See Methanex Corporation v. United States of America* (UNCITRAL) Final Award of the Tribunal on Jurisdiction and Merits, 3 August 2005, <www.italaw.com>, Part II, Chapter

25. There is authority for a possible exception, based on the doctrine of inherent powers, namely when a tribunal feels compelled to reopen an award and the proceedings in the face of colourable evidence of fraud (corruption of a tribunal member, forged evidence, etc.) that is likely to have affected the outcome. The contours of the remedy are well-known from Article 51 of the ICSID Convention,[52] which was based on an earlier codification by the ILC of inter-state arbitral procedure.[53] The tribunal in *Biloune v. Ghana* held that an–

> international Arbitral Tribunal has an inherent power to take cognizance of credible evidence, timely placed before it, that its previous determinations were the product of false testimony ... The present Tribunal would not hesitate to reconsider and modify its earlier award were it shown by credible evidence that it had been the victim of fraud and ... false testimony.[54]

The Iran-US Claims Tribunal has also alluded to such powers[55] but never actually exercised them.[56] More recently, an ILA study endorsed the existence of such powers.[57]

26. While one can see the force in giving a way to a tribunal to address a palpable, grave, and intentional affront to justice, the present authors agree with the view that such a power must be residual, i.e. available only when setting aside through the controlling courts is not possible.[58] The Rules contain exhaustively enumerated, targeted remedies; absent which, the tribunal should remain *functus officio*.

2. Binding force

27. Article 34(2) is principally directed to the binding force that a tribunal has 'on the parties', hence it contains a separate injunction to the effect that '[t]he parties shall carry out awards without delay'. Although it was noted in the revision process that the obligation to carry out an award goes without saying given an award's binding force, it was decided to retain that wording from the

---

E, para. 27 et seq. (tribunal rejected the proposition that a partial award could be reviewed following resignation of an arbitrator who had been subject to a challenge).

52 *See* Christoph H. Schreuer, Loretta Malintoppi, August Reinisch & Anthony Sinclair, *The ICSID Convention, A Commentary*, 879 et seq. (2nd ed., Cambridge University Press 2009); *see also Victor Pey Casado and President Allende Foundation v. Republic of Chile* (ICSID Case No. ARB/98/2) Decision (on Revision), 18 November 2009, <www.italaw.com> (request for revision found to be inadmissible).

53 *See* Article 38 of the International Law Commission's 1958 Model Rules on Arbitral Procedure, YBILC 86 (1958-II).

54 *Antoine Biloune and Marine Drive Complex Ltd v. Ghana Investments Centre and the Government of Ghana* (UNCITRAL) Award on Damages and Costs, 30 June 1990, XIX YCA 11 (1994), paras 33-34.

55 *Henry Morris v. Government of the Islamic Republic of Iran* (1983) 3 Iran-US CTR 364, 365.

56 Baker & Davis, *supra* fn 17, at 200.

57 ILA International Commercial Arbitration Committee Resolution No. 4/2016, 7-11 August 2016, Annex, <www.ila-hq.org>.

58 Caron & Caplan, *supra* fn 6, at 829.

1976 text on the basis that it made it plain that compliance with an award is a matter of 'urgency'.[59]

28. Nevertheless, it is clear that an award's binding force is also foundation for its preclusive effect on further litigation of issues decided (i.e. res judicata). That effect is also directed to the tribunal, which, after having issued an issue in a partial award, can no longer revisit its decision through subsequent awards.[60]

29. Article 34(2) provides that 'all' awards are binding, and therefore does not leave room for a process of an appeal on the merits to another arbitral tribunal. (That is a possibility envisaged in Article V(1)(e) of the New York Convention, which refers in material part to an award that 'has not yet become binding on the parties'.)[61] If the parties wish to cater for such a process (which is exceedingly rare in general practice), they will have to make special provision for it and define when an award will become binding.

3. Waiver of recourse against the award

30. From the outset of the revision process, it was noted that the quality of finality stated in the 1976 Rules (and reiterated *verbatim* in the 2010 Rules) did 'not fully convey that the award was subject to no appeal in the courts'.[62] It was therefore proposed that the revised Rules should expressly state that 'the award shall be subject to no appeal'. Such a rule, found in the ICC Rules and LCIA Rules,[63] was primarily intended to exclude appeals on points of law (notably under section 69 of the English Arbitration Act 1996) but not the remedy of setting aside.[64]

31. There was initially general consensus on such a rule,[65] and several draft iterations of article 34 included it.[66] For example, an early draft provided that 'appeal, review

---

59 *See* UNCITRAL Summary Record of the 17th Meeting, 26 April 1976, UN Doc A/CN.9/9/C.2/SR.17, para. 16, Mr Boston (Sierra Leone).

60 *See* fns 1 and 18 and the accompanying text, *supra*.

61 Article V(1)(e) of the New York Convention.

62 Jan Paulsson & Georgios Petrochilos, *Revision of the UNCITRAL Rules* (September 2006), para. 250, fn 244, <www.uncitral.org> ('In particular, the French text of the Rules renders the term "final" as: "Elle [la sentence] n'est pas susceptible d'appel *devant une instance arbitrale*" (emphasis added). It is not clear from the *travaux* why this formulation was preferred to alternative, broader ones' (citing also UNCITRAL Summary Record of the 10th Meeting, 21 April 1976, UN Doc A/CN.9/9/C.2/SR.10, paras 76-77 ('[sentence] rendue en dernier ressort'); and UNCITRAL Summary Record of the 17th Meeting, 26 April 1976, UN Doc A/CN.9/9/C.2/SR.17, paras 18-19 ('[sentence] qui n'est plus susceptible de voie de recours')).

63 *Ibid.*, (noting that the proposed wording is formulated 'as a positive rule ... rather than as a constructive waiver of the right to appeal'); *see also* Article 26.9 of the 1998 LCIA Rules; Article 28(6) of the 1998 ICC Rules.

64 *Ibid.*, at paras 250-251.

65 UNCITRAL Report of 47th Session, 25 September 2007, UN Doc A/CN.9/641, paras 85-90; UNCITRAL Report of 51st Session, 10 November 2009, UN Doc A/CN.9/684, paras 71-86.

66 *See*, e.g., UNCITRAL Note by the Secretariat, 5 March 2010, UN Doc A/CN.9/703/Add.1, para. 16; and UNCITRAL Report of 51st Session, 10 November 2009, UN Doc A/CN.9/684,

or recourse' was excluded but 'set aside' explicitly safeguarded.[67] Gradually, concerns started being expressed. It was noted, for instance, that in some jurisdictions the notion of set-aside encompassed challenges on the merits.[68] Overall the difficulty perceived by some delegations was one of formulation, namely how to encapsulate appeals on questions of fact or law, as was intended,[69] without affecting the right to seek setting aside or resist recognition or enforcement.[70] The Working Group considered several drafting alternatives, but continued concern was expressed regarding the scope of the intended waiver and how it would operate in various jurisdictions.[71] To be sure, there was an air of unreality in this debate, as the corresponding provisions in other arbitration rules have never given rise to ambiguity, not least because setting aside cannot be excluded by agreement of the parties (and even in the very few jurisdictions where it can, specific agreement is required). In time, a further difficulty was added, namely a suggestion that sovereign immunity defences should be expressly carved out of a waiver rule.

32. In the end the Working Group was unable to arrive at a formulation attracting full consensus and catering to all concerns (real and perceived). It relegated the waiver to the Annex, where a 'possible waiver statement' is included as guidance to parties adopting the UNCITRAL Rules. This is drafted in very capacious terms, covering 'any form of recourse against an award'. A note included in the Annex rightly cautions the parties that the effectiveness of such an exclusion of recourse 'depend[s] on the applicable law'.

F. CONFIDENTIALITY OR PUBLICATION: ARTICLE 34(5)

33. As under many other sets of arbitration rules,[72] article 34(5) gives effect to confidentiality. The 1976 text was retained in that regard, and this is an important

para. 71.

67 UNCITRAL Working Paper for 46th Session, 6 December 2006, UN Doc A/CN.9/WG.II/WP.145/Add.1, 15-16.

68 *See* UNCITRAL Report of 51st Session, 10 November 2009, UN Doc A/CN.9/684, paras 79-82.

69 *Ibid.*, at para. 73; UNCITRAL Report of 47th Session, 25 September 2007, UN Doc A/CN.9/641, paras 87-90 (the drafters did not want a waiver of set-aside rights 'being given automatically or merely (and possibly inadvertently) through the submission of a dispute to the Rules').

70 *See* UNCITRAL Report of 51st Session, 10 November 2009, UN Doc A/CN.9/684, paras 71-73.

71 *See* UNCITRAL Summary Record of the 903rd Meeting, 22 June 2010, UN Doc A/CN.9/SR.903, XLI UNCITRAL Ybk 1220, 1226 para. 69, The Chairperson. *See also* Report of the Commission on its 43rd Session, 21 June-9 July 2010, UN Doc A/65/17, para. 143.

72 *See*, e.g., Article 30.1 of the LCIA Rules; Article 44 of the Swiss Rules; Article 9 of the SCC Rules; Article 37(1) of the AAA International Arbitration Rules. Note, however, that the 2010 Rules do not reflect the practice of the Iran-US Claims Tribunal, which allowed public access to its decisions since the Government of Iran was party to almost all cases and would have otherwise gained an unfair advantage over US claimants from its resultant knowledge. On this point, *see* Baker & Davis, *supra* fn 17, at 173-174.

provision when the *lex arbitri* does not provide for confidentiality as the default provision or, to the contrary, it provides for an absence of confidentiality. Parties may obviously derogate from confidentiality by agreement, and increasingly they do so in investor-state proceedings even where the Transparency Rules do not apply on their own terms.

34. The terms of article 34(5) – that the award 'may [not] be made public' – seem to confer broad confidentiality protection, covering both the text of the award but also its existence and content. Thus summaries of an award are prohibited by article 34(5), except perhaps if anonymized and excised/redacted of particulars that could identify the parties or the dispute. By contrast, the provision does not cover voluntary disclosure within the organization of a corporate entity that was a party in the arbitration, or to analogous recipients such as counsel, advisors, or consultants, provided that they, too, are under a duty of confidentiality.[73]

35. Also, article 34(5) covers only awards, just as article 28(3) covers only hearings. There is no express confidentiality protection for the existence of the arbitration and the identity of the parties, nor in respect of written pleadings, the evidential record, or tribunal decisions other than awards. It is arguable that these aspects of confidentiality are necessarily implied by articles 34(5) and 28(3), on grounds that these articles would be undermined by publicizing other aspects of the process. Such an argument, though analytically tenable, will be difficult to sustain in jurisdictions which start from a default rule of non-confidentiality, if the parties chose to site the proceedings in such a jurisdiction.

36. Although all other paragraphs in article 34 are directed to duties to be complied with by the tribunal, paragraph (5) is directed to both the tribunal and the parties. (Typically, confidentiality undertakings are included in acceptance forms prepared by arbitral institutions for arbitrators.) Thus both the parties and the tribunal are bound to preserve confidentiality, as are also third persons who participated in the process and may accordingly be said to have accepted relevant duties under the Rules, such as tribunal secretaries/assistants, witnesses, party or tribunal experts, court reporters, interpreters and translators.[74]

37. The unqualified confidentiality rule in article 32(5) of the 1976 Rules needed to be brought in line with modern realities. It was recognized that it caused practical difficulties where a party needed to rely on the award to enforce it or to protect its rights (e.g. as a defence in later proceedings with a third party, or to sustain a res judicata objection), or where other circumstances so required[75] (for example to comply with disclosure obligations of significant events for listed companies, or to satisfy duties vis-à-vis competition authorities). Article 34(5) of the 2010 Rules therefore provides exceptions to the confidentiality of awards in circumstances where and to the extent that disclosure is required (i) 'by legal duty' or (ii) 'to protect or pursue a legal right, or in relation to legal proceedings'.

---

73 Thomas H. Webster, *Handbook of UNCITRAL Arbitration*, para. 34-131 (2nd ed., Sweet & Maxwell 2015).

74 *See* Born, *supra* fn 17, at 2803-2804.

75 UNCITRAL Report of 47th Session, 25 September 2007, UN Doc A/CN.9/641, para. 96.

G. COMMUNICATION OF THE AWARD: ARTICLE 34(6)

38. Copies of the award must be transmitted to the parties in a prompt manner. No specific deadline is set down, although some national arbitration laws may impose time-limits in this respect.[76] Communication of the award does, however, trigger the 30-day time-limit provided in articles 37-39 of the Rules, which govern post-award proceedings.[77] Communication of the award also notifies the parties of their rights and obligations under the award; triggers their obligation to 'carry out all awards without delay' under article 34(2); and provides the parties with documentation necessary for enforcement.[78]

39. Article 32(7) of the 1976 Rules required that the tribunal comply with any requirement of the law of the country where the award was made that the award be filed or registered within the timeframe provided by that law.[79] This somewhat archaic requirement, found in few laws, was removed from article 34 of the 2010 Rules, on the basis that it was an 'onerous burden' for the tribunal 'in countries where registration requirements were ambiguous'.[80] It was also considered unnecessary, considering that tribunals are under an article 1(3) general duty to comply with mandatory requirements of national law.[81]

---

76 Castello, *supra* fn 18, at 251.

77 Including the interpretation and correction of an award, and additional awards. *See* discussion of articles 37, 38 and 39, *infra*.

78 *See* Article 35 of the UNCITRAL Model Law; and Article IV(1) of the New York Convention.

79 Article 32(7) of the 1976 Rules.

80 UNCITRAL Report of 45th Session, 5 October 2006, UN Doc A/CN.9/614, para. 117.

81 UNCITRAL Report of 47th Session, 25 September 2007, UN Doc A/CN.9/641, paras 101-105.

Article 35
Applicable law, *amiable compositeur*

1976 Rules Article 33: Applicable law, *amiable compositeur*	2010 Rules Article 35: Applicable law, *amiable compositeur*
1. The arbitral tribunal shall apply the law designated by the parties as applicable to the substance of the dispute. Failing such designation by the parties, the arbitral tribunal shall apply the law determined by the conflict of laws rules which it considers applicable.	1. The arbitral tribunal shall apply the rules of law designated by the parties as applicable to the substance of the dispute. Failing such designation by the parties, the arbitral tribunal shall apply the law which it determines to be appropriate.
2. The arbitral tribunal shall decide as *amiable compositeur* or *ex aequo et bono* only if the parties have expressly authorized the arbitral tribunal to do so and if the law applicable to the arbitral procedure permits such arbitration.	2. The arbitral tribunal shall decide as *amiable compositeur* or *ex aequo et bono* only if the parties have expressly authorized the arbitral tribunal to do so.
3. In all cases, the arbitral tribunal shall decide in accordance with the terms of the contract and shall take into account the usages of the trade applicable to the transaction.	3. In all cases, the arbitral tribunal shall decide in accordance with the terms of the contract, if any, and shall take into account any usage of trade applicable to the transaction.

1. Article 35 concerns the 'rules of law' or the law applicable to the substance of the dispute, which is a notion different from the law applicable to the arbitration (the *lex arbitri*).[1] Like most arbitration rules, article 35(1) gives effect to party autonomy in the choice of the rules that will apply on the merits of the dispute. It also provides for the situation where the parties have failed to make such a

1 Nigel Blackaby, Constantine Partasides, Alan Redfern & Martin J. Hunter, *Redfern and Hunter on International Arbitration*, para. 3.37 (6th ed., Kluwer 2015).

choice, in which case the tribunal will apply the law 'which it determines to be appropriate'. Article 35(2) addresses the tribunal's power to decide the case as *amiable compositeur* or *ex aequo et bono*, and article 35(3) stresses the importance of the terms of the contract, and, secondarily, of trade usages.[2]

2. These three components are addressed separately below.

A. APPLICABLE LAW: ARTICLE 35(1)

1. Party autonomy

3. The doctrine of party autonomy in the choice of law applicable to the substance of a dispute is recognized in both the 1976 Rules and the 2010 Rules, as well as in most other arbitration rules, international conventions and national laws.[3] The tribunal must accordingly give effect to the choice of the parties. This may in principle be a tacit but clear choice in the main contract or the arbitration agreement, or, alternatively, in a separate agreement after the commencement of the proceedings.[4] A choice of substantive law should not be inferred 'merely from the selection of the place of the arbitration', which 'can and often does reflect quite different considerations'.[5]

2. 'Rules of law' designated by the parties

4. Article 33(1) of the 1976 Rules provides that the tribunal 'shall apply the law designated by the parties'. In contrast, article 35(1) of the 2010 Rules states that the arbitral tribunal 'shall apply the *rules of law* designated by the parties' (emphasis added).[6] This is a major change, and it is consistent with the UNCITRAL Model Law.[7]

---

[2] *See* David D. Caron & Lee M. Caplan, *The UNCITRAL Arbitration Rules, A Commentary*, 111 (2nd ed., Oxford University Press 2013), citing UNCITRAL Report of the Secretary-General on the Preliminary Draft Set of Arbitration Rules, 4 November 1974, UN Doc A/CN.9/97, VI UNCITRAL Ybk 163, 178. *See also* W. Laurence Craig, William W. Park & Jan Paulsson, *International Chamber of Commerce Arbitration*, 319 et seq. (3rd ed., Oceana Publications 2000).

[3] *See* UNCITRAL Report of the Secretary General on the Draft UNCITRAL Arbitration Rules, 12 December 1975, UN Doc A/CN.9/112/Add.1, 178. *See also* Article 28(1) of the Model Law and Article 42 of the ICSID Convention. *See also*, e.g., Article 21(1) of the ICC Rules; Article 16.4 of the LCIA Rules; Article 33(1) of the Swiss Rules; and Article 61(a) of the WIPO Rules.

[4] Caron & Caplan, *supra* fn 2, at 113.

[5] *Ibid.*, citing Robert von Mehren, *Arbitration in Central and Eastern Europe*, Arb J 38, 40 (1992) and Ole Lando, *The Law Applicable to the Merits of the Dispute*, 2 Arb Intl 104, 107-108 (1986).

[6] Prior to its inclusion in the UNCITRAL Model Law, the term 'rules of law' was used only in the 1965 Washington Convention on the Settlement of Investment Disputes and the arbitration laws of France and Djibouti. *See* UNCITRAL Working Paper for 45th Session, 20 July 2006, UN Doc A/CN.9/WG.II/WP.143/Add.1, para. 30.

[7] *See*, e.g., UNCITRAL Report of 45th Session, 5 October 2006, UN Doc A/CN.9/614, para. 122; UNCITRAL Report of 47th Session, 25 September 2007, UN Doc A/CN.9/641, para.

5. The 2010 Rules employ the term 'rules of law' because of its broader scope, which enables the parties 'to designate as applicable to their case rules of more than one legal system, including rules of law which have been elaborated on the international level'.[8] This last source refers to international treaties (such as the Vienna Convention on the International Sale of Goods of 1980) or 'non-national sets of rules or principles', such as the UNIDROIT Principles of International Commercial Contracts.[9] Although the drafters of the Model Law appear to have intended that the expression be interpreted narrowly, exclusive of 'general legal principles' and 'law developed in arbitration awards',[10] the expression was given broader scope in the years following the Model Law's promulgation and it was interpreted as including 'legal rules pertaining to notions of a transnational law, *lex mercatoria* or general principles of law'.[11] The reference to 'rules of law' in the UNCITRAL Rules is therefore to be understood as meaning any body of legal rules.[12]

6. Although the application of the *lex mercatoria* has been subject to controversy, its application having been (rightly) criticised as 'uncertain' and 'elusive',[13] and seems to find little traction in contemporary arbitral practice, where the *lex arbitri* allows the parties to designate the *lex mercatoria* or general principles of commercial law as the substantive law applicable to the dispute, the tribunal

107; and UNCITRAL Report of 51st Session, 10 November 2009, UN Doc A/CN.9/684, para. 91. This modification also brought the Rules into line with a number of national arbitration laws: *see* Yves Derains & Eric A. Schwartz, *A Guide to the ICC Rules of Arbitration*, 235, fn 84 (2nd ed., Kluwer 2005) (offering a presentation of the chronological order in which various States have adopted the 'rules of law' notion into their national arbitration laws). *See also* Article 28 of the Model Law.

8 *See* UNCITRAL Working Paper for 45th Session, 20 July 2006, UN Doc A/CN.9/WG.II/WP.143/Add.1, para. 30. *See also* Jan Paulsson & Georgios Petrochilos, *Revision of the UNCITRAL Rules* (September 2006), para. 259, <www.uncitral.org>.

9 Jason Fry, Simon Greenberg & Francesca Mazza, *The Secretariat's Guide to ICC Arbitration*, para. 3-761 (ICC 2012) (noting that 'rules of law' may also include, for example, 'the Principles of European Contract Law, INCOTERMS, model laws prepared by UNCITRAL, and any principles of public international law that may be applicable (e.g. in investment treaty arbitration)'); *see also* ICC, *The UNIDROIT Principles of International Commercial Contracts in ICC Arbitration, 1999-2001*, 12(2) ICA Bulletin 49 (2001).

10 Derains & Schwartz, *supra* fn 7, at 235, citing Howard M. Holtzmann & Joseph E. Neuhaus, *A Guide to the UNCITRAL Model Law on International Commercial Arbitration, Legislative History and Commentary*, 768 (2nd ed., Kluwer 1995). When drafting the Model Law, which heavily influenced article 35 of the 2010 Rules, the Working Group specifically refused to accept an interpretation of the term 'rules of law' that included general principles of law or case law developed in arbitral awards; *see* UNCITRAL Report of 6th Session, 22 September 1983, UN Doc A/CN.9/245, XV UNCITRAL Ybk 155, 165 para. 94.

11 Marc Blessing, 'Regulations in Arbitration Rules on Choice of Law' in Albert Jan van den Berg (ed), *Planning Efficient Arbitration Proceedings: The Law Applicable in International Arbitration*, 7 ICCA Congress Series 391 (1996).

12 *See* Report of the Commission on its 43rd Session, 21 June-9 July 2010, UN Doc A/65/17, para. 155.

13 Derains & Schwartz, *supra* fn 7, at 236.

should respect that choice.[14] Although the Iran-US Claims Tribunal did not always specify the source of the law it applied, it did often apply *lex mercatoria* or general principles of law, even in the face of the parties' choice of law.[15]

7. The designated 'rules of law' need not be in force at the time of designation. In fact, a specific intention in Article 28(1) of the UNCITRAL Model Law was to allow the parties to designate conventions not yet in force.[16] Caron and Caplan argue that the parties' choice of a law not yet in force should be respected, adding the reservation – which does not seem to have an obvious foundation – that its application should not be inconsistent with the domestic law otherwise applicable.[17] As already noted, the notion of 'rules of law' also promotes party autonomy in that it respects the will of the parties to elect different legal systems to govern various aspects of their relationships (*dépeçage*).[18] Finally, the new article 35(1) more clearly allows tribunals to give effect to 'stabilized' choices of national law in agreement between investors and States.[19] Absent stabilization a choice of law is of course taken to mean the law of the State designated as it evolves over time.[20]

8. It was considered during the revision process whether the 2010 Rules should clarify that the parties' choice should be interpreted as referring only to 'the

14 *See* Caron & Caplan, *supra* fn 2, at 115, fn 21 (referring to, e.g., *Pabalk Ticaret Limited Sirketi v. Norsolor SA* (ICC Case No. 3131), 26 October 1979, IX YCA 109 (1984), where an award applying principles of *lex mercatoria* was enforced by the French courts; *Deutsche Schachtbau-und Tiefbohrgesellschaft mbH (DST) v. Ras Al Khaimah National Oil Co (Rakoil)* 3 WLR 1023 (1987), where an award applying internationally accepted principles of law was held by the Swiss courts as enforceable under the New York Convention).

15 *See* John R. Crook, *Applicable Law In International Commercial Arbitration: The Iran-US-Claims Tribunal Experience*, 83 AJIL 278 et seq. (1989). *See also* Stewart A. Baker & Mark D. Davis, *The UNCITRAL Arbitration Rules in Practice – The Experience of the Iran-United States Claims Tribunal*, 178-179 (Kluwer 1992) (referring in particular to *CMI International Inc v. Iran* (1983) 4 Iran-US CTR 263, 267-268, where 'the Tribunal ignored purchase order provisions that made the Idaho Uniform Commercial Code the law governing the contract ... stat[ing] that it preferred to analyze the issue in accordance with general principles of law'). *See also*, e.g., *Gould Marketing, Inc v. Ministry of National Defense of Iran* (1983) 3 Iran-US CTR 147, 152-153; *Starrett Housing Corporation v. Government of the Islamic Republic of Iran* (1983) 4 Iran-US CTR Rep 122, 155; *Sylvania Technical Systems Inc v. Islamic Republic of Iran* (1985) 8 Iran-US CTR 298, 308-309; and *International Technical Products Corp v. Government of the Islamic Republic of Iran* (1985) 9 Iran-US CTR 10, 23-24.

16 *See* Holtzmann & Neuhaus, *supra* fn 10, at 766-768; Caron & Caplan, *supra* fn 2, at 116.

17 Caron & Caplan, *supra* fn 2, at 116 (stating, more specifically, that 'a convention not in force, but which has been designated as applicable law, should be applied along the same principle and with similar reservations as applicable to lex mercatoria'); *see also* Crook, *supra* fn 15.

18 Paulsson & Petrochilos, *supra* fn 8, at para. 259, citing Holtzmann & Neuhaus, *supra* fn 10, at 766-768 (where the authors note that use of the term 'rules of law' allows parties to 'choose the national law of any State and [to] choose the national laws of different States to govern various aspects of their relationship' under a single contract, or to 'have a given national law apply but exclude the provisions on a specific topic').

19 *See*, e.g., *Mobil Oil Iran Inc v. Islamic Republic of Iran* (1987) 16 Iran-US CTR 3, 20-28.

20 Caron & Caplan, *supra* fn 2, at 114.

substantive law of that State and not to its conflict-of-law rules', as provided in Article 28(1) of the UNCITRAL Model Law.[21] The Working Group concluded that this was unnecessary as the formulation 'designated by the parties as applicable to the substance of the dispute' left no room for ambiguity and excluded the possibility of *renvoi*,[22] unless the parties expressly state otherwise.

9. The autonomy of the parties to designate the rules of law applicable to their dispute is, however, limited by mandatory laws from which they cannot derogate,[23] to the extent the tribunal recognizes such as applicable. Mandatory rules apply on a unilateral basis, i.e. by determining the scope and circumstances of their application. Thus such mandatory rules may originate both from a legal system from which the parties selected 'rules of law' (e.g. the law on sales contracts of country X) and from the legal systems of other States or international organizations (such as the EU). For instance, the parties cannot choose the law applicable to their capacity or escape provisions of an applicable law that have status of public policy (including competition law).[24] Disregarding mandatory laws may render the award unenforceable or incapable of recognition under Article V(2) of the New York Convention.[25]

---

21 UNCITRAL Report of 51st Session, 10 November 2009, UN Doc A/CN.9/684, para. 92. *See also* Article 28(1) of the Model Law, which provides: '(1) The arbitral tribunal shall decide the dispute in accordance with such rules of law as are chosen by the parties ... Any designation of the law or legal system of a given State shall be construed, unless otherwise expressed, as directly referring to the substantive law of that State and not to its conflict of laws rules'.

22 UNCITRAL Report of 51st Session, 10 November 2009, UN Doc A/CN.9/684, para. 92. *See also* Peter Binder, *Analytical Commentary to the UNCITRAL Arbitration Rules*, para. 35-011 (Sweet & Maxwell 2013).

23 Blackaby, Partasides, Redfern & Hunter, *supra* fn 1, at paras 3.128-3.130 ('Thus, by way of example, Russian law may feature in the determination of corporate governance issues relating to a Russian company even if the arbitration arises from a shareholders agreement governed by Swedish law. In the same way, again by way of example, US-quoted companies cannot exclude the application of the Foreign Corrupt Practices Act of 1977 from the operations simply by concluding an investment agreement in Kazakhstan that is subject to Kazakh law').

24 This is also consistent with certain restrictions on 'freedom of choice' set out under the Rome Convention. *See* in particular Article 1(2)(a) (status or legal capacity of natural persons) and Article 3(3) (mandatory rules of law). *See* UNCITRAL Summary Record of the 906th Meeting, 23 June 2010, UN Doc A/CN.9/SR.906, XLI UNCITRAL Ybk 1242, 1244 para. 41, (Greece): 'There were matters of applicable law that were not dependent on the parties' choice, including the parties' capacity to enter into a transaction'.

25 *See* Report of the Commission on its 43rd Session, 21 June-9 July 2010, UN Doc A/65/17, para. 156; *see also* UNCITRAL Summary Record of the 906th Meeting, 23 June 2010, UN Doc A/CN.9/SR.906, XLI UNCITRAL Ybk 1242, 1244 para. 40, Ms Moss (Norway) ('It was also stated that, in any case, parties and the arbitral tribunal were not completely free to choose the applicable law. It was explained that the validity and enforceability of the award depended on the applicable law and on the Convention on the Recognition and Enforcement of Foreign Arbitral Awards (1958) (the New York Convention). For instance, under Article V of the New York Convention, an award was invalid or unenforceable if a party to the arbitration agreement was under some incapacity under its law, if the award

10. It is also the case that the parties' designation may not, on its true construction, cover all of the legal issues that pertain to the 'substance of the dispute'. Capacity and status, domicile, authority of agents, tortious liability are all examples of issues which are often not covered by designations of applicable law in commercial contracts. The conclusion is that while article 35(1) compels the application of the rules designated by the parties (again, subject to mandatory law), it does not compel the exclusive application of these rules: a host of other rules/laws may need to be applied to resolve the substantive dispute.

3. Applicable law in the absence of a designation

11. If the parties fail to designate the rules of law applicable to the substance of the dispute, the second limb of article 35(1) of the 2010 Rules provides that the arbitral tribunal is to apply the law that it deems appropriate. In contrast to article 33(1) of the 1976 Rules, and Article 28(2) of the UNCITRAL Model Law, tribunals are therefore no longer constrained to apply the conflict-of-laws rules that they consider applicable in order to identify the applicable law.[26] They may instead resort directly to a legal system that they consider appropriate – the so-called *voie directe*.

12. The revision process opened debates on a number of issues, which are helpful in understanding the provision that was ultimately adopted. The first was whether the provision should refer to 'law' or 'rules of law'.[27] One proposal, influenced by the ICC, LCIA and Swiss Rules, was to use the notion of 'rules of law', as used in the first limb of article 35(1) of the 2010 Rules.[28] The Working Group did not adopt this proposal, preferring to maintain consistency with the Model Law[29] and considering also that the removal of the reference to the conflict-of-laws rules, coupled with the reference to 'rules of law' in the first limb of paragraph 1, had sufficiently extended the parties' and tribunal's flexibility.[30]

13. A second issue was whether the reference to the conflict-of-laws rules should be replaced with a reference to the rules of law 'most closely connected to the

---

was on a matter that was not arbitrable under the law applied by the court or if it conflicted with the public policy of the forum. It was highlighted that relevant laws regarding legal capacity, arbitrability and public policy should be taken into consideration').

26 This is consistent with the practice of the Iran-US Claims Tribunal, which, when applying the 1976 Rules, 'effectively skipped the step of identifying an applicable system of choice of law rules and proceeded directly to choose the substantive body of law it found most appropriate to each dispute': *see* Baker & Davis, *supra* fn 15, at 180.

27 *See* UNCITRAL Report of 47th Session, 25 September 2007, UN Doc A/CN.9/641, paras 106-107.

28 *See* Article 17(1) of the 1998 ICC Rules; Article 22.3 of the 1998 LCIA Rules; and Article 33(1) of the 2004 Swiss Rules.

29 *See* UNCITRAL Report of 47th Session, 25 September 2007, UN Doc A/CN.9/641, paras 108-109.

30 *See* Report of the Commission on its 43rd Session, 21 June-9 July 2010, UN Doc A/65/17, para. 155. *See also* Binder, *supra* fn 22, at para. 35-014.

dispute'[31] (or a different wording ensuring that the law ultimately chosen would be the national law of a State).[32] The Working Group also debated whether the tribunal's discretion should be limited by reference to conflict-of-laws rules or, alternatively, by a requirement that the tribunal base its determination on 'objective criteria'.[33] However, it concluded that the tribunal's discretion was sufficiently constrained by the requirement that the award contain reasons, making express wording to that effect unnecessary.[34]

14. Ultimately, the proposal that attracted consensus, as reflected in the formulation adopted, was that the Rules should afford the tribunal broad discretion in determining the applicable law, equivalent to that found in article 17 of the 1998 ICC Rules (i.e., '[i]n the absence of any such agreement, the Arbitral Tribunal shall apply the rules of law which it determines to be appropriate').[35]

15. The reference merely to 'the law', in the second limb of paragraph 1, may appear potentially to exclude the application of a multitude of laws in one dispute. However, the intention was merely to make a distinction with 'rules of law'. As one author puts it, 'tribunals (in default of any party choice) may only choose to apply ... national law', because it is likely that, 'when parties cannot agree on a choice of law ... they nonetheless expect their dispute to be governed by a national law, rather than by the arbitrator's own determination, for example, of *lex mercatoria*'.[36] The *travaux* reveal that it is intended for the tribunal to be able to apply different laws:

> [I]n international arbitration, it was not unusual that more than one law had to be applied to deal with different issues, such as capacity or corporate matters. After discussion, the Working Group was of the view that the

31 *See* UNCITRAL Working Paper for 46th Session, 6 December 2006, UN Doc A/CN.9/WG.II/WP.145/Add.1, para. 38. In support of this proposal, it was noted that it would 'offer the opportunity to modernize the Rules by allowing the arbitral tribunal to decide directly on the applicability of such instruments as e.g., the United Nations Convention on Contracts for the International Sale of Goods, the Unidroit Principles of International Commercial Contracts, texts adopted by the International Chamber of Commerce, such as the Incoterms and the Uniform Customs and Practices for Documentary Credit, or *lex mercatoria*': *see* UNCITRAL Report of 47th Session, 25 September 2007, UN Doc A/CN.9/641, para. 110.

32 There was also a suggested variant of the wording of article 33(1) of the 1976 Rules, which maintained the reference to conflict-of-laws rules, but provided that this 'could only result in the application of a national law and placed the arbitral tribunal in the same situation as a State court having to determine which law should govern a dispute in the absence of designation by the parties, with the additional obligation for the arbitral tribunal to choose the conflict-of-laws rules to be used for that determination'. However, this variant did not find broad support; in particular, it was emphasized that the wording 'did not provide guidance to the arbitral tribunal in its determination of the conflict-of-laws rules': *see* UNCITRAL Report of 47th Session, 25 September 2007, UN Doc A/CN.9/641, para. 110.

33 *See* UNCITRAL Report of 51st Session, 10 November 2009, UN Doc A/CN.9/684, para. 95.

34 *Ibid.*

35 *Ibid.*, at para. 94; UNCITRAL Report of 47th Session, 25 September 2007, UN Doc A/CN.9/641, para. 111.

36 James E. Castello, 'UNCITRAL Arbitration Rules, Section IV, Article 35' in Loukas A. Mistelis (ed), *Concise International Arbitration*, 252 (2nd ed., Kluwer 2015).

provision was drafted in sufficiently broad terms and it was understood that *the tribunal might apply different laws*, depending on the issues at stake. (emphasis added)[37]

16. A major intention was, as noted, to set forth a 'flexible solution' that 'would modernize the Rules by allowing the arbitral tribunal to decide directly on the applicability of the appropriate law'.[38] The *Sapphire* arbitration is an early example of this '*voie directe*' method, which 'gives arbitrators the freedom to choose as they please'.[39] In *Sapphire*, the tribunal held that–

> [c]ontrary to a State judge, who is bound to conform to the conflict law rules of the State in whose name he metes out justice, the arbitrator is not bound by such rules. He must look for the common intention of the parties, and use the connecting factors generally used in doctrine and in case law and must disregard national peculiarities.[40]

B. *AMIABLE COMPOSITEUR/EX AEQUO ET BONO*: ARTICLE 35(2)

17. Both notions, *amiable compositeur* and an *ex aequo et bono* decision, release a tribunal from observing rules of law and allow it to rely on equitable considerations.[41] These terms appear as separate, alternate concepts in both the 1976 and 2010 Rules, because the Working Group hoped to accommodate the different terms existing in various legal systems and literature.[42] Despite this, 'the increasing practice of international arbitral tribunals' is to view the concepts together as a reference to general principles of equity.[43]

18. Authorisation by the parties for the tribunal to decide as *amiable compositeur* or *ex aequo et bono* 'does not mean that an arbitrator cannot apply rules of substantive law, it simply removes the imperative or obligatory character of such law and allows the arbitrator to choose that which he wishes to apply'.[44] And '[t]o the extent that they do agree, commentators seem to suggest that even

---

37 UNCITRAL Report of 51st Session, 10 November 2009, UN Doc A/CN.9/684, para. 96.

38 *Ibid.*, at para. 94.

39 Blackaby, Partasides, Redfern & Hunter, *supra* fn 1, at para. 3.213.

40 *Sapphire International Petroleum Ltd v. The National Iranian Oil Company*, 13 ICLQ 1011 (1964).

41 Blackaby, Partasides, Redfern & Hunter, *supra* fn 1, at para. 3.195; Caron & Caplan, *supra* fn 2, at 119-121.

42 *See* Report of the Commission on its 9th Session, 12 April-7 May 1976, UN Doc A/31/17, para. 175; UNCITRAL Summary Record of the 14th Meeting, 23 April 1976, UN Doc A/CN.9/9/C.2/SR.14, para. 19, Mr Holtzmann (United States of America) (noting that 'different legal systems [place] different interpretations on the two terms. Furthermore, there [is] disagreement among legal scholars as to their exact meaning. Consequently, the sponsors of the proposal [have] decided to include both terms in the text so that parties would be free to use either, depending on the legal system to be applied').

43 Blackaby, Partasides, Redfern & Hunter, *supra* fn 1, at para. 3.196.

44 Bernard G. Poznanski, *The Nature and Extent of an Arbitrator's Powers in International Commercial Arbitration*, 4(3) J Int Arb 71, 78 (1987).

an arbitral tribunal that decides "in equity" must act in accordance with some generally accepted legal principles'.[45]

19. Article 33 of the 1976 Rules subjected the authority of the arbitral tribunal to decide as *amiable compositeur* or *ex aequo et bono* to two cumulative conditions: (i) the express authorization of the parties; and (ii) the permission to do so by 'the law applicable to the arbitral procedure' (which meant the 'law applicable to the arbitration', as in article 1(2) of the 1976 Rules).[46] In line with other sets of arbitration rules,[47] the only explicit condition retained in the 2010 Rules is that the tribunal be expressly authorized to do so by the parties.[48] The parties may provide this authorization in the arbitration agreement or in a separate agreement. Although case-law examples under the 1976 Rules or the 2010 Rules which demonstrate a tribunal's determination of a dispute either as *amiable compositeur* or *ex aequo et bono* are scant, the practice of other tribunals indicates that such express authorization may be provided orally before the arbitrators, for example, at a pre-hearing conference or at a hearing.[49]

20. The Rules are emphatic that the parties' authorization must be 'express' – a requirement conspicuously absent in respect of the parties' choice of law or rules – but they do not spell out the consequences of a tribunal's proceeding to resolve the dispute as an *amiable compositeur* without such authorization. The burden of showing that this was the case is of course high: it would require a clear showing that the tribunal failed altogether to apply the law, or subordinated the law to the equities of the case; and much would likely turn on the role, if any, that the parties' agreement or the applicable law/rules grant to equitable considerations. But if such a transgression is proved, there can be no doubt in the authors' submission that it should be regarded as a grave one. Nevertheless, it is not entirely clear – although decided cases are scarce – on what basis the resulting award should be set aside. One can make a cogent case for treating this is as a failure by the tribunal to comply with the parties' agreed procedure,

45 Blackaby, Partasides, Redfern & Hunter, *supra* fn 1, at para. 3.193.

46 Pieter Sanders, *Commentary on UNCITRAL Arbitration Rules*, II YCA 172, 210 (1977). Sanders notes that it is the law applicable to the arbitration, which is 'well distinguished from the law applicable to the substance of the dispute', that determines whether the tribunal may exercise this power.

47 *See*, e.g., Article 21(3) of the ICC Rules; Article 22.4 of the LCIA Rules; Article 27(3) of the SCC Rules.

48 For guidance as to what may constitute the parties' express authorization, *see Liberty Reinsurance Canada v. QBE Insurance and Reinsurance (Europe) Ltd* [2002] CanLII 6636 (ON SC) (where the Canadian Court, applying Article 28(3) of the UNCITRAL Model Law, held that there had been no express authorization by the parties with respect to an arbitration clause which provided that the contract should be interpreted as an 'honourable agreement', and that the tribunal was to be relieved of 'all judicial formalities' in reaching its decision).

49 *See*, e.g., *Benvenuti & Bonfant v. People's Republic of the Congo* (ICSID) Award of 8 August 1980, 21 ILM 740 (1982), para. 122 (where the agreement of the parties to allow the tribunal to decide *ex aequo et bono* was presented to the arbitrators in the form of minutes of meeting).

i.e. the need for an express authorization, or as an excess of jurisdiction (cf. Article 34(2)(a)(iv) and (iii) of the Model Law, respectively).[50] But it must be recognized that one would be asking the reviewing court to go into the merits of the tribunal's decision, which is in principle impermissible. Indeed, the Swiss Supreme Court seems to dither on this issue, having at times considered it either as a reviewable jurisdictional issue or a non-reviewable issue of the merits.[51]

21. The condition in article 33(2) of the 1976 Rules that 'the law applicable to the arbitral procedure permits such arbitration' was not included in article 35(2) of the 2010 Rules, as the Working Group intended to align the formulation of the revised provision with those found in other arbitration rules, and also viewed this phrase as unnecessary given that a conflicting mandatory provision of the *lex arbitri* would prevail pursuant to article 1(2) in any event.[52]

C. TERMS OF THE CONTRACT AND USAGES OF TRADE: ARTICLE 35(3)

22. Article 33(3) of the 1976 Rules provided that the arbitral tribunal 'shall decide in accordance with the terms of the contract and shall take into account the usages of the trade applicable to the transaction'. A similar provision is found in Article 28(4) of the UNCITRAL Model Law.[53] As noted by Sanders, article 33(3) prioritizes the terms of the contract over trade usages, in that the tribunal's decision 'must be made "in accordance with" the contract, whilst trade usages must be "taken into account"'; as such, 'the contract ranks first'.[54] This remains true of article 35(2) of the 2010 Rules.

23. Two changes were made in article 35(3) of the 2010 Rules. First, the wording 'if any' was added after the reference to the terms of the contract in order to recognize that, in cases proceeding under a treaty, a contract may not be the legal basis of the claim. Second, 'the usages of the trade' was replaced with 'any usage of trade' in the 2010 Rules, which makes it clearer that the tribunal is not directed

---

50 For the latter view *see*, e.g., Gary B. Born, *International Commercial Arbitration*, 3555 (2nd ed., Kluwer 2014).

51 *See* Tobias Zuberbühler, Christoph Müller & Philipp A. Habegger, *Swiss Rules of International Arbitration: Commentary*, 372 (2nd ed., Juris Publishing 2013); and Gabrielle Kaufmann-Kohler & Antonio Rigozzi, *International Arbitration: Law and Practice in Switzerland*, para. 7.80 and the references (Oxford University Press 2015).

52 *See* UNCITRAL Working Paper for 45th Session, 20 July 2006, UN Doc A/CN.9/WG.II/WP.143/Add.1, para. 31 (noting that 'certain arbitration centres (article 17.3 of the ICC Rules, article 22.4 of the LCIA Rules and article 28.3 of the AAA International Arbitration Rules) require authorization by the parties for the arbitral tribunal to decide as amiable compositeur or *ex aequo et bono* and do not include a requirement that the law applicable to the arbitral procedure permit an arbitration to be decided *ex aequo et bono*'); Caron & Caplan, *supra* fn 2, at 120.

53 Article 28(4) of the Model Law states: 'In all cases, the arbitral tribunal shall decide in accordance with the terms of the contract and shall take into account the usages of the trade applicable to the transaction'.

54 *See* Sanders, *supra* fn 46, at 210 (further noting that '[t]his distinction, after long discussions, was made on purpose' by the drafters of the 1976 Rules).

to ascertain the corpus of trade usages but simply to identify any one that may fall to be taken account of.[55] Nevertheless, the *travaux* of both the 1976 and 2010 Rules offer no particular guidance as to what falls within the notion of 'usage of trade',[56] probably because it was thought self-evident in 1976. Commentators have suggested that the determination should be informed by Article 1(9) of the UNIDROIT Principles of International Contracts.[57]

24. Both article 35(3) and its predecessor provide that the tribunal must decide in accordance with the terms of the contract and take any usages of trade into account 'in all cases', irrespective of whether the law was designated by the parties, by the tribunal, or whether the tribunal is deciding as *amiable compositeur* or *ex aequo et bono*. The intention was to give effect to the parties' expectations, consistent with similar provisions in arbitration texts.[58] The tribunal must therefore first apply the terms of the contract.[59]

25. One issue which arose during the 2010 revision process was whether the word 'contract' was broad enough to encompass all types of agreement which might form the basis of a transaction.[60] With a view to broadening the scope of this provision, one proposal was to replace 'contract' with 'agreement' as, in some jurisdictions, the term 'contract' was narrowly defined, whereas the term 'agreement' was understood to include contracts and other forms of agreements. The proposal failed in the face of three objections. The first was

---

55 UNCITRAL Report of 47th Session, 25 September 2007, UN Doc A/CN.9/641, para. 113.

56 *See Mesa Power Group LLC v. Government of Canada* (UNCITRAL) Award, 24 March 2016, < www.italaw.com > (where the claimant argued, pursuant to article 33(3) of the 1976 Rules, that the tribunal should consider the WTO Agreement on Government Procurement and the General Agreement on Tariffs and Trade when determining the meaning of 'procurement' under NAFTA. Canada did not refer to the 1976 Rules when putting forth its definition of 'procurement', but opposed the use of the GATT as an interpretive tool (at para. 381). In arriving at its decision, the tribunal did not rely on article 33 of the Rules, but instead relied on principles of interpretation set out in section 231 of the Treaty (para. 406). It did, however take into account the GATT).

57 Article 1(9) of the UNIDROIT Principles of International Contracts 2010 provides as follows: '(1) The parties are bound by any usage to which they have agreed and by any practice which they have established between themselves. (2) The parties are bound by a usage that is widely known to and regularly observed in international trade by parties in the particular trade concerned except where the application of such usage would be unreasonable'. *See also* Derains & Schwartz, *supra* fn 7, at 242-244 (addressing Article 17(2) of the 1998 ICC Rules (now Article 21(2) of the 2017 ICC Rules). The authors are careful to distinguish between trade usages on one hand and *lex mercatoria* on the other, stating that *lex mercatoria* 'is ordinarily intended to refer to legal rules arising out of international commerce. Trade usage, on the other hand, normally constitutes part of the parties' agreement … parties expect that the contracts they conclude, unless specifically agreed otherwise, will be performed in accordance with the usual practices observed in their area of business. Thus, unlike *lex mercatoria*, trade usage is generally internal, not external, to the parties' agreement'.

58 *See* UNCITRAL Report of the Secretary General on the Draft UNCITRAL Arbitration Rules, 12 December 1975, UN Doc A/CN.9/112/Add.1, 179, para. 7.

59 Caron & Caplan, *supra* fn 2, at 122-123.

60 *See* UNCITRAL Report of 51st Session, 10 November 2009, UN Doc A/CN.9/684, para. 99.

that in some jurisdictions only 'contracts' are legally enforceable.[61] The second was that consistency required maintaining the term 'contract', which was used in the corresponding provision of the UNCITRAL Model Law and the European Convention on International Commercial Arbitration of 1961; and that using different language could create difficulties for countries having enacted arbitration laws based on these instruments. The third objection was that the term 'contract' was used consistently throughout the Rules.[62] A further proposal to add the words 'or any other legal instrument' after the word 'contract' was also rejected, as 'legal instruments' could be taken to include investment treaties and other international instruments, to which article 35(3) may not apply at all, or with diminished effect.[63]

61 *Ibid.*
62 *Ibid.*
63 *Ibid.*

Article 36
Settlement or other grounds for termination

1976 Rules Article 34: Settlement or other grounds for termination	2010 Rules Article 36: Settlement or other grounds for termination
1. If, before the award is made, the parties agree on a settlement of the dispute, the arbitral tribunal shall either issue an order for the termination of the arbitral proceedings or, if requested by both parties and accepted by the tribunal, record the settlement in the form of an arbitral award on agreed terms. The arbitral tribunal is not obliged to give reasons for such an award. 2. If, before the award is made, the continuation of the arbitral proceedings becomes unnecessary or impossible for any reason not mentioned in paragraph 1, the arbitral tribunal shall inform the parties of its intention to issue an order for the termination of the proceedings. The arbitral tribunal shall have the power to issue such an order unless a party raises justifiable grounds for objection. 3. Copies of the order for termination of the arbitral proceedings or of the arbitral award on agreed terms, signed by the arbitrators, shall be communicated by the arbitral tribunal to the parties. Where an arbitral award on agreed terms is made, the provisions of article 32, paragraphs 2 and 4 to 7, shall apply.	1. If, before the award is made, the parties agree on a settlement of the dispute, the arbitral tribunal shall either issue an order for the termination of the arbitral proceedings or, if requested by the parties and accepted by the arbitral tribunal, record the settlement in the form of an arbitral award on agreed terms. The arbitral tribunal is not obliged to give reasons for such an award. 2. If, before the award is made, the continuation of the arbitral proceedings becomes unnecessary or impossible for any reason not mentioned in paragraph 1, the arbitral tribunal shall inform the parties of its intention to issue an order for the termination of the proceedings. The arbitral tribunal shall have the power to issue such an order unless there are remaining matters that may need to be decided and the arbitral tribunal considers it appropriate to do so. 3. Copies of the order for termination of the arbitral proceedings or of the arbitral award on agreed terms, signed by the arbitrators, shall be communicated by the arbitral tribunal to the parties. Where an arbitral award on agreed terms is made, the provisions of article 34, paragraphs 2, 4 and 5 shall apply.

1. Article 36 deals with situations where it becomes unnecessary or impossible for the tribunal to resolve the dispute by way of a final award, principally settlement and discontinuance. In so doing, it retains the substance of article 34 of the 1976 version and updates it in certain respects.

2. Parties to arbitration may resolve their dispute in the course of the arbitration. Like other sets of arbitration rules, the UNCITRAL Rules provide a procedure for the tribunal to follow in such cases.[1] Where the parties settle their dispute, the arbitral tribunal has two options under article 36(1) of the 2010 Rules, the text of which was originally inspired by Rule 43 of the ICSID Rules.[2] First, it may issue an order for the termination of the arbitral proceedings, in case the parties are content for their settlement to be memorialised only in a settlement agreement. Second, the tribunal may record the settlement in the form of an arbitral award on agreed terms, where (i) the parties have requested that it do so and (ii) the tribunal accepts the request.[3] A settlement award may be partial, i.e. cover some of the claims in dispute. This follows by parity of reasoning from article 39(1), which allows the tribunal to make an 'award' (as opposed to an 'additional award') if a termination order has left remaining matters undecided.

3. Article 36(2) of the 2010 Rules provides for the power of the tribunal to terminate the proceedings in situations other than settlement between the parties, where the continuation of the arbitral proceedings becomes impossible or unnecessary. This is principally the case where the claimant withdraws its claim.[4]

4. Article 36(3) sets out technical requirements for termination orders and awards on agreed terms, and subjects the latter to paragraphs 2, 4 and 5 of article 34 of the 2010 Rules, which set out formal and content-based requirements for arbitral awards.[5] The tribunal does not, however, have an obligation to provide reasons in an award on agreed terms.

---

[1] *See*, e.g., Article 34 of the Swiss Rules; Article 45 of the SCC Rules; Article 33 of the ICC Rules; and Article 26.9 of the LCIA Rules.

[2] *See* UNCITRAL Report of the Secretary General on the Draft UNCITRAL Arbitration Rules, 12 December 1975, UN Doc A/CN.9/112/Add.1, 179 para. 2.

[3] Note that the tribunal has discretion to refuse the parties' request: *see* Pieter Sanders, *Commentary on UNCITRAL Arbitration Rules*, II YCA 172, 211 (1977). Sanders notes that, as a general rule, arbitrators will be prepared to satisfy a request to incorporate the settlement into an award. *See also* Peter Turner & Reza Mohtashami, *A Guide to the LCIA Arbitration Rules*, para. 7.30 (Oxford University Press 2009) (noting that, under Article 26.8 of the 1998 LCIA Rules (now Article 26.9 of the 2014 LCIA Rules), the tribunal 'has discretion in deciding whether to accede to the parties' request for the issuance of a consent award').

[4] David D. Caron & Lee M. Caplan, *The UNCITRAL Arbitration Rules, A Commentary*, 788 (2nd ed., Oxford University Press 2013).

[5] *See* comments on article 34 of the 2010 Rules, *supra*. Paragraphs 2, 4 and 5 of article 34 address the 'final and binding' nature of awards, the signature and other formal requirements, and publication of the award, respectively.

A. SETTLEMENT OF THE DISPUTE: ARTICLE 36(1)

1. Termination order or award on agreed terms

(i) Termination orders

5. If the parties do not request to have their settlement agreement recorded in an award, the enforceability of their settlement is dependent on the applicable national law. In practice, parties may choose not to record their agreement if, for example, they are confident that its terms are easily enforceable or are self-executing (e.g. all claims are withdrawn and the status quo remains).[6] Although some authors (reasonably) argue that the parties should inform the tribunal of their settlement promptly, both as a matter of courtesy and in order to avoid incurring additional costs,[7] the Rules impose no time restrictions on the parties for informing the tribunal of such an agreement. It is difficult to conceive a strict procedural duty in that regard.

6. In any event, once informed, the tribunal will issue a termination order. A termination order is not intended to generate res judicata effect on the substance of the parties' claims.[8]

(ii) Advantages of awards on agreed terms

7. Recording the settlement through an award may consist in (a) merely recording that there has been a comprehensive or partial settlement and setting forth agreed dispositions accordingly; or (b) recording the terms of the settlement in the form of dispositions that can be enforced as an award. This has clear benefits. First, the settlement terms will be embodied in an instrument that constitutes an 'award' within the meaning of the Rules (and of course national law and the New York Convention).[9] Consequently, the settlement will acquire the same status as any other award rendered under the Rules, becoming enforceable and acquiring res judicata status.[10] Although settlement agreements are in principle

---

6 *See Government of the United States v. Islamic Republic of Iran*, Case No. B-25, Chamber One, Order of 17 November 1987, as referenced in Caron & Caplan, *supra* fn 4, at 782 (where the United States was content to withdraw its claim once the Tribunal received notification that the funds sought by the US Government had been transferred into its possession. Thereafter, enforcement was not required and neither was an award).

7 *See* Nigel Blackaby, Constantine Partasides, Alan Redfern & Martin J. Hunter, *Redfern and Hunter on International Arbitration*, para. 9.38 (6th ed., Kluwer 2015); Caron & Caplan, *supra* fn 4, at 782.

8 Thomas H. Webster, *Handbook of UNCITRAL Arbitration*, para. 36-15 (2nd ed., Sweet & Maxwell 2015). *See also* the commentary on article 30(1)(a), *supra*.

9 Caron & Caplan, *supra* fn 4, at 783.

10 Sanders, *supra* fn 3, at 212; *see also* Article 30(2) of the UNCITRAL Model Law (noting that '[s]uch an award has the same status and effect as any other award on the merits of the case'); and Albert Jan van den Berg, *The New York Arbitration Convention of 1958, Towards a Uniform Judicial Interpretation*, 49-50 (Kluwer 1981).

binding and enforceable, this will normally require court (or arbitral) intervention, as opposed to the straightforward execution of an award proper. That is why cautious parties often choose not to rely solely on a settlement agreement.[11] Second, the recording of the settlement in the form of an award, as well as the exercise of writing such an award, may grant the arbitrators an opportunity to review the settlement agreement and offer suggestions where necessary for a comprehensive settlement.

8. When the tribunal records the settlement in the form of an award on agreed terms, article 36(1) of the 2010 Rules provides that it is not obliged to provide reasons. During the revision process, the Working Group considered incorporating language expressly to account for situations in which a tribunal might legitimately refuse to issue an award on agreed terms, by adding the wording 'or for refusing to issue it' after 'the tribunal is not obligated to give reasons for such an award'. However, the Working Group considered that this addition was unnecessary, given that a tribunal in such a case may elect to issue an order for the termination of the proceedings, for which no reasons are required.[12] There can be no question that the tribunal will wish to hear the parties (in writing, orally, or both) before deciding.

(iii) Requesting an award on agreed terms

9. The term 'both parties' in article 34(1) of the 1976 Rules was substituted with 'the parties' in article 36(1) of the 2010 Rules in order to reflect the application of the Rules in multiparty disputes, as explicitly recognized by article 10(1) of the 2010 Rules. An issue that remains open after the 2010 revision is whether all parties must request the award on agreed terms, as suggested by the text of the provision ('if requested by *the parties*' (emphasis added)). The question whether a request by one party would suffice for this purpose was intensely debated during the drafting of Article 30(1) of the UNCITRAL Model Law, which corresponds to article 36(1) of the Rules.[13] Supporters of a single-party request argued that the party receiving payment had a clear interest in obtaining an award that would be fully enforceable,[14] and that requiring a joint request would make it possible for one party to prevent the tribunal from recording a settlement in the form of an award.[15] Opponents argued that 'there were fewer dangers of injustice by

---

11 *See* Peter Binder, *Analytical Commentary to the UNCITRAL Arbitration Rules*, para. 36-006 (Sweet & Maxwell 2013).

12 UNCITRAL Report of 51st Session, 10 November 2009, UN Doc A/CN.9/684, para. 101. *See also* Binder, *supra* fn 11, at para. 36-013.

13 *See* UNCITRAL Note by the Secretariat, 31 August 1982, UN Doc A/CN.9/WG.II/WP.38, article 33, fn 28.

14 UNCITRAL Report on 4th Session, 10 November 1982, UN Doc A/CN.9/232, XIV UNCITRAL Ybk 33, 49 para. 174. In response to this argument, Binder notes that 'it may be questioned whether a settlement, the enforcement of which one party does not intend to accept, will in fact hold in the long run': *see* Binder, *supra* fn 11, at para. 36-009.

15 *See* UNCITRAL Report of the Secretary General, 15 April 1985, UN Doc A/CN.9/263/Add.1, XVI UNCITRAL Ybk 83, 92 article 30, para. 1.

requiring both parties to request an award on agreed terms'.[16] After deliberation, the Commission agreed that there should be 'the dual will of the two parties' for the settlement to be recorded as an award, but that 'the formal request needed to be made by only one of them'.[17]

10. Although this is not provided for expressly in the Rules, a request for the tribunal to record a settlement agreement as an award on agreed terms should be in writing and signed, with the settlement agreement 'typically attached to the joint request for the arbitral tribunal's review'.[18]

2. The tribunal's discretion

11. In order for the parties' settlement to be recorded as an award on agreed terms under article 36(1) of the 2010 Rules, the request must be 'accepted' by the arbitral tribunal. Whether the tribunal should retain the discretion to reject the parties' request for an award on agreed terms was disputed at the time of drafting of the 1976 Rules, as well as the UNCITRAL Model Law. One concern was that this requirement violated party autonomy.[19] However, supporters of the requirement argued that the tribunal should retain discretion to refuse to record the settlement in the form of an award if the terms of the settlement are unlawful.[20] They also argued that the right of the parties to terminate the arbitral proceedings through settlement (certainly covered by party autonomy in absolute terms) should be distinguished from their right to have that settlement recorded as an award; and that the arbitrators should not be forced to sign any settlement agreement the parties have reached.[21] As most delegates desired, the tribunal's discretion was maintained.[22]

12. The circumstances in which a tribunal would elect a termination order are of course limited. One must start from the principle that the tribunal's mandate

---

16 *See* UNCITRAL Report on 4th Session, 10 November 1982, UN Doc A/CN.9/232, XIV UNCITRAL Ybk 33, 49 para. 175.

17 *See* Report of the 18th Session, 21 August 1985, UN Doc A/40/17, XVI UNCITRAL Ybk 3, 31 para. 250. *See also* Howard M. Holtzmann & Joseph E. Neuhaus, *A Guide to the UNCITRAL Model Law on International Commercial Arbitration, Legislative History and Commentary*, 822-823 (Kluwer 1989); Caron & Caplan, *supra* fn 4, at 783.

18 Caron & Caplan, *supra* fn 4, at 786; *see also* Klaus P. Berger, *International Economic Arbitration*, 585-586 (Kluwer 1993).

19 *See* UNCITRAL Report of the Secretary General, 19 March 1985, UN Doc A/CN.9/263, XVI UNCITRAL Ybk 53, 75 article 30; Report of 8th Session, 1-17 April 1975, UN Doc A/10017, VI UNCITRAL Ybk 9, 42, para. 194; and UNCITRAL Summary Record of the 11th Meeting, 21 April 1976, UN Doc A/CN.9/9/C.2/SR.11, para. 79, Mr Melis (Australia).

20 *See* Report of 8th Session, 1-17 April 1975, UN Doc A/10017, VI UNCITRAL Ybk 9, 42, para. 195; UNCITRAL Report of the Secretary General on the Draft UNCITRAL Arbitration Rules, 12 December 1975, UN Doc A/CN.9/112/Add.1, 179 para. 4.

21 *See* Report of the 18th Session, 21 August 1985, UN Doc A/40/17, XVI UNCITRAL Ybk 3, 31 para. 249.

22 *See* Report of 8th Session, 1-17 April 1975, UN Doc A/10017, VI UNCITRAL Ybk 9, 42, para. 194.

is to resolve the parties' dispute in an 'efficient' manner (cf. article 17(1)), and this mandate encompasses issuing an award on agreed terms giving effect to a settlement. Thus a tribunal would be justified in refusing to do so in rare cases, notably where it considers the terms of the agreement illegal on their face or concealing an improper/unlawful purpose.[23] The tribunal is most likely to exercise its discretion to refuse the parties' request where the agreement is manifestly unlawful or contrary to public policy.[24] This may be the case, for example, where the settlement violates anti-trust or income tax laws or foreign exchange policies,[25] or in cases of 'suspected fraud, illicit or utterly unfair settlement terms'.[26] Commentators have provided further examples, such as where the award on agreed terms could encourage or facilitate the performance of an illegal act, such as the manufacturing of an internationally banned substance or the smuggling of contraband.[27]

13. However, the tribunal's discretion is not unlimited. The drafters intended the tribunal's discretion to be limited to exceptional circumstances.[28] Holtzmann and Neuhaus note that the arbitrator's duty in this regard is not to investigate the parties' reasons for settlement, but to determine whether its terms are valid and enforceable under the applicable law and policy.[29] This is further confirmed by the practice of the Iran-US Claims Tribunal. When establishing the circumstances in which it would be appropriate for it to refuse to record a settlement agreement as an award, and after having analysed the *travaux préparatoires* of the 1976 Rules, the Tribunal concluded that 'the power to refuse to record a settlement cannot be exercised in an arbitrary manner', and that the arbitrators 'should not attempt to review the reasonableness of the settlement in the place of the arbitrating parties'.[30]

---

23 *Soleimany v. Soleimany* [1999] QB 785 (settlement award an instrument of bypassing currency-export regulations).

24 *See* Report of 8th Session, 1-17 April 1975, UN Doc A/10017, VI UNCITRAL Ybk 9, 42 para. 194; UNCITRAL Summary Record of the 11th Meeting, 21 April 1976, UN Doc A/CN.9/9/C.2/SR.11, para. 82, Mr Sanders (Special Consultant to the UNCITRAL secretariat).

25 *See* UNCITRAL Summary Record of the 11th Meeting, 21 April 1976, UN Doc A/CN.9/9/C.2/SR.11, para. 82, Mr Sanders (Special Consultant to the UNCITRAL secretariat).

26 *See* UNCITRAL Report of the Secretary-General, Analytical commentary on draft text of a model law on international commercial arbitration, 25 March 1985, UN Doc A/CN.9/264, XVI UNCITRAL Ybk 104, 65 para. 2.

27 Blackaby, Partasides, Redfern & Hunter, *supra* fn 7, at para. 9.39.

28 Caron & Caplan, *supra* fn 4, at 785. *See also* Holtzmann & Neuhaus, *supra* fn 17, at 824-825 (noting that such a refusal should occur only in exceptional circumstances, such as violations of law and public policy or where the settlement conflicts with 'fundamental notions of fairness and justice').

29 Holtzmann & Neuhaus, *supra* fn 17, at 824-825. *See also* Caron & Caplan, *supra* fn 4, at 785.

30 *See Iran v. United States (Case A/1)* (1981-1982) 1 Iran-US CTR 144, para. 153 (where Iran argued that the Tribunal should make an award on agreed terms whenever the claim is found to be prima facie within the Tribunal's jurisdiction, whereas the US argued that the Tribunal's discretion should be broader, ensuring that the settlement represents a 'reasonable resolution' of the claim).

14. A further limitation on the tribunal's discretion is that it may only record as an award a settlement agreement that falls within its jurisdiction, as determined by the arbitration agreement.[31] It cannot include in the award a matter that is outside the scope of the arbitration agreement, except by construing the settlement agreement as an implied amendment of the arbitration agreement.[32] Moreover, if the settlement agreement involves third parties who are not signatories to the original arbitration agreement, it would be necessary for such additional parties to accede to the arbitration agreement in order for the tribunal to be able to record the settlement as an award.[33]

3. The arbitrator's role in settlement negotiations

15. Both the 1976 and the 2010 Rules are silent on the role of the arbitrator as regards settlement negotiations, and do not address whether the arbitrator may facilitate settlement discussions between the parties.[34] That was the right approach as a matter of policy, given that there are deep-seated differences in that regard among the various national procedural traditions (as noted below). But there is nothing in the Rules to preclude such a role being undertaken by a tribunal – it being necessary for the tribunal to determine how such a role would comport with the *lex arbitri*, the arbitration agreement of the parties, procedural orders and directions that may already be in place, and its duties as a fair and impartial adjudicator under article 17(1). It is clear at the very least that the parties must agree upon such a role, whether at their initiative or that of the tribunal. The drafters did, however, envisage the possibility of the tribunal's assisting the parties in formalising a settlement agreement reached orally in the course of a hearing.[35] However, settlement negotiations often fail, and the risk that the arbitral proceedings will continue after an unsuccessful attempt at settlement could have a chilling effect on any settlement discussions in which arbitrators are involved. Parties may, for instance, be reluctant to make settlement proposals that could

---

31 The Iran-US Claims Tribunal was similarly clear that it may only record as an award on agreed terms those settlements which fell within the jurisdiction conferred to it by the Iran-United States Claims Settlement Declaration (19 January 1981): *see Iran v. United States (Case A/1)* (1981-1982) 1 Iran-US CTR 144, para. 152.

32 Berger, *supra* fn 18, at 586.

33 *Ibid.*; *see also* Caron & Caplan, *supra* fn 4, at 784.

34 However, *see* Rule 8 of the 1987 IBA Rules of Ethics for International Arbitrators: 'Where the parties have so requested, or consented to a suggestion to this effect by the arbitral tribunal, the tribunal as a whole (or the presiding arbitrator where appropriate), may make proposals for settlement to both parties simultaneously, and preferably in the presence of each other. Although any procedure is possible with the agreement of the parties, the arbitral tribunal should point out to the parties that it is undesirable that any arbitrator should discuss settlement terms with a party in the absence of the other parties since this will normally have the result that any arbitrator involved in such discussions will become disqualified from any future participation in the arbitration'.

35 *See* UNCITRAL Report of the Secretary General on the Draft UNCITRAL Arbitration Rules, 12 December 1975, UN Doc A/CN.9/112/Add.1, 179 para. 3; and UNCITRAL Report of 8th Session, 4 November 1974, UN Doc A/CN.9/97, VI UNCITRAL Ybk 163, 178-179 para. 2.

be interpreted as admissions or which may generally undermine their position before the arbitrators, should the arbitration ultimately proceed.[36] While both the ICJ and the Iran-US Claims Tribunal have taken the stance that proposals and concessions made by the parties in the course of settlement negotiations should not be taken into account by the tribunal,[37] the parties may reasonably be reluctant to engage in these discussions in the presence of the arbitrators.

16. Participation by an arbitrator in settlement negotiations could also serve as a basis for a party to claim that the arbitrator was biased or prejudiced.[38] This problem is further complicated by the fact that civil- and common-law jurisdictions have different perspectives on the extent to which it is appropriate for arbitrators to facilitate settlement discussions; in some civil law systems, the arbitrator's role as a facilitator rises to the level of a 'noble obligation',[39] whereas common law systems traditionally have reservations regarding arbitrators' facilitating of settlements, as likely to cause loss of impartiality.[40]

17. The 2010 Rules do not shed any light on these issues. However, the UNCITRAL Notes state that:

> In some jurisdictions, the arbitration law permits facilitation of a settlement by the arbitral tribunal with the agreement of the parties. In other jurisdictions, it is not permissible for the arbitral tribunal to do more than raise the prospect of a settlement that would not involve the arbitral tribunal. Where the applicable arbitration law permits the arbitral tribunal to facilitate a settlement, it may, if so requested by the parties, guide or assist the parties

---

36 *See* Caron & Caplan, *supra* fn 4, at 787. *See also*, more generally, Robert B. Davidson & David Plant, 'ADR and Arbitration' in Lawrence W. Newman & Richard D. Hill (eds), *The Leading Arbitrator's Guide to International Arbitration*, 73 et seq. (3rd ed., Juris 2014); Michael E. Schneider, 'Combining Arbitration with Conciliation' in Albert Jan van den Berg (ed), *International Dispute Resolution: Towards an International Arbitration Culture*, 8 ICCA Congress Series 57, 94-95 (1998); Berger, *supra* fn 18, at 581.

37 *See*, e.g., *Mobil Oil Iran Inc v. Government of the Islamic Republic of Iran* (1987) 16 Iran-US CTR 55 ('It is well settled that a tribunal, which must decide a case subsequent to the failure of the parties to arrive at a settlement by way of negotiations, need not take into account the proposals and concessions that either party might have made in the course of such negotiations. The reason for this rule is obvious: such proposals and concessions have no purpose other than to allow an agreement to be attained and may well be very far from what each party considered to be its rights. Since such proposals were rejected, they have lost all validity and have become meaningless'). *See also Case Concerning the Factory at Chorzow (Germany v. Poland)*, PCIJ Series A No 9 (1927), 51.

38 *See* generally Catherine A. Rogers & Jeffrey C. Jeng, 'The Ethics of International Arbitrators' in Lawrence W. Newman & Richard D. Hill (eds), *The Leading Arbitrator's Guide to International Arbitration*, 204-205 (3rd ed., Juris 2014).

39 Daniele Favalli and Max K. Hasenclever, *The Role of Arbitrators in Settlement Proceedings*, 23(7) Mealey's International Arbitration Report 2 (2008).

40 *See* Bernd Ehle, 'The Arbitrator as a Settlement Facilitator' in Olivier Caprasse et al., *Walking a Thin Line: what an Arbitrator can do, must do or must not do: Recent Developments and Trends*, 80 (Colloquium CEPANI40 2010).

in their negotiations. Certain sets of arbitration rules provide for facilitation of a settlement by the arbitral tribunal.[41]

18. Some of the concerns mentioned above may be avoided by full disclosure of the tribunal's role in the settlement process and a well-crafted agreement on the process which addresses the role of 'all involved'.[42] Furthermore, the parties may enlist the services of a third-party conciliator under the UNCITRAL Conciliation Rules, which offer a higher degree of confidentiality than the Arbitration Rules.[43] A standard mechanism in any event is for the parties to adopt a rule to the effect that that any materials put forward in the settlement negotiations would be inadmissible in the arbitration proceedings.[44]

B. CONTINUATION OF PROCEEDINGS IMPOSSIBLE OR UNNECESSARY: ARTICLE 36(2)

1. Termination of the proceedings

19. Article 36(2) of the 2010 Rules addresses any other situation where the proceedings are to be terminated because their continuation has become 'unnecessary or impossible'. As noted, a tribunal faced with this situation will either (i) order the termination of the proceedings (which, as mentioned above, is not intended to have res judicata effect) after having informed the parties and heard them; or (ii) continue the proceedings because, after having heard the parties, it considers that 'there are remaining matters that may need to be decided and the arbitral tribunal considers it appropriate to do so'. The provision is similar in its conception and operation with article 30(1)(a).

20. The *travaux préparatoires* of the 1976 Rules and of the Model Law provide little guidance as to how the tribunal should make the determination that continuation of the proceedings has become unnecessary or impossible. Nor did the Working Group discuss the meaning of the terms 'unnecessary' or 'impossible', or the

---

41 UNCITRAL, *Notes on Organizing Arbitral Proceedings*, para. 72 (United Nations 2016). The 1996 Notes provided as follows: 'Attitudes differ as to whether it is appropriate for the arbitral tribunal to bring up the possibility of settlement. Given the divergence of practices in this regard, the arbitral tribunal should only suggest settlement negotiations with caution. However, it may be opportune for the arbitral tribunal to schedule the proceedings in a way that might facilitate the continuation or initiation of settlement negotiations'; *see* UNCITRAL, *Notes on Organizing Arbitral Proceedings*, para. 47 (United Nations 1996).

42 *See* Caron & Caplan, *supra* fn 4, at 787.

43 *Ibid.*

44 Cf. Article 20 of the UNCITRAL Conciliation Rules, which provides as follows: 'The parties undertake not to rely on or introduce as evidence in arbitral or judicial proceedings, whether or not such proceedings relate to the dispute that is the subject of the conciliation proceedings; (a) Views expressed or suggestions made by the other party in respect of a possible settlement of the dispute; (b) Admissions made by the other party in the course of the conciliation proceedings; (c) Proposals made by the conciliator; (d) The fact that the other party had indicated his willingness to accept a proposal for settlement made by the conciliator'.

distinction between them. It appears that they are used as compendious terms intended to cover a variety of possible circumstances. As a notion, the term 'unnecessary' encompasses situations where the parties have no legitimate interest in continuing the proceedings – for example, where the dispute has become moot – whereas the term 'impossible' implies a legal or material barrier to the continuation of the proceedings (for example, a party has ceased to exist and there is no successor).

21. Some instances of 'unnecessary or impossible' continuation are specifically mentioned in the Rules. These include: (i) the parties reaching a settlement, but not requesting an award on agreed terms, or such a request being denied by the tribunal pursuant to article 36(1); (ii) the tribunal ordering the termination of the proceedings as a result of the claimant's failure to communicate its statement of claim pursuant to article 30(1)(a); and (iii) the parties failing to pay the required deposit on costs in full within 30 days of receipt of the request pursuant to article 43(4).[45] Situations akin to those, amounting to a want of prosecution which seriously prejudices the respondent, may also be envisaged.

22. As noted above, a claimant's decision to withdraw its claim is a common situation addressed under article 36(2).[46] Faced with a strong defence from the respondent or a substantial counterclaim, and a costs claim as a result, a claimant may decide to abandon the arbitral process. A claimant may also withdraw due to its inability to obtain documents or to secure the witnesses required for a successful presentation of the case.[47] Other possible scenarios where article 36(2) may apply include the parties' resolving their dispute in another forum,[48] or the tribunal's finding that it lacks jurisdiction over a substantial part of the dispute.[49]

23. In such cases, the arbitral tribunal should in principle terminate the proceedings unless there are any 'remaining matters'. Although the phrase 'considers it appropriate to do so' suggests that the tribunal has complete discretion in determining whether there are indeed remaining matters to be decided, it goes without saying that the tribunal should nevertheless seek in advance the parties' views on such an important matter.[50]

2. Remaining matters

24. Under article 36(2) of the 2010 Rules, the tribunal's power to issue a termination order is no longer restricted by a party's ability to '[raise] justifiable grounds for objection', as was the case under article 34(2) of the 1976 Rules. Under the

---

45 *See* Caron & Caplan, *supra* fn 4, at 789.

46 *Ibid.*, at 788.

47 *Ibid.*, at 788-789; *see also*, e.g., *W Jack Buckamier v. Islamic Republic of Iran* (1992) 28 Iran-US CTR 53, 75-76.

48 *See* UNCITRAL Summary Record of 167th Meeting, 14 April 1975, UN Doc A/CN.9/SR.167, 203, Mr Krispis (Greece).

49 *See*, e.g., *Bank Markazi Iran v. Rainier National Bank*, Case No. 738, Chamber Two, Order of 29 November 1985.

50 Caron & Caplan, *supra* fn 4, at 790.

2010 Rules, a tribunal that considers the continuation of the proceedings to have become unnecessary or impossible is prevented from issuing a termination order only where 'there are remaining matters that may need to be decided and the arbitral tribunal considers it appropriate to do so'. The *travaux* of the 2010 Rules reveal that the primary purpose of this revision was to align article 36 with other revised provisions, such as article 30(1)(a) regarding the claimant's failure to submit its statement of claim.[51] Article 28(1) of the 1976 Rules compelled the tribunal to terminate the proceedings where the claimant failed to communicate its statement of claim. Under article 30(1)(a) of the 2010 Rules, the tribunal retains discretion to continue the proceedings if it considers that there are 'remaining matters', such as counterclaims[52] or a claim for costs raised by the respondent.[53] More generally, therefore, the 2010 formulation indicates what are the valid grounds for an 'objection' to termination.

C. TECHNICAL AND FORMAL REQUIREMENTS

25. The changes made in article 36(3) of the 2010 Rules during the revision process are of a mechanical nature. Both article 36(3) and its predecessor in the 1976 Rules provide that any award shall be subject to article 34(2) (article 32(2) of the 1976 Rules) as regards the final and binding nature of the award.

26. Article 36(3) of the 2010 Rules also states that '[c]opies of the order for termination of the arbitral proceedings or of the arbitral award on agreed terms' must be signed by the arbitrators and communicated to the parties. Whereas article 34(3) of the 1976 Rules provides that an award on agreed terms must satisfy the requirements of articles 32(2) and 32(4)-(7), article 36(3) provides that it must comply with the corresponding articles, 34(4) and 34(5). The minor change results from the drafters' decision to delete the 1976 article 32(7) from the 2010 Rules.[54]

27. An award on agreed terms should therefore comply with the formal requirements of an ordinary award: it must be made in writing, be signed by the arbitrators, and

51 *See* UNCITRAL Working Paper for 52nd Session, 10 December 2009, UN Doc A/CN.9/WG.II/WP.157/Add.2, para. 10; and UNCITRAL Report of 51st Session, 10 November 2009, UN Doc A/CN.9/684, para. 102.

52 Caron & Caplan, *supra* fn 4, at 790. For further details on the meaning of 'remaining matters', *see also* commentary on article 30 of the 2010 Rules, *supra*.

53 *See Forminster Enterprises Limited (Cyprus) v. Czech Republic* (UNCITRAL) Final Award, 15 December 2014, < www.italaw.com >, para. 88 (where, after the claimant had attempted to withdraw its notice of arbitration, the tribunal refused to terminate the proceedings pursuant to article 34(2) of the 1976 Rules because the respondent had a claim for costs: 'Therefore, the Arbitral Tribunal is driven to the conclusion that the Claimant was not entitled to terminate the arbitral proceedings unilaterally on 17 February 2014. The proceedings cannot be terminated under Art. 34(2) of the UNCITRAL Rules as being "unnecessary" since the Respondent had reserved a claim for costs which it has properly presented in accordance with the procedural timetable. The proceedings shall therefore continue until the Arbitral Tribunal has determined the Respondent's claim for costs').

54 *See* Caron & Caplan, *supra* fn 4, at 792; *see also* UNCITRAL Working Paper for 48th Session, 30 November 2007, UN Doc A/CN.9/WG.II/WP.149, para. 69.

contain the date and the place of arbitration, etc. Article 34(3) does not apply to awards on agreed terms as this would contradict article 36(1), which states that 'the arbitral tribunal is not obliged to give reasons' for an award under article 36.

Article 37
Interpretation of the award

1976 Rules Article 35: Interpretation of the award	2010 Rules Article 37: Interpretation of the award
1. Within thirty days after the receipt of the award, either party, with notice to the other party, may request that the arbitral tribunal give an interpretation of the award.	1. Within 30 days after the receipt of the award, a party, with notice to the other parties, may request that the arbitral tribunal give an interpretation of the award.
2. The interpretation shall be given in writing within forty-five days after the receipt of the request. The interpretation shall form part of the award and the provisions of article 32, paragraphs 2 to 7, shall apply.	2. The interpretation shall be given in writing within 45 days after the receipt of the request. The interpretation shall form part of the award and the provisions of article 34, paragraphs 2 to 6, shall apply.

1 In contrast to a number of arbitration rules,[1] the UNCITRAL Rules expressly allow for interpretation of the award, although one could also view this as an inherent power of the tribunal.[2] Along with articles 38 and 39, article 37 represents a limited exception to the finality of an award under article 34(2).[3] This provision

1 *See*, e.g., Article 27 of the LCIA Rules (providing only for correction of the award and additional awards) and Article 68 of the WIPO Rules. For examples of arbitration rules that do provide for interpretation, *see*, e.g., Article 36 of the ICC Rules; Article 35 of the Swiss Rules; and Article 47 of the SCC Rules.

2 *See* Gary B. Born, *International Commercial Arbitration*, 3147 (2nd ed., Kluwer 2014). *See also* John Savage & Emmanuel Gaillard (eds), *Fouchard, Gaillard, Goldman on International Commercial Arbitration*, para. 1415 (Kluwer 1999). *See also* ILA International Commercial Arbitration Committee Resolution No. 4/2016, 7-11 August 2016, <www.ila-hq.org> (inherent powers of the tribunal).

3 *See* Jan Paulsson & Georgios Petrochilos, *Revision of the UNCITRAL Rules* (September 2006), para. 262, <www.uncitral.org> ('An award is final and *res judicata*. In principle it is not subject to review or challenge in the courts in respect of its legal or factual reasoning. It follows that a legitimate request for interpretation of an award can only concern a failure on the tribunal's part to articulate its dispositive ruling in a way that is comprehensible

is substantially unchanged from the equivalent provision in the 1976 Rules, with minor amendments made to align it with new provisions in the 2010 Rules regarding multiparty arbitrations.[4]

A. THE INTERPRETATION PROCESS

2. Articles 37-39 of the Rules provide the tribunal with the opportunity to address ambiguities, errors, or omissions, better to ensure that the award is enforceable and not susceptible to annulment.[5] In particular, interpretation 'provides a vehicle for one or both parties to secure clarification of the award',[6] 'resolving any ambiguity and vagueness in its terms',[7] as opposed to modifying or supplementing the original decision.[8] The central goal is to dispel any doubts over the way in which the award is to be performed.[9] The line between interpretation and supplementation or revision is not invariably a bright one. It is always a case of applying a general test (and the corresponding distinction from other remedies) in particular circumstances. Certain commentators define interpretation as restoring 'the true meaning of the original decision where it was badly expressed in the holdings, be it because the latter seem to be at odds with the reasons or to contain obscurities or ambiguities'.[10] The drafters of the 1976 Rules also contemplated 'interpretation' in a more literal sense, identifying that clarification of the language of the award may be necessary where the language of the proceedings is not the native language of all the arbitrators.[11] While interpretations are not frequent in practice,[12] that a party should resort to such an exceptional mechanism will usually in itself indicate the importance of the issue in the context of the dispute.

---

and unambiguous, and so permits the parties to carry it out in accordance with article 32(2) [of the 1976 Rules]').

4 The wording 'either party' and 'other party' in article 35(1) of the 1976 Rules has been replaced with 'a party' and 'other parties' in article 37(1) of the 2010 Rules. *See also* discussion of article 17 of the 2010 Rules, *supra*.

5 *See* Born, *supra* fn 2, at 3113 (noting that 'awards containing serious errors or omissions may be subject to annulment or non-recognition').

6 UNCITRAL Report of the Secretary General on the Draft UNCITRAL Arbitration Rules, 12 December 1975, UN Doc A/CN.9/112/Add.1, 180 para. 3.

7 David D. Caron & Lee M. Caplan, *The UNCITRAL Arbitration Rules, A Commentary*, 802 (2nd ed., Oxford University Press 2013).

8 Clyde E. Croft, Christopher Kee & Jeffrey Waincymer, *A Guide to the UNCITRAL Arbitration Rules*, 412 (Cambridge University Press 2013).

9 *See* Nigel Blackaby, Constantine Partasides, Alan Redfern & Martin J. Hunter, *Redfern and Hunter on International Arbitration*, para. 10.18 (6th ed., Kluwer 2015). For the practice of the Iran-US Claims Tribunal, *see also American Bell International Inc v. Iran* (1987) 14 Iran-US CTR 173 (where the tribunal rejected a request for interpretation as there was no ambiguity impeding execution of the award).

10 Croft, Kee & Waincymer, *supra* fn 8, at 412, citing Jean-François Poudret & Sébastien Besson, *Comparative Law of International Arbitration*, 693-694 (2nd ed., Sweet and Maxwell 2007).

11 *See* Report of 8th Session, UN Doc A/10017, VI UNCITRAL Ybk 9, 43, para. 206 (1975).

12 *See* Born, *supra* fn 2, at 3141. *See also* Stewart A. Baker & Mark D. Davis, *The UNCITRAL Arbitration Rules in Practice – The Experience of the Iran-United States Claims Tribunal*, 194 (Kluwer 1992) ('Given its narrow interpretation of the arbitrating parties' rights to an

In particular, interpretation may indeed be pivotal in clarifying the parties' future obligations in an ongoing commercial relationship.

3. All remedies provided for in articles 37-39 are exceptional. They are not meant to provide losing parties with an opportunity to submit additional evidence, advance new arguments, or obtain a review or reconsideration by the tribunal of its decision.[13] Thus interpretation under article 37 should be directed to 'a specific point or part of the award'.[14] In particular, it should be directed to the dispositive part of the award, or parts of the award directly affecting the parties' rights and obligations,[15] as opposed to merely the reasoning behind the award.[16]

4. Interpretation is clearly distinguishable from correction under article 38; the latter alters the award, while the former by definition cannot. Moreover, while the tribunal may make corrections of its own initiative, interpretations and additional awards may only be made at the request of a party. Nevertheless, the boundary between interpretation under article 37 and the making of additional awards under article 39 of the 2010 Rules is somewhat more difficult to draw. The *Wintershall* arbitration illustrates this: the tribunal doubted whether the law applicable to the arbitration barred interpretative decisions, and found that the substance of what it had to do, which it regarded as an interpretation, could simply be characterized as an additional award in which it clarified certain provisions of the agreement.[17]

5. Although the mandatory language of article 37(2) ('interpretation shall be given') on its face may suggest that the tribunal has no discretion, the practice of the

interpretation, it should come as no surprise that the Tribunal received few requests under Article 35 [of the Tribunal Rules of Procedure] – and granted none').

13 *See* Caron & Caplan, *supra* fn 7, at 803; and Baker & Davis, *supra* fn 12, at 194 (noting that, '[i]n general, the Tribunal correctly regarded requests for interpretation as not-so-subtle requests that it reconsider its award on the merits ... a form of review well outside the scope of Article 35 [of the Tribunal Rules of Procedure]').

14 *See* Article 33(1)(b) of the Model Law (providing that 'if so agreed by the parties, a party, with notice to the other party, may request the arbitral tribunal to give an interpretation of a specific point or part of the award'). However, note that a suggestion to align article 37 of the 2010 Rules with the Model Law in this respect was rejected; *see* UNCITRAL Report of 51st Session, 10 November 2009, UN Doc A/CN.9/684, para. 104. Cf., e.g., the decision of the Iran-US Claims Tribunal in *American Bell International Inc v. Iran* (1987) 14 Iran-US CTR 173, 174 (where the request was rejected as it '[did] not identify any aspect of the Award where the Tribunal's interpretation [was] necessary').

15 *See* Born, *supra* fn 2, at 3143 and the references.

16 *See* Baker & Davis, *supra* fn 12, at 192-194. *See*, e.g., *Pepsico Inc v. Iran* (1986) 13 Iran-US CTR 328, 329-330 (where the tribunal rejected the party's request for interpretation based on the ambiguous reasoning of the award, stating that the *travaux* to the 1976 Rules revealed that the purpose of the provision was to clarify any ambiguous language in an award).

17 *See Wintershall AG v. The Government of Qatar* (UNCITRAL) Interpretation by Tribunal of its Partial Award on Liability, 31 May 1988, 28 ILM 795 (1989).

Iran-US Claims Tribunal demonstrates that an interpretation falls to be given only if the tribunal is satisfied that there is a sound basis for the relevant request.[18]

6. The tribunal may not charge additional fees for an interpretative decision, but additional costs may be charged.[19]

B. SCOPE OF APPLICATION

7. Article 37 expressly provides for the tribunal to give an interpretation of 'the award'. This should be read as inclusive of 'separate awards on different issues [made] at different times' (article 34(1)). Thus the post-award remedies provided in articles 37-39 of the Rules will apply not only to final awards but also to partial awards,[20] interim awards,[21] and interlocutory awards (cf. article 32(1) of the 1976 Rules).

8. The position is less clear in respect of decisions made by the tribunal in forms other than that of an award. Tribunals have, however, applied the post-award powers contained in articles 37-39 in this context. For example, a NAFTA tribunal relied on article 36 of the 1976 Rules in order to correct a termination order.[22] On certain occasions, the Iran-US Claims Tribunal has also corrected termination orders, deriving its power to do so 'by analogy' from its power under article 36 of the 1976 Rules.[23] This practice seems unimpeachable. However, avoidance of doubt may prove a compelling reason for a tribunal to elect to render a decision, e.g. an order for interim measures, explicitly as an award (in accordance with article 34).

---

18 *See* James E. Castello, 'UNCITRAL Arbitration Rules, Section IV, Article 37' in Loukas A. Mistelis (ed), *Concise International Arbitration*, 255 (2nd ed., Kluwer 2015), citing to *Ford Aerospace & Communications Corp et al v. Air Force of the Islamic Republic of Iran* (1986) 12 Iran-US CTR 304, 307. *See also* Croft, Kee & Waincymer, *supra* fn 8, at 412.

19 *See* article 40(3) of the 2010 Rules.

20 *Methanex Corporation v. United States of America* (UNCITRAL) Tribunal's Letter re Request for Interpretation of Award, 25 September 2002, <www.italaw.com> (Request for Interpretation made under article 35 of the 1976 Rules).

21 *See*, e.g., *Paul Donin de Rosiere v. Islamic Republic of Iran* (1987) 14 Iran-US CTR 100, 101-102; *see also Aaron C. Berkowitz, Brett E. Berkowitz and Trevor B. Berkowitz (formerly Spence International Investments and others) v. Republic of Costa Rica* (ICSID Case No. UNCT/13/2) Interim Award of the Tribunal (Corrected), 30 May 2017, <www.italaw.com>.

22 *Melvin J Howard, Centurion Health Corp & Howard Family Trust v. The Government of Canada* (UNCITRAL) Correction of Order for the Termination of Proceedings and Award on Costs, 9 August 2010, <www.italaw.com>, para. 3. *See also* Caron & Caplan, *supra* fn 7, at 813.

23 *See Bank Markazi Iran v. European American Banking Corp*, Case No. 679, Chamber Two, Order of 22 January 1986 cited in Caron & Caplan, *supra* fn 7, at 817 ('In view of the above-mentioned circumstances and in order to avoid any prejudice to the Claimant, the Tribunal using by analogy its power under Article 36 of the [1983 Tribunal Rules of Procedure] ... hereby corrects its order').

C. INTERPRETATION AND FINALITY OF AWARDS

9. The notion that a tribunal can issue an interpretation appears inconsistent with the fact that, in most legal systems,[24] the tribunal becomes *functus officio* when it issues its final award, and its mandate is terminated. When drafting the 1976 Rules, it was clarified that article 35 (article 37 of the 2010 Rules) constitutes an express agreement by the parties to extend the tribunal's jurisdiction to the post-award phase for the limited purpose of interpretation.[25]

10. In order to ensure that the interpretation of the award is as binding and enforceable as the award itself, article 37(2) expressly provides that 'the interpretation shall form part of the award' – thus placing it within the ambit of the New York Convention[26] – and that the requirements for the making of an award provided in articles 34(2)-(6) apply. This is a deeming provision, and it has the merit of being entirely clear-cut: it is not simply the case that the interpretative decision has status equal to the award; rather, it is an integral part of it. (By contrast, a decision rejecting a request for interpretation does not of course partake of the award.) Another consequence of article 37(2) is that the interpretative decision is to be made by a majority of the arbitrators, thereby complying with article 33(1).[27] However, the enforceability of an interpretation as part of an award will ultimately depend on any mandatory provisions of the *lex arbitri*.[28]

11 Article 37 also does not offer guidance as to the instrument through which to effect a correction, in contrast to, for example, the ICC Rules, which provide that the decision to interpret the award shall 'take the form of an addendum'.[29] 'Restated Award' or simply 'Award Interpretation' are possible forms.

---

24 *See*, e.g., Article 32 of the Model Law. *See also* Born, *supra* fn 2, at 3123 (suggesting that, post-award, the tribunal does not lose its mandate, but rather has a limited mandate to interpret, correct or supplement awards, which is eventually extinguished over time).

25 *See* UNCITRAL Report of the Secretary General on the Draft UNCITRAL Arbitration Rules, 12 December 1975, UN Doc A/CN.9/112/Add.1, 180 para. 3.

26 *See* Report of the Commission on its 9th Session, 12 April-7 May 1976, UN Doc A/31/17, 79 para. 191 (this provision was originally added to article 35 of the 1976 Rules '[i]n recognition of the fact that, when given, an interpretation by the arbitral tribunal of its award was necessarily and authoritatively linked to the award').

27 *See* Pieter Sanders, *Commentary on UNCITRAL Arbitration Rules*, II YCA 172, 212 (1977) (noting that '[a]lthough Article 31 [of the 1976 Rules] is not expressly referred to, the interpretative award is also made on the basis of a majority decision', and that, further, '[a] n arbitrator may even refuse to sign, and attach a dissenting opinion' to the interpretation).

28 *See* Born, *supra* fn 2, at 3146 (the parties' agreement to apply institutional rules which permit interpretations of arbitral awards 'should be given effect, even where applicable law in the arbitral seat is silent regarding the subject of interpretations'). *See also* Castello, *supra* fn 18, at 256.

29 Article 36(3) of the ICC Rules.

D. TIME-LIMITS

12. One question left unanswered by article 37 is 'whether a request for interpretation, correction or an additional award suspends the time-limit for challenging the primary award'.[30] Although the UNCITRAL Model Law positively answers this question at Article 34(3), not all national arbitration laws address this matter, and therefore 'simultaneous filing may be the only sensible course of conduct'.[31] The better view must nevertheless be that pending a request for interpretation that may ultimately lead to the award's being materially affected in its content, deadlines for setting-aside and enforcement are in abeyance – at least so far as the possible interpretation may have a bearing on such post-award actions.

13. Under article 37(1) of the 2010 Rules, a party has 30 days from the receipt of the award to request an interpretation, so that 'arbitrators would know reasonably quickly that some further action in respect of the award would be requested of them'.[32] The same time-limit applies to requests for correction under article 38 as well as for additional awards under article 39.[33]

14. Article 37(2) provides that the tribunal has 45 days to provide its interpretation after receipt of the request. The drafters considered that this left arbitrators sufficient time to hold new deliberations, if necessary.[34] This may be contrasted with the 60-day time-period provided in respect of an additional award (under article 39 of the 2010 Rules), which understandably may necessitate further deliberations.[35] And unlike article 39, article 37 does not explicitly allow the tribunal to extend the time in which it must render the interpretation; it is therefore open to argument whether a tribunal has the power to extend or abridge this period of time as provided for by article 17(2).[36] According to one commentary, such time-limits should be 'strictly adhered to' because the tribunal is 'traditionally considered to be *functus officio* after rendering a final award' and 'the power in article 37 is an exception to this principle'.[37] That is right so far as it goes; but there may well be exceptional cases requiring extensive briefing and deliberation, or simply very busy schedules. On the face of article 17(2), it is possible to argue that a tribunal may extend the time-periods set out in articles

---

30 Croft, Kee & Waincymer, *supra* fn 8, at 413.

31 *Ibid.*

32 Report of the Commission on its 9th Session, 12 April-7 May 1976, UN Doc A/31/17, 66, 79 para. 190.

33 *See* the recommendation by Paulsson & Petrochilos, *supra* fn 3, at para. 266.

34 *See* Sanders, *supra* fn 23, at 212.

35 *Ibid.*, at 213.

36 Article 17(2) of the 2010 Rules provides as follows: 'The arbitral tribunal may, *at any time*, after inviting the parties to express their views, extend or abridge any period of time prescribed under these Rules or agreed by the parties' (emphasis added). *See also* commentary on article 17 of the 2010 Rules, *supra*.

37 Croft, Kee & Waincymer, *supra* fn 8, at 412.

37-39.[38] Moreover, the parties may modify this provision pursuant to article 1(1) of the Rules, provided that the *lex arbitri* permits this.[39]

15. The time-limit for making a request for interpretation or correction of the award or for an additional award in articles 37-39 begins to run when the award is received. These time-limits are not cumulative, even if a party joins several requests. Thus, while nothing in the Rules prevents a party from making a request for interpretation and correction of the award, or a request for correction and an additional award, such requests must be made within 30 days from the issuance of the award. The applicable time-limit for the tribunal to respond to the request also remains unchanged. Thus, in the latter situation, the tribunal would have 45 days from receipt of the 'double request' to provide its correction, and 60 days to provide the additional award. However, a party is perfectly entitled to require an interpretation or correction of an additional award. In this case, the time-limit to make the request would start to run from the date of the additional award.

16. There may be differences between the time-limits provided for in the *lex arbitri* and the Rules. For example, the time-limit for interpretation set out in the Rules is 45 days (article 37(2)), whereas Article 33 of the Model Law provides for a 30-day time-limit. Where the time-limit provided in the *lex arbitri* is shorter, the correct interpretation is that, by agreeing to apply the Rules, 'the parties have agreed to an extension' of the shorter time-limit,[40] provided of course that the provision of national law is not a mandatory norm.

17. An interpretation is 'necessarily and authoritatively linked' to the award.[41] As such, the date of the interpretation has no legal effect on the original date of the award, a question ultimately determined by the law governing the award. As is also the case for a request for correction of the award (article 38), the tribunal should give the other party a reasonable opportunity to comment on and raise any arguments in respect of a request for interpretation of the award.

---

38 *See* comments relating to article 17(2) of the 2010 Rules, *supra*.

39 *See* Peter Binder, *Analytical Commentary to the UNCITRAL Arbitration Rules*, para. 38-011 (Sweet & Maxwell 2013).

40 Croft, Kee & Waincymer, *supra* fn 8, at 412.

41 *See* fn 26, *supra*.

Article 38
Correction of the award

1976 Rules Article 36: Correction of the award	2010 Rules Article 38: Correction of the award
1. Within thirty days after the receipt of the award, either party, with notice to the other party, may request the arbitral tribunal to correct in the award any errors in computation, any clerical or typographical errors, or any errors of similar nature. The arbitral tribunal may within thirty days after the communication of the award make such corrections on its own initiative.	1. Within 30 days after the receipt of the award, a party, with notice to the other parties, may request the arbitral tribunal to correct in the award any error in computation, any clerical or typographical error, or any error or omission of a similar nature. If the arbitral tribunal considers that the request is justified, it shall make the correction within 45 days of receipt of the request.
2. Such corrections shall be in writing, and the provisions of article 32, paragraphs 2 to 7, shall apply.	2. The arbitral tribunal may within 30 days after the communication of the award make such corrections on its own initiative.
	3. Such corrections shall be in writing and shall form part of the award. The provisions of article 34, paragraphs 2 to 6, shall apply.

1. In order to ensure accuracy and ultimately enforceability of the award,[1] article 38 of the 2010 Rules allows the tribunal to correct 'any error in computation, any clerical or typographical error, or any error or omission of a similar nature'. This captures unintentional errors or omissions, such as a misplaced decimal point, misspelled names, incorrect dates or the omission of a signature.[2] Most major sets of arbitration rules provide that the tribunal may correct or rectify such errors or

1 *See* Gary B. Born, *International Commercial Arbitration*, 3113 (2nd ed., Kluwer 2014) (noting that 'awards containing serious errors or omissions may be subject to annulment or non-recognition').

2 David D. Caron & Lee M. Caplan, *The UNCITRAL Arbitration Rules, A Commentary*, 811-812 (2nd ed., Oxford University Press 2013).

omissions, although these powers are generally limited to minor errors.[3] Indeed, 'correction' of the award is intended to '"restor[e]" the award's 'proper contents': it does not provide a means by which to revisit the substantive holding of the award.[4] To illustrate, if the tribunal arrives at a sum awarded by erroneously performing the underlying arithmetical calculation, which is also set out in the award, it is plain that this was an unintentional error. It is more difficult to say the same of decisions that rely on criticizable inputs or adopt mathematically/practically unsound price formulae, for example. These are just poor decisions, but it is not clear that they may be categorized as '*erreurs materielles*'.

2. Under both the 1976 and the 2010 Rules, the parties may request that the tribunal correct the award within 30 days of its receipt, and the tribunal may make such corrections of its own initiative within 30 days after the communication of the award.[5] If a party requests a correction, notice must be given to the other parties.[6] The correction must be made in writing and the provisions relating to the technical requirements applicable to awards also apply to corrections.[7] The tribunal's power of correction extends to 'awards' as provided in article 34(1) of the 2010 Rules, and therefore includes partial, interim or interlocutory awards.[8]

3. However, the 1976 Rules did not provide a time-limit within which the tribunal was to make the correction requested by the parties, which might invite dilatory requests for correction. The 2010 Rules address these issues by providing that the tribunal must issue a correction requested by the parties within 45 days of that request, provided, however, that it considers the request 'justified'. The 2010 provisions also now explicitly state that any corrections form part of the award, in the same way as article 37 provides for interpretative decisions.

A. ERRORS AND OMISSIONS

4. During the revision process, members of the Working Group were concerned that the scope of the phrase 'or any errors of similar nature' in article 36(1) of the 1976 Rules may not encompass formal but important omissions such as the failure

3 *See*, e.g., Article 27.1 of the LCIA Rules; Article 36(1) of the ICC Rules; Article 47(1) of the SCC Rules. *See also* Nigel Blackaby, Constantine Partasides, Alan Redfern & Martin J. Hunter, *Redfern and Hunter on International Arbitration*, para. 10.17 (6th ed., Kluwer 2015); and Jason Fry, Simon Greenberg & Francesca Mazza, *The Secretariat's Guide to ICC Arbitration*, para. 3-1264 (ICC 2012) (discussing 'an unusual case from 2009' in which the tribunal accidentally signed an earlier version of the award, and had to subsequently revoke it and request that the Secretariat send the final, correct version to the parties).

4 Caron & Caplan, *supra* fn 2, at 811, citing to *Harold Birnbaum v. Islamic Republic of Iran* (1995) 31 Iran-US CTR 286.

5 *See* article 36(1) of the 1976 Rules; article 38(2) of the 2010 Rules. The provision underwent a merely structural change, with the tribunal's power to issue corrections of its own initiative moving from the first paragraph to a separate, second paragraph.

6 The right of other parties 'to comment on or contest' the request for correction is implied by the requirement of notification: *see* Caron & Caplan, *supra* fn 2, at 813.

7 Articles 32(2)-(7) of the 1976 Rules; articles 34(2)-(6) of the 2010 Rules.

8 *See* discussion of article 37, section B, *supra*.

by an arbitrator to sign the award or provide the date or place of the arbitration (as required by article 34(4)).[9] It is particularly important for the tribunal to be able to correct such errors, as they could otherwise constitute a basis for the setting-aside of the award.[10] The Working Group resolved this matter by amending the wording to read, in article 38(1) of the 2010 Rules, 'or any error *or omission* of a similar nature' (emphasis added). The Working Group noted, however, that this revised wording was not intended to cover omissions of substance.[11]

5. All three categories of error described in article 38(1) fall within the notion of inadvertent slips. This point is important in construing the last part of the first sentence of this paragraph, which speaks of 'any error or omission *of a similar nature*' (emphasis added) to computational, clerical or typographical errors. The error must thus be of a material nature rather than an intellectual error in the tribunal's judgment. To illustrate, identifying in an award a witness by a wrong name is an error; but misconstruing the witness's testimony is not. Nevertheless, errors are not confined to the purely mechanical. This is clear from the inclusion of omissions in article 38(1). If it is evident on the face of the award that the tribunal did decide a point in a certain way but failed to record its decision (whether at all or in part) on this point in the dispositive section of the award, then the omission can be rectified through an article 38 correction. The correction may amount to an explicit ruling that a certain claim has been dismissed. If, by contrast, there is no foundation in the award for concluding that the tribunal merely failed to record something that it had decided, the situation must be characterized as a substantive omission falling within article 39 (additional award). To illustrate, if the tribunal's award leaves no doubt that default interest at a certain annual rate should be awarded for two years but the dispositive portion of the award only computes one year's worth of interest, this is an error. By contrast, if the tribunal failed altogether to decide either way on a claim for post-award interest, that is a matter calling for an additional award.

6. It is clear that there can be cases where the line between correction and other remedies is less than bright. It is also clear that the remedy of correction – and to a lesser extent also interpretation and additional awards – may serve as an opportunity to reconsider and modify portions of an award. It is less clear that such questionable uses of post-award remedies can attract setting-aside. There is authority for the proposition that they cannot, on grounds that only the tribunal

---

9 *See* UNCITRAL Report of 45th Session, 5 October 2006, UN Doc A/CN.9/614, para. 127.

10 *See* Jan Paulsson & Georgios Petrochilos, *Revision of the UNCITRAL Rules* (September 2006), para. 269, <www.uncitral.org>; *see also* Pieter Sanders, *Has the Moment Come to Revise the Arbitration Rules of UNCITRAL?*, 20(3) Arb Int 243, 256 (2004) (where Sanders argues that the phrase 'errors of similar nature' would not cover the eventuality 'in case arbitrators omitted to sign their award or omitted to state the date or place of the award', and that an award may be set aside as a result).

11 *See* UNCITRAL Report of 51st Session, 10 November 2009, UN Doc A/CN.9/684, paras 109-110; and UNCITRAL Working Paper for 46th Session, 6 December 2006, UN Doc A/CN.9/WG.II/WP.145/Add.1, para. 41.

can interpret the scope of its post award remedies.[12] In manifest and grave cases, it may however be open to the reviewing court to find that the tribunal's approach was a violation of the parties' agreed procedure (cf. Article 34(2)(a)(iv) of the Model Law).

B. TIME-LIMITS

7. As already mentioned, the drafters of the 2010 Rules decided to set a specific time-limit within which the arbitral tribunal must make a correction requested by one of the parties. The tribunal must make the correction 'within 45 days of receipt of the request'. This is consistent with the time-limit provided in article 37(2) of the 2010 Rules (interpretation of the award). However, unlike article 39(2) of the 2010 Rules (additional award) and Article 33(4) of the UNCITRAL Model Law, article 38 does not expressly allow the tribunal to extend the 45-day time-limit on its own motion. This matter has been discussed above in connection with the remedy of interpretation.[13] The 45-day time-limit applies only where the request for correction originates from a party; the 30-day time-limit provided in article 38(2), which starts as of the communication of the award, applies where the tribunal makes corrections 'on its own initiative'.

8. The 2010 Rules do not provide for a specific procedure under article 38. Nevertheless, when a party requests that the tribunal make a correction, article 17(1) requires that the tribunal give the other party a reasonable opportunity to comment on the request. As one commentator notes, even if the correction appears evident or is limited in scope, the tribunal should hear any arguments any other parties may wish to raise before making the correction.[14] If the tribunal instigates a correction, it should likewise inform the parties of its intention and invite views from them before deciding how to proceed.[15]

---

12 *See T.Co Metals LLC v. Dempsey Pipe & Supply Inc.*, 592 F.3d (2d Cir. 2010) (refusing to vacate an 'Amended Final Award' which was based on reconsideration of the record evidence on grounds that the power to assess the permitted scope of correction rested with the tribunal, 'irrespective of whether it decided the issue correctly').

13 *See* comments regarding article 17(2), *supra*.

14 *See* Thomas H. Webster, *Handbook of UNCITRAL Arbitration*, para. 38-6 (2nd ed., Sweet & Maxwell 2015), citing to *Ed Bulley Ventures Ltd v. Eton-West Construction Inc* [2002] BCSC 826 (where a challenge to the arbitrator's additional award, on the basis that it constituted a reconsideration of issues addressed in his initial award, was rejected by the Canadian Court. The British Columbia Supreme Court found that, in his initial award, the arbitrator had clearly left open the contested issue and invited the parties to advise him should any corrections be required).

15 *Ibid.*, at para. 38-24.

C. JUSTIFYING THE REQUEST FOR CORRECTION

9. The *travaux préparatoires* do not elaborate on the circumstances in which a request for correction under article 38(1) of the 2010 Rules would be justified.[16] However, the intentions of the drafters of the 1976 Rules demonstrate the discretion the tribunal retains in this regard:

> Even in cases where the arbitrators receive a timely request from one or both parties that an error in the award [be] corrected, the arbitrators have full discretion to decide whether or not they wish to issue such a correction (e.g., the arbitrators may decide that the alleged error whose correction was requested was not an error at all).[17]

10. As Baker and Davis explain:

> [T]he number of requests to the [Iran-US Claims] Tribunal for reconsideration disguised as requests for corrections, interpretations, and additional awards clearly demonstrates the irresistible temptation for disappointed parties to allege whatever it takes to get the arbitrators to reconsider.[18]

This is precisely the situation that the 2010 provision seeks to address by providing, in article 38(1), that the tribunal shall determine whether the request for correction is 'justified'. This is ultimately a question for the tribunal's judgment. In this respect, the Iran-US Claims Tribunal has 'interpreted its authority to make corrections narrowly and its discretion to refuse requests for corrections broadly', for instance by deciding that 'an alleged error in identifying the claimant' which had no impact on the payment of the award 'did not fall within the category of mistakes for which a correction may be issued'.[19] Conversely, mistakes requiring corrections included the confusion of Georgian and Persian dates, a failure to account for an amount that should have been accounted for in a calculation, and mathematical errors.[20] In practice, a request is likely to be considered unjustified where the party is seeking to correct a reasoned conclusion, as opposed to an

---

16 *See* UNCITRAL Working Paper for 52nd Session, 10 December 2009, UN Doc A/CN.9/WG.II/WP.157/Add.2, paras 13-14. Article 33(1) of the Model Law contains identical wording as regards justification.

17 *See* UNCITRAL Report of the Secretary General on the Draft UNCITRAL Arbitration Rules, 12 December 1975, UN Doc A/CN.9/112/Add.1, 180 para. 2.

18 Stewart A. Baker & Mark D. Davis, *The UNCITRAL Arbitration Rules in Practice – The Experience of the Iran-United States Claims Tribunal*, 204 (Kluwer 1992).

19 *See*, e.g., *Bank Markazi Iran v. European American Banking Corp*, Case No. 679, Chamber Two, Order of 22 January 1986; *Component Builders, Inc v. Islamic Republic of Iran* (1985) 9 Iran-US CTR 404, 404-405; and *Paul Donin de Rosiere v. Islamic Republic of Iran* (1987) 14 Iran-US CTR 100, 101. *See also* Baker & Davis, *supra* fn 19, at 195-196.

20 *See* Baker & Davis, *supra* fn 19, at 195-196. Outside the practice of the Iran-US Claims Tribunal, *see Melvin J Howard, Centurion Health Corp & Howard Family Trust v. The Government of Canada* (UNCITRAL) Correction of Order for the Termination of Proceedings and Award on Costs, 9 August 2010, < www.italaw.com > (providing, *inter alia*, that the words 'The Hague' in the dispositive section of the award shall be struck and replaced with the word 'Toronto'); and *Guaracachi America Inc and Rurelec PLC v. The Plurinational State of Bolivia* (UNCITRAL) Letter from Tribunal to Parties on Correction of Award, 3 March 2014,

unintentional error made by the tribunal.[21] It is also possible that the request concerns an immaterial detail (for example, in a factual narrative set out by way of background) which the tribunal may come to regard as not justifying supplementing its award and possibly diluting its force.

D. CORRECTION FORMS PART OF THE AWARD

11. Although corrections may have implicitly formed part of the award under the 1976 Rules,[22] article 38(3) of the 2010 Rules now explicitly states that they do so.

12. The discussions preceding the adoption of the 1976 Rules do not shed light on why article 36 did not explicitly state that corrections were part of the award. However, the *travaux préparatoires* for article 35 of the 1976 Rules (interpretation of the award) do reveal that the legal effect of corrections or interpretations was considered a matter regulated by national arbitration law, which may explain why the 1976 Rules did not directly address this issue.[23] During the 2010 revision process, the Working Group decided to align the relevant provisions, and to clarify that any correction shall form part of the award.[24] The provision also serves as 'an agreement between the parties to extend the arbitral tribunal's authority beyond the date of the award' for the purposes of the correction.[25]

13. The new wording also prevents a party from attempting to resist enforcement and recognition of the corrected award. This is confirmed by the second sentence of article 38(3), which subjects corrections to the technical requirements of awards. Further, the correction is also subject to the majority rule provided in article 33 of the 2010 Rules.[26] As with interpretations of the award, the ultimate status of the correction will, however, depend on the applicable national arbitration law.[27]

14. As noted in our commentary on article 37, article 38(3) does not offer guidance as to the instrument through which to effect a correction. In contrast, the ICC Rules provide that the '[a] decision to correct ... the award shall take the form of

---

< www.italaw.com > (concerning, *inter alia*, the correction of clerical and typographical errors in the Spanish version of the award).

21 *See* Caron & Caplan, *supra* fn 2, at 813, citing to *Picker International Corporation v. Islamic Republic of Iran* (1986) 12 Iran-US CTR 306, 307 (where the tribunal denied a request for correction of the wording used to identify the claimant); and *Petrolane Inc v. Islamic Republic of Iran* (1991) 27 Iran-US CTR 264 (where the tribunal denied a request for correction of its characterisation of an earlier decision as an 'award').

22 David D. Caron, Lee M. Caplan & Matti Pellonpää, *The UNCITRAL Arbitration Rules, A Commentary*, 895-896 (Oxford University Press 2006) (noting that, in respect of article 36 of the 1976 Rules, '[a] correction forms part of the award and thus may be enforced domestically and internationally along with the award'). *See also* Caron & Caplan, *supra* fn 2, at 815.

23 *See* commentary on article 35 of the 2010 Rules, *supra*.

24 *See* UNCITRAL Report of 51st Session, 10 November 2009, UN Doc A/CN.9/684, paras 111-112.

25 Caron & Caplan, *supra* fn 2, at 812.

26 *Ibid*.

27 *Ibid*.

an addendum and shall constitute part of the award'.[28] The WIPO Rules provide that '[a]ny correction, which shall take the form of a separate memorandum, signed by the Tribunal ... shall become part of the award'.[29] Similarly, the LCIA Rules also state that the correction 'shall take the form of a memorandum by the Arbitral Tribunal'.[30] As noted in discussion of article 37, although the 'Correction to Award' is dated, that date 'is not intended under the Rules to have any legal effect on the original date of the award, a question that ultimately is determined by the law governing the award'.[31]

15. Tribunals have developed their own practices. For example, the Iran-US Claims Tribunal issues a 'Correction to Award', setting out its decision on the alleged errors, with the corrected pages of the award and a signature page, including the signatures of the majority of arbitrators in favour of the correction, provided in an appendix.[32]

E. COSTS

16. Article 40(4) of the 1976 Rules states that no additional fees may be charged by an arbitral tribunal for the correction of its award. Article 40(3) of the 2010 Rules sets out the same rule: the arbitral tribunal may only charge the parties for the incidental costs in relation to the correction of an award, such as the reasonable travel and other expenses of the arbitrators, as provided in article 40(2)(b)-(f). It is possible that necessary costs may include fees and expenses of the tribunal-appointed expert (article 29) whom the tribunal may need to consult in respect of an error of a technical nature. The rationale underlying the no-fees rule is that, if the need arises to cure ambiguities, errors or omissions in order to prevent annulment and ensure the enforceability of the award, additional work by the tribunal should not come at a cost to the parties.

28 *See* Article 36(3) of the ICC Rules.
29 *See* Article 68(a) of the WIPO Rules.
30 *See* Article 27.1 of the LCIA Rules.
31 Caron & Caplan, *supra* fn 2, at 814.
32 *Ibid.*, citing to *Harold Birnbaum v. Islamic Republic of Iran*, Correction to Award No 549-967-2, 19 July 1993.

Article 39
Additional award

1976 Rules Article 37: Additional award	2010 Rules Article 39: Additional award
1. Within thirty days after the receipt of the award, either party, with notice to the other party, may request the arbitral tribunal to make an additional award as to claims presented in the arbitral proceedings but omitted from the award. 2. If the arbitral tribunal considers the request for an additional award to be justified and considers that the omission can be rectified without any further hearings or evidence, it shall complete its award within sixty days after the receipt of the request. 3. When an additional award is made, the provisions of article 32, paragraphs 2 to 7, shall apply.	1. Within 30 days after the receipt of the termination order or the award, a party, with notice to the other parties, may request the arbitral tribunal to make an award or an additional award as to claims presented in the arbitral proceedings but not decided by the arbitral tribunal. 2. If the arbitral tribunal considers the request for an award or additional award to be justified, it shall render or complete its award within 60 days after the receipt of the request. The arbitral tribunal may extend, if necessary, the period of time within which it shall make the award. 3. When such an award or additional award is made, the provisions of article 34, paragraphs 2 to 6, shall apply.

1. After interpretation and correction (articles 37-38), article 39 provides a further, exceptional post-award extension of the tribunal's authority where this is necessary to ensure that the award has its proper effect. It empowers the tribunal to 'make an award or an additional award' where a claim presented during the proceedings was left undecided by the tribunal.[1] This provision reflects the drafters' concerns that, in many jurisdictions, an award which does not address all

---

[1] This is also referred to as *infra petita*. *See* Peter Binder, *Analytical Commentary to the UNCITRAL Arbitration Rules*, para. 39-005 (Sweet & Maxwell 2013).

the claims raised in the arbitration may not be recognized or enforced,[2] or possibly even set aside (as opposed to being remitted to the tribunal for reconsideration). The corrective mechanism in article 39 therefore prevents the neutralisation of a lengthy, costly arbitration where the arbitrators have 'inadvertently failed to rule in their award on each part of every claim raised during the arbitral proceedings'.[3] Thus, the tribunal's jurisdiction is extended where a party makes a 'justified' request for an additional award.[4]

2. The three prongs of article 39 of the 2010 Rules, as well as the modifications to the 1976 corresponding provision, are addressed below.

A. REQUEST FOR AN AWARD OR AN ADDITIONAL AWARD: ARTICLE 39(1)

3. Article 37 of the 1976 Rules provides that, within 30 days of having received the award, and giving notice to the other party, a party may request that the tribunal make an additional award. This provision therefore does not provide for the situation where the arbitral tribunal has issued a termination order pursuant to article 34 of the 1976 Rules (article 36 of the 2010 Rules) despite having failed to address certain of the parties' claims. Under the 2010 Rules, article 39 provides that the tribunal may issue an 'award' (as opposed to an 'additional award'), where it has issued a termination order but must subsequently address claims that it has left undecided.[5] This change is also reflected in the new wording of article 39(1), which was revised from 'claims presented in the arbitral proceedings but omitted from the award' to 'claims presented in the arbitral proceedings *but not decided by the arbitral tribunal*' (emphasis added).[6]

4. Under both the 1976 and 2010 versions of the Rules, the scope of an additional award should be limited to claims that were in fact presented in the arbitral

---

2 *See* UNCITRAL Report of the Secretary General on the Draft UNCITRAL Arbitration Rules, 12 December 1975, UN Doc A/CN.9/112/Add.1, 180 para. 1 ('Most national arbitration laws provide that the arbitrators' failure or omission to deal with all the claims raised in the arbitration is sufficient reason for setting aside or refusing to enforce an award'). Note, however, that this is not a ground for refusal of recognition or enforcement of the award under Article V(1)(c) of the New York Convention. *See also* David D. Caron & Lee M. Caplan, *The UNCITRAL Arbitration Rules, A Commentary*, 821 (2nd ed., Oxford University Press 2013); Nicola C. Port, Scott E. Bowers, et al., 'Article V(1)(c)' in Herbert Kronke, Patricia Nacimiento, et al. (eds), *Recognition and Enforcement of Foreign Arbitral Awards: A Global Commentary on the New York Convention*, 276 (Kluwer 2010); and John Savage & Emmanuel Gaillard (eds), *Fouchard, Gaillard, Goldman on International Commercial Arbitration*, para. 1700 (Kluwer 1999).

3 *See* UNCITRAL Report of the Secretary General on the Draft UNCITRAL Arbitration Rules, 12 December 1975, UN Doc A/CN.9/112/Add.1, 180 para. 1.

4 *See* Stewart A. Baker & Mark D. Davis, *The UNCITRAL Arbitration Rules in Practice – The Experience of the Iran-United States Claims Tribunal*, 196 (Kluwer 1992). Similar provisions allowing for an additional award can be found in, e.g., Article 37 of the Swiss Rules, Article 48 of the SCC Rules and Article 27.3 of the LCIA Rules.

5 *See* UNCITRAL Report of 51st Session, 10 November 2009, UN Doc A/CN.9/684, para. 113.

6 *Ibid.*, at para. 115.

proceedings. The relevant provisions are not to serve as a means by which a party, having failed to raise an issue or submit evidence, may go back to correct such failings.[7] In short, these provisions do not permit the tribunal to revisit its final awards.[8] Article 39 was intended to address instances of obvious omissions where arbitrators have 'failed to render a complete award'; for example, by failing to fix or apportion arbitration costs or to rule on a particular claim.[9] This provision was not intended to apply, however, where the tribunal deliberately elects not to address a particular claim or issue in the award because it regards it as unnecessary to do so given their decisions on other issues which render further consideration moot.[10] In order to avoid any ambiguity on this score, tribunals may well document the disposition of all claims in the award, 'no matter how small or inconsequential their bearing is on the outcome of the case'.[11] A formula which tribunals sometimes employ to that end is to record in the dispositive part of their decision that they thereby reject all other claims and submissions.

5. Under both article 37(1) of the 1976 Rules and article 39(1) of the 2010 Rules, a party must request the additional award: the tribunal may not act on its own initiative. However, one may argue with considerable force that the tribunal may (or even should) inform the parties of any important omissions it may discover, pursuant to its duty to ensure the enforceability and validity of the award.[12] The decision whether or not to make a request for an additional award will then rest with the parties.

B. RENDERING OF THE AWARD OR ADDITIONAL AWARD: ARTICLE 39(2)

6. Under article 39(2) of the 2010 Rules, it is for the tribunal to determine whether a request for an additional award is 'justified'. This was also the position under article 37(2) of the 1976 Rules,[13] and, in practice, tribunals have exercised their authority to reject requests for additional awards on a number of grounds.[14] For

---

7 Baker & Davis, *supra* fn 4, at 197. *See also* Pieter Sanders, *Commentary on UNCITRAL Arbitration Rules*, II YCA 172, 176, 213 (1977).

8 James E. Castello, 'UNCITRAL Arbitration Rules, Section IV, Article 39' in Loukas A. Mistelis (ed), *Concise International Arbitration*, 257-258 (2nd ed., Kluwer 2015).

9 Caron & Caplan, *supra* fn 2, at 822; *see also* Sanders, *supra* fn 7, at 213.

10 *See* Baker & Davis, *supra* fn 4, at 197; *see also* UNCITRAL Summary Record of the 12th Meeting, 22 April 1976, UN Doc A/CN.9/9/C.2/SR.12, para. 25, Mr Pirrung (Federal Republic of Germany).

11 *See* Caron & Caplan, *supra* fn 2, at 823.

12 *Ibid.*

13 *See* UNCITRAL Report of the Secretary General on the Draft UNCITRAL Arbitration Rules, 12 December 1975, UN Doc A/CN.9/112/Add.1, 181 para. 4; *see also* Baker & Davis, *supra* fn 4, at 197; and *Harris International Telecommunications Inc v. Islamic Republic of Iran* (1988) 18 Iran-US CTR 76 (where the tribunal rejected a request by indicating that the award had been 'expressly restricted' to the issue in question; i.e., that the tribunal's omission of the point in question had been intentional).

14 Caron & Caplan, *supra* fn 2, at 823. *See also* Baker & Davis, *supra* fn 4, at 198 (noting one 'archetypical case' in which the Iran-US Claims Tribunal did grant a request under article 37 as a result of its failure to rule on a request for costs).

example, tribunals in some cases have considered that, contrary to a party's allegations, no claims had been omitted,[15] or that the alleged omissions had in fact been sufficiently addressed in the award.[16] For example, in *British Caribbean Bank,* the respondent requested an additional award on the basis that the tribunal had failed to rule on the question of whether the general methodology, as articulated in the *Chorzow Factory* case[17] applied, or if compensation could be calculated according to special requirements in the relevant investment treaty. The claimant argued that the respondent was merely attempting to challenge the tribunal's reasoning on compensation, and that the tribunal had fully and finally disposed of the issue of compensation in its final award. The tribunal agreed with the claimant and rejected the request for an additional award.[18]

7. Under article 37(2) of the 1976 Rules, the tribunal could only 'complete its award' if the request was justified and the omission 'c[ould] be rectified without any further hearings or evidence'.[19] Article 39(2) of the 2010 Rules removes this requirement, recognizing that arbitrators should be free to convene fresh hearings or call for further evidence if they consider that this is necessary for the tribunal to render or complete an award. This change was inspired by Article 33(3) of the UNCITRAL Model Law. The drafters of the Model Law considered that the entire award could be at risk of being set aside if the tribunal was denied the possibility of an adversarial process,[20] and the drafters of the 2010 Rules agreed.[21]

C. TIME-LIMITS

8. Article 39 of the 2010 Rules lays down two time-limits. First, parties have 30 days from the receipt of the award or termination order to submit a request. Second, the tribunal has 60 days from the receipt of such a request 'to render or complete its award'.

9. In contrast to article 37(2) of the 1976 Rules, article 39(2) of the 2010 Rules now expressly allows the tribunal to extend, 'if necessary', the time-limit for making

---

15 *See*, e.g., *Woodward-Clyde Consultants v. Islamic Republic of Iran*, Case No. 67, Chamber Three, Order of 30 December 1983; *Flexi-Van Leasing Inc v. Islamic Republic of Iran* (1986) 13 Iran-US CTR 325, 327; *Exxon Research and Engineering Co v. Islamic Republic of Iran* (1987) 16 Iran-US CTR 110, 111.

16 *See*, e.g., *Harris International Telecommunications Inc v. Islamic Republic of Iran* (1988) 18 Iran-US CTR 76, 77.

17 *See Case Concerning the Factory at Chorzow (Germany v. Poland)*, PCIJ Series A No 9 (1927).

18 *See British Caribbean Bank Limited v. The Government of Belize* (PCA Case No. 2010-18) Decision on the Respondent Motion pursuant to the UNCITRAL Arbitration Rules, Articles 36 and 37, 7 March 2015, < www.italaw.com >.

19 *See* UNCITRAL Report of the Secretary General on the Draft UNCITRAL Arbitration Rules, 12 December 1975, UN Doc A/CN.9/112/Add.1, 181 para. 4; Caron & Caplan, *supra* fn 2, at 823; Sanders, *supra* fn 7, at 213.

20 Caron & Caplan, *supra* fn 2, at 823.

21 *Ibid.*; *see also* UNCITRAL Report of 45th Session, 5 October 2006, UN Doc A/CN.9/614, para. 128.

the award. In practice, the possibility for extension will facilitate briefing and also adequate consultation between the arbitrators in preparing the additional award, particularly in complex cases. This revision, which is consistent with the UNCITRAL Model Law,[22] was not without controversy in the Working Group. In fact, the terms 'if necessary' were the result of a compromise, signalling that tribunals should not unhesitatingly grant themselves extensions.[23] In the absence of good reasons justifying the extension, the arbitral tribunal 'shall' render or complete its award within the time-limit provided. The use of the term 'shall' implies more than a best-efforts undertaking; it implies that the tribunal has a duty to render or complete the award within the stipulated time-limit.[24] This is also consistent with the statement of availability provided in the Annex to the 2010 Rules,[25] and the tribunal's duty, under article 17(1) of the 2010 Rules, to provide a fair and efficient arbitral process.

D. TECHNICAL REQUIREMENTS: ARTICLE 39(3)

10. Although this may or may not be necessary, depending on the *lex arbitri*,[26] article 39 of the 2010 Rules nevertheless serves as an agreement between the parties to prolong the tribunal's jurisdiction over the dispute. Therefore, the additional award is an award within the meaning of the Rules and must comply with the requirements in article 34(2)-(6), as provided by article 39(3). The additional award must also comply with the majority-vote requirement stipulated in article 33(1).[27]

---

22 *See* Article 33(4) of the Model Law (providing, in pertinent part, that '[t]he arbitral tribunal may extend, if necessary, the period of time within which it shall make a correction, interpretation or an additional award'). *See also* Pieter Sanders, *Has the Moment Come to Revise the Arbitration Rules of UNCITRAL?*, 20(3) Arb Int 243, 256 (2004).

23 Cf. article 25 of the 2010 Rules, which requires the application of a standard of justifiability – as opposed to necessity – in determining whether a time-limit extension should be permitted for the communication of written statements.

24 For an example of the distinction between 'undertake' and 'shall', *see Avena and Other Mexican Nationals (Mexico v. United States of America)*, Judgment, ICJ Rep 12, 50 (2004). The ICJ concluded that the 'shall' found in article 36, paragraph 1 (*b*) of the Vienna Convention on Consular Relations imposed more than a best-efforts undertaking upon the United States. According to the Court, 'shall' was to be understood as imposing an 'obligation incumbent upon [the United States]'.

25 The statement of availability is listed in the Annex to the 2010 Rules as an 'addition to the statement of independence'. It provides: 'I confirm, on the basis of the information presently available to me, that I can devote the time necessary to conduct this arbitration diligently, efficiently and in accordance with the time limits in the Rules'.

26 *See* Caron & Caplan, *supra* fn 2, at 822 (explaining that, '[i]n some jurisdictions, an award that fails to address all claims is not a final award; thus the arbitral tribunal's jurisdiction over the dispute remains in force until all outstanding claims are resolved').

27 *Ibid.*

Article 40
Definition of costs

1976 Rules Article 38: Costs	2010 Rules Article 40: Definition of costs
The arbitral tribunal shall fix the costs of arbitration in its award. The term 'costs' includes only:	1. The arbitral tribunal shall fix the costs of arbitration in the final award and, if it deems appropriate, in another decision.
	2. The term 'costs' includes only:
(a) The fees of the arbitral tribunal to be stated separately as to each arbitrator and to be fixed by the tribunal itself in accordance with article 39;	(a) The fees of the arbitral tribunal to be stated separately as to each arbitrator and to be fixed by the tribunal itself in accordance with article 41;
(b) The travel and other expenses incurred by the arbitrators;	(b) The reasonable travel and other expenses incurred by the arbitrators;
(c) The costs of expert advice and of other assistance required by the arbitral tribunal;	(c) The reasonable costs of expert advice and of other assistance required by the arbitral tribunal;
(d) The travel and other expenses of witnesses to the extent such expenses are approved by the arbitral tribunal;	(d) The reasonable travel and other expenses of witnesses to the extent such expenses are approved by the arbitral tribunal;
(e) The costs for legal representation and assistance of the successful party if such costs were claimed during the arbitral proceedings, and only to the extent that the arbitral tribunal determines that the amount of such costs is reasonable;	(e) The legal and other costs incurred by the parties in relation to the arbitration to the extent that the arbitral tribunal determines that the amount of such costs is reasonable;
(f) Any fees and expenses of the appointing authority as well as the expenses of the Secretary-General of the Permanent Court of Arbitration at The Hague.	(f) Any fees and expenses of the appointing authority as well as the fees and expenses of the Secretary-General of the PCA.
	3. In relation to interpretation, correction or completion of any award under articles

	37 to 39, the arbitral tribunal may charge the costs referred to in paragraphs 2 (b) to (f), but no additional fees.

1. An international arbitration is often a costly affair for the parties. Compared to litigation before national courts, there are additional costs (the hiring of the hearing facilities, costs of interpretation, transcription services, travel and accommodation etc.) and the arbitrators' fees and expenses[1] (normally defrayed in the form of advance monetary deposits).[2] Articles 40 and 41 of the 2010 Rules were drafted against the background of increasing pressure on the arbitration community to demonstrate cost-effectiveness.[3]

2. Article 40 of the 2010 Rules determines the method for fixing costs and defines the notion of (recoverable) 'costs'. Specifically: article 40(1) provides that the costs should be fixed in the final award or, where appropriate, any other decision; article 40(2) provides a definition of costs; and article 40(3) addresses the costs of the correction, interpretation or completion of awards. These three components are addressed in turn below.

A. FIXING THE COSTS OF ARBITRATION: ARTICLE 40(1)

3. Article 40(1) of the 2010 Rules differs from its predecessor in article 38 of the 1976 Rules in that it allows the tribunal to fix costs at any stage of the proceedings, including in a termination order and in decisions made under articles 37-39.[4] Whereas article 38 of the 1976 Rules provides that the arbitral tribunal '*shall* fix the costs of arbitration in its award' (emphasis added), article 40(1) of the 2010 Rules recognizes the need for flexibility.[5] The tribunal may therefore decide on the costs of a discrete phase of the proceedings that led to (for example) a

---

1 *See* Nigel Blackaby, Constantine Partasides, Alan Redfern & Martin J. Hunter, *Redfern and Hunter on International Arbitration*, paras 9.87-9.90 (6th ed., Kluwer 2015).

2 *See* David D. Caron & Lee M. Caplan, *The UNCITRAL Arbitration Rules, A Commentary*, 840 (2nd ed., Oxford University Press 2013).

3 *See* Thomas H. Webster, *Handbook of UNCITRAL Arbitration*, para. 40-4 (2nd ed., Sweet & Maxwell 2015); *see also* Blackaby, Partasides, Redfern & Hunter, *supra* fn 1, at paras 9.85-9.86; and Queen Mary University of London & White & Case LLP, *2015 International Arbitration Survey: Improvements and Innovations in International Arbitration* (2015), < www.arbitration.qmul.ac.uk >, 24-32 (noting that respondents to a user survey ranked 'cost and lack of speed ... amongst the worst characteristics of international arbitration', and illustrating arbitration users' favourable views towards expedited procedures and emergency arbitrator provisions).

4 UNCITRAL Report of 52nd Session, 19 February 2010, UN Doc A/CN.9/688, para. 16. *See also* Webster, *supra* fn 3, at para. 40-8.

5 Article 40(1) of the 2010 Rules therefore grants the tribunal greater freedom regarding decisions on costs than is seen in other sets of arbitration rules: *see*, e.g., Article 38 of the Swiss Rules; Article 73 of the WIPO Rules (providing that costs are to be fixed in the award). Cf. Article 38(3) of the ICC Rules (providing that, '[a]t any time during the arbitral proceedings, the arbitral tribunal may make decisions on costs ... and order payment').

jurisdictional decision or an order on interim measures, or issue one or more separate awards on costs,[6] or fix the costs in a termination order pursuant to article 36(1).[7] For example, the tribunal in *HICEE BV v. Slovak Republic* allocated the costs of the arbitration in a partial award, subsequently addressing, in a final and supplementary award, the additional costs incurred by the tribunal and the PCA in the course of the claimant's challenge to an arbitrator.[8] Nevertheless, in the majority of cases it is sensible for the arbitral tribunal to fix the costs in its final award,[9] and it is generally good practice for tribunals to render their decisions on costs in the form of an 'award' – as opposed to 'another decision' pursuant to article 40(1) – in order to ensure enforceability.[10]

4. In sum, article 40(1) *requires* the tribunal to fix the costs in its final award ('shall fix the costs') and *permits* it to do so in other decisions if possible and appropriate to fix costs in respect of earlier, discrete phases of the proceedings. Thus the conjunctive 'and' in paragraph (1) of article 40 effectively means *and/or* (and the wording 'or' was in fact also considered in earlier drafts).[11]

B. DEFINING COSTS: ARTICLE 40(2)

5. Article 40(2) provides an exhaustive list of expenditures incurred by either the parties or the arbitral tribunal which constitute recoverable 'costs'.[12] The list includes arbitrator fees and their travel and other expenses ((a) and (b)); the costs of expert advice and other assistance required by the tribunal (c); travel and other expenses of witnesses if approved by the tribunal in its cost decision (d); legal and other costs incurred by the parties (e); and any fees and expenses of the appointing authority and of the Secretary-General of the PCA

---

6 *See*, e.g., *S D Myers Inc v. Government of Canada* (UNCITRAL) Final Award on Costs, 30 December 2002, < www.italaw.com >; *Pope & Talbot Inc v. The Government of Canada* (UNCITRAL) Award in Respect of Costs, 26 November 2002, < www.italaw.com >. *See also* UNCITRAL Report of 51st Session, 10 November 2009, UN Doc A/CN.9/684, para. 120 (noting that 'the arbitral tribunal might fix the costs of the arbitration in more than one award').

7 *See*, e.g., *Canfor Corporation v. United States of America and Tembec et al. v. United States of America and Terminal Forest Products Ltd v. United States of America* (UNCITRAL) Joint Order on the Costs of Arbitration and for the Termination of Certain Arbitral Proceedings, 19 July 2007, < www.italaw.com >. *See also* UNCITRAL Report of 52nd Session, 19 February 2010, UN Doc A/CN.9/688, para. 16.

8 *See HICEE BV v. The Slovak Republic* (UNCITRAL) Partial Award, 23 May 2011, < www.italaw.com >, para. 151; *HICEE BV v. The Slovak Republic* (UNCITRAL) Supplementary and Final Award, 17 October 2011, < www.italaw.com >, paras 7-8.

9 Caron & Caplan, *supra* fn 2, at 842.

10 *Ibid.*

11 *See* UNCITRAL Report of 52nd Session, 19 February 2010, UN Doc A/CN.9/688, para. 16.

12 *See* UNCITRAL Report of 45th Session, 5 October 2006, UN Doc A/CN.9/614, para. 130 ('It was stated that the word "only" used in the chapeau resulted in the list being exhaustive'). According to one commentator, where a cost does not fall under articles 40(2)(a)-(f), the tribunal must decide whether it has authority to award additional costs (which could be done either pursuant to the arbitration agreement or under the law applicable to the arbitration). *See* Webster, *supra* fn 3, at para. 40-13.

(f). Defining 'costs' is important as it gives rise to certain rights and obligations under articles 41 and 42 of the 2010 Rules, notably the ability to recover costs as the prevailing party.[13]

6. The list provided in articles 38(a)-(f) of the 1976 Rules has remained largely unchanged in the 2010 Rules, although the term 'reasonable' has been inserted in the 2010 Rules as an important qualifier to the provisions of articles 40(2)(b)-(e).[14] In fact, the 1976 Rules required only that the amount of arbitrators' fees be 'reasonable' (pursuant to article 39), while there was no such requirement for the other costs listed in article 38. The Working Group undertook to address this issue from the very outset of the revision process.[15] While it is evident from the *travaux* of the 1976 Rules that the drafters were mostly concerned with the reasonableness of the arbitrators' fees,[16] the 2010 Rules drafters considered it necessary to include the reasonableness standard throughout article 40(2), particularly in light of the tribunal's duties under article 17(1) of the 2010 Rules.[17]

7. The tribunal has authority and must exercise judgement, in a judicial manner, to determine the 'reasonableness' of costs. To this end, article 41(1) of the 2010 Rules, which addresses arbitrators' fees and expenses, provides considerable guidance by stating that the amount in dispute, the complexity of the subject-matter, the time spent by the arbitrators and any other relevant circumstances of the case, should all be taken into account.

1. Fees of the arbitral tribunal: article 40(2)(a)

8. The remuneration for the arbitrators' services in resolving the dispute obviously forms part of costs. Both versions of the Rules require that the amount of each arbitrator's remuneration be indicated by the tribunal itself in its final award (or in 'another decision', under the 2010 Rules). The drafters intended for this requirement to ensure that the arbitrators do not 'run up the costs of arbitral

---

13 *See*, e.g., *Khan Resources Inc et al. v. Government of Mongolia* (UNCITRAL) Award on the Merits, 2 March 2015, <www.italaw.com>, para. 442 (where the tribunal considered that the costs of keeping certain entities running, i.e. 'salaries, insurance, office expenses, investor relations costs etc.' during the arbitration did not fall within any of the categories set out in article 40 of the 2010 Rules and were therefore unrecoverable).

14 *See* UNCITRAL Report of 45th Session, 5 October 2006, UN Doc A/CN.9/614, para. 132; UNCITRAL Report of 48th Session, 29 February 2008, UN Doc A/CN.9/646, para. 18. Note also that the scope of article 40(2)(e) has been broadened, as further discussed *infra*.

15 *See* UNCITRAL Working Paper for 45th Session, 20 July 2006, UN Doc A/CN.9/WG.II/WP.143/Add.1, para. 36. *See also* Jan Paulsson & Georgios Petrochilos, *Revision of the UNCITRAL Rules* (September 2006), para. 275, <www.uncitral.org> (qualifying articles 38(b)-(d) of the 1976 Rules with the word 'reasonable' would be a desirable amendment).

16 *See* Report of the Commission on its 9th Session, 12 April-7 May 1976, UN Doc A/31/17, 80 para. 210. The Working Group made it clear, however, that the explicit use of the term in these provisions did not imply that other costs could be unreasonable; *see* Peter Binder, *Analytical Commentary to the UNCITRAL Arbitration Rules*, para. 40-014 (Sweet & Maxwell 2013).

17 *See* Binder, *supra* fn 16, at para. 40-014.

proceedings'.[18] During the 2010 revision process, the Working Group noted that stating each arbitrator's fees separately 'had proven useful ... in disciplining arbitrators and avoiding exaggerated costs'.[19]

2. Costs incurred by the arbitrators: article 40(2)(b)-(c)

9. It was uncontroversial in the revision process that the costs of 'travel and other expenses', as well as those of 'expert advice and of other assistance' should be retained within the definition of costs under article 40(2) of the 2010 Rules. The term 'expert advice' in article 40(2)(c) may refer to experts appointed by the tribunal (pursuant to article 29): although all experts, including those retained by the parties as independent experts, testify to and provide 'advice' to the tribunal with an overriding duty of providing their best professional opinion, the costs associated with party-retained experts fit more naturally within article 40(2)(e) which refers to 'legal and other costs incurred by the parties'. The term 'other expenses' refers to expenses for administrative support, such as secretarial and court-reporting services, translation and interpretation, and services requested of the appointing authority.[20] The practice of various arbitral institutions varies as to the determination of the reasonableness of expenses.[21]

3. Witness expenses: article 40(2)(d)

10. In the process of preparing the 1976 Rules, some delegates argued that travel and other expenses of witnesses should not be included in the definition of costs, as a party may, for example, 'produce so many witnesses that the costs of arbitration [become] an unbearable burden'.[22] However, the Commission retained the provision on witness expenses on the view that 'a successful party should be compensated for the expenses incurred in calling the witnesses who were instrumental in establishing the correctness of his position'.[23] Importantly, both the 1976 Rules and the 2010 Rules provide that the inclusion of witness expenses

---

18 *See* Stewart A. Baker & Mark D. Davis, *The UNCITRAL Arbitration Rules in Practice – The Experience of the Iran-United States Claims Tribunal*, 208 (Kluwer 1992).

19 *See* UNCITRAL Report of 51st Session, 10 November 2009, UN Doc A/CN.9/684, para. 121.

20 Caron & Caplan, *supra* fn 2, at 844.

21 *See* Webster, *supra* fn 3, at paras 40-16–40-18. *See also* the ICC Note on Personal and Arbitral Tribunal Expenses (1 September 2013), available at <www.iccwbo.org>.

22 *See* UNCITRAL Summary Record of the 12th Meeting, 22 April 1976, UN Doc A/CN.9/9/C.2/SR.12, para. 71, Mr Guevara (Philippines); *see also* Report of the Commission on its 9th Session, 12 April-7 May 1976, UN Doc A/31/17, 81 para. 213.

23 Report of the Commission on its 9th Session, 12 April-7 May 1976, UN Doc A/31/17, 81 para. 214. *See also* UNCITRAL Summary Record of the 12th Meeting, 22 April 1976, UN Doc A/CN.9/9/C.2/SR.12, para. 72, Mr Sanders (Special Consultant to the UNCITRAL secretariat) (noting that the wording 'to the extent such expenses are approved [by the arbitral tribunal]' had been added to article 38(d) of the 1976 Rules 'in order to avoid abuse of the right to call witnesses').

is subject to the arbitral tribunal's 'approval'.[24] Where witness expenses are found to be unreasonable – either because the witness's evidence was not germane or not probative,[25] or because the cost was excessive[26] – they may therefore be unrecoverable. Finally, the term 'other expenses' has been interpreted as referring to the subsistence costs of witnesses and other costs in connection with witness testimony.[27]

4. Parties' legal and 'other' costs: article 40(2)(e)

11. Article 38(e) of the 1976 Rules limited the costs under this heading to legal costs. Only the costs of the 'successful party' were recoverable, to the extent that these were (i) determined by the tribunal to be reasonable, and (ii) 'claimed during the arbitral proceedings'. Under the 2010 Rules, the definition of costs is extended to include 'legal or other costs incurred by the parties'. The costs of non-legal assistance, such as expert opinions, are included in this broad definition.[28] The requirement of reasonableness in relation to these costs is retained in article 40(2)(e) of the 2010 Rules, which adds that recoverable costs must have been incurred 'in relation to the arbitration' – which seems (subject to the overall requirement of reasonableness) to be broader than costs incurred in the pursuit of the arbitration and may thus (but not always will) encompass pre-arbitration advice. It is certainly the case that 'the arbitration' comprises all steps, including decisions rendered under articles 37-39.

12. Costs are no longer limited to those that the parties 'claimed' in the course of the proceedings. Naturally, the parties must claim costs for them to be awarded and for the tribunal to allocate them as between the parties pursuant to article 42.[29] The deletion of the requirement that party costs must have been claimed simply reflects that conceptually the notion of costs does not include such a requirement. The requirement of a claim operates as a prerequisite for a decision pursuant to article 42.

13. The requirement that 'legal and other costs' be incurred 'in relation to the arbitration' means that they must have 'a reasonable nexus to the preparation

---

24 *See* Report of the Commission on its 9th Session, 12 April-7 May 1976, UN Doc A/31/17, 81 para. 215.

25 Webster, *supra* fn 3, at para. 40-25 (citing to a Final Award, rendered on 21 December 1998, in an unreported UNCITRAL arbitration, where the tribunal stated that it '[was] not convinced that it was necessary to call all the witnesses who have been called', and therefore fixed the amount of costs at USD 1,250,000 where USD 1,797,571 was claimed).

26 Webster, *supra* fn 3, at para. 40-23.

27 Caron & Caplan, *supra* fn 2, at 845. *See also* UNCITRAL Summary Record of the 12th Meeting, 22 April 1976, UN Doc A/CN.9/9/C.2/SR.12, para. 77, Mr Sanders (Special Consultant to the UNCITRAL secretariat).

28 For example, the parties may seek expert opinions as to the calculation of quantum or damages. *See* Caron & Caplan, *supra* fn 2, at 845; *see also* UNCITRAL Report of 48th Session, 29 February 2008, UN Doc A/CN.9/646, para. 19.

29 Webster, *supra* fn 3, at para. 40-28.

and presentation' of the case to qualify as 'costs'.[30] This is reflected in the practice of the Iran-US Claims Tribunal, although it is possible to say that the Tribunal's practice is possibly over-restrictive and not necessarily indicative of what may be expected in a more commercial setting several decades later. In one case, for example, the Tribunal refused to award costs for a claimant's expenditures which were incurred prior to the preparation of its statement of claim.[31] The Tribunal also held that expenses incurred in litigation against Iran in US courts before the establishment of the Tribunal were not legitimate costs of a subsequent arbitration.[32] It further held that expenses incurred in relation to challenging or enforcing awards were not legitimate costs of arbitration.[33] However, in cases where litigation and arbitration expenses were closely intertwined (e.g. court-ordered provisional measures relating to the arbitral proceedings), commentators have argued that a tribunal should consider such expenses as 'costs'.[34]

14. In assessing reasonableness, the tribunal will exercise its discretion and compare the parties' respective costs, many tribunals having an inclination to regard such a comparison as almost dispositive. It will consider further, notably: the complexity of the case; the use of experts and whether such experts were helpful to the tribunal; (arguably) the parties' managers' or officials' time; and the use of in-house counsel and the effect of this on the overall cost.[35]

5. Fees and expenses of the appointing authority and Secretary-General of the PCA: article 40(2)(f)

15. Fees incurred by the appointing authority, or fees charged by the Secretary General of the PCA, are included in the costs of arbitration.[36] The PCA, for example, charges an administrative fee for analysing a request for the designation of an appointing authority.[37] Costs charged by an administering institution are also part of the costs.

---

30 Caron & Caplan, *supra* fn 2, at 846.

31 *See Granite State Machine Co Inc v. Islamic Republic of Iran* (1982) 1 Iran-US CTR 442, 448; *see also McCollough & Co Inc v. Ministry of Post, Telegraph and Telephone* (1986) 11 Iran-US CTR 44.

32 *See Sylvania Technical Systems Inc v. Islamic Republic of Iran* (1985) 8 Iran-US CTR 329, 24; and *Computer Sciences Corp v. Government of Islamic Republic of Iran* (1986-I) 10 Iran-US CTR 269, 316.

33 *See Sylvania Technical Systems Inc v. Government of Islamic Republic of Iran* (1985) Separate Opinion of Judge Holtzmann, 8 Iran-US CTR 329, 334.

34 *See* Jacomijn J. van Hof, *Commentary on the UNCITRAL Arbitration Rules, The Application by the Iran-U.S. Claims Tribunal*, 296 (Kluwer 1991).

35 Webster, *supra* fn 3, at para. 40-33.

36 *See* Report of the Commission on its 9th Session, 12 April-7 May 1976, UN Doc A/31/17, 81 para. 220.

37 Caron & Caplan, *supra* fn 2, at 846.

C. COSTS INCURRED FOR INTERPRETATION, CORRECTION OR COMPLETION OF AWARDS: ARTICLE 40(3)

16. Article 40(4) of the 1976 Rules prohibited the arbitral tribunal from charging 'additional fees' for interpretation, correction or completion of an award, but was silent as to the tribunal's ability to charge to the parties other arbitration costs, such as those enumerated under articles 38(b)-(f).[38] In contrast, the corresponding article 40(3) of the 2010 Rules maintains the prohibition on additional arbitrator fees, but now explicitly allows the arbitral tribunal to charge the costs referred to in articles 40(2)(b)-(f).

17. The argument underpinning the inclusion of article 40(4) of the 1976 Rules was founded in 'the belief that arbitrators would not deserve additional fees because the need for correction or completion of their award was due to their own fault'.[39] A debate arose during the revision process as to whether the provision should be retained: some delegates suggested that it would encourage tribunals to draft their awards 'with optimal clarity', whereas others were of the opinion that 'additional work by the tribunal could legitimately result in additional fees being charged'.[40]

18. One of the proposed solutions drew inspiration from Article 33(1)(b) of the UNCITRAL Model Law, which distinguishes unanimous party requests for interpretation, correction and completion from unilateral requests.[41] The suggestion was that arbitrators should not charge additional fees in the former case, as the unanimous nature of the request suggested that the deficiency is rooted in the tribunal's failure to render a complete and clear award. By contrast, unilateral requests were to be considered more likely to constitute attempts to delay the proceedings, thereby justifying additional arbitrator fees.[42] Another suggestion was to grant the tribunal discretion to decide whether it should charge additional fees in the circumstances of each case; but unsurprisingly, this raised the concern that the tribunal would be placed in the insidious position of appearing to be a judge in its own cause, and resulted in a stalemate.[43]

19. The Working Group therefore decided that article 40(3) of the 2010 Rules would maintain the prohibition, while explicitly allowing the tribunal to charge the costs

---

38 Such recoverable costs of the arbitral tribunal under article 38 include, inter alia, the travel and other expenses incurred, and the costs of expert advice and of other assistance required by the arbitral tribunal. *See* Caron & Caplan, *supra* fn 2, at 847-848.

39 *See* UNCITRAL Report of 48th Session, 29 February 2008, UN Doc A/CN.9/646, para. 31; Report of the Commission on its 9th Session, 12 April-7 May 1976, UN Doc A/31/17, 79 para. 192.

40 *See* UNCITRAL Report of 48th Session, 29 February 2008, UN Doc A/CN.9/646, paras 31-32; *see also* Caron & Caplan, *supra* fn 2, at 847.

41 *See* Article 33(1)(b) of the Model Law; UNCITRAL Report of 48th Session, 29 February 2008, UN Doc A/CN.9/646, paras 33-34 ('A distinction could thus be drawn between collective requests for interpretation, correction or completion of the award (which should entail no additional fees) and unilateral requests (where fees could be charged)').

42 *See* UNCITRAL Report of 48th Session, 29 February 2008, UN Doc A/CN.9/646, para. 33.

43 *Ibid.*, at paras 34-36.

enumerated in articles 40(2)(b)-(f) (corresponding to the costs enumerated under articles 38(b)-(f) of the 1976 Rules), where these were incurred in connection with the interpretation, correction or completion of the award. This decision is in some ways an unhappy compromise, in that it is possible for parties, but not for the tribunal, to claim and be awarded costs in respect of processes instigated under articles 37-39, however frivolous and/or involved such a process (or a combination thereof) may be. One hopes that the prospect of an adverse costs award will be a sufficient deterrent against frivolous or repeat applications under articles 37-39.

Article 41
Fees and expenses of arbitrators

1976 Rules Article 39: Costs	2010 Rules Article 41: Fees and expenses of arbitrators
1. The fees of the arbitral tribunal shall be reasonable in amount, taking into account the amount in dispute, the complexity of the subject-matter, the time spent by the arbitrators and any other relevant circumstances of the case.	1. The fees and expenses of the arbitrators shall be reasonable in amount, taking into account the amount in dispute, the complexity of the subject matter, the time spent by the arbitrators and any other relevant circumstances of the case.
2. If an appointing authority has been agreed upon by the parties or designated by the Secretary-General of the Permanent Court of Arbitration at The Hague, and if that authority has issued a schedule of fees for arbitrators in international cases which it administers, the arbitral tribunal in fixing its fees shall take that schedule of fees into account to the extent that it considers appropriate in the circumstances of the case.	2. If there is an appointing authority and it applies or has stated that it will apply a schedule or particular method for determining the fees for arbitrators in international cases, the arbitral tribunal in fixing its fees shall take that schedule or method into account to the extent that it considers appropriate in the circumstances of the case.
3. If such appointing authority has not issued a schedule of fees for arbitrators in international cases, any party may at any time request the appointing authority to furnish a statement setting forth the basis for establishing fees which is customarily followed in international cases in which the authority appoints arbitrators. If the appointing authority consents to provide such a statement, the arbitral tribunal in fixing its fees shall take such information into account to the extent that it considers appropriate in the circumstances of the case.	3. Promptly after its constitution, the arbitral tribunal shall inform the parties as to how it proposes to determine its fees and expenses, including any rates it intends to apply. Within 15 days of receiving that proposal, any party may refer the proposal to the appointing authority for review. If, within 45 days of receipt of such a referral, the appointing authority finds that the proposal of the arbitral tribunal is inconsistent with paragraph 1, it shall make any necessary adjustments thereto, which shall be binding upon the arbitral tribunal.

4. In cases referred to in paragraphs 2 and 3, when a party so requests and the appointing authority consents to perform the function, the arbitral tribunal shall fix its fees only after consultation with the appointing authority which may make any comment it deems appropriate to the arbitral tribunal concerning the fees.

4.

(a) When informing the parties of the arbitrators' fees and expenses that have been fixed pursuant to article 40, paragraphs 2 (a) and (b), the arbitral tribunal shall also explain the manner in which the corresponding amounts have been calculated;

(b) Within 15 days of receiving the arbitral tribunal's determination of fees and expenses, any party may refer for review such determination to the appointing authority. If no appointing authority has been agreed upon or designated, or if the appointing authority fails to act within the time specified in these Rules, then the review shall be made by the Secretary-General of the PCA;

(c) If the appointing authority or the Secretary-General of the PCA finds that the arbitral tribunal's determination is inconsistent with the arbitral tribunal's proposal (and any adjustment thereto) under paragraph 3 or is otherwise manifestly excessive, it shall, within 45 days of receiving such a referral, make any adjustments to the arbitral tribunal's determination that are necessary to satisfy the criteria in paragraph 1. Any such adjustments shall be binding upon the arbitral tribunal;

(d) Any such adjustments shall either be included by the arbitral tribunal in its award or, if the award has already been issued, be implemented in a correction to the award, to which the procedure of article 38, paragraph 3, shall apply.

5. Throughout the procedure under paragraphs 3 and 4, the arbitral tribunal shall proceed with the arbitration, in accordance with article 17, paragraph 1.

6. A referral under paragraph 4 shall not affect any determination in the award other than the arbitral tribunal's fees and expenses; nor shall it delay the recognition and enforcement of all parts of the award other than those relating to the determination of the arbitral tribunal's fees and expenses.

1. Article 41 of the 2010 Rules and its predecessor, article 39 of the 1976 Rules, govern the fees and expenses of arbitrators. The purpose of this provision has always been to set certain limits on the arbitrators' discretion in incurring and then fixing their own fees,[1] a particularly important function given the operation of the Rules in ad hoc proceedings, where there is no administering institution to exercise oversight.[2] The major change in the 2010 version is precisely this – to insert a degree of scrutiny and oversight, better to protect both the parties and also arbitrators from criticism (or perceptions) of runaway costs and self-dealing. Each limb of article 41 is discussed in turn below, with a particular focus on the four provisions that were added in 2010 (articles 41(3)-(6)).

A. FEES UNDER THE 1976 RULES

2. Under the 1976 Rules, the appointing authority played a minor role in policing arbitrators' fees. Article 39(2) provided that any schedule of fees the appointing authority had issued for arbitrators in international cases that it administered should be taken into account by the arbitral tribunal in fixing its fees, 'to the extent that [the tribunal] considers [this] appropriate'.[3] If the appointing authority had not issued a schedule of fees, a party might request that the appointing authority provide a statement 'setting forth the basis for establishing fees which is customarily followed in international cases in which the authority appoints arbitrators'.[4] In both cases, and where the (i) appointing authority consents to perform this function and (ii) a party so requests, the appointing authority may also 'make any comment it deems appropriate to the arbitral tribunal concerning the fees' before these are fixed by the arbitral tribunal.[5] These mechanisms were hardly ever used in practice.

3. The 1976 Rules therefore afforded the tribunal considerable discretion in establishing its fees, opening the door to perceptions of possible abuse or self-dealing.[6] To complicate matters, the 1976 Rules did not require that the tribunal be transparent from the outset regarding its calculation methods, and the parties may not have an incentive to keep arbitrators in check: a claimant seeking to ingratiate itself with the arbitral tribunal, for example, may choose to condone exorbitant hourly or daily fees. National courts were the only available recourse against tribunal

---

1 *See* David D. Caron & Lee M. Caplan, *The UNCITRAL Arbitration Rules, A Commentary*, 853 (2nd ed., Oxford University Press 2013).

2 James E. Castello, 'UNCITRAL Arbitration Rules, Section IV, Article 41' in Loukas A. Mistelis (ed), *Concise International Arbitration*, 262 (2nd ed., Kluwer 2015).

3 *See* article 39(2) of the 1976 Rules.

4 *See* article 39(3) of the 1976 Rules.

5 *See* article 39(4) of the 1976 Rules.

6 *See* Jan Paulsson & Georgios Petrochilos, *Revision of the UNCITRAL Rules* (September 2006), para. 277, < www.uncitral.org > . *See also* UNCITRAL Summary Record of the 12th Meeting, 22 April 1976, UN Doc A/CN.9/9/C.2/SR.12, para. 45, Mr Jenard (Belgium).

determinations of fees, and it is easy to see how it may be possible to castigate such determinations as scandalous in certain such fora.[7]

B. THE REVISION PROCESS

4. During the revision process, the Working Group ultimately came to the view that tighter regulation of arbitrators' fees and expenses was required, and that additional safeguards would enhance the legitimacy and integrity of the arbitral process, avoiding situations where parties would be forced to resort to national courts.[8] Some delegates considered that the UNCITRAL Rules may otherwise fall in disuse.[9]

5. Three principles guided the Working Group during the revision process: (i) the need for increased transparency as regards the fixing of the arbitrators' fees;[10] (ii) the need for a 'neutral mechanism' (such as the appointing authority or the Secretary-General of the PCA) with power to resolve issues concerning fees in a definitive manner – mostly as a safeguard deterring abuse[11] and to promote confidence in arbitration and make the Rules attractive;[12] and (iii) the need to ensure that such a process would not unduly delay the arbitral proceedings.[13]

6. In light of these principles, the voluntary procedures set out in articles 39(2) and 39(4) of the 1976 Rules were replaced with 'a more robust and effective mechanism'.[14] Article 41 of the 2010 Rules regulates the setting of the arbitrators' fees and the determination of expenses at two different stages of the proceedings: (i) at the outset, when the tribunal is to make a proposal regarding the manner in which it will determine its fees and expenses (pursuant to article 41(3)); and (ii) at the conclusion of the proceedings, where the tribunal determines the quantum of its fees and expenses in the final award or other decision (pursuant to article 41(4)).[15] Thus, the 2010 Rules remedy the above problems by allowing the appointing authority to provide guidance, and, where necessary, exercise decisive oversight in respect of arbitrators' fees and expenses.

---

7 *See* UNCITRAL Report of 48th Session, 29 February 2008, UN Doc A/CN.9/646, para. 20; *see also* UNCITRAL Summary Record of the 12th Meeting, 22 April 1976, UN Doc A/CN.9/9/C.2/SR.12, para. 49, Mr Holtzmann (United States of America) (noting that 'the only way in which [the parties] could appeal against the amount of such fees would be through costly litigation proceedings').

8 *See* UNCITRAL Report of 48th Session, 29 February 2008, UN Doc A/CN.9/646, para. 20.

9 *See* UNCITRAL Report of 45th Session, 5 October 2006, UN Doc A/CN.9/614, para. 133.

10 *See* UNCITRAL Working Paper for 52nd Session, 10 December 2009, UN Doc A/CN.9/WG.II/WP.157/Add.2, para. 24.

11 *See* Paulsson & Petrochilos, *supra* fn 6, at para. 277.

12 *See* UNCITRAL Report of 48th Session, 29 February 2008, UN Doc A/CN.9/646, para. 21.

13 *Ibid.*, at paras 24-26.

14 Caron & Caplan, *supra* fn 1, at 855.

15 *See* UNCITRAL Report of 52nd Session, 19 February 2010, UN Doc A/CN.9/688, paras 31-33.

C. THE REVISED RULES

1. 'Reasonableness' requirement: articles 41(1) and 41(2)

7. Article 39 of the 1976 Rules provides that arbitrators' fees and expenses 'shall be reasonable in amount', taking into account the amount in dispute, the complexity of the subject matter and the time spent by the arbitrators.[16] This reflects the drafters' expectations that arbitrators selected 'based on faith in their expertise and in their readiness to adjudicate the dispute with impartiality and fairness may be expected to act reasonably in setting their own fees'.[17] Article 41(1) of the 2010 Rules is unchanged in this regard; and the text calls for no particular observation.

8. Although the Rules do not incorporate a fixed schedule of fees, the parties may do so by modifying article 41(1), providing for fees to be calculated in accordance with a fee schedule chosen by the parties or provided by an arbitral institution.[18] The appointing authority may also offer guidance by providing a schedule or other method for determining the fees pursuant to article 41(2). The tribunal may take this into account 'to the extent that it considers appropriate'. Here, too, the position remains as under the 1976 version.

2. Tribunal's fee proposal and its review: article 41(3)

9. The 1976 Rules do not encourage (though of course they do not prevent) the tribunal to inform the parties of how it intends to calculate its fees and expenses. The 2010 Rules address this by expressly requiring that the tribunal inform the parties, '[p]romptly after its constitution', as to how it proposes to determine its fees and expenses, 'including any rates it intends to apply' (article 41(3)). Such 'rates' may include *ad valorem*, time-based, or fixed-fee methods, as well as cancellation or commitment fees, as long as the result yielded is reasonable.[19] This provision thus demands full disclosure from the outset, ensuring in the light of all circumstances set forth in article 41(1) that any disagreements can be addressed, and – as in institutional arbitration – that the parties are not surprised

---

16 Cf. Appendix III of the ICC Rules (listing the scales of arbitrator's fees, minimum and maximum amounts of which are fixed as a percentage of the amount in dispute).

17 *See* UNCITRAL Report of the Secretary General on the Draft UNCITRAL Arbitration Rules, 12 December 1975, UN Doc A/CN.9/112/Add.1, 181 para. 2.

18 Castello, *supra* fn 2, at 262-263. *See*, e.g., *Glamis Gold Ltd v. The United States of America* (UNCITRAL) Award, 8 June 2009, <www.italaw.com>, para. 187 (where the tribunal noted that the parties, by agreement, had modified article 39 of the 1976 Rules to provide that the arbitrators' fees would be determined in accordance with the ICSID Schedule of Fees).

19 *See* Caron & Caplan, *supra* fn 1, at 857; and UNCITRAL Report of 48th Session, 29 February 2008, UN Doc A/CN.9/646, para. 25. *See* further Nigel Blackaby, Constantine Partasides, Alan Redfern & Martin J. Hunter, *Redfern and Hunter on International Arbitration*, paras 4.204-4.214 (6th ed., Kluwer 2015).

by the method in accordance with which the tribunal will have fixed its fees and expenses when they come to the end of the arbitral process.[20]

10. The obligation is incumbent upon the 'arbitral tribunal' as a whole, and not upon individual arbitrators. The obligation should be discharged in relation to all parties. This calls for one further comment. The provision speaks of the tribunal's fees and expenses, envisaging that there be a single proposal, formulated by the tribunal as a collegial formation at the time mandated by the provision, addressed to all parties for their acceptance. This makes it plain that there can be no question of a separate fee agreement between a party and its appointee on the tribunal in advance of an appointment. Such arrangements are purported to be made in ad hoc proceedings from time to time, and in the submission of the present authors they are always problematic, principally because *all* parties are liable for costs, and the costs include the fees of the *entire* tribunal: fee arrangements must therefore be agreed *by all*. That is the position even where the parties have agreed that each is to bear the costs 'of the arbitrator appointed by itself'.[21] That is an agreement on the *allocation* of part of the tribunal's fees and costs (leaving those of the presiding arbitrator to be decided under article 42(1)); it is *not* an agreement that displaces the rules on the determination of arbitrators' fees and expenses in article 41. That is not to exclude the possibility – rare though it is – of different arrangements for individual tribunal members, provided that these are agreed by and known to all at the outset.

11. Within 15 days of having received the tribunal's proposal, a party who is unsatisfied with the rates or other method proposed may ask the appointing authority to review the proposal for consistency with the reasonableness standard provided for in article 41(1).[22] The appointing authority may make any adjustments it considers necessary; and as provided in article 41(3), such adjustments 'shall be binding upon the arbitral tribunal'. In the event that no appointing authority has been agreed upon or designated, the 15-day time-period is suspended until an authority is selected.[23] Practice will show whether parties regard this remedy as significant enough to warrant the designation of an appointing authority.

---

20 *See* Caron & Caplan, *supra* fn 1, at 857.

21 Articles 12(9) and 8(2) of the Netherlands–Poland BIT (7 September 1992; in force 1 February 1994).

22 *See* Castello, *supra* fn 2, at 263. Early drafts of the 2010 Rules demonstrate that the initial standard of review proposed for article 41(3) was whether the tribunal's proposal was 'manifestly inconsistent', as opposed to 'inconsistent', with article 41(1): *see* UNCITRAL Note by the Secretariat, 5 March 2010, UN Doc A/CN.9/703/Add.1, para. 24. However, the Working Group concluded that this would set too high a threshold for review: *see* UNCITRAL Report of 52nd Session, 19 February 2010, UN Doc A/CN.9/688 para. 120. Note also that article 41(4)(b) of the 2010 Rules provides that where the appointing authority fails to act within the time specified in the Rules, the Secretary-General of the PCA shall conduct the review.

23 Castello, *supra* fn 2, at 263 (noting that the party seeking referral must initiate the process for choosing an appointing authority during those 15 days). *See* article 6(3) of the 2010 Rules. *See also* UNCITRAL Report of 52nd Session, 19 February 2010, UN Doc A/CN.9/688 paras 26 and 127.

12. Unlike article 41(4) of the 2010 Rules, article 41(3) does not address the situation where the appointing authority fails to act after the request for review. Referring the request to the Secretary-General of the PCA is therefore not an option, unlike under article 41(4). In such cases, the parties must designate, or cause the designation of, a substitute appointing authority.[24]

3. Final determination of fees and review: article 41(4)

13. A need to review the arbitrators' fees and expenses may also appear at a later stage of the proceedings. For example, even where the tribunal's methodology for determining its fees and expenses was acceptable to the parties under article 41(3) of the 2010 Rules, the tribunal's application of it in the actual calculation in any costs decision may nevertheless appear unreasonable. Article 41(4) addresses this situation and provides a process for the review and revision of fees and expenses as fixed in the final award or other decision.[25] Article 41(4)(a) speaks of the tribunal's 'informing the parties of the arbitrators' fees and expenses that have been fixed' (emphasis added), and in practice this means that the parties will see the information in the 'final award' or other 'decision' in which costs are fixed pursuant to article 40(1). It is true that article 41(4)(d) envisages that there may be a separate information exchange and possible adjustments to fee amounts before an award has been issued, but such a process is difficult to reconcile with the plain language of articles 41(4)(a) and 40(1).

14. The process is facilitated by the requirement provided in article 41(4)(a): when informing the parties of the fees and expenses it has fixed pursuant to article 40(2)(a)-(b), the tribunal must 'explain the manner in which the corresponding amounts have been calculated'. This requires the tribunal to explain how the final fees and expenses were derived 'in accordance with the manner of their determination that was previously announced'.[26] Particulars given may range from daily activity sheets or, more likely in order to protect the secrecy of deliberations, a condensed narrative of the work and other activity (notably travel) of the arbitrators.

15. As a second step, article 41(4)(b) provides that if a party nevertheless objects to the tribunal's determination, it can refer it to the appointing authority for review within 15 days of receipt. If no appointing authority has been designated, or if the authority fails to act within the 45-day time-limit, a party may refer the review of the fees to the Secretary-General of the PCA. This avoids delay at this (usually last) stage of the process, which might otherwise deter a meritorious request for review. There are two possible standards of review. First, the fees may be compared against the original or adjusted proposal provided under article 41(3). This exercise is limited to determining whether the methodology employed is the

---

[24] *See* UNCITRAL Note by the Secretariat, 5 March 2010, UN Doc A/CN.9/703/Add.1, para. 25.

[25] Castello, *supra* fn 2, at 263.

[26] *Ibid.*

same as that provided in the proposal rather than for reasonableness.[27] Second, the fees must not be 'manifestly excessive'. This standard was meant to prevent abuses by arbitrators, covering situations where, for example, an arbitrator's final fees technically complied with the proposal but 'were based on a questionably high number of hours'.[28]

16. Pursuant to article 41(4)(c), the appointing authority or the Secretary-General of the PCA, as applicable, is authorized to make any adjustments to the tribunal's determination of its fees and expenses. As for article 41(3), these adjustments are expressly stated to be 'binding upon the arbitral tribunal'. Furthermore, the tribunal is obliged to incorporate the adjustments in its award, or, where an award has already been rendered, through a correction to the award and they therefore become part of the award pursuant to article 38.[29] The tribunal has no power to disagree with, alter, or seek a revision/reconsideration of the adjustment.

17. While article 41(3) and 41(4) both allow the parties to request a review of the tribunal's fees and expenses by the appointing authority, only article 41(4) allows the request to be sent to the Secretary-General of the PCA, under article 41(4)(c). As noted, this approach is sound,[30] as the appointing authority's failure to act at an early stage of the proceedings can be easily resolved through the ordinary procedures set out by the Rules (i.e. by the parties agreeing on a substitute appointing authority), where article 41(3) is most likely to find application. However, under article 41(4), if the only recourse available to the parties was to initiate the procedure for designating a substitute appointing authority, the arbitral process could easily be extended for weeks.

D. TIME-LIMITS

18. The aim of the time-limits set out in article 41(3) is to ensure an expeditious determination of the tribunal's fees and expenses. The first requirement is that the tribunal make its proposal for the determination of its fees and expenses 'promptly after its constitution'. The language differs from that of article 17(2), which requires the tribunal to establish a provisional timetable 'as soon as practicable after its constitution'. If anything, however, 'promptly' in the present context must logically mean at the very latest by the time of the provisional

---

27 The Working Group chose this narrower standard in order to '[avoid] unnecessary duplication of reviews previously conducted'. *See* UNCITRAL Report of 52nd Session, 19 February 2010, UN Doc A/CN.9/688, para. 121.

28 *See* UNCITRAL Report of 52nd Session, 19 February 2010, UN Doc A/CN.9/688, para. 121. *See also* Castello, *supra* fn 2, at 264.

29 Article 41(4)(d) of the 2010 Rules. *See* UNCITRAL Working Paper for 52nd Session, 10 December 2009, UN Doc A/CN.9/WG.II/WP.157/Add.2, para. 19. *See also* Caron & Caplan, *supra* fn 1, at 861, fn 105 (noting that, where an adjustment on fees is ordered after the 30-day time-limit for correcting an issued award (as provided in article 38 of the 2010 Rules), article 41(4)(d) should be read as extending the time-limit for the purpose of effecting the adjustment).

30 *See* UNCITRAL Report of 52nd Session, 19 February 2010, UN Doc A/CN.9/688, paras 117-118.

timetable. The parties are entitled to advance certainty on fees and expenses before settling the procedural schedule.

19. Second, the parties may request that the appointing authority review the tribunal's proposal under article 41(3) '[w]ithin 15 days of receiving the proposal'. Third, the appointing authority must make its determination 'within 45 days of receipt of such referral'. Article 41(5) also promotes the efficiency of the fee-determination procedure by requiring that the arbitral tribunal 'proceed with the arbitration' in accordance with article 17(1) throughout the steps set out in articles 41(3) and 41(4).

20. Furthermore, the time-limits established by article 41(4) also encourage the speedy resolution of any concerns relating to the calculation of the tribunal's fees and expenses, without delaying the conclusion of the proceedings.[31] Indeed, the parties must refer the matter to the appointing authority or the Secretary-General of the PCA '[w]ithin 15 days of receiving the arbitral tribunal's determination of fees and expenses', and the review must be completed 45 days from receipt of the referral.

21. Most importantly, and in order to assuage concerns that the review mechanism might be abused by parties seeking to delay enforcement of the award, article 41(6) of the 2010 Rules specifically provides that the review process in article 41(4) shall not 'delay the recognition and enforcement' of the award, except insofar as concerns the determination of the tribunal's fees and expenses.[32]

22. Turning, finally, to the possibility to shorten or (more likely) extend the time-limits set out in article 41(3)-(4) for the review functions of the appointing authority or the PCA, there is no provision to that effect in the Rules. A proposal to grant an explicit power to extend this deadline was not passed,[33] as was the case for a proposal to grant an equivalent power under article 6(4). As already discussed in the context of article 17(2), the general power of the tribunal to 'extend or abridge any period of time prescribed under these Rules' on its face covers articles 41(3)-(4). But it would be somewhat incongruous with the function of independent review of the tribunal's work for the tribunal to have that power (without suggesting in any way that tribunals would exercise such a power unreasonably). One may expect that if any extension is needed, the appointing authority and the PCA will turn to the parties and seek their agreement.

---

31 *See* UNCITRAL Working Paper for 52nd Session, 10 December 2009, UN Doc A/CN.9/WG.II/WP.157/Add.2, para. 24.

32 *See* Report of the Commission on its 43rd Session, 21 June-9 July 2010, UN Doc A/65/17, paras 176-177. The Working Group decided that it was not necessary to include a deposit for the costs of the reviewing authorities, but that the report should indicate that the Commission expected the reviewing authority to charge a fee, which, together with article 41(6), was thought sufficient to deter frivolous requests for review. *See* Report of the Commission on its 43rd Session, 21 June-9 July 2010, UN Doc A/65/17, paras 173-174. *See also* UNCITRAL Summary Record of the 908th Meeting, 24 June 2010, UN Doc A/CN.9/SR.908, XLI UNCITRAL Ybk 1256, 1257 para 15, The Chairperson.

33 *See* UNCITRAL Note by the Secretariat, 5 March 2010, UN Doc A/CN.9/703/Add.1, para. 25.

Article 42
Allocation of costs

1976 Rules Article 40: Costs	2010 Rules Article 42: Allocation of costs
1. Except as provided in paragraph 2, the costs of arbitration shall in principle be borne by the unsuccessful party. However, the arbitral tribunal may apportion each of such costs between the parties if it determines that apportionment is reasonable, taking into account the circumstances of the case. 2. With respect to the costs of legal representation and assistance referred to in article 38, paragraph (e), the arbitral tribunal, taking into account the circumstances of the case, shall be free to determine which party shall bear such costs or may apportion such costs between the parties if it determines that apportionment is reasonable. 3. When the arbitral tribunal issues an order for the termination of the arbitral proceedings or makes an award on agreed terms, it shall fix the costs of arbitration referred to in article 38 and article 39, paragraph 1, in the text of that order or award. 4. No additional fees may be charged by an arbitral tribunal for interpretation or correction or completion of its award under articles 35 to 37.	1. The costs of the arbitration shall in principle be borne by the unsuccessful party or parties. However, the arbitral tribunal may apportion each of such costs between the parties if it determines that apportionment is reasonable, taking into account the circumstances of the case. 2. The arbitral tribunal shall in the final award or, if it deems appropriate, in any other award, determine any amount that a party may have to pay to another party as a result of the decision on allocation of costs.

1. Article 42 of the 2010 Rules authorizes the tribunal to allocate the costs of the arbitration between the parties. In principle, costs are borne by the unsuccessful party, reflecting the practice adopted by 'the majority of arbitral tribunals' applying institutional arbitration rules, and the well-established principle that 'costs follow the event'.[1] Article 40(1) of the 1976 Rules, which Article 42(1) of the 2010 faithfully follows in that regard, was an early and very major contributor to the establishment of the practice. Article 42 of the 2010 Rules (as its predecessor) also recognizes that apportionment may be more appropriate in some circumstances. Subject to any mandatory requirements regarding cost apportionment under the applicable arbitration law, the tribunal therefore enjoys discretion in departing from the starting position that one party should bear all the costs of the arbitration, dividing the costs between the parties where and to the extent that 'it determines that apportionment is reasonable'.

2. The drafters made significant changes to article 40 of the 1976 Rules during the revision process leading to the adoption of article 42 of the 2010 Rules. The commentary below starts with an overview of the 1976 provision before discussing the revised text in article 42.

A. ARTICLE 40 OF THE 1976 RULES

3. Article 40(1) of the 1976 Rules starts from the principle that costs are to be borne by the unsuccessful party, i.e. that 'costs follow the event',[2] as opposed to letting them lie where they fall. If there is no clearly 'successful' party, tribunals applying the 1976 Rules have tended to divide the costs evenly among the parties.[3] Under article 40(1), the arbitral tribunal also has discretion to apportion

---

1 *See* ICC Commission Report, *Decisions on Costs in International Arbitration*, 4-5 (ICC 2015) (where the Commission found that, '[d]espite the fact that the ICC and at least half of the other major institutional rules contain no presumption in favour of the recovery of costs by the successful party, it appears that the majority of arbitral tribunals broadly adopt that approach as a starting point, thereafter adjusting the allocation of costs as considered appropriate. This was the approach in the majority of ICC awards examined, in 91% of HKIAC awards, in the majority of ICDR awards, in 90% of SIAC awards and in more than half of the SCC awards. This was also the case in most LCIA and PCA awards, which is not surprising as LCIA and PCA Rules contain a rebuttable presumption in favour of recovery of costs by the successful party'). *See also*, e.g., Article 40(1) of the Swiss Rules; Article 28.4 of the LCIA Rules; Article 52(2) of the CIETAC Rules; section 61(2) of the English Arbitration Act 1996 (England & Wales); sections 91 and 1057 of the German Zivilprozessordnung.

2 *See* Report of the Commission on its 9th Session, 12 April-7 May 1976, UN Doc A/31/17, para. 222 (where it was stated that 'the rule that normally the costs of arbitration be borne by the unsuccessful party was fair and correct, and it gave a good indication to the parties of the way in which the costs of arbitration would be apportioned in most cases'). *See also Jan Oostergetel and Theodora Laurentius v. The Slovak Republic* (UNCITRAL) Final Award, 23 April 2012, <www.italaw.com>, para. 337; and *Petrobart Limited v. The Kyrgyz Republic* (UNCITRAL) Award, 13 February 2003, <www.italaw.com>, 51-52.

3 *See Chevron Corporation (USA) and Texaco Petroleum Company (USA) v. The Republic of Ecuador* (UNCITRAL) Final Award, 31 August 2011, <www.italaw.com>, para. 376 ('in the present case the Claimants have been largely successful on jurisdiction and liability,

the costs between the parties if, after taking into account the circumstances of the case, it considers that such apportionment would be reasonable. It is crucial in understanding article 40 to bear in mind that the notion of 'costs of the arbitration' in article 40(1) excludes the costs of the parties' legal representation and assistance. Although the tribunal has in respect of such costs no starting rule or principle, the same standard of reasonableness is set out, pursuant to which the tribunal may (i) determine which party should bear the costs of legal representation and assistance or (ii) apportion these costs between the parties if it considers such apportionment reasonable in the circumstances of the case. That there was no starting principle in respect of the parties' costs was made rather emphatic by the use of the words 'the arbitral tribunal ... shall be free to determine' in article 40(2), compared to the words 'shall in principle be borne' in article 40(1).

4. Thus the tribunal in *Gallo v. Canada*, for example, held that the costs of legal representation were not subject to the general principle articulated in article 40(1), holding instead that the parties would bear their own costs in this respect.[4] In *Oostergetel v. Slovak Republic*, the tribunal exercised its 'free' discretion under article 40(2) of the 1976 Rules in deciding that the unsuccessful claimants should pay EUR 2,000,000 of the respondent's legal costs, which amounted to EUR 12,400,000 (the claimant's legal costs were also approximately EUR 2,000,000). In coming to its decision, the tribunal considered that 'the deficiencies in the presentation of the Claimants' case [had] made the resolution of this dispute unusually burdensome for the Tribunal and presumably also for the Respondent'.[5] It was therefore considered appropriate in the circumstances that the claimants bear part of the respondent's legal costs.

5. Article 40(3) of the 1976 Rules provides that where the proceedings are terminated by a termination order or an award on agreed terms, the arbitral tribunal must fix the costs of arbitration 'in the text of that order or award'. That feature has been in essence retained, but revised in the light of other changes in respect of awards (article 34(1) of the 2010 Rules) and other decisions (article 40(1)).

6. Finally, article 40(4) of the 1976 Rules prohibits the arbitral tribunal from charging any additional fees for the interpretation, correction or completion of its award. During the revision process, this provision was relocated and amended to allow tribunals to charge certain costs, as set out in articles 40(2)(b)-(f) of the 2010 Rules.[6]

---

but the Respondents have been mostly successful on damages. The Tribunal finds therefore that there is no clearly successful Party and consequently decides that each side shall bear its own costs of legal representation and assistance (as well as the expenses of witnesses referred to in Article 38(d)) and divide tribunal costs evenly').

4 *See Vito G. Gallo v. The Government of Canada* (UNCITRAL) Award, 15 September 2011, < www.italaw.com >, paras 356-358.

5 *See Jan Oostergetel and Theodora Laurentius v. The Slovak Republic* (UNCITRAL) Final Award, 23 April 2012, < www.italaw.com >, paras 339-340.

6 *See* discussion of article 40 of the 2010 Rules, *supra*. *See also* David D. Caron & Lee M. Caplan, *The UNCITRAL Arbitration Rules, A Commentary*, 877 (2nd ed., Oxford University

B. ARTICLE 42 OF THE 2010 RULES

7. Article 42(1) of the 2010 Rules establishes the same principle as article 40(1) of the 1976 Rules: the costs of the arbitration are in principle 'borne by the unsuccessful party or parties'.[7] As under the 1976 Rules, the tribunal is authorized to apportion the costs differently if it considers this reasonable 'taking into account the circumstances of the case'. Not all arbitral rules contain such a principle, which is an emphatic feature of UNCITRAL arbitration.[8] Crucially, the article 42(1) principle applies to *all* costs within the meaning of article 40(2); that is to say, the principle has been made more encompassing compared to the 1976 version.

8. During the revision process, the Working Group considered removing the notion of 'the unsuccessful party', given that 'it might not be easy in all instances to determine which party was to be considered the successful party'.[9] One suggestion for a more 'neutral formulation', based on article 31(3) of the 1998 ICC Rules, did not receive support.[10] The 2010 provision features a clear preference for the 'loser pays' rule as a matter of principle.[11] As practitioners know well, determining which party is 'successful' and to what extent is not a matter of precise science; but that is indeed an advantage of the rule rather than the opposite. A claimant that is successful in establishing one investment-treaty breach among several claimed in the circumstances of a novel case may be more 'successful' than a claimant in a straightforward debt-collection case who recovers just over 50% of its dues. The broader point is that 'success' is to be considered comprehensively, encompassing more than a mechanical determination as to which party has prevailed in the final outcome. For example, a claimant may succeed in the arbitration, but nevertheless fail to establish the vast majority of

---

Press 2013).

7 The additional wording 'or parties' reflects the possibility of multiparty arbitration under the 2010 Rules.

8 *See*, e.g., Article 38 of the ICC Rules; Article 49 of the SCC Rules; Article 33 of the HKIAC Rules (although cf. Article 36.4 of the 2008 HKIAC Rules). *See also* ICC Commission Report, *supra* fn 1, at 4-5 (noting that 'an alternative starting point' to the principle of 'costs follow the event' is that each party will be responsible for paying its own costs, with recovery of such costs from other parties permitted only in 'rare circumstances'). The ICSID Rules also do not contain a presumption that the losing party should bear the costs of the arbitration: *see* Articles 59-61 of the ICSID Convention. *See also*, e.g., *EDF International SA, SAUR International SA and León Participaciones Argentinas SA v. Argentine Republic* (ICSID Case No. ARB/03/23) Decision on Annulment, 5 February 2016, <www.italaw.com>, para. 389 ('There is no general rule in ICSID proceedings that the losing party should pay the successful party's costs, nor is there even a presumption in favour of such an outcome', further providing in fn 445: 'In contrast to the position under Article 40 of the UNCITRAL Rules, under which the starting point is a presumption that the unsuccessful party must bear the whole costs of the tribunal').

9 *See* UNCITRAL Report of 48th Session, 29 February 2008, UN Doc A/CN.9/646, para. 29.

10 *Ibid*. Article 31(3) of the 1998 ICC Rules provides as follows: 'The final Award shall fix the costs of the arbitration and decide which of the parties shall bear them or in what proportion they shall be borne by the parties'.

11 *See* Caron & Caplan, *supra* fn 6, at 866.

its claims, or it may have presented evidence at great expense that was rejected by the tribunal.[12] The respondent will be able to say that it was successful in the vast majority of its defences. It is important to keep all these perspectives in mind of what may count as a 'success' rather than regarding 'success' as a mechanical outcome-determined notion and then coming to consider factors such as multiplicity of claims and inflated amounts in a separate subsequent inquiry of 'apportionment' under article 42(1). In sum, one may say that success is to be determined by reference to the major components of the case that drove the costs of the arbitration: which party was successful in respect of each component?

9. Although the Working Group discussed the possibility of separating among various categories of costs, it ultimately decided that a single standard was preferable.[13] Article 42(1) of the 2010 Rules therefore combines articles 40(1) and 40(2) of the 1976 Rules, now providing a single, unified standard applicable to all costs of the arbitration. The principle is therefore that the unsuccessful party bears all costs listed in article 40(2) of the 2010 Rules, including the other side's legal costs,[14] unless the tribunal decides that it is 'reasonable' to apportion such costs (either as a percentage of the overall sum or by categories) in a different manner. Circumstances relevant to this decision include principally procedural conduct (as illustrated by the *Oostergetel* award, above) and in particular

---

12 *See Windstream Energy LLC v. Government of Canada* (UNCITRAL) PCA Case No. 2013-22, Award, 27 September 2016, < www.italaw.com >, para. 514 (where the claimant prevailed in the arbitration, despite only one of its four claims being granted by the tribunal. Further, the tribunal did not accept the claimant's principal method of valuation, 'to which much of the evidence, in particular expert evidence related, and on which much of the time at the hearing was spent'. Accordingly, the tribunal ordered the respondent to reimburse the claimant only 50% of its legal and other costs. The tribunal also held that each party was to bear its share of the arbitration costs (para. 513)). *See also The Renco Group Inc v. The Republic of Peru* (ICSID Case No. UNCT/13/1) Final Award, 9 November 2016, < www.italaw.com >, paras 31 and 50-56 (where the tribunal held that 'the fact that Peru has only achieved a relative, rather than an absolute, measure of success' constituted a circumstance justifying departure from the presumption in article 42(1) of the 2010 Rules, and ordered each party to bear its own legal and other costs). *See also* Pieter Sanders, *Commentary on UNCITRAL Arbitration Rules*, II YCA 172, 214-215 (1977) (noting that '[i]f, for example, the claim is only partially awarded, an apportionment seems to be indicated').

13 *See* UNCITRAL Report of 48th Session, 29 February 2008, UN Doc A/CN.9/646, para. 28.

14 *See* for example *Khan Resources Inc et al. v. Government of Mongolia* (UNCITRAL) Award on the Merits, 2 March 2015, < www.italaw.com >, paras 432 and 445-449 (where the tribunal, constituted under the 2010 Rules, concluded that the claimants were successful on the merits phase of the arbitration, and that, as such, it was appropriate that 'costs should follow the event' as provided in article 42. The tribunal also considered that the claimants should be able to recover their legal fees from the unsuccessful party, including the costs of a success fee payable to the claimants' counsel). Cf. *European American Investment Bank AG (EURAM) v. Slovak Republic* (UNCITRAL) ('*EURAM v. Slovak Republic*') Award on Costs, 20 August 2014, < www.italaw.com >, para. 40 (where the tribunal, constituted under the 1976 Rules, refused to approach the question of legal costs under article 40(2) of the 1976 Rules in the same manner as the question of the costs of the arbitration under article 40(1) as this would serve to 'assimilate' the two articles, in spite of the clear difference in language).

inefficiencies/wasted costs caused, general procedural disloyalty including dilatoriness, impropriety (such as causing the resignation of one's appointee on the tribunal), failure to comply with tribunal directions and orders, oppressive or repeat applications, and the like. Tribunals must be mindful that one of the most effective disciplinary tools at their disposal is a full award on costs. Thus, it is not inconceivable that a party who has had a measure of 'success', in the result may deserve little or no costs relief. As illustrated by several awards, tribunals do consider the reasonableness of legal costs claimed by parties, and will not hesitate to let them lie where they fall if they are unreasonable.[15]

10. Authors have raised concerns regarding the broad discretion granted to arbitral tribunals under article 42(1) of the 2010 Rules,[16] especially considering the many different approaches tribunals have adopted in the apportionment of arbitration costs.[17] The practice of the Iran-US Claims Tribunal illustrates the realm of possibilities in this regard: each Chamber of the Tribunal adopted a different approach to apportioning costs. Chamber Two, for example, 'never awarded legal costs to a successful party', whereas Chambers One and Three 'awarded legal costs on many occasions, but with little explanation of their reasoning and usually in amounts that fell far short of full compensation'.[18]

11. There is force in the criticisms and concerns. Nevertheless, the clarity of article 42(1) compared to the dual position under article 40(1)-(2) of the 1976 Rules should enhance consistent outcomes. Ultimately, it may be unrealistic to expect tribunals to reach mechanistically consistent outcomes. The spectrum of costs-related considerations will differ from one case to the next, as will the individual weight of each consideration. Realistically, all that one should expect

---

15 *See*, e.g., *Detroit International Bridge Company v. Government of Canada* (UNCITRAL) Award on Costs, 17 August 2015, <www.italaw.com>, paras 42-53 (the tribunal having declined jurisdiction, the respondent submitted that article 42 of the 2010 Rules contained a presumption that the unsuccessful party will bear both the costs of the arbitral and institutional fees and the reasonable legal representation costs, and that it should be awarded these costs as the only successful party (given that jurisdiction was declined). The tribunal agreed and held that the claimant was to bear all the costs of the arbitration, but only two thirds of the respondent's legal costs, as the tribunal considered that the number of lawyers working on the case for the respondent had been excessive).

16 *See* Caron & Caplan, *supra* fn 6, at 868.

17 *See* Thomas H. Webster, *Efficiency in Investment Arbitration: Recent Decisions on Preliminary and Costs Issues*, 25(4) Arb Int 469, 507 et seq. (2009).

18 Caron & Caplan, *supra* fn 6, at 868-869 and the references. *See also* Stewart A. Baker & Mark D. Davis, *The UNCITRAL Arbitration Rules in Practice – The Experience of the Iran-United States Claims Tribunal*, 215 (Kluwer 1992) ('In some cases, the Tribunal explicitly grounded an award of partial costs on the claimant's partial success. Usually, however, it appeared to treat the extent of a claimant's success as one of many factors implicitly weighed in selecting a "reasonable" cost award figure'); and Jacomijn J. van Hof, *Commentary on the UNCITRAL Arbitration Rules, The Application by the Iran-U.S. Claims Tribunal*, 302-303, and 310 (Kluwer 1991) (noting the 'highly divergent' practice of the Iran-US Claims Tribunal Chambers, and citing to *McCollough & Co Inc v. Ministry of Post, Telegraph and Telephone* (1986) 11 Iran-US CTR 17, where 'the Tribunal awarded $20,000 (15% of the amount claimed), without giving any justification').

from tribunals is an assessment made in a judicial fashion, rather than in pure discretion and in broad-brush terms, setting out their reasoning in a 'transparent and logical manner', respecting any agreement between the parties which may modify article 42(1), and taking into account the parties' expectations.[19]

1. Circumstances considered when allocating costs: article 42(1)

12. Article 42 provides no guidance as to the 'circumstances of the case' to be taken into account by the tribunal when apportioning costs. The *travaux préparatoires* are also silent on this matter. However, the practice of tribunals applying the UNCITRAL Rules establishes certain recurring considerations, namely: (i) the success of the parties on their claims; (ii) the conduct of the parties during the arbitral proceedings; (iii) the nature of the parties; and (iv) the nature of the dispute resolution mechanism.[20] These factors are further discussed below.

(i) The success of the parties on their claims

13. When determining how to apportion costs between the parties, tribunals typically take the relative success of the parties' claims into account.[21] Indeed, support for this approach was recently expressed in the *EURAM* case, in which the tribunal went so far as to state that 'the parties' relative degree of success is the principal consideration' for a tribunal when exercising its discretion to apportion costs.[22] The tribunal in this case also endorsed the rationale underpinning this approach as identified in the *SD Myers v. Canada* case – that 'the successful party "has in effect been forced to go through the process in order to achieve success, and should not be penalised by having to pay for the process itself"'.[23]

---

19 Caron & Caplan, *supra* fn 6, at 869, citing to *Association of Service Industry Firms v. Service Industry Firm* (UNCITRAL) Award, 27 May 1991, reprinted in XVII YCA 11, 26-27 (1992); and *Himpurna California Energy Ltd v. PT (Persero) Perusahaan Listruik Negara* (UNCITRAL) Final Award, 4 May 1999 reprinted in XXV YCA 13, 106, para. 390 (2000).

20 *Ibid.*, at 870.

21 *See* fn 12, *supra*. *See also*, e.g., *Canfor Corporation v. United States of America and Tembec et al. v. United States of America and Terminal Forest Products Ltd v. United States of America* (UNCITRAL) ('*Canfor, Tembec, Terminal v. US*') Joint Order on Costs and Termination, 19 July 2007, <www.italaw.com>, paras 149-152 (where the tribunal, interpreting the reference to 'the unsuccessful party' in article 40(1) of the 1976 Rules as inclusive of a claimant that unilaterally withdrew its claim, ordered the claimant 'to bear the costs of arbitration referred to in articles 38 and 39' of the 1976 Rules); and *Robert Azinian, Kenneth Davitian & Ellen Baca v. The United Mexican States* (ICSID Case No. ARB (AF)/97/2) ('*Azinian v. Mexico*') Award, 1 November 1999, <www.italaw.com>, para. 125 (where the tribunal noted that, in ordinary circumstances, ordering a losing claimant 'to bear the costs of the arbitration, as well as to contribute to the prevailing respondent's reasonable costs of representation ... serves the dual function of reparation and dissuasion').

22 *See EURAM v. Slovak Republic*, *supra* fn 14, at para. 41.

23 *Ibid.*, citing to *S D Myers Inc v. Government of Canada* (UNCITRAL) Final Award on Costs, 30 December 2002, <www.italaw.com>, para. 15.

14. In the *Sylvania* arbitration before the Iran-US Claims Tribunal, Judge Holtzmann offered two examples of situations in which the degree of the parties' relative success may have a bearing on the tribunal's apportionment of costs.[24] First, apportionment between the parties may be appropriate in cases where the success of the parties is split – for example, where the claimant prevails on the claim while the respondent prevails on the counterclaim.[25] In these cases, tribunals may split costs evenly, each party bearing its own legal costs.[26] Second, cases involving 'quite separate and independent causes of action' may warrant apportionment if the claimant succeeds on one claim but not on the other.[27] This method and reasoning have been applied by numerous arbitral tribunals.[28]

15. In the *Guaracachi America* case, the tribunal considered that apportionment was justified on grounds that there was no 'clearly successful' party.[29] Although the respondent was found liable to pay compensation to one of the claimants, the respondent was nevertheless 'largely successful on quantum', reducing the compensation awarded to less than a quarter of the amount claimed.[30] The respondent had also been forced to defend itself on 'certain elements of quantum which were ultimately unfounded'.[31] The tribunal therefore determined that each side should bear its own legal and other costs incurred in connection with the

---

24 *See Sylvania Technical Systems Inc v. Government of the Islamic Republic of Iran* (1985) 8 Iran-US CTR 329, Separate Opinion of Judge Holtzmann, 331-333; and van Hof, *supra* fn 18, at 303-306. *See also*, adopting a similar approach to that outlined by Judge Holtzmann, *Yukos Universal Limited (Isle of Man) v. The Russian Federation* (UNCITRAL) Final Award, 18 July 2014, < www.italaw.com >, para. 1887.

25 *Sylvania Technical Systems Inc v. Government of the Islamic Republic of Iran* (1985) 8 Iran-US CTR 329, Separate Opinion of Judge Holtzmann, 333.

26 *See*, e.g., *Oxus Gold plc v. Republic of Uzbekistan, the State Committee of Uzbekistan for Geology & Mineral Resources, and Navoi Mining & Metallurgical Kombinat* (UNCITRAL) Award, 17 December 2015, < www.italaw.com >, para. 1043.

27 *Sylvania Technical Systems Inc v. Government of the Islamic Republic of Iran* (1985) 8 Iran-US CTR 329, Separate Opinion of Judge Holtzmann, 333.

28 *See*, e.g., *Pope & Talbot Inc v. Government of Canada* (UNCITRAL) Award in Respect of Costs, 26 November 2002, < www.italaw.com >, paras 8-11; *S D Myers Inc v. Government of Canada* (UNCITRAL) Final Award on Costs, 30 December 2002, < www.italaw.com >, paras 15-19; and *International Thunderbird Gaming Corporation v. The United Mexican States* (UNCITRAL) Award, 26 January 2006, < www.italaw.com >, paras 219-221. *See also* Caron & Caplan, *supra* fn 6, at 871.

29 *Guaracachi America Inc and Rurelec PLC v. The Plurinational State of Bolivia* (UNCITRAL) Award, 31 January 2014, < www.italaw.com >, para. 619 ('In this case, however, there is no clearly successful party. The Tribunal has upheld its jurisdiction in respect of Rurelec and found the Respondent liable to pay compensation. Yet, in reaching that result, the Tribunal has upheld two of the Respondent's jurisdictional objections. One of these objections ... resulted in a total lack of jurisdiction over the claims of one of the two Claimants, GAI. Moreover, the Respondent has also been largely successful on quantum, reducing the compensation ultimately awarded to less than a quarter of the original claim. From a technical point of view, GAI has thus been wholly unsuccessful in these proceedings and Rurelec only partially successful').

30 *Ibid.*

31 *Ibid.*

arbitration, splitting the tribunal's, the PCA's, and the appointing authority's fees and expenses equally.[32]

(ii) The conduct of the parties during the arbitral proceedings

16. The conduct of the parties was a relevant factor under 1976 Rules,[33] and of course it remains relevant under the 2010 Rules, as already noted above. A number of tribunals have in this way 'estimated compensation' for expenses incurred as a direct result of another party's conduct where it was frivolous, demonstrated bad faith, or was unnecessarily burdensome.[34] Examples of poor conduct that may lead to an apportionment of costs include a party's failure to attend a hearing without cause,[35] a party's repeated failure to file a submission requested by the tribunal, a party's initiation of unjustified parallel proceedings,[36] or a party's unsolicited submissions.[37]

(iii) The nature of the parties

17. Another factor that tribunals tend to consider is the legal status of the parties; namely, whether the party is a sovereign or a private entity. Where both parties are sovereign states, the conventional practice is for each side to bear its own costs (following the ICJ practice, where no costs claims are possible, the rationale being that resolving a dispute peacefully in the Court is a service to both parties).[38] That kind of rationale would not be regarded as valid by most practitioners in commercial cases between states and private parties. By contrast, the status of

32 *Ibid.*, at para. 620. *See also Hesham T M Al-Warraq v. Republic of Indonesia* (UNCITRAL) Final Award, 15 December 2014, <www.italaw.com>, paras 680-682 (where the tribunal, constituted under the 2010 Rules, considered it reasonable that each party bear its own legal expenses and costs, as well as half of the costs of the arbitration, based on their relative success and pursuant to article 42(1) of the 2010 Rules).

33 *See* UNCITRAL Summary Record of the 13th Meeting, 22 April 1976, UN Doc A/CN.9/9/C.2/SR.13, para. 4, Mr Holtzmann (United States of America).

34 Caron & Caplan, *supra* fn 6, at 872. *See*, e.g., *Behring International Inc v. Islamic Republic of Iran Air Force* (1991) 27 Iran-US CTR 218, 246-256.

35 *See* Baker & Davis, *supra* fn 18, at 214-215, citing to, inter alia, *Sedco Inc v. National Iranian Oil Co* (1985) 8 Iran-US CTR 28, 38-39; van Hof, *supra* fn 18, at 311.

36 *See*, e.g., *EURAM v. Slovak Republic, supra* fn 14, at paras 56-57 (where the tribunal concluded that the parties' conduct ultimately was not sufficient 'to make a significant difference for the purpose of apportionment of costs', but nevertheless addressed 'the lack of candour shown by the Claimant in relation to its decision to pursue proceedings in the Bratislava Court at the same time that it was pursuing its arbitration claim').

37 *See* Caron & Caplan, *supra* fn 6, at 872, citing to *Link-Trading Joint Stock Company v. Department for Customs Control of the Republic of Moldova* (UNCITRAL) Final Award, 18 April 2002, <www.italaw.com>, para. 96.

38 *Ibid.*, at 873. *See also* James E. Castello, 'UNCITRAL Rules' in Frank-Bernd Weigand (ed.), *Practitioner's Handbook on International Commercial Arbitration*, 1530 (2nd ed., Oxford University Press 2009).

an impecunious or economically stressed party may well entitle it to preferential costs protection.[39]

(iv) The nature of the dispute resolution mechanism

18. Caron and Caplan argue that, '[i]nvestor-state arbitration is a unique form of dispute resolution, the nature of which may inform an arbitral tribunal's decision whether to apportion costs'.[40] Two principal arguments are invoked in support of the thesis that investor-state arbitration calls for a different costs-apportionment model to the 'cost follows the event' approach in article 42(1) of the 2010 Rules. First, the proliferation of international investment instruments has given rise to a substantial number of novel, often complex issues of international law. As recognized by the tribunal in *Azinian v. Mexico*, 'the legal constraints on such causes of action' may be 'unfamiliar' to a party, which may be taken into account by the tribunal when determining the reasonableness of apportionment.[41] The validity of this argument of course fast diminishes in line with the increasing learning available in respect of such cases. Second, it has been asserted that apportioning costs in investor-state cases 'is inconsistent with the aims of international investment agreements because it discourages investors ... from "seek[ing] judicial review of administrative conduct"'.[42] That approach does not seem to find favour with the majority of investment-treaty tribunals,[43] at least as a rule of principle from which one should start. Indeed, the *Eureko* tribunal felt able to decide on the allocation of costs in two sentences: 'Claimant has prevailed. Consequently, its costs and those of the Tribunal shall be borne by the Respondent'.[44] But there may well be appropriate cases where the 'judicial-review' aspect of the dispute is to be accorded special weight, displacing at least to an extent the loser-pays principle.

2. Determination of the costs in the final or other award: article 42(2)

19. Whereas article 40(3) of the 1976 Rules provided that the costs of the arbitration may be 'fixed' in an award or a termination order, article 42(2) of the 2010 Rules

---

39 *Dr. Horst Reineccius et al. v. Bank for International Settlements* (PCA Case No. 2000-04) Final Award, 19 September 2003 (tribunal found it necessary to require the respondent bank to pay the legal expenses of a claimant, invoking human rights law and 'the principle of effective access to justice' (para. 126)).

40 Caron & Caplan, *supra* fn 6, at 874.

41 *See Azinian v. Mexico, supra* fn 21, at para. 126.

42 *See* Caron & Caplan, *supra* fn 6, at 874, citing to *International Thunderbird Gaming Corporation v. The United Mexican States* (UNCITRAL) Separate Opinion of Thomas Wälde, 1 December 2005, <www.italaw.com>, para. 139 (where the late Thomas Wälde also refers, at para. 140, fn 204, to the situation in WTO dispute settlement proceedings whereby, for an 'investor with limited financial resources', 'considerations of access to justice may play a role').

43 *See*, e.g., *Canfor, Tembec, Terminal v. US, supra* fn 21, at paras 149-152.

44 *Eureko BV v. Republic of Poland* (UNCITRAL) Partial Award, 19 August 2005, <www.italaw.com>, para. 261.

states that the tribunal shall 'determine' costs 'in the final award or ... in any other award'. Thus, the wording of article 42(2) indicates that the allocation of costs under the 2010 Rules must be made in an instrument called an award. However, article 40 of the 2010 Rules expressly states that the arbitral tribunal may 'fix' the costs of the arbitration 'if it deems appropriate, in another decision', which must be read to include not only termination orders but also interim-measures and other decisions, even if not titled 'awards'.[45] The wording of article 42(2) is simply explicable by reference to article 34(1), which states in broad terms that the tribunal is at liberty to decide in the form of 'separate awards ... different issues at different times'. That provision expands the range of issues that may be decided by way of an award. It does not limit the tribunal's power to fix costs when it chooses to issue rulings in the form of 'another decision'.

20 To understand the interplay between articles 40(1) and 42(2), one must appreciate the different functions that these play, a difference which is indicated by the terms 'fix' and 'determine'. Article 40(1) addresses the tribunal's decision as to which heads of cost and in what amount are to be regarded as the costs of the arbitration. These are then 'fixed'. Article 42(2) deals with the tribunal's decision as to which party and to what extent is to bear the costs. That the Rules call a 'determination', and it is clear that it must be ultimately expressed in the form of an 'amount' that either or both of the parties have to bear, i.e. a monetary award that is enforceable in a straightforward manner. This was a concern of the Working Group[46] and is generally good practice.[47] Thus, following an inquiry from a delegate during the 2010 revision process as to whether the wording of article 42(2) should read 'any other decision' instead of 'any other award',[48] the Working Group concluded that the tribunal's decision as to the allocation of costs is ultimately to be included in an award.[49]

21. The position is therefore in short as follows. Under the Rules, fixing the costs is an exercise notionally separate from the subsequent exercise of allocating or

45 *See also* discussion of article 40 of the 2010 Rules, *supra*.

46 *See* UNCITRAL Report of 52nd Session, 19 February 2010, UN Doc A/CN.9/688, para. 123 (where the Working Group noted that 'difficulties with the execution of the decision on costs had frequently arisen in certain jurisdictions, where the final order or award had not made specific reference to the amount that one party had to pay to the other party').

47 Caron & Caplan, *supra* fn 6, at 870. *See also* Thomas H. Webster, *Handbook of UNCITRAL Arbitration*, para. 42-31 (2nd ed., Sweet & Maxwell 2015) (noting that a costs order would generally only satisfy the conditions for recognition and enforceability under the New York Convention if contained in an award).

48 *See* UNCITRAL Summary Record of the 906th Meeting, 23 June 2010, UN Doc A/CN.9/SR.906, XLI UNCITRAL Ybk 1242, 1245 para. 48, Mr Chung (Republic of Korea).

49 *See* Report of the Commission on its 43rd Session, 21 June-9 July 2010, UN Doc A/65/17, para. 178 ('The question was raised whether the words "any other award" appearing in paragraph 2 should be replaced with the words "any other decision", so as to align the wording of that paragraph with the term used in draft article 40, paragraph 1. In response, it was explained that draft article 42 dealt with the determination of amounts that a party might have to pay to another party as a result of the decision on allocation of costs, and that decision was to be found in an award').

'determining' them as between the parties. The latter must be in the form of a (monetary) award; the former need not. The two exercises must be made together at the latest in the tribunal's final award; but costs-fixing may also be done earlier (in an earlier award or other decision) and there may also be earlier awards.

22. Note, as a practical matter, that as the costs falling in the categories spelt out in article 42(2)(d)-(f) cannot be covered by party advances under article 43(1), an award of costs in respect of these categories has to be implemented through a payment between the parties. By contrast, an award of costs falling within article 42(2)(a)-(c) may be implemented in part by returning to the successful party any unused portion of the costs advances made pursuant to article 43(1).

Article 43
Deposit of costs

1976 Rules Article 41: Deposit of Costs	2010 Rules Article 43: Deposit of Costs
1. The arbitral tribunal, on its establishment, may request each party to deposit an equal amount as an advance for the costs referred to in article 38, paragraphs (a), (b) and (c).	1. The arbitral tribunal, on its establishment, may request the parties to deposit an equal amount as an advance for the costs referred to in article 40, paragraphs 2 (a) to (c).
2. During the course of the arbitral proceedings the arbitral tribunal may request supplementary deposits from the parties.	2. During the course of the arbitral proceedings the arbitral tribunal may request supplementary deposits from the parties.
3. If an appointing authority has been agreed upon by the parties or designated by the Secretary-General of the Permanent Court of Arbitration at The Hague, and when a party so requests and the appointing authority consents to perform the function, the arbitral tribunal shall fix the amounts of any deposits or supplementary deposits only after consultation with the appointing authority which may make any comments to the arbitral tribunal which it deems appropriate concerning the amount of such deposits and supplementary deposits.	3. If an appointing authority has been agreed upon or designated, and when a party so requests and the appointing authority consents to perform the function, the arbitral tribunal shall fix the amounts of any deposits or supplementary deposits only after consultation with the appointing authority, which may make any comments to the arbitral tribunal that it deems appropriate concerning the amount of such deposits and supplementary deposits.
4. If the required deposits are not paid in full within thirty days after the receipt of the request, the arbitral tribunal shall so inform the parties in order that one or another of them may make the required payment. If such payment is not made, the arbitral tribunal may order the suspension or termination of the arbitral proceedings.	4. If the required deposits are not paid in full within 30 days after the receipt of the request, the arbitral tribunal shall so inform the parties in order that one or more of them may make the required payment. If such payment is not made, the arbitral tribunal may order the suspension or termination of the arbitral proceedings.
	5. After a termination order or final award has been made, the arbitral tribunal shall

5. After the award has been made, the arbitral tribunal shall render an accounting to the parties of the deposits received and return any unexpended balance to the parties.	render an accounting to the parties of the deposits received and return any unexpended balance to the parties.

1. Somewhat paradoxically, the last provision in the Rules deals with an issue that falls to be addressed in the early stages of the arbitral process. A particular feature of ad hoc arbitration is that the tribunal itself (rather than an arbitral institution) is responsible for ensuring that sufficient funds are at its disposal in the form of advances on costs by the parties.[1] Such advances may cover only the categories of costs comprised in article 40(2)(a)-(c), and thus exclude heads of costs that are not tribunal-related, namely those that relate to witnesses, the parties' legal and other costs, and the fees and expenses of the appointing and designating authorities. These latter heads of costs therefore must be covered by one or all of the parties directly and claimed/allocated accordingly pursuant to article 42. In fact, it happens on occasion that the reason for the termination of arbitral proceedings pursuant to article 36(2) is the failure or inability of the parties to provide the required deposits.[2] Article 43 of the 2010 Rules empowers the tribunal to request advance and supplementary monetary deposits from the parties, failing which the proceedings may be suspended or terminated.

2. Except for certain adjustments accommodating multiparty arbitrations and other minor changes discussed below, article 43 of the 2010 Rules is virtually identical to its predecessor, article 41 of the 1976 Rules.

3. Article 43(1) addresses initial deposits required upon establishment of the tribunal; article 43(2) provides for supplementary deposits throughout the proceedings; article 43(3) provides for consultation between the tribunal and the appointing authority regarding the amount of the deposits; article 43(4) sets out the consequences of the parties failing to pay the request deposits; and, finally, article 43(5) addresses the 'accounting' to be rendered by the tribunal, and the return of any unexpended balance to the parties. These components are addressed in turn below.

A. ADVANCE DEPOSITS: ARTICLE 43(1)

4. Article 43 provides that deposits may be requested from the parties at two different stages of the arbitral proceedings: (i) when the tribunal is established (article 43(1)); and (ii) '[d]uring the course of the arbitral proceedings' (article 43(2)).

---

[1] *See* Peter Binder, *Analytical Commentary to the UNCITRAL Arbitration Rules*, para. 43-002 (Sweet & Maxwell 2013); *see also* Nigel Blackaby, Constantine Partasides, Alan Redfern & Martin J. Hunter, *Redfern and Hunter on International Arbitration*, paras 4.221-4.222 (6th ed., Kluwer 2015).

[2] Thomas H. Webster, *Handbook of UNCITRAL Arbitration*, para. 43-4 (2nd ed., Sweet & Maxwell 2015).

5. According to article 43(1), the tribunal may request monetary deposits from the parties as advances for the costs outlined in articles 40(2)(a)-(c), which include the fees of the arbitrators, their travel and other expenses, and the costs of expert advice and other assistance required by the tribunal. As Sanders acknowledges, 'this may be one of the first steps of the arbitrators': deposits are typically required at the outset of the proceedings as security for the arbitrators' fees and expenses.[3] Deposits at the start of the arbitral proceedings may also be used to cover the costs of administrative support,[4] and the tribunal will typically request such advance deposits shortly after it is constituted[5] but obviously after the article 41(3) process has been completed. The parties are each required to pay 'an equal amount', and contributions will be proportionate in multiparty arbitrations.[6]

6. Article 43(1) of the 2010 Rules does not address how deposits should be paid or held. Arbitrators may open trust accounts to hold the deposits, and parties may make transfers to such accounts.[7] Arbitral institutions typically provide the service of holding and releasing deposits for ad hoc arbitrations that they administer.[8] In administered cases, the arbitral institution may provide detailed information regarding the amount of deposits that will be required, the currency or currencies that the institution is prepared to use, and they will typically assist with managing the deposited funds.[9] In unadministered proceedings, the UNCITRAL Notes advise that 'it is useful to clarify matters, such as the type and the location of the account in which the deposit will be kept, how the deposit will be managed and whether interest on the deposit will accrue'.[10] This is consistent with the parties' right to a refund of unused funds and to 'any excess interest generated by their deposits'.[11]

---

3 *See* Pieter Sanders, *Commentary on UNCITRAL Arbitration Rules*, II YCA 172, 192 (1977); *see also* Blackaby, Partasides, Redfern & Hunter, *supra* fn 1, at para. 4.220 ('The fact that arbitrators may become *functus officio* instantly at the joint will of the parties emphasises the importance for the arbitrators of obtaining adequate security for payment of their fees and expenses').

4 *See* David D. Caron & Lee M. Caplan, *The UNCITRAL Arbitration Rules, A Commentary*, 898 (2nd ed., Oxford University Press 2013). *See also Gulf Associates v. Islamic Republic of Iran*, Case No. 385, Chamber Two, Order of 11 December 1997, 1.

5 Webster, *supra* fn 2, at para. 43-5.

6 *See*, e.g., *Guaracachi America Inc and Rurelec PLC v. The Plurinational State of Bolivia* (UNCITRAL) Procedural Order No. 1, 9 December 2011, <www.italaw.com>, 7; and *S D Myers Inc v. Government of Canada* (UNCITRAL) Final Award on Costs, 30 December 2002, <www.italaw.com>, 11. *See also* Webster, *supra* fn 2, at para. 43-9; and Caron & Caplan, *supra* fn 4, at 897.

7 Blackaby, Partasides, Redfern & Hunter, *supra* fn 1, at para. 4.222.

8 *See*, for example, the LCIA fundholding procedures and conditions for non-LCIA arbitrations, available online at <www.lcia.org>. *See also* Webster, *supra* fn 2, at para. 43-11.

9 *See* UNCITRAL, *Notes on Organizing Arbitral Proceedings*, para. 45 (United Nations 2016).

10 *Ibid.*

11 Caron & Caplan, *supra* fn 4, at 898.

B. SUPPLEMENTARY DEPOSITS: ARTICLE 43(2)

7. It is not always possible for the tribunal to determine at the outset of proceedings what amount will be a sufficient deposit for the entire arbitration, notably because there are a number of gateway issues (of jurisdiction or admissibility, for example) or contingencies (such as interim measures). Alternatively, the tribunal may also decide to provide a schedule for further deposits. It may also be forced to request additional costs as the proceedings advance.[12] Article 43(2) therefore allows the tribunal to request supplementary deposits at any stage of the arbitral proceedings. The drafters of the original provision, article 41(2) of the 1976 Rules (which was included without modification as article 43(2) of the 2010 Rules), envisaged two particular situations in which supplementary deposits may be necessary: (i) where the tribunal considers that an expert witness is needed; and (ii) where the proceedings take longer than expected.[13] Supplementary deposit requests should be made 'well in advance of the procedural steps for which they are requested' to ensure that the procedural timetable is respected.[14]

C. OVERSIGHT BY THE APPOINTING AUTHORITY: ARTICLE 43(3)

8. Article 43(3) is identical to article 41(3) of the 1976 Rules. The appointing authority retains its consultative function in protecting the parties from unreasonable (whether unrealistically high or unrealistically low) demands for deposits by the arbitral tribunal. This function complements those to be found in article 41(2)-(4) in respect of tribunal fees and expenses. When an appointing authority has been designated and agrees to perform this function, a party may request that the tribunal confer with the appointing authority before fixing the deposit amounts required from the parties.[15] The appointing authority may make any comments 'that it deems appropriate' concerning the pending request for a deposit. However, the utility of this consultative mechanism has been called into question,[16] and there is no evidence that article 41(3) of the 1976 Rules has ever been applied.[17]

9. The 2010 revision process did not envision a complete overhaul of the provisions concerning the deposit of costs. The role of the appointing authority in this regard remains a consultative one: unlike for the fees and expenses of arbitrators under article 41 of the 2010 Rules, the appointing authority has no authority to impose

---

[12] Webster, *supra* fn 2, at paras 43-16–43-17.

[13] *See* UNCITRAL Report of the Secretary General on the Draft UNCITRAL Arbitration Rules, 12 December 1975, UN Doc A/CN.9/112/Add.1, 181 para. 1.

[14] Webster, *supra* fn 2, at para. 43-18.

[15] James E. Castello, 'UNCITRAL Arbitration Rules, Section IV, Article 43' in Loukas A. Mistelis (ed), *Concise International Arbitration*, 267 (2nd ed., Kluwer 2015).

[16] Professor Sanders, for example, queried whether the appointing authority would ever provide comments on a matter falling within the arbitral tribunal's discretion. *See* Pieter Sanders, *The Work of UNCITRAL on Arbitration and Conciliation*, 22 (Kluwer 2001).

[17] Caron & Caplan, *supra* fn 4, at 899 (further noting that '[t]he Iran-US Claims Tribunal appears to have found little value in Article 41(3) of the 1983 Tribunal Rules, choosing not to adopt this provision, or any modification of it').

its assessment of the reasonableness of the deposits on the arbitral tribunal. This is logical, as the deposit of costs does not require the same oversight as the determination of the tribunal's fees and expenses, and the potential for abuse is limited.

D. FAILURE TO PAY DEPOSITS: ARTICLE 43(4)

10. Article 43(4), which is also identical to its predecessor, article 41(4) of the 1976 Rules, regulates situations where a party fails to make the deposit required of it. If a party fails to make the deposit within 30 days of the receipt of the request, the tribunal must inform the other parties and give them an opportunity to cover the outstanding balance (and, we would add, to express views as to the appropriate course of action generally). By allowing another party to cover the required deposit, article 43(4) accounts for 'one of the risks assumed by parties in international arbitration' and provides a way to preclude that a recalcitrant party be able to halt the dispute resolution process merely by refusing to pay its share of the costs.[18] If the other parties refuse to do so, the tribunal may order the suspension or termination of the proceedings.

11. No guidance is given as to when termination is warranted rather than suspension. It must be the case that if a tribunal has reasons to believe that the failure is temporary (e.g. because the defaulting party has indicated that it faces temporary financial difficulties or currency-export restrictions), suspension will be the sensible course of action.[19] Termination will be reasonable and appropriate where there can be no certainty as to if and when a deposit may be made. One recalls in that connection that termination by means of an order pursuant to article 36(2) is envisaged as a procedural closure that is not intended to produce res judicata in respect of the substantive claims before the tribunal. So the sanction of termination under article 43(4) should not be perceived as a draconian measure which tribunals should almost never use.

12. Although the Rules do not regulate this matter, there is practice under both the 1976 and 2010 Rules to the effect that a party that has covered the other side's required advance may obtain a separate (partial) award for reimbursement.[20] This may be framed as an action for breach of the procedural duty set out in article 43(3) or one for reimbursement following from article 43(4). Either way, the salient point is that the recovering party need not await the next opportunity for an award on the substantive dispute but rather seek a separate award pursuant to article 42(2) ('any other award').

---

[18] Webster, *supra* fn 2, at 43-24.

[19] *See ibid.*, at 43-28.

[20] *Parties Not Indicated*, Partial Award (2008), XXXIV YCA 15 (2009); *Investors v. State*, PCA Case No. 2013-29 (unreported).

E. ACCOUNTING: ARTICLE 43(5)

13. Article 43(5) provides that after the termination order or final award has been made, the arbitral tribunal must 'render an accounting to the parties of the deposits received and return any unexpended balance to the parties'. The 'accounting' to which this provision refers may include 'information on the amount of deposits obtained from a particular party and how each portion of those deposits was spent', as well as 'any relevant account information and the applicable interest rates'.[21]

14. The wording of article 41(5) of the 1976 Rules was amended to form article 43(5) of the 2010 Rules. Instead of providing for accounting '[a]fter the award has been made', the 2010 Rules now provide for accounting '[a]fter a termination order or final award has been made'. This clarifies that the accounting and return of unexpended deposits is required not only where the proceedings are brought to a close through the issuance of a final award, but also where the arbitral tribunal terminates the arbitral proceedings (e.g. pursuant to article 30(1)(a) or article 36), without rendering a final award.[22]

---

21 Castello, *supra* fn 15, at 267.
22 *See* Caron & Caplan, *supra* fn 4, at 900-901.

PART II

UNCITRAL RULES ON TRANSPARENCY IN TREATY-BASED INVESTOR-STATE ARBITRATION

Transparency Rules

Article 1(1)-(2)
Scope of application

Article 1(1)-(2)

Applicability of the Rules

1. The UNCITRAL Rules on Transparency in Treaty-based Investor-State Arbitration ('Rules on Transparency') shall apply to investor-State arbitration initiated under the UNCITRAL Arbitration Rules pursuant to a treaty providing for the protection of investments or investors ('treaty')* concluded on or after 1 April 2014 unless the Parties to the treaty** have agreed otherwise.

2. In investor-State arbitrations initiated under the UNCITRAL Arbitration Rules pursuant to a treaty concluded before 1 April 2014, these Rules shall apply only when:

(a) The parties to an arbitration (the 'disputing parties') agree to their application in respect of that arbitration; or

(b) The Parties to the treaty or, in the case of a multilateral treaty, the State of the claimant and the respondent State, have agreed after 1 April 2014 to their application.

* For the purposes of the Rules on Transparency, a 'treaty' shall be understood broadly as encompassing any bilateral or multilateral treaty that contains provisions on the protection of investments or investors and a right for investors to resort to arbitration against Parties to the treaty, including any treaty commonly referred to as a free trade agreement, economic integration agreement, trade and investment framework or cooperation agreement, or bilateral investment treaty.

** For the purposes of the Rules on Transparency, any reference to a 'Party to the treaty' or a 'State' includes, for example, a regional economic integration organization where it is a Party to the treaty.

---

1. Mirroring article 1 of the Arbitration Rules, article 1 of the UNCITRAL Rules on Transparency in Treaty-based Investor-State Arbitration (the 'Transparency Rules') addresses their scope and applicability, as well as their relative position

with respect to other arbitration rules and national arbitration laws. Article 1 (scope of application) contains nine paragraphs, the first two relating to the applicability of the Transparency Rules.

I. ARTICLE 1(1): TREATIES CONCLUDED ON OR AFTER 1 APRIL 2014

A. Preconditions for application

2. Article 1(1) sets out clear conditions to the automatic application of the Transparency Rules, materially and temporally limiting their scope as follows:[1]

   (i) The Transparency Rules apply only to 'investor-State arbitration initiated ... pursuant to a treaty providing for the protection of investments or investors'. There should be little difficulty recognizing when a treaty is to be characterized as 'providing for the protection of investments or investors'; and of course that a treaty may also deal with other matters (e.g. trade) does not detract from this characterization; see paragraph 5 below. Thus, disputes under a contract or national law are also excluded, which has given rise to some criticism at the policy level.[2]

   (ii) The treaty in question must have been concluded on or after the entry into force of the Transparency Rules (i.e. 1 April 2014), thus precluding their retroactive application. The relevant date is the date of a treaty's conclusion, not of its entering into force. Note, however, that article 1(2) of the Transparency Rules allows the disputing parties, or the Parties to the treaty, to agree to apply the Transparency Rules to an arbitration arising out of a treaty concluded before 1 April 2014.[3]

   The Transparency Rules 'shall apply' where conditions (i) and (ii) above are satisfied and the arbitration has been initiated under the Arbitration Rules.[4] The mandatory wording of this provision affords no latitude to ignore the applicability of the Transparency Rules when the conditions for their application are met.[5] Thus a general reference to the 'UNCITRAL Arbitration Rules' in the underlying

---

1 *See* Krista N. Schefer, 'Article 1. Scope of Application' in Dimitrij Euler, Markus Gehring & Maxi Scherer (eds), *Transparency in International Investment Arbitration: A Guide to the UNCITRAL Rules on Transparency in Treaty-Based Investor-State Arbitration*, 41 (Cambridge University Press 2015).

2 *Ibid.*, at 49 (arguing that '[o]ne significant omission is the failure of the Rules to apply to contract-based arbitrations. The prevailing view of the drafters appeared to be that most investor-State arbitrations are arising – and will continue to arise – from treaty-based claims ... This is an empirical issue the accuracy of which is difficult to ascertain on available evidence. As such, the limitation may be ill-advised ... Unaffected by the Rules, ad hoc arbitrations in particular ... will remain intransparent. This leaves the public's knowledge about these most confidential arbitrations lacking').

3 *See* section II, *infra*.

4 Note, however, that the Transparency Rules may also be used in non-UNCITRAL arbitrations; *see* discussion of article 1(9), *infra*.

5 *See* Schefer, *supra* fn 1, at 41.

treaty (if concluded on or after 1 April 2014) is to be read as including the Transparency Rules.[6]

B. Opting out

3. Aside from the above conditions, article 1(1) is clear that the Parties to the treaty (but not the parties to the arbitration, called 'the disputing parties') may '[agree] otherwise', thereby extending or excluding the application of the Transparency Rules. They may, for example, explicitly refer to the 1976 or 2010 Arbitration Rules.[7]

4. One of the thorniest issues was whether the Transparency Rules would apply by default (unless the parties agreed to exclude them), or only where the Parties to the treaty specifically agreed to their application. This issue was from the outset of the preparatory process tied to the temporal scope of the Transparency Rules: if they were to apply unless excluded by agreement ('opt out'), extending them to prior investment treaties posed both legal and policy issues, given that arbitration rules are in principle not apt to lay down hard-and-fast 'dynamic interpretation' norms for treaties. By contrast, if they were to apply only by specific agreement ('opt in'), extending them to prior treaties was straightforward.[8] The final formulation of article 1(1) is therefore a product of compromise: whereas Parties to treaties concluded before the entry into effect of the Transparency Rules must 'opt in' to the regime by agreeing to the application of the Transparency Rules, Parties to treaties concluded on or after 1 April 2014 must 'opt out' in order to exclude the Transparency Rules.[9]

C. 'Treaty'

5. The term 'treaty' for the purposes of the Transparency Rules is specifically defined in a footnote. It incorporates bilateral and multilateral treaties, free trade agreements and economic integration agreements, insofar as these instruments contain provisions on the protection of investments or investors, and, importantly, 'a right for investors to resort to arbitration against Parties to the treaty'. As noted by commentators, the statement in the footnote that 'a "treaty" shall

---

[6] Lise Johnson & Nathalie Bernasconi-Osterwalder, *New UNCITRAL Arbitration Rules on Transparency: Application, Content and Next Steps*, 10 (CIEL, IISD, CCSI, August 2013), <http://ccsi.columbia.edu>. *See also* UNCITRAL Report of 56th Session, 16 February 2012, UN Doc A/CN.9/741, para. 14; and Schefer, *supra* fn 1, at 51 ('The assumption behind the acceptability of the opt-out mechanism is that by 1 April 2014, States will know of the Rules and decide whether to accept or reject them. If they do nothing, the Rules will apply "as an extension of the UNCITRAL Arbitration Rules"').

[7] *See* UNCITRAL Report of 56th Session, 16 February 2012, UN Doc A/CN.9/741, para. 54.

[8] *See* fn 10 below.

[9] UNCITRAL Report of 56th Session, 16 February 2012, UN Doc A/CN.9/741, para. 54; UNCITRAL Report of 58th Session, 13 February 2013, UN Doc A/CN.9/765, para. 17. *See also* Julia Salasky & Corinne Montineri, *UNCITRAL Rules on Transparency in Treaty-Based Investor-State Arbitration*, 31(4) ASA Bulletin 774, 781-783 (2013).

be understood broadly' was unnecessary; indeed, the Vienna Convention on the Law of Treaties already defines a 'treaty' broadly.[10] Thus, by listing specific agreements, the drafters may in fact have suggested 'a more limited definition than ... silence would have permitted',[11] but clarity in that regard was necessary in reaching consensus on the text.

D. 'Party' or 'State'

6. The second footnote to article 1(1) specifies that 'Party' or 'State' includes 'for example, a regional economic integration organization' where it is a Party to the treaty in question. This has particular significance in the EU context, given 'the Commission's competence to conclude investment agreements between the EU and other States', such as the EU-Canada Comprehensive Economic Trade Agreement.[12]

E. The right to exclude the application of the Transparency Rules

7. The question as to whether the investor should have a right to exclude the application of the Transparency Rules was also extensively discussed.[13] However, 'there was broad consensus in the Working Group that the legal standard on transparency should not include a right for the investor to derogate from the offer for transparent arbitration'.[14] A minority of delegations relied on the principle of party autonomy to argue that disputing parties should be able to agree between themselves not to apply the Transparency Rules;[15] however, by that stage of the drafting process, it had become clear that–

> [t]here was broad support for the suggestion that there should not be a provision allowing the disputing parties to vary the offer for transparent arbitration for the policy reason that it would not be appropriate for the disputing parties to reverse a decision [by the Parties to the treaty] on that matter.[16]

---

10 *See* Schefer, *supra* fn 1, at 47-49. Article 2(1)(a) of the Vienna Convention on the Law of Treaties (23 May 1969) provides that: '"Treaty" means an international agreement concluded between States in written form and governed by international law, whether embodied in a single instrument or in two or more related instruments and whatever its particular designation'.

11 Schefer, *supra* fn 1, at 48.

12 *Ibid.*, at 51 and the references.

13 UNCITRAL Report of 53rd Session, 20 October 2010, UN Doc A/CN.9/712, paras 30 and 95-96.

14 UNCITRAL Report of 54th Session, 25 February 2011, UN Doc A/CN.9/717, para. 53 (noting that 'providing the investor with the last word on the application of the legal standard on transparency would unduly privilege the investor, lead to a decrease in transparency and would be contrary to the Commission's mandate to enhance transparency in treaty-based investor-State arbitration').

15 UNCITRAL Report of 55th Session, 17 October 2011, UN Doc A/CN.9/736, para. 36.

16 *Ibid.*, at para. 33.

By contrast – and again as a policy choice – disputing parties may agree to apply the Transparency Rules where they would otherwise be inapplicable.

II. ARTICLE 1(2): TREATIES CONCLUDED BEFORE 1 APRIL 2014

A. Opting in

8. Article 1(2) pertains to treaties in force prior to 1 April 2014. There are only two circumstances in which the Transparency Rules will apply to such treaties:

(i) if the disputing parties 'agree to their application in respect of that arbitration'; or

(ii) if the State Parties to a bilateral treaty (or the State of the claimant and the respondent State, in the case of a multilateral treaty) reach an agreement on their application after 1 April 2014.

B. The opt-in versus opt-out approach

9. As noted above, article 1(1)-(2) of the Transparency Rules represents a compromise between the 'opt-in' and 'opt-out' approaches advanced during the drafting process.[17] The finalised text applies an opt-out approach for treaties concluded on or after 1 April 2014 (article 1(1)) and an opt-in approach for treaties already in existence by this date (article 1(2)).

10. With respect to pre-existing treaties, the Working Group considered two opposing views. On the one hand, and in light of the Working Group's mandate, the scope of article 1 should permit wide application of the Transparency Rules. On the other hand, this application must be in line with international law and the principle that States cannot be bound without their consent.[18] There were also diverging views as to how such consent should be expressed, i.e. whether it should be explicit or whether 'dynamic interpretation' of existing treaties should be permitted, or even presumed.[19]

C. No dynamic interpretation of existing treaties

11. A number of proposals favoured incorporating a provision for the dynamic interpretation of extant treaties into the Transparency Rules. Under such interpretation,

---

17 *See* UNCITRAL Report of 56th Session, 16 February 2012, UN Doc A/CN.9/741, para. 54; *see also* UNCITRAL Report of 58th Session, 13 February 2013, UN Doc A/CN.9/765, para. 17.

18 UNCITRAL Report of 56th Session, 16 February 2012, UN Doc A/CN.9/741, para. 16.

19 *Ibid.*, paras 16 and 42 (noting that the Working Group's diverging views 'fell into three categories: those in favour of including a provision to the effect that the transparency rules would not apply to existing treaties by a dynamic interpretation of those investment treaties; those expressing preference for permitting application of the rules on transparency to existing investment treaties, where so permitted, by a dynamic interpretation of the investment treaties; and lastly, those in support of not providing any rules on that matter').

references in existing treaties to the 1976 or 2010 Arbitration Rules as in force at the commencement of the arbitration, or envisaging the potential evolution of the applicable Arbitration Rules over time, were to be interpreted as allowing for the application of the Transparency Rules (in accordance with applicable rules of treaty interpretation).[20] It was similarly suggested that consent to arbitration under the Arbitration Rules could be interpreted as consent to the application of the Arbitration Rules as they develop over time.[21]

12. Dynamic interpretation, it was argued, is well-recognized under public international law and even accepted as standard practice. As such, it would be regrettable to deprive States of such an interpretation, especially since it would allow for wider application of the Transparency Rules, thus furthering the Working Group's mandate.[22]

13. Several delegations proposed that the Transparency Rules remain silent with respect to treaties pre-dating 1 April 2014. Application would therefore be determined 'in accordance with internationally accepted rules of treaty interpretation' to be found outside the Transparency Rules.[23] It was said by these delegations that the opt-in approach would thwart a reasonable expectation of States who intended to benefit from dynamic clauses in their treaties, and would 'send a negative message regarding the virtues of transparency'.[24]

14. Reflecting the consensus view that was ultimately reached, the final text of article 1(2) of the Transparency Rules deliberately excludes ('shall apply only') the dynamic interpretation of existing treaties.[25] Consent to apply the Transparency Rules must be clearly given by the disputing parties or by the State Parties to a treaty concluded before 1 April 2014. This is in line with the prevailing view that States cannot be forced to accept the application of the Transparency Rules without a reasonably express consent, such consent being able to arise only after the Transparency Rules came into effect.[26]

---

20 UNCITRAL Report of 55th Session, 17 October 2011, UN Doc A/CN.9/736, para. 24; UNCITRAL Report of 56th Session, 16 February 2012, UN Doc A/CN.9/741, para. 20; UNCITRAL Working Paper for 54th Session, 9 December 2010, UN Doc A/CN.9/WG.II/WP.162, para. 30. *See also* UNCITRAL Working Paper for 57th Session, Proposal by Governments of Argentina, Australia, Canada, Mexico, Norway, South Africa, and the United States of America, 2 August 2012, UN Doc A/CN.9/WG.II/WP.174, 2-4; and UNCITRAL Report of 58th Session, 13 February 2013, UN Doc A/CN.9/765, para. 19.

21 UNCITRAL Report of 53rd Session, 20 October 2010, UN Doc A/CN.9/712, para. 89.

22 UNCITRAL Report of 56th Session, 16 February 2012, UN Doc A/CN.9/741, para. 49; UNCITRAL Report of 57th Session, 12 October 2012, UN Doc A/CN.9/760, para. 135. The Working Group's mandate was to 'prepare a legal standard on transparency that would reflect best practices in the field of transparency in the context of investor-State arbitration': *see* UNCITRAL Report of 55th Session, 17 October 2011, UN Doc A/CN.9/736, para. 41.

23 UNCITRAL Report of 57th Session, 12 October 2012, UN Doc A/CN.9/760, para. 140.

24 *Ibid.*

25 *See* UNCITRAL Report of 56th Session, 16 February 2012, UN Doc A/CN.9/741, para. 55.

26 *Ibid.*, at para. 46; and UNCITRAL Report of 57th Session, 12 October 2012, UN Doc A/CN.9/760, para. 135.

15. The question was briefly considered whether an investor could claim that it had a right or at least a legitimate expectation that there would be no transparency regime under a pre-existing treaty.[27] It was considered 'doubtful' that any investment treaty could be thus interpreted,[28] and this is in the authors' submission plainly the right answer. On any view, investors' rights are derived from a treaty which is concluded between States without the investors' participation. A treaty may be varied or terminated, again without any participation, let alone consent, by investors. While it is right to say that investor rights already vested and invoked cannot be modified subsequently,[29] no such vesting occurs in respect of the arbitral process before an investor has resorted to arbitration.

D. Agreement to apply the Transparency Rules under existing treaties

1. *Agreements between disputing parties*

16. The first possible method of application of the Transparency Rules in the context of an investor-state arbitration pursuant to a treaty concluded before 1 April 2014 is where the disputing parties so agree. At the time of writing this has occurred in two cases.

17. In the first case, *Iberdrola SA v. Bolivia*,[30] an investor initiated the arbitration pursuant to the Bolivia-Spain BIT, alleging expropriation by Bolivia of four companies operating in the electricity distribution sector. Pursuant to the BIT, which entered into force in 2001, the 1976 Arbitration Rules applied to the proceedings.[31] The parties agreed that the PCA would administer the case, and that the Transparency Rules would apply. The PCA therefore assumed the role of 'repository' under article 8 of the Transparency Rules and the parties agreed that the information and documents relating to the arbitration, as well as the hearings, would be accessible to the public. Accordingly, the notice of arbitration, the terms of appointment of the arbitral tribunal, and the award on agreed terms rendered pursuant to article 34(1) of the 1976 Arbitration Rules are all available on the website of the PCA.[32]

---

27 UNCITRAL Working Paper for 54th Session, 9 December 2010, UN Doc A/CN.9/WG.II/WP.162, para. 41.

28 *Ibid.*

29 *Pope & Talbot Inc v. The Government of Canada* (UNCITRAL) Award in Respect of Damages, 31 May 2002, <www.italaw.com>.

30 *Iberdrola SA and Iberdrola Energia SAU v. Plurinational State of Bolivia* (PCA Case No. 2015-05), <www.italaw.com>.

31 *See* Article 11(2) of the Bolivia-Spain BIT (*Acuerdo para la Promoción y la Protección Recíproca de Inversiones entre el Reino de España y la República de Bolivia*) (2001), <www.investmentpolicyhub.unctad.org>.

32 *See* the *Notificación de Arbitraje*, the *Acta de Constitución*, and the *Orden de Conclusión*, available at <www.pcacases.com/web/view/115>.

18. The second case is *BSG Resources Limited v. Guinea.*[33] The claimant, a multinational British mining company, initiated arbitration against Guinea alleging, inter alia, the illegal withdrawal of its mining titles. The dispute did not arise out of a treaty and was brought under the ICSID Convention rather than the UNCITRAL Rules.[34] The parties agreed to apply a modified version of the Transparency Rules (as permitted by article 1(9) and the ICSID Convention) and, crucially, ICSID confirmed its willingness to administer the arbitration in accordance with the Transparency Rules.[35]

19. The *Iberdrola* and *BSG* cases demonstrate the flexibility available in the application of the Transparency Rules, particularly as regards the disputing parties' ability to 'opt-in' under article 1(2)(a). The *BSG* case further demonstrates the first application of the Transparency Rules in non-UNCITRAL arbitration proceedings, as further discussed below.

2. *Agreements between State Parties*

20. The Working Group wished to facilitate the opt-in process for treaties concluded before 1 April 2014, particularly in light of the large number of investment treaties concluded before that date.[36] In particular, the Working Group considered the following instruments as possible means by which the Transparency Rules may be applied to existing treaties:

    (i) a recommendation urging States to apply the Transparency Rules to investor-state dispute settlement;
    (ii) an international convention (as a general statement of applicability);
    (iii) joint interpretative declarations by State Parties pursuant to Article 31(3)(a) of the Vienna Convention; and/or
    (iv) an amendment or modification of the relevant treaty pursuant to Articles 39-41 of the Vienna Convention.[37]

---

33 *BSG Resources Limited, BSG Resources (Guinea) Limited and BSG Resources (Guinea) SARL v. Republic of Guinea* (ICSID Case No. ARB/14/22), <www.italaw.com>.

34 *See ibid.*, Request for Arbitration of BSG Resources Limited, 1 August 2014, paras 108-112 (addressing Guinea's consent to arbitration in accordance with the ICSID Convention, pursuant to Article 28(2) of the Guinean Investment Code and Article 184 of the 1995 Mining Code).

35 *See ibid.*, Procedural Order No. 2 on Transparency, 17 September 2015, paras 9-10.

36 *See* Briefing of the European Parliamentary Research Service, *UN Convention on Transparency in Treaty-based Investor-State Arbitration*, 1 February 2016, <www.europarl.europa.eu/thinktank/en/document.html?reference=EPRS_ATA(2016)573948> (noting that over 3000 BITs had been concluded prior to 1 April 2014).

37 UNCITRAL Report of 55th Session, 17 October 2011, UN Doc A/CN.9/736, para. 134. *See also* UNCITRAL Working Paper for 55th Session, 29 July 2011, UN Doc A/CN.9/WG.II/WP.166/Add.1, paras 15-23; UNCITRAL Working Paper for 54th Session, 9 December 2010, UN Doc A/CN.9/WG.II/WP.162, paras 22-40.

21. It was also suggested that unilateral declarations by States could be used to render the Transparency Rules applicable to existing treaties.[38] However, a declaration by one State would not be sufficient: all State Parties to an investment treaty would need to issue unilateral declarations to the same effect in order to allow for the application of the Transparency Rules under an existing treaty.[39]

22. Ultimately, the UN decided to opt for the legally safest and most solemn route. Thus came about the United Nations Convention on Transparency in Treaty-based Investor-State Arbitration (the 'Transparency Convention')[40] in order to facilitate the opt-in process for State Parties to investment treaties concluded before 1 April 2014. This instrument provides for the application of the Transparency Rules to disputes between contracting States and investors of other signatory States, irrespective of whether or not the arbitration is initiated under the UNCITRAL Arbitration Rules.[41] Nevertheless, article 3 of the Transparency Convention allows States to formulate certain reservations.[42] If the respondent State is a party to the Transparency Convention but the claimant is a national of a State which is not, the Transparency Rules will apply if the claimant agrees by way of a 'unilateral offer of application' in accordance with article 2(2). The broader objective is for States 'to supplement or supplant existing investment treaties and require arbitration pursuant to rules requiring transparency'.[43]

23. At the time of writing, the Transparency Convention has been signed by 19 States and ratified by three – Mauritius, Canada and, most recently, Switzerland.[44] This last ratification will allow the Transparency Convention to enter into force on 18 October 2017.[45] The Transparency Convention will apply only prospectively, to

---

[38] UNCITRAL Report of 53rd Session, 20 October 2010, UN Doc A/CN.9/712, para. 93; UNCITRAL Working Paper for 54th Session, 9 December 2010, UN Doc A/CN.9/WG.II/WP.162, para. 36.

[39] *Ibid.*, at para. 37.

[40] The United Nations Convention on Transparency in Treaty-based Investor-State Arbitration, also known as the Mauritius Convention on Transparency, was adopted on 10 December 2014 and is due to enter into force on 18 October 2017.

[41] *See* articles 1(1) and 2 of the Transparency Convention.

[42] Article 3(1) of the Transparency Convention provides as follows: 'A Party may declare that: (a) It shall not apply this Convention to investor-State arbitration under a specific investment treaty, identified by title and name of the contracting parties to that investment treaty; (b) Article 2(1) and (2) shall not apply to investor-State arbitration conducted using a specific set of arbitration rules or procedures other than the UNCITRAL Arbitration Rules, and in which it is a respondent; (c) Article 2(2) shall not apply in investor-State arbitration in which it is a respondent'.

[43] Johnson & Bernasconi-Osterwalder, *supra* fn 6, at 5.

[44] *See* the status of the Transparency Convention at < www.uncitral.org >.

[45] Article 9(1) of the Transparency Convention provides that it shall enter into force 'six months after the date of deposit of the third instrument of ratification, acceptance, approval or accession'. As Switzerland became the third country to ratify the Transparency Convention on 18 April 2017, this instrument shall enter into force on 18 October 2017. *See also* article 9(2) of the Transparency Convention, which provides that: 'When a State or a regional economic integration organization ratifies, accepts, approves or accedes to this Convention after the deposit of the third instrument of ratification, acceptance, approval or accession,

arbitrations commenced after the entry into force of the Transparency Convention for the party concerned.

this Convention enters into force in respect of that State or regional economic integration organization six months after the date of the deposit of its instrument of ratification, acceptance, approval or accession'.

Article 1(3)
Scope of application

Article 1(3)

Application of the Rules

3. In any arbitration in which the Rules on Transparency apply pursuant to a treaty or to an agreement by the Parties to that treaty:

(a) The disputing parties may not derogate from these Rules, by agreement or otherwise, unless permitted to do so by the treaty;

(b) The arbitral tribunal shall have the power, besides its discretionary authority under certain provisions of these Rules, to adapt the requirements of any specific provision of these Rules to the particular circumstances of the case, after consultation with the disputing parties, if such adaptation is necessary to conduct the arbitration in a practical manner and is consistent with the transparency objective of these Rules.

1. Article 1(3)(a) establishes that, in an arbitration where the Transparency Rules apply, the disputing parties may not derogate from them.[1] This is a derogation from the ordinary rule in article 1(3) of the Arbitration Rules. Article 1(3)(b) affords flexibility to the tribunal to adapt the Transparency Rules in order 'to conduct the arbitration in a practical manner'. Exercise of the tribunal's 'discretionary authority' in this regard must take into account the considerations contained in article 1(4) and must, per article 1(3)(b), be 'consistent with the

[1] There was support throughout the negotiations for such a provision, which prevents the disputing parties from varying the Transparency Rules and from derogating from the offer for transparent arbitration. *See* UNCITRAL Report of 55th Session, 17 October 2011, UN Doc A/CN.9/736, para. 33; UNCITRAL Working Paper for 57th Session, 2 August 2012, UN Doc A/CN.9/WG.II/WP.172, para. 19; and UNCITRAL Report of 56th Session, 16 February 2012, UN Doc A/CN.9/741, para. 61.

transparency objective'.[2] It is clear that while the tribunal is given considerable latitude through the term 'discretion', it is to decide on the matter judicially, both in a procedural sense (duty to consult with the disputing parties) and in a substantive sense (duty to consider what may be 'necessary' in a manner 'consistent with the transparency objective'). It is simply the case that, as with the tribunal's general procedural powers under article 17(1) of the Arbitration Rules, one cannot satisfactorily regulate detailed procedural issues in advance in a manner that is efficient or practical for all cases. Article 1(3)(b) recognizes this, and clarifies that the tribunal has a power of adaptation. This is useful, perhaps necessary even, to spell out, given that article 17(1) does not contain a similar stipulation, and the Arbitration Rules seem to grant similar powers only in respect of time-periods and -limits (see articles 17(2) and 25). Absent article 1(3)(b), tribunals would have to resort to the doctrine of inherent powers, the limitations of which are a matter of debate, as discussed in the context of article 17(1).

2. The phrase 'unless permitted to do so by the treaty' in article 1(3)(a) clarifies that provisions of the treaty will prevail in cases of conflict with the Transparency Rules.[3] This is consistent with article 1(7) (applicable instrument in case of conflict).[4] The Transparency Rules do not stipulate that the permission to derogate in the treaty must be explicit, or whether more general provisions authorizing the disputing parties (or the tribunal) to regulate the arbitral process will suffice for this purpose. It is submitted that the analysis would have to be conducted under the ordinary rules of treaty interpretation in Section 3 of the Vienna Convention on the Law of Treaties.[5] The question will be whether a post-2014 treaty which incorporates the Transparency Rules by reference (including the non-derogation rule in article 1(3)(a)) also authorizes the parties to trump article 1(3)(a). One may expect tribunals to require a degree of specificity in the wording of the putative authorization in the treaty: after all, article 1(3)(b) is quite a central provision of the Transparency Rules.

A. Limits to party autonomy

1. *Investors*

3. The Working Group initially considered whether an investor should be able to refuse an offer contained in a treaty to arbitrate under the Transparency Rules

---

[2] *See* Lise Johnson & Nathalie Bernasconi-Osterwalder, *New UNCITRAL Arbitration Rules on Transparency: Application, Content and Next Steps*, 12 (CIEL, IISD, CCSI, August 2013), <http://ccsi.columbia.edu>.

[3] UNCITRAL Report of 56th Session, 16 February 2012, UN Doc A/CN.9/741, para. 64.

[4] Article 1(7) of the Transparency Rules provides in pertinent part that '[n]otwithstanding any provision in these Rules, where there is a conflict between the Rules on Transparency and the treaty, the provisions of the treaty shall prevail'.

[5] *See* Section 3 of the Vienna Convention (comprising Articles 31-33, and addressing general rules of treaty interpretation, supplementary means of interpretation, and the interpretation of treaties authenticated in two or more languages, respectively).

and propose a different regime.[6] The final formulation of article 1(3), however, reflects the view that an investor would be unduly privileged if allowed to have what was regarded as the 'last word' with respect to the application of the Transparency Rules, which the Working Group believed might also lead to a decrease in transparency, contrary to its mandate and the objective of the Transparency Rules.[7] It was said that such an arbitration is based on 'an underlying treaty between State Parties, which limited the ability of the investor to depart from offers made by the host State'.[8]

4. As also noted above, the view that the disputing parties should have the freedom to agree not to apply the Transparency Rules was ultimately rejected, on the basis that the arbitrants, unless permitted to do so by the relevant treaty, should not be entitled to reverse the agreement of the State Parties to the treaty to apply the Transparency Rules.[9] The purpose of article 1(3) is to 'prohibit derogation by the disputing parties from the offer for transparent arbitration, for the policy reason that it would not be appropriate for the disputing parties to reverse a decision made by Parties to the investment treaty on that matter'.[10] The policy premise is that the Transparency Rules were intended to benefit 'not only the investor and the host State but also the general public'.[11]

5. To implement this policy decision, it was necessary explicitly to state, in article 1(3)(a), that the Transparency Rules may not be modified by the disputing parties.[12] Absent such a provision, where the Transparency Rules operate as part of the Arbitration Rules, article 1(1) of the latter would have permitted such modification.[13] This does not, however, prevent States from providing for the possibility to derogate from the Transparency Rules in a treaty, or, in respect of a treaty concluded on or after 1 April 2014, agreeing to opt out of the Transparency Rules altogether.[14]

---

6 UNCITRAL Report of 53rd Session, 20 October 2010, UN Doc A/CN.9/712, paras 30 and 95.

7 *Ibid.*, at para. 96; UNCITRAL Report of 54th Session, 25 February 2011, UN Doc A/CN.9/717, para. 50.

8 UNCITRAL Report of 53rd Session, 20 October 2010, UN Doc A/CN.9/712, para. 96; and UNCITRAL Working Paper for 54th Session, 9 December 2010, UN Doc A/CN.9/WG.II/WP.162, para. 50.

9 *See* UNCITRAL Report of 55th Session, 17 October 2011, UN Doc A/CN.9/736, paras 32-33; UNCITRAL Working Paper for 57th Session, 2 August 2012, UN Doc A/CN.9/WG.II/WP.172, para. 19; and UNCITRAL Report of 56th Session, 16 February 2012, UN Doc A/CN.9/741, para. 61.

10 UNCITRAL Report of 56th Session, 16 February 2012, UN Doc A/CN.9/741, para. 61.

11 UNCITRAL Report of 55th Session, 17 October 2011, UN Doc A/CN.9/736, para. 33; UNCITRAL Report of 56th Session, 16 February 2012, UN Doc A/CN.9/741, para. 61.

12 *Ibid.*, at para. 63.

13 *Ibid.* Article 1(1) of the 1976 and 2010 Arbitration Rules provides that 'disputes shall be settled in accordance with these Rules subject to such modification as the parties may agree'. *See* discussion of article 1 of the Arbitration Rules, *supra*.

14 *See* article 1(1) of the Transparency Rules. *See also* Krista N. Schefer, 'Article 1. Scope of Application' in Dimitrij Euler, Markus Gehring & Maxi Scherer (eds), *Transparency in*

6. The non-derogation rule in article 1(3)(a) is irrelevant in article 1(2)(a) cases where the Transparency Rules have been agreed upon by the disputing parties in the context of a pre-existing treaty. In such cases, the application of the Transparency Rules is purely voluntary and may be as extensive or reduced or modified as the parties desire.

7. At the time of writing, the only known derogation from the Transparency Rules has served to expand their scope of application. In *BSG Resources Limited v. Guinea* the parties to an ICSID arbitration agreed to the application of the Transparency Rules. The tribunal laid out the applicable transparency regime in its second procedural order, providing as follows:

> Although elaborated in the framework of UNCITRAL, the Transparency Rules are available for use in non-UNCITRAL arbitrations such as this ICSID arbitration (Art. 1(9)). Where the Contracting States to an investment treaty have not provided for the application of the Transparency Rules, the disputing parties (in the present case: the "Parties") may agree to apply the Transparency Rules (Art. 1(2)(a) by analogy and combined with Art. 1(9)). The ICSID legal framework allows the Parties to agree on a degree of transparency that is greater than the one required by the ICSID Convention and Arbitration Rules.
>
> In the present case, the Parties have agreed on the application of the Transparency Rules, expanded their scope in some respects, and provided for specific rules for their implementation. ICSID has confirmed its willingness to administer this arbitration in accordance with the rules set forth in this Order and to act as repository as defined in the Transparency Rules and in this Order.[15]

8. More specifically, the parties agreed that:

   (i) all written submissions, exhibits, legal authorities, witness statements and expert reports, as well as any transcripts of hearings, orders, decisions and awards of the Tribunal would be made available to the public;
   (ii) hearings would made accessible to the public through video link on the ICSID website, with physical attendance by third persons at hearings subject to the Tribunal's approval;
   (iii) each party should give notice within 21 days from the filing of any document 'that it seeks protection for confidential or protected information in that document';
   (iv) the broadcast would be delayed by thirty minutes in order to protect confidential or protected information during hearings.[16]

International Investment Arbitration: A Guide to the UNCITRAL Rules on Transparency in Treaty-Based Investor-State Arbitration, 54 (Cambridge University Press 2015).

15 *BSG Resources Limited, BSG Resources (Guinea) Limited and BSG Resources (Guinea) SARL v. Republic of Guinea* (ICSID Case No. ARB/14/22), Procedural Order No. 2 on Transparency, 17 September 2015, < www.italaw.com >, paras 9-10.

16 *Ibid.*, at paras 12-15.

B. Tribunal's discretion under article 1(3)(b)

9. Article 1(3)(b) gives the tribunal the power to adapt the Transparency Rules if and to the extent 'necessary' to ensure the efficiency of proceedings by way of 'adaptation' but, signally, without permitting derogation from them.[17] The final version of article 1(3) contains careful wording intended to ensure that such power does not amount to (notably) additional exceptions (i.e. exceptions over and above those contained in article 7).[18] This reflects the view that allowing deviations would have risked 'eroding the rules by creating opportunities to depart from them'.[19] In simple terms, the Transparency Rules were adopted as a negotiated package, and there was understandably a desire to ensure that all elements of it, including qualifications and exceptions, would apply *en bloc* where the Transparency Rules apply by virtue of an interstate agreement.

10. However, article 1(3)(b) is not intended to be so inflexible as to prevent the tribunal from ensuring the efficiency of the proceedings.[20] Adaptation is permitted if 'necessary to conduct the arbitration in a practical manner'. What counts as 'adaptation' as opposed to 'derogation' is not all that clear-cut. It is clear that, as just noted, exceptions of the nature of those contained in article 7 are beyond the remit of adaptation. It is also clear that more extensive transparency measures will fall within the remit. It may well be that 'adaptation' covers any alteration which is 'consistent with the transparency objective of the[] Rules', excluding only alterations which negate that objective. This includes, for example, addressing 'practical issues, such as the adjustment of a time period'.[21] Factors such as cost, the risk of disruption to the arbitral proceedings and unfair prejudice to a disputing party will also be relevant considerations.[22] In exercising its discretion under article 1(3)(b), and in accordance with article 1(4), as discussed below, the tribunal is able to ensure the 'procedural efficiency' required to maintain the benefits of UNCITRAL arbitration over court proceedings.[23] Nevertheless, the gateway requirement of necessity means that the Transparency Rules may not be adapted by a tribunal 'for mere convenience', and consideration must be given to whether any adaptations 'justify the avoidance of requirements that would offer enhanced transparency'.[24]

11. The discretionary power of the tribunal under article 1(3)(b) requires consultation with the parties, but does not specify whether variation of the Transparency Rules is to be at the tribunal's or the parties' initiative. It was suggested in the debates (apparently without opposition) that the tribunal has the power to adapt the

[17] UNCITRAL Working Paper for 57th Session, 2 August 2012, UN Doc A/CN.9/WG.II/WP.172, para. 19.
[18] UNCITRAL Report of 58th Session, 13 February 2013, UN Doc A/CN.9/765, para. 35.
[19] UNCITRAL Report of 56th Session, 16 February 2012, UN Doc A/CN.9/741, para. 72.
[20] *Ibid.*, at paras 67-68.
[21] *Ibid.*, at para. 67.
[22] *Ibid.*
[23] *See* Schefer, *supra* fn 14, at 56.
[24] *Ibid.*

Transparency Rules either of its own initiative or at the request of the parties.[25] At any rate, the duty to *consult* the parties suggests that, while their interests must be taken into account, the tribunal is not bound to obtain the parties' consent before making a decision; the tribunal may decide to act 'against the disputing parties' views' if it considers this appropriate.[26]

12. One issue left open by this provision is the specific meaning of the 'transparency objective' as described in article 1(3)(b). Although a preamble to the Transparency Rules may have been helpful in establishing this, the Working Group did discuss the broader policy 'aims' on several occasions: '[t]he goals as set forth in the documents include fostering good governance and supporting due process and the public's right to access information, and enhancing the legitimacy of and public interest in investor-State arbitration through greater public participation'.[27] In the submission of the authors, while the broader policy aims are to be borne in mind, the tribunal's task is to identify the more specific purposes served by the concrete provisions of the Transparency Rules and, indeed, the manner and degree to which such purposes are served.

---

25 UNCITRAL Report of 56th Session, 16 February 2012, UN Doc A/CN.9/741, para. 77.

26 *See* Schefer, *supra* fn 14, at 55 (noting that '[w]hile such decisions are certain to be rare, the possibility that a tribunal can act on its own belief in what is best opens the possibility of a new set of challenges for the traditional practice of party-led arbitration').

27 *Ibid.*, at 56. *See also* UNCITRAL Report of 55th Session, 17 October 2011, UN Doc A/CN.9/736, para. 14.

Article 1(4)-(6)
Scope of application

Article 1(4)-(6)

Discretion and authority of the arbitral tribunal

4. Where the Rules on Transparency provide for the arbitral tribunal to exercise discretion, the arbitral tribunal in exercising such discretion shall take into account:

(a) The public interest in transparency in treaty-based investor-State arbitration and in the particular arbitral proceedings; and

(b) The disputing parties' interest in a fair and efficient resolution of their dispute.

5. These Rules shall not affect any authority that the arbitral tribunal may otherwise have under the UNCITRAL Arbitration Rules to conduct the arbitration in such a manner as to promote transparency, for example by accepting submissions from third persons.

6. In the presence of any conduct, measure or other action having the effect of wholly undermining the transparency objectives of these Rules, the arbitral tribunal shall ensure that those objectives prevail.

I. ARTICLE 1(4)

1. Article 1(4) establishes that, where the Transparency Rules provide discretion to the tribunal, the exercise of that discretion should account for (i) the public interest in transparency, and (ii) the disputing parties' interest in 'a fair and efficient resolution of their dispute'.[1] The text implies a juxtaposition of these two

1 *See* UNCITRAL Report of 55th Session, 17 October 2011, UN Doc A/CN.9/736, para. 13 (stating that 'discretion should be exercised by the arbitral tribunal taking into account both the legitimate public interest in transparency in the field of treaty-based investor-State arbitration and in the arbitral proceedings as well [as] the arbitrating parties' own legitimate interest in an efficient resolution of their dispute'). *See also* UNCITRAL Working Paper for

sets of interests pulling in opposite directions, e.g. procedural efficiency tending to favour confining the process to the disputing parties and public interest tending to favour amici participation – with the tribunal balancing the two.

2. Portions of the final text of article 1(4) were at one point included in a draft preamble to the Transparency Rules.[2] In light of this initial positioning, article 1(4) should be understood as representing the broader, overarching aims of the Transparency Rules, i.e. to foster the public interest inherent in treaty-based investor-state arbitration, to balance the disputing parties' interests in a fair and efficient resolution of their dispute and, more generally, to enhance the legitimacy of such arbitrations.[3] Proposals to include references to human rights, and, specifically, a right to information, did not receive support.[4]

3. In particular, views were expressed against including a preamble since its legal force would be uncertain.[5] By moving the content of the preamble into the body of the Transparency Rules, the Working Group established the binding nature of the aims contained therein.

II. ARTICLE 1(5)

4. Article 1(5) pertains to the tribunal's 'authority' to direct transparency measures in UNCITRAL arbitrations in which the Transparency Rules do not apply. As discussed above, such authority would principally derive from article 17(1). The aim of article 1(5) was to 'counter any potential presumption *against* transparency that might have otherwise been interpreted to arise' from the exclusion in article 1(2).[6] That is to say, whatever transparency measures may be available under the Arbitration Rules will, 'at the very least, not be lower than [they] would be without the [Transparency] Rules'.[7]

5. Following this line of reasoning, one may also argue that article 1(5) can also serve a separate but related function: to permit a tribunal to adopt, by virtue

56th Session, 13 December 2011, UN Doc A/CN.9/WG.II/WP.169/Add.1, para. 24. The exercise of the tribunal's discretion must be consistent with the underlying principles of article 17(1) of the 2010 Rules.

2 *See* UNCITRAL Working Paper for 56th Session, 13 December 2011, UN Doc A/CN.9/WG.II/WP.169, para. 7.

3 *Ibid.*; UNCITRAL Report of 55th Session, 17 October 2011, UN Doc A/CN.9/736, paras 14-16 and 38-40; UNCITRAL Report of 56th Session, 16 February 2012, UN Doc A/CN.9/741, para. 82; and UNCITRAL Working Paper for 57th Session, 2 August 2012, UN Doc A/CN.9/WG.II/WP.172, para. 22.

4 *See* UNCITRAL Report of 56th Session, 16 February 2012, UN Doc A/CN.9/741, para. 83.

5 UNCITRAL Report of 55th Session, 17 October 2011, UN Doc A/CN.9/736, para. 14.

6 Lise Johnson & Nathalie Bernasconi-Osterwalder, *New UNCITRAL Arbitration Rules on Transparency: Application, Content and Next Steps*, 12 (CIEL, IISD, CCSI, August 2013), <http://ccsi.columbia.edu>.

7 Krista N. Schefer, 'Article 1. Scope of Application' in Dimitrij Euler, Markus Gehring & Maxi Scherer (eds), *Transparency in International Investment Arbitration: A Guide to the UNCITRAL Rules on Transparency in Treaty-Based Investor-State Arbitration*, 59 (Cambridge University Press 2015).

of article 17(1) or inherent powers, measures which may not be found in the Transparency Rules in cases that are in fact governed by these Rules; for example addressing a request for a consultative opinion to an IGO or international court. One will riposte that the Transparency Rules were prepared as a comprehensive package such that by necessary implication they exclude additional measures (as opposed to 'adopted' measures; see article 1(3)(b)). As to this, it is possible to counter that notions and requirements of public interest will evolve over time; and that the procedural powers that tribunals have exercised in UNCITRAL proceedings have also evolved over time. At the very least, this is a legitimate issue for debate in an appropriate case.

6. The powers of the tribunal and the direction in which they should be exercised are also discussed immediately below.

III. ARTICLE 1(6)

7. Article 1(6) gives the tribunal facially unbridled power to address 'any conduct, measure or other action' that wholly undermines the transparency objectives of the Transparency Rules in order to ensure that such objectives prevail.

8. In the light of the drafting history, article 1(6) reflects a compromise intended notably to counterbalance some of the exceptions set out in article 7, which provide respondent States with 'a measure of latitude to invoke their own law as a basis for avoiding disclosure'.[8] In this sense, article 1(6) acts as 'a sort of emergency provision'[9] to prevent, for example, a respondent State imposing national legislation completely to prohibit the disclosure of information in investor-state disputes, or invoking its essential security interests in order to 'wholly undermine' the Transparency Rules.[10]

9. Nevertheless, the provision speaks of 'any conduct, measure or other action', a formulation which can clearly encapsulate the investor or even a tribunal member. It is more difficult to suggest that third parties are covered: the word 'any' includes them textually, and one can see that in appropriate cases a tribunal must be able to do something about third-party actions. It is clear, however, that a tribunal has no authority over third parties. One may thus conceive of measures by the tribunal directed to the disputing parties calling for them to interact with third parties (e.g. to secure information or materials) or unilateral statements by the tribunal (e.g. to correct misinformation in certain media about the proceedings).

10. The provision is unusual in being drafted in basically disciplinary terms. While tribunals applying the Arbitration Rules not infrequently face mala fide conduct, there is no analogously-worded provision in the Rules. Tribunals have to rely on article 17(1) and discrete powers such as in respect of costs (article 42(1)) and

---

[8] Johnson & Bernasconi-Osterwalder, *supra* fn 6, at 12. *See also* discussion of article 7 of the Transparency Rules, *infra*.

[9] Schefer, *supra* fn 7, at 59.

[10] *See*, e.g., UNCITRAL Report of 57th Session, 12 October 2012, UN Doc A/CN.9/760, para. 103; UNCITRAL Report of 58th Session, 13 February 2013, UN Doc A/CN.9/765, para. 62.

replacement of arbitrators (article 14(2), which grants powers to the appointing authority). It cannot be suggested that the powers of a tribunal under article 1(6) should not include those already available under the Arbitration Rules, such as the power to issue binding directions in the form of an order (see article 33(1)) or interim measures, including various injunctions (see article 26(1)-(2)(b)). Indeed, article 1(6) should be read as pointing to the circumstances in which a tribunal may take action and to the purpose to be achieved by the tribunal's action. What kind of action may be taken and in what form must perforce find a foundation in the Arbitration Rules and the *lex arbitri*.

11. Article 1(6) appears to grant unlimited authority to take any action that 'shall ensure that [the Transparency Rules'] objectives prevail'. This calls for two observations. First, there can be no question of an *obligation de resultat*: all a tribunal may do is to deploy the measures at its disposal which are in its judgement best-suited and necessary to achieve the goal mandated by article 1(6). Secondly, while it is clear that preservation of the objectives of the Transparency Rules is stated as a consideration of special importance, and therefore one that would satisfy the requirement of necessity under article 26 of the Arbitration Rules (interim measures), it is questionable whether article 1(6) trumps all other considerations that the Rules require for various measures or actions – such as urgency, proportionality, fairness, due process, efficiency, etc.

Article 1(7)-(9)
Scope of application

Article 1(7)-(9)

Applicable instrument in case of conflict

7. Where the Rules on Transparency apply, they shall supplement any applicable arbitration rules. Where there is a conflict between the Rules on Transparency and the applicable arbitration rules, the Rules on Transparency shall prevail. Notwithstanding any provision in these Rules, where there is a conflict between the Rules on Transparency and the treaty, the provisions of the treaty shall prevail.

8. Where any of these Rules is in conflict with a provision of the law applicable to the arbitration from which the disputing parties cannot derogate, that provision shall prevail.

Application in non-UNCITRAL arbitrations

9. These Rules are available for use in investor-State arbitrations initiated under rules other than the UNCITRAL Arbitration Rules or in ad hoc proceedings.

1. Articles 1(7) and 1(8) address cases of conflict between the Transparency Rules and:

   (i) the applicable arbitration rules;[1]
   (ii) the relevant treaty; or
   (iii) provisions of the law applicable to the arbitration (the *lex arbitri*).[2]

---

1 *See* Lise Johnson & Nathalie Bernasconi-Osterwalder, *New UNCITRAL Arbitration Rules on Transparency: Application, Content and Next Steps*, 12-13 (CIEL, IISD, CCSI, August 2013), <http://ccsi.columbia.edu>. For example, if the applicable arbitration rules allow the disputing parties to agree to modify the rules governing the dispute (e.g. through article 1(1) of the Arbitration Rules), the Transparency Rules will prevail and prevent such modification.

2 UNCITRAL Report of 56th Session, 16 February 2012, UN Doc A/CN.9/741, para. 96; UNCITRAL Working Paper for 57th Session, 2 August 2012, UN Doc A/CN.9/WG.II/

2. Article 1(9) clarifies that use of the Transparency Rules is not limited to arbitrations conducted under the 1976 or 2010 Arbitration Rules and may be used in investor-state (i.e. treaty or contract-based) arbitrations initiated under other arbitration rules or in ad hoc proceedings.[3]

I. PREVALENCE OF THE TREATY

3. The prevailing view in the Working Group was that treaty provisions in conflict with the Transparency Rules should prevail, regardless of whether they provided for a greater or lesser degree of transparency.[4] This consensus (which one sees in article 1(3)(a) as well) is reflected in the last sentence of article 1(7), which clearly establishes the prevalence of treaty provisions in the event of a conflict.

4. Earlier drafts of article 1(7) aimed to ensure that the Transparency Rules would not supersede provisions in a treaty that required a greater degree of transparency.[5] One draft, for example, referred to the 'level of transparency' provided by the treaty,[6] though it was quickly pointed out that a methodology would be required to determine how that level would be assessed.[7] The final text abandoned this formulation, avoiding an assessment of the 'level' of transparency and instead confirming the general prevalence of treaty provisions in cases of conflict with the Transparency Rules.[8] As pointed out above in connection with article 1(3)(a), the degree of specificity required of the treaty text to establish a conflict will be a matter of treaty interpretation.

5. The entry into force of the Transparency Convention will remove the primacy of treaty provisions for contracting States. Article 2(4) of the Transparency Convention expressly excludes the final sentence of article 1(7) of the Transparency Rules. The effect is to increase transparency for treaties concluded before 1 April 2014; otherwise, as Johnson notes, 'if Article 1(7) of the Transparency Rules were to apply, it would allow an investment treaty with a lower standard of transparency to prevail over the Transparency Rules'.[9]

WP.172, para. 21. Article 1(8) reflects the Working Group's recognition of the possibility that, depending on the applicable domestic legal provisions addressing transparency and/or treaty law, the parties may derogate from the Transparency Rules. *See also* Johnson & Bernasconi-Osterwalder, *supra* fn 1, at 13 ('If, however, the Rules on Transparency are incorporated in a convention on transparency … then domestic law would have to be brought into conformity with the convention'). *See also id.*, at 23, Part IV.

3 *Ibid.*, at 13.

4 UNCITRAL Report of 56th Session, 16 February 2012, UN Doc A/CN.9/741, para. 89. *See also* UNCITRAL Report of 58th Session, 13 February 2013, UN Doc A/CN.9/765, para. 31.

5 UNCITRAL Report of 56th Session, 16 February 2012, UN Doc A/CN.9/741, para. 86. *See also* UNCITRAL Report of 55th Session, 17 October 2011, UN Doc A/CN.9/736, para. 27.

6 *See* UNCITRAL Working Paper for 56th Session, 13 December 2011, UN Doc A/CN.9/WG.II/WP.169, para. 8, draft article 1(4).

7 UNCITRAL Report of 56th Session, 16 February 2012, UN Doc A/CN.9/741, para. 87.

8 *See* the proposal referenced *ibid.*

9 Lise Johnson, *The Mauritius Convention on Transparency: Comments on the treaty and its role in increasing transparency of investor-State arbitration*, 8 (CCSI Policy Paper 2014).

6. An issue has been said to arise from the Transparency Convention's silence as to the prevalence of the Transparency Rules in relation to mandatory provisions of domestic arbitration law.[10] There are different ways to understand the legal hierarchy where arbitration rules apply pursuant to a treaty:

> One interpretation is that the treaty merely states that application under certain procedural rules is permissible or required, but does not intend to alter the default status of procedural rules by elevating them to the treaty level where they could trump contrary domestic law.
>
> A second interpretation is that the treaty incorporates the procedural rules by reference in its text, and by doing so makes the rules an integral part of the treaty, elevating those rules to treaty status where they can override inconsistent domestic law.[11]

7. The former approach is the orthodox one generally: there has never been a suggestion that UNCITRAL arbitrations conducted pursuant to an investment treaty are different from ordinary proceedings under the *lex arbitri* of a state; see article 1(3) of the Arbitration Rules. There is no reason one can see for the position to be different when the Transparency Convention applies. This approach is consistent with article 1(8) of the Transparency Rules, which confirms that mandatory provisions of the *lex arbitri* prevail over the Transparency Rules in case of conflict. Granted, as the Working Group unanimously recognized, it is 'not permissible for a State to adopt in its investment treaties the rules on transparency and then to use its domestic laws to undermine the spirit of those rules'.[12] But that is a species of treaty breach, to be addressed on the international-law plane by application of the rules of State responsibility. It is not a matter that may be addressed through the application of arbitration rules, save for whatever measures a tribunal may feel able to take pursuant to article 1(6) of the Transparency Rules (discussed above). This was in fact recognized through the adoption of article 1(8) which preserves the primacy of the *lex arbitri*.

II. ARTICLE 1(7) IS NOT A RULE OF TREATY INTERPRETATION

8. It is clear from the drafting history that nothing in article 1(7) of the Transparency Rules should be construed as establishing rules on treaty interpretation.[13] As such, the final sentence of this provision should be viewed as procedural guidance as to how the Transparency Rules should be applied in the case of conflict, rather than a rule as to how the underlying treaty should be interpreted.

9. The earlier draft version of article 1(7), as mentioned above, provided that:

---

10 *Ibid.* (noting that, '[g]enerally, arbitration rules that apply in contractual disputes are subject to and cannot override contrary mandatory provisions of domestic law at the seat of the arbitration').

11 *Ibid.*

12 UNCITRAL Report of 58th Session, 13 February 2013, UN Doc A/CN.9/765, para 62.

13 *Ibid.*, at para. 31.

> Where the treaty provides in any respect for a higher level of transparency than the Rules on Transparency, the relevant provision(s) of the treaty shall prevail, so that this higher level of transparency shall apply to the arbitration.[14]

This provision was perceived by some delegations as touching on a matter of treaty interpretation, to be regulated not by the Transparency Rules but by the Vienna Convention on the Law of Treaties.[15] In particular, the question whether treaty provisions (as drafted by the State Parties) and the Transparency Rules (as incorporated into the treaty by reference) would fall to be interpreted by application of the same rules of interpretation proved controversial.[16] Eventually, the Working Group removed the draft version of article 1(7), concluding that there were different approaches to treaty interpretation and that it was not appropriate to provide a rule of treaty interpretation in the Transparency Rules.[17]

III. INTERPLAY BETWEEN TRANSPARENCY RULES AND APPLICABLE ARBITRATION RULES OR MANDATORY NORMS OF DOMESTIC LAW

10. There is a varied level of interplay between the Transparency Rules and the applicable arbitration rules, in that the transparency provisions either (i) modify, (ii) supplement (e.g. articles 4 and 5) or (iii) do not affect (e.g. articles 7 and 8) the applicable arbitration rules.[18] It was suggested that article 1(7) further clarify the relationship between the two sets of rules, taking into account the possibility that future arbitration rules may provide for more transparency than do the Transparency Rules.[19] Ultimately, however, this suggestion was not integrated into the final text, which simply reflects the Working Group's 'shared understanding' that the Transparency Rules prevail over any applicable conflicting provision of the applicable arbitration rules.[20]

11. By contrast, the law applicable to the arbitration may contain provisions relating to (notably) confidentiality, which, in accordance with article 1(8), will prevail over the Transparency Rules if they constitute '[provisions] of the law applicable to

---

[14] *See* UNCITRAL Working Paper for 56th Session, 13 December 2011, UN Doc A/CN.9/WG.II/WP.169, para. 8, draft article 1(4).

[15] *See* UNCITRAL Report of 56th Session, 16 February 2012, UN Doc A/CN.9/741, paras 89 and 91.

[16] *Ibid.*, at para. 92.

[17] *Ibid.*, at paras 93-94.

[18] UNCITRAL Working Paper for 56th Session, 13 December 2011, UN Doc A/CN.9/WG.II/WP.169/Add.1, para. 15. *See also* UNCITRAL Working Paper for 57th Session, 2 August 2012, UN Doc A/CN.9/WG.II/WP.172, para. 20 (noting that 'a large majority was in favour of including a provision on the relationship between the rules on transparency and the applicable arbitration rules in the rules on transparency').

[19] UNCITRAL Working Paper for 56th Session, 13 December 2011, UN Doc A/CN.9/WG.II/WP.169, para. 22.

[20] *See* UNCITRAL Report of 58th Session, 13 February 2013, UN Doc A/CN.9/765, para. 31 (referring expressly to 'any applicable provision in the UNCITRAL Arbitration Rules').

the arbitration from which the disputing parties cannot derogate'.[21] This effectively excludes as potential seats countries where confidentiality is mandatory and non-derogable; a circumstance doubtless to be taken into account in an article 18(1) decision.

IV. APPLICATION NOT LIMITED TO UNCITRAL ARBITRATIONS

12. A suggestion was made to limit the application of the Transparency Rules to arbitrations conducted under the 1976 or 2010 Arbitration Rules, with proponents of this limitation highlighting 'the legal uncertainties and difficulties' that might arise in applying the Transparency Rules to arbitrations under other sets of arbitration rules.[22] Arbitral institutions were invited to comment on whether they could envisage application of the Transparency Rules to disputes initiated under their arbitration rules: ICSID, the SCC, the ICC and the PCA all confirmed that, 'as a matter of principle, application of transparency rules in conjunction with their institutional rules was unlikely to create problems'.[23] As noted above, ICSID has accepted to administer an arbitration in which the parties agreed to apply the Transparency Rules. The salient point of principle is that for the Transparency Rules to apply with arbitration rules other than the UNCITRAL Arbitration Rules, there must be compatibility. It is likely that confidentiality provisions in arbitration rules are all subject to contrary agreement of the parties; the agreement to apply the Transparency Rules being just that. It may be more difficult to secure the consent of an arbitral institution to derogate from confidentiality obligations enshrined in their statutes or practice.

13. Matters as to the necessary content and form of an agreement to apply the Transparency Rules are regulated by the law applicable, in the normal way, rather than the Rules themselves.

---

[21] *See* Krista N. Schefer, 'Article 1. Scope of Application' in Dimitrij Euler, Markus Gehring & Maxi Scherer (eds), *Transparency in International Investment Arbitration: A Guide to the UNCITRAL Rules on Transparency in Treaty-Based Investor-State Arbitration*, 62 (Cambridge University Press 2015) ('[w]here confidentiality remains explicitly protected by States, the Rules will give way'). *See also ibid.*, at 96 (noting, in the context of the discretion granted to the tribunal under article 3 of the Transparency Rules, that '[v]ery few, if any, of these provisions would be considered mandatory, and so in the usual fashion that arbitral rules, as a manifestation of the parties' agreement, prevail over non-mandatory law, Article 3 would prevail and be applicable. The impact of a consideration of Article 3 against these laws may therefore be of limited relevance').

[22] UNCITRAL Report of 55th Session, 17 October 2011, UN Doc A/CN.9/736, para. 27.

[23] *Ibid.*, at para. 28.

Article 2
Publication of information at the commencement of arbitral proceedings

Article 2

> Once the notice of arbitration has been received by the respondent, each of the disputing parties shall promptly communicate a copy of the notice of arbitration to the repository referred to under article 8. Upon receipt of the notice of arbitration from the respondent, or upon receipt of the notice of arbitration and a record of its transmission to the respondent, the repository shall promptly make available to the public information regarding the name of the disputing parties, the economic sector involved and the treaty under which the claim is being made.

1. Article 2 provides for 'prompt and mandatory disclosure' of the fact that an arbitration has been initiated.[1] All disputing parties have an obligation to provide the notice of arbitration to the repository (see articles 2 and 8),[2] which practically means that the most diligent one will do so, but that legally there is a joint and several obligation on all of the parties to ensure that the dispatch occurs. This obligation is triggered as soon as the respondent has received it.[3]

[1] Lise Johnson & Nathalie Bernasconi-Osterwalder, *New UNCITRAL Arbitration Rules on Transparency: Application, Content and Next Steps*, 13 (CIEL, IISD, CCSI, August 2013), <http://ccsi.columbia.edu>. The aim of article 2 is to inform the general public of the commencement of a dispute early in the proceedings. *See* UNCITRAL Report of 55th Session, 17 October 2011, UN Doc A/CN.9/736, para. 43; UNCITRAL Working Paper for 56th Session, 13 December 2011, UN Doc A/CN.9/WG.II/WP.169, para. 27.

[2] UNCITRAL Working Paper for 57th Session, 2 August 2012, UN Doc A/CN.9/WG.II/WP.172, para. 26; UNCITRAL Working Paper for 58th Session, 30 November 2012, UN Doc A/CN.9/WG.II/WP.176, para. 23.

[3] The transmission of the notice of arbitration to the respondent takes place in accordance with article 3 of the 2010 Arbitration Rules. *See* Giuseppe Bianco, 'Article 2. Publication of information at the commencement of arbitral proceedings' in Dimitrij Euler, Markus

Indeed, to ensure that publication of the basic facts of the arbitration (i.e. the names of the parties, the relevant economic sector and the relevant treaty) does not occur before the respondent has been put on notice of the proceedings, article 2 requires the claimant to include with the notice of arbitration a record of its transmission to the respondent.[4] As noted, 'since both disputing parties are to act in good faith, the interval between the receipt by the respondent and the communication to the repository should be short'.[5] The repository in turn processes and 'promptly' publishes the basic facts specified in article 2 upon receipt of the notice of arbitration from either party.[6]

2. As discussed below, the UNCITRAL Secretariat administers the Transparency Registry as a repository on behalf of the Secretary-General of the United Nations.[7]

3. At the time of writing, there are two cases listed in the Transparency Registry.[8] There are also five NAFTA cases,[9] reproduced in the Transparency Registry pursuant to a proposal by the Government of Canada to 'illustrate the role to be played by the registry as a global reference on transparency in investor-State treaty-based arbitration'.[10]

Gehring & Maxi Scherer (eds), *Transparency in International Investment Arbitration: A Guide to the UNCITRAL Rules on Transparency in Treaty-Based Investor-State Arbitration*, 68 (Cambridge University Press 2015) ('In the absence of a designation by the respondent or an authorisation by the tribunal, the notice is received when it is physically delivered to the respondent, or is deemed to have been received when it is delivered at the place of business, habitual residence or mailing address of the respondent').

4 *See* UNCITRAL Working Paper for 57th Session, 2 August 2012, UN Doc A/CN.9/WG.II/WP.172, para. 27; UNCITRAL Working Paper for 58th Session, 30 November 2012, UN Doc A/CN.9/WG.II/WP.176, para. 24.

5 *See* Bianco, *supra* fn 3, at 69.

6 UNCITRAL Working Paper for 58th Session, 30 November 2012, UN Doc A/CN.9/WG.II/WP.176, para. 23; Jan H. Nedden & Friedrich Rosenfeld, 'The new UNCITRAL Transparency Rules: How the trend towards transparency differs in investment and commercial arbitration' in Christoph Muller & Antonio Rigozzi (eds), *New Developments in International Commercial Arbitration 2013*, 41, 43 (2013). *See also* UNCITRAL Report of 56th Session, 16 February 2012, UN Doc A/CN.9/741, para. 109.

7 *See* Bianco, *supra* fn 3, at 71; *see also* discussion of article 8 of the Transparency Rules, *infra*.

8 *See* discussion of *Iberdrola SA and Iberdrola Energia SAU v. Plurinational State of Bolivia* (PCA Case No. 2015-05) and *BSG Resources Limited, BSG Resources (Guinea) Limited and BSG Resources (Guinea) SARL v. Republic of Guinea* (ICSID Case No. ARB/14/22) in relation to article 1 of the Transparency Rules, *supra*. Note, however, that the UNCITRAL Secretariat is yet to exercise its function as a repository, as these two cases designated, respectively, the PCA and ICSID as the repository.

9 *Pope & Talbot Inc v. The Government of Canada*; *Dow AgroSciences LLC v. The Government of Canada*; *Ethyl Corporation v. The Government of Canada*; *S D Myers Inc v. The Government of Canada*; and *Merrill & Ring Forestry L P v. The Government of Canada*.

10 *See* Report of the Commission on its 47th Session, 7-18 July 2014, UN Doc A/69/17, para. 108. *See also* the web page of the Transparency Registry: <www.uncitral.org/transparency-registry>.

A. Limited scope of disclosure obligations at initiation of proceedings

4. In the Working Group's deliberations, the main issue with respect to article 2 was whether the notice of arbitration and response should be published before the constitution of the tribunal (option 1) or thereafter (option 2).[11] The majority of delegations favoured option 2, while a minority advocated prompt publication of these documents immediately following the initiation of proceedings.[12] This latter view was also held by various NGOs.[13]

5. The delegations in favour of option 1 argued that it would best serve the interests of transparency,[14] allowing the public to be informed of the dispute and 'to express their views at an early stage of the proceedings'.[15] They argued that waiting until after the tribunal had been formed could result in lengthy delays between service of the notice of arbitration and disclosure of the dispute and, furthermore, if the case settled before a tribunal was empanelled, the existence of the dispute would remain unknown.[16]

6. Those favouring option 2 emphasized that the notice of arbitration and response may contain sensitive or confidential information, and the tribunal, once constituted, would be in a better position than the repository to screen the documents prior to disclosure.[17] It was further noted that early publication could compromise settlement of the dispute;[18] lead to the publication of frivolous claims;[19] make the disputing parties vulnerable to the pressures of civil society (in particular

---

11 UNCITRAL Report of 54th Session, 25 February 2011, UN Doc A/CN.9/717, para. 62. *See also* UNCITRAL Report of 55th Session, 17 October 2011, UN Doc A/CN.9/736, para. 52 ('Support was expressed for the proposition that if the notice of arbitration was to be published, the response thereto should also be published. With a view to ensuring fairness, it was suggested that details of the dispute contained in the notice should be made public only when the respondent State had an opportunity to present its own position in the response to the notice').

12 UNCITRAL Working Paper for 56th Session, 13 December 2011, UN Doc A/CN.9/WG.II/WP.169, para. 28; UNCITRAL Report of 55th Session, 17 October 2011, UN Doc A/CN.9/736, paras 42 and 53; UNCITRAL Report of 56th Session, 16 February 2012, UN Doc A/CN.9/741, paras 103 and 108.

13 *See* Bianco, *supra* fn 3, at 67.

14 UNCITRAL Report of 54th Session, 25 February 2011, UN Doc A/CN.9/717, para. 64.

15 UNCITRAL Report of 55th Session, 17 October 2011, UN Doc A/CN.9/736, para. 48. *See* UNCITRAL Report of 53rd Session, 20 October 2010, UN Doc A/CN.9/712, para. 34.

16 Johnson & Bernasconi-Osterwalder, *supra* fn 1, at 13.

17 UNCITRAL Report of 55th Session, 17 October 2011, UN Doc A/CN.9/736, para. 50; UNCITRAL Report of 54th Session, 25 February 2011, UN Doc A/CN.9/717, para. 65. *See also* Johnson & Bernasconi-Osterwalder, *supra* fn 1, at 13.

18 UNCITRAL Report of 56th Session, 16 February 2012, UN Doc A/CN.9/741, para. 106; UNCITRAL Report of 55th Session, 17 October 2011, UN Doc A/CN.9/736, para. 49.

19 UNCITRAL Working Paper for 54th Session, 9 December 2010, UN Doc A/CN.9/WG.II/WP.162/Add.1, para. 4.

on matters such as arbitrator appointment);[20] and affect the reliability of the information published.[21]

7. The finalised text of article 2 reflects a compromise, requiring as it does the prompt disclosure of limited basic facts, but withholding publication of the notice of arbitration and response until after the tribunal has been constituted (see article 3(1)).[22] The decision to exclude the notice of arbitration and response from article 2 'is a departure from a number of treaty provisions on transparency in investor-State arbitration, as well as from several delegations' [domestic] policies' that require prompt disclosure of the notice of arbitration.[23] It does, however, reflect the prevailing view amongst the delegations that publication prior to the constitution of the tribunal would be premature for the reasons noted above.[24]

B. Disagreement does not suspend obligations

8. Article 2 is triggered as soon as the arbitration commences, i.e. the date on which the notice of arbitration is received by the respondent in accordance with article 3(2) of the 2010 Arbitration Rules.[25] It was recognized that the disputing parties may disagree on the application of the Transparency Rules under article 1 and that, prior to the constitution of the tribunal, there would be no authority to resolve such disagreement. For this reason, disagreement does not suspend the disclosure obligations contained in article 2, on the premise that the limited scope of information disclosed would not have any significant consequences, nor would it risk confidential information becoming public.[26]

---

20 UNCITRAL Report of 54th Session, 25 February 2011, UN Doc A/CN.9/717, para. 63.

21 UNCITRAL Report of 53rd Session, 20 October 2010, UN Doc A/CN.9/712, para. 34. *See also* UNCITRAL Working Paper for 55th Session, 29 July 2011, UN Doc A/CN.9/WG.II/WP.166, para. 25; UNCITRAL Report of 54th Session, 25 February 2011, UN Doc A/CN.9/717, para. 62 (noting that, where the Transparency Rules applied to ad hoc UNCITRAL arbitrations, option 1 would leave the disputing parties with neither a tribunal nor an institution to handle any issues that might arise as a result of an early publication obligation').

22 UNCITRAL Report of 56th Session, 16 February 2012, UN Doc A/CN.9/741, para. 109. *See* UNCITRAL Report of 53rd Session, 20 October 2010, UN Doc A/CN.9/712, para. 33; Nedden & Rosenfeld, *supra* fn 6, at 44; UNCITRAL Report of 54th Session, 25 February 2011, UN Doc A/CN.9/717, para. 66.

23 Johnson & Bernasconi-Osterwalder, *supra* fn 1, at 14; *see also* Nathalie Bernasconi-Osterwalder & Lise Johnson, *Bulletin #2: Transparency in the dispute settlement process: Country best practices*, 4 International Institute for Sustainable Development (2011), <www.iisd.org>.

24 Nedden & Rosenfeld, *supra* fn 6, at 43; UNCITRAL Report of 53rd Session, 20 October 2010, UN Doc A/CN.9/712, para. 33.

25 Article 3(2) of the 2010 Arbitration Rules provides that '[a]rbitral proceedings shall be deemed to commence on the date on which the notice of arbitration is received by the respondent'.

26 *Ibid.*

C. No sanctions to address non-compliance

9. The disclosure obligations in articles 2 and 3 are mandatory. This raised questions as to how to address non-compliance.[27] The disputing parties, for example, could agree to refrain from disclosing the basic information required by article 2, despite their obligations under the Transparency Rules.[28] The predominant view in the Working Group, however, was that the nature of the Transparency Rules made it difficult to include sanctions.[29] In accordance with this view, non-compliance was not extensively discussed and is not a matter addressed in the final version of the Transparency Rules. It is a matter that a tribunal may have regard to in its decision on costs under article 42(1), as part of the parties' procedural conduct.

D. Disclosure does not require subjective judgement by the repository

10. The basic facts disclosed pursuant to article 2 of the Transparency Rules should not require any exercise of subjective judgement or discretion by the repository.[30] Publication of the names of the parties and the field of economic activity involved in the dispute was considered relatively uncontroversial, and in line with current ICSID practice (which was referenced during the negotiations and which was said to be familiar to many States).[31] It was agreed that information such as the nationalities of the parties and a description of the claim should not be published at the initiation of proceedings, since this information may prove contentious.[32] One may see for example how an investor's contested or unproved nationality, if communicated as asserted by the investor, could create unnecessary difficulties.

11. The Transparency Registry has also published guidelines on the submission of documents. These include templates for the disputing parties to submit, for example, the notice of arbitration, to the Transparency Registry.[33] Section A of these guidelines provides as follows:

> (1) Under article 2 of the Transparency Rules, both the claimant and the respondent shall promptly communicate a copy of the notice of arbitration to the Registry, or the claimant shall send the notice and a record of its transmission to the respondent. The notice of arbitration shall be accompanied with information on the name of the disputing parties, the economic sector

---

27 UNCITRAL Report of 55th Session, 17 October 2011, UN Doc A/CN.9/736, para. 45; UNCITRAL Report of 54th Session, 25 February 2011, UN Doc A/CN.9/717, para. 73.

28 UNCITRAL Report of 53rd Session, 20 October 2010, UN Doc A/CN.9/712, para. 36.

29 UNCITRAL Report of 55th Session, 17 October 2011, UN Doc A/CN.9/736, para. 45.

30 Johnson & Bernasconi-Osterwalder, *supra* fn 1, at 13.

31 UNCITRAL Report of 53rd Session, 20 October 2010, UN Doc A/CN.9/712, para. 33; UNCITRAL Report of 55th Session, 17 October 2011, UN Doc A/CN.9/736, para. 43; UNCITRAL Working Paper for 55th Session, 8 August 2011, UN Doc A/CN.9/WG.II/WP.167, paras 5-7; UNCITRAL Report of 54th Session, 25 February 2011, UN Doc A/CN.9/717, paras 66 and 68. *See also* UNCITRAL Working Paper for 54th Session, 9 December 2010, UN Doc A/CN.9/WG.II/WP.162/Add.1, para. 2.

32 UNCITRAL Report of 55th Session, 17 October 2011, UN Doc A/CN.9/736, para. 43.

33 Available at <www.uncitral.org/transparency-registry/en/guidelines.html>.

of the dispute and the treaty under which the claim arises, as specified in the template for disputing parties.

(2) If either disputing party challenges the application of the Transparency Rules, that party shall advise the Registry immediately.

(3) Once the arbitral tribunal is constituted, it shall be exclusively responsible for the submission of documents to the Registry. Submissions by others will not be accepted.

E. Potential exceptions to article 2

12. Unlike article 3 of the Transparency Rules, article 2 does not contain a reference to article 7 (exceptions to transparency). Indeed, it will only be in highly exceptional cases (e.g. a classified contract) that the basic information to be published pursuant to article 2 (i.e., the names of the parties, their economic sector of activity, and the relevant treaty) could qualify as 'confidential or protected information' for the purposes of article 7(2), or fall within the other exceptions listed.[34] Nevertheless, a question arises as to how such an issue might be dealt with and by whom, given that the tribunal will not have been constituted by this stage. Certainly the parties may make representations to the repository on the issue, but the information-dissemination duties of the repository are stated in unqualified terms in article 2. One author posits that article 7 of the Transparency Rules cannot be applied to article 2, and that the basic information required under article 2 should therefore be promptly published, without screening by the repository; and that the (unlikely) prejudice caused by any confidential or protected information contained therein simply cannot not be prevented.[35]

13. Yet article 7 of the Transparency Rules does contain references to article 2.[36] The drafting history of article 2 shows that the Working Group once considered providing for the notice of arbitration to be published at the outset of the proceedings,[37] which may explain why these references were included in article 7.[38] Lest one conclude this was by oversight – which cannot be presumed – article 7 does on its face apply and may need to apply, albeit in highly exceptional cases. Nevertheless, article 2 appears to afford no room for the repository not to disseminate all the information 'promptly'. In what must be (again) highly exceptional cases, it is perhaps possible for the repository to take the view that guidance from the tribunal is required once an article 7 issue is raised, and that given high risks some delay is warranted, 'promptly' meaning 'as promptly as possible in the circumstances'.

---

34 *See* discussion of article 7 of the Transparency Rules, *infra*.

35 *See* Bianco, *supra* fn 3, at 77, citing UNCITRAL Report of 57th Session, 12 October 2012, UN Doc A/CN.9/760, para. 50.

36 *See* articles 7(1) and 7(6).

37 UNCITRAL Working Paper for 55th Session, 29 July 2011, UN Doc A/CN.9/WG.II/WP.166, para. 24.

38 For discussion on this point, *see* Bianco, *supra* fn 3, at 78.

Article 3
Publication of documents

Article 3

1. Subject to article 7, the following documents shall be made available to the public: the notice of arbitration, the response to the notice of arbitration, the statement of claim, the statement of defence and any further written statements or written submissions by any disputing party; a table listing all exhibits to the aforesaid documents and to expert reports and witness statements, if such table has been prepared for the proceedings, but not the exhibits themselves; any written submissions by the non-disputing Party (or Parties) to the treaty and by third persons, transcripts of hearings, where available; and orders, decisions and awards of the arbitral tribunal.

2. Subject to article 7, expert reports and witness statements, exclusive of the exhibits thereto, shall be made available to the public, upon request by any person to the arbitral tribunal.

3. Subject to article 7, the arbitral tribunal may decide, on its own initiative or upon request from any person, and after consultation with the disputing parties, whether and how to make available exhibits and any other documents provided to, or issued by, the arbitral tribunal not falling within paragraphs 1 or 2 above. This may include, for example, making such documents available at a specified site.

4. The documents to be made available to the public pursuant to paragraphs 1 and 2 shall be communicated by the arbitral tribunal to the repository referred to under article 8 as soon as possible, subject to any relevant arrangements or time limits for the protection of confidential or protected information prescribed under article 7. The documents to be made available pursuant to paragraph 3 may be communicated by the arbitral tribunal to the repository referred to under article 8 as they become available and, if applicable, in a redacted form in accordance with article 7. The repository shall make all documents available in a timely manner, in the form and in the language in which it receives them.

5. A person granted access to documents under paragraph 3 shall bear any administrative costs of making those documents available to that person, such as the costs of photocopying or shipping documents to that person, but not the costs of making those documents available to the public through the repository.

1. Article 3 provides for the disclosure of documents submitted to or issued by the tribunal, subject to the exceptions listed in article 7. The precise scope of the article 3 disclosure obligations depends on the type of document, which will fall into one of three categories:[1]

   (i) specific documents that are mandatorily and automatically disclosed, identified in the closed list contained in article 3(1),[2] including, notably, arbitral awards;[3]
   (ii) documents that are mandatorily disclosed upon request to the tribunal by a third person, e.g. expert reports and witness statements, as provided by article 3(2); or
   (iii) documents that may be made available to the public by decision of the tribunal under article 3(3).[4] In exercising its judgement, the tribunal will be guided by article 1(4) of the Transparency Rules, which requires balancing the public interest in transparency with the disputing parties' interest in fair and efficient proceedings.[5]

---

1 Lise Johnson & Nathalie Bernasconi-Osterwalder, *New UNCITRAL Arbitration Rules on Transparency: Application, Content and Next Steps*, 15 (CIEL, IISD, CCSI, August 2013), <http://ccsi.columbia.edu>. *See also* Jan H. Nedden & Friedrich Rosenfeld, 'The new UNCITRAL Transparency Rules: How the trend towards transparency differs in investment and commercial arbitration' in Christoph Muller & Antonio Rigozzi (eds), *New Developments in International Commercial Arbitration 2013*, 41, 44-45 (2013); UNCITRAL Working Paper for 58th Session, 30 November 2012, UN Doc A/CN.9/WG.II/WP.176, paras 25-26.

2 *See* UNCITRAL Report of 54th Session, 25 February 2011, UN Doc A/CN.9/717, para. 84.

3 *See* UNCITRAL Report of 53rd Session, 20 October 2010, UN Doc A/CN.9/712, para. 62 (noting that '[m]any delegations expressed support for the establishment of a general provision under which awards rendered by arbitral tribunals in treaty-based investor-state arbitration should be published'). *See also* Nedden & Rosenfeld, *supra* fn 1, at 44-45 (noting that publication of awards not only contributes to the public interest in transparency, but also aims to develop a body of case law in treaty-based investor-State arbitration intended to increase predictability and reduce transaction costs). *See also* UNCITRAL Working Paper for 54th Session, 9 December 2010, UN Doc A/CN.9/WG.II/WP.162/Add.1, para. 16; UNCITRAL Report of 54th Session, 25 February 2011, UN Doc A/CN.9/717, para. 93.

4 UNCITRAL Working Paper for 58th Session, 30 November 2012, UN Doc A/CN.9/WG.II/WP.176, para. 26; UNCITRAL Working Paper for 56th Session, 13 December 2011, UN Doc A/CN.9/WG.II/WP.169, para. 30; Johnson & Bernasconi-Osterwalder, *supra* fn 1, at 16. *See also* UNCITRAL Report of 55th Session, 17 October 2011, UN Doc A/CN.9/736, paras 58 and 65 (noting that this formulation 'was seen as establishing a good balance between the documents to be published and the exercise by the arbitral tribunal of its discretion in managing the process').

5 *See* article 1(4) of the Transparency Rules; Johnson & Bernasconi-Osterwalder, *supra* fn 1, at 16.

The rationale is that certain categories of documents – such as exhibits, expert reports and witness statements – do not lend themselves to automatic publication, such that either upon-request or discretionary publication (as provided for in articles 3(2) and 3(3)) is more appropriate.[6]

2. Transcripts are treated separately from hearings, which are addressed in article 6 of the Transparency Rules. Thus, even where a hearing is closed to the public, any non-confidential portions of the transcripts (if available) will be mandatorily and automatically disclosed in accordance with article 3(1).[7]

3. Article 3(4) addresses the timing of documentary disclosure, in non-mechanical terms such as 'as soon as possible', 'as [the documents] become available' and 'in a timely manner'. Nevertheless, this provision provides for disclosure of relevant documents during the course of proceedings, thereby clearly rejecting the view expressed during the Working Group's negotiations that publication should only occur after the proceedings so as not to endanger their integrity.[8]

A. Overarching aims

4. Article 3 seeks to strike a balance between, on the one hand, the public interest in transparency and, on the other hand, 'the legitimate need to ensure manageability and efficiency of the arbitral procedure'.[9] The structure of article 3, and most notably the exclusion of exhibits, expert reports and witness statements from mandatory and automatic disclosure, reflects the importance that the Working Group placed on keeping proceedings manageable and 'preserving the disputing parties' right of effective access to justice'.[10] This emphasis is largely a product of practical considerations, and is not intended to limit disclosure but rather to avoid the 'cumbersome', time-consuming and costly exercise of automatically producing entire evidential records.[11]

---

6 *See* UNCITRAL Report of 57th Session, 12 October 2012, UN Doc A/CN.9/760, para. 27; Christopher Kee, 'Article 3. Publication of documents' in Dimitrij Euler, Markus Gehring & Maxi Scherer (eds), *Transparency in International Investment Arbitration: A Guide to the UNCITRAL Rules on Transparency in Treaty-Based Investor-State Arbitration*, 114 (Cambridge University Press 2015). *See also* Johnson & Bernasconi-Osterwalder, *supra* fn 1, at 16 (noting that '[m]any delegations felt that mandatory disclosure of all exhibits could be unduly burdensome, and that the burdens of such disclosure may not … be outweighed by the public interest in such information'); UNCITRAL Report of 55th Session, 17 October 2011, UN Doc A/CN.9/736, para. 60.

7 UNCITRAL Working Paper for 56th Session, 13 December 2011, UN Doc A/CN.9/WG.II/WP.169, para. 31; Johnson & Bernasconi-Osterwalder, *supra* fn 1, at 15.

8 UNCITRAL Report of 54th Session, 25 February 2011, UN Doc A/CN.9/717, para. 78.

9 UNCITRAL Report of 53rd Session, 20 October 2010, UN Doc A/CN.9/712, para. 42.

10 UNCITRAL Working Paper for 55th Session, 29 July 2011, UN Doc A/CN.9/WG.II/WP.166, para. 39; UNCITRAL Report of 54th Session, 25 February 2011, UN Doc A/CN.9/717, paras 75 and 145.

11 *See* UNCITRAL Report of 54th Session, 25 February 2011, UN Doc A/CN.9/717, para. 82.

B. Disclosure of exhibits by decision of the tribunal

5. There was considerable debate as to whether exhibits should be mandatorily and automatically disclosed under article 3(1).[12] Many delegations argued that this would be unduly burdensome for the disputing parties (given the voluminous nature of exhibits and the likely need for redaction) and that this would not be outweighed by the public interest in transparency.[13] Ultimately, this view prevailed; exhibits were removed from the ambit of article 3(1), but remain subject to disclosure under article 3(3) by decision of the tribunal.[14]

6. Nevertheless, article 3(1) of the Transparency Rules does provide for disclosure of a table of exhibits, despite opposition from a number of delegations that preparation of such a table would itself be burdensome, particularly for developing States or for those with limited resources.[15] The final text of this provision reflects a sensible compromise: a table of exhibits must be produced only where such a table 'has been prepared for the proceedings', i.e., where it already exists,[16] as it invariably does in practice. Though a disputing party not wishing to disclose such information could simply try to ensure that a table of this nature is never created during the proceedings, such behaviour is mitigated by the tribunal's discretionary powers contained in article 3(3). At any rate, procedural directions issued in the ordinary course commonly require such tables to be included with each evidential submission.

7. The tribunal must consult the parties with respect to exhibits or documents which it considers should be made available pursuant to article 3(3). Although the subject was not explicitly addressed during the Working Group's deliberations, article 3(3) could not have been intended to include draft awards or other 'deliberation documents'. These do not constitute 'documents provided to, or issued by, the arbitral tribunal', and the confidentiality of deliberations is essential to the integrity of the arbitral process.[17]

8. A tribunal's discretion under article 3(3) may be affected by freedom of information laws, which are becoming an increasingly relevant feature in confidentiality orders by tribunals.[18] Indeed, depending on the status and

---

[12] *See* UNCITRAL Report of 55th Session, 17 October 2011, UN Doc A/CN.9/736, para. 60.

[13] UNCITRAL Report of 57th Session, 12 October 2012, UN Doc A/CN.9/760, para. 15; Johnson & Bernasconi-Osterwalder, *supra* fn 1, at 15-16.

[14] Johnson & Bernasconi-Osterwalder, *supra* fn 1, at 15-16.

[15] UNCITRAL Report of 57th Session, 12 October 2012, UN Doc A/CN.9/760, para. 15.

[16] *Ibid.*, at para. 16; UNCITRAL Working Paper for 58th Session, 30 November 2012, UN Doc A/CN.9/WG.II/WP.176, para. 27.

[17] *See* Kee, *supra* fn 6, at 119; and the analysis of article 33 of the Arbitration Rules, *supra*.

[18] *See*, e.g., *Merrill & Ring Forestry L P v. Government of Canada* (ICSID Case No. UNCT/07/1) Investor's Submission on Confidentiality, 9 November 2007, < www.italaw.com >, para. 1 ('The disputing parties have been unable to agree upon the terms of a Confidentiality Order governing this arbitration. Canada has insisted that any Confidentiality Order governing the arbitration contain a provision permitting Canada to disclose information protected by the Order to applicants under Canada's *Access to Information Act* ('ATIA'). Counsel for Merrill & Ring has objected that making an Order subject to the express provisions of Canada's

applicability[19] of such laws (whether taking effect through treaties[20] or as mandatory provisions of the national arbitration law), they could, in theory, prevail over article 3(3).[21]

C. Mandatory disclosure upon request

9. Two views shaped the disclosure regime pertaining to expert reports and witness statements. On the one hand, these documents form a critical part of the evidential record and are key to understanding the documentary evidence, the issues, arguments and outcomes of a dispute; as such, they should be disclosed in order to fully promote the goal of enhancing transparency in investor-state arbitration.[22] On the other hand, there is an argument that the public 'should not be put on the same footing as the parties', and that reasonably detailed information regarding the subject of the dispute will suffice.[23] Moreover, and equally importantly, publicising expert reports and witness statements may lead to witness or expert intimidation and threaten the intellectual property protection of experts' work.[24]

10. The balance struck between these considerations led to the exemption of expert reports and witness statements from mandatory and automatic disclosure under article 3(1), but nevertheless permitted their release upon request by a third

---

ATIA effectively ensures Canada has no obligations of confidentiality while imposing strict obligations of confidentiality on Merrill & Ring. Such inequality of treatment is inconsistent with the NAFTA and could never guarantee the equality of the parties enshrined by Article 15 of the UNCITRAL Arbitration Rules'). The tribunal in this case ultimately rejected the investor's argument: *see ibid.*, Confidentiality Order, 21 January 2008, para. 15. For a more in depth discussion of this issue, *see* Kee, *supra* fn 6, at 96-99.

19 There is, of course, a question as to whether the freedom of information legislation in question constitutes a mandatory 'provision of the law applicable to the arbitration from which the disputing parties cannot derogate' pursuant to article 1(8) of the Transparency Rules. For discussion on this issue and legal and policy arguments, *see* Kee, *supra* fn 6, at 97-99 (noting that '[i]t would seem likely that the provisions of an FOI regime will almost always prevail over Article 3 of the Rules, based on the plain wording of the Rules themselves. However, a reasoned policy argument could be made that this should not necessarily be the case, and, as such, a determination would be needed on a case-by-case basis').

20 *Ibid.*, at 97-98 (referring to article 38(8) of the Canadian Model Foreign Investment Promotion and Protection Agreement, which provides that: 'To the extent that a Tribunal's confidentiality order designates information as confidential and a Party's law on access to information requires public access to that information, the Party's law on access to information shall prevail. However, a Party should endeavour to apply its law on access to information so as to protect information designated confidential by the Tribunal').

21 *Ibid.*, at 98 (noting that 'it is very unlikely that the FOI regime would not be considered a mandatory aspect of the *lex arbitri* and on that basis, pursuant to Article 1 paragraph 8 of the Rules, the FOI regime would also prevail').

22 UNCITRAL Report of 57th Session, 12 October 2012, UN Doc A/CN.9/760, para. 17; Johnson & Bernasconi-Osterwalder, *supra* fn 1, at 15.

23 UNCITRAL Report of 57th Session, 12 October 2012, UN Doc A/CN.9/760, para. 18.

24 *See* Johnson & Bernasconi-Osterwalder, *supra* fn 1, at 15.

party (exclusive of any attached exhibits) subject to the exceptions in article 7 of the Transparency Rules.[25] The article 7(2)(a)-(c) categories of 'confidential or protected information' in particular are likely to find application regularly.

D. Disclosure is not limited to specific recipients

11. Where article 3 provides for disclosure upon request or at the discretion of the tribunal, i.e. in articles 3(2) and 3(3), the Working Group deliberately rejected confining such disclosure to specific categories of recipients. In so doing, it emphasized that (i) there was 'no practical mechanism' to limit further disclosure once a document had been disclosed to a third party, and (ii) such limitations were potentially discriminatory and contrary to the goal of transparency.[26] Thus, once a request is made under article 3(2) or 3(3), the repository will make documents publicly available as opposed to selectively disclosing them to the requesting third party.[27]

E. Disclosure obligations after the tribunal has ceased to exist

12. Disclosure other than that which is mandatory and automatic under article 3(1) requires the involvement of the tribunal, either in response to a third-party request under article 3(2) or in the exercise of its discretionary power under article 3(3). As such, there is no formal mechanism by which a third party may request disclosure of documents once the tribunal has become *functus officio* after termination of the proceedings by final award, order of termination, and post-award remedies (articles 30(1)(a), 34(2) and 36-39). Thus it has been suggested that 'disputing parties ... be encouraged to work out an arrangement' for the post-dispute disclosure of documents.[28]

F. Exceptions to the general rule on costs of transparency

13. The general position taken by UNCITRAL is that the public should not bear the costs associated with the disclosure of information in the interest of

---

25 UNCITRAL Report of 57th Session, 12 October 2012, UN Doc A/CN.9/760, paras 20-21. Several delegations objected to this mandatory and automatic disclosure upon request and 'in particular, queried how this would reduce the burden on an arbitral tribunal'. *See also* Johnson & Bernasconi-Osterwalder, *supra* fn 1, at 15.

26 UNCITRAL Report of 57th Session, 12 October 2012, UN Doc A/CN.9/760, paras 25-26 (where the Working Group further noted that, 'where a person had requested a document or information under article 3, and the tribunal had in the exercise of its discretion granted access to that document or information, it was difficult to anticipate a basis on which the tribunal would subsequently refuse access to another person requesting the same material').

27 Johnson & Bernasconi-Osterwalder, *supra* fn 1, at 15.

28 *See* UNCITRAL Report of 58th Session, 13 February 2013, UN Doc A/CN.9/765, para. 91. *See also* Kee, supra fn 6, at 124; Johnson & Bernasconi-Osterwalder, *supra* fn 1, at 16 (noting UNCITRAL's indication that the availability of documents after the conclusion of the dispute was an issue which 'could and should be addressed through development of relevant guidelines or procedures of the specific arbitration').

transparency.[29] Article 3(5) provides an exception, requiring a third party that has been granted access to documents pursuant to a decision by the tribunal under article 3(3) to bear the administrative costs of such access. The term 'administrative costs' in article 3(5) is limited to the specific logistical and material costs of making the documents available to the requesting third party, and does not include, for example, the fees and expenses of the tribunal and the parties, and the cost of reviewing and redacting the relevant documents, which is borne by the disputing parties.[30]

[29] Johnson & Bernasconi-Osterwalder, *supra* fn 1, at 16.

[30] *Ibid*. *See also* Kee, *supra* fn 6, at 123; UNCITRAL Report of 57th Session, 12 October 2012, UN Doc A/CN.9/760, paras 126-130.

Article 4
Submission by a third person

Article 4

1. After consultation with the disputing parties, the arbitral tribunal may allow a person that is not a disputing party, and not a non-disputing Party to the treaty ('third person(s)'), to file a written submission with the arbitral tribunal regarding a matter within the scope of the dispute.

2. A third person wishing to make a submission shall apply to the arbitral tribunal, and shall, in a concise written statement, which is in a language of the arbitration and complies with any page limits set by the arbitral tribunal:

(a) Describe the third person, including, where relevant, its membership and legal status (e.g., trade association or other non-governmental organization), its general objectives, the nature of its activities and any parent organization (including any organization that directly or indirectly controls the third person);

(b) Disclose any connection, direct or indirect, which the third person has with any disputing party;

(c) Provide information on any government, person or organization that has provided to the third person (i) any financial or other assistance in preparing the submission; or (ii) substantial assistance in either of the two years preceding the application by the third person under this article (e.g. funding around 20 per cent of its overall operations annually);

(d) Describe the nature of the interest that the third person has in the arbitration; and

(e) Identify the specific issues of fact or law in the arbitration that the third person wishes to address in its written submission.

3. In determining whether to allow such a submission, the arbitral tribunal shall take into consideration, among other factors it determines to be relevant:

(a) Whether the third person has a significant interest in the arbitral proceedings; and

(b) The extent to which the submission would assist the arbitral tribunal in the determination of a factual or legal issue related to the arbitral proceedings by bringing a perspective, particular knowledge or insight that is different from that of the disputing parties.

4. The submission filed by the third person shall:

(a) Be dated and signed by the person filing the submission on behalf of the third person;

(b) Be concise, and in no case longer than as authorized by the arbitral tribunal;

(c) Set out a precise statement of the third person's position on issues; and

(d) Address only matters within the scope of the dispute.

5. The arbitral tribunal shall ensure that any submission does not disrupt or unduly burden the arbitral proceedings, or unfairly prejudice any disputing party.

6. The arbitral tribunal shall ensure that the disputing parties are given a reasonable opportunity to present their observations on any submission by the third person.

A. Overview

1. The Working Group expressed widespread support for allowing submissions by third persons, which were regarded (within a number of parameters) as useful to the tribunal as well as promoting the 'legitimacy of the arbitral process'.[1] Thus, article 4(1) of the Transparency Rules explicitly affirms the tribunal's authority to allow written submissions by third persons (amici curiae)[2] falling within the

[1] UNCITRAL Report of 53rd Session, 20 October 2010, UN Doc A/CN.9/712, para. 46. *See also* Mariel Dimsey, 'Article 4. Submission by a third person' in Dimitrij Euler, Markus Gehring & Maxi Scherer (eds), *Transparency in International Investment Arbitration: A Guide to the UNCITRAL Rules on Transparency in Treaty-Based Investor-State Arbitration*, 132-133 (Cambridge University Press 2015) (stating that '[t]he purpose of allowing third persons to participate in arbitral proceedings is that the tribunal and the parties should benefit from the special knowledge of the third person and its perspective on the issues', and citing to *Suez, Sociedad General de Aguas de Barcelona SA and Vivendi Universal SA v. Argentine Republic* (ICSID Case No. ARB/03/19) Order in Response to a Petition for Participation as Amicus Curiae, 19 May 2005, <www.italaw.com>. *See* generally Sophie Lamb, Daniel Harrison & Jonathan Hew, *Recent Developments in the Law and Practice of Amicus Briefs in Investor-State Arbitration*, V(2) Indian Journal of Arbitration Law 72-92 (2016).

[2] *See* UNCITRAL Report of 55th Session, 17 October 2011, UN Doc A/CN.9/736, para. 71 (where the Working Group considered using the term 'amicus curiae' but concluded that, in the interest of creating 'rules that would be understood in the same manner in all legal systems', use of this specific term should be avoided). *See* Jan H. Nedden & Friedrich Rosenfeld, 'The new UNCITRAL Transparency Rules: How the trend towards transparency

scope of the dispute.[3] Largely codifying emergent practice, it provides detailed procedures regarding: (i) the information to be provided by the third person (article 4(2)); (ii) the matters to be considered by the tribunal (articles 4(3), 4(5) and 4(6)); and (iii) the submission itself (article 4(4)).[4] The authorization of a third-person submission under article 4(1) presupposes the information referred to in article 4(2) and that the submission meets the requirements set out in article 4(4).[5]

2. Article 4(2) provides that a third person wishing to participate in the proceedings must apply to the tribunal.[6] It is rightly pointed out that the wording of this provision does not exclude the possibility that the tribunal may invite third persons to participate.[7] On the face of article 4(1), the tribunal's role is limited to 'allow[ing]' an application made by a prospective amicus pursuant to article 4(2). When the Transparency Rules envisage a tribunal initiative, they use the verb 'to invite'; see article 5(1) and cf. article 5(2). In any event, the prospect that a tribunal will invite an amicus to come forth or (perhaps more realistically) the parties to invite the amicus is very low. It is difficult to say that such a step will tend to show bias or prejudgement and is *a priori* impermissible. There may be rare cases where some expertise or perspective is felt by the tribunal to be absent and the parties are unable to supply it (e.g. because they lack the resources). But more often than not an amicus will have a certain perspective and also its contribution may be material to the outcome of the case. It will take very careful handling and very rare circumstances for a tribunal to be proactive in inviting an amicus request, risking a charge of unfair treatment of the parties.

---

differs in investment and commercial arbitration' in Christoph Muller & Antonio Rigozzi (eds), *New Developments in International Commercial Arbitration 2013*, 41, 46 (2013).

3 *See* Lise Johnson & Nathalie Bernasconi-Osterwalder, *New UNCITRAL Arbitration Rules on Transparency: Application, Content and Next Steps*, 17-18, (CIEL, IISD, CCSI, August 2013), <http://ccsi.columbia.edu> (noting that this is in line with the previous practice of arbitral tribunals); UNCITRAL Working Paper for 53rd Session, 5 August 2010, UN Doc A/CN.9/WG.II/WP.160/Add.1, para. 21. Note that, despite earlier suggestions, there is no indication that the tribunal is required by the Transparency Rules to provide grounds for refusal of a third-person submission. *See also* Nedden & Rosenfeld, *supra* fn 2, at 46.

4 *See* UNCITRAL Working Paper for 55th Session, 29 July 2011, UN Doc A/CN.9/WG.II/WP.166, para. 48; UNCITRAL Working Paper for 58th Session, 30 November 2012, UN Doc A/CN.9/WG.II/WP.176, para. 37; UNCITRAL Report of 55th Session, 17 October 2011, UN Doc A/CN.9/736, para. 70. *See also* UNCITRAL Report of 54th Session, 25 February 2011, UN Doc A/CN.9/717, paras 121-122 (the final formulation of article 4 of the Transparency Rules draws its inspiration from Rule 37(2) of the ICSID Arbitration Rules, as complemented by elements addressed in section B of the NAFTA Free Trade Commission's 'Statement of the Free Trade Commission on non-disputing party participation', 7 October 2003 (the 'NAFTA FTC Statement')).

5 *See* Nedden & Rosenfeld, *supra* fn 2, at 46.

6 This is also the case for Rule 37(2) of the ICSID Arbitration Rules and the procedure established in section B(1) of the NAFTA FTC Statement. *See also* Dimsey, *supra* fn 1, at 165.

7 Dimsey, *supra* fn 1, at 165.

3. Article 4(2) also outlines self-reporting disclosure obligations for any third person wishing to make a submission.[8] Although the Transparency Rules do not specifically address the consequences of a third person's failure to comply with the disclosure requirements of article 4(2), these are likely to depend on the nature of the case and the submission in question.[9] If relevant information is missing or, worse, withheld, the natural course of action is for the amicus request to be dismissed.

4. Article 4(3) provides 'a non-exhaustive list of factors' to be considered by the tribunal in determining whether or not to allow a third-person submission.[10] Nevertheless, the main ones are included, and they are well-recognized in practice. These include whether the third person has a 'significant interest'[11] in the arbitral proceedings (article 4(3)(a)) and the extent to which the submission would assist the arbitral tribunal in making a factual or legal determination 'by bringing a perspective, particular knowledge or insight that is different from that of the disputing parties' (article 4(3)(b)).[12] The requirement, as experience shows, which is likely to raise delicate issues is that of an interest in the proceedings – i.e. one

---

8 *See* UNCITRAL Report of 57th Session, 12 October 2012, UN Doc A/CN.9/760, paras 43-51. Note that these reporting requirements largely correspond to those set out in section B(2) of the NAFTA FTC Statement. For a more detailed discussion of each requirement, *see* Dimsey, *supra* fn 1, at 167-177.

9 *See* Dimsey, *supra* fn 1, at 177-178. *See also Apotex Holdings Inc and Apotex Inc v. United States of America* (ICSID Case No. ARB(AF)/12/1) ('*Apotex v. USA*') Procedural Order on the Participation of Applicant Mr. Barry Appleton as a Non-Disputing Party, 4 March 2013, <www.italaw.com>, para. 45 (where, in applying the disclosure requirements of section B(2) of the NAFTA FTC Statement, the tribunal found the applicant's non-disclosure of an indirect relationship with one of the claimant companies to be 'inconsequential').

10 Johnson & Bernasconi-Osterwalder, *supra* fn 3, at 18. On the factors to be considered by the tribunal in determining whether to allow the submission, cf. Article 3(3) in Appendix III of the SCC Rules; Rule 29.3 of the SIAC Investment Arbitration Rules.

11 As noted by Dimsey, *supra* fn 1, at 179, 'whether a third person has a significant interest in the arbitral proceedings can be a double-edged sword. On the one hand, the arbitral tribunal will only wish to allow those third persons access to the proceedings that have a genuine interest in contributing to the solution of the dispute ... On the other hand, the arbitral tribunal will not wish for third persons to participate who are "interested" in the dispute, i.e. who have an incentive or are otherwise motivated to influence the outcome through financial assistance or a close connection to one of the parties'. *See ibid.*, at 180 et seq. for awards applying the similar provisions of the ICSID Arbitration Rules and the provisions of the NAFTA FTC Statement.

12 Previously, petitioners have pointed out the difficulty of providing 'particular knowledge ... that is different from that of the disputing parties' without the benefit of access to the disputing parties' pleadings: *see*, in the context of Article 41(3) of the ICSID Additional Facility Rules, *Piero Foresti, Laura de Carli & Others v. The Republic of South Africa* (ICSID Case No. ARB(AF)/07/01) Petition for Limited Participation as non-Disputing Parties, 17 July 2009, <www.italaw.com>, paras 6.16-6.22 (noting that, '[w]ithout such access, the Petitioners are compelled to make any submissions on the basis of assumptions and speculation'). In this case, the tribunal took the view that the non-disputing parties must be allowed access to those pleadings which were necessary for them to focus their submissions.

that is significant and appropriate. There is considerable literature and practice in a number of jurisdictions on this matter, but it is not necessarily the case that domestic procedural practices should be transported into investment-treaty cases without more. Lest this requirement be read down and lead to all and sundry putative amici being admitted, proper meaning has to be given to it. It must be recognized that a prospective amicus will more often than not have a perspective (e.g. because of its statutory mission) that will tend to favour, in the result, one party's case or the other's. That is not per se an impermissible interest. What is impermissible is for an amicus to be just one more advocate because it has an interest in the outcome that is in substance indistinguishable from that of a party. That is why the special 'perspective, knowledge or insight' requirement operates very closely together with the 'interest' requirement: an amicus must be able to contribute something new and different from the parties. The wording 'among other factors' permits the tribunal to exercise its discretion to consider other relevant criteria.[13] One such can be whether one prospective amicus is 'balanced out' by another with a competing perspective. Further, article 4(3)(b) encompasses both factual and legal issues, as it was acknowledged that third persons 'frequently provide important factual information', the exclusion of which 'would do a disservice to the tribunal'.[14]

5. Article 4(4) lists the form and content requirements for third-person submissions. As for article 4(3), it is not intended to contain an exhaustive list of criteria.[15] Contrary to the NAFTA FTC Statement on which this provision is partly based,[16] article 4(4)(b) does not set a specific page-limit for third-person submissions, leaving this matter to the discretion of the tribunal.[17]

6. Article 4(5) allows the tribunal to balance transparency with the manageability of the arbitral process.[18] The tribunal must ensure that a third-person submission

---

13 UNCITRAL Report of 55th Session, 17 October 2011, UN Doc A/CN.9/736, para. 76.

14 UNCITRAL Report of 57th Session, 12 October 2012, UN Doc A/CN.9/760, para. 52. Cf. *Apotex v. USA*, *supra* fn 9, paras 30-34 (where the tribunal considered that the applicant's knowledge and expertise of investment treaty obligations would not surpass that of the disputing parties' counsel to the arbitration, and, as such, found it 'most unlikely' that the applicant would provide the tribunal with a particular perspective or insight different to that of the disputing parties). *See also* Dimsey, *supra* fn 1, at 183-185.

15 *See* Johnson & Bernasconi-Osterwalder, *supra* fn 3, at 18 (noting that '[t]ribunals may also impose separate conditions on the form and content of the submissions').

16 *See* UNCITRAL Report of 54th Session, 25 February 2011, UN Doc A/CN.9/717, paras 119-121. As noted *infra*, the Working Group also drew inspiration from Rule 37(2) of the ICSID Arbitration Rules.

17 *See* UNCITRAL Report of 55th Session, 17 October 2011, UN Doc A/CN.9/736, para. 75 (acknowledging that 'setting a specific page limit might not be appropriate for each case'). Cf. section B(3)(b) of the NAFTA FTC Statement, which provides that: 'The submission filed by a non-disputing party will: ... (b) be concise, and in no case longer than 20 typed pages, including any appendices'.

18 UNCITRAL Working Paper for 54th Session, 9 December 2010, UN Doc A/CN.9/WG.II/WP.162/Add.1, para. 24.

'does not disrupt or unduly burden the arbitral proceedings'[19] or 'unfairly prejudice any disputing party'.[20] The disruption and burden considerations are self-evident: additional submissions will require more work and resources by all participants, and almost invariably lead to changes in the procedural timetable. And as commentators point out, this provision therefore implicitly recognizes that third-person submissions may negatively affect one or both of the disputing parties' positions. Thus the additional burden or prejudice imposed is acceptable insofar as it is not 'undue' or 'unfair'.[21]

7. Finally, article 4(6) provides the disputing parties with an opportunity to present their observations on the third-person submission.[22] The mandatory wording of this provision affords the tribunal no discretion beyond ensuring that the opportunity for such observations is 'reasonable' (though not 'full'), which reflects the importance of safeguarding the disputing parties' due-process rights.

8. Article 4 of the Transparency Rules draws heavily on the provisions for third-party participation contained in Rule 37(2) of the ICSID Arbitration Rules and the NAFTA FTC Statement.[23] Nevertheless, there are some subtle differences: for example, article 4(5) of the Transparency Rules requires the tribunal to ensure that submissions do not, inter alia, unduly burden the proceedings as a whole, whereas pursuant to the ICSID Arbitration Rules and the NAFTA FTC Statement, it is the disputing parties that must not be unduly burdened by such submissions.[24]

B. Third-person submissions require authorization by the tribunal

9. Article 4 of the Transparency Rules makes it clear that third persons do not have an automatic right to have their submissions accepted,[25] and that the decision

---

19 UNCITRAL Report of 55th Session, 17 October 2011, UN Doc A/CN.9/736, para. 77. Relevant considerations will include, for example, compliance with timelines and costs issues.

20 *See* Dimsey, *supra* fn 1, at 191-193, noting a substantive element to such prejudice ('a situation in which a third person [makes] a submission that [is] highly detrimental to the arguments being presented by one party) and a procedural element ('a situation in which ... a detailed and lengthy response by the party of whose case the third person submission had been critical' is necessary). *See also* UNCITRAL Report of 53rd Session, 20 October 2010, UN Doc A/CN.9/712, para. 47; Nedden & Rosenfeld, *supra* fn 2, at 47.

21 Johnson & Bernasconi-Osterwalder, *supra* fn 3, at 18.

22 *Ibid. See also* Nedden & Rosenfeld, *supra* fn 2, at 47.

23 Cf. e.g., article 4(5) of the Transparency Rules and Rule 37(2) of the ICSID Arbitration Rules (in pertinent part: '[t]he Tribunal shall ensure that the non-disputing party submission does not disrupt the proceeding or unduly burden or unfairly prejudice either party, and that both parties are given an opportunity to present their observations on the non- disputing party submission'); section B(7) of the NAFTA FTC Statement ('The Tribunal will ensure that: (a) any non-disputing party submission avoids disrupting the proceedings; and (b) neither disputing party is unduly burdened or unfairly prejudiced by such submissions').

24 *See* Lamb, Harrison & Hew, *supra* fn 1, at 76.

25 *See* UNCITRAL Report of 54th Session, 25 February 2011, UN Doc A/CN.9/717, para. 120; UNCITRAL Working Paper for 55th Session, 29 July 2011, UN Doc A/CN.9/WG.II/WP.166, para. 45.

rests with the tribunal. At a relatively early stage of the drafting process, the Working Group rejected a proposal permitting the disputing parties to determine whether to allow third-person submissions.[26] Instead, acknowledging that 'the purpose of amicus curiae submissions was to enlighten the arbitral tribunal in its decision-making process', the Working Group considered that the tribunal would be best placed to assume a 'gate-keeping role' in deciding whether to allow third-person submissions.[27] It will be unusual of course for the tribunal to oppose a view held by all disputing parties that amici generally or specific amici should or should not be admitted, for after all the parties know more about the case than the tribunal at that stage. But one can see the wisdom of the tribunal's having the authority to prevent inappropriate situations of generalized proxy litigation through amici.

10. The words 'may allow' in article 4(1) do not necessarily refer directly to the tribunal's general discretion pursuant to article 1(4) of the Transparency Rules.[28] Though the tribunal must indeed take into account the factors listed in article 1(4),[29] the Working Group rejected any implicit or explicit reference to that provision, finding that articles 4(3) and 4(5) already provided specific guidance for the tribunal in respect of third-person submissions.[30] This, it is true, reflects in specific criteria the more general precepts in article 1(4). The tribunal should first refer to this specific guidance when making a determination under article 4(1), before turning to the factors in article 1(4) as may be necessary.

11. Furthermore, the third person bears the burden of demonstrating that its submission is relevant to the dispute, and that it addresses only matters 'within the scope of the dispute', as provided for in articles 4(1) and 4(4)(d).[31]

C. Guidelines for third-person submissions

12. The guidelines and 'certain restricting criteria' exhibited in article 4 of the Transparency Rules set out distinct parameters for both the tribunal's discretion to allow third-person submissions and the nature of these submissions.[32] This is

---

26 UNCITRAL Report of 53rd Session, 20 October 2010, UN Doc A/CN.9/712, para. 47.

27 *Ibid.*

28 UNCITRAL Report of 57th Session, 12 October 2012, UN Doc A/CN.9/760, para. 40.

29 *See* Johnson & Bernasconi-Osterwalder, *supra* fn 3, at 18.

30 *See* UNCITRAL Report of 57th Session, 12 October 2012, UN Doc A/CN.9/760, para. 40 (where the Working Group rejected the addition of the wording 'in the exercise of its discretion' between 'may' and 'allow' in article 4(1), which elsewhere in the Transparency Rules is used to indicate a reference to article 1(4)).

31 *See* Dimsey, *supra* fn 1, at 164 (citing to *United Parcel Service of America Inc v. Government of Canada* (UNCITRAL) Direction of the Tribunal on the Participation of Amici Curiae, 1 August 2003, <www.italaw.com>, para. 5 (where the tribunal stated that third-person submissions must 'relate to issues raised by the disputing parties and cannot introduce new issues in the litigation or go beyond the scope of the case as defined by the disputing parties').

32 *See* UNCITRAL Report of 54th Session, 25 February 2011, UN Doc A/CN.9/717, para. 117; UNCITRAL Report of 55th Session, 17 October 2011, UN Doc A/CN.9/736, para. 70;

a compromise derived from the Working Group's decision to give the tribunal, as opposed to the disputing parties, discretion to allow third-person submissions. For example, article 4(1) requires that the tribunal consult with the disputing parties before allowing such submissions, which reflects the view that this decision should not be left to the tribunal alone.[33] Similarly, article 4(6) requires that the disputing parties be given a reasonable opportunity to present their observations on any third-person submissions.

13. The detailed provisions of article 4 are a departure from the vague provisions on third-party submissions contained in certain investment treaties.[34] They represent a conscious decision taken by the Working Group to provide 'sufficient guidance' as to how to deal with third-person submissions, particularly 'taking account of the fact that a number of States had little experience in the field'.[35]

D. Form of third-person participation limited to written submissions

14. Article 4 does not address any form of third-person participation other than written submissions. Participation through statements at oral hearings, for example, is excluded from the scope of the Transparency Rules[36] (though it has on occasion occurred in practice). Despite this, the arbitral tribunal may nevertheless have the power under article 1(5) to allow other forms of third-person participation – for example, under article 15 of the 1976 Arbitration Rules or article 17 of the 2010 Arbitration Rules.[37] Moreover, cases such as *Foresti v. South Africa* suggest that third-person participation in the proceedings may, in some circumstances, extend to their having sight of certain documents submitted in the arbitration.[38] Of course,

UNCITRAL Working Paper for 53rd Session, 5 August 2010, UN Doc A/CN.9/WG.II/WP.160/Add.1, para. 21.

33 UNCITRAL Report of 54th Session, 25 February 2011, UN Doc A/CN.9/717, paras 120 and 125. *See also* Dimsey, *supra* fn 1, at 160 ('It is noteworthy here that the Rules do not require the consent of the parties; the requirement is deliberately limited to an obligation to consult with the parties. Of course, if one party were to make strong objections to the participation of third persons in the proceedings, the tribunal would be obliged to give these due weight and then to exercise its discretion').

34 UNCITRAL Report of 55th Session, 17 October 2011, UN Doc A/CN.9/736, para. 69. *See also* Johnson & Bernasconi-Osterwalder, *supra* fn 3, at 18.

35 UNCITRAL Report of 54th Session, 25 February 2011, UN Doc A/CN.9/717, paras 119-120; UNCITRAL Working Paper for 55th Session, 29 July 2011, UN Doc A/CN.9/WG.II/WP.166, paras 46-47.

36 Johnson & Bernasconi-Osterwalder, *supra* fn 3, at 17.

37 *Ibid*. For a recent example of an arbitral tribunal applying article 15 of the 1976 Arbitration Rules to written amicus curiae submissions, *see Eli Lilly and Company v. The Government of Canada* (UNCITRAL) (ICSID Case No. UNCT/14/2) Procedural Order No. 4, 23 February 2016, <www.italaw.com> (where the tribunal decided the admissibility of nine applications submitted by a total of 25 parties).

38 *See Piero Foresti, Laura de Carli & Others v. The Republic of South Africa* (ICSID Case No. ARB(AF)/07/01) Award, 4 August 2010, <www.italaw.com>, para. 27 (where the tribunal acknowledged its previous decision to permit non-disputing parties ('NDPs') to file submissions, noting that '[i]n order that the NDPs might do so, the Tribunal asked that

where the Transparency Rules apply, such documents may be available to third persons pursuant to article 3 (publication of documents). However, where these documents have yet to be filed, there is a temporal question as to the possibility of delaying third-person submissions so that the third persons in question may have the benefit of reading, e.g., the parties' pleadings in advance of filing their own submissions.[39]

E. Funding of third persons

15. The Working Group delegations debated whether to require disclosure of the third person's funding assistance where this reached a material percentage threshold of the third person's total revenue.[40] That, too, is a measure of transparency, and one that is imposed on investor claimants under certain investment treaties (e.g. the CETA). The argument was advanced that a specific percentage would provide clear guidance on the requirements of article 4(2)(c)(ii) and would be a relevant indicator of whether the funder's influence could be significant.[41] Others observed that a percentage may not always be a useful indicator, as it would not reflect substantial assistance in cases where a large organization had received a large sum without reaching the requisite percentage of its total revenue.[42]

16. The compromise contained in article 4(2)(c)(ii) mandates disclosure of any 'substantial assistance' (i.e. funding or otherwise, which likely includes contributions made in kind)[43] in either of the two years preceding the application. In light of the decision not to specify a percentage figure, the guidance in this provision ('funding around 20 per cent of its overall operations annually') was 'provided by way of illustrative example' and not as a threshold below which disclosure is not required.[44] Of course, where the third person has received *direct* financial or

---

the Parties agree on and file with the Centre by 16 November 2009: (i) redacted versions of the Memorial and Counter-Memorial; (ii) redacted versions of legal opinions; and (iii) a list of witnesses and experts that had provided evidence on facts and quantum (without any description of the content of the report or statement)'). *See also Glamis Gold Ltd v. The United States of America* (UNCITRAL) Procedural Order No. 6, 15 October 2005, < www.italaw.com >, paras 11-12; *Infinito Gold Ltd v. Costa Rica* (ICSID Case No. ARB/14/5) Procedural Order No. 2, 1 June 2016, < www.italaw.com >, paras 40-45.

39 *See Glamis Gold Ltd v. The United States of America* (UNCITRAL) Procedural Order No. 6, 15 October 2005, < www.italaw.com >, paras 11-12; and Award, 8 June 2009, paras 278-279. For an overview of UNCITRAL and ICSID cases in which amicus curiae briefs have been admitted under the applicable arbitral rules (and not under the Transparency Rules), *see* Dimsey, *supra* fn 1, at 143 et seq. and Lamb, Harrison & Hew, *supra* fn 1, at 79-84.

40 UNCITRAL Report of 57th Session, 12 October 2012, UN Doc A/CN.9/760, paras 47-48.

41 *Ibid.*, at para. 48.

42 *Ibid.* (further noting the argument that 'expressing assistance as a percentage of income might preclude reporting in circumstances where assistance, even of a significant nature, had been given "in kind", or where the assistance fell just below the threshold').

43 *Ibid.*, at paras 48-50. *See also* Dimsey, *supra* fn 1, at 173.

44 UNCITRAL Report of 57th Session, 12 October 2012, UN Doc A/CN.9/760, para. 50.

other assistance for the preparation of its submission, information on the funder must be provided pursuant to article 4(2)(c)(i).

F. Supplement to UNCITRAL Arbitration Rules

17. Articles 4 and 5 of the Transparency Rules supplement Section III of the Arbitration Rules, which are silent on third-person submissions.[45] The Working Group noted that tribunals have not considered article 25(4) of the 1976 Arbitration Rules or article 28(3) of the 2010 Arbitration Rules (requiring closed hearings) to preclude third-person submissions, and, in practice, such submissions have been accepted pursuant to tribunals' discretionary powers, as noted above.[46] Articles 4 and 5 of the Transparency Rules effectively codify the procedure by which tribunals in treaty-based investor-state arbitrations should handle submissions by third persons and by non-disputing Parties to the treaty,[47] thus filling lacunae in the 1976 and 2010 Arbitration Rules.

18. It is clear that the amici provisions in article 4 serve a purpose different from joinder under article 17(5) of the 2010 Arbitration Rules. It would be an abuse of article 4 for it to be relied upon to bring in the proceedings a person that is a party to the arbitration agreement.

---

45 UNCITRAL Working Paper for 56th Session, 13 December 2011, UN Doc A/CN.9/WG.II/WP.169/Add.1, paras 27-28.

46 *Ibid.*, at para. 27.

47 *Ibid.*, at para. 28.

Article 5
Submission by a non-disputing Party to the treaty

Article 5

1. The arbitral tribunal shall, subject to paragraph 4, allow, or, after consultation with the disputing parties, may invite, submissions on issues of treaty interpretation from a non-disputing Party to the treaty.

2. The arbitral tribunal, after consultation with the disputing parties, may allow submissions on further matters within the scope of the dispute from a non-disputing Party to the treaty. In determining whether to allow such submissions, the arbitral tribunal shall take into consideration, among other factors it determines to be relevant, the factors referred to in article 4, paragraph 3, and, for greater certainty, the need to avoid submissions which would support the claim of the investor in a manner tantamount to diplomatic protection.

3. The arbitral tribunal shall not draw any inference from the absence of any submission or response to any invitation pursuant to paragraphs 1 or 2.

4. The arbitral tribunal shall ensure that any submission does not disrupt or unduly burden the arbitral proceedings, or unfairly prejudice any disputing party.

5. The arbitral tribunal shall ensure that the disputing parties are given a reasonable opportunity to present their observations on any submission by a non-disputing Party to the treaty.

A. Overview

1. Article 5(1) of the Transparency Rules requires the tribunal to accept submissions from non-disputing Parties to the treaty ('non-disputing Parties'), i.e. States or

international organizations, on matters of treaty interpretation.[1] The provision is modelled on NAFTA Article 1128. It also partly reflects and partly develops practice under BITs, albeit rare.[2] Article 5(1) does not spell this out, but one may well expect to see in support of legal observations primary and other documents from the negotiation of a treaty. (Analogous functions may be served by a party being joined under article 17(5) of the 2010 Rules, but article 5(1) is *lex specialis* and excludes article 17(5).) By decision of the tribunal, after consultation with the parties, article 5(2) permits submissions from non-disputing Parties on 'further matters within the scope of the dispute'.[3] In deciding whether the latter submissions should be allowed, the tribunal must consider, among other relevant factors, the factors identified in article 4(3) concerning amici, as well as the need to 'avoid submissions which would support the claim of the investor in a manner tantamount to diplomatic protection'.[4] On a purely textual reading, the tribunal may only 'invite' – rather than 'compel' – non-disputing-Party submissions on matters of treaty interpretation.[5] Thus an interested State must secure a formal invitation, which one of the parties may ask the tribunal to extend.

2. Article 5(3) prevents the tribunal from drawing adverse inferences from the absence of non-disputing-Party submissions,[6] the obvious rationale being that an investor should not be perceived as shunned by its State in these circumstances. This is entirely consistent with the no-support rule in article 5(2). Article 5(4), replicating the wording of article 4(5), acts as a safeguard to establish that non-disputing Party submissions shall not (i) disrupt or unduly burden the proceedings, or (ii) unfairly prejudice any of the disputing parties.[7]

---

1 *See* Lise Johnson & Nathalie Bernasconi-Osterwalder, *New UNCITRAL Arbitration Rules on Transparency: Application, Content and Next Steps*, 19 (CIEL, IISD, CCSI, August 2013), <http://ccsi.columbia.edu> (noting that, in contrast to article 4 of the Transparency Rules, article 5 is not limited to written submissions).

2 *See* UNCITRAL Report of 55th Session, 17 October 2011, UN Doc A/CN.9/736, para. 83.

3 *Ibid. See also* UNCITRAL Report of 54th Session, 25 February 2011, UN Doc A/CN.9/717, para. 124; UNCITRAL Report of 53rd Session, 20 October 2010, UN Doc A/CN.9/712, para. 49; UNCITRAL Report of 55th Session, 17 October 2011, UN Doc A/CN.9/736, paras 86 and 94. Article 5 of the Transparency Rules refers to 'a non-disputing Party to the treaty' as opposed to 'a non-disputing State Party to the treaty' (which was used extensively during the negotiations), thereby recognizing that a non-disputing Party may not be a State; *see* UNCITRAL Report of 55th Session, 17 October 2011, UN Doc A/CN.9/736, para. 95.

4 *See* article 4(3) of the Transparency Rules, which refers to the existence of a third person's 'significant interest' in the arbitral proceedings, as well as 'the extent to which the submission would assist the arbitral tribunal in the determination of a factual or legal issue ... by bringing a perspective, particular knowledge or insight that is different from that of the disputing parties'.

5 Johnson & Bernasconi-Osterwalder, *supra* fn 1, at 19.

6 UNCITRAL Report of 55th Session, 17 October 2011, UN Doc A/CN.9/736, para. 91; Johnson & Bernasconi-Osterwalder, *supra* fn 1, at 19.

7 Johnson & Bernasconi-Osterwalder, *supra* fn 1, at 19. *See also* discussion of article 4(5) of the Transparency Rules, *supra*.

3. Finally, article 5(5) protects the disputing parties' due-process rights by affording them the opportunity to present their observations on submissions by non-disputing Parties.[8] This right is extremely important in the present context. An investor, as the only non-State participant, should have a fair opportunity to address what it may regard as the concerted effort of two States, who after all will have numerous matters of common interest, to gang up against it. It is important in this context to bear in mind that the States may choose to present a partial negotiating history, while the investor may not have full access to the relevant sources, i.e. documents and witnesses. That, too, is a matter which may require careful procedural handling by the tribunal. Article 27(3) directions for production of documents may be an appropriate mechanism; evidential inferences (see article 27(4)) may be an alternative mechanism.

4. In the light of existing investment treaties which provide for non-disputing-Party submissions with respect to treaty interpretation, as well as investment cases where tribunals have allowed such submissions in the absence of an express provision in the treaty, it may be argued that the tribunal already had the inherent power to ask a non-disputing Party for its views.[9] (The authors would add that article 17(1) of the 2010 Rules seems a more straightforward foundation.) Suggestions to this effect were discussed in the Working Group, which nevertheless determined that article 5 should be retained in order to clarify 'the legal regime applicable to that category of [non-disputing-Party] submissions'.[10]

5. As further discussed below, article 5 of the Transparency Rules was kept separate from article 4 (relating to third-person submissions), as the non-disputing Party's status as a contracting State to the treaty was considered to engender particular legal implications and sensitivities.[11]

---

[8] *See* UNCITRAL Working Paper for 58th Session, 30 November 2012, UN Doc A/CN.9/WG.II/WP.176, para. 39; UNCITRAL Working Paper for 56th Session, 13 December 2011, UN Doc A/CN.9/WG.II/WP.169, para. 38.

[9] Martins Paparinskis & Jessica Howley, 'Article 5. Submission by a non-disputing Party to the treaty' in Dimitrij Euler, Markus Gehring & Maxi Scherer (eds), *Transparency in International Investment Arbitration: A Guide to the UNCITRAL Rules on Transparency in Treaty-Based Investor-State Arbitration*, 206-208 (Cambridge University Press 2015) (noting at fn 35 that, '[i]n a number of cases, tribunals have asked for submissions from the home State of the investor', and citing to, inter alia, *Aguas del Tunari, SA v. Republic of Bolivia* (ICSID Case No. ARB/02/3) Decision on Respondent's Objections to Jurisdiction, 21 October 2005, <www.italaw.com>, Appendix IV).

[10] *See* UNCITRAL Report of 55th Session, 17 October 2011, UN Doc A/CN.9/736, paras 81 and 83 (it was suggested that 'a State Party to a treaty might issue statements on treaty interpretation, or unilateral declarations on its understanding of a treaty provision'). *See also* UNCITRAL Report of 58th Session, 13 February 2013, UN Doc A/CN.9/765, para. 46 (suggesting that 'a non-disputing Party could make submissions on its own initiative' and that the tribunal could 'deal with them as it deemed appropriate'). *See also* Paparinskis & Howley, *supra* fn 9, at 207-208.

[11] *See* UNCITRAL Report of 55th Session, 17 October 2011, UN Doc A/CN.9/736, para. 83.

B. Right of non-disputing Parties to make submissions

6. In the Working Group, views diverged as to whether non-disputing Parties should have a right to make submissions, or whether the tribunal should have the discretion to determine their admissibility.[12] Those favouring the discretionary power of the tribunal argued that it would provide valuable flexibility, for example by allowing the tribunal to reject submissions made late in the proceedings when they could be disruptive.[13]

7. As the Working Group observed, most treaties are either silent on this issue or afford non-disputing Parties a right to make submissions.[14] The Working Group therefore acknowledged that replacing this right with the discretionary power of the tribunal 'would potentially diverge from current practice and dilute future standards'.[15] Moreover, a non-disputing Party is, by definition, a Party to the treaty, and any interpretation of the treaty by the tribunal may affect the non-disputing Party's rights in future proceedings. It was argued that non-disputing-Party submissions could enhance the tribunal's understanding of the treaty by providing 'balanced and comprehensive information', and that the tribunal 'could in any event accord whatever weight to that submission as it saw fit'.[16]

8. The potential significance of non-disputing Party submissions is evident:

> Given the importance for the proper interpretation of the relevant treaty of the intention and agreement of the Parties, a non-disputing Party's views can be of significance for an arbitral tribunal ... if the views of the treaty Parties coincide, this may be demonstrative of an agreement as to the treaty's proper

---

12 *See* UNCITRAL Working Paper for 58th Session, 30 November 2012, UN Doc A/CN.9/WG.II/WP.176, para. 40 ('Matter for further consideration: "[shall] [may]"'). The debate ultimately saw the 'shall' formulation adopted. *See also* UNCITRAL Report of 57th Session, 12 October 2012, UN Doc A/CN.9/760, paras 59-61; UNCITRAL Report of 55th Session, 17 October 2011, UN Doc A/CN.9/736, paras 90-92 (noting also that the suggestion that a non-disputing Party should only be entitled to make a submission 'if so requested by the arbitral tribunal' received little support).

13 UNCITRAL Report of 58th Session, 13 February 2013, UN Doc A/CN.9/765, paras 43 and 48. *See also*, for instruments providing to non-disputing Parties to a treaty the right to make submissions, Article 1128 of NAFTA; Article 10.20(2) of the 2004 Dominican Republic-Central America Free Trade Agreement; Article 35 of the 2004 Canada Model FIPA; Article 28(2) of the 2012 US Model BIT.

14 UNCITRAL Report of 58th Session, 13 February 2013, UN Doc A/CN.9/765, para. 45.

15 *Ibid.* For an overview of case law and practice with respect to submissions by non-disputing Parties to treaties in investment arbitration (the main practice having developed in NAFTA cases pursuant to article 1128), *see* Paparinskis & Howley, *supra* fn 9, at 198-207. *See also* Gabrielle Kaufmann-Kohler, 'Non-Disputing State Submissions in Investment Arbitration: Resurgence of Diplomatic Protection?' in Laurence Boisson de Chazournes, Marcelo G. Kohen & Jorge E. Viñuales (eds), *Diplomatic and Judicial Means of Dispute Settlement*, 305, 312 et seq. (Martinus Nijhoff 2012).

16 UNCITRAL Report of 57th Session, 12 October 2012, UN Doc A/CN.9/760, para. 60; UNCITRAL Report of 58th Session, 13 February 2013, UN Doc A/CN.9/765, para. 44. Moreover, it was observed that it would be unusual for the tribunal to reject a submission from a non-disputing Party.

interpretation. But even in the absence of such agreement, a non-disputing Party may well have an alternative perspective on the treaty than that put forward by the respondent State. It may also, on a more practical level, have materials available to it that are relevant to the treaty's interpretation, such as documents relating to the drafting history, but to which the parties to the arbitration proceedings do not have access. As the [Working Group] noted, allowing non-disputing Party submissions can therefore help to avoid treaty interpretation being "one-sided".[17]

9. A mandatory 'shall' wording for article 5(1) ultimately prevailed. However, as a compromise between the opposing views outlined above, the Working Group elected to address concerns as to a perceived lack of flexibility by including, in article 5(1), an express reference to article 5(4), which protects the proceedings and disputing parties from undue burdens and unfair prejudice, respectively.[18] In contrast, third-person submissions pursuant to article 4(1) of the Transparency Rules are subject to the tribunal's discretion.[19] The Working Group recognized that a submission by a non-disputing Party on treaty interpretation could affect and arguably prejudice one disputing party's position.[20] The threshold in the second limb of article 5(4) (i.e. *unfair* prejudice) is therefore not met if a submission merely prejudices one of the disputing parties.[21] It must be recognized that article 5(4) refers to procedural prejudice, such as tardiness for example. However, as commentators note, the requirements of procedural fairness contained in article 5(4) require that the tribunal reach an 'appropriate balance' in cases where, for instance, non-disputing Parties attempt to 'interfere with the arbitral process by making use of their powers to interpret the treaty under consideration to the disadvantage of the investor while proceedings are ongoing'.[22]

10. There is a broader issue, which concerns the weight to be given to a submission by a State. In the NAFTA system, there is a clear distinction between (a) binding interpretations (which are authentic interpretations or agreed amendments in terms of legal effect, and which bind the issuing States in applying NAFTA generally)[23] and (b) legal submissions in the context of cases, which do not involve the proffering States as disputing parties.[24] The former are binding legal

17 Paparinskis & Howley, *supra* fn 9, at 210 and 222-223. *See* generally *ibid.*, 209-212; and Anthea Roberts, *Power and Persuasion in Investment Treaty Interpretation: The Dual Role of States*, 104(2) American Journal of International Law 179, 180 and 200 (2010) (noting that a subsequent agreement by the treaty parties as to interpretation, as well as subsequent practice, is determinative as to the parties' intentions in terms of treaty interpretation).

18 *See* UNCITRAL Report of 58th Session, 13 February 2013, UN Doc A/CN.9/765, paras 49 and 51.

19 *See* discussion of article 4 of the Transparency Rules, *supra*.

20 UNCITRAL Report of 58th Session, 13 February 2013, UN Doc A/CN.9/765, para. 48.

21 *Ibid.*, at para. 49.

22 Paparinskis & Howley, *supra* fn 9, at 225.

23 Article 1131(2) of NAFTA ('An interpretation by the Commission of a provision of this Agreement shall be binding on a Tribunal established under this Section').

24 Article 1128 of NAFTA ('On written notice to the disputing parties, a Party may make submissions to a Tribunal on a question of interpretation of this Agreement').

instruments, the latter argument in one case. The two must not be conflated. It may not be permissible, or fair, for two States to suggest through pleadings a concordant legal position (authentic interpretation) which there is no evidence that they have accepted in their treaty practice though they could just as easily have already accepted – any more than it would be fair for such a submission to be 'tantamount to diplomatic protection'. That is not a matter which the Transparency Rules do or indeed can address. It is a matter for the tribunal, in assessing the weight of an article 5(2) submission.

C. Scope of submissions not limited to treaty interpretation

11. Article 5(2) of the Transparency Rules clarifies that the scope of submissions from non-disputing Parties is not limited to treaty interpretation and may also encompass, for example, matters of fact and law (i.e. 'further matters within the scope of the dispute').[25] While non-disputing Parties have the right to make submissions on treaty interpretation pursuant to article 5(1), submissions on other matters are subject to the authorisation of the tribunal, which acts 'as a filter' to determine which submissions it finds useful.[26] Article 5(2) further requires that the tribunal consult with the disputing parties prior to allowing a submission on matters beyond treaty interpretation.[27] One can see for example how it may be helpful for the tribunal to have authoritative information on (say) the nationality law of the investor's home State, corporate-residence requirements, the status of a company, etc.

D. Tribunal's ability to invite submissions

12. The delegations disagreed on whether the tribunal should have the ability to invite submissions from non-disputing Parties.[28] The final text of article 5 approaches this issue differently depending on the nature of the submission: whereas article 5(1) permits the tribunal to invite submissions on issues of treaty interpretation after consultation with the disputing parties (in contrast to article 4, which

---

25 UNCITRAL Report of 57th Session, 12 October 2012, UN Doc A/CN.9/760, paras 65 and 67 (noting that the word 'further' in article 5(2) distinguishes matters under this provision from issues of treaty interpretation dealt with in article 5(1) and encompasses both legal and factual matters). *See also* UNCITRAL Working Paper for 56th Session, 13 December 2011, UN Doc A/CN.9/WG.II/WP.169, para. 40; UNCITRAL Working Paper for 58th Session, 30 November 2012, UN Doc A/CN.9/WG.II/WP.176, para. 41.

26 *See* UNCITRAL Report of 57th Session, 12 October 2012, UN Doc A/CN.9/760, para. 65.

27 *See* UNCITRAL Working Paper for 58th Session, 30 November 2012, UN Doc A/CN.9/WG.II/WP.176, para. 39; UNCITRAL Working Paper for 56th Session, 13 December 2011, UN Doc A/CN.9/WG.II/WP.169, para. 38.

28 UNCITRAL Report of 57th Session, 12 October 2012, UN Doc A/CN.9/760, paras 69-70 (the delegations arguing against allowing the tribunal to invite submissions stated that doing so (i) risked the politicisation of the dispute and could introduce elements of diplomatic protection and (ii) would place the non-disputing Party in a more privileged position than a third party to the dispute, which was unjustified in relation to issues outside the scope of treaty interpretation).

provides no such power to the tribunal), article 5(2), as finally worded, does not explicitly permit the tribunal to invite (but rather only to 'allow') submissions on 'further matters within the scope of the dispute'.[29]

13. Although commentators have suggested that the omission of the invitation provision in article 5(2) should not be interpreted as implying that the tribunal does not have such authority,[30] the majority and correct view has come to the opposite conclusion, citing to the Working Group's deliberate removal of the tribunal's authority on this point.[31] However, under article 1(5), such restriction should not impact 'on any power the tribunal might otherwise have under the arbitration rules or otherwise'.[32]

E. Addressing concerns over diplomatic protection

14. During the Working Group's work, concerns were raised that article 5(2) could be used by the investor's home State to facilitate diplomatic protection.[33] Essentially, '[t]he concern was that if the non-disputing Party is the home State of the investor and is able to make broad factual and legal submissions', this may 'enable that State to engage in diplomatic protection with respect to its nationals'.[34] Article 5(2) explicitly addresses this concern by (i) making legal or factual non-disputing-Party submissions subject to the discretion of the tribunal, and (ii) expressly directing the tribunal to consider 'the need to avoid submissions which would support the claim of the investor in a manner tantamount to diplomatic protection' in exercising its discretion.[35] The latter requirement is to be policed by the tribunal at the outset, when an application is made to it. It is thus incumbent on the tribunal to ensure that it knows precisely what the applicant State proposes to address in its submission (and why); and to reject a proposed submission

[29] *Ibid.*, at para. 70.

[30] Johnson & Bernasconi-Osterwalder, *supra* fn 1, at 19.

[31] *See*, e.g., Paparinskis & Howley, *supra* fn 9, at 215 ('As with Article 4 [of the Transparency Rules], the tribunal is not obliged to accept such submissions, and it may not invite them'). *See also* UNCITRAL Report of 57th Session, 12 October 2012, UN Doc A/CN.9/760, paras 68-70.

[32] *See* UNCITRAL Report of 57th Session, 12 October 2012, UN Doc A/CN.9/760, para. 70.

[33] UNCITRAL Report of 53rd Session, 20 October 2010, UN Doc A/CN.9/712, para. 49; Johnson & Bernasconi-Osterwalder, *supra* fn 1, at 19. *See also* UNCITRAL Report of 55th Session, 17 October 2011, UN Doc A/CN.9/736, paras 79 and 87; UNCITRAL Report of 57th Session, 12 October 2012, UN Doc A/CN.9/760, paras 61 and 67.

[34] Paparinskis & Howley, *supra* fn 9, at 216 (citing the Report of the International Law Commission on its 58th Session, 1 May-9 June and 3 July-11 August 2006, UN Doc A/61/10, Chapter IV, Article 1: 'diplomatic protection consists of the invocation by a State, through diplomatic action or other means of peaceful settlement, of the responsibility of another State for an injury caused by an internationally wrongful act of that State to a natural or legal person that is a national of the former State with a view to the implementation of such responsibility').

[35] Johnson & Bernasconi-Osterwalder, *supra* fn 1, at 19.

'regarding both the content of rules as well as their application to facts in the context of the particular dispute'.[36]

15. The final formulation of article 5(2) recognizes that, in practice, non-disputing home States rarely intervene merely to protect the interests of their nationals as investors.[37] Further, it reflects the understanding that non-disputing Party submissions on issues of fact and law may benefit the tribunal, as described above. In such situations, the non-disputing (home) State Party may be best-placed to provide authoritative information.[38]

---

36 Paparinskis & Howley, *supra* fn 9, at 220 (concluding, at 222, that '[t]he key difficulty will lie in distinguishing those kinds of submissions that are sufficiently close to a diplomatic protection claim to be regarded as "tantamount" thereto from those that are not, including distinguishing submissions on questions of interpretation from broader submissions on other legal and factual matters').

37 UNCITRAL Report of 57th Session, 12 October 2012, UN Doc A/CN.9/760, para. 60.

38 UNCITRAL Report of 55th Session, 17 October 2011, UN Doc A/CN.9/736, para. 88.

Article 6
Hearings

Article 6

1. Subject to article 6, paragraphs 2 and 3, hearings for the presentation of evidence or for oral argument ('hearings') shall be public.

2. Where there is a need to protect confidential information or the integrity of the arbitral process pursuant to article 7, the arbitral tribunal shall make arrangements to hold in private that part of the hearing requiring such protection.

3. The arbitral tribunal shall make logistical arrangements to facilitate the public access to hearings (including where appropriate by organizing attendance through video links or such other means as it deems appropriate). However, the arbitral tribunal may, after consultation with the disputing parties, decide to hold all or part of the hearings in private where this becomes necessary for logistical reasons, such as when the circumstances render any original arrangement for public access to a hearing infeasible.

A. Overview

1. Article 6 establishes the rule that all evidential and legal hearings shall be public and then goes on to set out three circumstances in which there must be private ('in camera') hearings: (i) to protect confidential information; (ii) to protect the integrity of the arbitral process; and (iii) for eventual logistical reasons.[1] Public or 'open' hearings are understood to allow the public to attend hearings, 'but

[1] Lise Johnson & Nathalie Bernasconi-Osterwalder, *New UNCITRAL Arbitration Rules on Transparency: Application, Content and Next Steps*, 20 (CIEL, IISD, CCSI, August 2013), < http://ccsi.columbia.edu >. Note that hearing transcripts are addressed in article 3 of the Transparency Rules pertaining to the publication of documents; *see* discussion of article 3 of the Transparency Rules, *supra*.

not to actively participate in them'.[2] Article 6(1) does not apply to hearings on procedural matters,[3] such as the procedural timetable or document production. There are hearings which partake of both legal argument and procedural discourse, such as hearings on whether there should be a preliminary-objections phase, but there too the object is a procedural one and unrelated to the merits of the case.

2. Article 6(3) authorizes the tribunal, after consultation with the parties, to hold all or part of a hearing in private where necessary for logistical reasons.[4] Where hearings are held in private for any of the reasons listed in paragraphs (2) and (3), they are closed only to the extent necessary.[5]

B. Public hearing as the default rule

3. There was debate in the Working Group on whether public hearings, which are undeniably a possible feature of investment-treaty arbitrations, should form an exception or the general rule.[6] Delegations arguing against public hearings put forward the view that the concept was 'contrary to the very nature of arbitration'.[7] Article 28(3) of the 2010 Rules was cited in that connection. They further noted that investor-state arbitrations often raised political issues, with public hearings likely to place additional pressure on the respondent State, which could 'adversely affect settlement of the dispute'.[8]

4. The compromise in the final text adopts open hearings as the default rule, subject to narrow exceptions aimed at addressing valid objections such as the

---

2 *See* UNCITRAL Report of 53rd Session, 20 October 2010, UN Doc A/CN.9/712, paras 52-57 and 60 (discussing whether third parties should be permitted to participate in oral hearings, and noting that the general practice with amici curiae had been to allow written submissions but not to permit participation in hearings. Some delegations argued that third-party participation should not be precluded, as tribunals may wish to question these parties on their submissions and thus, a provision on hearings should allow the tribunal such discretion. Nevertheless, the final formulation of article 6 does not address this issue).

3 *See* UNCITRAL Report of 57th Session, 12 October 2012, UN Doc A/CN.9/760, paras 86-88; UNCITRAL Working Paper for 58th Session, 30 November 2012, UN Doc A/CN.9/WG.II/WP.176, para. 47 (substantive hearings include 'jurisdictional hearings and hearings in which evidence by witnesses or experts ... [is] presented'). *See also* Jan H. Nedden & Friedrich Rosenfeld, 'The new UNCITRAL Transparency Rules: How the trend towards transparency differs in investment and commercial arbitration' in Christoph Muller & Antonio Rigozzi (eds), *New Developments in International Commercial Arbitration 2013*, 41, 46 (2013).

4 UNCITRAL Report of 54th Session, 25 February 2011, UN Doc A/CN.9/717, para. 109; UNCITRAL Report of 55th Session, 17 October 2011, UN Doc A/CN.9/736, para. 104; UNCITRAL Working Paper for 58th Session, 30 November 2012, UN Doc A/CN.9/WG.II/WP.176, para. 46.

5 Johnson & Bernasconi-Osterwalder, *supra* fn 1, at 20.

6 *See* UNCITRAL Report of 57th Session, 12 October 2012, UN Doc A/CN.9/760, paras 77-82.

7 UNCITRAL Report of 53rd Session, 20 October 2010, UN Doc A/CN.9/712, para. 57; UNCITRAL Report of 54th Session, 25 February 2011, UN Doc A/CN.9/717, para. 101.

8 UNCITRAL Report of 53rd Session, 20 October 2010, UN Doc A/CN.9/712, para. 57.

need to protect confidential information and logistical feasibility.[9] This solution reflects the view that open hearings are a fundamental feature of transparent arbitration and essential for enhancing the public's confidence in treaty-based investor-state arbitration.[10] It was also seen as establishing a balanced regime with room for the tribunal to exercise its discretionary powers under article 1(4) of the Transparency Rules.[11]

5. Adopting public hearings as the default rule, though a 'notable departure' from arbitration rules,[12] was in line with the Working Group's mandate to create a different and higher transparency-standard than that which is available under the 1976 or 2010 Arbitration Rules.[13] Article 6 reverses the presumption that hearings will be held in camera unless otherwise agreed by the parties, as provided in article 25(4) of the 1976 Arbitration Rules and article 28(3) of the 2010 Arbitration Rules.[14]

C. No veto power for disputing parties to close hearings

6. Whether alone or acting together, the disputing parties cannot veto open hearings: such a right was considered during the drafting process but was ultimately removed.[15] Delegations in favour of retaining it argued that it was necessary in order to address issues of national security; confidential information; the politicisation of disputes; the concern that open hearings might become 'logistically unworkable'; and possible cost implications.[16] Ultimately, however, a veto power – whether unilateral or by agreement of all disputing parties – was seen as squarely contrary to transparency and therefore incompatible with the mandate of the Working Group.[17] Indeed, such a power would be incompatible with article 1(3)(a), which prohibits the disputing parties from derogating from

---

9 This compromise was adopted in the Working Group's penultimate session; *see* UNCITRAL Report of 57th Session, 12 October 2012, UN Doc A/CN.9/760, para. 82; UNCITRAL Report of 58th Session, 13 February 2013, UN Doc A/CN.9/765, paras 53, 55 and 57; UNCITRAL Working Paper for 58th Session, 30 November 2012, UN Doc A/CN.9/WG.II/WP.176, para. 45. *See also* Nedden & Rosenfeld, *supra* fn 3, at 46.

10 UNCITRAL Report of 54th Session, 25 February 2011, UN Doc A/CN.9/717, para. 103; and UNCITRAL Report of 53rd Session, 20 October 2010, UN Doc A/CN.9/712, para. 53.

11 UNCITRAL Report of 58th Session, 13 February 2013, UN Doc A/CN.9/765, para. 55; UNCITRAL Working Paper for 56th Session, 13 December 2011, UN Doc A/CN.9/WG.II/WP.169, para. 42.

12 Johnson & Bernasconi-Osterwalder, *supra* fn 1, at 20.

13 UNCITRAL Report of 58th Session, 13 February 2013, UN Doc A/CN.9/765, para. 55.

14 *Ibid.*; UNCITRAL Report of 53rd Session, 20 October 2010, UN Doc A/CN.9/712, para. 54.

15 UNCITRAL Working Paper for 56th Session, 13 December 2011, UN Doc A/CN.9/WG.II/WP.169/Add.1, para. 17; UNCITRAL Report of 55th Session, 17 October 2011, UN Doc A/CN.9/736, para. 100; Johnson & Bernasconi-Osterwalder, *supra* fn 1, at 20. *See also* UNCITRAL Report of 54th Session, 25 February 2011, UN Doc A/CN.9/717, paras 101, 104-105 and 114.

16 UNCITRAL Report of 57th Session, 12 October 2012, UN Doc A/CN.9/760, para. 79.

17 UNCITRAL Working Paper for 55th Session, 29 July 2011, UN Doc A/CN.9/WG.II/WP.166, para. 54; UNCITRAL Report of 55th Session, 17 October 2011, UN Doc A/CN.9/736, para.

the Transparency Rules, by agreement or otherwise, unless permitted to do so by provisions of the relevant treaty.[18] Moreover, it was said, a veto power may have created a discrepancy with the level of transparency provided for in article 3: disputing parties capable of vetoing open hearings may have circumvented the Transparency Rules by not submitting written evidence under article 3 but rather presenting such evidence in closed hearings.[19]

7. Articles 6(2), 6(3) and 7 address the concerns noted above. By referring to article 7, which defines 'confidential or protected information', article 6(2) thus governs the circumstances in which portions of the hearing should be held in private.[20] The tribunal has a good amount of flexibility; for example, it may refuse public access to a hearing pursuant to article 6(2) of the Transparency Rules, but 'allow delayed access in the form of transcripts' pursuant to article 3(1) – for example, where full and/or immediate disclosure of the information would 'impede law enforcement'.[21] Alternatively the tribunal may, 'after consultation with the disputing parties, establish procedures for the designation and redaction of certain confidential information in documents presented at the hearing, [or] suggest technical solutions, available under Article 6(3)'.[22] The tribunal may also close the hearing to the public where this is necessary to protect 'the integrity of the arbitral process'; for example, where the collection or production of evidence would be undermined,[23] where there could be interruptions by protesters, etc.

8. In practice, it will be noted, hearings are scarcely attended by the general public, at least not in person (it is difficult to know how much interest webcast footage attracts). But that of course is not the point; the point is that hearings are open and *may* be attended.

D. Limited authority of the tribunal to close hearings

9. As part of the compromise establishing public hearings as the default rule,[24] articles 6(2) and 6(3) allow the tribunal to close the hearings to the public under specific,

---

100. *See also* UNCITRAL Report of 54th Session, 25 February 2011, UN Doc A/CN.9/717, para. 114.

18 *See* UNCITRAL Report of 58th Session, 13 February 2013, UN Doc A/CN.9/765, para. 55.

19 *Ibid.*

20 *See* discussion of article 7 of the Transparency Rules, *infra.*

21 *See* Klint Alexander, 'Article 6. Hearings' in Dimitrij Euler, Markus Gehring & Maxi Scherer (eds), *Transparency in International Investment Arbitration: A Guide to the UNCITRAL Rules on Transparency in Treaty-Based Investor-State Arbitration*, 238 (Cambridge University Press 2015); and article 7(2)(d) of the Transparency Rules.

22 *Ibid.*, at 239.

23 *Ibid.*, at 240 (providing the example of a situation in which 'the information could hamper the collection or production of evidence, [or] lead to the intimidation of witnesses, lawyers or arbitrators, or members of the arbitral tribunal'). *See also ibid.*, at 241 et seq. for discussion of *Glamis Gold Ltd v. The United States of America* (UNCITRAL) which, Alexander asserts, 'reveals the philosophy behind Article 6(3)'.

24 *See*, regarding the Working Group's 'compromise proposal', Julia Salasky & Corinne Montineri, *UNCITRAL Rules on Transparency in Treaty-Based Investor-State Arbitration*,

limited circumstances. This is in line with the view that the tribunal is best-placed to balance the public interest in transparency 'with countervailing interests such as the need to ensure that the hearings [remain] manageable, and avoid aggravation of the dispute'.[25] However, the limitations imposed on the tribunal's exercise of its discretion under article 6 reflect the view that a wider scope of discretion risked being ambiguously open-ended, 'leaving the tribunal open to pressure from the parties and thus jeopardizing the principle of transparency'.[26]

10. The wording 'where this becomes necessary for logistical reasons' establishes a 'necessity' threshold for deviating from the default rule of public hearings. This is a higher bar than one of mere convenience for the parties or the tribunal.[27] This threshold addresses concerns that the tribunal's discretion to close 'the entire hearing' for logistical reasons might be too broad and could potentially give rise to abuse.[28] However, article 6(3) also gives the arbitral tribunal the authority to determine how to make hearings open by way of 'logistical arrangements', and contemplates that public access to hearings may be facilitated through online tools.[29]

11. That the tribunal's power to hold hearings in private may be exercised in limited circumstances is indicated by the sole example provided in article 6(3) as an illustration of necessity: 'such as when the circumstances render any original arrangement for public access to a hearing infeasible'. The implication is that logistical matters should be arranged prior to the hearing to facilitate public access and minimise practical challenges.[30] It is therefore only where (i) unexpected circumstances subsequently arise and (ii) those circumstances render a closed hearing 'necessary (as opposed to merely convenient)' that a hearing should be closed to the public.[31]

E. Media attendance and broadcasting of hearings

12. Article 6 does not address whether public access to hearings encompasses, or may be provided only through, mass-media attendance, and, if so, whether the

31(4) ASA Bulletin 774, 781 and 787 (2013).

25 UNCITRAL Report of 53rd Session, 20 October 2010, UN Doc A/CN.9/712, para. 56.

26 UNCITRAL Report of 57th Session, 12 October 2012, UN Doc A/CN.9/760, para. 78.

27 *See* Alexander, *supra* fn 22, at 241.

28 UNCITRAL Report of 55th Session, 17 October 2011, UN Doc A/CN.9/736, para. 104 ('Some views were expressed that paragraph (3) might be too broad as it permitted closing the entire hearing for logistical reasons which, in certain instances, might give rise to abuse. In reply, it was said that the words "where this is or becomes necessary for logistical reasons" might take sufficient account of that concern').

29 *See* Johnson & Bernasconi-Osterwalder, *supra* fn 1, at 20. *See also* Alexander, *supra* fn 22, at 241 (noting that the Working Group identified 'from the very beginning of the debate that webcast or other technological solutions may ... facilitate public access to the hearings even where physical attendance was impossible'); and UNCITRAL Working Paper for 54th Session, 9 December 2010, UN Doc A/CN.9/WG.II/WP.162/Add.1, para. 29.

30 Johnson & Bernasconi-Osterwalder, *supra* fn 1, at 20.

31 *Ibid.*

proceedings may be broadcast worldwide.[32] A number of delegations argued that, should the mass media be permitted to attend, they should follow the practice of 'ordinary court proceedings' in several jurisdictions and not be allowed to broadcast the hearings.[33] However, others pointed out that the public's ability physically to attend a hearing would depend on geographical location and thus broadcasting would ensure the widest possible public access.[34] Moreover, at least one tribunal has allowed the broadcasting of hearings pursuant to article 15(1) of the 1976 Arbitration Rules (which do not expressly provide for any such possibility),[35] and this is standard practice in NAFTA arbitrations and in the ICJ.

13. Absent any explicit restriction, it may be concluded from the drafting history that media attendance and broadcasting (organized by an arbitral institution, the tribunal, the parties, or a third-party provider) were foreseen and are permitted, and may indeed be the most practical and economical way of granting access to the public. This freedom would be tempered by the tribunal's exercise of its discretion under articles 6(2) and 6(3), and also under article 1(4). During the Working Group's deliberations, for example, it was suggested that public hearings could be organized 'through webcast, or other means that would not necessarily require the physical presence of the public in the hearing room'.[36] Certain delegations also raised a concern regarding oral submissions that may unexpectedly touch on confidential information; in response to this concern, it was said that such difficulties had not arisen in practice, including in cases of the live broadcasting of hearings.[37]

---

32 Note that this question was nevertheless raised at an early stage of the Working Group's deliberations: *see* UNCITRAL Report of 53rd Session, 20 October 2010, UN Doc A/CN.9/712, para. 55.

33 UNCITRAL Report of 53rd Session, 20 October 2010, UN Doc A/CN.9/712, para. 55.

34 *Ibid.*

35 *See United Parcel Service of America Inc v. Government of Canada* (UNCITRAL) Tribunal's Procedural Directions for Amicus Submissions, 4 April 2003, <www.italaw.com>; and Alexander, *supra* fn 22, at 232 ('the arbitral tribunal in the *United Parcel Service (UPS)* case against Canada emphasised the broader public policy implications of anti-competitive conduct in the use of courier and parcel services to make hearings open to the public, subject to the protection of confidential information. The arbitral tribunal based its decision on Article 15(1) of the Arbitration Rules (1976) ... The public hearing in the *UPS* case was broadcast live in the World Bank Headquarters'). *See also* discussion of the *BSG v. Guinea* case in relation to article 1 of the Transparency Rules, *supra*.

36 UNCITRAL Working Paper for 54th Session, 9 December 2010, UN Doc A/CN.9/WG.II/WP.162/Add.1, para. 29.

37 UNCITRAL Report of 55th Session, 17 October 2011, UN Doc A/CN.9/736, para. 105. In practice a time-delay is often applied to the webcast in order to protect any confidential information. For example, the ICSID News Release regarding the webcast of the *BSG v. Guinea* case, available on the ICSID website at <www.icsid.worldbank.org>, provides, in pertinent part: 'The parties have agreed to make the hearing open to the public via webcast, except for those parts involving confidential or sensitive information. A video of the hearing will be streamed online in English and French *with a one-hour delay*' (emphasis added).

Article 7
Exceptions to transparency

Article 7

Confidential or protected information

1. Confidential or protected information, as defined in paragraph 2 and as identified pursuant to the arrangements referred to in paragraphs 3 and 4, shall not be made available to the public pursuant to articles 2 to 6.

2. Confidential or protected information consists of:

(a) Confidential business information;

(b) Information that is protected against being made available to the public under the treaty;

(c) Information that is protected against being made available to the public, in the case of the information of the respondent State, under the law of the respondent State, and in the case of other information, under any law or rules determined by the arbitral tribunal to be applicable to the disclosure of such information; or

(d) Information the disclosure of which would impede law enforcement.

3. The arbitral tribunal, after consultation with the disputing parties, shall make arrangements to prevent any confidential or protected information from being made available to the public, including by putting in place, as appropriate:

(a) Time limits in which a disputing party, non-disputing Party to the treaty or third person shall give notice that it seeks protection for such information in documents;

(b) Procedures for the prompt designation and redaction of the particular confidential or protected information in such documents; and

(c) Procedures for holding hearings in private to the extent required by article 6, paragraph 2. Any determination as to whether information is confidential or protected shall be made by the arbitral tribunal after consultation with the disputing parties.

4. Where the arbitral tribunal determines that information should not be redacted from a document, or that a document should not be prevented from being made available to the public, any disputing party, non-disputing Party to the treaty or third person that voluntarily introduced the document into the record shall be permitted to withdraw all or part of the document from the record of the arbitral proceedings.

5. Nothing in these Rules requires a respondent State to make available to the public information the disclosure of which it considers to be contrary to its essential security interests.

Integrity of the arbitral process

6. Information shall not be made available to the public pursuant to articles 2 to 6 where the information, if made available to the public, would jeopardize the integrity of the arbitral process as determined pursuant to paragraph 7.

7. The arbitral tribunal may, on its own initiative or upon the application of a disputing party, after consultation with the disputing parties where practicable, take appropriate measures to restrain or delay the publication of information where such publication would jeopardize the integrity of the arbitral process because it could hamper the collection or production of evidence, lead to the intimidation of witnesses, lawyers acting for disputing parties or members of the arbitral tribunal, or in comparably exceptional circumstances.

A. Overview

1. Article 7 defines the exceptions to the Transparency Rules, which are limited to the protection of (i) confidential or protected information ('confidential information'; see article 7(1)-(5)) and (ii) the integrity of the arbitral process (article 7(6)-(7)).[1] The tribunal decides on a case-by-case basis whether information falls under either of these exceptions 'based on the nature of the information and the applicable law' to which law the relevant provisions expressly refer.[2]

1 *See* UNCITRAL Report of 54th Session, 25 February 2011, UN Doc A/CN.9/717, paras 129-147; UNCITRAL Report of 55th Session, 17 October 2011, UN Doc A/CN.9/736, paras 110-130; UNCITRAL Report of 57th Session, 12 October 2012, UN Doc A/CN.9/760, paras 89-119; UNCITRAL Working Paper for 58th Session, 30 November 2012, UN Doc A/CN.9/WG.II/WP.176/Add.1, para. 2; UNCITRAL Working Paper for 56th Session, 13 December 2011, UN Doc A/CN.9/WG.II/WP.169, para. 46; UNCITRAL Working Paper for 55th Session, 29 July 2011, UN Doc A/CN.9/WG.II/WP.166/Add.1, para. 2.

2 Lise Johnson & Nathalie Bernasconi-Osterwalder, *New UNCITRAL Arbitration Rules on Transparency: Application, Content and Next Steps*, 22 (CIEL, IISD, CCSI, August 2013), <http://ccsi.columbia.edu>.

2. Article 7(1) establishes that confidential information will not be disclosed to the public pursuant to articles 2[3] to 6 of the Transparency Rules.[4] Where the tribunal decides that certain information must be protected, all parties involved in the proceedings, and the repository, are obligated to keep the information confidential.[5]

3. Article 7(2) defines confidential information, listing four 'potentially overlapping' categories.[6] Pursuant to article 7(2)(c), the respondent State's laws govern the question whether information submitted by that State is protected from disclosure.[7] The substantive-law question as to the confidentiality of all 'other information' referred to in article 7(2)(c) – e.g., information provided by the claimant, a non-disputing Party, or a third party – is otherwise left open, allowing the tribunal to determine which law applies to this question.[8]

4. Article 7(3) clarifies that any determination as to the confidential nature of information is to be made by the tribunal after consulting (or hearing) the parties. Article 7(3)(a)-(c) provides guidance to the tribunal regarding arrangements for the protection of confidential information.

5. Article 7(4) allows any party to withdraw voluntarily-submitted documents from the record if the tribunal determines that no redactions should be made or that the document as a whole should be disclosed. This provision applies only to documents submitted voluntarily and does not apply to documents that the tribunal has compelled a party to produce.[9] It leaves open the possibility, however,

---

3 *See* the applicability of article 7 to article 2 in discussion of article 2 of the Transparency Rules, *supra*.

4 Jan H. Nedden & Friedrich Rosenfeld, 'The new UNCITRAL Transparency Rules: How the trend towards transparency differs in investment and commercial arbitration' in Christoph Muller & Antonio Rigozzi (eds), *New Developments in International Commercial Arbitration 2013*, 41, 48 (2013).

5 *See* Thierry P. Augsburger, 'Article 7. Exceptions to transparency' in Dimitrij Euler, Markus Gehring & Maxi Scherer (eds), *Transparency in International Investment Arbitration: A Guide to the UNCITRAL Rules on Transparency in Treaty-Based Investor-State Arbitration*, 264 (Cambridge University Press 2015).

6 Johnson & Bernasconi-Osterwalder, *supra* fn 2, at 22; Nedden & Rosenfeld, *supra* fn 4, at 48, fn 22.

7 UNCITRAL Working Paper for 56th Session, 13 December 2011, UN Doc A/CN.9/WG.II/WP.169, para. 49. *See also* Johnson & Bernasconi-Osterwalder, *supra* fn 2, at 22.

8 Augsburger, *supra* fn 5, at 268: 'Article 7(2)(c) thus directs the arbitral tribunal to apply two different standards when evaluating the law applicable to exceptions to transparency. If the information was provided by the respondent State, the arbitral tribunal must apply the law of that State. If, on the other hand, the information was provided by any other party, e.g., the claimant, a non-disputing Party to the treaty or a third party, the arbitral tribunal has the discretion to determine which law is applicable to the exception'. *See also* Johnson & Bernasconi-Osterwalder, *supra* fn 2, at 22; Julia Salasky & Corinne Montineri, *UNCITRAL Rules on Transparency in Treaty-Based Investor-State Arbitration*, 31(4) ASA Bulletin 774, 793 (2013) (noting that article 7(2)(c) 'was the subject of heavy debate' during the drafting process).

9 UNCITRAL Report of 57th Session, 12 October 2012, UN Doc A/CN.9/760, para. 113.

of a party's withdrawing 'a self-determined confidential part of the document', with the resultant effect of distorting the meaning of the document as a whole.[10]

6. Article 7(5) provides the disputing State Party with 'a self-judging exception' to prevent disclosure that it considers contrary to its essential security interests.[11]

7. Article 7(6) establishes that information 'which would jeopardize the integrity of the arbitral process' will not be made available to the public.[12] Article 7(7) permits the tribunal to 'restrain or delay' mandatory publication of such information; it does not necessarily permanently bar disclosure.[13] Furthermore, the Working Group acknowledged that a tribunal 'already enjoyed wide discretionary power' under article 15 of the 1976 Arbitration Rules or article 17 of the 2010 Arbitration Rules, which allow it to conduct the arbitral proceedings in a manner that preserves their integrity.[14] However, the converse is not true: article 7 does not affect the UNCITRAL Arbitration Rules, as it pertains solely to the implementation of the Transparency Rules.[15]

B. Exceptions are narrowly defined

8. In order to balance the disclosure provisions in the Transparency Rules and the compromise reached as to their scope of application (article 1), there was consensus for a regime of exceptions.[16] The general principle guiding the crafting of these exceptions was that they should be tightly defined in order to address concerns relating to confidential information and the integrity of the arbitral process without weakening the objectives of increased transparency.[17]

---

10 UNCITRAL Report of 57th Session, 12 October 2012, UN Doc A/CN.9/760, para. 115.

11 *Ibid.*, at para. 106; UNCITRAL Working Paper for 58th Session, 30 November 2012, UN Doc A/CN.9/WG.II/WP.176/Add.1, para. 6.

12 *See* UNCITRAL Report of 53rd Session, 20 October 2010, UN Doc A/CN.9/712, para. 72; UNCITRAL Report of 57th Session, 12 October 2012, UN Doc A/CN.9/760, paras 118-119; UNCITRAL Working Paper for 58th Session, 30 November 2012, UN Doc A/CN.9/WG.II/WP.176/Add.1, paras 7-8.

13 Johnson & Bernasconi-Osterwalder, *supra* fn 2, at 23.

14 UNCITRAL Report of 54th Session, 25 February 2011, UN Doc A/CN.9/717, para. 142; UNCITRAL Report of 53rd Session, 20 October 2010, UN Doc A/CN.9/712, para. 72. *See* UNCITRAL Working Paper for 55th Session, 29 July 2011, UN Doc A/CN.9/WG.II/WP.166/Add.1, paras 6-7.

15 UNCITRAL Working Paper for 56th Session, 13 December 2011, UN Doc A/CN.9/WG.II/WP.169/Add.1, para. 30.

16 Johnson & Bernasconi-Osterwalder, *supra* fn 2, at 22.

17 UNCITRAL Report of 54th Session, 25 February 2011, UN Doc A/CN.9/717, para. 137. *See also* UNCITRAL Report of 53rd Session, 20 October 2010, UN Doc A/CN.9/712, para. 70: 'General comments were made to the effect that while exceptions for reasons of protecting confidential or sensitive information were necessary, they should not be so wide as to weaken the main rules on transparency. It was also suggested that exceptions to transparency to protect confidential or sensitive information should provide clarity and guidance, in order to avoid disputes between the parties on that matter'.

C. Definition, scope and categorisation of confidential information

9. The definition of 'confidential or protected information' was extensively debated.[18] These terms were preferred to the term 'privileged information', as it was felt that the latter 'might not be understood in the same manner in all jurisdictions'.[19] Moreover, the express reference in article 7(1) to the concept defined in article 7(2) clarifies that the tribunal cannot 'define additional circumstances under which an exception shall be granted'.[20]

10. It was suggested that the term 'confidential business information' in article 7(2)(a) be defined in greater detail, although there was no support for incorporating a list of possible categories into this provision.[21] This is consistent with the Working Group's decision that the 'carve outs' for confidential information should avoid 'the need to envisage all possible circumstances, but rather [leave] a large degree of discretion to the arbitral tribunal'.[22] Although the tribunal will have to base its determinations on the facts of each particular case, these may be informed by the sub-categories of 'confidential business information' accepted by tribunals in the context of NAFTA disputes.[23] These include:

- trade secrets;
- financial, commercial, scientific or technical information that is treated consistently in a confidential manner by the disputing party or third party to which it relates, including pricing and costing information, marketing and strategic planning documents, market share data, or detailed accounting or financial records not otherwise disclosed in the public domain;
- information the disclosure of which could result in financial loss or gain to the disputing party or third party to which it relates;
- information the disclosure of which could interfere with contractual or other negotiations of the disputing party or third party to which it relates; and
- other communications treated as confidential in furtherance of settlement between the disputing parties.[24]

11. Article 7(2)(b) provides that any information protected from publication by the underlying treaty qualifies as confidential information and shall not be disclosed

---

18 Nedden & Rosenfeld, *supra* fn 4, at 48, fn 22. *See also* UNCITRAL Working Paper for 58th Session, 30 November 2012, UN Doc A/CN.9/WG.II/WP.176/Add.1, paras 4-6; Salasky & Montineri, *supra* fn 8, at 792-793 (noting that the definition of 'confidential or protected information' was inspired by definitions in existing investment treaties and investment treaty frameworks, and 'was the subject of much debate in the Working Group').

19 UNCITRAL Report of 54th Session, 25 February 2011, UN Doc A/CN.9/717, para. 132.

20 *See* Augsburger, *supra* fn 5, at 263; Salasky & Montineri, *supra* fn 8, at 793.

21 UNCITRAL Report of 55th Session, 17 October 2011, UN Doc A/CN.9/736, para. 125.

22 UNCITRAL Report of 53rd Session, 20 October 2010, UN Doc A/CN.9/712, para. 67.

23 *See* Augsburger, *supra* fn 5, at 265-266.

24 *Ibid.*, citing to *William Ralph Clayton, William Richard Clayton, Douglas Clayton, Daniel Clayton and Bilcon of Delaware Inc v. Government of Canada* (UNCITRAL), PCA Case No. 2009-04, Procedural Order No. 2 (Confidentiality Order), 4 May 2009, < www.italaw.com >; and *Mercer International Inc v. Government of Canada* (ICSID Case No. ARB(AF)/12/3) Confidentiality Order, 24 January 2013, < www.italaw.com >.

to the public. This provision is consistent with article 1(7), which states that the provisions of the underlying treaty shall prevail over the Transparency Rules in case of a conflict.[25]

12. Article 7(2)(c), as further discussed below, provides that information protected under the law of the respondent State, or the law otherwise applicable (in respect of 'other information' not provided by the respondent State), shall not be made available to the public.

13. Article 7(2)(d) provides that 'information the disclosure of which would impede law enforcement' shall not be disclosed. The *travaux préparatoires* provide little insight as to the specific concerns or fact-patterns that this exception, which was included at a late stage of the drafting process,[26] addresses. The broad rationale is fairly obvious, and in an investment-treaty context it may well find application in cases of fraud in the establishment or performance of an investment. One notes, however, the proliferation of criminal prosecutions to deter or oppress claimant investors, as may be seen in a series of recent decisions enjoining such reactions by States. There is therefore a risk that a State will suppress the relevant information invoking the very instrument that it is claimed to have abused – law enforcement. One commentator suggests that 'law enforcement' 'relates to institutions, principles, operations and arrangements with the duty to enforce the application of the laws of a State and engage with the pursuit and prosecution of crime'.[27]

14. In terms of scope, articles 7(1)-(5) of the Transparency Rules are not restricted to documents submitted by the disputing parties: rather, they are intended to apply to all documents, including documents submitted by third parties and non-disputing Parties as well as documents issued by the tribunal or any tribunal-appointed experts.[28]

15. The tribunal has discretion to decide how the parties should proceed when categorising information as confidential for the purposes of article 7.[29] Designations are subject to review by the tribunal, either on a request by a disputing party or, crucially, at the tribunal's own initiative. The ability of the tribunal to review designations of its own motion was included in the Transparency Rules in response to the concern that the disputing parties may otherwise circumvent

[25] *See* article 1(7) of the Transparency Rules. *See also* Augsburger, *supra* fn 5, at 267 and the references (setting out a range of contexts in which information may be protected under a treaty, for example, in respect of national security or public interest issues).

[26] *See* Augsburger, *supra* fn 5, at 273. Note that the Working Group intended article 7(2)(d) to act UNCITRAL Report of 57th Session, 12 October 2012, UN Doc A/CN.9/760, paras 106-109.

[27] Augsburger, *supra* fn 5, at 274-275.

[28] *See* UNCITRAL Report of 55th Session, 17 October 2011, UN Doc A/CN.9/736, para. 129.

[29] Johnson & Bernasconi-Osterwalder, *supra* fn 2, at 22; Salasky & Montineri, *supra* fn 8, at 793.

article 7 through express or implied agreement (e.g., to redact or withhold information that the tribunal would regard as non-confidential).[30]

16. Though suggested during the drafting process, there is no provision allowing a party to challenge the classification of a document as confidential information in light of a change in circumstances.[31] It was argued that such a mechanism would create uncertainty.[32] It is not clear from the *travaux*, however, that a classification is made once and for all, nor is there any intrinsic reason why it should be so. Article 7(3)-(4) appears to be drafted in terms which allow a re-classification in such unusual circumstances.

D. Law applicable to confidentiality of information[33]

17. Under article 7(2)(c), information of the respondent State that is considered confidential under that State's national law is protected from disclosure.[34] A number of delegations suggested that this self-referential provision could be easily abused by introducing legislation and would dilute the objectives of the Transparency Rules.[35] It was further pointed out that the respondent State would in any event be bound by its own laws and that, in this regard, there should be consistency between the Transparency Rules and domestic laws.[36] The Working Group unanimously agreed that a State may not be permitted to adopt the Transparency Rules and subsequently use domestic legislation to evade or

---

30 UNCITRAL Report of 55th Session, 17 October 2011, UN Doc A/CN.9/736, para. 129 (where the Working Group stated that 'the arbitral tribunal should be entitled to oversee the process of redaction … in order to avoid that parties through implied or express agreement on confidentiality, defeated the whole purpose of the transparency rules'). The final formulation of article 7 of the Transparency Rules therefore does not permit the parties to agree to withhold non-confidential information; a draft provision permitting the disputing parties to do so in cases where the information constituted a breach of the public interest was deleted. *See* UNCITRAL Report of 58th Session, 13 February 2013, UN Doc A/CN.9/765, paras 63-64.

31 UNCITRAL Report of 55th Session, 17 October 2011, UN Doc A/CN.9/736, para. 130. Cf. article 19(3) of the Norwegian Draft Model BIT 2007 (withdrawn), which provided for the arbitral tribunal to decide on designations of information as confidential where the other party objected thereto. *See also* Augsburger, *supra* fn 5, at 255.

32 UNCITRAL Report of 55th Session, 17 October 2011, UN Doc A/CN.9/736, para. 130.

33 Even by a late stage of the drafting process, there remained three options for this provision as follows: '(i) … the tribunal is given discretion to conduct a conflict of law analysis for all information; (ii) … the tribunal is directed to the law of the respondent for the respondent's information, and a conflict of law analysis for all other information; and (iii) … the tribunal is given guidance for its conflict of law analysis that on issues of respondent information, it should take respondent law particularly into account'. *See* UNCITRAL Working Paper for 58th Session, 30 November 2012, UN Doc A/CN.9/WG.II/WP.176/Add.1, para. 4.

34 UNCITRAL Report of 58th Session, 13 February 2013, UN Doc A/CN.9/765, para. 61.

35 UNCITRAL Report of 57th Session, 12 October 2012, UN Doc A/CN.9/760, para. 103.

36 UNCITRAL Report of 58th Session, 13 February 2013, UN Doc A/CN.9/765, para. 61. *See* UNCITRAL Report of 55th Session, 17 October 2011, UN Doc A/CN.9/736, para. 127.

undermine them.[37] Article 1(6) of the Transparency Rules specifically addresses and frustrates such behaviour.[38]

18. A proposal was also put forward to remove the reference in article 7(2)(c) to the law of the respondent State, which was viewed as infringing on the tribunal's discretion to determine the applicable law.[39] In response, however, delegations argued that this would not provide 'sufficient guidance, in particular to a respondent, as to whether decisions of the arbitral tribunal might put it in breach of its own law'.[40] As recognized by the Working Group, the final provision is therefore a product of compromise; it protects the regime of the Transparency Rules 'whilst giving comfort to States that confidential and protected information (of all parties to a dispute) will be adequately safeguarded thereunder'.[41] Whereas the law of the respondent State is mandatorily applied to determinations of the confidentiality of information emanating from that State, the tribunal has discretion to determine the applicable law in respect of all 'other information'.[42]

E. Arrangements to prevent disclosure of confidential information

19. Article 7(3) deals with the logistical measures a tribunal may take in order to prevent the disclosure of confidential information. As an initial step, the tribunal is required to consult with the disputing parties,[43] after which it may implement, for example, the time-limits or procedures outlined in articles 7(3)(a)-(c). The inevitable costs consequences of any such procedures were considered by the Working Group to form 'a necessary part of implementing transparency proceedings' in furtherance of its mandate.[44]

20. The wording preceding the examples listed in article 7 – '*including* by putting in place, *as appropriate*' (emphasis added) – demonstrates the tribunal's latitude in determining the arrangements necessary to protect confidential information. As such, the examples provided should be considered 'neither exhaustive nor mandatory', the tribunal being 'free to adapt them or replace them' as

37 UNCITRAL Report of 58th Session, 13 February 2013, UN Doc A/CN.9/765, para. 62; UNCITRAL Report of 57th Session, 12 October 2012, UN Doc A/CN.9/760, para. 103.

38 However, such behaviour is only addressed to the extent that the national law in question does not constitute 'a provision of the law applicable to the arbitration from which the disputing parties cannot derogate' pursuant to article 1(8) of the Transparency Rules. *See supra*, fn 35.

39 UNCITRAL Report of 57th Session, 12 October 2012, UN Doc A/CN.9/760, para. 102.

40 *Ibid.*

41 Salasky & Montineri, *supra* fn 8, at 793; *see also* UNCITRAL Report of 57th Session, 12 October 2012, UN Doc A/CN.9/760, para. 102.

42 UNCITRAL Report of 57th Session, 12 October 2012, UN Doc A/CN.9/760, para. 102.

43 *See* Augsburger, *supra* fn 5, at 275 (noting that '[o]ther possible parties to the arbitration, such as non-disputing parties to the treaty or third parties, are not part of the consultation process. This includes, for example, that they have neither any veto right, nor any right to be heard when it comes to the arrangements made').

44 *See* UNCITRAL Report of 57th Session, 12 October 2012, UN Doc A/CN.9/760, para. 128; Salasky & Montineri, *supra* fn 8, at 791.

appropriate.[45] This is in line with a suggestion advocating 'a more flexible and simplified drafting approach' which would permit the tribunal to adopt suitable procedures in accordance with the specific facts of the case.[46]

21. Article 7(3) further provides that, after consulting with the disputing parties, the arbitral tribunal is responsible for deciding 'whether information is confidential or protected'.[47] This provision clarifies that determinations as to the existence of confidential information under article 7(2) are to be made by the tribunal; in so doing, article 7(3) 'explicitly elevates the arbitral tribunal to the sole decision maker'.[48] Accordingly, the disputing parties must defer to the authority of the tribunal for such decisions (theoretically, even where they agree as to the coverage of a document under article 7(2) or as to appropriate measures).[49]

F. Withdrawal of documents from the record

22. Article 7(4) provides any party to the arbitration with the opportunity to remove all or part of a document from the record where (i) that party has 'voluntarily introduced the document' in question, and (ii) the tribunal has concluded that the information contained therein is not covered by article 7(2). Initially, the Working Group did not distinguish between information volunteered by a party and information produced pursuant to an order by the arbitral tribunal.[50] However, it was subsequently agreed that the scope of application of article 7(4) was limited to volunteered information, in order to avoid the situation 'whereby a party compelled to produce a document by the arbitral tribunal could subsequently withdraw that document on grounds of confidentiality',[51] thereby frustrating disclosure.

23. There is an important trade-off to be considered when a party withdraws a document pursuant to article 7(4). Withdrawal from the record means that the material cannot be relied upon – indeed, it has to be regarded as never having

45 Augsburger, *supra* fn 5, at 277; *see also* Laurence Boisson De Chazournes & Rukia Baruti Dames, *Transparency in Investor-State Arbitration: An Incremental Approach*, 2(1) BCDR International Arbitration Review 59, 70-71 (2015).

46 UNCITRAL Report of 57th Session, 12 October 2012, UN Doc A/CN.9/760, para. 92.

47 *See* article 7(3) of the Transparency Rules; Salasky & Montineri, *supra* fn 8, at 793.

48 Augsburger, *supra* fn 5, at 283 (noting that, in this sense, article 7(3) of the Transparency Rules is 'highly unusual' as it may require a tribunal, having determined that a certain document does not constitute confidential information, to circumvent the disputing parties' contrary agreement on this point and order its disclosure. The question as to how well this prospect sits with the fundamental principle of party autonomy may lead to uncomfortableness on the part of the tribunal ; *see ibid.*, at 283-284).

49 *Ibid.*, at 284.

50 UNCITRAL Report of 55th Session, 17 October 2011, UN Doc A/CN.9/736, para. 129; UNCITRAL Working Paper for 56th Session, 13 December 2011, UN Doc A/CN.9/WG.II/WP.169, para. 45. *See also* Augsburger, *supra* fn 5, at 285 (noting that '[t]his solution is, basically, the one retained in Article 10.21 CAFTA-DR and Article 29 of the US Model BIT 2012').

51 UNCITRAL Report of 57th Session, 12 October 2012, UN Doc A/CN.9/760, para. 113.

been relied upon, and prior pleadings may have to be redacted/reformulated accordingly.

24. It stands to reason also that other parties to the arbitration must refrain from reintroducing the same information in their own submissions, which would otherwise negate article 7(4). Nevertheless, the *Philip Morris* tribunal has reached the opposite conclusion, apparently considering that the other side may effectively recharacterize a de-characterized document unilaterally and reintroduce it into the record.[52]

G. Self-judging security exception for respondent State

25. Security interests were of 'sufficiently critical' concern for some State delegations to be regarded by the Working Group as warranting a specific carve-out in article 7(5). This is exceptional in three respects: first, it is self-enforced in that it provides an absolute bar to any disclosure: '[n]othing in these Rules requires a respondent State to make available to the public information ...'; secondly, it is stated as self-judging: 'information the disclosure of which it considers to be contrary to its essential security interests'; thirdly, such information does not come within the ambit of 'confidential or protected information' under article 7(1)-(6) but rather attracts separate protection. These features attracted criticism by a number of delegations, on grounds that they leave room for abuse.[53] That is doubtless true on the face of the text, though there is authority for the proposition that 'essential security interests'[54] comprise very few, fundamental interests, as well as for the proposition that the doctrine of good faith excludes the possibility of there being any purely self-judging entitlement.[55]

26. These delicate issues need not be considered at any length here. Experience shows that article 7(5) is likely to be invoked in practice extremely rarely. In

---

52 *See* Augsburger, *supra* fn 5, at 286-287, citing to *Philip Morris Asia Limited v. The Commonwealth of Australia* (UNCITRAL) PCA Case No. 2012-12, Procedural Order No. 5 Regarding Confidentiality, 30 November 2012, <www.italaw.com>, para. 53(B)(5)(f); cf. *Biwater Gauff (Tanzania) Ltd v. United Republic of Tanzania* (ICSID Case No. ARB/05/22) Procedural Order No. 3, 29 September 2006, <www.italaw.com>, para. 158. *See also* Article 10.21(4)(d) of the 2004 Dominican Republic-Central America Free Trade Agreement (providing that where a disputing party withdraws all or part of its submission, or submits redacted documents, 'the other disputing party shall ... resubmit complete and redacted documents which either remove the information withdrawn ... by the disputing party that first submitted the information or redesignate the information consistent with the designation ... of the disputing party that first submitted the information').

53 UNCITRAL Report of 58th Session, 13 February 2013, UN Doc A/CN.9/765, paras 65-66.

54 The phraseology is used in a number of WTO texts, US FCN treaties and BITs, including the US-Argentina BIT, Article XI of which was invoked by Argentina in the *CMS v. Argentina* case. *See* further William J. Moon, *Essential Security Interests in International Investment Agreements*, 15(2) Journal of International Economic Law 481 (2012); and UNCTAD, *Investor-State Dispute Settlement: UNCTAD Series on Issues in International Investment Agreements II*, 44-46 (United Nations 2014).

55 *See*, e.g., Augsburger, *supra* fn 5, at 288-289 and the references.

the first place, highly-classified and still-sensitive materials very rarely feature in investment-treaty cases. In the second place, States are generally loath to place such materials into the record even when ordered to produce them (which is also a rarity). Thus article 7(5) may find application in cases whose subject-matter directly implicates State security (e.g. a classified military system or facility) or where the respondent State seeks to justify its conduct as necessary for national security (e.g. expelling individuals engaged in espionage and seizing their property). Of necessity, in such cases the evidential record will centrally feature materials involving national security. Where a tribunal perceives abuse in a State's characterization of such materials under article 7(5), the remedy available is to be found in article 1(6). It may be that a reasonable course of action for the tribunal would be to review a State's classification and invite it to de-characterize the document or portions thereof (redacting portions that were properly characterized). It will be difficult for a tribunal to go further, for article 7(5) states in unqualified terms that 'nothing in these Rules requires a respondent State' to heed to the tribunal: *nothing* includes article 1(6). A tribunal would therefore have to find authority outside the Transparency Rules to force disclosure. It would be an extreme case where the tribunal would find that necessary or prudent.

27. We note for completeness that the scope of the article 7(5) exception was at one point broader, including information that would impede law enforcement or whose divulgation was contrary to the public interest.[56] Ultimately, however, article 7(5) was whittled down to include only essential security interests, responding to fears that, especially in the aggregate, such broad notions could take on practically any meaning a State might choose to ascribe them.[57]

H. Scope of the 'integrity of the arbitral process' exception[58]

28. The 'integrity of the arbitral process' exception is a narrow category, intended to prevent or delay disclosure only under the exceptional circumstances listed in article 7(7).[59] The scope of this exception was debated in the Working Group, with concerns expressed that it should not be overly broad or vague, in order to avoid 'inappropriately limit[ing] transparency'.[60] Indeed, 'language referring to

---

56 *See* UNCITRAL Working Paper for 58th Session, 30 November 2012, UN Doc A/CN.9/WG.II/WP.176/Add.1, para. 1. Note that an exception for 'information the disclosure of which would impede law enforcement' was retained in the Transparency Rules as article 7(2)(d); however, the provision is subject to the tribunal's discretion, whereas 'essential security interests' was retained as a self-judging exception for respondent States.

57 UNCITRAL Report of 57th Session, 12 October 2012, UN Doc A/CN.9/760, para. 106.

58 *See* UNCITRAL Report of 53rd Session, 20 October 2010, UN Doc A/CN.9/712, para. 72; UNCITRAL Working Paper for 55th Session, 29 July 2011, UN Doc A/CN.9/WG.II/WP.166/Add.1, para. 6.

59 Johnson & Bernasconi-Osterwalder, *supra* fn 2, at 23. *See also* Augsburger, *supra* fn 5, at 290 et seq. (citing to pre-Transparency Rules case-law examples in which the arbitral tribunal imposed restrictions on the dissemination of information).

60 UNCITRAL Report of 54th Session, 25 February 2011, UN Doc A/CN.9/717, para. 139.

"the risk of aggravation of the dispute" or "rendering the resolution of the dispute difficult or impossible"' was viewed as too expansive, and thus rejected.[61] The final text makes it plain that the 'integrity of the arbitral process' and the likely 'jeopard[y]' to it are notions that are fairly tightly-defined: article 7(6) expressly requires that the necessary determinations be made pursuant to article 7(7). The latter provision, in turn, spells out serious risks pertaining to evidence, intimidation, and 'comparably exceptional circumstances'.[62] It is clear that the *ejusdem generis* rule applies.

29. Articles 7(6) and 7(7) do not appear to encompass broader issues of due process or disturbance of hearings, which were understood by some of the delegations to fall outside the scope of this category of protection.[63] The examples provided in article 7(7) are specific, and the non-inclusion of other circumstances considered by the Working Group – such as the general politicisation of the proceedings, manipulation by the mass media and the disruption of hearings[64] – indicates that these would be unlikely to come within the article 7(7) exception except if they rise to the highest intensity.

I. No sanctions for breach of confidentiality obligations

30. The Working Group briefly discussed the issue of sanctions to address breaches of the confidentiality obligations contained in article 7 (e.g. instances where protected information is disclosed in contravention of the Transparency Rules).[65] One possible sanction discussed related to costs, drawing on the example of Article 9.7 of the 2010 IBA Rules on the Taking of Evidence in International Arbitration.[66] There was considered to be a risk, however, that disputing State Parties would invoke State immunity as a defence to such sanctions.[67]

---

61 UNCITRAL Report of 54th Session, 25 February 2011, UN Doc A/CN.9/717, para. 139.

62 *See ibid.*, at paras 138-139. This reflects the view that a high threshold should be set in respect of any exceptions to the Transparency Rules for the protection of the integrity of the arbitral process; *see* UNCITRAL Report of 55th Session, 17 October 2011, UN Doc A/CN.9/736, para. 114 (providing that publication restrictions would only be acceptable under articles 7(6) and 7(7) 'in circumstances that met the threshold of exceptional circumstances'). *See also* Johnson & Bernasconi-Osterwalder, *supra* fn 2, at 23 (noting that 'the Working Group was unable to agree on any other circumstances that would serve as an example of a "comparably exceptional" case warranting a restriction on transparency under the "integrity of the process" exception'); Augsburger, *supra* fn 5, at 295-297.

63 UNCITRAL Report of 54th Session, 25 February 2011, UN Doc A/CN.9/717, para. 140.

64 *Ibid.*, at para. 138.

65 UNCITRAL Report of 53rd Session, 20 October 2010, UN Doc A/CN.9/712, para. 71.

66 *See ibid.* Article 9.7 of the IBA Rules on the Taking of Evidence in International Arbitration states: 'If the Arbitral Tribunal determines that a Party has failed to conduct itself in good faith in the taking of evidence, the Arbitral Tribunal may, in addition to any other measures available under these Rules, take such failure into account in its assignment of the costs of the arbitration, including costs arising out of or in connection with the taking of evidence'.

67 UNCITRAL Report of 53rd Session, 20 October 2010, UN Doc A/CN.9/712, para. 71.

Article 8
Repository of published information

Article 8

The repository of published information under the Rules on Transparency shall be the Secretary-General of the United Nations or an institution named by UNCITRAL.

A. Overview

1. Article 8 provides for the establishment of a repository of published information ('repository'), which will be the Secretary-General of the United Nations or an institution named by UNCITRAL.[1] The repository receives documents from the parties or the tribunal pursuant to articles 2 and 3(4) and is obliged to promptly make them available to the public.[2] Although the repository communicates predominantly with the tribunal (article 3), it also accepts information directly from the parties before the tribunal has been constituted (article 2).[3]

---

1 *See* UNCITRAL Working Paper for 56th Session, 13 December 2011, UN Doc A/CN.9/WG.II/WP.169/Add.1, paras 31 and 33 (noting that article 8 of the Transparency Rules does not affect the Arbitration Rules, as its sole purpose is 'to deal with the means of publication'). *See also* UNCITRAL Working Paper for 58th Session, 30 November 2012, UN Doc A/CN.9/WG.II/WP.176/Add.1, para. 10; UNCITRAL Report of 54th Session, 25 February 2011, UN Doc A/CN.9/717, para. 150; and UNCITRAL Note by the Secretariat, 13 December 2012, UN Doc A/CN.9/WG.II/WP.177, para. 2. The UNCITRAL repository is known as the Transparency Registry, and is available at: <www.uncitral.org/transparency-registry>.

2 *See* Jan H. Nedden & Friedrich Rosenfeld, 'The new UNCITRAL Transparency Rules: How the trend towards transparency differs in investment and commercial arbitration' in Christoph Muller & Antonio Rigozzi (eds), *New Developments in International Commercial Arbitration 2013*, 41, 43 (2013).

3 *See* article 2 of the Transparency Rules; and UNCITRAL Working Paper for 56th Session, 13 December 2011, UN Doc A/CN.9/WG.II/WP.169/Add.1, para. 31.

2. Article 3(4) of the Transparency Rules provides that documents are to be made available to the public 'in a timely manner, in the form and in the language in which [the repository] receives them'.[4] This is in line with the view that providing translation would only be feasible for an international repository system 'in very limited contexts' – for example, in respect of the title of the treaty upon which the claim is based.[5]

3. An effective repository, assuming the Transparency Rules are widely used in coming years, will likely establish a structured body of international investment arbitration jurisprudence, allowing parties to consult an increasing number of tribunal decisions when preparing their arguments. According to one commentator, this may contribute to 'the increasing consistency in decision-making that has become a systemic value and has been heralded as enhancing the system's legitimacy both within the profession and towards the public at large'.[6] In any event, the repository will be especially useful as UNCITRAL cases have typically been made public only after their issuance by one of the disputing parties, or where parties have agreed in advance to make the award public. Successful use of the repository would therefore replace the scattered methods of information collection currently in place.[7]

B. Form of the repository

4. The delegations examined two options with respect to the form of the repository: (i) a single entity to undertake all functions, and (ii) a system in which arbitral institutions would maintain their own registries.[8] A third option analogous to the procedure for designating an appointing authority was briefly examined, pursuant to which the disputing parties would choose a repository and, if they could not agree, an institution would designate the repository.[9]

---

4 *See* article 3(4) of the Transparency Rules.

5 UNCITRAL Note by the Secretariat, 13 December 2012, UN Doc A/CN.9/WG.II/WP.177, para. 16.

6 Kathleen Claussen, 'Article 8: Repository of published information' in Dimitrij Euler, Markus Gehring & Maxi Scherer (eds), *Transparency in International Investment Arbitration: A Guide to the UNCITRAL Rules on Transparency in Treaty-Based Investor-State Arbitration*, 308 (Cambridge University Press 2015).

7 For a more detailed discussion of the databases collecting decisions in an ad hoc manner, *see ibid.*, at 309-311.

8 UNCITRAL Report of 58th Session, 13 February 2013, UN Doc A/CN.9/765, para. 81. *See also* UNCITRAL Note by the Secretariat, 13 December 2012, UN Doc A/CN.9/WG.II/WP.177, paras 4-5 (noting that the second option had two variants (the complexity of which likely served as a further incentive to opt for the first option of a single repository): (i) all institutions would operate under 'a common umbrella website with a single interface for external users'; or (ii) each institution would maintain its own repository system, with one institution hosting a website with links to each of the other institutions' repository websites where documents from arbitral proceedings would be published).

9 UNCITRAL Report of 55th Session, 17 October 2011, UN Doc A/CN.9/736, para. 132. *See* UNCITRAL Working Paper for 56th Session, 13 December 2011, UN Doc A/CN.9/WG.II/WP.169/Add.1, para. 32.

5. Ultimately, the delegations opted for a single repository.[10] This choice appears to have been driven by (i) technical considerations, (ii) cost considerations and (iii) the effects on transparency. From a technical perspective, a single repository was the most attractive option because only one system would need to be created; a single set of technical guidelines could be easily implemented and maintained; there would be no need for technical integration between multiple registries; and it could easily facilitate a uniform standard for document searches.[11] It was considered that these factors would also lead to greater cost-efficiency in comparison to a multiple-registry system.[12] In terms of transparency, a single, uniform system with 'free text search functionality and filtering function' would make it easy for the public to locate documents of interest, thus maintaining a higher level of transparency than a system of multiple repositories, which would be more time-consuming and onerous to search.[13]

C. UN Secretary-General as preferred repository

6. It was noted that the UNCITRAL Arbitration Rules and Transparency Rules are United Nations instruments and that it would thus be logical for the UN Secretariat to provide the repository services.[14] Accordingly, the final version of the Transparency Rules identifies the UN Secretary-General as the repository, giving UNCITRAL the authority to select an alternative institution.

7. Only late in the negotiations was it unanimously agreed that the best institution to serve as the repository was UNCITRAL itself,[15] should it have the capacity to do so by 1 April 2014, the date of entry into force of the Transparency Rules.[16]

---

[10] UNCITRAL Report of 58th Session, 13 February 2013, UN Doc A/CN.9/765, para. 83: The delegations expressed a strong preference that the repository be a single institution.

[11] UNCITRAL Note by the Secretariat, 13 December 2012, UN Doc A/CN.9/WG.II/WP.177, paras 6-7 and 13.

[12] *See ibid.*, at para. 9 (noting that, 'apart from the PCA and ICSID ... other arbitral institutions do not have the requisite technical systems or servers in place, and ... start-up costs in addition to maintenance and staffing costs ... could be disproportionately high should an institution receive only a fraction of the global case load per year'). *See also* UNCITRAL Report of 58th Session, 13 February 2013, UN Doc A/CN.9/765, para. 83.

[13] *See* UNCITRAL Note by the Secretariat, 13 December 2012, UN Doc A/CN.9/WG.II/WP.177, paras 6-8 and 13-14 (in contrast to the single repository option, multiple repositories risked diluting transparency since they were less conducive to global searches).

[14] UNCITRAL Report of 53rd Session, 20 October 2010, UN Doc A/CN.9/712, paras 73 and 75 ('It was further noted that the Office of Legal Affairs of the United Nations, to which the UNCITRAL Secretariat belongs, had experience in handling comparable types of services, including the publication of instruments of deposits of ratifications, access or acceptance of international conventions'). *See also* UNCITRAL Working Paper for 58th Session, 30 November 2012, UN Doc A/CN.9/WG.II/WP.176/Add.1, para. 10.

[15] UNCITRAL Report of 58th Session, 13 February 2013, UN Doc A/CN.9/765, para. 84. *See* UNCITRAL Working Paper for 58th Session, 30 November 2012, UN Doc A/CN.9/WG.II/WP.176/Add.1, para. 11.

[16] UNCITRAL Report of 57th Session, 12 October 2012, UN Doc A/CN.9/760, para. 121; Lise Johnson & Nathalie Bernasconi-Osterwalder, *New UNCITRAL Arbitration Rules on*

Notably, the PCA and ICSID also expressed their willingness and readiness to act as a single repository in the event that UNCITRAL was unable to do so (e.g. due to insufficient resources) by 1 April 2014.[17] At the time of writing, the PCA and ICSID have each served as the repository on one occasion, whereas the UNCITRAL Secretariat is yet to exercise this function.[18]

D. Little or no discretion rests with the repository

8. The Transparency Rules are designed to limit any discretion that the repository might need to exercise with respect to the receipt and publication of documents. Under article 3(2), for example, requests for the publication of documents not subject to mandatory and automatic disclosure are directed to the tribunal, and any exceptions to publication requirements are determined at the tribunal's discretion in accordance with article 7.[19] Even the limited information disclosed by the parties prior to the constitution of the tribunal is not intended to require the exercise of judgement or discretion on the part of the neutral repository,[20] although a possible exception has been identified and is discussed at paragraphs 12-13 of the section on article 2 of the Transparency Rules, supra.

E. Limited guidance on the purpose and operation of the repository

9. Article 8 of the Transparency Rules refers only to the identity of the repository and does not address its purpose or provide guidelines for its operation. It also omits a number of issues that were touched upon during the drafting process. For example, it was suggested that the Working Group may wish to consider a waiver of liability clause with respect to the repository and the tribunal, and/or to consider how to address liability claims that might be brought 'in case of violation of data privacy'.[21]

Transparency: Application, Content and Next Steps, 23 (CIEL, IISD, CCSI, August 2013), <http://ccsi.columbia.edu>. *See also ibid.*, at 11 (noting that 'UNCITRAL chose April 1, 2014 as the effective date of the Rules on Transparency … in order to give UNCITRAL time to secure necessary resources and develop the capabilities in order to serve as the repository').

17 UNCITRAL Report of 53rd Session, 20 October 2010, UN Doc A/CN.9/712, para. 75; UNCITRAL Working Paper for 58th Session, 30 November 2012, UN Doc A/CN.9/WG.II/WP.176/Add.1, para. 10; UNCITRAL Report of 58th Session, 13 February 2013, UN Doc A/CN.9/765, para. 85; UNCITRAL Report of 54th Session, 25 February 2011, UN Doc A/CN.9/717, para. 148. *See also* Johnson & Bernasconi-Osterwalder, *supra* fn 16, at 23.

18 The PCA was designated the repository in *Iberdrola SA and Iberdrola Energia SAU v. Plurinational State of Bolivia* (PCA Case No. 2015-05), <www.italaw.com>. ICSID was designated the repository in *BSG Resources Limited, BSG Resources (Guinea) Limited and BSG Resources (Guinea) SARL v. Republic of Guinea* (ICSID Case No. ARB/14/22), <www.italaw.com>. For discussion of these cases, *see* discussion of article 1 of the Transparency Rules, *supra*.

19 *See* discussion of articles 3 and 7 of the Transparency Rules respectively, *supra*.

20 Johnson & Bernasconi-Osterwalder, *supra* fn 16, at 13.

21 UNCITRAL Note by the Secretariat, 13 December 2012, UN Doc A/CN.9/WG.II/WP.177, para. 26.

10. In the light of the *travaux préparatoires*, however, it is clear that the repository's sole purpose is to receive, store and make public documents in accordance with – and thereby serving the objectives of – the Transparency Rules.[22] It remains possible that guidelines separate from the Transparency Rules may emerge as the UNCITRAL repository becomes operational and practical issues pertaining to document collection, storage and publication become more salient.

[22] *See* UNCITRAL Working Paper for 56th Session, 13 December 2011, UN Doc A/CN.9/WG.II/WP.169/Add.1, para. 33.

Annex I
UNCITRAL Arbitration Rules, UNCITRAL Transparency Rules

Resolution adopted by the General Assembly on 16 December 2013

[on the report of the Sixth Committee (A/68/462)]

68/109. United Nations Commission on International Trade Law Rules on Transparency in Treaty-based Investor-State Arbitration and Arbitration Rules (as revised in 2010, with new article 1, paragraph 4, as adopted in 2013)

The General Assembly,

Recalling its resolution 2205 (XXI) of 17 December 1966, by which it established the United Nations Commission on International Trade Law with a mandate to further the progressive harmonization and unification of the law of international trade and in that respect to bear in mind the interests of all peoples, in particular those of developing countries, in the extensive development of international trade,

Recognizing the value of arbitration as a method of settling disputes that may arise in the context of international relations and the wide use of arbitration for the settlement of treaty-based investor-State disputes,

Recalling its resolutions 31/98 of 15 December 1976 and 65/22 of 6 December 2010, in which it recommended the use of the Arbitration Rules of the United Nations Commission on International Trade Law,[1]

Bearing in mind that the Arbitration Rules are widely used for the settlement of treaty-based investor-State disputes,

Recognizing the need for provisions on transparency in the settlement of such treaty-based investor-State disputes to take account of the public interest involved in such arbitrations,

---

1 *Official Records of the General Assembly, Thirty-first Session, Supplement No. 17* (A/31/17), chap. V, sect. C; and ibid., *Sixty-fifth Session, Supplement No. 17* (A/65/17), chap. III and annex I.

Believing that rules on transparency in treaty-based investor-State arbitration would contribute significantly to the establishment of a harmonized legal framework for a fair and efficient settlement of international investment disputes, increase transparency and accountability and promote good governance,

Noting that the Commission, at its forty-sixth session, adopted the Rules on Transparency in Treaty-based Investor-State Arbitration[2] and amended the Arbitration Rules as revised in 2010 to include, in a new article 1, paragraph 4, a reference to the Rules on Transparency,[3]

Noting also that the Rules on Transparency are available for use in investor-State arbitrations initiated under rules other than the Arbitration Rules or in ad hoc proceedings,

Noting further that the preparation of the Rules on Transparency was the subject of due deliberation in the Commission and that they benefited from consultations with Governments and interested intergovernmental and international non-governmental organizations,

1. *Expresses its appreciation* to the United Nations Commission on International Trade Law for having prepared and adopted the Rules on Transparency in Treaty-based Investor-State Arbitration2 and the Arbitration Rules (as revised in 2010, with new article 1, paragraph 4, as adopted in 2013),3 as annexed to the report of the Commission on the work of its forty-sixth session;[4]

2. *Requests* the Secretary-General to publish, including electronically, and disseminate broadly the text of the Rules on Transparency, both together with the Arbitration Rules (as revised in 2010, with new article 1, paragraph 4, as adopted in 2013) and as a stand-alone text, and to transmit them to Governments and organizations interested in the field of dispute settlement;

3. *Recommends* the use of the Rules on Transparency in relation to the settlement of investment disputes within the scope of their application as defined in article 1 of the Rules, and invites Member States that have chosen to include the Rules in their treaties to inform the Commission accordingly;

4. *Also recommends* that, subject to any provision in relevant treaties that may require a higher degree of transparency than that provided in the Rules on Transparency, the Rules be applied through appropriate mechanisms to investor-State arbitration initiated pursuant to treaties providing for the protection of investors or investments concluded before the date of coming into effect of the Rules, to the extent that such application is consistent with those treaties.

68th plenary meeting
16 December 2013

---

2 Ibid., *Sixty-eighth Session, Supplement No. 17* (A/68/17), chap. III and annex I.
3 Ibid., chap. III and annex II.
4 *Official Records of the General Assembly, Sixty-eighth Session, Supplement No. 17* (A/68/17).

UNCITRAL ARBITRATION RULES

(with new article 1, paragraph 4, as revised in 2013)

Section I. Introductory rules

Scope of application[5]

Article 1

1. Where parties have agreed that disputes between them in respect of a defined legal relationship, whether contractual or not, shall be referred to arbitration under the UNCITRAL Arbitration Rules, then such disputes shall be settled in accordance with these Rules subject to such modification as the parties may agree.

2. The parties to an arbitration agreement concluded after 15 August 2010 shall be presumed to have referred to the Rules in effect on the date of commencement of the arbitration, unless the parties have agreed to apply a particular version of the Rules. That presumption does not apply where the arbitration agreement has been concluded by accepting after 15 August 2010 an offer made before that date.

3. These Rules shall govern the arbitration except that where any of these Rules is in conflict with a provision of the law applicable to the arbitration from which the parties cannot derogate, that provision shall prevail.

4. For investor-State arbitration initiated pursuant to a treaty providing for the protection of investments or investors, these Rules include the UNCITRAL Rules on Transparency in Treaty-based Investor-State Arbitration ("Rules on Transparency"), subject to article 1 of the Rules on Transparency.

Notice and calculation of periods of time

Article 2

1. A notice, including a notification, communication or proposal, may be transmitted by any means of communication that provides or allows for a record of its transmission.

2. If an address has been designated by a party specifically for this purpose or authorized by the arbitral tribunal, any notice shall be delivered to that party at that address, and if so delivered shall be deemed to have been received. Delivery by electronic means such as facsimile or e-mail may only be made to an address so designated or authorized.

3. In the absence of such designation or authorization, a notice is:

(a) Received if it is physically delivered to the addressee; or
(b) Deemed to have been received if it is delivered at the place of business, habitual residence or mailing address of the addressee.

---

[5] A model arbitration clause for contracts can be found in the annex to the Rules.

4. If, after reasonable efforts, delivery cannot be effected in accordance with paragraphs 2 or 3, a notice is deemed to have been received if it is sent to the addressee's last-known place of business, habitual residence or mailing address by registered letter or any other means that provides a record of delivery or of attempted delivery.

5. A notice shall be deemed to have been received on the day it is delivered in accordance with paragraphs 2, 3 or 4, or attempted to be delivered in accordance with paragraph 4. A notice transmitted by electronic means is deemed to have been received on the day it is sent, except that a notice of arbitration so transmitted is only deemed to have been received on the day when it reaches the addressee's electronic address.

6. For the purpose of calculating a period of time under these Rules, such period shall begin to run on the day following the day when a notice is received. If the last day of such period is an official holiday or a non-business day at the residence or place of business of the addressee, the period is extended until the first business day which follows. Official holidays or nonbusiness days occurring during the running of the period of time are included in calculating the period.

Notice of arbitration

Article 3

1. The party or parties initiating recourse to arbitration (hereinafter called the "claimant") shall communicate to the other party or parties (hereinafter called the "respondent") a notice of arbitration.

2. Arbitral proceedings shall be deemed to commence on the date on which the notice of arbitration is received by the respondent.

3. The notice of arbitration shall include the following:

(a) A demand that the dispute be referred to arbitration;
(b) The names and contact details of the parties;
(c) Identification of the arbitration agreement that is invoked;
(d) Identification of any contract or other legal instrument out of or in relation to which the dispute arises or, in the absence of such contract or instrument, a brief description of the relevant relationship;
(e) A brief description of the claim and an indication of the amount involved, if any;
(f) The relief or remedy sought;
(g) A proposal as to the number of arbitrators, language and place of arbitration, if the parties have not previously agreed thereon.

4. The notice of arbitration may also include:

(a) A proposal for the designation of an appointing authority referred to in article 6, paragraph 1;
(b) A proposal for the appointment of a sole arbitrator referred to in article 8, paragraph 1;

(c) Notification of the appointment of an arbitrator referred to in article 9 or 10.

5. The constitution of the arbitral tribunal shall not be hindered by any controversy with respect to the sufficiency of the notice of arbitration, which shall be finally resolved by the arbitral tribunal.

Response to the notice of arbitration

Article 4

1. Within 30 days of the receipt of the notice of arbitration, the respondent shall communicate to the claimant a response to the notice of arbitration, which shall include:

(a) The name and contact details of each respondent;
(b) A response to the information set forth in the notice of arbitration, pursuant to article 3, paragraphs 3 (c) to (g).

2. The response to the notice of arbitration may also include:

(a) Any plea that an arbitral tribunal to be constituted under these Rules lacks jurisdiction;
(b) A proposal for the designation of an appointing authority referred to in article 6, paragraph 1;
(c) A proposal for the appointment of a sole arbitrator referred to in article 8, paragraph 1;
(d) Notification of the appointment of an arbitrator referred to in article 9 or 10;
(e) A brief description of counterclaims or claims for the purpose of a set-off, if any, including where relevant, an indication of the amounts involved, and the relief or remedy sought;
(f) A notice of arbitration in accordance with article 3 in case the respondent formulates a claim against a party to the arbitration agreement other than the claimant.

3. The constitution of the arbitral tribunal shall not be hindered by any controversy with respect to the respondent's failure to communicate a response to the notice of arbitration, or an incomplete or late response to the notice of arbitration, which shall be finally resolved by the arbitral tribunal.

Representation and assistance

Article 5

Each party may be represented or assisted by persons chosen by it. The names and addresses of such persons must be communicated to all parties and to the arbitral tribunal. Such communication must specify whether the appointment is being made for purposes of representation or assistance. Where a person is to act as a representative of a party, the arbitral tribunal, on its own initiative or at the request of any party, may at any time require proof of authority granted to the representative in such a form as the arbitral tribunal may determine.

Designating and appointing authorities

Article 6

1. Unless the parties have already agreed on the choice of an appointing authority, a party may at any time propose the name or names of one or more institutions or persons, including the Secretary-General of the Permanent Court of Arbitration at The Hague (hereinafter called the "PCA"), one of whom would serve as appointing authority.

2. If all parties have not agreed on the choice of an appointing authority within 30 days after a proposal made in accordance with paragraph 1 has been received by all other parties, any party may request the Secretary-General of the PCA to designate the appointing authority.

3. Where these Rules provide for a period of time within which a party must refer a matter to an appointing authority and no appointing authority has been agreed on or designated, the period is suspended from the date on which a party initiates the procedure for agreeing on or designating an appointing authority until the date of such agreement or designation.

4. Except as referred to in article 41, paragraph 4, if the appointing authority refuses to act, or if it fails to appoint an arbitrator within 30 days after it receives a party's request to do so, fails to act within any other period provided by these Rules, or fails to decide on a challenge to an arbitrator within a reasonable time after receiving a party's request to do so, any party may request the Secretary-General of the PCA to designate a substitute appointing authority.

5. In exercising their functions under these Rules, the appointing authority and the Secretary-General of the PCA may require from any party and the arbitrators the information they deem necessary and they shall give the parties and, where appropriate, the arbitrators, an opportunity to present their views in any manner they consider appropriate.All such communications to and from the appointing authority and the Secretary-General of the PCA shall also be provided by the sender to all other parties.

6. When the appointing authority is requested to appoint an arbitrator pursuant to articles 8, 9, 10 or 14, the party making the request shall send to the appointing authority copies of the notice of arbitration and, if it exists, any response to the notice of arbitration.

7. The appointing authority shall have regard to such considerations as are likely to secure the appointment of an independent and impartial arbitrator and shall take into account the advisability of appointing an arbitrator of a nationality other than the nationalities of the parties.

Section II. Composition of the arbitral tribunal

Number of arbitrators

Article 7

1. If the parties have not previously agreed on the number of arbitrators, and if within 30 days after the receipt by the respondent of the notice of arbitration the parties have not agreed that there shall be only one arbitrator, three arbitrators shall be appointed.

2. Notwithstanding paragraph 1, if no other parties have responded to a party's proposal to appoint a sole arbitrator within the time limit provided for in paragraph 1 and the party or parties concerned have failed to appoint a second arbitrator in accordance with article 9 or 10, the appointing authority may, at the request of a party, appoint a sole arbitrator pursuant to the procedure provided for in article 8, paragraph 2, if it determines that, in view of the circumstances of the case, this is more appropriate.

Appointment of arbitrators (articles 8 to 10)

Article 8

1. If the parties have agreed that a sole arbitrator is to be appointed and if within 30 days after receipt by all other parties of a proposal for the appointment of a sole arbitrator the parties have not reached agreement thereon, a sole arbitrator shall, at the request of a party, be appointed by the appointing authority.

2. The appointing authority shall appoint the sole arbitrator as promptly as possible. In making the appointment, the appointing authority shall use the following list-procedure, unless the parties agree that the list-procedure should not be used or unless the appointing authority determines in its discretion that the use of the list-procedure is not appropriate for the case:

(a) The appointing authority shall communicate to each of the parties an identical list containing at least three names;
(b) Within 15 days after the receipt of this list, each party may return the list to the appointing authority after having deleted the name or names to which it objects and numbered the remaining names on the list in the order of its preference;
(c) After the expiration of the above period of time the appointing authority shall appoint the sole arbitrator from among the names approved on the lists returned to it and in accordance with the order of preference indicated by the parties;
(d) If for any reason the appointment cannot be made according to this procedure, the appointing authority may exercise its discretion in appointing the sole arbitrator.

Article 9

1. If three arbitrators are to be appointed, each party shall appoint one arbitrator. The two arbitrators thus appointed shall choose the third arbitrator who will act as the presiding arbitrator of the arbitral tribunal.

2. If within 30 days after the receipt of a party's notification of the appointment of an arbitrator the other party has not notified the first party of the arbitrator it has appointed, the first party may request the appointing authority to appoint the second arbitrator.

3. If within 30 days after the appointment of the second arbitrator the two arbitrators have not agreed on the choice of the presiding arbitrator, the presiding arbitrator shall be appointed by the appointing authority in the same way as a sole arbitrator would be appointed under article 8.

Article 10

1. For the purposes of article 9, paragraph 1, where three arbitrators are to be appointed and there are multiple parties as claimant or as respondent, unless the parties have agreed to another method of appointment of arbitrators, the multiple parties jointly, whether as claimant or as respondent, shall appoint an arbitrator.

2. If the parties have agreed that the arbitral tribunal is to be composed of a number of arbitrators other than one or three, the arbitrators shall be appointed according to the method agreed upon by the parties.

3. In the event of any failure to constitute the arbitral tribunal under these Rules, the appointing authority shall, at the request of any party, constitute the arbitral tribunal and, in doing so, may revoke any appointment already made and appoint or reappoint each of the arbitrators and designate one of them as the presiding arbitrator.

Disclosures by and challenge of arbitrators[6] (articles 11 to 13)

Article 11

When a person is approached in connection with his or her possible appointment as an arbitrator, he or she shall disclose any circumstances likely to give rise to justifiable doubts as to his or her impartiality or independence. An arbitrator, from the time of his or her appointment and throughout the arbitral proceedings, shall without delay disclose any such circumstances to the parties and the other arbitrators unless they have already been informed by him or her of these circumstances.

Article 12

1. Any arbitrator may be challenged if circumstances exist that give rise to justifiable doubts as to the arbitrator's impartiality or independence.

---

6 Model statements of independence pursuant to article 11 can be found in the annex to the Rules.

2. A party may challenge the arbitrator appointed by it only for reasons of which it becomes aware after the appointment has been made.

3. In the event that an arbitrator fails to act or in the event of the de jure or de facto impossibility of his or her performing his or her functions, the procedure in respect of the challenge of an arbitrator as provided in article 13 shall apply.

Article 13

1. A party that intends to challenge an arbitrator shall send notice of its challenge within 15 days after it has been notified of the appointment of the challenged arbitrator, or within 15 days after the circumstances mentioned in articles 11 and 12 became known to that party.

2. The notice of challenge shall be communicated to all other parties, to the arbitrator who is challenged and to the other arbitrators. The notice of challenge shall state the reasons for the challenge.

3. When an arbitrator has been challenged by a party, all parties may agree to the challenge. The arbitrator may also, after the challenge, withdraw from his or her office. In neither case does this imply acceptance of the validity of the grounds for the challenge.

4. If, within 15 days from the date of the notice of challenge, all parties do not agree to the challenge or the challenged arbitrator does not withdraw, the party making the challenge may elect to pursue it. In that case, within 30 days from the date of the notice of challenge, it shall seek a decision on the challenge by the appointing authority.

Replacement of an arbitrator

Article 14

1. Subject to paragraph 2, in any event where an arbitrator has to be replaced during the course of the arbitral proceedings, a substitute arbitrator shall be appointed or chosen pursuant to the procedure provided for in articles 8 to 11 that was applicable to the appointment or choice of the arbitrator being replaced. This procedure shall apply even if during the process of appointing the arbitrator to be replaced, a party had failed to exercise its right to appoint or to participate in the appointment.

2. If, at the request of a party, the appointing authority determines that, in view of the exceptional circumstances of the case, it would be justified for a party to be deprived of its right to appoint a substitute arbitrator, the appointing authority may, after giving an opportunity to the parties and the remaining arbitrators to express their views: (a) appoint the substitute arbitrator; or (b) after the closure of the hearings, authorize the other arbitrators to proceed with the arbitration and make any decision or award.

Repetition of hearings in the event of the replacement of an arbitrator

Article 15

If an arbitrator is replaced, the proceedings shall resume at the stage where the arbitrator who was replaced ceased to perform his or her functions, unless the arbitral tribunal decides otherwise.

Exclusion of liability

Article 16

Save for intentional wrongdoing, the parties waive, to the fullest extent permitted under the applicable law, any claim against the arbitrators, the appointing authority and any person appointed by the arbitral tribunal based on any act or omission in connection with the arbitration.

Section III. Arbitral proceedings

General provisions

Article 17

1. Subject to these Rules, the arbitral tribunal may conduct the arbitration in such manner as it considers appropriate, provided that the parties are treated with equality and that at an appropriate stage of the proceedings each party is given a reasonable opportunity of presenting its case. The arbitral tribunal, in exercising its discretion, shall conduct the proceedings so as to avoid unnecessary delay and expense and to provide a fair and efficient process for resolving the parties' dispute.

2. As soon as practicable after its constitution and after inviting the parties to express their views, the arbitral tribunal shall establish the provisional timetable of the arbitration. The arbitral tribunal may, at any time, after inviting the parties to express their views, extend or abridge any period of time prescribed under these Rules or agreed by the parties.

3. If at an appropriate stage of the proceedings any party so requests, the arbitral tribunal shall hold hearings for the presentation of evidence by witnesses, including expert witnesses, or for oral argument. In the absence of such a request, the arbitral tribunal shall decide whether to hold such hearings or whether the proceedings shall be conducted on the basis of documents and other materials.

4. All communications to the arbitral tribunal by one party shall be communicated by that party to all other parties. Such communications shall be made at the same time, except as otherwise permitted by the arbitral tribunal if it may do so under applicable law.

5. The arbitral tribunal may, at the request of any party, allow one or more third persons to be joined in the arbitration as a party provided such person is a party to the arbitration agreement, unless the arbitral tribunal finds, after giving all parties,

including the person or persons to be joined, the opportunity to be heard, that joinder should not be permitted because of prejudice to any of those parties. The arbitral tribunal may make a single award or several awards in respect of all parties so involved in the arbitration.

Place of arbitration

Article 18

1. If the parties have not previously agreed on the place of arbitration, the place of arbitration shall be determined by the arbitral tribunal having regard to the circumstances of the case. The award shall be deemed to have been made at the place of arbitration.

2. The arbitral tribunal may meet at any location it considers appropriate for deliberations. Unless otherwise agreed by the parties, the arbitral tribunal may also meet at any location it considers appropriate for any other purpose, including hearings.

Language

Article 19

1. Subject to an agreement by the parties, the arbitral tribunal shall, promptly after its appointment, determine the language or languages to be used in the proceedings. This determination shall apply to the statement of claim, the statement of defence, and any further written statements and, if oral hearings take place, to the language or languages to be used in such hearings.

2. The arbitral tribunal may order that any documents annexed to the statement of claim or statement of defence, and any supplementary documents or exhibits submitted in the course of the proceedings, delivered in their original language, shall be accompanied by a translation into the language or languages agreed upon by the parties or determined by the arbitral tribunal.

Statement of claim

Article 20

1. The claimant shall communicate its statement of claim in writing to the respondent and to each of the arbitrators within a period of time to be determined by the arbitral tribunal. The claimant may elect to treat its notice of arbitration referred to in article 3 as a statement of claim, provided that the notice of arbitration also complies with the requirements of paragraphs 2 to 4 of this article.

2. The statement of claim shall include the following particulars:

(a) The names and contact details of the parties;
(b) A statement of the facts supporting the claim;
(c) The points at issue;
(d) The relief or remedy sought;

(e) The legal grounds or arguments supporting the claim.

3. A copy of any contract or other legal instrument out of or in relation to which the dispute arises and of the arbitration agreement shall be annexed to the statement of claim.

4. The statement of claim should, as far as possible, be accompanied by all documents and other evidence relied upon by the claimant, or contain references to them.

Statement of defence

Article 21

1. The respondent shall communicate its statement of defence in writing to the claimant and to each of the arbitrators within a period of time to be determined by the arbitral tribunal. The respondent may elect to treat its response to the notice of arbitration referred to in article 4 as a statement of defence, provided that the response to the notice of arbitration also complies with the requirements of paragraph 2 of this article.

2. The statement of defence shall reply to the particulars (b) to (e) of the statement of claim (art. 20, para. 2). The statement of defence should, as far as possible, be accompanied by all documents and other evidence relied upon by the respondent, or contain references to them.

3. In its statement of defence, or at a later stage in the arbitral proceedings if the arbitral tribunal decides that the delay was justified under the circumstances, the respondent may make a counterclaim or rely on a claim for the purpose of a set-off provided that the arbitral tribunal has jurisdiction over it.

4. The provisions of article 20, paragraphs 2 to 4, shall apply to a counterclaim, a claim under article 4, paragraph 2 (f), and a claim relied on for the purpose of a set-off.

Amendments to the claim or defence

Article 22

During the course of the arbitral proceedings, a party may amend or supplement its claim or defence, including a counterclaim or a claim for the purpose of a set-off, unless the arbitral tribunal considers it inappropriate to allow such amendment or supplement having regard to the delay in making it or prejudice to other parties or any other circumstances. However, a claim or defence, including a counterclaim or a claim for the purpose of a set-off, may not be amended or supplemented in such a manner that the amended or supplemented claim or defence falls outside the jurisdiction of the arbitral tribunal.

Pleas as to the jurisdiction of the arbitral tribunal

Article 23

1. The arbitral tribunal shall have the power to rule on its own jurisdiction, including any objections with respect to the existence or validity of the arbitration agreement. For that purpose, an arbitration clause that forms part of a contract shall be treated as an agreement independent of the other terms of the contract. A decision by the arbitral tribunal that the contract is null shall not entail automatically the invalidity of the arbitration clause.

2. A plea that the arbitral tribunal does not have jurisdiction shall be raised no later than in the statement of defence or, with respect to a counterclaim or a claim for the purpose of a set-off, in the reply to the counterclaim or to the claim for the purpose of a set-off. A party is not precluded from raising such a plea by the fact that it has appointed, or participated in the appointment of, an arbitrator. A plea that the arbitral tribunal is exceeding the scope of its authority shall be raised as soon as the matter alleged to be beyond the scope of its authority is raised during the arbitral proceedings. The arbitral tribunal may, in either case, admit a later plea if it considers the delay justified.

3. The arbitral tribunal may rule on a plea referred to in paragraph 2 either as a preliminary question or in an award on the merits. The arbitral tribunal may continue the arbitral proceedings and make an award, notwithstanding any pending challenge to its jurisdiction before a court.

Further written statements

Article 24

The arbitral tribunal shall decide which further written statements, in addition to the statement of claim and the statement of defence, shall be required from the parties or may be presented by them and shall fix the periods of time for communicating such statements.

Periods of time

Article 25

The periods of time fixed by the arbitral tribunal for the communication of written statements (including the statement of claim and statement of defence) should not exceed 45 days. However, the arbitral tribunal may extend the time limits if it concludes that an extension is justified.

Interim measures

Article 26

1. The arbitral tribunal may, at the request of a party, grant interim measures.

2. An interim measure is any temporary measure by which, at any time prior to the issuance of the award by which the dispute is finally decided, the arbitral tribunal orders a party, for example and without limitation, to:

(a) Maintain or restore the status quo pending determination of the dispute;
(b) Take action that would prevent, or refrain from taking action that is likely to cause,
  (i) current or imminent harm or
  (ii) prejudice to the arbitral process itself;
(c) Provide a means of preserving assets out of which a subsequent award may be satisfied; or
(d) Preserve evidence that may be relevant and material to the resolution of the dispute.

3. The party requesting an interim measure under paragraphs 2 (a) to (c) shall satisfy the arbitral tribunal that:

(a) Harm not adequately reparable by an award of damages is likely to result if the measure is not ordered, and such harm substantially outweighs the harm that is likely to result to the party against whom the measure is directed if the measure is granted; and
(b) There is a reasonable possibility that the requesting party will succeed on the merits of the claim. The determination on this possibility shall not affect the discretion of the arbitral tribunal in making any subsequent determination.

4. With regard to a request for an interim measure under paragraph 2 (d), the requirements in paragraphs 3 (a) and (b) shall apply only to the extent the arbitral tribunal considers appropriate.

5. The arbitral tribunal may modify, suspend or terminate an interim measure it has granted, upon application of any party or, in exceptional circumstances and upon prior notice to the parties, on the arbitral tribunal's own initiative.

6. The arbitral tribunal may require the party requesting an interim measure to provide appropriate security in connection with the measure.

7. The arbitral tribunal may require any party promptly to disclose any material change in the circumstances on the basis of which the interim measure was requested or granted.

8. The party requesting an interim measure may be liable for any costs and damages caused by the measure to any party if the arbitral tribunal later determines that, in the circumstances then prevailing, the measure should not have been granted. The arbitral tribunal may award such costs and damages at any point during the proceedings.

9. A request for interim measures addressed by any party to a judicial authority shall not be deemed incompatible with the agreement to arbitrate, or as a waiver of that agreement.

Evidence

Article 27

1. Each party shall have the burden of proving the facts relied on to support its claim or defence.

2. Witnesses, including expert witnesses, who are presented by the parties to testify to the arbitral tribunal on any issue of fact or expertise may be any individual, notwithstanding that the individual is a party to the arbitration or in any way related to a party. Unless otherwise directed by the arbitral tribunal, statements by witnesses, including expert witnesses, may be presented in writing and signed by them.

3. At any time during the arbitral proceedings the arbitral tribunal may require the parties to produce documents, exhibits or other evidence within such a period of time as the arbitral tribunal shall determine.

4. The arbitral tribunal shall determine the admissibility, relevance, materiality and weight of the evidence offered.

Hearings

Article 28

1. In the event of an oral hearing, the arbitral tribunal shall give the parties adequate advance notice of the date, time and place thereof.

2. Witnesses, including expert witnesses, may be heard under the conditions and examined in the manner set by the arbitral tribunal.

3. Hearings shall be held in camera unless the parties agree otherwise. The arbitral tribunal may require the retirement of any witness or witnesses, including expert witnesses, during the testimony of such other witnesses, except that a witness, including an expert witness, who is a party to the arbitration shall not, in principle, be asked to retire.

4. The arbitral tribunal may direct that witnesses, including expert witnesses, be examined through means of telecommunication that do not require their physical presence at the hearing (such as videoconference).

Experts appointed by the arbitral tribunal

Article 29

1. After consultation with the parties, the arbitral tribunal may appoint one or more independent experts to report to it, in writing, on specific issues to be determined by the arbitral tribunal. A copy of the expert's terms of reference, established by the arbitral tribunal, shall be communicated to the parties.

2. The expert shall, in principle before accepting appointment, submit to the arbitral tribunal and to the parties a description of his or her qualifications and a

statement of his or her impartiality and independence. Within the time ordered by the arbitral tribunal, the parties shall inform the arbitral tribunal whether they have any objections as to the expert's qualifications, impartiality or independence. The arbitral tribunal shall decide promptly whether to accept any such objections. After an expert's appointment, a party may object to the expert's qualifications, impartiality or independence only if the objection is for reasons of which the party becomes aware after the appointment has been made. The arbitral tribunal shall decide promptly what, if any, action to take.

3. The parties shall give the expert any relevant information or produce for his or her inspection any relevant documents or goods that he or she may require of them. Any dispute between a party and such expert as to the relevance of the required information or production shall be referred to the arbitral tribunal for decision.

4. Upon receipt of the expert's report, the arbitral tribunal shall communicate a copy of the report to the parties, which shall be given the opportunity to express, in writing, their opinion on the report. A party shall be entitled to examine any document on which the expert has relied in his or her report.

5. At the request of any party, the expert, after delivery of the report, may be heard at a hearing where the parties shall have the opportunity to be present and to interrogate the expert. At this hearing, any party may present expert witnesses in order to testify on the points at issue. The provisions of article 28 shall be applicable to such proceedings.

Default

Article 30

1. If, within the period of time fixed by these Rules or the arbitral tribunal, without showing sufficient cause:

(a) The claimant has failed to communicate its statement of claim, the arbitral tribunal shall issue an order for the termination of the arbitral proceedings, unless there are remaining matters that may need to be decided and the arbitral tribunal considers it appropriate to do so;
(b) The respondent has failed to communicate its response to the notice of arbitration or its statement of defence, the arbitral tribunal shall order that the proceedings continue, without treating such failure in itself as an admission of the claimant's allegations; the provisions of this subparagraph also apply to a claimant's failure to submit a defence to a counterclaim or to a claim for the purpose of a set-off.

2. If a party, duly notified under these Rules, fails to appear at a hearing, without showing sufficient cause for such failure, the arbitral tribunal may proceed with the arbitration.

3. If a party, duly invited by the arbitral tribunal to produce documents, exhibits or other evidence, fails to do so within the established period of time, without showing

sufficient cause for such failure, the arbitral tribunal may make the award on the evidence before it.

Closure of hearings

Article 31

1. The arbitral tribunal may inquire of the parties if they have any further proof to offer or witnesses to be heard or submissions to make and, if there are none, it may declare the hearings closed.

2. The arbitral tribunal may, if it considers it necessary owing to exceptional circumstances, decide, on its own initiative or upon application of a party, to reopen the hearings at any time before the award is made.

Waiver of right to object

Article 32

A failure by any party to object promptly to any non-compliance with these Rules or with any requirement of the arbitration agreement shall be deemed to be a waiver of the right of such party to make such an objection, unless such party can show that, under the circumstances, its failure to object was justified.

Section IV. The award

Decisions

Article 33

1. When there is more than one arbitrator, any award or other decision of the arbitral tribunal shall be made by a majority of the arbitrators.

2. In the case of questions of procedure, when there is no majority or when the arbitral tribunal so authorizes, the presiding arbitrator may decide alone, subject to revision, if any, by the arbitral tribunal.

Form and effect of the award

Article 34

1. The arbitral tribunal may make separate awards on different issues at different times.

2. All awards shall be made in writing and shall be final and binding on the parties. The parties shall carry out all awards without delay.

3. The arbitral tribunal shall state the reasons upon which the award is based, unless the parties have agreed that no reasons are to be given.

4. An award shall be signed by the arbitrators and it shall contain the date on which the award was made and indicate the place of arbitration. Where there is more than one arbitrator and any of them fails to sign, the award shall state the reason for the absence of the signature.

5. An award may be made public with the consent of all parties or where and to the extent disclosure is required of a party by legal duty, to protect or pursue a legal right or in relation to legal proceedings before a court or other competent authority.

6. Copies of the award signed by the arbitrators shall be communicated to the parties by the arbitral tribunal.

Applicable law, amiable compositeur

Article 35

1. The arbitral tribunal shall apply the rules of law designated by the parties as applicable to the substance of the dispute. Failing such designation by the parties, the arbitral tribunal shall apply the law which it determines to be appropriate.

2. The arbitral tribunal shall decide as amiable compositeur or ex aequo et bono only if the parties have expressly authorized the arbitral tribunal to do so.

3. In all cases, the arbitral tribunal shall decide in accordance with the terms of the contract, if any, and shall take into account any usage of trade applicable to the transaction.

Settlement or other grounds for termination

Article 36

1. If, before the award is made, the parties agree on a settlement of the dispute, the arbitral tribunal shall either issue an order for the termination of the arbitral proceedings or, if requested by the parties and accepted by the arbitral tribunal, record the settlement in the form of an arbitral award on agreed terms. The arbitral tribunal is not obliged to give reasons for such an award.

2. If, before the award is made, the continuation of the arbitral proceedings becomes unnecessary or impossible for any reason not mentioned in paragraph 1, the arbitral tribunal shall inform the parties of its intention to issue an order for the termination of the proceedings. The arbitral tribunal shall have the power to issue such an order unless there are remaining matters that may need to be decided and the arbitral tribunal considers it appropriate to do so.

3. Copies of the order for termination of the arbitral proceedings or of the arbitral award on agreed terms, signed by the arbitrators, shall be communicated by the arbitral tribunal to the parties. Where an arbitral award on agreed terms is made, the provisions of article 34, paragraphs 2, 4 and 5, shall apply.

Interpretation of the award

Article 37

1. Within 30 days after the receipt of the award, a party, with notice to the other parties, may request that the arbitral tribunal give an interpretation of the award.

2. The interpretation shall be given in writing within 45 days after the receipt of the request. The interpretation shall form part of the award and the provisions of article 34, paragraphs 2 to 6, shall apply.

Correction of the award

Article 38

1. Within 30 days after the receipt of the award, a party, with notice to the other parties, may request the arbitral tribunal to correct in the award any error in computation, any clerical or typographical error, or any error or omission of a similar nature. If the arbitral tribunal considers that the request is justified, it shall make the correction within 45 days of receipt of the request.

2. The arbitral tribunal may within 30 days after the communication of the award make such corrections on its own initiative.

3. Such corrections shall be in writing and shall form part of the award. The provisions of article 34, paragraphs 2 to 6, shall apply.

Additional award

Article 39

1. Within 30 days after the receipt of the termination order or the award, a party, with notice to the other parties, may request the arbitral tribunal to make an award or an additional award as to claims presented in the arbitral proceedings but not decided by the arbitral tribunal.

2. If the arbitral tribunal considers the request for an award or additional award to be justified, it shall render or complete its award within 60 days after the receipt of the request. The arbitral tribunal may extend, if necessary, the period of time within which it shall make the award.

3. When such an award or additional award is made, the provisions of article 34, paragraphs 2 to 6, shall apply.

Definition of costs

Article 40

1. The arbitral tribunal shall fix the costs of arbitration in the final award and, if it deems appropriate, in another decision.

2. The term "costs" includes only:

(a) The fees of the arbitral tribunal to be stated separately as to each arbitrator and to be fixed by the tribunal itself in accordance with article 41;
(b) The reasonable travel and other expenses incurred by the arbitrators;
(c) The reasonable costs of expert advice and of other assistance required by the arbitral tribunal;
(d) The reasonable travel and other expenses of witnesses to the extent such expenses are approved by the arbitral tribunal;
(e) The legal and other costs incurred by the parties in relation to the arbitration to the extent that the arbitral tribunal determines that the amount of such costs is reasonable;
(f) Any fees and expenses of the appointing authority as well as the fees and expenses of the Secretary-General of the PCA.

3. In relation to interpretation, correction or completion of any award under articles 37 to 39, the arbitral tribunal may charge the costs referred to in paragraphs 2 (b) to (f), but no additional fees.

Fees and expenses of arbitrators

Article 41

1. The fees and expenses of the arbitrators shall be reasonable in amount, taking into account the amount in dispute, the complexity of the subject matter, the time spent by the arbitrators and any other relevant circumstances of the case.

2. If there is an appointing authority and it applies or has stated that it will apply a schedule or particular method for determining the fees for arbitrators in international cases, the arbitral tribunal in fixing its fees shall take that schedule or method into account to the extent that it considers appropriate in the circumstances of the case.

3. Promptly after its constitution, the arbitral tribunal shall inform the parties as to how it proposes to determine its fees and expenses, including any rates it intends to apply. Within 15 days of receiving that proposal, any party may refer the proposal to the appointing authority for review. If, within 45 days of receipt of such a referral, the appointing authority finds that the proposal of the arbitral tribunal is inconsistent with paragraph 1, it shall make any necessary adjustments thereto, which shall be binding upon the arbitral tribunal.

4. (a) When informing the parties of the arbitrators' fees and expenses that have been fixed pursuant to article 40, paragraphs 2 (a) and (b), the arbitral tribunal shall also explain the manner in which the corresponding amounts have been calculated;
(b) Within 15 days of receiving the arbitral tribunal's determination of fees and expenses, any party may refer for review such determination to the appointing authority. If no appointing authority has been agreed upon or designated, or if the appointing authority fails to act within the time specified in these Rules, then the review shall be made by the Secretary-General of the PCA;

(c) If the appointing authority or the Secretary-General of the PCA finds that the arbitral tribunal's determination is inconsistent with the arbitral tribunal's proposal (and any adjustment thereto) under paragraph 3 or is otherwise manifestly excessive, it shall, within 45 days of receiving such a referral, make any adjustments to the arbitral tribunal's determination that are necessary to satisfy the criteria in paragraph 1. Any such adjustments shall be binding upon the arbitral tribunal;

(d) Any such adjustments shall either be included by the arbitral tribunal in its award or, if the award has already been issued, be implemented in a correction to the award, to which the procedure of article 38, paragraph 3, shall apply.

5. Throughout the procedure under paragraphs 3 and 4, the arbitral tribunal shall proceed with the arbitration, in accordance with article 17, paragraph 1.

6. A referral under paragraph 4 shall not affect any determination in the award other than the arbitral tribunal's fees and expenses; nor shall it delay the recognition and enforcement of all parts of the award other than those relating to the determination of the arbitral tribunal's fees and expenses.

Allocation of costs

Article 42

1. The costs of the arbitration shall in principle be borne by the unsuccessful party or parties. However, the arbitral tribunal may apportion each of such costs between the parties if it determines that apportionment is reasonable, taking into account the circumstances of the case.

2. The arbitral tribunal shall in the final award or, if it deems appropriate, in any other award, determine any amount that a party may have to pay to another party as a result of the decision on allocation of costs.

Deposit of costs

Article 43

1. The arbitral tribunal, on its establishment, may request the parties to deposit an equal amount as an advance for the costs referred to in article 40, paragraphs 2 (a) to (c).

2. During the course of the arbitral proceedings the arbitral tribunal may request supplementary deposits from the parties.

3. If an appointing authority has been agreed upon or designated, and when a party so requests and the appointing authority consents to perform the function, the arbitral tribunal shall fix the amounts of any deposits or supplementary deposits only after consultation with the appointing authority, which may make any comments to the arbitral tribunal that it deems appropriate concerning the amount of such deposits and supplementary deposits.

4. If the required deposits are not paid in full within 30 days after the receipt of the request, the arbitral tribunal shall so inform the parties in order that one or more of them may make the required payment. If such payment is not made, the arbitral tribunal may order the suspension or termination of the arbitral proceedings.

5. After a termination order or final award has been made, the arbitral tribunal shall render an accounting to the parties of the deposits received and return any unexpended balance to the parties.

ANNEX

Model arbitration clause for contracts

Any dispute, controversy or claim arising out of or relating to this contract, or the breach, termination or invalidity thereof, shall be settled by arbitration in accordance with the UNCITRAL Arbitration Rules.

Note. Parties should consider adding:

> (a) The appointing authority shall be . . . [name of institution or person];
> (b) The number of arbitrators shall be . . . [one or three];
> (c) The place of arbitration shall be . . . [town and country];
> (d) The language to be used in the arbitral proceedings shall be . . .

Possible waiver statement

Note. If the parties wish to exclude recourse against the arbitral award that may be available under the applicable law, they may consider adding a provision to that effect as suggested below, considering, however, that the effectiveness and conditions of such an exclusion depend on the applicable law.

Waiver

> The parties hereby waive their right to any form of recourse against an award to any court or other competent authority, insofar as such waiver can validly be made under the applicable law.

Model statements of independence pursuant to article 11 of the Rules

No circumstances to disclose

> I am impartial and independent of each of the parties and intend to remain so. To the best of my knowledge, there are no circumstances, past or present, likely to give rise to justifiable doubts as to my impartiality or independence. I shall promptly notify the parties and the other arbitrators of any such circumstances that may subsequently come to my attention during this arbitration.

Circumstances to disclose

> I am impartial and independent of each of the parties and intend to remain so. Attached is a statement made pursuant to article 11 of the UNCITRAL Arbitration Rules of (a) my past and present professional, business and other relationships with the parties and (b) any other relevant circumstances. [Include statement.] I confirm that those circumstances do not affect my independence and impartiality. I shall promptly notify the parties and the other arbitrators of any such further relationships or circumstances that may subsequently come to my attention during this arbitration.

Note. Any party may consider requesting from the arbitrator the following addition to the statement of independence:

> I confirm, on the basis of the information presently available to me, that I can devote the time necessary to conduct this arbitration diligently, efficiently and in accordance with the time limits in the Rules.

UNCITRAL RULES ON TRANSPARENCY IN TREATY-BASED INVESTOR-STATE ARBITRATION

Article 1. Scope of application

Applicability of the Rules

1. The UNCITRAL Rules on Transparency in Treaty-based Investor-State Arbitration ("Rules on Transparency") shall apply to investor-State arbitration initiated under the UNCITRAL Arbitration Rules pursuant to a treaty providing for the protection of investments or investors ("treaty")[7] concluded on or after 1 April 2014 unless the Parties to the treaty[8] have agreed otherwise.

2. In investor-State arbitrations initiated under the UNCITRAL Arbitration Rules pursuant to a treaty concluded before 1 April 2014, these Rules shall apply only when:

(a) The parties to an arbitration (the "disputing parties") agree to their application in respect of that arbitration; or
(b) The Parties to the treaty or, in the case of a multilateral treaty, the State of the claimant and the respondent State, have agreed after 1 April 2014 to their application.

Application of the Rules

3. In any arbitration in which the Rules on Transparency apply pursuant to a treaty or to an agreement by the Parties to that treaty:

(a) The disputing parties may not derogate from these Rules, by agreement or otherwise, unless permitted to do so by the treaty;
(b) The arbitral tribunal shall have the power, besides its discretionary authority under certain provisions of these Rules, to adapt the requirements of any specific provision of these Rules to the particular circumstances of the case, after consultation with the disputing parties, if such adaptation is necessary to conduct the arbitration in a practical manner and is consistent with the transparency objective of these Rules.

Discretion and authority of the arbitral tribunal

4. Where the Rules on Transparency provide for the arbitral tribunal to exercise discretion, the arbitral tribunal in exercising such discretion shall take into account:

---

7 For the purposes of the Rules on Transparency, a "treaty" shall be understood broadly as encompassing any bilateral or multilateral treaty that contains provisions on the protection of investments or investors and a right for investors to resort to arbitration against Parties to the treaty, including any treaty commonly referred to as a free trade agreement, economic integration agreement, trade and investment framework or cooperation agreement, or bilateral investment treaty.

8 For the purposes of the Rules on Transparency, any reference to a "Party to the treaty" or a "State" includes, for example, a regional economic integration organization where it is a Party to the treaty.

(a) The public interest in transparency in treaty-based investor-State arbitration and in the particular arbitral proceedings; and
(b) The disputing parties' interest in a fair and efficient resolution of their dispute.

5. These Rules shall not affect any authority that the arbitral tribunal may otherwise have under the UNCITRAL Arbitration Rules to conduct the arbitration in such a manner as to promote transparency, for example by accepting submissions from third persons.

6. In the presence of any conduct, measure or other action having the effect of wholly undermining the transparency objectives of these Rules, the arbitral tribunal shall ensure that those objectives prevail.

Applicable instrument in case of conflict

7. Where the Rules on Transparency apply, they shall supplement any applicable arbitration rules. Where there is a conflict between the Rules on Transparency and the applicable arbitration rules, the Rules on Transparency shall prevail. Notwithstanding any provision in these Rules, where there is a conflict between the Rules on Transparency and the treaty, the provisions of the treaty shall prevail.

8. Where any of these Rules is in conflict with a provision of the law applicable to the arbitration from which the disputing parties cannot derogate, that provision shall prevail.

Application in non-UNCITRAL arbitrations

9. These Rules are available for use in investor-State arbitrations initiated under rules other than the UNCITRAL Arbitration Rules or in ad hoc proceedings.

Article 2. Publication of information at the commencement of arbitral proceedings

Once the notice of arbitration has been received by the respondent, each of the disputing parties shall promptly communicate a copy of the notice of arbitration to the repository referred to under article 8. Upon receipt of the notice of arbitration from the respondent, or upon receipt of the notice of arbitration and a record of its transmission to the respondent, the repository shall promptly make available to the public information regarding the name of the disputing parties, the economic sector involved and the treaty under which the claim is being made.

Article 3. Publication of documents

1. Subject to article 7, the following documents shall be made available to the public: the notice of arbitration, the response to the notice of arbitration, the statement of claim, the statement of defence and any further written statements or written submissions by any disputing party; a table listing all exhibits to the aforesaid documents and to expert reports and witness statements, if such table has been prepared for the proceedings, but not the exhibits themselves; any written submissions by the

non-disputing Party (or Parties) to the treaty and by third persons, transcripts of hearings, where available; and orders, decisions and awards of the arbitral tribunal.

2. Subject to article 7, expert reports and witness statements, exclusive of the exhibits thereto, shall be made available to the public, upon request by any person to the arbitral tribunal.

3. Subject to article 7, the arbitral tribunal may decide, on its own initiative or upon request from any person, and after consultation with the disputing parties, whether and how to make available exhibits and any other documents provided to, or issued by, the arbitral tribunal not falling within paragraphs 1 or 2 above. This may include, for example, making such documents available at a specified site.

4. The documents to be made available to the public pursuant to paragraphs 1 and 2 shall be communicated by the arbitral tribunal to the repository referred to under article 8 as soon as possible, subject to any relevant arrangements or time limits for the protection of confidential or protected information prescribed under article 7. The documents to be made available pursuant to paragraph 3 may be communicated by the arbitral tribunal to the repository referred to under article 8 as they become available and, if applicable, in a redacted form in accordance with article 7. The repository shall make all documents available in a timely manner, in the form and in the language in which it receives them.

5. A person granted access to documents under paragraph 3 shall bear any administrative costs of making those documents available to that person, such as the costs of photocopying or shipping documents to that person, but not the costs of making those documents available to the public through the repository.

Article 4. Submission by a third person

1. After consultation with the disputing parties, the arbitral tribunal may allow a person that is not a disputing party, and not a non-disputing Party to the treaty ("third person(s)"), to file a written submission with the arbitral tribunal regarding a matter within the scope of the dispute.

2. A third person wishing to make a submission shall apply to the arbitral tribunal, and shall, in a concise written statement, which is in a language of the arbitration and complies with any page limits set by the arbitral tribunal:

(a) Describe the third person, including, where relevant, its membership and legal status (e.g., trade association or other non-governmental organization), its general objectives, the nature of its activities and any parent organization (including any organization that directly or indirectly controls the third person);

(b) Disclose any connection, direct or indirect, which the third person has with any disputing party;

(c) Provide information on any government, person or organization that has provided to the third person (i) any financial or other assistance in preparing the submission; or (ii) substantial assistance in either of the two years preceding the application by the third person under this article (e.g. funding around 20 per cent of its overall operations annually);

(d) Describe the nature of the interest that the third person has in the arbitration; and

(e) Identify the specific issues of fact or law in the arbitration that the third person wishes to address in its written submission.

3. In determining whether to allow such a submission, the arbitral tribunal shall take into consideration, among other factors it determines to be relevant:

(a) Whether the third person has a significant interest in the arbitral proceedings; and

(b) The extent to which the submission would assist the arbitral tribunal in the determination of a factual or legal issue related to the arbitral proceedings by bringing a perspective, particular knowledge or insight that is different from that of the disputing parties.

4. The submission filed by the third person shall:

(a) Be dated and signed by the person filing the submission on behalf of the third person;

(b) Be concise, and in no case longer than as authorized by the arbitral tribunal;

(c) Set out a precise statement of the third person's position on issues; and

(d) Address only matters within the scope of the dispute.

5. The arbitral tribunal shall ensure that any submission does not disrupt or unduly burden the arbitral proceedings, or unfairly prejudice any disputing party.

6. The arbitral tribunal shall ensure that the disputing parties are given a reasonable opportunity to present their observations on any submission by the third person.

Article 5. Submission by a non-disputing Party to the treaty

1. The arbitral tribunal shall, subject to paragraph 4, allow, or, after consultation with the disputing parties, may invite, submissions on issues of treaty interpretation from a non-disputing Party to the treaty.

2. The arbitral tribunal, after consultation with the disputing parties, may allow submissions on further matters within the scope of the dispute from a non-disputing Party to the treaty. In determining whether to allow such submissions, the arbitral tribunal shall take into consideration, among other factors it determines to be relevant, the factors referred to in article 4, paragraph 3, and, for greater certainty, the need to avoid submissions which would support the claim of the investor in a manner tantamount to diplomatic protection.

3. The arbitral tribunal shall not draw any inference from the absence of any submission or response to any invitation pursuant to paragraphs 1 or 2.

4. The arbitral tribunal shall ensure that any submission does not disrupt or unduly burden the arbitral proceedings, or unfairly prejudice any disputing party.

5. The arbitral tribunal shall ensure that the disputing parties are given a reasonable opportunity to present their observations on any submission by a non-disputing Party to the treaty.

Article 6. Hearings

1. Subject to article 6, paragraphs 2 and 3, hearings for the presentation of evidence or for oral argument ("hearings") shall be public.

2. Where there is a need to protect confidential information or the integrity of the arbitral process pursuant to article 7, the arbitral tribunal shall make arrangements to hold in private that part of the hearing requiring such protection.

3. The arbitral tribunal shall make logistical arrangements to facilitate the public access to hearings (including where appropriate by organizing attendance through video links or such other means as it deems appropriate). However, the arbitral tribunal may, after consultation with the disputing parties, decide to hold all or part of the hearings in private where this becomes necessary for logistical reasons, such as when the circumstances render any original arrangement for public access to a hearing infeasible.

Article 7. Exceptions to transparency

Confidential or protected information

1. Confidential or protected information, as defined in paragraph 2 and as identified pursuant to the arrangements referred to in paragraphs 3 and 4, shall not be made available to the public pursuant to articles 2 to 6.

2. Confidential or protected information consists of:

(a) Confidential business information;
(b) Information that is protected against being made available to the public under the treaty;
(c) Information that is protected against being made available to the public, in the case of the information of the respondent State, under the law of the respondent State, and in the case of other information, under any law or rules determined by the arbitral tribunal to be applicable to the disclosure of such information; or
(d) Information the disclosure of which would impede law enforcement.

3. The arbitral tribunal, after consultation with the disputing parties, shall make arrangements to prevent any confidential or protected information from being made available to the public, including by putting in place, as appropriate:

(a) Time limits in which a disputing party, non-disputing Party to the treaty or third person shall give notice that it seeks protection for such information in documents;
(b) Procedures for the prompt designation and redaction of the particular confidential or protected information in such documents; and

(c) Procedures for holding hearings in private to the extent required by article 6, paragraph 2.

Any determination as to whether information is confidential or protected shall be made by the arbitral tribunal after consultation with the disputing parties.

4. Where the arbitral tribunal determines that information should not be redacted from a document, or that a document should not be prevented from being made available to the public, any disputing party, non-disputing Party to the treaty or third person that voluntarily introduced the document into the record shall be permitted to withdraw all or part of the document from the record of the arbitral proceedings.

5. Nothing in these Rules requires a respondent State to make available to the public information the disclosure of which it considers to be contrary to its essential security interests.

Integrity of the arbitral process

6. Information shall not be made available to the public pursuant to articles 2 to 6 where the information, if made available to the public, would jeopardize the integrity of the arbitral process as determined pursuant to paragraph 7.

7. The arbitral tribunal may, on its own initiative or upon the application of a disputing party, after consultation with the disputing parties where practicable, take appropriate measures to restrain or delay the publication of information where such publication would jeopardize the integrity of the arbitral process because it could hamper the collection or production of evidence, lead to the intimidation of witnesses, lawyers acting for disputing parties or members of the arbitral tribunal, or in comparably exceptional circumstances.

Article 8. Repository of published information

The repository of published information under the Rules on Transparency shall be the Secretary-General of the United Nations or an institution named by UNCITRAL.

Annex II
Revision of the UNCITRAL Arbitration Rules

A REPORT BY JAN PAULSSON & GEORGIOS PETROCHILOS, SEPTEMBER 2006

INTRODUCTION

1. This report has been commissioned by the Secretariat as part of an initiative to spur discussion on the revision of the UNCITRAL Arbitration Rules,[1] which were adopted by the UNCITRAL and the UN General Assembly in 1976 (the *UNCITRAL Rules* or, where the context permits, simply the *Rules*).[2]

2. In 1976, the UN General Assembly felt able to "recommend[] the use of the [UNCITRAL Rules]" chiefly because it was:

> *Convinced* that the establishment of rules for *ad hoc* arbitration that are acceptable in countries with different legal, social and economic systems would significantly contribute to the development of harmonious international economic relations.[3]

The Rules have never been revised, notwithstanding the fact that the prospect of revisions was clearly envisaged in 1976: the text of the model arbitration clause accompanying article 1 of the Rules refers to the "UNCITRAL Arbitration Rules as *at present in force*" (emphasis added).

I. THE CASE FOR REVISION

3. The challenge is to ensure that the Rules continue to meet the needs of their users, reflecting best practice in the field of international arbitration. In the authors' view, a revision of the Rules

---

1 See the Annotated Provisional Agenda for the 44th Session of Working Group II (23-27 January 2006), UN Doc A/CN.9/WG.II/WP.140 (14 November 2005) para 31; and Note by the Secretariat: Settlement of Commercial Disputes – Possible Future Work in the field of settlement of commercial disputes: revision of the UNCITRAL Arbitration Rules, UN Doc A/CN.9/610/Add.1 (3 April 2006).

2 See General Assembly Resolution 31/98 (15 December 1976), UN Doc A/RES/31/98 (1976). The UNCITRAL Rules are reprinted at (1977) 8 UNCITRAL YB 7 and (1976) 15 ILM 701, together with GA Res 31/98

3 GA Res 31/98 (note 2 above), third preambular paragraph (emphasis in the original).

is overdue and indispensable. This view is shared by the principal draftsman of the original Rules,[4] Professor Sanders, who has written that: "UNCITRAL's Arbitration Rules were born in 1976 and grew up to everybody's satisfaction. However, after 30 years they are ready for their first facelift." Four principal reasons support this conclusion, in our view.

4. First, since 1976, there have been great advances in arbitral practice. This is unsurprising. The volume of international arbitrations has reached dimensions unknown prior to 1976; major international arbitration rules have emerged or been extensively revised; and UNCITRAL itself has adopted a Model Law on International Commercial Arbitration in 1985, after a long gestation process.[5] While some of the advances in international arbitration may be traced to the Rules themselves,[6] their drafters could not have anticipated all of the difficulties that have emerged in the international arbitral process, nor the responsive innovations that have appeared in contemporary arbitration statutes and rules.

5. Secondly, the Rules were largely inspired by arbitration rules that are no longer current.[7] Similarly, several recent sets of arbitration rules which were initially inspired by the UNCITRAL Rules have now departed substantially from them.[8] Naturally, the evolution of such other arbitration rules must be noted and analysed on its merits, and not out of a blind desire to "compete" against those texts.

6. Thirdly, the intrinsic merit of the Rules and the *imprimatur* they have received from the UN General Assembly have commended them to states for investment disputes (notably under Bilateral Investment Treaties (*BITs*),[9] Chapter 11 of the North American Free Trade Agreement (*NAFTA*), of 1992[10] and the Energy Charter Treaty of 1994[11]), the Iran-US Claims Tribunal (adjudicating claims both under contracts and under international law[12]), and mass-claims settlement

4 See *Sanders* (2004) 243, with references to the author's earlier works; and id, "Arbitration Rules of UNCITRAL: 30 Years", UNCITRAL/VIAC colloquium paper (April 2006).

5 Currently adopted in 57 jurisdictions; see www.uncitral.org (3 September 2006).

6 See, eg, the clear statements of principle on *compétence de la compétence* and the separability of the arbitration agreement in articles 21(1)-(2) of the Rules.

7 Principally the 1966 UN Economic Commission for Europe Rules (1966: UN Doc E/ECE/Trade 81 (1967)), and the former United Nations Economic Commission for Asia and the Far East (now the United Nations Economic and Social Commission for Asia and the Pacific) Rules (1966) amongst other provision of various arbitration rules; see Report of UNCITRAL Secretary General: Preliminary draft set of arbitration rules for optional use in *ad hoc* arbitration relating to international trade (Terms of Reference), UN Doc A/CN.9/97 (1975) 164.

8 See notably the LCIA Rules (adopted in 1981; revised in 1985 and 1998); the InterAmerican Commercial Arbitration Commission (IACAC) Rules (adopted in 1982; revised in 1988 and 2002: Annex to 22 Code of Federal Regulations 194.1); the Stockholm Chamber of Commerce (SCC) Rules (adopted in 1988; revised in 1999; with a revision currently under consideration); the World Intellectual Property Organization (WIPO) Rules (1994); and the Singapore International Arbitration Centre (SIAC) Rules (1997).

9 By November 2005, the cumulative number of treaty-based arbitrations launched since 1987 grew to approximately 219 cases, 132 of which were brought before the World Bank's International Centre for Settlement of Investment Disputes (ICSID) and 65 pursuant to the UNCITRAL Rules: Latest Developments in Investor-State Dispute Settlement, UNCTAD IIA MONITOR No 4 (2005) 1. By contrast, ICC arbitration is a rather uncommon feature of BITs: the few available examples include the France-Syria BIT of 1978, the US-Haiti BIT of 1983 (not in force), the Greece-Hungary BIT of 1989, the Switzerland-South Africa BIT of 1995, and the Portugal-Cuba BIT of 1998.

10 (1993) 32 ILM 605, Articles 1101-1138, in particular 1120(1)(c).

11 (1995) 34 ILM 381, Article 26(4).

12 See the Declaration of the Government of the Democratic and Popular Republic of Algeria concerning the Settlement of Claims by the Government of the United States of America and the Government of the Islamic Republic of Iran of 19 January 1981 (or "Claims Settlement Declaration"), (1981) 20 ILM 257, Articles II and III(2).

procedures.[13] While many claims brought under those instruments involve contracts,[14] claims for breach of customary or conventional international law are legally distinct from contractual claims.[15] Thus, claims asserting causes of action under international law will not always fit comfortably within the narrow language of article 1(1) of the Rules, which refers to "disputes in relation to [a] contract". More importantly from a procedural perspective, disputes under those instruments often raise questions of law or public interest calling for particular procedural arrangements, such as separate phases on jurisdiction and admissibility before the submission of a Statement of Claim, *amicus curiae* briefs, and consolidation of claims and hearings. Some of the international instruments mentioned above empower arbitral tribunals to amend the Rules as necessary,[16] or directly set forth particular procedural arrangements derogating from or supplementing the Rules.[17] But under the vast majority of BITs, parties and tribunals have to look for guidance outside the text of the Rules in relation to those issues.

7. The fact that the Rules have been effective in such varied circumstances attests not only to their malleability but also, and more importantly, to the forethought of parties who detected and corrected their shortcomings in various contexts,[18] and to the adroitness of a number of arbitrators (including in particular those of the Iran-US Claims Tribunal). There is thus no reason to be complacent about the need to revise the Rules. To the contrary, a revision would extend the benefit of accumulated experience to the widest possible audience of parties, arbitrators, and counsel.

8. A final consideration is the development of sets of guidelines on specific procedural matters. UNCITRAL itself has issued, in 1996, Notes on Organizing Arbitral Proceedings. These were initially conceived as practical guidelines on procedural matters to be decided by the tribunal in consultation with the parties in a pre-hearing conference,[19] but do have wider relevance in respect of significant procedural matters. The IBA Rules (1999) and the IBA Guidelines on Conflicts of Interest (2004) also reflect sound, generally accepted practices in the field. The UNCITRAL Rules ought to be consistent with the basic premises of these texts.

II. THE PURPOSE AND METHODOLOGY OF THIS REPORT

9. This report concludes unhesitatingly that a revision is necessary and urgent in order for the Rules to continue "significantly contribut[ing] to the development of harmonious international economic relations".[20] This demonstration may best be made by examining each of the provisions

---

13 As in the United Nations Compensation Commission (UNCC) established in 1991 pursuant to United Nations Security Council Resolution 692 to process claims and pay compensation stemming from the Gulf War; see UN Doc S/RES/692 (20 May 1991). The Provisional Rules for Claims Procedure adopted by the Governing Council of the UNCC in June 1992 (UN Doc S/AC.26/1992/10) provide in Article 43 that: "Subject to the provisions of these procedures, Commissioners may make such additional procedural rulings as may be necessary to complete work on particular cases or categories of cases. In so doing, the Commissioners may rely on the relevant UNCITRAL Rules for guidance."

14 Cf *Compañía de Aguas del Aconquija SA and Vivendi Universal (formerly Compagnie Générale des Eaux) v Argentina* (ARB/97/3) Decision on Annulment of 3 July 2002, (2002) 41 ILM 1135, para 60: "A particular investment dispute may at the same time involve issues of the interpretation and application of the BIT's standards and questions of contract".

15 See, eg, ibid, paras 112-113.

16 See Article III(1) of the Claims Settlement Declaration (note 12 above) and the Iran-US Claims Tribunal Final Rules of Procedure (1983), (1983) 2 Iran-US CTR 403.

17 See NAFTA Articles 1220 *et seq*.

18 See the *Brcko Area* arbitration discussed at paragraph 240 below.

19 UNCITRAL Notes on organizing Arbitral Proceedings (1996) para 1: "The stated purpose of the Notes is to "assist arbitration practitioners by listing and briefly describing questions on which appropriately timed decisions on organizing arbitral proceedings may be useful."

20 GA Res 31/98 (note 2 above), second preambular paragraph.

of the Rules in light of contemporary practice. The main body of this report (paragraphs 21 *et seq*) is devoted to that task. Given the magnitude of the task, we have endeavoured to set out our analysis succinctly. References to materials and works relevant to our analysis are, for the same reason, illustrative rather than exhaustive.

10. We would welcome that our conclusions and suggestions be subjected to scrutiny and discussion with the widest possible audience (including the Permanent Court of Arbitration (*PCA*) and other arbitral institutions that administer UNCITRAL proceedings).

11. Our premise is that the Rules should provide for an efficient process: leaving room for – and encouraging – specific arrangements to suit the circumstances of each case; and being able to deploy their effect as widely as possible under a variety of arbitration laws (including public international law). The Rules aim to help resolve difficult cases and provide guidance to parties and tribunals. There is clearly a balance to be drawn as to the degree of specificity required of the Rules in the various contexts in which they operate. This, too, is a matter for debate, on which views may legitimately differ.[21]

12. Yet two particular considerations suggest that the Rules should offer comprehensive guidance. First, the Rules are primarily designed for *ad hoc* proceedings without institutional guidance. Gaps or uncertainty tend to strengthen the existing impression that *ad hoc* arbitration is suitable for experienced parties only.[22] Secondly, the Rules are a universal text that should produce consistent and predictable outcomes in the hands of a wide spectrum of arbitrators and parties. Thus, while it is certainly true that experienced arbitrators are able to devise bespoke solutions for particular circumstances, this does not speak against comprehensive coverage in the Rules. Experienced and confident arbitrators would not be stifled by comprehensive guidance.

13. On the other hand, we are bound to recognize that the line between comprehensiveness and over-complication is not bright. Some questions arise more frequently than others. Concise texts can be user-friendly. We trust that informed and focused debate will reveal the right balance to be drawn.

III. MAIN LINES OF REVISION

14. It is useful to outline at the outset the principal suggestions for revision contained in this report. They are as follows:

(a) **Both parties to file opening submissions before the constitution of the arbitral tribunal**: Article 3 requires the claimant's Notice of Arbitration to indicate the "general nature" of its claim as well as the "remedy or relief sought." The next event is that the arbitral tribunal is constituted, without the respondent having an opportunity (or being required) to state its position with respect to (i) jurisdiction, (ii) the claim, or (iii) any counterclaim. The first occasion for the respondent to take a position on these matters is only after the arbitral tribunal has been constituted, and after a further Statement of Claim (or determination that its equivalent was "contained" in

21 By way of illustration, compare the few curt provisions that the French *Nouveau Code de Procédure Civile* of 1981 devotes on the arbitration proceedings proper (Articles 1492-1497) with the corresponding sections (ss 1-65) of the Arbitration Act 1996 (England & Wales). For an in-depth discussion of the policy issues involved see Park, "The 2002 Freshfields Lecture — Arbitration's Protean Nature: The Value of Rules and the Risks of Discretion", (2003) 19 Arb Int 279.

22 This is the conclusion of empirical research conducted by the School of International Arbitration at Queen Mary, University of London; see *International arbitration: Corporate attitudes and practices* (2006) 12 (only 24% of the corporations interviewed opt for *ad hoc* arbitration, which is perceived as appropriate for "primarily larger corporations with more experience of international arbitration").

the Notice of Arbitration) which must include the factual basis of the claim as well as "all documents [the claimant] deems relevant".[23] Not to determine the respondent's position – perhaps for six months – is wasteful. It does not promote reciprocal understanding of the dispute, and therefore impedes efficient preparation for both litigation and amicable settlement. Moreover, it is not good practice to constitute an arbitral tribunal without having any indication of the kind of case that will be mounted in defence, as this may bear on the required attributes of arbitrators, especially if any appointment is to be made by an Appointing Authority; this goes for *both* of the co-arbitrators as well as the presiding arbitrator. Furthermore, giving the respondent an opportunity to submit a Response to the claimant's Notice of Arbitration permits the inclusion of a requirement that the Response should contain any counterclaims that the respondent intends to raise. This would, in turn, permit the claimant to articulate in its Statement of Claim both its positive case (on its claim) and its defensive case (on the respondent's counterclaim). Finally, the exchange of a Notice of Arbitration and Response will permit the tribunal meaningfully to exercise its power under the proposed article 15(1) to issue the appropriate procedural directions for the conduct of the proceedings. Thus, the claimant's Notice of Arbitration and the respondent's Response are in principle not envisaged as substantive pleadings: they are to delineate the contours and complexion of the case, rather than fully articulate it.[24] In simpler cases, however, the parties may wish to submit a more substantial Notice of Arbitration and Response, and treat them as a Statement of Claim and a Statement of Defence respectively. Articles 18(1) and 19(1) are to preserve that option.

(b) **The claimant's Statement of Claim to follow the respondent's Response**: The present articles 3(4)(c) and 18(1) permit the claimant to include its Statement of Claim in its Notice of Arbitration. This option would serve no useful purpose. Indeed, it would be inconsistent with the requirement that the respondent submit a Response to the claimant's Notice of Arbitration. Further, in cases where the tribunal decides to devote a preliminary phase of the proceedings to its jurisdiction or to issues of admissibility, the claimant's notice/statement may well have been superseded by events that occurred during that preliminary phase (which may be lengthy). While the inclusion of the Statement of Claim in the Notice of Arbitration may expedite the proceedings, this may also be achieved in other ways, notably by an accelerated timetable and by giving both parties the option of treating their opening pleadings as their first memorials.

(c) **Composition of tribunal**: The present provisions (articles 5-7) are designed to give an opportunity to the parties to agree on (a) the number of arbitrators, (b) the identity of the Appointing Authority, and (c) the identity of the arbitrators. While this is laudable, it may be exploited by recalcitrant litigants. One improvement would be to allow any party to request the PCA to designate an Appointing Authority at any time. This would, further, permit an amendment to the present rule according to which the default number of arbitrators is three. While the rule is in principle sound, it has the potential to deter small claims from being brought to arbitration on considerations of cost. If an Appointing Authority can be designated at any time, as we propose, the decision on the number of arbitrators may be taken by that Authority in light of the nature and circumstances of the case. Finally, the provisions relating to the appointment of arbitrators may be grouped under a single article (rather than two, as is now the case under articles 6 and 7), for simplicity and consistency.

---

23 See article 18(2) of the Rules.

24 Contrast, for example, ss 6 and 9 of the DIS Rules, under which the proceedings are commenced by a "statement of claim" followed by a "statement of defence".

(d) **Multiparty arbitration**: Commercial agreements in the international sphere increasingly involve a multitude of contracting parties. The ICC's statistics indicate that multiparty cases, involving more than one claimant or respondent, have steadily increased from 20% in 1991-1998 and 25% in 1999 to 30% of the cases registered in 2001. This trend was consolidated in 2002-2005: in each of those years approximately one-third of the cases registered by the ICC were multiparty cases.[25] The implications of the landmark judgment of the French *Cour de cassation* in *Dutco* appears now to have been fully assimilated in principle and in practice.[26] The English Arbitration Act 1996 (s 16 and s 18), the ICC Rules (Article 10), the LCIA Rules (Article 8.1), and the WIPO Rules (Article 18) indicate the solution to be adopted: an external Appointing Authority is to appoint the entire tribunal when parties on the same side are unable to agree on one arbitrator to be appointed jointly by all of them.[27] There is no proper justification for the UNCITRAL Rules retaining the potential for paralysis; they are outdated in this respect.

(e) **General procedural duties and powers; procedural conferences; default provisions on specific procedural matters**: Article 15(1) expressly permits the arbitral tribunal to "conduct the arbitration in such manner as it considers appropriate". This is the hallmark of arbitration – that the format and timetable of the proceedings should be tailor-made to the circumstances of each particular case. While there is therefore no intention of detracting from the general rule in article 15(1), it seems appropriate in light of modern practice to include a general provision to the effect that the tribunal has a duty to take all steps necessary for an expeditious and efficient resolution of the dispute, and issue appropriate directions to the parties. The parties would have a corresponding duty to co-operate with (or among) each other and with the tribunal, including by complying with its directions; failure to do so would have costs consequences. These general rules would be supplemented by default provisions, subject to contrary party agreement, giving the tribunal specific powers on consolidation, joinder, and other matters.

(f) **Truncated tribunals and obstructing arbitrators**: This issue is touched upon in article 13, on substitute arbitrators; and in article 32(4), requiring the majority of the tribunal to state the reasons for the absence of one arbitrator's signature from an award. Clear rules are required to deal with two situations:

- *Where the tribunal decides to "proceed with the arbitration"*[28] *notwithstanding the absence of one of its members.* The *Himpurna* case, involving an arbitrator impeded from attending hearings by agents of the respondent state that had appointed him, was conducted under the UNCITRAL Rules.[29] The decision of the two remaining arbitrators to proceed to fulfil their mandate and render an award reflects what Judge Schwebel has called "the better, but not the only, view of the matter".[30] A clear rule would avoid the need to make controversial interpretations in the midst of a crisis.

---

25 The ICC statistics are to be found in the first issue of the *ICC Bull* for each year. The relevant figures for 1991-1999 are to found in (2003) 14:1 ICC Bull 8.

26 See Cass Civ 1re, 7 January 1992, *Sociétés Siemens & BKMI v Société Dutco* (1992) 119 JDI 707; and cf Case Ä 7197-01 (Stockholm District Court, 2001) noted Petrochilos, [2002:1] Stockholm Arb Rep 201.

27 Whitesell and Silva-Romero, "Multiparty and Multicontract Arbitration: Recent ICC Experience" (2003) ICC Bull (Special Supplement – Complex Arbitration) 7.

28 As article 28(2) provides in case of a party's failure to appear at a hearing.

29 See *Himpurna California Energy Ltd (Bermuda) v Republic of Indonesia* (2000) 25 YCA 186, para 59 (Final Award, UNCITRAL, 1999). The impeded arbitrator, Priyatna Abdurrasyid, has related his experience in a chapter of his memoirs entitled "They said I was going to be kidnapped", (2003) 18:6 Mealey's Int'l Arb Rep 29.

30 Schwebel, "Injunction of Arbitral Proceedings and Truncation of the Tribunal", (2003) 18:4 Mealey's Int'l Arb Rep 33, 38.

- *Where the tribunal perceives that one of its members is obstructing the progress of the case, including the tribunal's deliberations.* The parties are not privy to the internal workings of the tribunal, so they are not in a position to prove that it is appropriate to replace the obstructing arbitrator. A clear rule is required to give the tribunal the power to complete its mission and render an award.

(g) **Confidentiality**: Articles 25(4) and 32(5) deal with the confidentiality of hearings and awards respectively, but there are no rules regarding the confidentiality of the proceedings as such or of the materials (including pleadings) before the tribunal. An explicit provision is overdue in any event, but now becomes essential given the pressures generated in the context of investment arbitrations. The possibility of accepting *amicus* briefs (see the proposed article 15(5)) reinforces the need for clear provisions on confidentiality.

(h) **Majority decision**: Article 31(1), requiring that "any award or other decision of the arbitral tribunal shall be made by a majority of the arbitrators", is inconsistent with the better rule, that the presiding arbitrator may decide alone if no majority is formed. It is true that this rule is hardly ever applied. But it would be false to think that it is therefore unimportant. The co-arbitrators are aware of the existence of the rule, so each of them has a clear incentive to adopt a reasonable posture. Put otherwise, the value of the rule permitting awards to be made by the presiding arbitrator alone lies primarily in its deterrent force. By contrast, under the UNCITRAL Rules, the onus in difficult cases is on the presiding arbitrator to move toward the least unreasonable co-arbitrator. Judge Bellet was heard to say that article 31(1) was an important reason for his resignation from the Iran-US Claims Tribunal.[31]

(i) **Production of documents**: Article 24(3) is overly vague. It contains no hint of the criteria by reference to which a tribunal might "require" the production of "documents, exhibits, or other evidence". The width of the tribunal's power in this respect is in part due to the fact that articles 18(2) and 19(2), on the Statement of Claim and the Statement of Defence respectively, permit the claimant and the respondent to "add a reference to the documents or other evidence [they] will submit" at a later a stage, rather than produce that evidence with those submissions. This option does not comport with current practice, and ought to be corrected. This would also permit a reformulation of article 24(3), in line with Articles 3 and 9 of the IBA Rules.

(j) **Interim measures**: Article 26 is narrowly worded (it refers only to "measures ... necessary in respect of the subject-matter of the dispute"), and contains an illustrative enumeration of measures that does not cover contemporary needs. UNCITRAL's own (ongoing) efforts in this field ought to be taken into account in reformulating article 26 in a way that will permit tribunals to issue any provisional or conservatory measures properly required in the circumstances.

(k) **Interpretation of awards**: There has now been significant experience on article 35, notably in the Iran-US Claims Tribunal. The Rules should be clarified in the interest of predictability. The key concept is that this provision should apply only if there is a dispute as to what the award orders the parties to do.

(l) **Tribunal fees**: Article 39(1) of the Rules, requiring that fees be "reasonable in amount", is in itself unobjectionable. In most cases involving experienced practitioners, the issue of fees is handled properly. But there have been disturbing instances of "negotiations" regarding fees between arbitrators and the parties, especially where one party finds it tactically appealing to accept anything the arbitrators say. Such experiences can cause loss of respect for the process. (And of course the purpose of having rules is

---

31. The formal letter of resignation tendered by Judge Bellet on 1 December 1982 is described by Aldrich, *The Jurisprudence of the Iran – United States Claims Tribunal* (1996) 18. Judge Bellet formally cited the unexpectedly large amount of cases and delays encountered in the work of the Tribunal as the reasons for his resignation.

not for the easy cases, where the participants have similar expectations.) There is no simple solution in the context of *ad hoc* rules, but the subject deserves serious attention in order to avoid the spectre of self-dealing arbitrators.

15. The importance of these issues demonstrates, in our view, that the need for a revision is not neutralised by the consideration that the existing Rules have been incorporated in other legal instruments (eg, BITs) and therefore enshrine settled expectations. It cannot be assumed that the expectations of the users of the Rules are settled in any way. To the contrary, users expect rules to be revised to accommodate innovations that reflect best practice. Such revisions are routinely brought into effect using familiar techniques of transitional rules.

IV. STRUCTURE OF THIS REPORT

16. The main body of our analysis and conclusions is set out at paragraphs 21 *et seq* below. For ease of review, we have dealt separately with each article whose revision should be considered; this gives rise to crossreferencing, and explains a certain degree of repetition. In respect of each provision, we start with its current text before going on to set out the rationale for revision and ending with a possible revised wording. Provisions that, in our view, give rise to no revision (or only to minor changes, in capitalization of terms for the sake of consistency) have not been dealt with in the main body of this report.

17. Where we suggest the insertion of a new article, we have provisionally numbered it after the article preceding it, in order to maintain the current article numbering of the Rules: thus, the new article on the respondent's Response is article 3*bis*. This makes for a few awkward references ("article 15*bis*(2)"), but on the whole facilitates the comparison between proposed new articles and the existing articles. Similarly, we have followed – rather than altering – the existing structure of the Rules. Again, this was to facilitate review, and in no way to foreclose the question whether the existing structure of the Rules should be maintained – a question that in our submission requires serious consideration, but at a later stage. (For example, it is arguable that provisions dealing with multiplicity of parties (eg, proposed articles 7 and 15(8)) should be gathered in a discrete section.) We fully recognize that our approach results in an inelegant clustering of many important, and diverse, procedural powers in and around article 15;[32] but that can be easily corrected later.

18. For consistency, we have on the whole followed the nomenclature and style of the present Rules. Thus, where we propose new wording for an existing, or a new provision, we have tried to emulate as closely as possible relevant phraseology of existing provisions (eg "counter-claim" rather than "counterclaim"). However, it is undeniable that some of the terms of the 1976 text now appear quite outdated or inappropriate (eg exclusively masculine pronouns for arbitrators and parties, and "either" party rather than "any"), and the English syntax is sometimes odd. In addition, current usage is to capitalize certain terms as defined terms: eg, Statement of Claim, Claimant, Arbitral Tribunal. The importance of the UNCITRAL Rules is so great that they merit clear and elegant expression.

19. An annex to this report sets out the present text of the UNCITRAL Rules against the revised text proposed in this report.

32 Specifically, article 15(1) remains a principal, overarching provision, with two additional sentences; it is followed by several more detailed (and diverse) provisions in article 15(2)-(9). The existing article 15(2)-(3) is then incorporated in a new article 15*bis*, and there is also a new article 15*ter*, on confidentiality.

V. ACKNOWLEDGMENTS

20. An earlier "discussion draft" of this report (dated 31 March 2006) was considered by the Secretariat[33] and circulated by the authors to a limited number of colleagues.[34] We have received valuable input,[35] which we have endeavoured to reflect in the present text. Finally, we have sought to incorporate reports and discussions at a colloquium to honour the 30th anniversary of the Rules, which was held on 6-7 April 2006 in Vienna.

ARTICLE 1(1)

I. Present Rule

> Where the parties to a contract have agreed in writing* that disputes in relation to that contract shall be referred to arbitration under the UNCITRAL Arbitration Rules, then such disputes shall be settled in accordance with these Rules subject to such modification as the parties may agree in writing.

---

* MODEL ARBITRATION CLAUSE

Any dispute, controversy or claim arising out of or relating to this contract, or the breach, termination or invalidity thereof, shall be settled by arbitration in accordance with the UNCITRAL Arbitration Rules as at present in force.

Note – Parties may wish to consider adding:
(a) The appointing authority shall be ... (name of institution or person);
(b) The number of arbitrators shall be ... (one or three);
(c) The place of arbitration shall be ... (town or country);
(d) The language(s) to be used in the arbitral proceedings shall be ...

---

21. The issues that arise in respect of Article 1(1) concern:
- the twin requirement that an arbitration agreement be "in writing" and that modifications thereof also be "in writing";
- the applicable version of the Rules, in case they are revised; and
- the apparent limitation that disputes arbitrable under the Rules must be "in relation to [a] contract".

22. As to the "in writing" requirement, the *travaux* indicate that it was intended to serve two distinct purposes. First, there was (and is) the issue of conformity with Article II(1)-(2) of the New York Convention[36] and with national laws to same or similar effect. Secondly, there was a concern that the parties' agreement should clearly express – hence "in writing" – an intention to arbitrate under the Rules.[37] It was, however, decided that the Rules should make

---

33 See the Note by the Secretariat prepared for the September 2006 meeting of Working Group II, UN Doc A/CN.9/WG.II/WP.143 and Add.1 (20 July 2006).

34 Key conclusions of that discussion draft are outlined in a Note by the Secretariat, UN Doc A/CN.9/610/Add.1 (3 April 2006) paras 3-13. The preliminary report is now available electronically at *Transnational Dispute Management* (*TDM*), www.transnational-dispute-management.com/.

35 Notably from Professors van den Berg and Berger.

36 See UNCITRAL Discussions on Preliminary Draft Rules, para 18.

37 See Report of UNCITRAL Secretary General on Revised Draft Rules (Commentary on Article 1), para 7.

no attempt to define what is a "writing" and how it is formed, leaving this matter to the New York Convention and applicable national laws.[38]

23. As to the reference to disputes "in relation to [a] contract", it was recognized as a narrow formulation but was nonetheless intentionally retained, in preference to a wider reference to "defined legal relationships".[39]

II. Discussion

Agreement to arbitrate and modifications of the Rules "in writing"

24. The drafters of the Rules recognized a need for the "in writing" requirement to be formulated in simple and broad terms, allowing it to operate without difficulty under a variety of applicable laws and the New York Convention (and, one might add, Article 6 of the European Convention on Human Rights[40]). This remains a valid consideration, in light of UNCITRAL's ongoing work on arbitration agreements recorded or concluded electronically.[41] The text of article 1(1) as it stands seems to be capable of accommodating future legislative developments on the concept of "writing",[42] and should be retained on this basis.[43] (While we acknowledge the force of an argument that the requirement (if any) of an agreement in writing should be left to the law of the arbitration,[44] the approach in article 1(1) has the merit of permitting the tribunal to identify with more certainty an agreement to arbitrate "under the ... Rules".)

25. By contrast, article 1(1) is less compelling where it requires that the parties should set out any modifications they wish to make in a written agreement, or at least reduce those agreed modifications to writing. Either interpretation of the wording of article 1(1) would bring about unreasonable results in cases of *de minimis* modifications. For example, articles 18(1) and 19(1) call for the submission of ("*shall* communicate") a "statement of claim" and a "statement of defence", but the parties may prefer the terms "memorial" and "counter-memorial":[45] no agreement in writing should be required. More generally, the parties are better placed to evaluate

---

38 Hence a draft article 1(3) ("'Agreement in writing' means an arbitration clause in a contract or a separate agreement, including an exchange of letters, signed by the parties, or contained in an exchange of telegrams or telexes.") was omitted from the final text of the Rules; see UNCITRAL Discussions on Preliminary Draft Rules, para 21.

39 See Report of UNCITRAL Committee of the Whole II, para 13; and UNCITRAL Discussions on Preliminary Draft Rules, para 17.

40 See Petrochilos, *Procedural Law in International Arbitration* (2004) paras 4.13-4.14.

41 UNCITRAL's current proposals relate to a possible interpretative declaration in respect of Articles II(2) and VII(1) of the New York Convention and a revised Article 7 of the Model Law on International Commercial Arbitration; see Note by Secretariat, Preparation of Uniform Provisions on Written Form for Arbitration Agreements, UN Doc A/CN.9/WG.II/WP.139 (2005); Sorieul, "UNCITRAL'S Current Work in the Field of International Commercial Arbitration", (2005) 22:6 J Int'l Arb 543. Under the CIETAC Arbitration Rules (as revised in 2005), Article 5(3), an arbitration agreement must be "in the tangible form of a document [including] EDI [electronic data interchange], or Email".

42 For example, where the applicable law qualifies as "agreements in writing" agreements concluded "otherwise than in writing by reference to terms which are in writing" (Arbitration Act 1996 (England & Wales) s 5(3)), reference to standard terms providing for arbitration under the UNCITRAL Rules would satisfy the requirement of writing under both the applicable law and article 1(1) of the Rules. See further Landau, "The Requirement of a Written Form for an Arbitration Agreement: When 'Written' Means 'Oral'", in van den Berg (ed), *International Commercial Arbitration: Important Contemporary Questions* (ICCA Congress Series No 11, 2003) 19.

43 Professor Sanders has, however, taken a different view; see *Sanders* (2004) 262.

44 See, eg, Article 4(3)(d) of the ICC Rules.

45 In *Saluka Investments BV v Czech Republic*, the parties agreed to such a change in nomenclature, and this was part of the arrangements that the tribunal and the parties agreed upon at a procedural hearing; see the Partial Award of 17 March 2006, para 7(f).

whether the modifications they desire are of such importance or detail as to call for a written agreement or document. Rare cases of disputes between the parties on whether they have or have not agreed to modify the Rules in any way would be resolved by the arbitral tribunal on the basis of this general principle.

26. The foregoing considerations lead to the proposal that the second "in writing" requirement in article 1(1) be deleted, in favour of the formulation "subject to such modification as the parties may agree upon".

Which version of the Rules to apply?

27. As already noted, the model arbitration clause accompanying article 1(1) refers to the Rules "as at present in force", so catering for the eventuality of a revision. In practice, and in particular in investment-treaty practice, such language is found infrequently. Most investment treaties simply refer to the "arbitration rules of the United Nations Commission on International Trade Law".[46] Only a few treaties expressly stipulate that, in the event of a revision of the Rules, the applicable version will be the one in force at the time of the initiation of the arbitration.[47] Even rarer are examples of BITs qualifying this language by reference to General Assembly Resolution 31/98[48] or the year of adoption of the Rules (1976).[49]

28. The experience with the ICC Rules indicates that a revised version of the Rules should contain an express interpretative provision to the effect that when the parties have agreed to arbitrate under the UNCITRAL Rules, they shall be deemed to have submitted *ipso facto* to the Rules in effect on the date of the commencement of the arbitration proceedings[[50]] unless they have agreed to submit to the Rules in effect on the date of their arbitration agreement.[51]

29. A General Assembly Resolution on the revised version of the UNCITRAL Rules might additionally recommend that where the parties have agreed to the 1976 Rules they should consider expressly agreeing to arbitrate pursuant to the revised version of the Rules.

Arbitrable disputes "in relation to [the parties'] contract"

30. It is plain that the UNCITRAL Rules have been used, and will continue to be used, in investment disputes that either (a) do not relate to a contract at all[52] or (b) relate to a contract involving a person that is not a party in the arbitration.[53] This was also the case for several claims of "expropriation or other measures affecting property rights" before the Iran-US Claims Tribunal.[54]

---

46 See for example NAFTA Article 1120(1)(c); Article 10(3)(b) of the Greek Model BIT (2001), reprinted in UNCTAD, *International Investment Instruments: A Compendium* vol VIII (2003) 273; and Article 1 of the 2004 United States of America Model BIT.

47 See, eg, the Hong Kong SAR – Italy BIT (1995); United Kingdom of Great Britain and Northern Ireland – Bosnia and Herzegovina BIT (2002); and Article 8(2)(c) of the United Kingdom Model BIT (1991), reprinted in UNCTAD, *International Investment Instruments: A Compendium* vol III (1996) 185.

48 See, eg, the Egypt-Turkmenistan BIT (1995).

49 See, eg, the India-Portugal BIT (2000); and the Korea-Singapore BIT (2005).

50 As opposed to the version of the Rules in force at the time of the conclusion of the arbitration agreement.

51 ICC Rules, Article 6; on which see further *Derains & Schwartz* 74. The LCIA Rules contain an introductory statement referring not only to the current version of those Rules ("the following Rules") but also to "such amended rules as the LCIA may have adopted hereafter to take effect before the commencement of the arbitration".

52 For example, disputes on the withdrawal of a licence, under an investment treaty; see, eg, *International Thunderbird Gaming Corp v United Mexican States*, (Award of 26 January 2006).

53 As was the case in *CME* and *Lauder*: *CME Czech Republic BV v The Czech Republic* (Partial Award of 13 September 2001), and *Ronald S Lauder v The Czech Republic* (Final Award of 3 September 2001).

54 Claims Settlement Declaration (note 12 above) Article II(1). Accordingly, Article 1 of the Rules of Procedure of the Iran-US Claims Tribunal did not refer to "disputes in relation to [a] contract". See

31. Apart from investment disputes and similar cases, there is no cogent reason to limit the ambit of the Rules to "disputes in relation to [a] contract", if the applicable arbitration law contains no such requirement. Thus, Article 7(1) of the Model Law permits arbitration of disputes "in respect of a defined legal relationship, whether contractual or not". Consistently with this approach, other major sets of arbitration rules (such as the ICC Rules and the LCIA Rules) contain no reference to the classes of disputes that are arbitrable under them. The arbitrability of a dispute is properly a matter for the law of the arbitration, and there is nothing on the face of the UNCITRAL Rules to suggest that they are not suitable for the resolution of non-contractual disputes.

32. This issue did arise in the *Larsen v The Hawaiian Kingdom* case, which concerned a dispute about the alleged "unlawful imposition of American municipal laws over claimant's person within the territorial jurisdiction of the Hawaiian Kingdom." The arbitrability of the dispute under the UNCITRAL Rules (on the application of which the parties had agreed) was raised by the tribunal of its own motion as a preliminary matter.[55]

The tribunal held as follows:

> When regard is had to the non-prescriptive and non-coercive nature of the UNCITRAL Rules as a standard regime available for parties to apply to resolve disputes between them, however, there appears no reason why the UNCITRAL Rules cannot be adapted to apply to a non-contractual dispute. For example, the parties could agree that a dispute as to tort, or occupier's or environmental liability might be determined in an arbitration applying the UNCITRAL Rules. Moreover they could so agree in relation to a dispute which had already arisen independently of any contractual relationship between them. In this manner the parties to an arbitration may specifically or by implication adopt or apply the UNCITRAL Rules to any dispute.[56]

33. The *Larsen* tribunal felt the need to be satisfied that the dispute brought before it was arbitrable under the Rules; the parties had no such doubts. It would be good to resolve that question once for all, pre-empting possible preliminary objections on the arbitrability of non-contractual disputes under the Rules.

34. For the sake of consistency (see proposed article 16(5)) we recommend changing the model arbitration clause to refer to the "juridical seat", rather than the "place of arbitration".

III. Proposed Revision

35. Proposed revised text of article 1(1):

> Where the parties ~~to a contract~~ have agreed in writing* ~~that disputes in relation to that contract shall be referred~~ to arbitration of disputes under the UNCITRAL Arbitration Rules

---

also *The Republic Srpska v The Federation of Bosnia and Herzegovina*, Arbitration over inter-entity boundary in Brcko Area (Award on Control over the Brcko Corridor, 14 February 1997), (1997) 36 ILM 396, which was an arbitration brought under the Dayton Accords to settle an inter-entity boundary dispute.

55 *Larsen v The Hawaiian Kingdom*, Procedural Order No 3 (17 July 2000) para 8 (quoted at para 6.2 of the Award (2001), 119 ILR 566):

> On the face of the pleadings, however, it appears that the dispute referred to arbitration is not a dispute "in relation to a contract" between the parties, or a dispute that relates to any other contractual or quasicontractual relationship between them, or that it falls within the field of "international commercial relations" referred to in the preamble to the United Nations General Assembly resolution which adopted the Rules (General Assembly resolution 31/98, 15 December 1976). There is therefore a preliminary question whether the dispute identified in Article 1 of the [parties' arbitration] Agreement is an arbitrable dispute under the Rules.

56 *Larsen* Award, ibid, para 10.7.

in respect of a defined legal relationship, whether contractual or not, then such disputes shall be settled in accordance with these Rules subject to such modification as the parties may agree ~~in writing~~ upon. The parties shall be deemed to have submitted to the Rules in effect on the date of commencement of the arbitration proceedings, unless they have specified the Rules in effect on the date of their arbitration agreement.

---

* MODEL ARBITRATION CLAUSE

Any dispute, controversy or claim arising out of or relating to this contract, or the breach, termination or invalidity thereof, shall be settled by arbitration in accordance with the UNCITRAL Arbitration Rules as at present in force.

Note – Parties may wish to consider adding:

(a) The A~~a~~ppointing A~~a~~uthority shall be … (name of institution or person);
(b) The number of arbitrators shall be … (one or three);
(c) The ~~place of arbitration~~ juridical seat shall be … (~~town~~ city or country);
(d) The language(s) to be used in the arbitral proceedings shall be …

ARTICLE 1(2)

I. Present Rule

These Rules shall govern the arbitration except that where any of these Rules is in conflict with a provision of the law applicable to the arbitration from which the parties cannot derogate, that provision shall prevail.

36. Article 1(2) was added to the text of the Rules by the Committee on the Whole, in 1976, in order to make clear that the application of the Rules was subject to a controlling national arbitration law (the *lex arbitri*).[57] The Rules do not themselves define which law is the controlling law, nor the provisions of that law "from which the parties cannot derogate". These questions are left – and in our view properly so – to the arbitral tribunal.[58]

II. Discussion

37. There are two concerns in relation to article 1(2). The first is that there is a general reference to "the law applicable to the arbitration", without clarifying that the body of law that is relevant is *arbitration* law. The second concern is that it is often assumed that "law" can only be the law of a given state (ordinarily the law of the juridical seat of the arbitration[59]), as opposed to public international law. Doubtless this is valid in the vast majority of cases, including UNCITRAL arbitrations under BITs or the NAFTA.[60] But, where a state or international organization is involved as an arbitrating party, it need not be so; and in some cases it is not

---

57 See Report of UNCITRAL Committee of the Whole II, para 12. The initial text proposed read simply: "These Rules are subject to the law applicable to the arbitration"; see UNCITRAL Report on the work of its 9th Session, para 53. For further details see Petrochilos (note 40 above) para 5.39 and the references.

58 See further ibid Chapters 2-3 and in particular 5, with references.

59 Cf article 32(7), requiring an award to be "filed or registered" if this is a requirement of the law "of the country where the award is made".

60 See Petrochilos (note 40 above) paras 6.60-6.62 and the references. Indeed, two NAFTA awards have been challenged (one successfully, in part) in the courts of the seat; see *United Mexican States v Metalclad Corp* [2001] BCSC 664; (2002) 119 ILR 647, (2002) 5 ICSID Rep 238 (Supreme Court of British Columbia, 2 May 2001); and *United Mexican States v Marvin Roy Feldman Karpa* (Court of Appeal for Ontario, 11 January 2005).

so.[61] (Note in that regard that the current practice of UN bodies and agencies is to agree to arbitration under the UNCITRAL Rules, in the expectation that such proceedings will *not* be governed by the national arbitration law of any state.[62])

38. The uncertainty in that regard has led to well-known problems in the early years of the Iran-US Claims Tribunal.[63] There is a straightforward way of eliminating it, by explicitly referring to "international law" in article 1(2). There would otherwise be no need to go further than article 1(2) currently does, in order to include a conflicts-of-laws provision defining which law it is that supplies the provisions from which the parties cannot derogate.[64]

III. Proposed Revision

39. Proposed revised text of article 1(2):

> These Rules shall govern the arbitration except that where any of these Rules is in conflict with a provision of the applicable arbitration law ~~applicable to the arbitration~~ (including, where applicable, international law) from which the parties cannot derogate, that provision shall prevail.

ARTICLE 2

I. Present Rule

> 1. For the purposes of these Rules, any notice, including a notification, communication or proposal, is deemed to have been received if it is physically delivered to the addressee or if it is delivered at his habitual residence, place of business or mailing address, or, if none of these can be found after making reasonable inquiry, then at the addressee's last-known residence or place of business. Notice shall be deemed to have been received on the day it is so delivered.
>
> 2. For the purposes of calculating a period of time under these Rules, such period shall begin to run on the day following the day when a notice, notification, communication or proposal is received. If the last day of such period is an official holiday or a non-business day at the residence or place of business of the addressee, the period is extended until the first business day which follows. Official holidays or non-business days occurring during the running of the period of time are included in calculating the period.

40. Both paragraphs in article 2 are based on the 1974 UNCITRAL Convention on the Limitation Period in the International Sale of Goods,[65] and embrace the so-called "effective receipt" theory.[66] They are intended to set forth default provisions, which the parties may vary.[67]

---

61 See Petrochilos (note 40 above) Chapter 6.

62 Ibid, paras 6.81-6.89.

63 Ibid, paras 6.09-6.49.

64 Cf Article 16.3 of the LCIA Rules and Article 59(b) of the WIPO Rules, both referring primarily to the "arbitration law of the seat of the arbitration".

65 See Report of UNCITRAL Secretary General on Revised Draft Rules (ad Article 3) para 1; and UNCITRAL Discussions on Preliminary Draft Rules, para 24.

66 See van Hof, *Commentary on the UNCITRAL Arbitration Rules: The Application by the Iran-US Claims Tribunal* (1991) 19.

67 See *Caron/Caplan/Pellonpää* 379.

II. Discussion

41. The existing text of article 2 is satisfactory in what it says. It does not, however, deal with three issues: (a) delivery by electronic means;[68] (b) service on states; and (c) the tribunal's ability to extend or abbreviate the time-periods stipulated in other provisions of the Rules.

42. Taking each of those matters in turn:

(a) The terms "physically delivered" in article 2(1) may be read as excluding electronic communications, contrary to contemporary practice.[69]
(b) In practice, claimants initiating arbitrations against states variously serve Notices of Arbitration to the respondent state's Ministry of Foreign Affairs, the Head of the Government, other Ministries, an ambassador of the respondent state, or (less frequently) autonomous state agencies.[70] This incoherent practice is prone to cause confusion, and does not assist states in receiving notice of proceedings in a timely fashion. A rule setting forth the state organs capable of receiving service would clarify matters.[71]
(c) The orderly conduct of the arbitral proceedings is primarily the responsibility of the arbitral tribunal, which has the power, and duty, to issue all appropriate directions in that regard.[72] In discharge of that power and duty, arbitral tribunals ought to have an express power to extend or abbreviate the time-periods stipulated under the Rules,[73] as necessary for a "fair and efficient process of resolving the parties' dispute". The practical value of such a power would of course arise in cases where the parties fail to agree on these matters. The wording we propose in this regard contains the essential elements of Article 4.7 of the LCIA Rules.

III. Proposed Revision

43. Proposed revised text of article 2:

> 1. For the purposes of these Rules, any notice, including a notification, communication or proposal, is deemed to have been received if it is physically delivered to the addressee or if it is delivered at his, her or its habitual residence, place of business or mailing address, or, if none of these can be found after making reasonable inquiry, then at the addressee's last-known residence or place of business. Notice shall be deemed to have been received on the day it is so delivered.
>
> 2. <u>Delivery pursuant to paragraph 1 may be made by facsimile, telex, e-mail or any other electronic means of communication that provides a durable record of dispatch and receipt.</u>

---

68 *Sanders* (2004) 246.

69 See, eg, Article 3(2) of the ICC Rules; Article 4.1 of the LCIA Rules; and cf Article 23(2) of the "Brussels Regulation" on Jurisdiction and Recognition of Judgments in Civil and Commercial Matters (Council Regulation (EC) No 44/2001, [2001] OJ L12/1). See also Article 9(2) of the proposed UN Convention on the Use of Electronic Communications in International Contracts, reprinted in UN Doc A/60/515 (2005) 7: Where the law requires that a communication or contract should be in writing, or provides consequences for the absence of a writing, that requirement is met by an electronic communication if the information contained therein is accessible so as to be usable for subsequent reference.

70 See, for the last-mentioned possibility, *Link-Trading v Department of Customs Control of the Republic of Moldova* (Jurisdiction) (16 March 2001). In that case, the intention in naming a Department of the Republic was to "su[e] the Republic in the name of its Customs Department": ibid, 4. The tribunal upheld its jurisdiction against the Republic.

71 Parties would naturally be free to agree otherwise. Thus, Article 2(3) of the Iran-US Claims Tribunal Rules of Procedure required service on the Agent of the government concerned.

72 Proposed revised article 15(1) makes this clear: see paragraphs 115 *et seq* below.

73 See, eg, Article 4.7 of the LCIA Rules; in exceptional cases, Article 38(c) of the WIPO Rules.

3. Any notice, including a notification, communication or proposal, is deemed to have been received by a state if it is delivered to an organ of that state that is competent, under the law of that state, to receive such notices. Unless the parties have agreed otherwise, the head of a diplomatic mission of a state shall be deemed a competent organ for the purposes of the present article.

4. For the purposes of calculating a period of time under these Rules, such period shall begin to run on the day following the day when a notice, notification, communication or proposal is received. If the last day of such period is an official holiday or a non-business day at the residence or place of business of the addressee, the period is extended until the first business day which follows. Official holidays or non-business days occurring during the running of the period of time are included in calculating the period.

5. In discharge of its duties under article 15, paragraph 1, the Arbitral Tribunal may at any time extend or abridge any period of time prescribed under or pursuant to these Rules.

ARTICLE 3

I. Present Rule

44. Article 3 reads:

1. The party initiating recourse to arbitration (hereinafter called the "claimant") shall give to the other party (hereinafter called the "respondent") a notice of arbitration.

2. Arbitral proceedings shall be deemed to commence on the date on which the is received by the respondent.

3. The notice of arbitration shall include the following:
(a) A demand that the dispute be referred to arbitration;
(b) The names and addresses of the parties;
(c) A reference to the arbitration clause or the separate arbitration agreement that is invoked;
(d) A reference to the contract out of or in relation to which the dispute arises;
(e) The general nature of the claim and an indication of the amount involved, if any;
(f) The relief or remedy sought;
(g) A proposal as to the number of arbitrators (i.e. one or three), if the parties have not previously agreed thereon.

4. The notice of arbitration may also include: (a) The proposals for the appointments of a sole arbitrator and an appointing authority referred to in article 6, paragraph 1; (b) The notification of the appointment of an arbitrator referred to in article 7; (c) The statement of claim referred to in article 18.

II. Discussion

45. The purpose of a Notice of Arbitration generally is to "apprise the respondent of the general context of the claim that will be asserted against him and is useful in selecting qualified arbitrators".[74] Article 3(3)-(4) distinguishes between the necessary elements of the Notice of Arbitration and the optional elements thereof. One of the optional elements (article 3(4)(c)) is an inclusion of the claimant's Statement of Claim, as a means of expediting the proceedings.[75]

---

[74] See Report of UNCITRAL Secretary General on Preliminary Draft Rules (Commentary on Article 3) para 3.

[75] See Report of UNCITRAL Committee of the Whole II, paras 22-23.

46. Article 3 may be streamlined in two ways. First, it is important to separate the Notice of Arbitration from the Statement of Claim, consistently with the notion that the respondent should have an opportunity (and a duty) to express its views prior to the constitution of the arbitral tribunal.[76] Secondly, it would be useful for the Notice of Arbitration, being the claimant's initial pleading commencing the arbitration (article 3(2)), to contain all of the elements necessary to permit the respondent to take a position on (a) the claimant's claim, (b) the validity and scope of the arbitration agreement invoked, (c) counterclaims, and (d) the constitution of the tribunal. Article 1.1 of the LCIA Rules reflects that approach, and our proposed revised wording for article 3(3) of the Rules is consistent with the LCIA Rules in that regard.

47. We propose that article 3(4) be deleted: all elements set out in article 3(3), as amended below, would be obligatory, and the possibility for the claimant to treat its Notice of Arbitration as a Statement of Claim would be preserved by article 18(1). Our suggestions as to each sub-paragraph of article 3(3) are as follows:

(a) No amendment.
(b) The Notice should also set out the names and contact details of the claimant's counsel (if any).[77] This would lead to the deletion, in part, of the present article 4.
(c) There appears to be no cogent reason to permit the claimant simply to refer to – rather than provide a copy of – the arbitration agreement on which it relies. Indeed, one would imagine that receiving a copy of the arbitration agreement with the Notice of Arbitration would be particularly useful to the respondent in cases where, for example, the respondent is a successor to the person or entity that has concluded the arbitration agreement, or where the claimant and the respondent have several ongoing contracts on the basis of different standard terms, which contain different arbitration clauses.
(d) Consistently with article 1(1), provision should be made for disputes which do not arise "out of or in relation to" a contract. Where the dispute does arise out of a contract, a copy of that contract (rather than merely a reference to it) should be provided.
(e) To be retained, with a minor clarification: the claimant would provide "a brief description of the claim", rather than an indication of "[t]he general nature of the claim" as the current article 3(3)(e) provides.
(f) No amendment.
(g) The existing sub-paragraph (g) would be re-numbered (i). Subparagraph (g) would be drafted along the lines of Article 1.1(e) of the LCIA Rules, and require the claimant to make the appointment called for under the arbitration agreement (if the arbitration agreement calls for such an appointment); see the proposed article 6(3)(a).
(h) This would be the existing sub-paragraph (g), which is sound as far as it goes; see also the proposed article 5(2). However, if the claimant proposes that the tribunal consist of a sole arbitrator, it should also propose the name of one or more sole arbitrators: it is possible that the *identity* of a sole arbitrator proposed will make the sole arbitrator formation acceptable to the respondent.
(i) Consistent with the LCIA Rules[78] and the ICC Rules,[79] the claimant should also be required, under article 3(3), to make proposals on the juridical seat and language of the arbitration, if these matters have not already been agreed upon.

---

76 See paragraph 14(a) above; and paragraphs 49 *et seq* below, in respect of the proposed new article 3*bis*.

77 See Article 1.1(a) of the LCIA Rules; Article 9(ii) of the WIPO Rules; and Article 5(i) of the SCC Rules.

78 Article 1.1(d).

79 Article 4(3)(f).

III. Proposed Revision

48. Proposed revised text of article 3:

> 1. The party initiating recourse to arbitration (hereinafter called the "C~~c~~laimant") shall send to the other party (hereinafter called the "R~~r~~espondent") ~~a notice of arbitration~~Notice of Arbitration. If the parties have agreed that the case is to be administered by an institution a copy of the Notice of Arbitration shall be sent to that institution.
>
> 2. Arbitral proceedings shall be deemed to commence on the date on which the ~~notice of arbitration~~Notice of Arbitration is received by the R~~r~~espondent.
>
> 3. The ~~notice of arbitration~~Notice of Arbitration shall include the following:
> (a) A demand that the dispute be referred to arbitration;
> (b) The names, ~~and~~ addresses and other known contact details of the parties and of the person or persons (if any) representing or assisting the Claimant in the arbitration;
> (c) A copy of the ~~reference to the arbitration clause or the separate~~ arbitration agreement or other instrument ~~that is~~ invoked by the Claimant as the basis for commencing arbitration under the Rules;
> (d) A copy of ~~reference to~~ the contract, if any, out of or in relation to which the dispute arises;
> (e) ~~The general nature~~ A brief description of the dispute and the claim and an indication of the amount involved, if any;
> (f) The relief or remedy sought;
> (g) The identify of the Claimant's appointee, if the parties' agreement requires the parties to appoint arbitrators;
> (h) A proposal as to the number of arbitrators (i.e. one or three), if the parties have not ~~previously~~ agreed thereon. Where the Claimant proposes that the Arbitral Tribunal consist of a Sole Arbitrator, it shall also propose the names of one or more persons, one of whom would serve as the Sole Arbitrator;
> (i) The Claimant's proposals as to the juridical seat and language of the arbitration, if the parties have not already agreed on these matters.
>
> 4. ~~The notice of arbitration may also include:~~
> ~~(a) The proposals for the appointments of a sole arbitrator and an appointing authority referred to in article 6, paragraph 1.;~~
> ~~(b) The notification of the appointment of an arbitrator referred to in article 7;~~
> ~~(c) The statement of claim referred to in article 18.~~

NEW ARTICLE 3*bis*

I. Discussion

49. The rationale for requiring the submission of a brief "Response" (or, if that term is preferred, "Answer") by the respondent is straightforward and has been set out at paragraph 14(a) above. In essence, the Response would be a brief pleading in which the respondent would take a position on the claimant's Notice of Arbitration before the constitution of the tribunal and the submission of the claimant's Statement of Claim.[80] Thus, a Response would serve to indicate from the outset the respondent's views on:

- the existence or scope of the arbitration agreement invoked by the claimant;
- any other issues relating to the admissibility of the claimant's claim (which may be relevant to the timetable and format of the arbitration proceedings);

80 At present, the ICSID Rules, the UNCITRAL Rules, and the WIPO Rules are the only major sets of arbitration rules that do not require the respondent to submit a brief opening pleading before the constitution of a tribunal.

- the nature (character and magnitude) of the dispute, and the respondent's position on the claimant's claim;
- potential counterclaims;
- the constitution of the tribunal; and
- the juridical seat and language of the arbitration.

50. In other words, the exchange of the Notice of Arbitration and the Response would serve to set the stage for the subsequent phases of the arbitration, and to give a possibility to the respondent to have a measure of influence on the constitution of the tribunal. The Response is intended as a short document, mirroring the Notice of Arbitration. As stated in the Introduction to the Rules of the Netherlands Arbitration Institute (*NAI*) (at para 6.5):

> The request for arbitration and the short answer may be brief. Once the arbitrators are appointed, the parties will have a full opportunity to present their case. The request for arbitration and short answer should not be confused with the statements of claim and defence. These memorials are not submitted until after the arbitrators are appointed ... The request for arbitration and the short answer are meant primarily to inform the Administrator of the nature and circumstances of the dispute so as to facilitate the designation of the arbitrators.

51. Accordingly, the Response, as its name implies, would be a purely responsive pleading. It would incorporate elements that are under the current article 19(2) necessary parts of the Statement of Defence.

52. Our proposal proceeds on the basis that 30 days is a reasonable period for the submission of the respondent's Response.[81] This would lead to a consequential amendment in article 5, which at present provides that a three member tribunal is to be formed if within 15 days of the Notice of Arbitration the parties have not agreed on the principle of a single-member tribunal.

53. Finally, it would be appropriate to specify (on the example of Article 2.3 of the LCIA Rules) that the respondent's failure to submit a Response should not later preclude that party from denying the claimant's claims or from advancing its own counterclaims. This is consistent with article 19(3) of the present text of the Rules (requiring the respondent in principle to submit any counterclaims with its Statement of Defence).

II. Proposed Rule

54. Article 3*bis* would read as follows:

> RESPONSE TO THE NOTICE OF ARBITRATION
>
> <u>Article 3*bis*</u>
>
> <u>1. Within thirty days of receipt of the Notice of Arbitration, the Respondent shall send to the Claimant a written Response.</u>
>
> <u>2. The Response shall include the following:</u>
> <u>(a) A statement of the Respondent's position on particulars (a)-(f) and (h)-(i) of the Notice of Arbitration;</u>
> <u>(b) A brief description of any counter-claims advanced by the Respondent, including an indication of the amounts involved (if any), and the relief or remedy sought in respect of such counter-claims; and</u>
> <u>(c) If the parties' agreement requires the parties to appoint arbitrators, and the Respondent has not already made such an appointment, the identity of the Respondent's appointee.</u>

81 Cf Article 2.1 of the LCIA Rules; Article 5(6) of the ICC Rules; and Articles 11-12 of the WIPO Rules.

3. Failure to communicate a Response shall not preclude the Respondent from denying any claim or from advancing a counter-claim in the arbitration.

ARTICLE 4

I. Present Rule

The parties may be represented or assisted by persons of their choice. The names and addresses of such persons must be communicated in writing to the other party; such communication must specify whether the appointment is being made for purposes of representation or assistance.

II. Discussion

55. The "communications" provided for in article 4 would be made in the Notice of Arbitration and the Response, under articles 3(3)(b) and 3*bis*(2)(a), making the second part of article 4 redundant.

III. Proposed Revision

56. Proposed revised text of article 4:

> The parties may be represented andor assisted by persons of their choice. The names and addresses of such persons must be communicated in writing to the other party; such communication must specify whether the appointment is being made for purposes of representation or assistance.

SECTION II. COMPOSITION OF THE TRIBUNAL

57. The Rules devote four articles (articles 5-9) to the constitution of the arbitral tribunal. Those provisions are organized in a conceptually clear-cut way. First, the parties are given an opportunity to agree on the number of arbitrators, which is to be one or three, the default position being three (article 5). Secondly, there are separate provisions dealing respectively with sole-arbitrator formations (article 6) and three-member tribunals (article 7). Finally, article 8 complements articles 6 and 7 by some further procedural provisions.

58. Our preliminary report of March 2006 made three observations of considerable, in our view, importance:

- First, while the Rules give an opportunity to the parties to agree on the number of arbitrators, an Appointing Authority, and the identity of that Authority, the process for reaching agreement on all these matters is not explicitly set out in the Rules. In our March preliminary report, we organized the exchange of proposals between the parties in the Notice of Arbitration and the Response, and new provisions (in articles 5-7*quater*) were included in an attempt to cover all eventualities and sequences of possible agreement and disagreement.[82] The resulting provisions might have been comprehensive but, practically, they were too complex to be satisfactory.
- Secondly, the Rules do not at present address the question of multiparty cases at all. A specific provision is required in that regard.
- Finally, the present Rules do not deal with agreements pursuant to which an Appointing Authority is to appoint the entire tribunal. Again, a specific provision is called for.

---

[82] See paragraphs 40-51 of the March preliminary report; and the four-page flowchart describing the constitution of the tribunal at Annex 2 of the March report.

59. The present report proposes a simpler organization of the necessary provisions. In addition, it proposes a more prominent role for the Appointing Authority than is now the case: this is one of the reasons for which we propose that any party should have the right to request the Secretary-General of the PCA to designate an Appointing Authority at any time.

- Article 5 deals (as the present article 5) with the number of arbitrators. We propose a provision whereby if by the time the Response is due the parties have been unable to agree on the number of arbitrators (ie, in principle one or three), the Appointing Authority would decide on the matter. In addition, article 5 incorporates the text of the present article 8(2).
- A new article 5*bis* deals with the designation of the Appointing Authority, and incorporates in substance the present article 8(1).
- A new article 6 deals in one provision (instead of two, as is now the case, under articles 6-7) with the constitution of the tribunal, whether it consist of a sole arbitrator or three.
- A new article 7 sets forth rules for cases involving multiple parties.
- Article 8 deals with the situation where the constitution of the entire tribunal has been entrusted to an Appointing Authority.

60. We set out in the following paragraphs the reasoning for our approach in more detail.

ARTICLE 5

I. Present Rule

61. Article 5 reads:

> If the parties have not previously agreed on the number of arbitrators (i.e. one or three), and if within fifteen days after the receipt by the respondent of the notice of arbitration the parties have not agreed that there shall be only one arbitrator, three arbitrators shall be appointed.

II. Discussion

62. Four issues may be raised. First, whether the Rules should permit (and if so, cater for the constitution of) tribunals consisting of a number of arbitrators other than one or three. Secondly, whether the default number of arbitrators should be one or three. Thirdly, if the default number is to remain three, whether the Secretary-General of the PCA or the Appointing Authority should, on application of a party, nevertheless have the power to decide that "the dispute is such as to warrant the appointment" of a sole arbitrator.[83] Finally, the maintenance of the 15-day time period in which the parties may reach agreement on the number of arbitrators, in light of the 30-day period for the submission of the Response under proposed article 3*bis*.

63. The present text of article 5 makes it clear that a tribunal of a format other than a sole or three arbitrators – which undoubtedly represent less than 1% of intentional practice – requires the parties to agree to derogate from the Rules. We agree that there is no good reason to encourage parties to agree on two-member tribunals (with recourse to an umpire), fourmember tribunals (with one member having a casting vote), or tribunals comprising five or more members. This is not, however, to say that such formations are impermissible under the Rules. The text of

[83] Cf Article 8(2) of the ICC Rules (where the default position is that a sole arbitrator shall be appointed). See to the same effect Article 5 of the AAA Rules, according to which: "If the parties have not agreed on the number of arbitrators, one arbitrator shall be appointed unless the administrator determines in its discretion that three arbitrators are appropriate because of the large size, complexity or other circumstances of the case."

article 5 should reflect that such formations are possible under the Rules but that it is for the parties to make provision for the constitution of such tribunals.

64. Article 5 proceeds on the premise that the default, "safe" composition for arbitral tribunals sitting in international disputes should be three members.[84] Article 10 of the Model Law is to the same effect. However, claims involving relatively small sums have on occasion been heard by three-member tribunals simply because the respondent defaulted in the constitution of the tribunal. With a three-member tribunal as the default position, a respondent can force up costs by refusing to agree on a sole arbitrator where the claim does not warrant three. Though this would be a risky strategy, it may deter some claimants with good cases but limited resources. These problems would have been avoided if the Appointing Authority had the power to appoint a sole arbitrator when the circumstances justify this.

65. As to the 15-day period within which the parties may agree on a single- or three-member tribunal, it would simplify matters if the respondent expressed its views on the matter in the Response. This would permit the respondent more fully to articulate the reasons for its proposals on the constitution of the tribunal – for example, how counterclaims affect the nature and magnitude of the dispute, and any particular expertise or qualifications that a sole arbitrator should have. For this reason, we propose that the time-period in article 5 be harmonized with the 30-day period in which the respondent should submit its Response.

66. We also consider that the rule in current article 8(2) would appear more natural in the context of article 5, and recommend moving it to article 5(3).

III. Proposed Rule

67. Proposed text of the new article 5:

> 1. These Rules contemplate that the Arbitral Tribunal will be comprised of either a sole arbitrator or three arbitrators. The parties may agree otherwise, but in that case they shall also agree on the method by which the tribunal is to be constituted. If the Arbitral Tribunal has not been constituted within [ninety] days of receipt of the Notice of Arbitration, any party may request the Appointing Authority to make all necessary appointments. The Appointing Authority shall make the necessary appointments following the procedure in article 6, paragraphs 3-5, and select one arbitrator as the presiding arbitrator.
>
> 2. If the parties have not agreed on the number of arbitrators, the Notice of Arbitration shall contain a proposal for a Sole Arbitrator or a three-member tribunal. If any Respondent has not agreed to that proposal by the time at which it is required to communicate its Response, any party may request the Appointing Authority to decide, in light of such observations by the parties as the Appointing Authority may invite, whether a Sole Arbitrator or a threemember tribunal is to be appointed.
>
> 3. Whenever the names of one or more persons are proposed for appointment as arbitrators, their full names, contact details and nationalities shall be indicated, together with a description of their qualifications.

NEW ARTICLE 5*bis*

I. Discussion

68. Given the nature of the Rules as *ad hoc* rules, the availability of an Appointing Authority is crucial. The model arbitration clause accompanying article 1 encourages the parties to make

---

[84] See Report of UNCITRAL Committee of the Whole II, para 28; and UNCITRAL Discussions on Preliminary Draft Rules, para 39.

agreement on the Appointing Authority. Article 6(2)(b) (and article 7(2)(b)) provide a safety net: if the parties have not agreed, and are unable to agree, on an "institution or person" to perform the functions of an Appointing Authority, the Secretary-General of the PCA is to designate such an authority.

69. The *travaux* indicate that the "designating authority" role of the Secretary-General of the PCA was envisaged in the preliminary draft text of the Rules.[85] Experience shows that the dual structure of the Rules (designating authority and Appointing Authority) works well. The PCA has an experienced and professional secretariat of specialized lawyers, and considerable track record in identifying the institution or person who should serve as Appointing Authority in a given case.[86] The role of the PCA should therefore be retained. Indeed, it may be useful in the interest of efficiency that the possibility be given to the parties directly to designate the PCA as Appointing Authority.

70. Similarly, the list-procedure provided for in the current article 6(3) (and article 7(3)) seems to work well, in line with the intentions of its drafters.[87] (Indeed, it is on occasion used in discussions between parties attempting to reach agreement on a sole or presiding arbitrator in arbitrations under other rules.) On the other hand, it is in our experience unnecessary to require the Appointing Authority always and exclusively to resort to that procedure; our proposed article 6(3) spells this out.

71 We propose that a new article 5*bis* be included in the Rules to deal exclusively with the designation of an Appointing Authority, by the parties or the Secretary-General of the PCA. To discourage dilatory tactics and increase efficiency, we propose that the parties should have the ability to seek the designation of an Appointing Authority at any time: in other words, such designation would no longer be contingent on a failure in the constitution of the tribunal and the passage of a 60-day period (as is now the case under articles 6(2) and 7(2)). The minor incidental cost involved in such an advance designation is more than offset by the efficiency gains.

72. Recourse to the Secretary-General of the PCA is separately provided for in cases where the Appointing Authority fails to make an appointment within 30 (not 60, as is now the case) days of a request to do so; see article 6(6).

73. The proposed article 5*bis* would also incorporate two procedural provisions (in paragraphs (3) and (4)) reflecting in substance the existing article 8(1) of the Rules.

II. Proposed Rule

74. Proposed text of new article 5*bis*:

> 1. The parties may agree on a person or institution, including the Secretary-General of the Permanent Court of Arbitration at The Hague, to exercise the functions of the Appointing Authority under these Rules.
>
> 2. In the event that the parties have not agreed on the identity of an Appointing Authority, any party may, with or at any time following the Notice of Arbitration, request the Secretary-General of the Permanent Court of Arbitration at The Hague to designate another person or institution as the Appointing Authority.

85 See Report of UNCITRAL Secretary General on Preliminary Draft Rules, 169, para 2.

86 See, eg, PCA Annual Report (2004) 10.

87 "This procedure ... gives the parties an opportunity to raise objections against certain candidates, which may avoid challenge proceedings after an appointment has been made": *Sanders* (1977) 186.

3. When a party requests the Appointing Authority or the Secretary-General of the Permanent Court of Arbitration at The Hague to exercise their functions under these Rules, it shall supply with its request copies of the Notice of Arbitration and (if available) the Response, together with the supporting materials required under article 3, paragraph 3 and article 3*bis*, paragraph 2. The Appointing Authority or the Secretary-General of the Permanent Court of Arbitration at The Hague may require from any of the parties such further information as they deem necessary to exercise their functions.

4. All requests or other communications between a party and the Appointing Authority or the Secretary-General of the Permanent Court of Arbitration at The Hague shall also be provided, in copy, to all other parties.

ARTICLE 6 (OLD ARTICLES 6-7)

I. Present Rule

75. Article 6 reads:

1. If a sole arbitrator is to be appointed, either party may propose to the other:
   (a) The names of one or more persons, one of whom would serve as the sole arbitrator; and
   (b) If no appointing authority has been agreed upon by the parties, the name or names of one or more institutions or persons, one of whom would serve as appointing authority.

2. If within thirty days after receipt by a party of a proposal made in accordance with paragraph 1 the parties have not reached agreement on the choice of a sole arbitrator, the sole arbitrator shall be appointed by the appointing authority agreed upon by the parties. If no appointing authority has been agreed upon by the parties, or if the appointing authority agreed upon refuses to act or fails to appoint the arbitrator within sixty days of the receipt of a party's request therefore, either party may request the Secretary-General of the Permanent Court of Arbitration at The Hague to designate an appointing authority.

3. The appointing authority shall, at the request of one of the parties, appoint the sole arbitrator as promptly as possible. In making the appointment the appointing authority shall use the following list-procedure, unless both parties agree that the list-procedure should not be used or unless the appointing authority determines in its discretion that the use of the list-procedure is not appropriate for the case:
   (a) At the request of one of the parties the appointing authority shall communicate to both parties an identical list containing at least three names;
   (b) Within fifteen days after the receipt of this list, each party may return the list to the appointing authority after having deleted the name or names to which he objects and numbered the remaining names on the list in the order of his preference;
   (c) After the expiration of the above period of time the appointing authority shall appoint the sole arbitrator from among the names approved on the lists returned to it and in accordance with the order of preference indicated by the parties;
   (d) If for any reason the appointment cannot be made according to this procedure, the appointing authority may exercise its discretion in appointing the sole arbitrator.

4. In making the appointment, the appointing authority shall have regard to such considerations as are likely to secure the appointment of an independent and impartial arbitrator and shall take into account as well the advisability of appointing an arbitrator of a nationality other than the nationalities of the parties.

76. Article 7 reads:

1. If three arbitrators are to be appointed, each party shall appoint one arbitrator. The two arbitrators thus appointed shall choose the third arbitrator who will act as the presiding arbitrator of the tribunal.

2. If within thirty days after the receipt of a party's notification of the appointment of an arbitrator the other party has not notified the first party of the arbitrator he has appointed:
(a) The first party may request the appointing authority previously designated by the parties to appoint the second arbitrator; or
(b) If no such authority has been previously designated by the parties, or if the appointing authority previously designated refuses to act or fails to appoint the arbitrator within thirty days after receipt of a party's request therefore, the first party may request the Secretary-General of the Permanent Court of Arbitration at The Hague to designate the appointing authority. The first party may then request the appointing authority so designated to appoint the second arbitrator. In either case, the appointing authority may exercise its discretion in appointing the arbitrator.

3. If within thirty days after the appointment of the second arbitrator the two arbitrators have not agreed on the choice of the presiding arbitrator, the presiding arbitrator shall be appointed by an appointing authority in the same was as a sole arbitrator would be appointed under article 6.

II. Discussion

77. We propose a new article 6, amalgamating the provisions of the present articles 6 and 7. The salient features of the proposed article are:

- The operative time limit for appointments is 30 (not 60) days, and this applies not only to the parties but also to the Appointing Authority (whether it be designated by the parties or the PCA[88]).
- In the event the parties have agreed that the tribunal is to consist of a sole arbitrator, article 6(1) gives the parties an opportunity to agree on his or her identity within 30 days, failing which any party may request the Appointing Authority to select the sole arbitrator. In the event the decision that there is to be a sole arbitrator is made by the Appointing Authority (by application of article 5(2)), the 30-day deadline cannot apply. The words "upon the request of any party" in article 6(1) give the parties an opportunity to (i) attempt to select a sole arbitrator jointly or (ii) unilaterally request the Appointing Authority to make that selection.
- Similarly, when a three-member formation has been decided by the Appointing Authority (see article 5(2)), the parties are given 15 days each to appoint two arbitrators.
- It is now explicit that "hav[ing] regard to such considerations as are likely to secure the appointment of independent and impartial arbitrators" is necessary in all appointments by the Appointing Authority.
- Consistent with the present article 6(4), third-state nationality is one of the criteria for the selection of presiding and sole arbitrators by the Appointing Authority – provided, however, that a party has indicated such a preference.
- The nationality of corporations may, for the purposes of the Rules, be determined by having regard to beneficial ownership (rather than the state of incorporation, *siège social*, etc).
- The existing articles 6(3) and 7(3) provide for a list-procedure to be followed as a mandatory and exclusive mechanism for the selection of arbitrators by the Appointing Authority, and that procedure is set out in detail in article 6(3). We propose that the list-procedure be explicitly referenced in the Rules, but as an option: the general rule

88 Cf Baker & Davis, *The UNCITRAL Arbitration Rules in Practice* (1992) 26.

in the proposed article 6(4) is that the Appointing Authority should adopt "such procedures as it deems appropriate".
- The Secretary-General of the PCA is given a larger role than under the present Rules; see the proposed article 6(6).

III. Proposed Rule

78. Proposed text of new article 6:

1. If a Sole Arbitrator is to be appointed, and if by the time the Response is due to be communicated there has been no agreement as to his or her identity, the Sole Arbitrator shall, upon the request of any party, be appointed by the Appointing Authority.

2. If a three-member tribunal is to be appointed, the following procedure shall be followed, unless the parties have agreed otherwise.
(a) The Claimant shall appoint an arbitrator in the Notice of Arbitration.
(b) At the latest by the time the Response is to be communicated, the Respondent shall appoint a second arbitrator, failing which any party may request the Appointing Authority to make that appointment.
(c) In the event the decision to appoint a three-member tribunal has been made the Appointing Authority (article 5, para. 2), the Claimant shall appoint an arbitrator within 15 days of the Appointing Authority's decision; and the Respondent shall appoint an arbitrator within 15 days of the Claimant's appointment, failing which any party may request the Appointing Authority to make the relevant appointment.
(d) The two arbitrators appointed in accordance with paragraphs (a)-(c) shall appoint the third and presiding arbitrator within thirty days of the appointment of the second arbitrator, failing which any party may request the Appointing Authority to make that appointment.

3. In exercising its functions under this article, the Appointing Authority shall use such procedures as it deems appropriate, which may include the use of lists of proposed arbitrators whom the parties are invited to rank in order of preference.

4. In making any appointment under this article, the Appointing Authority shall have regard to such considerations as are likely to secure the appointment of independent and impartial arbitrators.

5. In appointing the presiding arbitrator or a Sole Arbitrator, the Appointing Authority shall in principle accept requests by a party that the nationality of that arbitrator should not be that of any of the parties. For that purpose, the Appointing Authority shall take account of such indications as it may have received as to the dominant beneficial ownership of corporate entities.

6. If the Appointing Authority, howsoever designated, has not made an appointment pursuant to this article within thirty days of being requested to do so, the Secretary-General of the Permanent Court of Arbitration at The Hague may, upon the request of any party and unless he or she deems it appropriate to extend the time limit, make that appointment or designate another Appointing Authority to do so.

7. Any disagreement with respect to compliance with time limits under this article shall be resolved by the Secretary-General of the Permanent Court of Arbitration at The Hague.

NEW ARTICLE 7

I. Discussion

79. The present Rules do not expressly envisage the possibility of an arbitration agreement providing for the appointment of the entire tribunal by an Appointing Authority.[89] Such agreements do exist and, as discussed below, have given rise to problems in practice. The problems that may arise are the following:

- The parties have not agreed on an institution or person to serve as the Appointing Authority, and are unable to reach agreement on this point after the commencement of the proceedings.
- The Appointing Authority agreed upon by the parties refuses or fails to make the necessary appointments.

80. The latter issue arose in the recently reported *Econet* case (2005),[90] involving Zimbabwean, South African, and Nigerian parties. The dispute arose out of a shareholders' agreement involving multiple parties. Perhaps because of the multiplicity of parties, the arbitration clause in that agreement provided that a three-member tribunal would be empanelled by decision of a senior judge in Nigeria. The respondents opposed the appointment of arbitrators by the Appointing Authority, and the judge declined to appoint a tribunal. Two months thereafter, the claimant requested the Secretary-General of the PCA to designate another Appointing Authority, under article 7(2)(b) of the Rules. The Appointing Authority designated by the Secretary-General proceeded to appoint all three arbitrators, selecting one of them as the presiding arbitrator.

81. The tribunal dismissed the case on jurisdictional grounds, holding that it had not been appointed in accordance with the agreement of the parties. Article 7 was held inapplicable where the parties had agreed that the entire tribunal would be appointed by an Appointing Authority; and it was not possible to apply article 7 by analogy without rewriting the parties' agreement.[91] (The defect in the present Rules is that they do not contemplate a default mechanism in the event the *first* of three arbitrators is not appointed; it may have been assumed that a claimant would never fail to make the first appointment, but this assumption is irrelevant when all three arbitrators are to be named by the Appointing Authority and the latter refuses to act.)

II. Proposed Rule

82. The proposed new article 7 would read as follows:

> 1. Where the parties have agreed that the Arbitral Tribunal in its entirety is to be appointed by an Appointing Authority and have agreed on the identity of that authority, any party may request that authority to make the necessary appointments.
>
> 2. Where the Appointing Authority refuses or fails to make the necessary appointments within thirty days of a request to that effect, any party may request the Secretary-General of the Permanent Court of Arbitration at The Hague to designate a replacement Appointing Authority.
>
> 3. The Appointing Authority designated in accordance with paragraph 1 or 2 shall make the necessary appointments following the procedure in article 6, paragraphs 3-5, and select one arbitrator as the presiding arbitrator.

---

89 Nor do any of the other commonly used institutional rules specifically cater for such a possibility.

90 (2006) 21:6 Mealey's Int'l Arb Rep, with a note by Sinclair.

91 In this case, the law of the seat of the arbitration did contain provisions by which another Appointing Authority (a court) could be seised of a request to appoint the tribunal. That procedure had not been used.

NEW ARTICLE 8

I. Discussion

83. In the well known *Dutco* case,[92] the French *Cour de cassation* declined to uphold the validity of an appointment made under Article 2(6) of the 1975/1988 ICC Rules. Pursuant to that Article, the ICC Court had appointed an arbitrator on behalf of two co-respondents who had been unable to select an arbitrator. The Court held that "the principle of the equality of the parties in the appointment of arbitrators is a matter of public policy and can be waived only after a dispute has arisen".

84. The lesson of *Dutco* directly influenced the 1998 revisions of the ICC and LCIA Rules. Article 10 of the ICC Rules (entitled "Multiple Parties") reads:

> 1. Where there are multiple parties, whether as Claimant or as Respondent, and where the dispute is to be referred to three arbitrators, the multiple Claimants, jointly, and the multiple Respondents, jointly, shall nominate an arbitrator for confirmation pursuant to Article 9.
>
> 2. In the absence of such a joint nomination and where all parties are unable to agree to a method for the constitution of the Arbitral Tribunal, the Court may appoint each member of the Arbitral Tribunal and shall designate one of them to act as chairman. In such case, the Court shall be at liberty to choose any person it regards as suitable to act as arbitrator, applying Article 9 when it considers this appropriate.

85. In practice, the ICC Court exercises its discretion in Article 10(2) ("the Court *may* appoint") where it appears that the multiple claimants or respondents do not form a single group with common rights and obligations – as was the case in *Dutco*.[93]

86. Article 8.1 of the LCIA Rules is clearly expressed in that regard (with emphasis added):

> Where the Arbitration Agreement entitles each party howsoever to nominate an arbitrator, the parties to the dispute number more than two and such parties *have not all agreed in writing that the disputant parties represent two separate sides for the formation of the Arbitral Tribunal as Claimant and Respondent respectively,* the LCIA Court shall appoint the Arbitral Tribunal without regard to any party's nomination.[94]

87. The current text of the Rules does not accommodate *Dutco* in any way. This is a serious lacuna. The solution adopted in the ICC and LCIA Rules is sound and workable, and should be part of a revised text of the UNCITRAL Rules. A proposed new article 8 would deal with multiparty cases, and expressly give the Appointing Authority the ability to either constitute the entire tribunal or confirm an existing appointment and make the appointment that the multiple claimants or respondents are unable to make jointly.

II. Proposed Rule

88. Proposed text of new article 8:

---

92 Cass Civ 1re, 7 January 1992, *Sociétés Siemens & BKMI v Société Dutco* (1992) 119 JDI 707.

93 See *Derains & Schwartz* 177; and Whitesell and Silva-Romero, "Multiparty and Multicontract Arbitration: Recent ICC Experience" (2003) ICC Bull (Special Supplement – Complex Arbitration) 7.

94 Note that the tenor of *Dutco* was recognized as sound by the Departmental Advisory Committee which had principal drafting responsibility for the Arbitration Act 1996 (England & Wales); see UK Department of Trade and Industry, Departmental Advisory Committee on Arbitration Law, *Report on The Arbitration Bill* (February 1996) para 88, reprinted in Mustill & Boyd, *Commercial Arbitration (Companion Volume to the 2nd edition)* (2001) 395 *et seq*; and s 18 of the Arbitration Act 1996 (England & Wales).

1. Where there are multiple Claimants or Respondents, and where the Arbitral Tribunal is to be constituted pursuant to article 6, paragraph 2, the multiple Claimants, jointly, and the multiple Respondents, jointly, shall appoint an arbitrator.

2. In the absence of such joint appointments and where all parties are unable to agree on a method for the constitution of the Arbitral Tribunal by the time the Response is due to be communicated, any party may request the Appointing Authority to make the necessary appointment or appointments, pursuant to paragraph 3.

3. The Appointing Authority, having heard the parties' views, may:
(a) revoke an appointment already made, and appoint each of the arbitrators and designate one of them as the presiding arbitrator; or
(b) confirm an appointment already made and make a further appointment, acting in either case in accordance with article 6, paragraphs 3-5.

ARTICLE 9

I. Present Rule

A prospective arbitrator shall disclose to those who approach him in connexion with his possible appointment any circumstances likely to give rise to justifiable doubts as to his impartiality or independence. An arbitrator, once appointed or chosen, shall disclose such circumstances to the parties unless they have already been informed by him of these circumstances.

II. Discussion

89. Article 9 sets forth a two-step disclosure process in clear and effective language that is broadly consistent with Article 12(1) of the Model Law. Article 9 may, however, be improved in three respects:

- by making it explicit that the duty of impartiality and independence is a continuing one, consistently with Article 12(1) of the Model Law;[95]
- by clarifying that disclosure should be in the form of a written declaration;[96] and
- by providing guidance (in a note) on the required content of the disclosure.

III. Proposed Revision

90. Proposed revised text of article 9:

A prospective arbitrator shall disclose to those who approach him in connexion with his or her possible appointment any circumstances likely to give rise to justifiable doubts as to his or her impartiality or independence. From the time of his or her appointment and throughout the arbitral proceedings, an arbitrator~~, once appointed or chosen,~~ shall without delay disclose such circumstances to the parties and to the Appointing Authority that has appointed him or her, unless they have already been informed by him or her of these circumstances. Upon acceptance of his or her appointment, an arbitrator shall provide to the parties and to the Appointing Authority that has appointed him or her a signed statement of independence.*

---

* PROPOSED TEXTS OF STATEMENT OF INDEPENDENCE

---

95 See also Article 7(3) of the ICC Rules, and Article 5.2-5.3 of the LCIA Rules.
96 As is the case in ICC, LCIA, and ICSID arbitrations, for example.

(A) UNQUALIFIED

I am independent of each of the parties and intend to remain so. To the best of my knowledge, there are no circumstances, past or present, likely to give rise to justifiable doubts as to my impartiality. I hereby undertake promptly to notify the parties and the other members of the Arbitral Tribunal of any such circumstance that may subsequently come to my attention during this arbitration.

(B) QUALIFIED

I am independent of each of the parties and intend to remain so. Attached is a statement of (a) my past and present professional, business and other relationships with the parties and (b) any other circumstance that might cause my reliability for independent and impartial judgment to be questioned by a party.[97] I hereby undertake promptly to notify the parties and the other members of the Arbitral Tribunal of any such further relationship or circumstance that may subsequently come to my attention during this arbitration.

NEW ARTICLE 9*bis*

I. Discussion and Proposed Rule

91. Neither the Rules nor the Model Law contain any provision on the liability of arbitrators.[98] This must be recognized as a lacuna; the question is whether this question should be answered in the Rules or the law of the arbitration. The sets of arbitration rules that do deal with the question answer it by setting forth limitation-of-liability clauses, leaving the establishment of liability, if any, to the law of the arbitration (or, possibly, the national law of the arbitrator concerned, or the law of the place where the act has been committed that is said to give rise to liability).[99]

92. Existing arbitration rules offer two possible approaches. The first, adopted in the ICC Rules (Article 34), is an unqualified exclusion of liability:

> Neither the arbitrators, nor the Court and its members, nor the ICC and its employees, nor the ICC National Committees shall be liable to any person for any act of omission in connection with the arbitration.

93. The second, and more common, is reflected in the Introductory Note to the IBA Rules of Ethics for International Arbitrators (1987),[100] which states the general rule that "international arbitrators should in principle be granted immunity from suit under national laws, except in extreme case of wilful or reckless disregard of their legal obligations". The LCIA Rules (Article 31.1) and the AAA Rules (Article 35) similarly refer to "conscious and deliberate wrongdoing".[101]

---

97 This sentence is inspired from the declaration required of ICSID arbitrators; see ICSID Administrative Council Resolution (AC/C/RES/2006) (Amendment of Arbitration Rule 6: Constitution of the Tribunal).

98 On the Model Law states that have adopted specific provisions on this matter see Sanders, *The Work of UNCITRAL on Arbitration and Conciliation* (2004) 161 *et seq.*

99 See *Derains & Schwartz* 383; and Lew, Mistelis and Kröll, *Comparative International Commercial Arbitration* (2003) 294.

100 In this respect, the 1987 text has not been superseded by the IBA Guidelines on Conflicts of Interest in International Arbitration of 2004.

101 The importance of safeguarding the arbitrators' immunity is highlighted by a recent case in Texas, where a litigant unhappy with the outcome of the arbitration filed a suit against (among others) the arbitrators, alleging corruption. The arbitrators, all highly respected in the international arbitration community, refused to take part in the proceedings, and the claim was dismissed for lack of jurisdiction: *Gulf Petro Trading Company, Inc et al v Nigerian National Petroleum Corporation et al*, (Order on Defendant's Motion to Dismiss, United States District Court, Eastern District of Texas, Beaumont Division, 15 March 2006) (Case No. 1:05CV619) 14.

94. The term "wrongdoing", however, suggests that liability may be established if the act in question is shown to be not only "conscious and deliberate" but also a "wrong" within the technical meaning of the applicable law. If this is so, then the term "wrongdoing" has little practical value in itself, at least in terms of establishing liability. What would be required is a possibility to hold an arbitrator liable not under the common law of torts but for grave and deliberate misconduct in the performance on his or her duties as an arbitrator. The English Arbitration Act 1996 (s 29(1)) and the Irish International Commercial Arbitration Act 1998 (s 12(1)) more aptly refer to an "act or omission shown to have been in bad faith" and "in the discharge or purported discharge of [one's] functions as an arbitrator". Bad-faith conduct would include, but not be limited to, a "deliberate violation of the arbitration agreement or the [arbitration] rules".[102]

95. In light of the foregoing, a new article 9*bis* might be considered, with the following wording:

> No arbitrator (including his or her employees and assistants), secretary to the Arbitral Tribunal appointed in accordance with article 15, paragraph 9, or expert to the Arbitral Tribunal shall be liable to any party for any act or omission in connexion with the performance of his or her tasks under these Rules except if that act or omission was manifestly in bad faith.

96 Consideration may also be given to extending the immunity of article 9*bis* to persons or institutions performing the function of an Appointing Authority under the Rules, and even the Secretary-General of the PCA (although the question is at present probably purely theoretical, given his immunity from suit in the courts).

ARTICLE 10(2)

I. Present Rule

> A party may challenge the arbitrator appointed by him only for reasons of which he becomes aware after the appointment has been made.

II. Discussion and Proposed Revision

97. Article 10(2) should read:

> A party may challenge the arbitrator appointed by it~~him~~ only for reasons of which it~~he~~ becomes aware after the appointment has been made.

ARTICLE 11

I. Present Rule

> 1. A party who intends to challenge an arbitrator shall send notice of his challenge within fifteen days after the appointment of the challenged arbitrator has been notified to the challenging party or within fifteen days after the circumstances mentioned in articles 9 and 10 became known to that party.
>
> 2. The challenge shall be notified to the other party, to the arbitrator who is challenged and to the other members of the arbitral tribunal. The notification shall be in writing and shall state the reasons for the challenge.
>
> 3. When an arbitrator has been challenged by one party, the other party may agree to the challenge. In both cases the procedure provided in article 6 or 7 shall be used in full for

102 Cf Article 10.2 of the LCIA Rules.

the appointment of the substitute arbitrator, even if during the process of appointing the challenged arbitrator a party had failed to exercise his right to appoint or to participate in the appointment.

II. Discussion and Proposed Revision

98. Article 11 should read:

> 1. A party who intends to challenge an arbitrator shall send notice of ~~his~~its challenge within fifteen days after the appointment of the challenged arbitrator has been notified to the challenging party or within fifteen days after the circumstances mentioned in articles 9 and 10 became known to that party.
>
> 2. The challenge shall be notified to the other party, to the arbitrator who is challenged and to the other members of the A~~a~~rbitral T~~t~~ribunal. The notification shall be in writing and shall state the reasons for the challenge.
>
> 3. When an arbitrator has been challenged by a ~~one~~ party, the other parties~~y~~ may agree to the challenge. In both cases the procedure provided in article 6 ~~or 7~~ shall be used in full for the appointment of the substitute arbitrator, even if during the process of appointing the challenged arbitrator a party had failed to exercise ~~his~~its right to appoint or to participate in the appointment.

ARTICLE 12(1)

I. Present Rule

99. Article 12(1) reads: If the other party does not agree to the challenge and the challenged arbitrator does not withdraw, the decision on the challenge will be made: (a) When the initial appointment was made by an appointing authority, by that authority; (b) When the initial appointment was not made by an appointing authority, but an appointing authority has been previously designated, by the authority; (c) In all other cases, by the appointing authority to be designated in accordance with the procedure for designating an appointing authority as provided for in article 6.

II. Discussion and Proposed Revision

100. The provision is drafted on the assumption that a party that has unsuccessfully invited an arbitrator to withdraw has an interest in seizing the Appointing Authority of a challenge application as soon as possible. Hence, Article 12(1) sets forth no time-limit by which the party making the challenge must seek a decision by the Appointing Authority (and, if necessary, seek the designation of an Appointing Authority).

101. In the hands of parties given to dilatory tactics, this has on occasion led to delay and, worse, uncertainty on the part of the tribunal, which may feel hesitant to proceed, in the shadow of a possible or likely challenge.

102. The possibility for mischief could be eliminated by the addition of the following words in the opening part of article 12(1):

> If the other party does not agree to the challenge and the challenged arbitrator does not withdraw, within [fifteen/thirty] days from the date of the notice of challenge the party making the challenge may seek a ~~the~~ decision on the challenge, which will be made: …

ARTICLE 13

I. Present Rule

103. Article 13 reads:

> 1. In the event of the death or resignation of an arbitrator during the course of the proceedings, a substitute arbitrator shall be appointed or chosen pursuant to the procedure provided for in articles 6 to 9 that was applicable to the appointment or choice arbitrator being replaced.
>
> 2. In the event that an arbitrator fails to act or in the event of the *de jure* or *de facto* impossibility of his performing his functions, the procedure in respect of the challenge and replacement of an arbitrator as provided in the preceding articles shall apply.

II. Discussion

104. This crucial provision has given rise to several important questions:

(a) Should an arbitrator's ability to resign be conditional on a showing of "serious reasons";[103] and if so, how would such a limitation be policed and by whom?
(b) In the same vein, is a resignation always to take effect immediately?
(c) Does the peremptory language of article 13 ("*shall* be appointed", "the procedure in respect of the challenge and replacement ... *shall apply*"[104]) preclude the remaining arbitrators from continuing with the proceedings and possibly issuing an award?
(d) What is the threshold of "impossibility" in article 13(2)? Does this provision adequately deal with obstruction – intentional or not – of the deliberations of the arbitral tribunal, unbeknownst to the parties?

105. The *travaux* provide little guidance on those questions. They indicate that care was taken to formulate article 13 in a way to dissuade vexatious, ill-grounded challenges to arbitrators. Thus, the Commission was careful to choose the terms "*de jure* or *de facto* impossibility"[105] for article 13(2), as providing a more objective test than the term "incapacity".[106] On the other hand, Article 13(2) *was* intended to cater for an arbitrator's "failure to act" – a situation that the Commission felt could not be regarded as, in effect, a "resignation" under article 13(1).[107] Moreover, although it was recognized that an arbitrator should be able to resign only for exceptional "good reasons",[108] it was felt that such an obligation could not be effectively enforced.[109]

106. Practice under the Rules, in particular that of the Iran-US Claims Tribunal, furnishes some further answers.[110] More importantly for present purposes, the available practice highlights the limitations of the present text of article 13.

---

103 Cf *Sanders* (2004) 247.

104 Practically, in cases of resignation of party-appointed arbitrators, application of the appointment process under article 7 means that the relevant party has 30 days in which to make a substitute appointment, failing which the designating authority/Appointing Authority process is to take its course. The potential for delay and disruption is obvious, especially where a hearing, deliberations, or the signature of an award are imminent.

105 The terms "*de jure* or *de facto*" are also to be found in Article 14(1) of the Model Law, in Article 12 (2) of the ICC Rules, and in Article 10 of IACAC Rules.

106 See Report of UNCITRAL Committee of the Whole II, 71, para 70.

107 See UNCITRAL Discussions on Preliminary Draft Rules, 34, paras 89-91.

108 See UN Doc A/CN.9/9/C.2/SR.5 (1976) 5, para 31; and *Sanders* (1977) 191.

109 Ibid.

110 For a detailed analysis and extensive references see *Caron/Caplan/Pellonpää* Chapter 6.

107. Clear rules are necessary to give effect to the principle that "an arbitrator shall not, through his deliberate absence, be able to frustrate the rendering of an award".[111] It is possible and desirable to dissuade spurious resignations, or at least contain their consequences. This might be achieved by rules to the effect described below.

- In multi-member arbitral tribunals, a resignation is to be approved by the other arbitrators: Requiring an arbitrator to articulate his reasons for resigning (however unverifiable these may in some cases be), and to submit to his colleagues' scrutiny and judgment, may be an effective deterrent against ill-considered or plainly tactical resignations.[112] This practice ultimately prevailed in the Iran-US Claims Tribunal,[113] and it is entirely consistent with the general rule that the arbitral tribunal is responsible for the conduct of the proceedings.[114] Such a rule should function well in multi-member tribunals, especially given the proposed power for the presiding arbitrator to decide alone when no majority can be formed.[115] On the other hand, difficulties would arise in the unusual hypothesis that the two party-appointed arbitrators might wish to force the presiding arbitrator to remain on the tribunal.[116] And it is clear that the rule could not apply in single-member tribunals – where the risk of spurious resignations is inherently limited, however.
- A resignation is to take effect on a date decided upon by the arbitral tribunal: This rule would permit arbitral tribunals to continue with the proceedings in an orderly way.[117]
- A non-approved resignation, or an arbitrator's failure to comply with the decisions of the arbitral tribunal as to the date on which his resignation is to take effect, will not prevent the tribunal from continuing with the case: This is one manifestation of the more general rule that absences without a valid excuse (i.e., by way of resignation, plain absence, or failure to co-operate in advancing the proceedings) will not prevent the majority of the tribunal from continuing with the proceedings. This eliminates

---

[111] International Law Commission, Report to the General Assembly, [1958-II] ILCYB 83, 88, para 38. This comment expressed the rationale of Article 27(2) of the ILC Model Rules on Arbitral Procedure, endorsed by GA Res 1262 (XIII) (1958), reprinted in [1958-II] ILCYB 83. Article 27(2) of those Rules requires the replacement of an arbitrator only when the parties' agreement so provides or an arbitrator absents himself *with* the permission of the tribunal president; in other cases the tribunal proceeds minus the absentee member.

[112] One particular type of tactical resignations, identified by Mr Daly, the Deputy Secretary-General of the PCA, at the 30th Anniversary UNCITRAL/VIAC colloquium in April 2006, is a series of revolving resignations followed by successive appointments within the 30-day period stipulated in article 7(2), so preventing the appointing authority from intervening. It is both difficult and delicate to set out the circumstances in which the appointing authority (if one has been designated) would be authorized to take the matter in its own hands. The requirement of approval for all resignations would be a more straightforward solution to the problem, assuming that a tribunal has been fully constituted and is therefore in a position to approve a putative resignation.

[113] See Aldrich, *The Jurisprudence of the Iran – United States Claims Tribunal* (1998) 13. In institutional arbitration, as under the ICC and the LCIA Rules, resignations are subject to approval by the respective Courts of Arbitration; see Article 12(1) of the ICC Rules, and Article 10.1 of the LCIA Rules.

[114] See article 15(1) of the Rules.

[115] See article 31(1), paragraphs 232 *et seq* below.

[116] In fact, either of the two party-appointed arbitrators might cause deadlock by refusing to approve a reasonable resignation request by the presiding arbitrator. Consideration may be given to the idea of referring such (surely exceptional) cases, where the two party-appointed arbitrators fail to reach consensus, to the Appointing Authority.

[117] Cf Article 13(5) of the Iran-US Claims Tribunal Rules of Procedure (the "Mosk Rule"), which requires an arbitrator who has resigned to "continue to serve … with respect to all cases in which he had participated in a hearing on the merits".

the possibility of making tactical gain by absences that are unjustified or timed to cause maximum disruption and delay.

The Iran-US Claims Tribunal experienced several different instances of truncated chambers. The Tribunal relied on an inherent power to proceed – that is, a jurisdictional empowerment outside the Tribunal Rules of Procedure.[118] The tribunal in the *Himpurna* case, sitting in an *ad hoc* arbitration under the UNCITRAL Rules, expressly relied upon the earlier practice of the Iran-US Claims Tribunal. In *Himpurna*, the respondent state was found to have prevented its appointed arbitrator from attending a scheduled hearing, shortly before its commencement. The tribunal held that, given the timing of the arbitrator's absence and the lack of a valid excuse, awaiting the replacement of the missing arbitrator would be "manifestly inappropriate". In material part, the tribunal held:

> This text [article 12(1)] was the subject of specific comment in the Iran-United States Claims Tribunal decision in *Uiterwyk Corp, et al v Islamic Republic of Iran, et al* (6 July 1988). In response to a dissenting decision by the absent Iranian arbitrator Mostafavi, the two remaining arbitrators, Böckstiegel and Holtzmann, issued a Supplemental Opinion which concluded that Art. 13(2) of the UNCITRAL Rules "is not the exclusive procedure for dealing with failure of an arbitrator to act", and that it "cannot be invoked to disrupt the orderly process of the Tribunal or to obstruct its functions". This Arbitral Tribunal concurs with that conclusion. A possible course may be to remove and replace an arbitrator who has withdrawn, if the withdrawal takes place at a sufficiently early stage that his replacement would cause only limited disruption. Such a solution is, however, manifestly inappropriate when an arbitrator withdraws at an advanced stage in the proceedings and that withdrawal is found by the Arbitral Tribunal to be without valid excuse.[119]

108. In Judge Schwebel's view the *Himpurna* tribunal's decision reinforces further "the better, but not the only, view of the matter".[120]

109. Connivance between an arbitrator and a party which appointed him is to be severely discouraged. One of the few truly effective disincentives to this kind of behaviour is to deprive the party which has appointed an arbitrator whose resignation is not approved of the right to name his replacement. (In pathological cases, this could otherwise lead to a series of inappropriate appointments, and effectively sabotage the process.) Such a sanction has always been part of the ICSID system.[121] It was applied in the very first ICSID case in favour of the State of Morocco.[122] This may have contributed to the near-absence of any such instances in

118 See *Caron/Caplan/Pellonpää* 287-298.

119 *Himpurna California Energy Ltd (Bermuda) v Republic of Indonesia* (2000) 25 YCA 186 (Final Award, UNCITRAL, 1999) paras 58-59.

120 Schwebel, "Injunction of Arbitral Proceedings and Truncation of the Tribunal", (2003) 18:4 Mealey's Int'l Arb Rep 33, 38. See also Schwebel, *International Arbitration: Three Salient Problems* (1987) Chapter III.

121 See Article 56(3) of the ICSID Convention; commented upon as follows by its principal drafter: "[t]his provision reflects the suspicion that the party [that made the original appointment] may not be a stranger to the resignation": Broches, "Convention on the Settlement of Investment Disputes Between States and Nationals of Other States of 1965: Explanatory Notes and Survey of Its Application", (1993) 18 YCA 627, 766.

122 In respect of the rejected resignation of the claimants' joint nominee, Sir John Foster QC, *see Holiday Inns v Morocco*, summarized in Lalive, "The First World Bank Arbitration (*Holiday Inns v Morocco*) – Some Legal Problems", (1980) 51 BYIL 123.

ICSID arbitrations over the subsequent decades.[123] ICSID's example is implicitly followed in the 1998 LCIA revision[124] and is proposed for adoption in the revision of article 13 of the Rules.

110. This leaves one further question, whether the terms "*de jure* or *de facto* impossibility of performing [an arbitrator's] functions" are sufficiently clear and comprehensive. The LCIA Rules (Article 10.1) use the rather clearer terms "unable or unfit", but the Model Law (Article 14(1)) retains the terms "*de jure* or *de facto* unable to perform [an arbitrator's] functions". In order to maintain consistency between the Rules and the Model Law, the "*de jure* or *de facto*" terminology might be retained. On the other hand, the terms "*de jure* or *de facto* impossibility" are overly narrow inasmuch as they fail to cover cases where an arbitrator effectively "refuses ... to act" (LCIA Rules, Article 10.1) or "for other reasons fails to act without undue delay" (Model Law, Article 14(1)). This should be corrected.

III. Proposed Revision

111. Proposed revised text of article 13:

> 1. Where the Arbitral Tribunal consists of more than one arbitrator, a resignation by an arbitrator shall require the approval of a majority of the other arbitrators. The presiding arbitrator shall have the casting vote. The decision approving the resignation of an arbitrator shall be in writing. It may stipulate that the resignation shall take effect on a future date.
>
> 2. In the event of the death or approved resignation of an arbitrator during the course of the arbitral proceedings, a substitute arbitrator shall be appointed [or chosen] pursuant to the procedure provided for in articles 6 to 9 8 that was applicable to the appointment [or choice] of the arbitrator being replaced. In the event an arbitrator's resignation is not approved pursuant to paragraph 1, he or she shall be replaced by a direct selection by the Appointing Authority.
>
> 3. In the event that an arbitrator refuses or fails to act, or in the event of the *de jure* or *de facto* impossibility of his or her performing his or her functions, or if he or she for other reasons fails to act without undue delay, the procedure in respect of the challenge and replacement of an arbitrator as provided in the preceding articles shall apply, subject to paragraph 4. Unless the Appointing Authority finds that the reasons for the arbitrator's non-performance of his or her functions are beyond his or her control, the Appointing Authority shall directly appoint the replacement arbitrator.
>
> 4. Where the other arbitrators unanimously determine that paragraph 3 applies to an arbitrator, or if he or she has tendered a resignation which is not accepted pursuant to paragraph 1, they shall have the power, upon written notice to the third arbitrator and the parties, to continue the arbitration and make any direction, decision, or award, if the circumstances of the case so warrant. For the purposes of this paragraph, the circumstances of the case include the stage of the arbitration and any explanation given by the third arbitrator.

---

123 Although a second instance involving Mr Galo Leoro Franco was resolved with similar effect in March 2006: *Casado and President Allende Foundation v Republic of Chile* (ARB/98/2).

124 Article 11.1 gives the LCIA Court "complete discretion to decide whether or not to follow the original nominating process."

ARTICLE 14

I. Present Rule

> If under articles 11 to 13 the sole or presiding arbitrator is replaced, any hearings held previously shall be repeated; if any other arbitrator is replaced, such prior hearings may be repeated at the discretion of the arbitral tribunal.

II. Discussion

112. While it may be appropriate in most cases where a sole arbitrator or presiding arbitrator is replaced for hearings to be repeated, there is no compelling reason to lay down a peremptory rule. Not all hearings are essential for the disposition of a claim: repetition may not justify the expense. In addition, verbatim transcripts of hearings are commonly held, and a newly appointed presiding arbitrator having confidence in his coarbitrators may be content with such a transcript. In short, whether or not to repeat a hearing should be decided by the tribunal in light of all circumstances; no rigid rule appears necessary.

113. For this reason, Article 14 of the Rules of Procedure of the Iran-US Claims Tribunal and Article 12(4) of the ICC Rules leave this decision entirely to the tribunal without attempting to lay down any rigid rules.[125]

III. Proposed Revision

114. Proposed revised text of article 14:

> If under articles 11 to 13 ~~the sole or presiding arbitrator is replaced,~~ any arbitrator is replaced, the reconstituted Arbitral Tribunal, having consulted the parties, shall determine if and to what extent any hearings held previously shall be repeated~~; if any other arbitrator is replaced, such prior hearings may be repeated at the discretion of the arbitral tribunal~~.

ARTICLE 15(1)

I. Present Rule

115. Article 15(1) reads: Subject to these Rules, the arbitral tribunal may conduct the arbitration in such manner as it considers appropriate, provided that the parties are treated with equality and that at any stage of the proceedings each party is given a full opportunity of presenting his case.

II. Discussion

116. The *travaux* to article 15(1) highlight flexibility in the conduct of the proceedings and reliance on the expertise of the arbitrators as "two of the hallmarks of arbitration".[126] Arbitrators must thus be entrusted with wide powers to regulate the conduct of the proceedings, provided that the parties receive equal treatment[127] and a full opportunity of presenting their case, as

---

125 See to the same effect SCC Rules, Article 25; ICSID Rules, Article 12.

126 Report of UNCITRAL Secretary General on Revised Draft Rules (Commentary on Article 14) 172, para 1.

127 It should not be assumed however, that treating parties with equality means meeting out identical treatment to the parties in all circumstances. (This is relevant, in particular, to costs issues, including deposits.) For an example see *Howe v BIS* (Order of 31 August 2001) para H.2, discussed by Petrochilos (note 40 above) para 4.48. More generally, the intention in article 15(1) was to permit the tribunal

specified in Article 18 of the Model Law, a provision which the Secretary of UNCITRAL has called the *Magna Carta* of arbitration.[128]

117. Where article 15(1) perhaps falls short is that it does not spell out the tribunal's duty to ensure that arbitral proceedings are dealt with without unnecessary delay;[129] nor does it spell out the specific power of arbitral tribunals to issue directions in that regard. It is within those limits that tribunals have to organize proceedings in the most efficacious way in the circumstances of the case.[130]

118. Further, we consider that indicating the potential cost consequences of a failure to comply with such directions would assist in ensuring the efficacy of the arbitral process.[131]

III. Proposed Revision

119. Proposed revised text of article 15(1):

> Subject to these Rules, the A~~a~~rbitral T~~t~~ribunal may conduct the arbitration in such manner as it considers appropriate, provided that the parties are treated with equality and that at any stage of the proceedings each party is given a full opportunity of presenting ~~his~~its case. The Arbitral Tribunal shall take all action and issue all necessary directions to the parties in order to avoid unnecessary delay and expense and to provide a fair and efficient process for resolving the parties' dispute. The parties shall comply with and carry out any directions issued by the Arbitral Tribunal; failure to do so may be taken into account by the Arbitral Tribunal in allocating the costs of the arbitration pursuant to article 40.

---

to conduct the arbitral process "with fairness" eschewing absolute equality when circumstances so required; see ibid para 4.87 and the references.

128 Quoted in *Holzmann & Neuhaus* 550. Article 18 of the Model Law states: "The parties shall be treated with equality and each party shall be given a full opportunity of presenting his case."

129 Such a rule is provided for under Article 14.1(ii) of the LCIA Rules, Article 20(3) of the SCC Rules, Article 38(c) of WIPO Rules and Article 16(2) of the AAA Rules. See also the UNCITRAL Model Law, Article 14(1) which cautions against the failure of an arbitrator to act "without undue delay"; and section 1(a) of the Arbitration Act 1996 (England & Wales), which states that "the object of arbitration is to obtain the fair resolution of disputes by an impartial tribunal without unnecessary delay or expense". Article 14.1(ii) of the LCIA rules is perhaps the most comprehensive by imposing the general duty on tribunals at all times "to adopt procedures suitable to the circumstances of the arbitration, avoiding unnecessary delay or expense, so as to provide a fair and efficient means for the final resolution of the parties' dispute."

130 This general principle is also reflected in article 32(1) of the Rules, authorizing a tribunal to make "interim, interlocutory, or partial awards" at various stages of the proceedings. Thus, the general rule in article 15(1) would allow a tribunal to tailor its proceedings as necessary to deal with a manifestly unmeritorious claim (see the new ICSID Rule 41(5)), a question that created some difficulty in the *Occidental v Ecuador* case. The arbitral tribunal under the UNCITRAL Rules dismissed a claim of expropriation on grounds of "admissibility", finding that "it is ... evident that there is no expropriation in this case": *Occidental Exploration and Production Co v Republic of Ecuador, Final Award* (1 July 2004) para 80. Occidental challenged this holding before the English courts, on the basis that article 21(4) of the Rules does not authorize a tribunal to deal summarily with the merits of a claim. The High Court dismissed that challenge for reasons of English law not relevant here: *Republic of Ecuador v Occidental Exploration and Production Co* [2006] EWHC 345, paras 130-137. Questions of English law aside, the difficulty that Occidental identified with article 21(4) of the Rules would have been remedied if appropriate directions had been made under the proposed article 15(1) of the Rules.

131 A draft revised text for the SCC Rules (August 2006) would go further, and permit the tribunal to "draw such inferences as it considers appropriate" if a party fails to comply with (*inter alia*) the tribunal's directions "without showing good cause": draft Article 30(3).

NEW ARTICLE 15(2)-(3)

I. Discussion

120. Preparatory meetings are increasingly viewed as serving a useful purpose, particularly in more complex international arbitration proceedings. Preparatory meetings are expressly provided for under the Iran-US Claims Tribunal Notes to Article 15.[132] Further, arbitral tribunals are expressly empowered to hold such meetings in WIPO, ICSID as well as in AAA arbitrations.[133]

121. There are three specific instances where holding preparatory meetings may be particularly recommended: at the beginning of the arbitration (to decide on the schedule and format of the proceedings), when witnesses are to be heard (to decide on the matters described in article 25(2)) and when the tribunal considers the appointment of one or more experts under article 27 of the Rules.[134]

122. While the general rule contained in the current article 15(1) does not preclude tribunals from holding preparatory meetings, a provision should usefully be included in the Rules expressly conferring the power on the tribunal to hold such meetings "at an appropriate stage of the proceedings", whether following a request by the parties or at its own initiative.[135]

123. The UNCITRAL Notes provide guidance to both the arbitral tribunal and the parties on matters to be discussed in a preparatory meeting. These are, in particular, defining the points at issue, the order in which issues are to be decided and defining any relief or remedy sought; possible settlement negotiations and their effect on scheduling proceedings; the language to be used in the proceedings; the juridical seat of the arbitration and the possibility of meeting outside that place; administrative services that may be needed for the arbitral tribunal to carry out its functions (eg hearing arrangements or secretarial assistance); deposits in respect of costs; confidentiality of information relating to the arbitration; arrangements for the exchange of written submissions; other practical details concerning written submissions and evidence (eg copies, numbering, references); issues relating to documentary evidence, including time-limits for their submission; disclosure and exceptions (eg whether certain classes of documents should be immune from requests to produce); joint submission of a single set of documentary evidence and the possibility of submitting summaries of voluminous documentary evidence; physical evidence other than documents; issue regarding witnesses (eg the manner of taking oral evidence, the order in which the witnesses will be called); experts and expert witnesses; matters relating to the holding of hearings; and possible requirements concerning the filing or delivery the award.

II. Proposed Rules

124. Articles 15(2)-(3) would read as follows:

> <u>2. As soon as practicable after its constitution, the Arbitral Tribunal shall establish a provisional timetable for the conduct of the proceedings, in consultation with the parties.</u>

---

[132] The Iran-US Claims Tribunal adopted article 15 of the UNCITRAL Rules but provided in Note 4 to that article that "[t]he arbitral tribunal may make an order directing the arbitrating parties to appear for a pre-hearing conference. The pre-hearing conference will normally be held only after the Statement of Defence in the case had been received. The order will state the matters to be considered at the pre-hearing conference."

[133] Article 47 of the WIPO Rules (1994); Article 21(1) of the ICSID Rules; and Article 16(2) of the AAA Rules. Under article 18 the ICC Rules, the Tribunal must in all cases draw up its terms of reference and a timetable for the proceedings. However, the ICC Rules do not in this regard reflect general international arbitration practice.

[134] Sanders, *The Work of UNCITRAL on Arbitration and Conciliation* (2004) 11-13.

[135] See ibid 10; *Sanders* (2004) 247.

3. At any appropriate stage of the proceedings, the Arbitral Tribunal may meet or confer with the parties on any issue relating to the conduct of the proceedings, having due regard to the UNCITRAL Notes on Organizing Arbitral Proceedings.

NEW ARTICLE 15(4)

I. Discussion

125. Disputes occasionally arise between the same parties under separate contracts (eg, related contracts or a chain of contracts) containing separate arbitration clauses, and for one of the parties to refuse that all such disputes be resolved in the same proceedings. It may also occur that, pending proceedings in respect of a contract, a party should initiate a separate arbitration in respect of a distinct claim under the same contract in order to gain a tactical advantage.[136] Consolidation in such situations might ensure an efficient resolution of the disputes between the (same) parties, consistently with the general principle in article 15(1). Consolidation would also reduce the possibility of inconsistent awards in parallel arbitrations.[137]

126. Consolidation of claims would be especially desirable where the claims are part of the same overall transaction (or a chain of transactions) between the same parties or, at least, where the claims are closely related.[138]

127. Under the present Rules consolidation is possible only where the parties specifically agree.[139] Moreover, a counterclaim arising out of a different, but closely related, contract is inadmissible.[140]

128. The Departmental Advisory Committee which was principally responsible for the elaboration of the English Arbitration Act 1996 "concluded that the problem [of consolidation] was

---

136 See *Derains & Schwartz* 60.

137 The *cause célèbre* for consolidation is the contrasting outcomes of the awards in *CME Czech Republic BV v The Czech Republic* (Partial Award of 13 September 2001), and *Ronald S Lauder v The Czech Republic* (Final Award of 3 September 2001) – although it must be noted that the revision proposed here would not necessarily have assisted in the particular circumstances of the *CME* and *Lauder* arbitrations, because the claimants in those two proceedings were different.

138 Consolidation is permitted under the Swiss Rules (Article 4(1)) and under the CEPANI Rules (Article 11). The NAFTA not only demonstrates that consolidation feasible in *ad hoc* arbitration under the Rules, but actually goes so far as to permit consolidation even when the parties are not the same (Article 1126(2)). The NAFTA provisions are remarkably far-reaching, as demonstrated by the decision of the NAFTA Consolidation Tribunal to accede to the United States' request to consolidate the three "Softwood Lumber" arbitrations initiated by Canfor Corporation, various companies of the Tembec group, and Terminal Forest Products Inc; see *Canfor Corp et al v US*, Order of the Consolidation Tribunal (7 September 2005). The claimants in all three cases had objected to consolidation, and while two of them have proceeded with the arbitration, the Tembec claimants have withdrawn their claims and, in February 2006, moved to vacate the consolidation Order in the District Court for the District of Columbia (Case No 05-2345 (RMC)).

139 See Aldrich, *The Jurisprudence of the Iran-United States Claims Tribunal* (1998) 434435 for the means by which the Iran-US Claims Tribunal "combine[d] separate claims in a single proceeding for reasons of economy and efficiency".

140 Article 19(3) of the Rules states that the respondent can bring a counterclaim "arising out of the same contract". There is, however, no reason why counterclaims should in principle be restricted to those that arise from the same contract, especially in light of the modern trend to arbitrate several different kinds of non-contractual disputes under the UNCITRAL Rules. The *travaux* show that while considering the draft article 19 (on counterclaims) the Commission noted that it would be normal arbitration practice to consolidate the hearings of two claims that arose out of separate, but connected, contracts (see UNCITRAL Discussions on Preliminary Draft Rules, paras 136-137), but no provision catering for this was included in the final text of the Rules. Such a provision should be considered for inclusion in the revised Rules.

best left to be solved by consent, and expressed the hope that those responsible for drafting standard forms of contract and institutional arbitration rules would include clauses enabling the tribunal to order consolidation or concurrent hearings in appropriate cases".[141]

129. Consolidation is allowed under the ICC Rules,[142] when all proceedings relate to the same "legal relationship", on the premise that the parties have consented to give a tribunal the power to consolidate claims by choosing to arbitrate in accordance with the ICC Rules. This serves also as the justification for including the proposed consolidation provision in the UNCITRAL Rules.

130. Note that our proposed wording is based on NAFTA (Article 1126(2)).

II. Proposed Rule

131. Article 15(4) would read as follows:

> Where two or more claims which involve the same (and no other) parties and have a question of law or fact in common are the subject of separate arbitration proceedings under these Rules, the Arbitral Tribunal may, after hearing the parties, by reasoned order:
> (a) assume jurisdiction over, and hear and determine together, all or part of the claims; or
> (b) assume jurisdiction over, and hear and determine one or more of the claims, the determination of which it believes would assist in the resolution of the others.

NEW ARTICLE 15(5)

I. Discussion

132. Under the Rules, the question whether the arbitral tribunal may allow third parties to participate in arbitral proceedings, and to what extent it may do so, is controversial.[143] Third parties, for example nongovernmental organisations, often ask for an opportunity to explain their concerns (or offer a particular insight) in relation to a claim in investment-treaty arbitrations.

133. Article 15(1) of the Rules, providing that the "tribunal may conduct the arbitration in such manner as it considers appropriate", has been held to confer the power on the tribunal to accept *amicus curiae* briefs in written form.[144] Especially in light of the frequent use of

---

141 Reprinted in Mustill and Boyd, *Commercial Arbitration (Companion Volume to the 2nd edition)* (2001) 309.

142 Article 4(6) of the ICC Rules provides: "When a party submits a Request in connection with a legal relationship in respect of which arbitration proceedings between the same parties are already pending under these Rules, the Court may, at the request of a party, decide to include the claims contained in the Request in the pending proceedings provided that the Terms of Reference have not been signed or approved by the Court. Once the Terms of Reference have been signed or approved by the Court, claims may only be included in the pending proceedings subject to the provisions of Article 19." Note that this provision has rarely been applied: *Derains & Schwartz* 59.

143 In the *travaux préparatoires*, "[i]t was suggested that a provision should be included in the Rules defining the circumstances in which a person not a party ... might participate in an arbitral proceeding, since in certain circumstances the participation of such persons might be desirable": UNCITRAL Discussions on Preliminary Draft Rules, para 19.

144 See *Methanex Corporation v United States of America* (Decision on Jurisdiction of 15 January 2001) (NAFTA) para 47. See also *United Parcel Service of America Inc v Government of Canada* (Decision on Jurisdiction of 17 October 2001) (NAFTA) para 72: the tribunal followed the *Methanex* decision, but added that "[t]he circumstances and the detail of the making of any *amicus* submissions would be the subject of consultation with the parties."

the UNCITRAL Rules in arbitrations under international investment treaties, we believe and propose that such a power should be made explicit in the Rules.[145]

134. The Iran-US Claims Tribunal, while accepting the text of article 15 without modifications in its Rules of Procedure, expressly allowed for *amicus* submissions from non-parties in its Note 5 to the Article:

> The Tribunal may, having satisfied itself that the statement of one of the two Governments – or, under special circumstances, any other person – who is not a party in a particular case is likely to assist the tribunal in carrying out its task, permit such Government or person to assist the Tribunal by presenting oral and written statements.[146]

135. In taking its decision on whether to accept *amicus curiae* briefs, the tribunal will have to consider a number of factors, including whether the case involves significant issues of public interest which might benefit from a wider scope of arguments than those of the disputants, whether such submissions would assist the tribunal in the determination of a factual or legal issue, and whether the purported *amicus* has a significant and legitimate interest.[147]

II. Proposed Rule

136. Article 15(5) would read as follows:

> Unless the parties have agreed otherwise, the Arbitral Tribunal may, after having consulted with the parties, and especially in cases raising issues of public interest, allow any person who is not a party to the proceedings to present one or more written statements, provided that the Tribunal is satisfied that such statements are likely to assist it in the determination of a factual or legal issue related to the proceeding by bringing a perspective, particular knowledge or insight which the parties are unable to present. The Arbitral Tribunal shall determine the mode and number of such statements after consulting with the parties.

NEW ARTICLE 15(6)-(9)

I. Discussion

137. The powers conferred on arbitral tribunals by article 15(1) are broad, ranging from permitting *amicus curiae* briefs,[148] to requesting the parties to submit specific briefs on certain

---

145 We also propose an amendment to article 25(4) that would enable the tribunal to allow third parties to attend or monitor hearings in appropriate circumstances: see paragraph 198 below.

146 On the practice under that provision see *Caron/Caplan/Pellonpää* 37, citing *The United States of America v The Islamic Republic of Iran*, Decision No DEC 37-A17-FT (13 May 1985), (1985) 8 Iran-US CTR 189.

147 As the new proposed ICSID Rule 37(2) provides:

> After consulting both parties, the Tribunal may allow a person or entity that is not a party to the dispute (in this Rule called the "non-disputing party") to file a written submission with the Tribunal regarding a matter within the scope of the dispute. In determining whether to allow such a filing, the Tribunal shall consider, among other things, the extent to which:
> (a) the non-disputing party submission would assist the Tribunal in the determination of a factual or legal issue related to the proceeding by bringing a perspective, particular knowledge or insight that is different from that of the disputing parties;
> (b) the non-disputing party submission would address a matter within the scope of the dispute;
> (c) the non-disputing party has significant interest in the proceeding.
> The Tribunal shall ensure that the non-disputing party submission does not disrupt the proceeding, unduly burden or unfairly prejudice either party, and that both parties are given an opportunity of presenting their observations on the non-disputing party submission.

148 *Methanex Corporation v United States of America* (Decision on Jurisdiction of 15 January 2001) (NAFTA) para 47. See above, note 144.

points.[149] The present proposals are not aimed at limiting those powers, but only at providing guidance and indications, from which the parties can derogate, should they wish to do so.

138. Several such powers are already discussed in the UNCITRAL Notes, to which the arbitral tribunal may have regard to under our proposed article 15(3). The following matters are not.

- *Conducting enquiries*: It sometimes occurs that the arbitrators have to intervene in order to put the parties on the right track as to necessary points at issue in the proceedings. Such a power should be expressed in the Rules, along the lines of Article 22.1(c) of the LCIA Rules.[150]
- *Ordering a party to make property available for inspection*: The Rules already provide for the carrying out of inspections by the tribunal. The site or property to be inspected is usually under the control of one of the parties. Like Article 22.1(d) of the LCIA Rules, the Rules should provide the tribunal with the further power "to order any party to make any property, site or thing under its control and relating to the subject matter of the arbitration available for inspection by the Arbitral Tribunal, any other party, its expert or any expert to the Arbitral Tribunal".
- *Allowing a third party to be joined in the proceedings*: It is in the interests of the efficiency of arbitration that a third party, most commonly an insurer, may be joined in the proceedings. This would require the consent of the parties to the main claim as well as that of the third party. The wording of Article 22.1(h) of the LCIA Rules is appropriate in this regard.[151]
- *Allowing tribunals to appoint secretaries*: Secretaries (or "administrative" or "legal" secretaries as they are sometimes called) perform useful functions, especially in complex cases, by assisting the tribunal in carrying out research and administrative tasks (for example, organizing hearings and meetings, co-ordinating communications among the members of the tribunal and with the parties, and organizing materials relevant to the tribunal's deliberations).[152] Following Professor Sanders' suggestion,[153] we propose that the Rules codify the tribunal's power to designate a secretary, which is well established in practice. The parties may naturally agree to exclude this power; and, in exercising its discretion to designate a secretary the tribunal would always take account of its duty to act efficiently and avoid unnecessary expense (see article 15(1)).

II. Proposed Rules

139. Articles 15(6)-(9) would read as follows:

> 6. After consulting with the parties, the Tribunal may conduct such enquiries as may appear to it to be necessary or expedient, including whether and to what extent the Arbitral Tribunal should itself take the initiative in identifying the issues and ascertaining the relevant facts and the law(s) or rules of law applicable to the arbitration, the merits of the parties' dispute, and the arbitration agreement.

---

149 *Larsen v The Hawaiian Kingdom*, Procedural Order No 3 (17 July 2000) para 16 (quoted at para 6.2 of the Award (2001) 119 ILR 566).

150 Article 22.1(c) provides the arbitrators with the power to conduct such enquiries as may appear to the Arbitral Tribunal to be necessary or expedient, including whether and to what extent the Arbitral Tribunal should itself take the initiative in identifying the issues and ascertaining the relevant facts and the law(s) or rules of law applicable to the arbitration, the merits of the parties' dispute and the Arbitration Agreement

151 The Swiss Rules (Article 4(1)) also permit joinder.

152 See generally Partasides, "The Fourth Arbitrator: The Role of Secretaries to Tribunals in International Arbitration", (2002) 18 Arb Int 147.

153 *Sanders* (2004) 265.

7. After consulting with the parties, the Tribunal may order any party to make any property, site, or thing under that party's control and relating to the subject matter of the arbitration available for inspection by the Arbitral Tribunal, another party, its expert, or any expert appointed by the Arbitral Tribunal.

8. After consulting with the parties, the Tribunal may allow, upon the application of a party, one or more third persons to be joined in the arbitration as a party provided any such third person and the applicant party have consented thereto in writing, and thereafter to make a single final award, or separate awards, in respect of all parties so implicated in the arbitration.

9. The Arbitral Tribunal may, having consulted with the parties, and determined that it would contribute to overall cost-effectiveness by relieving the arbitrators of certain tasks, designate a secretary to the Tribunal. Any such designation shall be by written notice to the parties, identifying the person concerned and describing the tasks that may be entrusted to him or her by the Tribunal and under its responsibility. The secretary to the Tribunal shall provide to the parties a signed statement of independence conforming to article 9.

NEW ARTICLE 15*bis* (INCORPORATING CURRENT ARTICLE 15(2)(3))

I. Present Rule

2. If either party so requests at any stage of the proceedings, the arbitral tribunal shall hold hearings for the presentation of evidence by witnesses, including expert witnesses, or for oral argument. In the absence of such a request, the arbitral tribunal shall decide whether to hold such hearings or whether the proceedings shall be conducted on the basis of documents and other materials.

3. All documents or information supplied to the arbitral tribunal by one party shall at the same time be communicated by that party to the other party.

II. Discussion

140. On its face article 15(2) may be read as obliging the arbitrators to hear oral testimony tendered by a party even if they consider such testimony immaterial or irrelevant to the resolution of the dispute.[154]

141. The concern over parties requesting hearings in order to disrupt proceedings or stall the issuance of an award is prevalent in the legislative history of Article 24 of the Model Law, a provision based on the wording of article 15(2) of the Rules.[155] The Working Group altered the phrase "at any stage of the proceedings" to "at an appropriate stage of the proceedings", which was accepted as the final formulation.[156] Therefore, under the Model Law, "a request presumably must come at such a time as to permit the arbitral tribunal to hold a hearing at an appropriate stage of the proceedings. It may not come, for example, on the eve of the award or after the time set by the tribunal for such requests has lapsed."[157] This better formulation should also be reflected in the UNCITRAL Rules.

142. The phrase "evidence by witnesses, including expert witnesses" is problematic in that in some legal systems (eg, Germany), the parties themselves, and their senior officers or

154 See Report of UNCITRAL Secretary General on Revised Draft Set of Rules (Commentary on article 13 [now article 15]), para 3.

155 *Holtzmann & Neuhaus* 673.

156 Ibid, 693-695. Article 24(1) of the Model Law formulates in general the rule in a better fashion than article 15(2) of the Rules, creating a need to harmonise the two provisions.

157 *Holtzmann & Neuhaus* 673.

employees, cannot be characterised as witnesses.[158] Accordingly, Article 24 of the Model Law was drafted so as to avoid any reference to the technical term "witnesses"; Instead, only the word "evidence" was retained.[159] Our proposals regarding this issue are included in article 25(2).

III. Proposed Revision

143. Proposed revised text of article 15*bis* (current article 15(2)-(3)):

> 1. Upon request of any ~~If either party so requests at any stage of the proceedings,~~ the A~~a~~rbitral T~~t~~ribunal shall hold hearings at an appropriate stage of the proceedings for the presentation of evidence by witnesses, including expert witnesses, or for oral argument. In the absence of such a request, the A~~a~~rbitral T~~t~~ribunal shall decide whether to hold such hearings or whether the proceedings shall be conducted exclusively on the basis of documents and other materials.
>
> 2. All documents or information supplied to the A~~a~~rbitral T~~t~~ribunal by one party shall at the same time be communicated by that party to the other party.

NEW ARTICLE 15*ter*

I. Discussion

144. Following substantial controversy on whether arbitral proceedings should be confidential, the ICC considered including an express provision on confidentiality in its Rules when it most recently revised them in 1998.[160] After extensive consideration, it was decided that a general confidentiality provision should not be included, and that the matter should be left to be addressed on a case-by-case basis by the arbitrators and the parties (for example, in the Tribunal's Terms of Reference).[161]

145. In arbitrations under the UNCITRAL Rules, the issue could be addressed in preparatory meetings,[162] having regard to paragraphs 31 and 32 of the UNCITRAL Notes.

146. Confidentiality of the materials used in the arbitration is a different matter. While Article 20(7) of the ICC Rules provides the tribunal with the power to "take measures for protecting trade secrets and confidential information",[163] the WIPO, LCIA, AAA and Swiss Rules all set forth a general rule that any materials used in the arbitration are confidential.[164] We believe that the Rules should adopt a similar provision, while making it clear that confidentiality may yield the countervailing legal rights or duties.[165]

147. We have also made a suggestion in the proposed rule that conforms with the power in revised article 15(5) to permit the submission of *amicus curiae* briefs. The broad language employed in the last sentence of the proposed article, dealing with exceptions to the duty of confidentiality, comports with our proposed article 32(2) on exclusion of appeals.

---

158 See, eg, Gaillard and Savage, *Fouchard Gaillard Goldman on International Commercial Arbitration* (1999) 698-699.
159 See below, at paragraphs 193-196.
160 *Derains & Schwartz* 284-285.
161 Ibid, 285.
162 See the commentary to the proposed new article 15(2)-(3) of the Rules above, at paragraphs 120-123.
163 Note that this rule was initially inspired by Article 52 of the WIPO Rules: *Derains & Schwartz* 285.
164 See Article 74(a) of the WIPO Rules; Article 30.1 of the LCIA Rules; Article 34 of the AAA Rules; and Article 43(1) of the Swiss Rules.
165 For an example of a provision that expressly requires open hearings and non-confidential materials, see Article 29 of the United States of America–Uruguay BIT (2004).

II. Proposed Rule

148. Article 15*ter* would read as follows:

> Unless the parties have agreed otherwise, all materials in the proceedings which are not otherwise in the public domain, including materials created for the purpose of the arbitration and all other documents or evidence given by a party, witness, expert, [or any other person,] shall be treated as confidential, save and to the extent that disclosure may be required of a party by legal duty, to protect or pursue a legal right, and in *bona fide* legal proceedings before a state court or other judicial authority in relation to an award.

ARTICLE 16(1)

I. Present Rule

> PLACE OF ARBITRATION
>
> 1. Unless the parties have agreed upon the place where the arbitration is to be held, such place shall be determined by the arbitral tribunal, having regard to the circumstances of the arbitration.

II. Discussion

149. According to Professor Sanders:

> This [rule] not only refers to practical considerations in connection with the arbitral proceedings, such as the least possible displacement of parties, witnesses and arbitrators, but also ... to the legal consequences of the choice, and more especially to the recognition and enforcement of the award.[166]
>
> [T]he decision of the arbitral tribunal on the place of arbitration is a majority decision. In view of the legal consequences of the choice of the place of arbitration, such a decision is not – like the decision on the language to be used in the arbitration proceedings – a decision on a "question of procedure", and Article 31 para 2 does not, therefore ... apply.[167]

150. For the avoidance of doubt, a requirement that such a decision should be taken by majority should be inserted in article 16(1) itself.

151. More importantly, the choice of the place of the arbitration imports, in the vast majority of national arbitration laws, the supervisory and support jurisdiction of the courts of that country, and the application of the national arbitration law.[168] The legal nature of the place of the arbitration is referred to, in s 3 of the Arbitration Act 1996, as the "juridical seat". This expression is to be preferred to the current one. The existing expression in many cases creates the mistaken impression that the place chosen for occasional meetings is also the formal place of arbitration.

III. Proposed Revision

152. Proposed revised text of article 16(1):

> PLACE OF ARBITRATION JURIDICAL SEAT

---

166 *Sanders* (1977) 194.

167 Ibid. See also *Caron/Caplan/Pellonpää* 93: "[I]t is advisable that an arbitral tribunal select the place of arbitration by a majority decision in accordance with Article 31(1)".

168 See Model Law, Article 1(2).

~~Unless the parties have agreed upon the place where the arbitration is to be held, such place shall be determined by the arbitral tribunal, having regard to the circumstances of the arbitration.~~

If the parties have agreed on a place of arbitration, that place shall be the juridical seat of the arbitration. Otherwise, this determination shall be made by the Arbitral Tribunal, in accordance with article 31, paragraph 1. The Arbitral Tribunal shall nevertheless have the discretion to conduct hearings or other meetings in any other place. With the exception of provisions which the national procedural law of the juridical seat of the arbitration explicitly defines as mandatory, the Arbitral Tribunal shall not be required to apply that national law to the conduct of the arbitration.

ARTICLES 16(2)-(3)

I. Present Rule

2. The arbitral tribunal may determine the locale of the arbitration within the country agreed upon by the parties. It may hear witnesses and hold meetings for consultation among its members at any place it deems appropriate, having regard to the circumstances of the arbitration.

3. The arbitral tribunal may meet at any place it deems appropriate for the inspection of goods, other property or documents. The parties shall be given sufficient notice to enable them to be present at such inspection.

4. The award shall be made at the place of arbitration.

II. Discussion

153. It has become apparent from contemporary practice[169] that the "limited flexibility" granted to the tribunal under the present Rules should be extended[170] to allow the tribunal to perform all of its functions outside the country which is the formal *place of arbitration*, "having regard to the circumstances of the arbitration".[171]

154. The formulation of the Model Law, Article 20(2), is more comprehensive and more useful:

> Notwithstanding the provisions of paragraph (1) of this article, the arbitral tribunal may, unless otherwise agreed by the parties, meet at any place it considers appropriate for consultation among its members, for hearing witnesses, experts or the parties, or for inspection of goods, other property or documents.

The wording of Article 20(2) of the Model Law "would seem to include ... all the possible stages of the arbitral proceeding."[172]

---

169 In *Himpurna California Energy Ltd (Bermuda) v Republic of Indonesia* (2000) 25 YCA 111, para 73 (Interim Award, UNCITRAL, 1999), the arbitral tribunal felt it necessary to move the hearing from Jakarta to The Hague as a result of an injunction ordered by the courts of Jakarta enjoining the arbitral proceedings and imposing a fine of USD $1 million per day for any breach of the injunction. See also *PT Garuda Indonesia v Birgen Air* [2002] 1 SLR 393 (CA).

170 Support can also be drawn from the stance taken by most modern institutional arbitration rules – see for example Article 14(2) of the ICC Rules, Article 13(2) of the AAA Rules, Article 16.2 of the LCIA Rules, Article 39(b) of the WIPO Rules, Article 16(2) of the Swiss Rules.

171 "Article 14(2) [of the ICC Rules] requires the Arbitral Tribunal to consult with the parties before deciding to conduct a hearing or meeting at a location other than the place of the arbitration. ... This obliges the arbitrators to explain to the parties why they consider their decision appropriate and this, in turn, should generally suffice to discourage the most blatant abuses": *Derains & Schwartz* 220.

172 *Holtzmann & Neuhaus* 596.

155. It thus seems possible to amalgamate and simplify articles 16(2) and (3) into a single paragraph.

156. Former article 16(4) should be changed for clarity,[173] consistency with Article 16(1), and to avoid any confusion as to which country's courts may exercise supervisory jurisdiction.

III. Proposed Revision

157. Proposed revised text of articles 16(2)-(4):

> ~~2. The arbitral tribunal may determine the locale of the arbitration within the country agreed upon by the parties. It may hear witnesses and hold meetings for consultation among its members at any place it deems appropriate, having regard to the circumstances of the arbitration.~~
>
> Having regard to the circumstances of the arbitration and subject to any specific contrary agreement of the parties, the Arbitral Tribunal may meet at any place it considers appropriate for consultation among its members, for hearing witnesses, experts or the parties, or for inspection of goods, other property or documents.
>
> ~~3. The arbitral tribunal may meet at any place it deems appropriate for the inspection of goods, other property or documents. The parties shall be given sufficient notice to enable them to be present at such inspection.~~
>
> 4. ~~The~~ Any award, decision or order of the Arbitral Tribunal shall be considered made at the ~~place~~ juridical seat ~~of arbitration~~, even if it is not physically signed there.

NEW ARTICLE 16(4)

I. Discussion

158. Although most institutional arbitration rules retain the term "place arbitration", we feel that this term creates unnecessary and avoidable confusion.[174] The Rules should be accessible to people with varying degrees of knowledge about arbitration proceedings and different linguistic skills. Using an obviously technical term, such as "juridical seat" will aid the parties' understanding that this term does not refer to the physical place where any hearings or meetings must take place, but is rather an expression that gives rise to certain legal consequences.

159. For the sake of clarity it is also desirable to set out expressly the connection between the technical term "juridical seat" and the more commonly used "place of arbitration". The presumption should be that the term "place of arbitration" does not require for any hearings to be conducted at that place.

II. Proposed Rule

160. Article 16(4) would read as follows:

> Reference to a place of arbitration shall ordinarily be construed as defining the juridical seat of arbitration, without any necessary implication hearings must be conducted in that place. Any controversy in this regard shall be resolved by the Arbitral Tribunal.

---

173 Article 25(3) of the ICC Rules; and s 53 of the Arbitration Act 1996 (England & Wales).

174 The *travaux* do not reveal any specific reason for using the term "place of arbitration". Indeed, during the consultations the terms "place of arbitration" and "seat of arbitration" appear to have been used interchangeably: see, eg, UN Doc A/CN.9/97, (1975) 6 UNCITRAL YB 182-3.

ARTICLE 17(1)

I. Present Rule

> Subject to an agreement by the parties, the arbitral tribunal shall, promptly after its appointment, determine the language or languages to be used in the proceedings. This determination shall apply to the statement of claim, the statement of defence, and any further written statements and, if oral hearings take place, to the language or languages to be used in such hearings.

II. Discussion

161. It was noted in the *travaux préparatoires* that in cases where the arbitrators selected the language or languages to be used in the arbitral proceedings, the arbitrators could consult with the parties before reaching their decision.[175] However, a suggestion to add this requirement to the text of article 17(1) was rejected because it was thought that any competent arbitrator would invariably consult with the parties before determining the language to be used. Given the occasional sensitivity of this issue, article 17(1) should expressly require consultation with the parties.[176]

162. It is understood that a determination under article 17(1) is a "question of procedure" in the sense of article 31(2).[177]

163. To avoid an impasse at the outset of the case, it would be useful to provide that the language to be used in initial stages of the case should be that of the arbitration agreement.

III. Proposed Revision

164. Proposed revised text of article 17(1):

> ~~Subject to an agreement by the parties, the arbitral tribunal shall, promptly after its appointment, determine the language or languages to be used in the proceedings, in consultation with the parties. This determination shall apply to the statement of claim, the statement of defence, and any further written statements and, if oral hearings take place, to the language or languages to be used in such hearings.~~
>
> The initial language of the arbitration shall be the language in which the agreement to arbitrate has been expressed. Upon the formation of the Arbitral Tribunal and unless the parties have reached agreement in that respect, the Arbitral Tribunal shall decide upon the language of the arbitration.

ARTICLE 17(2)

I. Present Rule

The arbitral tribunal may order that any documents annexed to the statement of claim or statement of defence, and any supplementary documents or exhibits submitted in the course of the proceedings, delivered in their original language, shall be accompanied by a translation into the language or languages agreed upon by the parties or determined by the arbitral tribunal.

---

175 Report of UNCITRAL Committee of the Whole II, para 90; *Caron/Caplan/Pellonpää* 354.

176 Article 14 of the AAA Rules, Article 17.3 of the LCIA Rules and Article 40 of the WIPO Rules all require the arbitral tribunal to have regard to the parties' views.

177 *Sanders* (1977) 194.

II. Proposed Revision

165. For clarity and consistency with our revisions, article 17(2) should read:

> The A~~a~~rbitral T~~t~~ribunal may order that ~~any documents annexed to the statement of claim or statement of defence, and any supplementary documents or exhibits submitted in the course of the proceedings, delivered~~ all texts relied upon by a party and submitted in their original language shall be accompanied by a translation into the language or languages agreed upon by the parties or determined by the A~~a~~rbitral T~~t~~ribunal pursuant to paragraph 1.

ARTICLE 18(1)

I. Present Rule

> Unless the statement of claim was contained in the notice of arbitration, within a period of time to be determined by the arbitral tribunal, the claimant shall communicate his statement of claim in writing to the respondent and to each of the arbitrators. A copy of the contract, and of the arbitration agreement if not contained in the contract, shall be annexed thereto.

II. Proposed Revision

166. In accordance with the revision of article 3(3), article 18(1) would now read:

> ~~Unless the statement of claim was contained in the notice of arbitration,~~ W~~w~~ithin a period of time to be determined by the A~~a~~rbitral T~~t~~ribunal, the C~~c~~laimant shall communicate ~~his~~its S~~s~~tatement of C~~c~~laim in writing to the R~~r~~espondent and to each of the arbitrators. ~~A copy of the contract, and of the arbitration agreement if not contained in the contract, shall be annexed thereto.~~ The Claimant may elect to treat its Notice of Arbitration (article 3, para. 3) as a Statement of Claim.

ARTICLE 18(2)

I. Present Rule

> The statement of claim shall include the following particulars:
> (a) The names and addresses of the parties;
> (b) A statement of the facts supporting the claim;
> (c) The points at issue;
> (d) The relief or remedy sought. The claimant may annex to his statement of claim all documents he deems relevant or may add a reference to the documents or other evidence he will submit.

II. Discussion

167. As indicated in the *travaux*:

> This paragraph describes the information that must be contained in a statement of claim ... [T]he claimant ... is not required to annex the documents which he deems relevant and on which he intends to rely [but] should he wish to do so, a claimant may annex to his statement of claim a list of the documents he intends to submit in support of his claim or he may even annex the relevant documents themselves.[178]

---

178 Report of UNCITRAL Secretary on Revised Draft Rules (Commentary on article 17), para 5.

168. There are no compelling reasons why this option should be maintained. Article 41(c) of the WIPO Rules[179] and Article 6.6 of the LCIA Rules[180] reflect good practice. We propose that article 18(2) of the Rules be reworded accordingly.

169. As a consequence of our revision of articles 3(3)(b) and 3*bis*(2)(a), paragraph (a) of article 18 should be deleted.

III. Proposed Revision

170. Proposed revised text of article 18(2):

> The S~~s~~tatement of C~~c~~laim shall include the following particulars:
> (a) ~~The names and addresses of the parties;~~
> ~~(b)~~ A statement of the facts and legal principles supporting the claim;
> ~~(c)~~(b) The points at issue;
> ~~(d)~~(c) The relief or remedy sought.
> ~~The claimant may annex to his statement of claim all documents he deems relevant or may add a reference to the documents or other evidence he will submit.~~ The Statement of Claim shall as far as possible be accompanied by all documents and other evidentiary materials relied upon by the Claimant, or by references to them. If the documentary evidence is especially voluminous, the Claimant may list any further documents it deems relevant.

ARTICLES 19(1)-(2)

I. Present Rule

> 1. Within a period of time to be determined by the arbitral tribunal, the respondent shall communicate his statement of defence in writing to the claimant and to each of the arbitrators.
>
> 2. The statement of defence shall reply to the particulars (b), (c) and (d) of the statement of claim (article 18, para. 2). The respondent may annex to his statement the documents on which he relies for his defence or may add a reference to the documents or other evidence he will submit.

II. Proposed Revision

171. Consistently with our revisions to article 18(1)-(2), the text of article 19(1)-(2) should read:

> 1. Within a period of time to be determined by the A~~a~~rbitral T~~t~~ribunal, the R~~r~~espondent shall communicate ~~his~~its S~~s~~tatement of D~~d~~efence ~~in writing~~ to the Cclaimant and to each of the arbitrators. The Respondent may elect to treat its Response to the Notice of Arbitration (article 3*bis*, para. 2) as a Statement of Defence.
>
> 2. The S~~s~~tatement of D~~d~~efence shall reply to the particulars (a), (b) ~~(c)~~ and ~~(d)~~ (c) of the S~~s~~tatement of C~~c~~laim (article 18, para. 2). ~~The respondent may annex to his statement the~~

---

179 Article 41(c) of the WIPO Rules provides: The Statement of Claim shall, to as large an extent as possible, be accompanied by the documentary evidence upon which the Claimant relies, together with a schedule of such documents. Where the documentary evidence is especially voluminous, the Claimant may add a reference to further documents it is prepared to submit.

180 Article 6.6 of the LCIA Rules reads: All Statements referred to in this Article shall be accompanied by copies (or, if they are especially voluminous, lists) of all essential documents on which the party concerned relies and which have not previously been submitted by any party, and (where appropriate) by any relevant samples.

~~documents on which he relies for his defence or may add a reference to the documents or other evidence he will submit.~~ The Statement of Defence shall as far as possible be accompanied by all documents and other evidentiary materials relied upon by the Respondent, or by references to them. If the documentary evidence is especially voluminous, the Respondent may list any further documents it deems relevant.

ARTICLES 19(3)-(4)

I. Present Rule

3. In his statement of defence, or at a later stage in the arbitral proceedings if the arbitral tribunal decides that the delay was justified under the circumstances, the respondent may make a counter-claim arising out of the same contract or rely on a claim arising out of the same contract for the purpose of a set-off.

4. The provisions of article 18, paragraph 2, shall apply to a counter-claim and a claim relied on for the purpose of a set-off.

II. Discussion

172. There appears to be no compelling reason to envisage explicitly that the respondent might submit counterclaims after the submission of his Statement of Defence, especially given that (a) counterclaims are in principle to be submitted with the Response (article 3*bis*); and (b) the respondent will have seen the claimant's full case as articulated in the Statement of Claim.[181]

173. The LCIA and the ICC Rules do not limit counterclaims to those arising out of the same contract. There appears to us to be no compelling reason for such a limitation; indeed, permitting counterclaims arising from separate but related agreements between the parties (provided they are all to be referred to arbitration under the UNCITRAL Rules) would enhance consistency and efficiency.[182] As the Rules stand at present, such counterclaims would require a specific *compromis* between the parties.[183] The relevant limitation is rather that the counterclaims must fall within the scope of an agreement to arbitrate under the UNCITRAL Rules.

174. The limitation to contracts is simply inappropriate to arbitrations arising under international treaties.

175. The distinction between counterclaims and claims in set-off is well understood, but contemporary arbitration parlance refers to all such claims generically as "counterclaims".[184] For simplicity, we propose to eliminate the distinction between counterclaims and claims in set-off.

---

181 It should be noted that at one stage in the *travaux préparatoires*, Article 18(2) governing the contents of the statement of claim also contained a provision dealing with any amendments to it. Later, the current article 20 governing amendments to the claim and defence was inserted in the Rules, and that provision was removed from Article 18(2) accordingly. It is not clear why the corresponding provision in Article 19(2) was not removed.

182 Note that Article II(1) of the Claims Settlement Declaration (note 12 above) gave the Iran-US Claims Tribunal jurisdiction over "any counterclaim which arises out of the same contract, transaction or occurrence that constitutes the subject matter of [the] national's claims."

183 "[T]he parties may agree, under special circumstances, that the respondent may assert as a counterclaim or set-off a claim that did not arise out of the same contract as where the disputes arise out of other contracts are also referred to arbitration under these Rules. Pursuant to article 2 of these Rules, such agreement of the parties would have to be in writing": Report of UNCITRAL Secretary on Revised Draft Rules (Commentary on article 18) para 4.

184 See, eg, the LCIA Rules, Article 15.4.

III. Proposed Revision

176. Proposed revised text of articles 19(3)-(4):

> 3. In ~~his~~its S~~s~~tatement of D~~d~~efence~~, or at a later stage in the arbitral proceedings if the arbitral tribunal decides that the delay was justified under the circumstances,~~ the R~~r~~espondent may make a counter-claim provided that it falls within the scope of an agreement between the parties to arbitrate under these Rules ~~arising out of the same contract or rely on a claim arising out of the same contract for the purpose of a set-off~~.
>
> 4. The provisions of article 18, paragraph 2, shall apply to a counter-claim ~~and a claim relied on for the purpose of a set-off~~.

NEW ARTICLE 19*bis*

I. Discussion and Proposed Rule

177. Article 21(3) assumes that the claimant will have an opportunity to reply to a counter-claim.[185] But article 21(3) gives no indication of the timelimits in which such reply should be submitted,[186] or its content.[187] Equally, there is no possibility under the Rules for an answer by the respondent to the claimant's reply to the counterclaim.[188]

178. We propose a provision modelled on Article 15.4 of the LCIA Rules, leaving it to the tribunal to determine the need for a further response by the respondent, under article 22.

179. Proposed text of article 19*bis*:

> Where the Respondent's Statement of Defence includes a counter-claim, the Claimant may, within thirty days, submit a reply to the counter-claim.

ARTICLE 20

I. Present Rule

> During the course of the arbitral proceedings either party may amend or supplement his claim or defence unless the arbitral tribunal considers it inappropriate to allow such amendment having regard to the delay in making it or prejudice to the other party or any other circumstances. However, a claim may not be amended in such a manner that the amended claim falls outside the scope of the arbitration clause or separate arbitration agreement.

---

185 "It is obvious that the claimant must get an opportunity to reply to the counter-claim. The Rules only say so indirectly when dealing with a plea as to the arbitrator's jurisdiction. The claimant should raise this plea with respect to a counter-claim 'not later that in the reply to the counter-claim' (Article 21, para 3)." *Sanders* (1977) 205.

186 It appears that under the Rules at present this matter would be dealt with by decision of the tribunal under article 22.

187 Cf Article 15.4 of the LCIA Rules:

> Within 30 days of receipt of the Statement of Defence, the Claimant shall send to the Registrar a Statement of Reply which, where there are any counterclaims, shall include a Defence to Counterclaim in the same manner as a defence is to be set out in the Statement of Defence.

188 Cf Article 15.5 of the LCIA Rules:

> If the Statement of Reply contains a Defence to Counterclaim, within 30 days of its receipt the Respondent shall send to the Registrar a Statement of Reply to Counterclaim.

II. Discussion and Proposed Revision

180. For consistency, article 20 should read as follows:

> During the course of the arbitral proceedings ~~either~~any party may amend or supplement ~~his~~its claim~~, or~~ defence or counterclaim unless the A~~a~~rbitral T~~t~~ribunal considers it inappropriate to allow such amendment having regard to the delay in making it or prejudice to the other party or any other circumstances. However, a claim may not be amended in such a manner that the amended claim or counter-claim falls outside the scope of the arbitration clause or separate arbitration agreement.

ARTICLE 21(1)

I. Present Rule

> The arbitral tribunal shall have the power to rule on objections that it has no jurisdiction, including any objections with respect to the existence or validity of the arbitration clause or of the separate arbitration agreement.

II. Discussion and Proposed Revision

181. On a literal interpretation of the paragraph, the arbitral tribunal does not have the power to rule on its jurisdiction if no objection to its jurisdiction is raised by the parties. This position does not reflect modern arbitration practice.[189] The tribunal should have the power of its own motion to raise and decide the existence and scope of its own jurisdiction (for example when the dispute is not arbitrable).[190]

182. This is reflected in Article 16(1) of the Model Law,[191] whose wording we propose should be adopted in article 21(1) of the Rules as follows:

> The A~~a~~rbitral T~~t~~ribunal ~~shall have the power to~~ may rule on its own jurisdiction, including ~~objections that it has no jurisdiction, including~~ any objections with respect to the existence or validity of the arbitration clause or of the separate arbitration agreement.

ARTICLE 21(3)

I. Present Rule

> A plea that the arbitral tribunal does not have jurisdiction shall be raised not later than in the statement of defence or, with respect to a counter-claim, in the reply to the counter-claim.

---

189 See, eg, *Larsen v The Hawaiian Kingdom*, Procedural Order No 3 (17 July 2000) para 7 (quoted at para 6.2 of the Award (2001), 119 ILR 566).

190 Professor Sanders also supports this view: "The [arbitral tribunal] may, in my opinion, *proprio motu*, decide it has no jurisdiction when the dispute is not arbitrable": Sanders, *The work of UNCITRAL on Arbitration and Conciliation* (2004) 15. Professor Sanders also recommends an addition clarifying that a party may challenge the tribunal's jurisdiction even though it has participated in the formation of that tribunal: Sanders, "Arbitration Rules of UNCITRAL: 30 years", paper presented at an UNCITRAL colloquium on 6 April 2006 4. With respect, we do not consider such an addition to be necessary.

191 Article 16(1) of the Model Law:

> The arbitral tribunal may rule on its own jurisdiction, including any objections with respect to the existence or validity of the arbitration agreement. For that purpose, an arbitration clause which forms part of a contract shall be treated as an agreement independent of the other terms of the contract. A decision by the arbitral tribunal that the contract is null and void shall not entail ipso jure the invalidity of the arbitration clause.

II. Discussion and Proposed Revision

183. The corresponding provision in the Model Law, Article 16(2), follows very closely the text of the Rules but, in addition, deals with two important points on which article 21(3) is silent. First, the admissibility of untimely objections ("pleas") to jurisdiction and, secondly, the admissibility of an objection "that the arbitral tribunal is exceeding the scope of its authority".[192] In addition, the Model Law makes clear that the objecting party has every interest in co-operating in the constitution of the tribunal, for such co-operation does not imply an acceptance of the tribunal's authority.

184. Thus, the revision proposed below follows almost word-for-word Article 16(2) of the Model Law, except for the first sentence, which is based on the existing article 21(3) of the Rules but clarifies that the "reply to the counter-claim" is not a separate submission specifically provided for in the Rules:

> A plea that the A~~a~~rbitral T~~t~~ribunal does not have jurisdiction shall be raised not later than in the S~~s~~tatement of D~~d~~efence or, with respect to a counter-claim, in the first opportunity to submit a reply to the counter-claim. A party is not precluded from raising such a plea by the fact that it has appointed, or participated in the appointment of, an arbitrator. A plea that the Arbitral Tribunal is exceeding the scope of its authority shall be raised as soon as the matter alleged to be beyond the scope of its authority is raised during the arbitral proceedings. The Arbitral Tribunal may, in either case, admit a later plea if it considers the delay justified.

ARTICLE 21(4)

I. Present Rule

> In general, the arbitral tribunal should rule on a plea concerning its jurisdiction as a preliminary question. However, the arbitral tribunal may proceed with the arbitration and rule on such a plea in their final award.

II. Discussion

185. This paragraph deals with the procedural aspect of objections to jurisdiction of the tribunal. It "stresses that 'in general' the arbitrators should rule on such objections as a preliminary question. On the other hand, the flexibility, corresponding also with the freedom allowed to arbitrators in article 15(1) has been maintained by adding the last sentence.[193]

186. The Rules do not prescribe the form of a decision on jurisdiction. It is good practice,[194] and conducive to certainty[195] that such decisions should ultimately be made in the form of a (reasoned) award on jurisdiction.

---

[192] See in detail *Holtzmann & Neuhaus* (1989) 482 *et seq*. For an example of an allegation that the tribunal has exceeded its authority or mandate see Svea Court of Appeal, 15 May 2003, *Czech Republic v CME Czech Republic BV* (Case No T 8735-03), (2003) 42 ILM 915: the Swedish court accepted that two challenges to the tribunal's award (cited at note 137 above) ought to have been raised as objections in the arbitration, and were subsequently inadmissible by operation of article 21(3) of the Rules and s 34 of the Swedish Arbitration Act. In other words, the Svea court did read a preclusion effect in article 21(3) of the Rules.

[193] *Sanders* (1977) 200.

[194] Article 23.3 of the LCIA Rules provides:

> The Arbitral Tribunal may determine the plea to its jurisdiction or authority in an award as to jurisdiction or later in an award on the merits, as it considers appropriate in the circumstances.

[195] CA Paris, 1 July 1999, *Braspetro Oil Services Company v The Management and Implementation Authority of the Great Man-Made River Project* (1999) 14:8 Mealey's Int'l Arb Rep G-1, 7:

187. In accordance with Article 16(3) of the Model Law,[196] recourse to domestic courts should only be had *after* the tribunal has pronounced on its jurisdiction, and such recourse should not delay the arbitral proceedings or prevent the tribunal from making a further award.[197] The revised text proposed below would not, however, comport with a (mandatory) national law provision expressly permitting a party to test the validity or scope of a putative arbitration agreement in the courts *before* an arbitral tribunal has been constituted.[198]

III. Proposed Revision

188. Proposed revised text of article 21(4):

> In general, the A~~a~~rbitral T~~t~~ribunal should rule on a plea concerning its jurisdiction as a preliminary question. However, the A~~a~~rbitral T~~t~~ribunal may proceed with the arbitration and rule on such a plea in the final award as it considers appropriate in the circumstances. Any request to a domestic court to decide on the Arbitral Tribunal's jurisdiction may only be made after the Arbitral Tribunal has rendered its award on jurisdiction. While such a request is pending, the Arbitral Tribunal may continue the arbitral proceedings and make an award.

ARTICLE 24

I. Present Rule

> 1. Each party shall have the burden of proving the facts relied on to support his claim or defence.
>
> 2. The arbitral tribunal may, if it considers it appropriate, require a party to deliver to the tribunal and to the other party, within such a period of time as the arbitral tribunal shall decide, a summary of the documents and other evidence which that party intends to present in support of the facts in issue set out in his statement of claim or statement of defence.
>
> 3. At any time during the arbitral proceedings the arbitral tribunal may require the parties to produce documents, exhibits or other evidence within such a period of time as the tribunal shall determine.

> [O]nly arbitral awards may be set aside [*faire l'objet d'un recours immédiat*], that is, decisions by arbitrators that conclusively liquidate, in whole or in part, the dispute that has been submitted to them, whether on the merits, or as a jurisdictional matter, or in connection with a procedural objection which terminates the case .... (authors' translation from the French original)

196 Article 16(3) of the Model Law provides:

> The arbitral tribunal may rule on a plea referred to in paragraph (2) of this article either as a preliminary question or in an award on the merits. If the arbitral tribunal rules as a preliminary question that it has jurisdiction, any party may request, within thirty days after having received notice of that ruling, the court specified in article 6 to decide the matter, which decision shall be subject to no appeal; while such a request is pending, the arbitral tribunal may continue the arbitral proceedings and make an award.

197 "The advantage of this procedure is that the arbitral tribunal can assess in each case and with regard to each jurisdictional question whether the risk of dilatory tactics is greater than the danger of wasting money and time in a useless arbitration:" *Holtzmann & Neuhaus* 486.

198 See s 1032(2) of the German Code of Civil Procedure (ZPO): "Prior to the constitution of the arbitral tribunal, an application may be made to the court to determine whether or not arbitration is admissible."

II. Discussion

189. This paragraph provides that the tribunal may, at any time during the proceedings, require a party to produce documents, exhibits or other evidence (again including evidence by witnesses).[199]

190. In the Iran-US Claims Tribunal[200] and under the LCIA[201] and WIPO Rules,[202] the power of the tribunal to require a party to produce evidence can be exercised on the tribunal's own motion. This should be clarified in Article 24(3) as well.

191. It is proposed that good practice, reflected in Articles 3.9[203] and 9.2[204] of the IBA Rules, be adopted in the UNCITRAL Rules.

III. Proposed Revision

192. Proposed revised text of article 24:

> 1. Each party shall have the burden of proving the facts relied on to support ~~his~~its claim or defence.
>
> 2. The A~~a~~rbitral T~~t~~ribunal may, if it considers it appropriate, require a party to deliver to the Ttribunal and to the other parties~~y~~, within such a period of time as the A~~a~~rbitral

---

199 *Sanders* (1977) 203.

200 See *Caron/Caplan/Pellonpää* 575.

201 Article 22 of the LCIA Rules reads:

> 22.1 Unless the parties at anytime agree otherwise in writing, the Arbitral Tribunal shall have the power, on the application of any party or of its own motion, but in either case only after giving the parties a reasonable opportunity to state their views ...
>
> (e) to order any party to produce to the Arbitral Tribunal, and to the other parties for inspection, and to supply copies of, any documents or classes of documents in their possession, custody or power which the Arbitral Tribunal determines to be relevant ....

202 WIPO Rules, Article 48(b) provides:

> At any time during the arbitration, the Tribunal may, at the request of a party or on its own motion, order a party to produce such documents or other evidence as it considers necessary or appropriate and may order a party to make available to the Tribunal or to an expert appointed by it or to the other party any property in its possession or control for inspection or testing.

203 IBA Rules, Article 3.6:

> The Arbitral Tribunal shall, in consultation with the Parties and in timely fashion, consider the Request to Produce and the objections. The Arbitral Tribunal may order the Party to whom such Request is addressed to produce to the Arbitral Tribunal and to the other Parties those requested documents in its possession, custody or control as to which the Arbitral Tribunal determines that (i) the issues that the requesting Party wishes to prove are relevant and material to the outcome of the case, and (ii) none of the reasons for objection set forth in Article 9.2 apply.

204 IBA Rules, Article 9.2:

> The Arbitral Tribunal shall, at the request of a Party or on its own motion, exclude from evidence or production any document, statement, oral testimony or inspection for any of the following reasons:
>
> (a) lack of sufficient relevance or materiality;
> (b) legal impediment or privilege under the legal or ethical rules determined by the Arbitral Tribunal to be applicable;
> (c) unreasonable burden to produce the requested evidence;
> (d) loss or destruction of the document that has been reasonably shown to have occurred;
> (e) grounds of commercial or technical confidentiality that the Arbitral Tribunal determines to be compelling;
> (f) grounds of special political or institutional sensitivity (including evidence that has been classified as secret by a government or a public international institution) that the Arbitral Tribunal determines to be compelling; or
> (g) considerations of fairness or equality of the Parties that the Arbitral Tribunal determines to be compelling.

Ttribunal shall decide, a summary of the documents and other evidence which that party intends to present in support of the facts in issue set out in hisits Sstatement of Celaim or Sstatement of Ddefence.

3. At any time during the arbitral proceedings the Aarbitral Ttribunal may, on the application of any party or of its own motion and having given the parties a reasonable opportunity to state their views, require any of the parties to produce documents, exhibitsmaterials or other evidence in their possession, custody or control within such a period of time as the Ttribunal shall determine. The Arbitral Tribunal's decision under this article shall be made pursuant to article 31, paragraph 1.

4. The Arbitral Tribunal may exercise its power under paragraph 3 when it determines that such documents, materials or other evidence are relevant and material to the outcome of the case, provided that none of the following reasons is extant:
(a) legal impediment or privilege under the legal or ethical rules determined by the Arbitral Tribunal to be applicable;
(b) unreasonable burden to produce the requested evidence;
(c) loss or destruction of the document that has been reasonably shown to have occurred;
(d) grounds of commercial or technical confidentiality that the Arbitral Tribunal determines to be compelling;
(e) grounds of special political or institutional sensitivity (including evidence that has been classified as secret by a government or a public international institution) that the Arbitral Tribunal determines to be compelling; or
(f) considerations of fairness or equality of the parties that the Arbitral Tribunal determines to be compelling.

ARTICLE 25(2)

I. Present Rule

If witnesses are to be heard, at least fifteen days before the hearing each party shall communicate to the arbitral tribunal and to the other party the names and addresses of the witnesses he intends to present, the subject upon and the languages in which such witnesses will give their testimony.

II. Discussion

193. In order to avoid the confusion, referred to in the commentary relating to our proposed article 15*bis*,[205] regarding the terms "witness" and "testimony" as used in the Rules,[206] article 25(2) should contain a definition of "witness".

---

205 At paragraphs 140-142 above. Note that the problem was resolved in the Iran-US Claims Tribunal by its adoption of Note 5 to Article 25, which reads:

> Notwithstanding the provisions of paragraph 4 of Article 25, the arbitral tribunal may at its discretion permit representatives of arbitrating parties in other cases which present similar issues of fact or law to the present to observe all or part of the hearing in a particular case, subject to the prior approval of the arbitrating parties in the particular case. The Agents of the two Governments are permitted to be present at pre-hearing conferences and hearings.

206 "[T]his issue has led to difficulties for the Iran-Us Claims Tribunal regarding, for example, the hearing of the parties themselves or their officers and employees .... While in the common law it is standard for a party to be called as a witness, the civil law tradition shows considerable reluctance to accept testimony from a party or a person who, because of his affiliation to a party, is likely to have a financial interest in the matter": *Caron/Caplan/Pellonpää* 611-612. Similar concerns were also expressed in the legislative history of Article 24(1) of the Model Law, and the conclusion was reached that no reference to "witness" should be made in that Article: *Holtzmann & Neuhaus* 673.

194. We consider that the definition offered by Article 20.7 of the LCIA Rules should be adopted.[207] That Article 20.7 states:

> Any individual intending to testify to the Arbitral Tribunal on any issue of fact or expertise shall be treated as a witness under these Rules notwithstanding that the individual is a party to the arbitration or was or is an officer, employee or shareholder of any party.

195. Furthermore, the tribunal controls the proceedings (article 15(1)), not the parties. It should have the power to decide whether to hear oral evidence, and if so, in what form, on what issues etc.[208]

III. Proposed Revision

196. Proposed revised text of article 25(2):

> ~~If witnesses are to be heard, at least fifteen days before the hearing each party shall communicate to the arbitral tribunal and to the other party the names and addresses of the witnesses he intends to present, the subject upon and the languages in which such witnesses will give their testimony.~~
>
> Witnesses may be heard under conditions set by the Arbitral Tribunal, including time limits for their identification and a requirement of prior submission of signed statements containing the substance of their testimony. Any individual testifying to the Arbitral Tribunal on any issue of fact or expertise shall be treated as a witness under these Rules notwithstanding that the individual is a party to the arbitration or was or is an officer, employee or shareholder of any party.

ARTICLE 25(4)

I. Present Rule

> Hearings shall be held *in camera* unless the parties agree otherwise. The arbitral tribunal may require the retirement of any witness or witnesses during the testimony of other witnesses. The arbitral tribunal is free to determine the manner in which witnesses are examined.

II. Discussion

197. The last sentence of the paragraph, dealing with the manner in which witnesses are examined should be deleted, since it is already covered by article 15 and is also dealt with in the UNCITRAL Notes, paragraph 63.

198. It should also be clarified in this article that the tribunal has the power, after consulting the arbitrating parties, to allow third parties to attend hearings and to issue directions for that purpose. Thus, a specific provision was added to the ICSID Rules in their most recent revision in April 2006. ICSID Rule 32(2) reads:

> (2) Unless either party objects, the Tribunal, after consultation with the Secretary-General, may allow other persons, besides the parties, their agents, counsel or advocates, witnesses

---

207 Note also that Article 4(2) of the IBA Rules states "Any person may present evidence as a witness, including a Party or a Party's officer, employee or other representative."

208 Professor Sanders recommends an addition to article 25 along the lines of article 4(8) of the IBA Rules providing that, as a general rule, the written statement of a witness that fails to appear before the tribunal when summoned should be disregarded: *Sanders* (2004) 263. With respect, we would prefer to leave the tribunal with more flexibility in this regard.

and experts during their testimony, and officers of the Tribunal, to attend or observe all or part of the hearings, subject to appropriate logistical arrangements. The Tribunal shall for such cases establish procedures for the protection of proprietary or privileged information.

199. Such a power would be particularly relevant when the tribunal decides to receive *amicus curiae* submissions pursuant to article 15(5) of the Rules.

III. Proposed Revision

200. Proposed revised text of article 25(4):

> Hearings shall be held *in camera* unless the parties agree otherwise. The A~~a~~rbitral T~~t~~ribunal may require the retirement of any witness or witnesses during the testimony of other witnesses. ~~The arbitral tribunal is free to determine the manner in which witnesses are examined~~After consulting the parties and having regard to the circumstances and article 15, paragraph 1, the Arbitral Tribunal may allow a third party to attend all or part of the hearings, subject to appropriate logistical arrangements. The Arbitral Tribunal shall for such cases issue necessary directions under article 15, paragraph 1 for the protection of proprietary or privileged information.

ARTICLE 25(5)

I. Present Rule

> Evidence of witnesses may also be presented in the form of written statements signed by them.

II. Discussion and Proposed Revision

201. We propose to delete article 25(5). A provision covering the same issue has been added to article 25(2), making 25(5) redundant.

> ~~Evidence of witnesses may also be presented in the form of written statements signed by them.~~

ARTICLE 26

I. Present Rule

> 1. At the request of either party, the arbitral tribunal may take any interim measures it deems necessary in respect of the subject-matter of the dispute, including measures for the conservation of the goods forming the subject-matter in dispute, such as ordering their deposit with a third person or the sale of perishable goods.
>
> 2. Such interim measures may be established in the form of an interim award. The arbitral tribunal shall be entitled to require security for the costs of such measures.
>
> 3. A request for interim measures addressed by any party to a judicial authority shall not be deemed incompatible with the agreement to arbitrate, or as a waiver of that agreement.

II. Discussion

202. It is clear that the term "interim measures" in article 26 was intended to encompass not only provisional measures but also conservatory measures. Article 26 proceeds on the assumption (which was perhaps valid in 1976) that a typical case would arise out of international trade; hence the emphasis on measures related to "the conservation of … goods". The Model Law,

following almost 20 years later, places no such emphasis: it speaks more generally of "interim measure[s] of protection ... in respect of the subject-matter of the dispute" (Article 17).

203. Today, article 26 of the Rules raises a number of difficult questions:

- Whether the types of measures available as "interim measures" are to be determined by reference to a particular law (including international law) or, rather, as an autonomous legal concept proper to international arbitration.
- Whether the terms "in respect of the subject-matter of the dispute" encompass measures to preserve the position of a party (eg injunctions, security for costs, or orders to refund part of an advance on costs that one party was forced to make in default of a payment by its opponent) or the integrity of the arbitral process (eg freezing orders to secure funds out of which an award may be satisfied, or anti-suit injunctions).
- In what circumstances (eg risk of irreparable harm, existing damage, or lack of another remedy), under what conditions (eg on a showing of a good arguable case on the merits) and in what procedure (after hearing both parties' views or ex parte) interim protection may be granted.
- Whether interim measures – in the form of an "interim award" or not – are binding and to be carried out without delay (as awards under article 32(2)).

204. With respect to some questions the Rules cannot, given their nature, provide an answer.[209] Notably, the Rules cannot answer the question whether tribunal-ordered interim measures are enforceable as "arbitral awards" under the New York Convention.[210]

205. On the other hand, the Commission's detailed treatment of the question, as part of an intended revision of Article 17 of the Model Law (proposed Chapter IV *bis*), comprehensively deals with the issues above.[211] The choice that presents itself is whether article 26 should mirror, in part at least, the proposed revised Article 17 of the Model Law or, rather, anticipate the *lignes directrices* of that proposed revision. This question involves not only practical considerations of timing, but also the question of legislative policy whether the Rules should go to the level of detail required of the Model Law.

206. Our suggestion is twofold:

- First, to maintain the basic structure and content of the existing article 26, making the clarifications that practice has shown are necessary or at least highly desirable. The necessary changes include language expanding the facially restrictive phraseology "measures ... in respect of the subject-matter of the dispute" in article 26(1).[212]

---

209 In addition, given the nature of the Rules as *ad hoc* rules, interim protection can be given only by the arbitral tribunal itself, and therefore not before the tribunal's constitution. Compare the "summary arbitral proceedings" procedure under Article 42a of the NAI Rules; and the revised Article 37 of the AAA Rules (effective 1 May 2006) providing for "emergency arbitrators" to deal with urgent requests for interim or conservatory measures.

210 This is a matter currently under consideration by the Commission; see Report of UNCITRAL Working Group on the Work of its 44th Session, UN Doc A/CN.9/592 (2006) paras 34-39; Note by the UNCITRAL Secretariat, UN Doc A/CN.9/WG.II/WP.141 (5 December 2005); and Articles 17 novies and 17 decies of the current draft Chapter IV *bis* for the Model Law, reprinted in ibid 5-6. For an assimilation of interim-measures orders to awards cf s 593(4) of the Austrian Code of Civil Procedure (ÖZPO).

211 The draft text currently under consideration is set out in a Note by the UNCITRAL Secretariat, UN Doc A/CN.9/WG.II/WP.141 (5 December 2005) 2-6. It consists of eleven detailed articles.

212 This would be entirely consistent with the significantly broader formulations to be found in Article 23(1) of the ICC Rules; Article 46(a) of the WIPO Rules; Article 26(1)-(2) of the Swiss Rules; and Article 21(1) of the AAA Rules.

- Secondly, to include in article 26 provisions containing broad guidance on the purposes of, and conditions for, interim measures to be granted thereunder. The current draft Articles 17 and 17 *bis* for Chapter IV *bis* of the Model Law (whose text has already been extensively debated and appears settled[213]) would serve both those purposes well (see "alternative one" below). Another possibility would be to preserve the existing text of article 26, making limited changes that would be consistent with – but not fully reflect the tenor of – the proposed revision of the Model Law (see "alternative two").

III. Proposed Revision

207. Article 26 would read as follows (following draft Articles 17, 17 *bis*, and 17 sexies (2) for Chapter IV *bis* of the Model Law):

Alternative One

1. ~~At the request of either party, the arbitral tribunal may take any interim measures it deems necessary in respect of the subject-matter of the dispute, including measures for the conservation of the goods forming the subject-matter in dispute, such as ordering their deposit with a third person or the sale of perishable goods.~~

Unless otherwise agreed by the parties, the Arbitral Tribunal may, at the request of a party, grant interim measures. An interim measure is any temporary measure, whether in the form of an [interim] award or in another form, by which, at any time prior to the issuance of the award by which the dispute is finally decided, the Arbitral Tribunal orders a party to:

(a) Maintain or restore the status quo pending determination of the dispute;
(b) Take action that would prevent, or refrain from taking action that is likely to cause, current or imminent harm or prejudice to the arbitral process itself;
(c) Provide a means of preserving assets out of which a subsequent award may be satisfied; or
(d) Preserve evidence that may be relevant and material to the resolution of the dispute.

2. ~~Such interim measures may be established in the form of an interim award. The arbitral tribunal shall be entitled to require security for the costs of such measures.~~

The party requesting an interim measure under subparagraphs (a), (b) and (c) of paragraph 1 shall satisfy the Arbitral Tribunal that:

(a) Harm not adequately reparable by an award of damages is likely to result if the measure is not ordered, and such harm substantially outweighs the harm that is likely to result to the party against whom the measure is directed if the measure is granted; and
(b) There is a reasonable possibility that the requesting party will succeed on the merits of the claim, provided that any determination on this possibility shall not affect the discretion of the Arbitral Tribunal in making any subsequent determination.

3. With regard to a request for an interim measure under paragraph 1(d), the requirements in sub-paragraphs (a) and (b) of paragraph 2 shall apply only to the extent the Arbitral Tribunal considers appropriate.

4. The Arbitral Tribunal may require the party requesting an interim measure to provide appropriate security in connexion with the measure.

---

213 See Report of UNCITRAL Working Group on the Work of it 37th Session, UN Doc A/CN.9/523 (2002) paras 15-76; Report of UNCITRAL Working Group on the Work of it 39th Session, UN Doc A/CN.9/545 (2003) paras 19-92; Report of UNCITRAL Working Group on the Work of its 43rd Session, UN Doc A/CN.9/589 (2005) paras 11-75; and Report of UNCITRAL Working Group on the Work of its 44th Session, UN Doc A/CN.9/592 (2006) paras 12-21.

5. A request for interim measures addressed by any party to a judicial authority shall not be deemed incompatible with the agreement to arbitrate, or as a waiver of that agreement.

208. A less ambitious text (following Article 23(1) of the ICC Rules) would be as follows:

Alternative Two

1. At the request of ~~either~~any party, the A~~a~~rbitral T~~t~~ribunal may ~~take~~ order any interim or conservatory measures it deems necessary ~~in respect of the subject-matter of the dispute, including measures for the conservation of the goods forming the subject-matter in dispute, such as ordering their deposit with a third person or the sale of perishable goods.~~

2. Such interim measures may be established in the form of an ~~interim~~ award. The A~~a~~rbitral T~~t~~ribunal shall be entitled to require security for ~~the costs of~~ in connexion with such measures.

3. A request for interim measures addressed by any party to a judicial authority shall not be deemed incompatible with the agreement to arbitrate, or as a waiver of that agreement.

ARTICLE 27(1)

I. Present Rule

The arbitral tribunal may appoint one or more experts to report to it, in writing, on specific issues to be determined by the tribunal. A copy of the expert's terms of reference, established by the arbitral tribunal, shall be communicated to the parties.

II. Discussion

209. The tribunal should consult the parties before appointing any expert to report to it. The ICC, WIPO and Swiss Rules so require.[214]

210. Consultation with the parties "should normally concern not only the question of whether an expert should be appointed, but the precise nature of the expert's mission ('terms of reference') as well as his identity and cost."[215]

211. It is not clear whether the decision under article 27(1) is to be made under article 31(1) or 31(2). Professor Sanders holds the view that it is "a matter of procedure and *Article 31, para. 2* applies".[216]

III. Proposed Revision

212. The revised text of article 27(1) reads:

The A~~a~~rbitral T~~t~~ribunal may, after consultation with the parties, appoint one or more experts to report to it, in writing, on specific issues to be determined by the T~~t~~ribunal. A copy of the expert's terms of reference, established by the A~~a~~rbitral T~~t~~ribunal, shall be communicated to the parties.

---

214 Article 20(4) of the ICC Rules; Article 55(a) of the WIPO Rules; and Article 27(2) of the Swiss Rules.

215 *Derains & Schwartz* 279. Under the ICC Rules, "although Article 20(4) might arguably be said to give the Arbitral Tribunal the right to appoint an expert even if none of the parties desires this, there is not any way in which the Arbitral Tribunal can, as a practical matter, impose an expert on the parties against all of their wishes, as the expert is required to be paid by the parties": ibid 279-280.

216 *Sanders* (1977) 203.

ARTICLE 27(2)

I. Present Rule

> The parties shall give the expert any relevant information or produce for his inspection any relevant documents or goods that he may require of them. Any dispute between a party and such expert as to the relevance of the required information or production shall be referred to the arbitral tribunal for decision.

II. Discussion

213. The arbitral tribunal should expressly be given the power to direct any experts appointed by the parties to meet with the tribunal-appointed expert in order to attempt to reach an agreement on contentious issues or, at least, to narrow them down.

214. The Civil Procedure Rules of England and Wales (1998, as amended) allow for such discussions among experts. CPR Rule 35.12 provides:

> 35.12
>
> (1) The court may, at any stage, direct a discussion between experts for the purpose of requiring the experts to
> (a) identify and discuss the expert issues in the proceedings; and
> (b) where possible, reach an agreed opinion on those issues.
>
> (2) The court may specify the issues which the experts must discuss.
>
> (3) The court may direct that following a discussion between the experts they must prepare a statement for the court showing
> (a) those issues on which they agree; and
> (b) those issues on which they disagree and a summary of their reasons for disagreeing.
>
> (4) The content of the discussion between the experts shall not be referred to at the trial unless the parties agree.
>
> (5) Where experts reach agreement on an issue during their discussions, the agreement shall not bind the parties unless the parties expressly agree to be bound by the agreement.

215. Our proposed provision is inspired by CPR Rule 35.12.

III. Proposed Revision

216. Proposed revised text of article 27(2):

> The parties shall give the expert any relevant information or produce for his or her inspection any relevant documents or goods that he or she may require of them. Any dispute between a party and ~~such~~ the expert as to the relevance of the required information or production shall be referred to the A~~a~~rbitral T~~t~~ribunal for decision. The Arbitral Tribunal may direct a meeting between the expert appointed by the Tribunal and any experts appearing for the parties for the purpose of identifying, discussing and, where possible, reaching an agreed opinion on, expert issues in the proceedings. The Arbitral Tribunal may also direct such a meeting between or among experts appearing for the parties.

217. It would also be possible to include this provision as a new article 27(3), renumbering the current article 27(3)-(4) as 27(4)-(5).

ARTICLE 27(4)

I. Present Rule

> At the request of either party the expert, after delivery of the report, may be heard at a hearing where the parties shall have the opportunity to be present and to interrogate the expert. At this hearing either party may present expert witnesses in order to testify on the points at issue. The provisions of article 25 shall be applicable to such proceedings.

II. Discussion and Proposed Revision

218. For clarity, article 27(4) should read:

> At the request of ~~either~~any party the expert, after delivery of the report, may be heard at a hearing where the parties shall have the opportunity to be present and to interrogate the expert. At this hearing ~~either~~any party may present expert witnesses in order to testify on the points at issue. The provisions of article 25 shall be applicable to such proceedings.

ARTICLE 28(1)

I. Present Rule

> If, within the period of time fixed by the arbitral tribunal, the claimant has failed to communicate his claim without showing sufficient cause for such failure, the arbitral tribunal shall issue an order for the termination of the arbitral proceedings. If, within the period of time fixed by the arbitral tribunal, the respondent has failed to communicate his statement of defence without showing sufficient cause for such failure, the arbitral tribunal shall order that the proceedings continue.

II. Discussion

219. The text needs to clarify that where the respondent has failed to communicate his Statement of Defence, such failure cannot and should not be treated by the tribunal as an admission of the claimant's allegation. Rather, some discretion should be given to a tribunal faced with such a situation.[217]

220. A provision to the same effect was added to Article 25 of the Model Law.[218] Article 25(a)-(b) of the Model Law provides:

> Unless otherwise agreed by the parties, if, without showing sufficient cause,
> (a) the claimant fails to communicate his Statement of Claim in accordance with article 23(1), the arbitral tribunal shall terminate the proceedings;
> (b) the respondent fails to communicate his Statement of Defence in accordance with article 23(1), the arbitral tribunal shall continue the proceedings without treating such failure in itself as an admission of the claimant's allegations;

III. Proposed Revision

221. Proposed revised text of article 28(1):

---

217 See *Sanders* (2004) 252.

218 Such a provision was added in order that the tribunal be provided with "certain discretion" in the event of default by the respondent in submitting his statement of defence. The tribunal, in such a case, would not be bound to treat such default as a full admission of the claim and of all the supporting facts. Nor would it be precluded from drawing inferences from such default. *Holtzmann & Neuhaus* 700.

If, within the period of time fixed by the <u>A</u>~~a~~rbitral <u>T</u>~~t~~ribunal, the Cclaimant has failed to communicate ~~his~~<u>its Statement of C</u>~~c~~laim without showing sufficient cause for such failure, the <u>A</u>~~a~~rbitral <u>T</u>~~t~~ribunal shall issue an order for the termination of the arbitral proceedings<u>, unless the Respondent has submitted a counter-claim</u>. If, within the period of time fixed by the <u>A</u>~~a~~rbitral <u>T</u>~~t~~ribunal, the <u>R</u>~~r~~espondent has failed to communicate ~~his~~<u>its</u> <u>S</u>~~s~~tatement of <u>D</u>~~d~~efence without showing sufficient cause for such failure, the <u>A</u>~~a~~rbitral <u>T</u>~~t~~ribunal shall order that the proceedings continue<u>, without treating such failure in itself as an admission of the Claimant's allegations</u>.

ARTICLE 28(2)

I. Present Rule

If one of the parties, duly notified under these Rules, fails to appear at a hearing, without showing sufficient cause for such failure, the arbitral tribunal may proceed with the arbitration.

II. Proposed Revision

222. The following revised text would be consistent with article 21(4), as we propose it be amended, in accordance with the Model Law:

If ~~one~~<u>any</u> of the parties, duly notified under these Rules, fails to appear at a hearing, without showing sufficient cause for such failure, the <u>A</u>~~a~~rbitral <u>T</u>~~t~~ribunal may proceed with the arbitration <u>and make an award</u>.

ARTICLE 28(3)

I. Present Rule

If one of the parties, duly invited to produce documentary evidence, fails to do so within the established period of time, without showing sufficient cause for such failure, the arbitral tribunal may make the award on the evidence before it.

II. Proposed Revision

223. For clarity, article 28(3) should read:

If <u>any</u>~~one~~ of the parties, duly invited to produce documentary evidence, fails to do so within the established period of time, without showing sufficient cause for such failure, the <u>A</u>~~a~~rbitral <u>T</u>~~t~~ribunal may make the award on the evidence before it.

ARTICLE 29

I. Present Rule

1. The arbitral tribunal may inquire of the parties if they have any further proof to offer or witnesses to be heard or submissions to make and, if there are none, it may declare the hearings closed.

2. The arbitral tribunal may, if it considers it necessary owing to exceptional circumstances, decide, on its own motion or upon application of a party, to reopen the hearings at any time before the award is made.

II. Discussion

224. It is unclear why, in relation to the closure of proceedings, a distinction needs to be drawn between the holding of hearings and the submission of written documents. While the current position under the UNCITRAL Rules provides separate procedural tracks for hearings and for written submissions,[219] it seems that the intention of the drafters of this article was to close proceedings *generally* (rather than hearings only) before the issuance of an award.[220]

225. There seems to be no reason why, in principle, written submissions and hearings should not be declared to be at an end at the same point in time.

226. ICSID Rule 38 expresses the better rule more clearly:

> (1) When the presentation of the case by the parties is completed, the proceeding shall be declared closed.
>
> (2) Exceptionally, the Tribunal may, before the award has been rendered, reopen the proceeding on the ground that new evidence is forthcoming of such a nature as to constitute a decisive factor, or that there is a vital need for clarification on certain specific points.[221]

227. We suggest revisions to article 29 in line with ICSID Rule 38.

III. Proposed Revision

228. Proposed revised text of article 29:

> 1. The <u>A</u>~~a~~rbitral <u>T</u>~~t~~ribunal may inquire of the parties if they have any further proof to offer or witnesses to be heard or submissions to make and, if there are none, it may declare the hearings closed. <u>When the parties have completed the presentation of the case, or of a phase of the case, the Tribunal shall declare the proceedings closed with respect to the whole case or its relevant phase.</u>
>
> 2. ~~The arbitral tribunal may, if~~ <u>If</u> it considers it necessary owing to exceptional circumstances, the <u>Arbitral Tribunal may</u> ~~decide~~, on its own motion or upon application of a party, to reopen the ~~hearings~~ <u>proceedings</u> at any time before ~~the~~ <u>an</u> award is made <u>pursuant to article 21, paragraph 4, article 31 or article 37, paragraph 2 and issue directions, pursuant to article 15, paragraph 1, with respect to further actions that the parties or the Arbitral Tribunal should take before an award is issued</u>.

ARTICLE 30

I. Present Rule

> A party who knows that any provision of, or requirement under, these Rules has not been complied with and yet proceeds with the arbitration without promptly stating his objection to such non-compliance, shall be deemed to have waived his right to object.

---

219 *Caron/Caplan/Pellonpää* 651.

220 In the *travaux préparatoires*, Report of UNCITRAL Committee of the Whole II, para 149, it was said:

> It was noted that the proposed article 25 *bis* would ensure that no party could unreasonably delay the arbitral proceedings by repeated requests for hearings *and the taking of further evidence*. (emphasis added)

It should also be noted that "Article 29 has no precedent in previous drafts of the Rules. It was added to the final version during the ninth session of UNCITRAL (1976)": *Sanders* (1977) 207.

221 See also Article 21 of the 1958 ILC Model Rules.

II. Discussion and Proposed Revision

229. First, consistently with Article 33 of the ICC Rules which imputes knowledge of a failure to comply on any party that proceeds notwithstanding such failure,[222] we would simply add the words "ought to know" in order to maintain, as much as possible, the current wording of article 30.

230. Secondly, directions of the arbitral tribunal should also be covered by this article.[223] Other changes are inspired by Article 32.1 of the LCIA Rules.[224]

231. Proposed revised text of article 30:

> A party that knows or ought to know that any provision of, or requirement under the arbitration agreement (including these Rules), or any directions given by the Arbitral Tribunal under these Rules, has not been complied with and yet proceeds with the arbitration without promptly stating ~~his~~its objection to such non-compliance, shall be deemed irrevocably to have waived ~~his~~its right to object.

ARTICLE 31(1)

I. Present Rule

> When there are three arbitrators, any award or other decision of the arbitral tribunal shall be made by a majority of the arbitrators.

II. Discussion

232. There can be no question that decisions (other than those on "questions of procedure", under article 31(2)) should in principle be taken by a majority of the tribunal. Article 31(1) is, in other words, unimpeachable so far as it goes; but it provides no fallback position where no majority exists. It is a well-documented fact that this is a real possibility.

233. The *RAKTA* arbitration[225] illustrates how deadlock may arise in such a way that the presiding arbitrator would have to sacrifice principle in order to render an award under the UNCITRAL Rules. The arbitration was brought by an Egyptian state-owned paper manufacturer, RAKTA, against a US construction company, Parsons & Whittemore. The tribunal, operating under the 1955 ICC Rules, was composed of two nationals of the disputing parties and Judge Lagergren of Sweden as chairman. A preliminary phase of the arbitration involved the determination of a *force majeure* defence advanced by Parsons & Whittemore as justification for having abandoned the construction site never to return. The Egyptian arbitrator would dismiss that defence entirely, while the American arbitrator would fully accept it. The chairman concurred in neither view:

---

222 Article 33 of the ICC Rules: A party which proceeds with the arbitration without raising its objection to a failure to comply with any provision of these Rules, or of any other rules applicable to the proceedings, any direction given by the Arbitral Tribunal, or any requirement under the arbitration agreement relating to the constitution of the Arbitral Tribunal, or to the conduct of the proceedings, shall be deemed to have waived its right to object.

223 Ibid. Article 58 of the WIPO Rules also provides: A party which knows that any provision of, or requirement under, these Rules, or any direction given by the Tribunal, has not been complied with, and yet proceeds with the arbitration without promptly recording an objection to such non-compliance, shall be deemed to have waived its right to object.

224 Article 32.1 LCIA Rules: A party who knows that any provision of the Arbitration Agreement (including these Rules) has not been complied with and yet proceeds with the arbitration without promptly stating its objection to such non-compliance, shall be treated as having irrevocably waived its right to object.

225 *RAKTA*, ICC 1703/1971, summarized in *Craig, Park & Paulsson*, *International Chamber of Commerce Arbitration* (3rd edn, 2000) 370.

he considered that *force majeure* could be invoked in respect of a limited period of time only, after which Parsons & Whittemore should have returned to the site. Under the ICC Rules, Judge Lagergren was not obliged to align himself with either of the two party-appointed arbitrators to form a majority. He was able to issue his ruling as an award by the chairman alone.

234. The present version of the ICC Rules formulates the relevant rule as follows (with added emphasis), in Article 25(1):

> When the Arbitral Tribunal is composed of more than one arbitrator, an Award is given by a majority decisions. *If there be no majority, the award shall be made by the chairman of the Arbitral Tribunal alone.*

Article 26.3 of the LCIA Rules, Article 61 of the WIPO Rules, Article 31 of the Swiss Rules and Article 28 of the IACAC Rules are to the same effect.

235. It is true that chairman-alone awards are rare.[226] It may be the very paucity of such awards that proves the value of permitting the presiding arbitrator to decide an issue alone, "as if acting as sole arbitrator".[227] Knowledge that unreasonable positions can yield no tactical benefit dissuades partisan conduct on the part of the co-arbitrators.[228] Conversely, the presiding arbitrator – presumptively the most neutral member of the panel – need not compromise his views and join with the *least unreasonable* of the co-arbitrators in order to form a majority.

236. Neither of those two aims can be achieved by the present article 31(1) of the UNCITRAL Rules, for it is clear that under that provision:

> arbitrators are forced to continue their deliberations until a majority, and probably a compromise solution, has been reached.[229]

237. The *travaux* indicate that the Commission considered giving the presiding arbitrator the power to make an award alone, to avoid forcing him "to agree to a juridically dubious solution in order to attain the necessary majority".[230] But that suggestion was dismissed,[231] principally on the considerations that the requirement of forming a majority would prevent coarbitrators from being reduced to "mere assessors" and emphasise the consultative process.[232]

238. Experience under article 31(1) suggests the provision should be reconsidered, and that the predominant approach led by the ICC Rules has not, in fact, had the result of marginalising co-arbitrators. (We note from the outset that the experience relevant here concerns tribunals operating in a highly contentious atmosphere; it is the test of such hard cases that the Rules must be able to withstand.)

239. The Iran-US Claims Tribunal saw several cases of jigsaw majorities being formed on an issue-by-issue basis, resulting in narrowly decided and worded awards followed by forceful

---

226 *Craig, Park & Paulsson*, ibid, records one further ICC award: ICC 3381/1984, [1986] JDI 1096, note Jarvin.

227 WIPO Rules, Article 61.

228 See *Derains & Schwartz* 306-307.

229 *Sanders* (1977) 208.

230 Sixth UNCITRAL Secretariat Note, UN Doc A/CN.9/263, (1985) 16 (1985) UNCITRAL YB 54, *ad* article 29(1).

231 See UNCITRAL Report, UN Doc A/31/17, (1976) 7 YB 9, paras 159-161.

232 Summary Record of the 11th Meeting of the Committee of the Whole (II), UNCITRAL 9th Session, UN Doc A/CN.9/9/C.2/SR.11, (1976) 3. The Model Law also requires majority awards, but the authors are aware of at least one instance where a state adopting the Model Law made a specific amendment to enable the arbitral tribunal Chair to rule without a majority: Act 2735/1999, 'On International Commercial Arbitration' (Greece) [1999] Government Gazette No A167, Article 31(1).

dissenting/concurring opinions by the Iranian and US judges.[233] Neither the dissentients nor the presiding judges thought this a happy experience. The first President of the Tribunal, Judge Pierre Bellet, was heard to say that one of the reasons he resigned that post was his lack of authority to disregard two extreme positions.[234] And, as to party-appointed judges, in the *Ultrasystems* case, Judge Mosk wrote:

> I concur in the Tribunal's Partial Award. I do so in order to form a majority, so that an award can be rendered.[235]

In the *Economy Forms* case, Judge Holtzmann made clear that the damages awarded were only half of what would have been proper, but went on:

> Why then do I concur in this inadequate award, rather than dissenting from it? The answer is based on the realistic old saying that there are circumstances in which "something is better than nothing".[236]

240. Roberts B. Owen, chairing the tribunal in the highly politicized *Dispute over Inter-entity Boundary in Brcko Area* between the Republika Srpska (area of Bosnia Herzegovina populated largely by ethnic Serbs) and the Federation of Bosnia and Herzegovina stated explicitly in the award he rendered without concurrence from either of his co-arbitrators that from the outset the positions of the two parties on the merits have been polar opposites and each party has explicitly refused to compromise. These polar positions and accompanying intense animosities, consistently in evidence from the opening of the Dayton conference onward, make clear from the outset that any party-appointed arbitrator would encounter significant difficulties in conducting himself with the usual degree of detachment and independence.[237]

Fortunately the parties to that dispute had been sensible enough to agree in advance to an amendment to article 31 of the UNCITRAL Rules making decisions by the presiding arbitrator binding in the absence of a majority.[238]

241. In sum, it would be useful to consider whether a fallback rule is not advisable, in the model of the ICC or LCIA Rules. The wording proposed below ("[i]f no majority is *formed*") purports to suggest that the arbitrators must make a good-faith reasonable effort to form a majority – but that they do not have to compromise their professional conscience to form a

---

233 See, eg, Foremost Teheran, Inc v Iran, (1986) 10 Iran-US CTR 229, 239 where the separate votes are recorded as follows:
[Judge] Ameli:
1. Joining as to denial of expropriation claims.
2. Concurring as to granting of claims for two unpaid dividends, except dissenting as to sub-paragraph 2(d) of the *dispositif*.
3. Dissenting as to granting of contractual claims.
4. Joining as to costs.
5. Dissenting as to award of interest.
6. Dissenting as to the existence of jurisdiction over certain of the claims and Parties. ...

[Judge] Holtzmann:
1. Dissenting as to denial of expropriation claims.
2. Joining as to granting of claims for two unpaid dividends.
3. Joining as to granting of contractual claims.
4. Dissenting as to denial of costs to the Claimants.
5. *Joining as to award of only 10% interest solely in order to form a majority.* (emphasis added)

234 The formal grounds Judge Bellet gave are summarized at note 31 above.

235 *Ultrasystems, Inc v Iran*, (1983) 2 Iran-US CTR 114, 123 (Op Mosk).

236 *Economy Forms Corp v Iran*, (1983) 3 Iran-US CTR 42, 55 (Conc Op Holtzmann).

237 *The Republic Srpska v The Federation of Bosnia and Herzegovina*, Arbitration over inter-entity boundary in Brcko Area (Award on Control over the Brcko Corridor of 14 February 1997) (1997) 36 ILM 396, para 5.

238 Ibid.

majority in every case. A provision to that effect would be entirely consistent with Article 29 of the Model Law, which requires "any decision of the arbitral tribunal" to be made by majority "unless otherwise agreed by the parties". The parties' agreement to arbitrate under the Rules, including article 31(1), would constitute an advance agreement by the parties within Article 29 of the Model Law.

III. Proposed Revision

242. Proposed revised text of article 31(1):

> When there are three <u>(or more)</u> arbitrators, any award or other decision of the <u>A</u>~~a~~rbitral <u>T</u>~~t~~ribunal shall be made by a majority of the arbitrators. <u>If no majority is formed, any award or other decision shall be made by the presiding arbitrator alone.</u>

ARTICLE 31(2)

I. PRESENT RULE

> In the case of questions of procedure, when there is no majority or when the arbitral tribunal so authorises, the presiding arbitrator may decide on his own, subject to revision, if any, by the arbitral tribunal.

II. DISCUSSION AND PROPOSED RULE

243. For clarity, article 31(2) should read:

> In the case of questions of procedure, when there is no majority or when the <u>A</u>~~a~~rbitral <u>T</u>~~t~~ribunal so authorises, the presiding arbitrator may decide on his <u>or her</u> own, subject to revision, if any, by the <u>A</u>~~a~~rbitral <u>T</u>~~t~~ribunal.

NEW ARTICLE 31(3)

I. Discussion

244. Secrecy of deliberations is a cardinal principle in international arbitration. Indeed, it is guaranteed by most major modern arbitration rules.[239] The rule is absolute and not subject to qualifications: "The deliberations of the tribunal shall remain secret."[240]

245. The principle also has a forward reach: it enjoins tribunal members from later divulging (eg, in a dissenting opinion) any information or materials concerning or produced in and for the deliberation process.

246. A qualification is required, however, for obstructionist arbitrators, as illustrated in the cases discussed in the context of "truncated" tribunals (article 13 above). Accordingly, Article 30.2 of the LCIA provides (with emphasis added):

> The deliberations of the Arbitral Tribunal are likewise confidential to its members, *save and to the extent* that disclosure of an arbitrator's refusal to participate in the arbitration is required of the other members of the Arbitral Tribunal under Articles 10, 12 and 26.

239 See Iran-US CTR Rule 31.2; Article 34 of the AAA Rules; Article 76 of the WIPO Rules; Article 20(3) of the SCC Rules; Article 30.2 of the LCIA Rules; Article 43(2) of the Swiss Rules.

240 Article 26 of the 1958 ILC Model Rules.

II. Proposed Rule

247. Proposed new article 31(3):

> The deliberations of the Arbitral Tribunal shall remain secret, save as may be necessary for a notice to be given pursuant to article 13, paragraph 5.

ARTICLE 32(1)

I. Present Rule

> In addition to making a final award, the arbitral tribunal shall be entitled to make interim, interlocutory, or partial awards.

II. Discussion

248. The Rules do not set forth criteria by which to distinguish between "final", "interim", "interlocutory", and "partial" awards.[241] The intention is to give the widest latitude to the arbitral tribunal to handle and ultimately liquidate the dispute in the most efficient way in the circumstances.[242] Without detracting in any way from that sound approach, minor clarifications to article 32(1) could be achieved by following the model set by section 47(1) of the Arbitration Act 1996[243] and ICSID Arbitration Rule 48(3). The latter provision is a useful reminder that the arbitrators must fully and efficiently determine all claims before them, so as to reduce the need of additional awards under article 37.

III. Proposed Revision

249. Proposed revised text of article 32(1):

> In addition to making a final award terminating the arbitral proceedings, the A~~a~~rbitral T~~t~~ribunal shall be entitled to make interim, interlocutory, or partial awards on the issues to be determined, as necessary to deal with every claim submitted to the Arbitral Tribunal.

ARTICLE 32(2)

I. Present Rule

> The award shall be made in writing and shall be final and binding on the parties. The parties undertake to carry out the award without delay.

II. Discussion

250. We propose adding a new sentence, modelled on Article 29(2) of the IACAC Rules of 2002, Article 28(6) of the ICC Rules, and Article 26.9 of the LCIA Rules. Unlike the ICC and LCIA

---

241 In addition, there are overlaps: a decision dismissing certain but not all of the claims on grounds of jurisdiction or admissibility may be both partial (for it does not dispose of the whole case) and final (terminating the proceedings in respect of the claims dismissed).

242 This latitude is mirrored in articles 34-38, which use the generic term "award" without qualification, although some of the provisions therein lend themselves more naturally to final awards.

243 "Unless otherwise determined by the parties, the tribunal may make more than one award at different times on different aspects of the matters to be determined."

Rules, however, the proposed text is formulated as a positive rule ("The award shall be subject to no appeal ..."), rather than as a constructive waiver of the right to appeal.[244]

In addition, the proposed text does not contain the self-evident limitation "insofar as such waiver [of any right to appeal, etc] can validly be made". Thus, the proposed new provision would operate to exclude, for example, an appeal on point of law.[245] However, the provision would not be construed as an "express" agreement excluding a challenge to the award (for example, on lack of jurisdiction, violation of due process, etc).[246]

III. Proposed Revision

251. Proposed revised text of article 32(2):

> The award shall be made in writing and shall be final and binding on the parties. The award shall be subject to no appeal or other recourse before any court or other authority [other than pursuant to articles 35, 36 and 37]. The parties undertake to carry out the award without delay.

ARTICLE 32(4)

I. Present Rule

An award shall be signed by the arbitrators and it shall contain the date on which and the place where the award was made. Where there are three arbitrators and one of them fails to sign, the award shall state the reason for the absence of the signature.

II. Discussion

252. Article 32(4) could benefit from limited modifications for the sake of consistency with our proposed revised articles 16(4) and 31(1) and Article 31(3) of the Model Law.[247] The "place of arbitration" is the "juridical seat" of the arbitral proceedings and should not vary depending as a result of the happenstance of signature at another place, for reasons of convenience,[248] which arise with even more force in three-member tribunals where the arbitrators are often based in different countries (cf articles 6(4) and 7(3)).

III. Proposed Revision

253. Proposed revised text of article 32(4):

---

[244] The term "final" does not fully convey that the award is subject to no appeal in the courts; see, eg, *Sanders* (1977) para 17.4. In particular, the French text of the Rules renders the term "final" as: "*Elle [la sentence] n'est pas susceptible d'appel devant une instance arbitrale*" (emphasis added). It is not clear from the *travaux* why this formulation was preferred to alternative, broader ones; see A/CN.9/9/C.2/SR.10 (21 April 1976) paras 76-77 ("*[sentence] rendue en dernier ressort*"); and A/CN.9/9/C.2/SR.17 (26 April 1976) paras 18-19 ("*[sentence] qui n'est pas susceptible de voie de recours*"). *Caron/Caplan/Pellonpää* 797-798 explain the French language formulation on the basis that the term "final" conveys the effect of *res judicata* which, in the context of the Rules, means that "an award is final when it is no longer capable of revision by the arbitral tribunal" (emphasis added, citation omitted).

[245] See Arbitration Act 1996 (England & Wales) s 69(1).

[246] Agreements to contract out of the supervisory jurisdiction of the courts are permitted by Swiss, Belgian, Swedish, Tunisian, and Turkish law. For details on the requirements for and effects of such agreements: Petrochilos (note 40 above) paras 3.87 *et seq*.

[247] See also ICC Rules, Article 25(3); AAA Rules, Article 27(3); LCIA Rules, Article 26(1); and WIPO Rules, Article 62.

[248] Sanders, "Arbitration Rules of UNCITRAL: 30 Years", paper presented at an UNCITRAL colloquium on 6 April 2006, 7.

> An award shall be signed by the arbitrators and ~~it~~ shall state~~ contain~~ the date on which it was made and the juridical seat of arbitration as determined in accordance with article 16, paragraph 3~~and the place where the award was made~~. Where there are three arbitrators and one of them fails to sign, the award shall state the reason for the absence of the signature.

ARTICLE 32(5)

I. Present Rule

> The award may be made public only with the consent of both parties.

II. Discussion

254. Article 32(5) as at present worded does not, on its face, cater for cases where a party is under a legal duty to disclose an award or its tenor. Our suggestions in that regard follow the clearly worded language of Article 30.1 of the LCIA Rules.

III. Proposed Revision

255. Proposed revised text of article 32(5):

> The award may be made public ~~only~~ with the consent of both the parties or where, and to the extent, disclosure is required of a party by legal duty, to protect or pursue a legal right or in relation to [*bona fide*] legal proceedings before a state court or other judicial authority.

ARTICLE 32(7)

I. Present Rule

> If the arbitration law of the country where the award is made requires that the award be filed or registered by the arbitral tribunal, the tribunal shall comply with this requirement within the period of time required by law.

II. Discussion and Proposed Revision

256. Article 32(7) should be amended to avoid an onerous burden being placed on the arbitral tribunal in countries where registration requirements are ambiguous:

> If the arbitration law of the country where the award is made requires that the award be filed or registered by the A~~a~~rbitral T~~t~~ribunal, the T~~t~~ribunal, at the timely request of any party, shall comply with this requirement within the period of time required by law

NEW ARTICLE 32(8)

I. Discussion

257. On the basis of Article 35 of the ICC Rules we propose a new article 32(8), which deals with the essential duty of arbitrators and parties to act in the spirit of the Rules even in circumstances where no specific provision covers the situation in question. We consider this to be a useful general provision, since – as has been said with respect to the ICC Rules – the "Rules are not intended to be a comprehensive code for the conduct of an arbitration."[249] We see no reason why this provision should leave out the parties, as the ICC Rules do. Parties

---

249 *Derains & Schwartz* 384.

as well as arbitrators would benefit if at least *some* guidance were given to indicate how the lacunae in the Rules – that will inevitably emerge from time to time – should be dealt with. We also regard it as appropriate that this general duty be linked to the enforceability of the award.

II. Proposed Rule

258. Proposed new article 32(8):

> In all matters not expressly provided for in these Rules, the Arbitral Tribunal and the parties shall act in the spirit of these Rules and shall make every effort to ensure that any decision or award is legally enforceable.

ARTICLE 33

I. Present Rule

> 1. The arbitral tribunal shall apply the law designated by the parties as applicable to the substance of the dispute. Failing such designation by the parties, the arbitral tribunal shall apply the law determined by the conflict of laws rules, which it considers applicable.
>
> 2. The arbitral tribunal shall decide as *amiable compositeur* or *ex aequo et bono* only if the parties have expressly authorized the arbitral tribunal to do so and if the law applicable to the arbitral procedure permits such arbitration.
>
> 3. In all cases, the arbitral tribunal shall decide in accordance with the terms of the contract and shall take into account the usages of the trade applicable to the transaction.

II. Discussion

259. A few minor amendments are recommended in respect of this provision, mainly to ensure consistency with article 1(1) of the Rules and Article 28(1) of the Model Law. The term "rules of law" has been preferred essentially because of its broad scope, respecting party autonomy to elect, for example, different legal systems to govern different aspects of the relationship.[250]

III. Proposed Revision

260. Proposed revised text of article 33:

> 1. The A~~a~~rbitral T~~t~~ribunal shall decide the dispute in accordance with such rules of law as are chosen ~~apply the law designated~~ by the parties as applicable to the substance of the dispute. Failing any~~such~~ designation by the parties, the A~~a~~rbitral T~~t~~ribunal shall apply the law determined by the conflict of laws rules, which it considers applicable.
>
> 2. The A~~a~~rbitral T~~t~~ribunal shall decide as *amiable compositeur* or *ex aequo et bono* only if the parties have expressly authorized the A~~a~~rbitral T~~t~~ribunal to do so and if the law applicable to the arbitration~~arbitral procedure~~ permits such arbitration.
>
> 3. In all cases, the A~~a~~rbitral T~~t~~ribunal shall decide in accordance with the terms of the parties' contract, if any, and ~~shall take into account~~ the usages of the trade applicable to the transaction.

---

[250] See, in more detail, *Holtzmann & Neuhaus* 766-768.

ARTICLE 34

I. Present Rule

1. If, before the award is made, the parties agree on a settlement of the dispute, the arbitral tribunal shall either issue an order for the termination of the arbitral proceedings or, if requested by both parties and accepted by the tribunal, record the settlement in the form of an arbitral award on agreed terms. The arbitral tribunal is not obliged to give reasons for such an award.

2. If, before the award is made, the continuation of the arbitral proceedings becomes unnecessary or impossible for any reason not mentioned in paragraph 1, the arbitral tribunal shall inform the parties of its intention to issue an order for the termination of the proceedings. The arbitral tribunal shall have the power to issue such an order unless a party raises justifiable grounds for objection.

3. Copies of the order for termination of the arbitral proceedings or of the arbitral award on agreed terms, signed by the arbitrators, shall be communicated by the arbitral tribunal to the parties. Where an arbitral award on agreed terms is made, the provisions of article 32, paragraphs 2 and 4 to 7, shall apply.

II. Discussion and Proposed Revision

261. Article 34(2) may be deleted. It is difficult to understand. If it concerns issues such as "failure to prosecute", these are best left to be governed by national law.

1. If, before the award is made, the parties agree on a settlement of the dispute, the A~~a~~rbitral T~~t~~ribunal shall either issue an order for the termination of the arbitral proceedings or, if requested by all~~both~~ parties and accepted by the T~~t~~ribunal, record the settlement in the form of an arbitral award on agreed terms. The A~~a~~rbitral T~~t~~ribunal is not obliged to give reasons for such an award.

2. If, before the award is made, the continuation of the arbitral proceedings becomes unnecessary or impossible for any reason not mentioned in paragraph 1, the arbitral tribunal shall inform the parties of its intention to issue an order for the termination of the proceedings. The arbitral tribunal shall have the power to issue such an order unless a party raises justifiable grounds for objection.

3. Copies of the order for termination of the arbitral proceedings or of the arbitral award on agreed terms, signed by the arbitrators, shall be communicated by the A~~a~~rbitral T~~t~~ribunal to the parties. Where an arbitral award on agreed terms is made, the provisions of article 32, paragraphs 2 and 4 to 7, shall apply.

ARTICLE 35

I. Present Rule

1. Within thirty days after the receipt of the award, either party, with notice to the other party, may request that the arbitral tribunal give an interpretation of the award.

2. The interpretation shall be given in writing within forty-five days after the receipt of the request. The interpretation shall form part of the award and the provisions of article 32, paragraphs 2 to 7, shall apply.

II. Discussion

262. An award is final and *res judicata*. In principle it is not subject to review or challenge in the courts in respect of its legal or factual reasoning.[251] It follows that a legitimate request for interpretation of an award can only concern a failure on the tribunal's part to articulate its dispositive ruling in a way that is comprehensible and unambiguous, and so permits the parties to carry it out in accordance with article 32(2).

263. As the Permanent Court of International Justice has stated, interpretation cannot "add" to a decision (and so cannot concern new points), and must relate to the "meaning and scope which the Court intended to give to the *judgment* in question".[252]

264. With the benefit of the extensive experience of the Iran-US Claims Tribunal,[253] it is clear that interpretation means "clarification" of an ambiguity[254] and must relate to the operative part (the "dispositif") of an award.[255] Article 33(1)(b) of the Model Law, stating that interpretation is permitted "on a specific point or part of the award" does not, in our view, fully reflect the practice outlined above.

265. Further, in order for a party to have a legitimate interest to seek an interpretation, a *dispute* must have arisen between the parties.[256]

266. The operative time period should be 30, rather than 45 days. This would align the provision with the tribunal's power, in article 36(1), to correct awards. If there is a need for clarification by the tribunal, it will be manifest on the face of the award and so immediately detectable by the parties.

267. Finally, to avoid the risk of obstruction, it should be specified that an arbitrator who has not joined in the award should not be involved in its interpretation.

III. Proposed Revision

268. Proposed revised text of article 35:

> 1. If a dispute arises between the parties as to the meaning or scope of the ruling contained in an award, ~~W~~within thirty days after the receipt of the award, ~~either~~any party, with notice to the other part~~y~~ies, may request that the A~~a~~rbitral T~~t~~ribunal give an interpretation of the specific point in the award in respect of which the dispute has arisen.
>
> 2. The Arbitral Tribunal, if it considers the request to be justified, shall give an interpretation ~~The interpretation shall be given~~ in writing within ~~forty-five~~thirty days after the receipt of the request. The interpretation shall form part of the award and the provisions of article 32, paragraphs 2 to 8~~7~~, shall apply, save that an arbitrator who has not agreed with an award shall not be involved in its interpretation under this article.

251 See eg Model Law, Article 34.

252 *Interpretation of Judgments Nos 7 and 8* (The Chorzów Factory) (Decision of 16 December 1927) PCIJ, Series A No 13, 1 at 10-11 and 21 (emphasis added). See thus Article 33(1) of the 1958 ILC Model Rules.

253 See *Caron/Caplan/Pellonpää* 880 *et seq*.

254 *Uiterwyk Corporation et al v The Government of the Islamic Republic of Iran et al*, (1988) 19 Iran-US CTR 107.

255 Fouchard, Gaillard, Goldman, *Traité de l'arbitrage international* (1996) 776.

256 See Article 50(1) of the ICSID Convention; and Schreuer, *The ICSID Convention: A Commentary* (2001) 858.

ARTICLE 36

I. Present Rule

1. Within thirty days after the receipt of the award, either party, with notice to the other party, may request the arbitral tribunal to correct in the award any errors in computation, any clerical or typographical errors, or any errors of similar nature. The arbitral tribunal may within thirty days after the communication of the award make such corrections on its own initiative.

2. Such correction shall be in writing, and the provisions of article 32, paragraph 2 to 7, shall apply.

II. Discussion

269. We agree with and endorse Professor Sanders' recommendations for widening the scope of article 36. We also agree with his proposal to introduce the possibility of repair in case arbitrators omitted to sign the award or omitted to state the date or place of the award. When the award has not been signed there is no award and if the date or place are omitted, which the award according to art. 32 "shall contain", the award may be set aside. All three omissions could be easily repaired by the [arbitral tribunal].[257]

III. Proposed Revision

270. Proposed revised text of article 36:

1. Within thirty days after the receipt of the award, ~~either~~any party, with notice to the other part~~y~~ies, may request the A~~a~~rbitral T~~t~~ribunal to correct in the award
(a) any errors in computation, any clerical or typographical errors, or any errors of similar nature;~~.~~ or
(b) the omission of the juridical seat, the date on which the award was made and the reasons for an arbitrator's failure to sign.

2. If the Arbitral Tribunal considers a request pursuant to paragraph 1 to be justified, it shall make the necessary corrections within thirty days of such request. The Arbitral Tribunal may, if and to the extent it considers it necessary, extend the period of time within which it shall make a correction, by giving written notice to the parties.

3. The A~~a~~rbitral T~~t~~ribunal may within thirty days after the communication of the award make ~~such~~ corrections such as described in paragraph 1 on its own initiative.

4. ~~Such c~~Corrections pursuant to paragraph 1 or 3 shall be in writing, and the provisions of article 32, paragraphs 2 to ~~7~~8, shall apply, save that an arbitrator who has not agreed with an award shall not be involved in its correction under this article.

ARTICLE 37

I. Present Rule

1. Within thirty days after the receipt of the award, either party, with notice to the other party, may request the arbitral tribunal to make an additional award as to claims presented in the arbitral proceedings but omitted from the award.

---

257 *Sanders* (2004) 252.

2. If the arbitral tribunal considers the request for an additional award to be justified and considers that the omission can be rectified without any further hearings or evidence, it shall complete its award within sixty days after the receipt of the request.

3. When an additional award is made, the provision of article 32, paragraphs 2 to 7, shall apply.

II. Discussion

271. Two possible revisions may be considered, and have been suggested by Professor Sanders:[258]

(a) elimination of the requirement that the arbitrators should be satisfied that "no further hearings or evidence are needed", on the basis that the arbitrators should be free to convene fresh hearings or request further evidence or pleadings; and
(b) allowing tribunals to extend the 60-day period, in line with Article 33(4) of the Model Law.

272. Both of these suggestions are sound.

III. Proposed Revision

273. Proposed revised text of article 37:

1. Within thirty days after the receipt of the award, ~~either~~<u>any</u> party, with notice to the other part~~y~~<u>ies</u>, may request the <u>A</u>~~a~~rbitral <u>T</u>~~t~~ribunal to make an additional award as to claims <u>(including counter-claims)</u> presented in the arbitral proceedings but omitted from the award.

2. If the <u>A</u>~~a~~rbitral <u>T</u>~~t~~ribunal considers the request for an additional award to be justified ~~and considers that the omission can be rectified without any further hearings or evidence~~, it shall complete its award within sixty days after the receipt of the request. <u>The Arbitral Tribunal may, if and to the extent it considers it necessary, extend the period of time within which it shall complete its award, by giving written notice to the parties.</u>

3. When an additional award is made, the provision of article 32, paragraphs 2 to <u>8</u>~~7~~, shall apply.

ARTICLE 38

I. Present Rule

The arbitral tribunal shall fix the costs of arbitration in its award. The term "costs" includes only:
(a) The fees of the arbitral tribunal to be stated separately as to each arbitrator and to be fixed by the tribunal itself in accordance with article 39;
(b) The travel and other expenses incurred by the arbitrators;
(c) The costs of expert advice and of other assistance required by the arbitral tribunal;
(d) The travel and other expenses of witnesses to the extent such expenses are approved by the arbitral tribunal;
(e) The costs for legal representation and assistance of the successful party if such costs were claimed during the arbitral proceedings, and only to the extent that the arbitral tribunal determines that the amount of such costs is reasonable;
(f) Any fees of the appointing authority as well as the expenses of the Secretary-General of the Permanent Court of Arbitration at The Hague.

---

[258] *Sanders* (2004) 256.

II. Discussion

274. Care must be taken to ensure that the list of the elements making up the costs of the arbitration is comprehensive. This is because "*only*" elements expressly listed under article 38 qualify as costs.[259]

275. We consider two amendments desirable. First, elements (b)-(d) should be qualified with the word "reasonable" as is already the case with element (e) (which refers to parties' legal costs): it would constitute a useful reminder to arbitrators that they must act efficiently in all respects in the conduct of the arbitration (as provided in article 15(1)). Secondly, fees and expenses of a secretary appointed by the arbitral tribunal should be expressly included in element (c).[260]

III. Proposed Revision

276. Proposed revised text of article 38:

> The A~~a~~rbitral T~~t~~ribunal shall fix the costs of arbitration in its award. The term "costs" includes only:
> (a) The fees of the A~~a~~rbitral T~~t~~ribunal to be stated separately as to each arbitrator and to be fixed by the T~~t~~ribunal itself in accordance with article 39;
> (b) The reasonable travel and other expenses incurred by the arbitrators;
> (c) The reasonable costs of expert advice and of other assistance required by the A~~a~~rbitral T~~t~~ribunal, including the fees and expenses of any secretary appointed pursuant to article 15, paragraph 9;
> (d) The reasonable travel and other expenses of witnesses to the extent such expenses are approved by the A~~a~~rbitral T~~t~~ribunal;
> (e) The costs for legal representation and assistance of the successful party if such costs were claimed during the arbitral proceedings, and only to the extent that the A~~a~~rbitral T~~t~~ribunal determines that the amount of such costs is reasonable;
> (f) Any fees of the A~~a~~ppointing A~~a~~uthority as well as the expenses of the Secretary-General of the Permanent Court of Arbitration at The Hague.

ARTICLE 39

I. Present Rule

> 1. The fees of the arbitral tribunal shall be reasonable in amount, taking into account the amount in dispute, the complexity of the subject-matter, the time spent by the arbitrators and any other relevant circumstances of the case.
>
> 2. If an appointing authority has been agreed upon by the parties or designated by the Secretary-General of the Permanent Court at The Hague, and if that authority has issued a schedule of fees for arbitrators in international cases which it administers, the arbitral tribunal in fixing its fees shall take that schedule of fees into account to the extent that it considers appropriate in the circumstances of the case.
>
> 3. If such appointing authority has not issued a schedule of fees for arbitrators in international cases, any party may at any time request the appointing authority to furnish a statement setting forth the basis for establishing fees which is customarily followed in international cases in which the authority appoints arbitrators. It the appointing authority consents to provide such a statement, the arbitral tribunal in fixing its fees shall take such

---

259 The word "only" was specifically added at the drafting stage of article 38: UNCITRAL Report on the Work of its 9th Session, para 57 (draft article 38(a)).

260 *Sanders* (2004) 257.

information into account to the extent that it considers appropriate in the circumstances of the case.

4 In cases referred to in paragraphs 2 and 3, when a party so requests and the appointing authority consents to perform the function, the arbitral tribunal shall fix its fees only after consultation with the appointing authority which may make any comment it deems appropriate to the arbitral tribunal concerning the fees.

II. Discussion

277. As already noted (paragraph 14(l) above), the core provision in article 39(1), is sound – as far as it goes. Given the nature of *ad hoc* arbitration, unsupervised by an arbitral institution, abuses have on occasion occurred. The issue merits serious consideration, because it detracts from the legitimacy of the process in the eyes of parties. There is no easy answer. Possible safeguards against abuse might be the following.

- The tribunal and the parties would be explicitly encouraged to agree on the method of calculating the tribunal's fees from the outset, at a preparatory meeting. Such a provision might be included in article 15.
- The Appointing Authority, or if none has been agreed upon or designated, the Secretary-General of the PCA, would have the power to resolve any objection by a party to a tribunal's decision on its fees pursuant to articles 39(1) and 38. (The value of such a provision would perhaps lie in its deterrent force, not in its actual application.)[261]

278. Professor Sanders suggests the deletion of paragraphs (3)-(4). We agree, for the reasons he gives:

> *Paragraph 3* deals with the situation that the A.A. [Appointing Authority] does not have a schedule for fees. In that case any party may at any time request the A.A. to furnish a statement setting forth 'the basis for establishing fees which is customarily followed in international cases in which the A.A. appoints arbitrators'. If the A.A. consents to do so, the A.T. [Arbitral Tribunal] shall take this statement into account, when fixing its fees.
>
> I doubt whether the A.A., in case it has no schedule for fees, which anyhow will be the case when a private person functions as A.A., will ever consent to furnish such statement and also doubt whether any party, when the A.T. arrives at the stage of fixing its fees, will make such request. The A.T. may consider such a request as expressing doubts about the reasonableness of the A.T. in fixing its fees.
>
> ...
>
> *Paragraph 4* even goes a step further than the obligation of the A.T. to take into account the schedule of the A.A. (para. 2) or the Statement of the A.A. (para. 3). According to para. 4 the A.T. shall fix its fees "only after consultation with the A.A.". The A.A., in this consultation, may make "any comment it deems appropriate to the A.T." in respect of the fees the A.T. envisages to fix.
>
> I doubt again whether a party, at the final stage of the arbitration proceedings when the A.T. is working on the draft of its award which will contain its decision on the fees, will make such request. I also doubt whether the A.A. will "consent to perform this function".

[261] The proposition that the PCA maintain and publish a range of hourly rates for UNCITRAL arbitrations was considered and rejected in 1976: Report of UNCITRAL Committee of the Whole II, paras 206-208. Given that the PCA has been performing crucial functions in the operation of the UNCITRAL Rules over 30 years, this role – rarely to be performed, but very important when it is – could usefully be added to its range of support services.

The request of a party to consult the A.A. on the fees the A.T. envisages to fix, may be regarded by the A.T. as expressing doubts about the reasonableness of the A.T. in fixing its fees. A party may, at this stage of the proceedings, prefer to avoid this reaction. On the other hand, consultation of the A.A. on the fees the A.T. has to fix in its award, requires full information of the A.A. about all the work done by the A.T. This consultation-intermezzo will also postpone the rendering of the award.[262]

III. Proposed Revision

279. Proposed revised text of article 39:

1. The fees of the <u>A</u>~~a~~rbitral <u>T</u>~~t~~ribunal shall be reasonable in amount, taking into account the amount in dispute, the complexity of the subject-matter, the time spent by the arbitrators and any other relevant circumstances of the case.

~~2. If an appointing authority has been agreed upon by the parties or designated by the Secretary-General of the Permanent Court of Arbitration at The Hague, and if that authority has issued a schedule of fees for arbitrators in international cases which it administers, the arbitral tribunal in fixing its fees shall take that schedule of fees into account to the extent that it considers appropriate in the circumstances of the case.~~

<u>If any party disagrees when the Arbitral Tribunal fixes its fees, the fees shall be fixed by the Appointing Authority. If the Appointing Authority is unwilling or unable to do so, the fees shall be fixed by the Secretary-General of the Permanent Court of Arbitration at The Hague or by another institution or person selected by the Secretary-General for that purpose.</u>

~~3. If such appointing authority has not issued a schedule of fees for arbitrators in international cases, any party may at any time request the appointing authority to furnish a statement setting forth the basis for establishing fees which is customarily followed in international cases in which the authority appoints arbitrators. It the appointing authority consents to provide such a statement, the arbitral tribunal in fixing its fees shall take such information into account to the extent that it considers appropriate in the circumstances of the case.~~

~~4. In cases referred to in paragraphs 2 and 3, when a party so requests and the appointing authority consents to perform the function, the arbitral tribunal shall fix its fees only after consultation with the appointing authority which may make any comment it deems appropriate to the arbitral tribunal concerning the fees.~~

ARTICLE 40

I. Present Rule

1. Except as provided in paragraph 2, the costs of arbitration shall in principle be borne by the unsuccessful party. However, the arbitral tribunal may apportion each of such costs between the parties if it determines that apportionment is reasonable, taking into account the circumstances of the case.

2. With respect to the costs of legal representation and assistance referred to in article 38, paragraph (e), the arbitral tribunal, taking into account the circumstances of the case, shall be free to determine which party shall bear such costs or may apportion such costs between the parties if it determines that apportionment is reasonable.

262 *Sanders* (2004) 258.

3. When the arbitral tribunal issues an order for the termination of the arbitral proceedings or makes an award on agreed terms, it shall fix the costs of arbitration referred to in article 38 and article 39, paragraph 1, in the text of that order or award.

4. No additional fees may be charged by an arbitral tribunal for interpretation or correction or completion of its award under articles 35 to 37.

II. Discussion

280. We propose to delete article 40(2), which fails to establish any meaningful distinction except a very vague indication that costs of legal representatives are less easily recoverable than other costs. Practice has shown that the discretion exercised by arbitral tribunals depends on the circumstances of each case; the current formulation adds confusion rather than predictability.

281. We also propose to delete article 40(4). That provision is implicitly premised on the belief that arbitrators do not deserve additional fees because the need for correction or completion of their award is due to their own fault. Whether one agrees or not with this rigorous premise, it does not account for legitimate work on unmeritorious requests for correction or completion of an award.

III. Proposed Revision

282. Proposed revised text of article 40:

1. ~~Except as provided in paragraph 2, t~~The costs of arbitration shall in principle be borne by the unsuccessful party. However, the A~~a~~rbitral T~~t~~ribunal may apportion each of such costs between the parties if it determines that apportionment is reasonable, taking into account the circumstances of the case.

~~2. With respect to the costs of legal representation and assistance referred to in article 38, paragraph (e), the arbitral tribunal, taking into account the circumstances of the case, shall be free to determine which party shall bear such costs or may apportion such costs between the parties if it determines that apportionment is reasonable.~~

3. When the A~~a~~rbitral T~~t~~ribunal issues an order for the termination of the arbitral proceedings or makes an award on agreed terms, it shall fix the costs of arbitration referred to in article 38 and article 39, paragraph 1, in the text of that order or award.

~~4. No additional fees may be charged by an arbitral tribunal for interpretation or correction or completion of its award under articles 35 to 37.~~

ARTICLE 41

I. Present Rule

1. The arbitral tribunal, on its establishment, may request each party to deposit an equal amount as an advance for the costs referred to in article 38, paragraphs (a), (b) and (c).

2. During the course of the arbitral proceedings the arbitral tribunal may request supplementary deposits from the parties.

3. If an appointing authority has been agreed upon by the parties or designated by the Secretary-General of the Permanent Court of Arbitration at The Hague, and when a party so requests and the appointing authority consents to perform the function, the arbitral tribunal shall fix the amounts of any deposits or supplementary deposits only after consultation with the appointing authority which may make any comments to the

arbitral tribunal which it deems appropriate concerning the amount of such deposits and supplementary deposits.

4. If the required deposits are not paid in full within thirty days after the receipt of the request, the arbitral tribunal shall so inform the parties in order that one or another of them may make the required payment. If such payment is not made, the arbitral tribunal may order the suspension or termination of the arbitral proceedings.

5. After the award has been made, the arbitral tribunal shall render an accounting to the parties of the deposits received and return any unexpended balance to the parties.

II. Discussion

283. Article 41(1) should be adjusted to cater for multi-party arbitration.

284. We also propose one consequential amendment in order to conform with our proposal to delete article 40(4) and, additionally, the deletion of article 40(3) for the reasons given by Professor Sanders:

> According to para. 3 the A.A., if requested by a party, may make "any comments to the A.T. it deems appropriate concerning the amount of such deposits and supplementary deposits". For making its comments on the amount for the deposits the A.T. has in view to require, the A.A. needs to be informed by the A.T. This information concerns its estimation of work to be done as well as the remuneration of the arbitrators for their work. It would be a time consuming procedure before the A.A. can make its comment. *Quid iuris*, if the A.T. and the A.A. do not reach agreement?
>
> I am not aware of any other Arbitration Rules requiring, if so requested by a party, comments of a third party on the amount of deposits, required by the A.T. Paragraph 3 requires consent of the A.A. to perform this function and make its comments subject to a request of a party. Neither the request nor the acceptance by the A.A. to make comments will in my opinion ever occur.[263]

285. Article 41(4) (renumbered 41(3)) could also benefit from widening the scope of the arbitral tribunal's discretion in dealing with a failure to pay a requested deposit.

III. Proposed Revision

286. Proposed revised text of article 41:

> 1. The A~~a~~rbitral T~~t~~ribunal, on its establishment [or thereafter], may request ~~each party~~the parties to deposit advances~~an equal amount as an advance~~ for the costs referred to in article 38, paragraphs (a), (b) and (c). In principle such advances shall be in equal shares, subject to different proportions if the Tribunal deems it appropriate, particularly in the case of multi-party arbitrations.
>
> 2. During the course of the arbitral proceedings the A~~a~~rbitral T~~t~~ribunal may request supplementary deposits from the parties.
>
> ~~3. If an appointing authority has been agreed upon by the parties or designated by the Secretary-General of the Permanent Court of Arbitration at The Hague, and when a party so requests and the appointing authority consents to perform the function, the arbitral tribunal shall fix the amounts of any deposits or supplementary deposits only after consultation with the appointing authority which may make any comments to the arbitral tribunal which it deems appropriate concerning the amount of such deposits and supplementary deposits.~~

---

263 *Sanders* (2004) 259-260.

4. If the required deposits are not paid in full within thirty days after the receipt of the request, the Aarbitral Ttribunal shall so inform the parties in order that one or another of them may make the required payment. If such payment is not made, the Aarbitral Ttribunal may order any sanctions it considers appropriate, including the suspension or termination of the arbitral proceedings.

5. After the award has been made, the Aarbitral Ttribunal shall render an accounting to the parties of the deposits received and return any unexpended balance to the parties.

Annex III
Summary guide to the *travaux préparatoires*

Summary Guide to the *Travaux Préparatoires* of the UNCITRAL Arbitration Rules 2010[1]

Session & subject-matter	*Documents consulted by the Working Group*	*Official Report and additional materials*
45th Session WG II (September 2006) Basic directions of revision; articles 1-40	– Working Paper for 45th Session, 20 July 2006, UN Doc A/CN.9/WG.II/WP.143 (articles 1-16) in (2007) XXXVIII UNCITRAL Ybk 1117 – Working Paper for 45th Session, 20 July 2006, UN Doc A/CN.9/WG.II/WP.143/Add.1 (articles 17-40) in (2007) XXXVIII UNCITRAL Ybk 1134 **Arbitration experts and their writings, as consulted by the Working Group in preliminary conference** – Pieter Sanders, *The Work of UNCITRAL on Arbitration and Conciliation* (Second and Expanded Edition, Kluwer 2004); *Has the Moment Come to Revise the Arbitration Rules of UNCITRAL?*, 20(3) Arb Int 243 (2004) – Jan Paulsson & Georgios Petrochilos, *Revision of the UNCITRAL Rules* (September 2006), <www.uncitral.org> (Paulsson & Petrochilos Report)	– Report of 45th Session, 5 October 2006, UN Doc A/CN.9/614 in (2007) XXXVIII UNCITRAL Ybk 1091 **Additional materials** – APRAG Report of 45th Session, 17 October 2006
46th Session WG II (February 2007) First reading of articles 1-21	– Working Paper for 46th Session, 6 December 2006, UN Doc A/CN.9/WG.II/WP.145 (articles 1-14) in (2007) XXXVIII UNCITRAL Ybk 1174 – Working Paper for 46th Session, 6 December 2006, UN Doc A/CN.9/WG.II/WP.145/Add.1 (articles 15-41) in (2007) XXXVIII UNCITRAL Ybk 1193	– Report of 46th Session, 20 March 2007, UN Doc A/CN.9/619 in (2007) XXXVIII UNCITRAL Ybk 1146 **Additional materials** – APRAG Report of 46th Session, 15 March 2007

[1] Numeration of draft articles refers to the numbering used in the corresponding Working Paper or Report.

Session & subject-matter	*Documents consulted by the Working Group*	*Official Report and additional materials*
47th Session WG II (September 2007) First reading of articles 22-37	– Working Paper for 46th Session, 6 December 2006, UN Doc A/CN.9/WG.II/WP.145/Add.1 (articles 15-41) in (2007) XXXVIII UNCITRAL Ybk 1193 – Working Paper for 47th Session, 3 August 2007, UN Doc A/CN.9/WG.II/WP.147 (articles 1-14) in (2008) XXXIX UNCITRAL Ybk 578; Corrigendum, 30 August 2007, UN Doc A/CN.9/WG.II/WP.147/Corr.1 (paras 10, 53) – Working Paper for 47th Session, 3 August 2007, UN Doc A/CN.9/WG.II/WP.147/Add.1 (articles 15-21) in (2008) XXXIX UNCITRAL Ybk 596; Corrigendum, 30 August 2007, UN Doc A/CN.9/WG.II/WP.147/Add.1/Corr.1 (paras 21, 25)	– Report of 47th Session, 25 September 2007, UN Doc A/CN.9/641 in (2008) XXXIX UNCITRAL Ybk 556 **Additional materials** – APRAG Report of 47th Session, 17 October 2007
48th Session WG II (February 2008) First reading of articles 38-41; Second reading of articles 1-2	– Working Paper for 46th Session, 6 December 2006, UN Doc A/CN.9/WG.II/WP.145/Add.1 (articles 15-41) in (2007) XXXVIII UNCITRAL Ybk 1193 – Working Paper for 47th Session, 3 August 2007, UN Doc A/CN.9/WG.II/WP.147 (articles 1-14) in (2008) XXXIX UNCITRAL Ybk 578; Corrigendum, 30 August 2007, UN Doc A/CN.9/WG.II/WP.147/Corr.1 (paras 10, 53) – Working Paper for 47th Session, 3 August 2007, UN Doc A/CN.9/WG.II/WP.147/Add.1 (articles 15-21) in (2008) XXXIX UNCITRAL Ybk 596; Corrigendum, 30 August 2007, UN Doc A/CN.9/WG.II/WP.147/Add.1/Corr. 1 (paras 21, 25) – Working Paper for 48th Session, 30 November 2007, UN Doc A/CN.9/WG.II/WP.149 (articles 22-37) in (2008) XXXIX UNCITRAL Ybk 629	– Report of 48th Session, 29 February 2008, UN Doc A/CN.9/646 in (2008) 39 UNCITRAL Ybk 606 **Additional materials** – Statements in respect of 'transparency' in investment arbitration, UNCITRAL Report of 48th Session, 29 February 2008, Annexes I-III, UN Doc A/CN.9/646 in (2008) XXXIX UNCITRAL Ybk 624 et seq. – APRAG Report of 48th Session, 28 February 2008

Session & subject-matter	*Documents consulted by the Working Group*	*Official Report and additional materials*
49th Session WG II (September 2008) Second reading of articles 1-17	– Working Paper for 49th Session, 6 August 2008, UN Doc A/CN.9/WG.II/WP.151 (articles 1-17) in (2009) XL UNCITRAL Ybk 497 – Working Paper for 49th Session, 6 August 2008, UN Doc A/CN.9/WG.II/WP.151/Add.1 (articles 18-41)in (2009) XL UNCITRAL Ybk 513 – Working Paper for 49th Session, 9 September 2008, UN Doc A/CN.9/WG.II/WP.152 (Swiss Proposal on articles 19 and 26) in (2009) XL UNCITRAL Ybk 532	– Report of 49th Session, 30 September 2008, UN Doc A/CN.9/665 in (2009) XL UNCITRAL Ybk 471 **Additional materials** – Report of the Secretary-General of the PCA on its activities under the UNCITRAL Arbitration Rules since 1976, 7 December 2006, UN Doc A/CN.9/634 in (2007) XXXVIII UNCITRAL Ybk 1215 – APRAG Report of 49th Session, 10 October 2008
50th Session WG II (February 2009) Second reading of articles 18-26	– Working Paper for 49th Session, 6 August 2008, UN Doc A/CN.9/WG.II/WP.151 (articles 1-17) in (2009) XL UNCITRAL Ybk 497 – Working Paper for 49th Session, 6 August 2008, UN Doc A/CN.9/WG.II/WP.151/Add.1 (articles 18-41) in (2009) XL UNCITRAL Ybk 513 – Working Paper for 49th Session, 9 September 2008, UN Doc A/CN.9/WG.II/WP.152 (Swiss Proposal on articles 19 and 26) in (2009) XL UNCITRAL Ybk 532 – Working Paper for 51st Session, 8 December 2008, UN Doc A/CN.9/WG.II/WP.154 (articles 1-19) in (2009) XL UNCITRAL Ybk 559	– Report of 50th Session, 9 March 2009, UN Doc A/CN.9/669 in (2009) XL UNCITRAL Ybk 534 **Additional materials** – APRAG Report of 50th Session, 27 February 2009
51st Session WG II (September 2009) Second reading of articles 27-39	– Working Paper for 49th Session, 6 August 2008, UN Doc A/CN.9/WG.II/WP.151/Add.1 (articles 18-41) in (2009) XL UNCITRAL Ybk 513 – Working Paper for 51st Session, 8 December 2008, UN Doc A/CN.9/WG.II/WP.154 (articles 1-19) in (2009) XL UNCITRAL Ybk 559 – Working Paper for 51st Session, 23 July 2009, UN Doc A/CN.9/WG.II/WP.154/Add.1 (articles 20-28) in (2010) XLI UNCITRAL Ybk 176	Report of 51st Session, 10 November 2009, UN Doc A/CN.9/684 in (2010) XLI UNCITRAL Ybk 149 **Additional materials** APRAG Report of 51st Session, 30 October 2009

Session & subject-matter	*Documents consulted by the Working Group*	*Official Report and additional materials*
52nd Session WG II (February 2010) Third reading of draft revised Rules	– Working Paper for 52nd Session, 10 December 2009, UN Doc A/CN.9/WG.II/WP.157 (articles 1-16) in (2010) XLI UNCITRAL Ybk 214 – Working Paper for 52nd Session, 10 December 2009, UN Doc A/CN.9/WG.II/WP.157/Add.1(articles 17-32) in (2010) XLI UNCITRAL Ybk 230 – Working Paper for 52nd Session, 10 December 2009, UN Doc A/CN.9/WG.II/WP.157/Add.2 (articles 33-43) in (2010) XLI UNCITRAL Ybk 244	– Report of 52nd Session, 19 February 2010, UN Doc A/CN.9/688 in (2010) XLI UNCITRAL Ybk 189
Committee of the Whole (21-25 June 2010) Articles 1-43	– Note by the Secretariat, 5 March 2010, UN Doc A/CN.9/703 (articles 1-19) – Note by the Secretariat, 5 March 2010, UN Doc A/CN.9/703/Add.1 (articles 20-43) – Compilation of comments by Governments and international organizations, 4 May 2010, UN Doc A/CN.9/704 and Add.1–Add.10	– Report of the Commission on its 43rd Session, 21 June-9 July 2010, UN Doc A/65/17, paras 16-186 in (2010) XLI UNCITRAL Ybk 11 – Summary Records of the 901st-910th meetings, 21-25 June 2010, UN Doc A/CN.9/SR.901-A/CN.9/SR.910 in (2010) XLI UNCITRAL Ybk 1207
910th meeting of the Commission (25 June 2010) Adoption of the UNCITRAL Arbitration Rules as revised in 2010	– Report of the Commission on its 43rd Session, 21 June-9 July 2010, UN Doc A/65/17, Annex I (UNCITRAL Arbitration Rules, as revised in 2010) in (2010) XLI UNCITRAL Ybk 91	– Report of the Commission on its 43rd Session, 21 June-9 July 2010, UN Doc A/65/17, para. 187 in (2010) XLI UNCITRAL Ybk 11

Draft Iterations of the UNCITRAL Arbitration Rules 2010[2]

Draft	*UNCITRAL document*
First Draft Used, together with the Paulsson & Petrochilos Report, for decisions on basic directions	– Working Paper for 45th Session, 20 July 2006, UN Doc A/CN.9/WG.II/WP.143 (articles 1-16) in (2007) XXXVIII UNCITRAL Ybk 1117 – Working Paper for 45th Session, 20 July 2006, UN Doc A/CN.9/WG.II/WP.143/Add.1 (articles 17-40) in (2007) XXXVIII UNCITRAL Ybk 1117
First Draft, *annotated* Used for Working Group, first reading	– Working Paper for 46th Session, 6 December 2006, UN Doc A/CN.9/WG.II/WP.145 (articles 1-14) in (2007) XXXVIII UNCITRAL Ybk 1174 – Working Paper for 46th Session, 6 December 2006, UN Doc A/CN.9/WG.II/WP.145/Add.1 (articles 15-41) in (2007) XXXVIII UNCITRAL Ybk 1193
First Draft, *annotated* Articles 1-21	– Working Paper for 47th Session, 3 August 2007, UN Doc A/CN.9/WG.II/WP.147 (articles 1-14) in (2008) XXXIX UNCITRAL Ybk 578; Corrigendum, 30 August 2007, UN Doc A/CN.9/WG.II/WP.147/Corr.1 (paras 10, 53) – Working Paper for 47th Session, 3 August 2007, UN Doc A/CN.9/WG.II/WP.147/Add.1 (articles 15-21) in (2008) XXXIX UNCITRAL Ybk 596; Corrigendum, 30 August 2007, UN Doc A/CN.9/WG.II/WP.147/Add.1/Corr. 1 (paras 21, 25)
First Draft, *annotated* Articles 22-37	– Working Paper for 48th Session, 30 November 2007, UN Doc A/CN.9/WG.II/WP.149 (2007) in (2008) XXXIX UNCITRAL Ybk 63
Second Draft Used for Working Group, second reading	– Working Paper for 49th Session, 6 August 2008, UN Doc A/CN.9/WG.II/WP.151 (articles 1-17) in (2009) XL UNCITRAL Ybk 497 – Working Paper for 49th Session, 6 August 2008, UN Doc A/CN.9/WG.II/WP.151/Add.1 (articles 18-41) in (2009) XL UNCITRAL Ybk 513

2 Numeration of draft articles refers to the numbering used in the corresponding Working Paper or Report.

Draft	*UNCITRAL document*
Second Draft, ***annotated*** Articles 1-28	– Working Paper for 51st Session, 8 December 2008, UN Doc A/CN.9/WG.II/WP.154 (articles 1-19) in (2009) XL UNCITRAL Ybk 559 – Working Paper for 51st Session, 23 July 2009, UN Doc A/CN.9/WG.II/WP.154/Add.1 (articles 20-28) in (2010) XLI UNCITRAL Ybk 176
Third Draft Used for Working Group, third reading	– Working Paper for 52nd Session, 10 December 2009, UN Doc A/CN.9/WG.II/WP.157 (articles 1-16) in (2010) XLI UNCITRAL Ybk 214 – Working Paper for 52nd Session, 10 December 2009, UN Doc A/CN.9/WG.II/WP.157/Add.1 (articles 17-32) in (2010) XLI UNCITRAL Ybk 230 – Working Paper for 52nd Session, 10 December 2009, UN Doc A/CN.9/WG.II/WP.157/Add.2 (articles 33-43) in (2010) XLI UNCITRAL Ybk 244
Third Draft, ***annotated*** Used for Committee of the Whole reading	– Note by the Secretariat, 5 March 2010, UN Doc A/CN.9/703 (articles 1-19) – Note by the Secretariat, 5 March 2010, UN Doc A/CN.9/703/Add.1 (articles 20-43)
Final Draft Adopted by the Commission	– Report of the Commission on its 43rd Session, 21 June-9 July 2010, UN Doc A/65/17, Annex I (UNCITRAL Arbitration Rules, as revised in 2010) in (2010) XLI UNCITRAL Ybk 91

Annex IV
Table of correspondence between 1976 and 2010 Rules

2010 UNCITRAL Arbitration Rules	1976 UNCITRAL Arbitration Rules
Section I. Introductory rules	*Section I. Introductory rules*
Scope of application* (article 1)	Scope of application (article 1) – Model arbitration clause
Notice and calculation of periods of time (article 2)	Notice, calculation of periods of time (article 2)
Notice of arbitration (article 3)	Notice of arbitration (article 3)
Response to the notice of arbitration (article 4)	–
Representation and assistance (article 5)	Representation and assistance (article 4)
Designating and appointing authorities (article 6)	–
Section II. Composition of the arbitral tribunal	*Section II. Composition of the arbitral tribunal*
Number of arbitrators (article 7)	Number of arbitrators (article 5)
Appointment of arbitrators (articles 8 to 10)	Appointment of arbitrators (articles 6 to 8)
Disclosures by and challenge of arbitrators** (articles 11 to 13)	Challenge of arbitrators (articles 9 to 12)

2010 UNCITRAL Arbitration Rules	1976 UNCITRAL Arbitration Rules
Replacement of an arbitrator (article 14)	Replacement of an arbitrator (article 13)
Repetition of hearings in the event of the replacement of an arbitrator (article 15)	Repetition of hearings in the event of the replacement of an arbitrator (article 14)
Exclusion of liability (article 16)	–
Section III. Arbitral proceedings	*Section III. Arbitral proceedings*
General provisions (article 17)	General provisions (article 15)
Place of arbitration (article 18)	Place of arbitration (article 16)
Language (article 19)	Language (article 17)
Statement of claim (article 20)	Statement of claim (article 18)
Statement of defence (article 21)	Statement of defence (article 19)
Amendments to the claim or defence (article 22)	Amendments to the claim or defence (article 20)
Pleas as to the jurisdiction of the arbitral tribunal (article 23)	Pleas as to the jurisdiction of the arbitral tribunal (article 21)
Further written statements (article 24)	Further written statements (article 22)
Periods of time (article 25)	Periods of time (article 23)
Interim measures (article 26)	Interim measures of protection (article 26)
Evidence (article 27) – Hearings (article 28)	Evidence and hearings (articles 24 and 25)
Experts appointed by the arbitral tribunal (article 29)	Experts (article 27)
Default (article 30)	Default (article 28)
Closure of hearings (article 31)	Closure of hearings (article 29)
Waiver of right to object (article 32)	Waiver of rules (article 30)
Section IV. The award	*Section IV. The award*
Decisions (article 33)	Decisions (article 31)

2010 UNCITRAL Arbitration Rules	1976 UNCITRAL Arbitration Rules
Form and effect of the award (article 34)	Form and effect of the award (article 32)
Applicable law, *amiable compositeur* (article 35)	Applicable law, *amiable compositeur* (article 33)
Settlement or other grounds for termination (article 36)	Settlement or other grounds for termination (article 34)
Interpretation of the award (article 37)	Interpretation of the award (article 35)
Correction of the award (article 38)	Correction of the award (article 36)
Additional award (article 39)	Additional award (article 37)
Definition of costs (article 40)	Costs (articles 38 to 40)
Fees and expenses of arbitrators (article 41)	–
Allocation of costs (article 42)	–
Deposit of costs (article 43)	Deposit of costs (article 41)
Annex	–

* Model arbitration clause for contracts.

** Model statements of independence pursuant to article 11 of the Rules.

Documents and Reports

ASIA PACIFIC REGIONAL ARBITRATION GROUP REPORTS

2008

APRAG Report of 48th Session, 28 February 2008

APRAG Report of 49th Session, 10 October 2008

2009

APRAG Report of 50th Session, 27 February 2009

APRAG Report of 51st Session, 30 October 2009

UNITED NATIONS DOCUMENTS

1974

UNCITRAL Report of 8th Session, 4 November 1974, UN Doc A/CN.9/97, VI UNCITRAL Ybk 163

UNCITRAL Report of the Secretary-General on the Preliminary Draft Set of Arbitration Rules, 4 November 1974, UN Doc A/CN.9/97, VI UNCITRAL Ybk 163

1975

Report of 8th Session, UN Doc A/10017, 1-17 April 1975, VI UNCITRAL Ybk 9

UNCITRAL Summary Record of 167th Meeting, 14 April 1975, UN Doc A/CN.9/SR.167

UNCITRAL Report of the Secretary General on the Draft UNCITRAL Arbitration Rules, 12 December 1975, UN Doc A/CN.9/112/Add.1

1976

Report of the Commission on its 9th Session, 12 April-7 May 1976, UN Doc A/31/17

UNCITRAL Report of 9th Session, 15 April 1976, UN Doc A/CN.9/9/C.2/SR.2

UNCITRAL Summary Record of the 6th Meeting, 19 April 1976, UN Doc A/CN.9/9/C.2/SR.6

UNCITRAL Summary Record of the 7th Meeting, 19 April 1976, UN Doc A/CN.9/9/C.2/SR.7

UNCITRAL Summary Record of the 10th Meeting, 21 April 1976, UN Doc A/CN.9/9/C.2/SR.10

UNCITRAL Summary Record of the 11th Meeting, 21 April 1976, UN Doc A/CN.9/9/C.2/SR.11

UNCITRAL Summary Record of the 12th Meeting, 22 April 1976, UN Doc A/CN.9/9/C.2/SR.12

UNCITRAL Summary Record of the 13th Meeting, 22 April 1976, UN Doc A/CN.9/9/C.2/SR.13

UNCITRAL Summary Record of the 17th Meeting, 26 April 1976, UN Doc A/CN.9/9/C.2/SR.17

1982

UNCITRAL Note by the Secretariat, 31 August 1982, UN Doc A/CN.9/WG.II/WP.38

UNCITRAL Report on 4th Session, 10 November 1982, UN Doc A/CN.9/232, XIV UNCITRAL Ybk 33

1983

UNCITRAL Report of 6th Session, 22 September 1983, UN Doc A/CN.9/245, XV UNCITRAL Ybk 155

1984

UNCITRAL Report of 7th Session, Note by the Secretariat, 6-17 February 1984, UN Doc A/CN.9/WG.II/WP.50, XV UNCITRAL Ybk 218

1985

UNCITRAL Report of the Secretary General, 19 March 1985, UN Doc A/CN.9/263, XVI UNCITRAL Ybk 53

UNCITRAL Report of the Secretary-General, Analytical commentary on draft text of a model law on international commercial arbitration, 25 March 1985, UN Doc A/CN.9/264, XVI UNCITRAL Ybk 104

UNCITRAL Report of the Secretary General, 15 April 1985, UN Doc A/CN.9/263/Add.1, XVI UNCITRAL Ybk 83

Report of the 18th Session, 21 August 1985, UN Doc A/40/17, XVI UNCITRAL Ybk 3

2000

UNCITRAL Report of 32nd Session, 10 April 2000, UN Doc A/CN.9/468, XXXI UNCITRAL Ybk 477

2003

UNCITRAL Report of 39th Session, 8 December 2003, UN Doc A/CN.9/545, XXXV UNCITRAL Ybk 463

2004

UNCITRAL Working Paper for 40th Session, 27 January 2004, UN Doc A/CN.9/WG.II/WP.127

2005

UNCITRAL Report of 43rd Session, 12 October 2005, UN Doc A/CN.9/589

2006

UNCITRAL Note by the Secretariat, 13 April 2006, UN Doc A/CN.9/606

UNCITRAL Recommendation regarding the interpretation of article II(2) and article VII(1) of the Convention on the Recognition and Enforcement of Foreign Arbitral Awards, 14 July 2006, UN Doc A/61/17

UNCITRAL Working Paper for 45th Session, 20 July 2006, UN Doc A/CN.9/WG.II/WP.143/Add.1

UNCITRAL Report of 45th Session, 5 October 2006, UN Doc A/CN.9/614

UNCITRAL Working Paper for 46th Session, 6 December 2006, UN Doc A/CN.9/WG.II/WP.145

UNCITRAL Working Paper for 46th Session, 6 December 2006, UN Doc A/CN.9/WG.II/WP.145/Add.1

UNCITRAL Report of the Secretary-General of the PCA on its activities under the UNCITRAL Arbitration Rules since 1976, 7 December 2006, UN Doc A/CN.9/634

2007

UNCITRAL Report of 46th Session, 20 March 2007, UN Doc A/CN.9/619

Report of the Commission on its 40th Session, 23 July 2007, UN Doc A/62/17 (Part I)

UNCITRAL Report of 47th Session, 25 September 2007, UN Doc A/CN.9/641

UNCITRAL Working Paper for 48th Session, 30 November 2007, UN Doc A/CN.9/WG.II/WP.149

2008

UNCITRAL Report of 48th Session, 29 February 2008, UN Doc A/CN.9/646

UNCITRAL Working Paper for 49th Session, 6 August 2008, UN Doc A/CN.9/WG.II/WP.151

UNCITRAL Working Paper for 49th Session, 6 August 2008, UN Doc A/CN.9/WG.II/WP.151/Add.1

UNCITRAL Working Paper for 49th Session, 9 September 2008, UN Doc A/CN.9/WG.II/WP.152

UNCITRAL Report of 49th Session, 30 September 2008, UN Doc A/CN.9/665

2009

UNCITRAL Report of 50th Session, 9 March 2009, UN Doc A/CN.9/669

UNCITRAL Working Paper for 51st Session, 23 July 2009, UN Doc A/CN.9/WG.II/WP.154/Add.1

UNCITRAL Report of 51st Session, 10 November 2009, UN Doc A/CN.9/684

UNCITRAL Working Paper for 52nd Session, 10 December 2009, UN Doc A/CN.9/WG.II/WP.157

UNCITRAL Working Paper for 52nd Session, 10 December 2009, UN Doc A/CN.9/WG.II/WP.157/Add.1

UNCITRAL Working Paper for 52nd Session, 10 December 2009, UN Doc A/CN.9/WG.II/WP.157/Add.2

2010

UNCITRAL Report of 52nd Session, 19 February 2010, UN Doc A/CN.9/688

UNCITRAL Note by the Secretariat, 5 March 2010, UN Doc A/CN.9/703/Add.1

Report of the Commission on its 43rd Session, 21 June-9 July 2010, UN Doc A/65/17

UNCITRAL Summary Record of the 902nd Meeting, 21 June 2010, UN Doc A/CN.9/SR.902, XLI UNCITRAL Ybk 1213

UNCITRAL Summary Record of the 903rd Meeting, 22 June 2010, UN Doc A/CN.9/SR.903, XLI UNCITRAL Ybk 1220

UNCITRAL Summary Record of the 904th Meeting, 22 June 2010, UN Doc A/CN.9/SR.904, XLI UNCITRAL Ybk 1228

UNCITRAL Summary Record of the 905th Meeting, 23 June 2010, UN Doc A/CN.9/SR.905, XLI UNCITRAL Ybk 1235

UNCITRAL Summary Record of the 906th Meeting, 23 June 2010, UN Doc A/CN.9/SR.906, XLI UNCITRAL Ybk 1242

UNCITRAL Summary Record of the 907th meeting, 24 June 2010, UN Doc A/CN.9/SR.907, XLI UNCITRAL Ybk 1249

UNCITRAL Summary Record of the 908th Meeting, 24 June 2010, UN Doc A/CN.9/SR.908, XLI UNCITRAL Ybk 1256

UNCITRAL Summary Record of the 909th Meeting, 25 June 2010, UN Doc A/CN.9/SR.909, XLI UNCITRAL Ybk 1262

UNCITRAL Working Paper for 53rd Session, 5 August 2010, UN Doc A/CN.9/WG.II/WP.160/Add.1

UNCITRAL Report of 53rd Session, 20 October 2010, UN Doc A/CN.9/712

UNCITRAL Working Paper for 54th Session, 9 December 2010, UN Doc A/CN.9/WG.II/WP.162

UNCITRAL Working Paper for 54th Session, 9 December 2010, UN Doc A/CN.9/WG.II/WP.162/Add.1

2011

UNCITRAL Report of 54th Session, 25 February 2011, UN Doc A/CN.9/717

UNCITRAL Working Paper for 55th Session, 29 July 2011, UN Doc A/CN.9/WG.II/WP.166

UNCITRAL Working Paper for 55th Session, 29 July 2011, UN Doc A/CN.9/WG.II/WP.166/Add.1

UNCITRAL Working Paper for 55th Session, 8 August 2011, UN Doc A/CN.9/WG.II/WP.167

UNCITRAL Report of 55th Session, 17 October 2011, UN Doc A/CN.9/736

UNCITRAL Working Paper for 56th Session, 13 December 2011, UN Doc A/CN.9/WG.II/WP.169

UNCITRAL Working Paper for 56th Session, 13 December 2011, UN Doc A/CN.9/WG.II/WP.169/Add.1

2012

UNCITRAL Report of 56th Session, 16 February 2012, UN Doc A/CN.9/741

UNCITRAL Working Paper for 57th Session, 2 August 2012, UN Doc A/CN.9/WG.II/WP.172

UNCITRAL Working Paper for 57th Session, Proposal by Governments of Argentina, Australia, Canada, Mexico, Norway, South Africa, and the United States of America, 2 August 2012, UN Doc A/CN.9/WG.II/WP.174

UNCITRAL Working Paper for 58th Session, 30 November 2012, UN Doc A/CN.9/WG.II/WP.176

UNCITRAL Working Paper for 58th Session, 30 November 2012, UN Doc A/CN.9/WG.II/WP.176/Add.1

UNCITRAL Report of 57th Session, 12 October 2012, UN Doc A/CN.9/760

UNCITRAL Note by the Secretariat, 13 December 2012, UN Doc A/CN.9/WG.II/WP.177

2013

UNCITRAL Report of 58th Session, 13 February 2013, UN Doc A/CN.9/765

Report of the Commission on its 46th Session, 8-26 July 2013, UN Doc A/68/17

2014

Report of the Commission on its 47th Session, 7-18 July 2014, UN Doc A/69/17

Bibliography

Gerald Aksen, 'The Iran-United States Claims Tribunal and the UNCITRAL Arbitration Rules, an early comment' in Jan C. Schultz & Albert Jan van den Berg (eds), *The Art of Arbitration* (Kluwer 1982)

Klint Alexander, 'Article 6. Hearings' in Dimitrij Euler, Markus Gehring & Maxi Scherer (eds), *Transparency in International Investment Arbitration: A Guide to the UNCITRAL Rules on Transparency in Treaty-Based Investor-State Arbitration* (Cambridge University Press 2015)

Richard C. Allison & Howard M. Holtzmann, 'The Tribunal's Use of Experts' in David D. Caron & John R. Crook (eds), *The Iran-United States Claims Tribunal and the Process of International Claims Resolution* (Transnational Publishers 2000)

Thierry P. Augsburger, 'Article 7. Exceptions to transparency' in Dimitrij Euler, Markus Gehring & Maxi Schrerer (eds), *Transparency in International Investment Arbitration: A Guide to the UNCITRAL Rules on Transparency in Treaty-Based Investor-State Arbitration* (Cambridge University Press 2015)

Stewart A. Baker & Mark D. Davis, *The UNCITRAL Arbitration Rules in Practice – The Experience of the Iran-United States Claims Tribunal* (Kluwer 1992)

James W. Barratt, 'Lost in Translation? The Independence of Experts under the 2010 IBA Rules' in *The European & Middle Eastern Arbitration Review 2012*, <www.globalarbitrationreview.com>

Denis Bensaude, *Malecki v. Long: Truncated Tribunals and Waivers of Dutco Rights*, 23(1) Journal of International Arbitration 81 (2006)

Albert Jan van den Berg, *The New York Arbitration Convention of 1958, Towards a Uniform Judicial Interpretation* (Kluwer 1981)

— *50 Years of the New York Convention: ICCA International Arbitration Conference* (Kluwer 2009)

— 'Dissenting Opinions by Party-Appointed Arbitrators in Investment Arbitration' in *Looking to the Future: Essays on International Law in Honor of W. Michael Reisman*, 820 (Brill 2010)

— *Charles Brower's problem with 100 per cent – dissenting opinions by party-appointed arbitrators in investment arbitration*, 31 Arb Int 381 (2015)

Klaus P. Berger, *International Economic Arbitration* (Kluwer 1993)

Nathalie Bernasconi-Osterwalder & Lise Johnson, *Bulletin #2: Transparency in the dispute settlement process: Country best practices*, International Institute for Sustainable Development (2011), < www.iisd.org >

Giuseppe Bianco, 'Article 2. Publication of information at the commencement of arbitral proceedings' in Dimitrij Euler, Markus Gehring & Maxi Scherer (eds), *Transparency in International Investment Arbitration: A Guide to the UNCITRAL Rules on Transparency in Treaty-Based Investor-State Arbitration* (Cambridge University Press 2015)

Peter Binder, *Analytical Commentary to the UNCITRAL Arbitration Rules* (Sweet & Maxwell 2013)

Nigel Blackaby, Constantine Partasides, Alan Redfern & Martin J. Hunter, *Redfern and Hunter on International Arbitration* (5th ed., Kluwer 2009)

— Constantine Partasides, Alan Redfern & Martin J. Hunter, *Redfern and Hunter on International Arbitration* (6th ed., Kluwer 2015)

Gordon Blanke, 'International Arbitration and ADR in Conditional EU Merger Clearance Decisions' in Gordon Blanke & Phillip Landolt (eds), *EU and US Antitrust Arbitration: A Handbook for Practitioners* (Kluwer 2011)

Marc Blessing, 'Regulations in Arbitration Rules on Choice of Law' in Albert Jan van den Berg (ed), *Planning Efficient Arbitration Proceedings: The Law Applicable in International Arbitration*, 7 ICCA Congress Series 391 (1996)

— *Comparison of the Swiss Rules with the UNCITRAL Arbitration Rules and Others*, Report submitted to ASA Conference in Zurich, 23 January 2004

Matthieu de Boisséson, Le Droit Français de l'Arbitrage National et International (GLN-éditions 1990)

Laurence Boisson De Chazournes & Rukia Baruti Dames, *Transparency in Investor-State Arbitration: An Incremental Approach*, 2(1) BCDR International Arbitration Review 59 (2015)

Gary B. Born, *International Commercial Arbitration* (2nd ed., Kluwer 2014)

Adrian Briggs, *Agreements on Jurisdiction and Choice of Law* (Oxford University Press 2008)

Charles N. Brower & Jason D. Brueschke, *The Iran-United States Claims Tribunal* (1998) (Martinus Nijhoff 1998)

— & Charles B. Rosenberg, *The Death of the Two-Headed Nightingale: Why the Paulsson – van den Berg Presumption that Party-Appointed Arbitrators are Untrustworthy is Wrongheaded*, 29(1) Arb Int 7 (2013)

Chester Brown, 'Inherent Powers in International Adjudication' in Cesare P. R. Romano, Karen Alter & Yuval Shany (eds), *The Oxford Handbook of International Adjudication* (Oxford University Press 2013)

David D. Caron, *Interim Measures of Protection: Theory and Practice in Light of the Iran-United States Claims Tribunal*, 46 ZaöRV 465 (1986)

— Lee M. Caplan & Matti Pellonpää, *The UNCITRAL Arbitration Rules, A Commentary* (Oxford University Press 2006)

— & Lee M. Caplan, *The UNCITRAL Arbitration Rules, A Commentary* (2nd ed., Oxford University Press 2013)

Jeremy Carver, *How to Avoid Conflicting Awards: the Lauder and CME Cases*, 5(1) J World Inv & Trade 28 (2004)

James E. Castello, Arbitral Ex Parte Interim Relief – The view in favour, 58(3) Dispute Resolution Journal 60 (2003)

— 'UNCITRAL Rules' in Frank-Bernd Weigand (ed.), *Practitioner's Handbook on International Commercial Arbitration* (2nd ed., Oxford University Press 2009)

— *Plus Ça Change, Plus C'est la Même Chose: Eight Revisions not Adopted in the 2010 UNCITRAL Rules*, 28(4) ASA Bull 855 (2010)

— *Unveiling the 2010 UNCITRAL Arbitration Rules*, 65(2) Dispute Resolution Journal 21 (2010)

— 'UNCITRAL Arbitration Rules' in Loukas A. Mistelis (ed), *Concise International Arbitration* (2nd ed., Kluwer 2015)

Kathleen Claussen, 'Article 8: Repository of published information' in Dimitrij Euler, Markus Gehring & Maxi Scherer (eds), *Transparency in International Investment Arbitration: A Guide to the UNCITRAL Rules on Transparency in Treaty-Based Investor-State Arbitration*, 308 (Cambridge University Press 2015)

W. Laurence Craig, William W. Park & Jan Paulsson, *International Chamber of Commerce Arbitration* (3rd ed., Oceana Publications 2000)

Clyde E. Croft, Christopher Kee & Jeffrey Waincymer, *A Guide to the UNCITRAL Arbitration Rules* (Cambridge University Press 2013)

John R. Crook, *Applicable Law In International Commercial Arbitration: The Iran-US Claims Tribunal Experience*, 83 AJIL 278 (1989)

Robert B. Davidson & David Plant, 'ADR and Arbitration' in Lawrence W. Newman & Richard D. Hill (eds), *The Leading Arbitrator's Guide to International Arbitration* (3rd ed., Juris 2014)

Yves Derains, *The View against Arbitral Ex Parte Interim Relief – Confirmation that the best may be the enemy of the good*, 58(3) Dispute Resolution Journal 61 (2003)

— & Eric A. Schwartz, *A Guide to the ICC Rules of Arbitration* (2nd ed., Kluwer 2005)

Mariel Dimsey, 'Article 4. Submission by a third person' in Dimitrij Euler, Markus Gehring & Maxi Scherer (eds), *Transparency in International Investment Arbitration: A Guide to the UNCITRAL Rules on Transparency in Treaty-Based Investor-State Arbitration* (Cambridge University Press 2015)

Zachary Douglas, *The International Law of Investment Claims* (Cambridge University Press 2009)

Bernd Ehle, 'The Arbitrator as a Settlement Facilitator' in Olivier Caprasse et al., *Walking a Thin Line: what an Arbitrator can do, must do or must not do: Recent Developments and Trends* (Colloquium CEPANI40 2010)

Dimitrij Euler, Markus Gehring & Maxi Scherer (eds), *Transparency in International Investment Arbitration: A Guide to the UNCITRAL Rules on Transparency in Treaty-Based Investor-State Arbitration* (Cambridge University Press 2015)

Daniele Favalli and Max K. Hasenclever, *The Role of Arbitrators in Settlement Proceedings*, 23(7) Mealey's International Arbitration Report 2 (2008)

Gerald Fitzmaurice, *The Law and Procedure of the International Court of Justice* (Grotius Publications 1986)

Philippe Fouchard, *Final Report on the Status of the Arbitrator*, 7/1 ICC Court Bull. 42 (1996)

Jason Fry, Simon Greenberg & Francesca Mazza, *The Secretariat's Guide to ICC Arbitration* (ICC 2012)

Emmanuel Gaillard & Yas Banifatemi, 'Negative Effect of Competence-Competence: The Rule of Priority in Favor of the Arbitrators' in Emmanuel Gaillard & Domenico Di Pietro (eds), *Enforcement of Arbitration Agreements and International Arbitral Awards – The New York Convention in Practice* (Cameron May 2008)

Bernard Hanotiau, *Complex Arbitrations: Multiparty, Multicontract, Multi-Issue and Class Actions* (Kluwer 2005)

Gerold Herrmann, *The UNCITRAL Model Law – Its Background, Salient Features, and Purposes*, 1(1) Arb Int 6 (1985)

Jacomijn J. van Hof, *Commentary on the UNCITRAL Arbitration Rules, The Application by the Iran-U.S. Claims Tribunal* (Kluwer 1991)

Howard M. Holtzmann & Joseph E. Neuhaus, *A Guide to the UNCITRAL Model Law on International Commercial Arbitration, Legislative History and Commentary* (Kluwer 1989)

— & Joseph E. Neuhaus, *A Guide to the UNCITRAL Model Law on International Commercial Arbitration, Legislative History and Commentary* (2nd ed., Kluwer 1995)

Norbert Horn, *Current Use of the UNCITRAL Arbitration Rules in the Context of Investment Arbitration*, 24 Arb Int 587 (2008)

ICC, *2015 ICC Dispute Resolution Statistics*, 1 ICC Dispute Resolution Bulletin (2016)

Lise Johnson, *The Mauritius Convention on Transparency: Comments on the treaty and its role in increasing transparency of investor-State arbitration* (CCSI Policy Paper, 2014)

— & Nathalie Bernasconi-Osterwalder, *New UNCITRAL Arbitration Rules on Transparency: Application, Content and Next Steps* (CIEL, IISD, CCSI, August 2013), < http://ccsi.columbia.edu >

Mark Kantor, *Valuation for Arbitration*, 17 Int Arb Law Library 304 (2008)

Gabrielle Kaufmann-Kohler, 'Non-Disputing State Submissions in Investment Arbitration: Resurgence of Diplomatic Protection?' in Laurence Boisson de Chazournes, Marcelo G. Kohen & Jorge E. Viñuales (eds), *Diplomatic and Judicial Means of Dispute Settlement*, 305 (Martinus Nijhoff 2012)

— & Antonio Rigozzi, *International Arbitration: Law and Practice in Switzerland* (Oxford University Press 2015).

Christopher Kee, 'Article 3. Publication of documents' in Dimitrij Euler, Markus Gehring & Maxi Scherer (eds), *Transparency in International Investment Arbitration: A Guide to the UNCITRAL Rules on Transparency in Treaty-Based Investor-State Arbitration* (Cambridge University Press 2015)

Kap-You Kim & John P. Bang, 'Commentary on Using Legal Experts in International Arbitration' in Albert Jan van den Berg (ed), *International Arbitration 2006: Back to Basics?*, 13 ICCA Congress Series 779 (2006)

Jennifer Kirby, *With Arbitrators, Less Can Be More: Why the Conventional Wisdom on the Benefits of Having Three Arbitrators May Be Overrated*, 26(3) J Int Arb 337 (2009)

Meg N. Kinnear, Andrea K. Bjorklund & John F.G. Hannaford, *Investment Disputes under NAFTA: An Annotated Guide To NAFTA Chapter 11* (Kluwer 2006)

Detlev Kühner & Gustav Flecke-Giammarco, 'Part IV: Selected Areas and Issues of Arbitration in Germany, ICC Arbitration in Germany' in Patricia Nacimiento, Stefan Michael Kröll, et al. (eds), *Arbitration in Germany: The Model Law in Practice* (2nd ed., Kluwer 2015)

Pierre Lalive, *Irresponsibility in International Commercial Arbitration*, 7(2) Asia Pacific Law Review 171 (1999)

Sophie Lamb, Daniel Harrison & Jonathan Hew, *Recent Developments in the Law and Practice of Amicus Briefs in Investor-State Arbitration*, V(2) Indian Journal of Arbitration Law 72 (2016)

Ole Lando, *The lex mercatoria in International Commercial Arbitration*, 34 ICLQ 747 (1985)
— *The Law Applicable to the Merits of the Dispute*, 2 Arb Intl 104 (1986)

LCIA, *Commentary on a Discussion Draft of the LCIA Rules*, 1(2) LCIA Newsletter 10 (1996)

Laurent Lévy, *Dissenting Opinions in International Arbitration in Switzerland*, 5 Arb Int 35 (1989)

Julian D. M. Lew, *Commentary on Interim and Conservatory Measures in ICC Arbitration Cases* 11(1) ICC Ct Bull 23 (2000)
— Loukas A. Mistelis & Stefan M. Kröll, *Comparative International Commercial Arbitration* (Kluwer 2003)

Sam Luttrell, *ICSID provisional measures 'in the round'*, 31(3) Arb Int 393 (2015)

Filip de Ly, Mark Friedman & Luca Radicati di Brozolo, *International Law Association International Commercial Arbitration Committee's Report and Recommendations on 'Confidentiality in International Commercial Arbitration'*, 28(3) Arb Int 355 (2012)

V.S. Mani, *International Adjudication: Procedural Aspects* (Martinus Nijhoff 1980)

Francis A. Mann, *Where is an award 'made'?*, 1(1) Arb Int 107 (1985)

Pierre Mayer, *L'autonomie de l'arbitre international dans l'appréciation de sa propre compétence*, 217 RdC 320 (1989-V)

Michael McIlwrath & John Savage, *International Arbitration and Mediation: A Practical Guide* (Kluwer 2010)

Mark S. McNeill & Ben Juratowitch, *Agora: Thoughts on Fiona Trust – The doctrine of separability and consent to arbitrate*, 24 Arb Int 475 (2008)

Robert von Mehren, *Arbitration in Central and Eastern Europe*, Arb J 38 (1992)

William J. Moon, *Essential Security Interests in International Investment Agreements*, 15(2) Journal of International Economic Law 481 (2012)

Sophie Nappert, *Commentary on the UNCITRAL Arbitration Rules 2010: A Practitioner's Guide*, 105 (Juris Publishing 2012)

Jan H. Nedden & Friedrich Rosenfeld, 'The new UNCITRAL Transparency Rules: How the trend towards transparency differs in investment and commercial arbitration' in Christoph Muller & Antonio Rigozzi (eds), *New Developments in International Commercial Arbitration 2013*, 41 (2013)

Martins Paparinskis & Jessica Howley, 'Article 5. Submission by a non-disputing Party to the treaty' in Dimitrij Euler, Markus Gehring & Maxi Scherer (eds), *Transparency in International Investment Arbitration: A Guide to the UNCITRAL Rules on Transparency in Treaty-Based Investor-State Arbitration* (Cambridge University Press 2015)

William W. Park, *The Arbitrator's Jurisdiction to Determine Jurisdiction*, 13 ICCA Congress Series 55 (Kluwer 2007)

Constantine Partasides, *The Fourth Arbitrator? The Role of Secretaries to Tribunals in International Arbitration*, 18(2) Arb Int 147 (2002)

Jan Paulsson (ed.), *International Handbook on Commercial Arbitration* (1984) as electronically available and updated at < www.kluwerarbitration.com >

— *Arbitration Without Privity*, 10 For Inv LJ 232 (1995)

— 'Jurisdiction and Admissibility' in *Global Reflections on International Law, Commerce and Dispute Resolution – Liber Amicorum in honour of Robert Briner* (ICC Publication 693) (2005)

— & Georgios Petrochilos, *Revision of the UNCITRAL Rules* (September 2006), < www.uncitral.org >

— *The Idea of Arbitration* (Oxford University Press 2013)

Marike R. P. Paulsson, *The 1958 New York Convention in Action* (Kluwer 2016)

Sebastian Perry & Kyriaki Karadelis, *Sun Rises on Czech Energy Claims*, GAR, 19 February 2014, < www.globalarbitrationreview.com >

Georgios Petrochilos, *Procedural Law in International Arbitration* (Oxford University Press 2004)

— *Interim Measures Under the Revised UNCITRAL Arbitration Rules*, 28(4) ASA Bulletin 878 (2010)

Nicola C. Port, Scott E. Bowers, et al., 'Article V(1)(c)' in Herbert Kronke, Patricia Nacimiento, et al. (eds), *Recognition and Enforcement of Foreign Arbitral Awards: A Global Commentary on the New York Convention* (Kluwer 2010)

Jean-François Poudret & Sébastien Besson, *Comparative Law of International Arbitration* (2nd ed., Sweet and Maxwell 2007)

Bernard G. Poznanski, *The Nature and Extent of an Arbitrator's Powers in International Commercial Arbitration*, 4(3) J Int Arb 71 (1987)

Jakob Ragnwaldh & Nils Eliasson, 'Security for Costs in Investment Arbitration' in Kaj Hobér, Annette Magnusson, Marie Öhrström & Christopher Goddard (eds), *Between East and West: Essays in Honour of Ulf Franke* (Juris 2010)

Alan Redfern, *Law and Practice of International Commercial Arbitration* (Sweet & Maxwell 2004)

— *The 2003 Freshfields – Lecture Dissenting Opinions in International Commercial Arbitration: The Good, the Bad, and the Ugly*, 20(3) Arb Int 223 (2004)

Lucy Reed, Jan Paulsson & Nigel Blackaby, *Guide to ICSID Arbitration* (2nd ed., Kluwer 2010)

August Reinisch, 'The Proliferation of International Dispute Settlement Mechanisms: The Threat of Fragmentation vs the Promise of a More Effective System? Some Reflections From the Perspective of Investment Arbitration' in Isabelle Buffard, James Crawford, Alain Pellet and Stephan Wittich (eds), *International Law Between Universalism and Fragmentation – Festschrift in Honour of Gerhard Hafner* (Brill 2008)

Jean Robert, *Administration of Evidence in International Commercial Arbitration*, I YCA 221 (1976)

Anthea Roberts, *Power and Persuasion in Investment Treaty Interpretation: The Dual Role of States*, 104(2) American Journal of International Law 179 (2010)

Catherine A. Rogers & Jeffrey C. Jeng, 'The Ethics of International Arbitrators' in Lawrence W. Newman & Richard D. Hill (eds), *The Leading Arbitrator's Guide to International Arbitration* (3rd ed., Juris 2014)

Noah Rubins, *In God We Trust, All Others Pay Cash: Security for Costs in International Commercial Arbitration*, 11(3) Am Rev Int Arb 307 (2000)

Julia Salasky & Corinne Montineri, *UNCITRAL Rules on Transparency in Treaty-Based Investor-State Arbitration*, 31(4) ASA Bulletin 774 (2013)

Pieter Sanders, *Model Rules for International Commercial Arbitration: UNCITRAL Arbitration Rules*, Report for 7th ICCA Congress (1974), <www.arbitration-icca.org>
— *Commentary on UNCITRAL Arbitration Rules*, II YCA 172 (1977)
— *Procedures and Practices under the UNCITRAL Rules*, 27 Am J Comp L 453 (1979)
— *The Work of UNCITRAL on Arbitration and Conciliation* (Kluwer 2001)
— *Has the Moment Come to Revise the Arbitration Rules of UNCITRAL?*, 20(3) Arb Int 243 (2004)
— *The Revision of the UNCITRAL Arbitration Rules* (August 2009) <www.arbitration-icca.org>

John Savage & Emmanuel Gaillard (eds), *Fouchard, Gaillard, Goldman on International Commercial Arbitration* (Kluwer 1999)

Krista N. Schefer, 'Article 1. Scope of Application' in Dimitrij Euler, Markus Gehring & Maxi Scherer (eds), *Transparency in International Investment Arbitration: A Guide to the UNCITRAL Rules on Transparency in Treaty-Based Investor-State Arbitration* (Cambridge University Press 2015)

Peter Schlosser, *The Decision of 27 February 1970 of the Federal Supreme Court of the Federal Republic of Germany (Bundesgerichtshof)*, 6 Arb Int 79 (1990)

Michael E. Schneider, 'Combining Arbitration with Conciliation' in Albert Jan van den Berg (ed), *International Dispute Resolution: Towards an International Arbitration Culture*, 8 ICCA Congress Series 57 (1998)
— *The Revision of the UNCITRAL Arbitration Rules – Some observations on the process and the results*, 4/2011 Les Cahiers de l'Arbitrage 903 (2011)

Christoph H. Schreuer, Loretta Malintoppi, August Reinisch & Anthony Sinclair, *The ICSID Convention, A Commentary* (2nd ed., Cambridge University Press 2009)

Georg von Segesser & Petra Rihar, *The Right to a Tribunal Appointed Expert*, <www.kluwerarbitrationblog.com>

Michael Straus, *The Practice of the Iran-U.S. Claims Tribunal in Receiving Evidence from Parties and from Experts*, 3 JIA 57 (1986)

Jerzy Sztucki, *Interim Measures in The Hague Court* (Kluwer 1983)

Rolf Trittmann, *When Should Arbitrators Issue Interim or Partial Awards and or Procedural Orders?*, 20(3) Journal of International Arbitration 255 (2003)

Peter Turner & Reza Mohtashami, *A Guide to the LCIA Arbitration Rules* (Oxford University Press 2009)

UNCITRAL, *Notes on Organizing Arbitral Proceedings* (United Nations 1996)
— *2012 Digest of Case Law on the Model Law on International Commercial Arbitration* (United Nations 2012)
— *Recommendations to assist arbitral institutions and other interested bodies with regard to arbitration under the UNCITRAL Arbitration Rules (as revised in 2010)*, (United Nations 2013)
— *Notes on Organizing Arbitral Proceedings* (United Nations 2016)

UNCTAD, *Investor-State Dispute Settlement: UNCTAD Series on Issues in International Investment Agreements II* (United Nations 2014)

Nathalie Voser, 'Multi-party Disputes and Joinder of Third Parties' in Albert Jan van den Berg (ed.), *50 Years of the New York Convention: ICCA International Arbitration Conference* (Kluwer 2009)

Jeffrey Waincymer, *Procedure and Evidence in International Arbitration* (Kluwer 2012)

Thomas H. Webster, *Efficiency in Investment Arbitration: Recent Decisions on Preliminary and Costs Issues*, 25(4) Arb Int 469 (2009)

— *Handbook of UNCITRAL Arbitration* (2nd ed., Sweet & Maxwell 2015)

Gillian M. White, *The Use of Experts by International Tribunals* (Syracuse University Press 1965)

Anne-Marie Whitesell & Eduardo Silva-Romero, 'Multiparty and Multicontract Arbitration: Recent ICC Experience' in *Complex Arbitrations: Perspectives on their Procedural Implications*, 7 ICC International Commercial Arbitration Bulletin Special Supplement (2003)

Markus Wirth, 'The Current Revision of the UNCITRAL Rules' in Christoph Müller (ed.), *New Developments in International Commercial Arbitration* (Schulthess 2007)

Ali Yesilirmak, *Provisional Measures in International Commercial Arbitration* (Kluwer 2005)

Tobias Zuberbühler, Christoph Müller & Philipp A. Habegger, *Swiss Rules of International Arbitration: Commentary* (Kluwer 2005)

— Christoph Müller & Philipp A. Habegger, *Swiss Rules of International Arbitration: Commentary* (2nd ed., Juris Publishing 2013)

Index

W